GUIDING CHILDREN'S SOCIAL DEVELOPMENT

Marjorie J. Kostelnik, Ph.D.
Associate Professor

Laura C. Stein, M.S.
Child Development Specialist

Alice Phipps Whiren, Ph.D.
Associate Professor

Anne K. Soderman, Ph.D.
Associate Professor

of the Department of Family and Child Ecology
Michigan State University

Published by

HE22   **SOUTH-WESTERN PUBLISHING CO.**

CINCINNATI   WEST CHICAGO, IL   DALLAS   LIVERMORE, CA

Consulting Editor:

Stephen R. Jorgensen, Ph.D.
 Associate Dean for Research and Graduate Studies and
 Professor, Department of Human Development and Family
 Studies
Texas Tech University

Cover Photo: © Ulrike Welsch

ISBN: 0-538-32220-9

Library of Congress Catalog Card Number: 86-61090

2 3 4 5 6 K 1 0 9 8

Printed in the United States of America

CONTENTS

FOREWORD

If you have ever marveled at the wisdom and ingenuity of a young child or muttered such expressions as "out of the mouths of babes," you know the feelings of surprise, wonder, and fulfillment that children sometimes can inspire in adults. Such experiences provide us the opportunity to look into a "peephole" that reveals exciting, mysterious, and seemingly elusive phenomena unavailable to us on a regular basis. We are awed momentarily, but our basic concepts about the everyday capabilities of children are not changed. We soon return to our usual adult ways of relating to children and snap back into our views of them as enormously limited in many important dimensions.

Now, how would you feel if you knew that there were conceptualizations of children and adult-child and child-child relationships, and methods available to translate these concepts into practice, that could enlarge that peephole into a picture window revealing capabilities in children of panoramic proportions? After some doubt and a little confusion about how all this could happen and how you would relate to it, you probably would be eager to learn more.

I hope this will be your attitude when you read this unique book, because it promises to help you acquire, as no book has before, the principles and skills that will allow you and all those you influence to relate to children in ways that do, indeed, maximize their potential. Observing a group of children responding to the methods espoused by the authors is an awesome experience. One begins to imagine that somehow, the children have been prompted to behave so impressively. On the contrary, an atmosphere has been created by their adult mentors that enables the children to blossom— all kinds of children, not just the "ideal student" types. Proof that these statements are grounded in reality can be gotten by observing any day in the Child Development Laboratories at Michigan State University, where the authors practice the methods they share in this book. Another benefit of employing the methods advocated here is that adults, too, are more satisfied in their relationships with children: troublesome power issues diminish, and feelings of accomplishment prevail.

To date, helping professionals have had difficulty developing effective, believable systems of communicating with and disciplining young children because there are two accepted but opposing views of children and how they are socialized. Proponents of either position generally ignore phenomena that their system does not readily deal with, which results in broad gaps in their approaches. A meaningful, comprehensive, empirically valid integration of both the humanistic and behavioral approaches to children is long overdue. Kostelnik, Stein, Whiren, and Soderman have seen the light and have adopted a consistent, integrative approach. Their work is no hodgepodge of concepts, no eclectic potpourri, but a truly integrated, comprehensive system for relating to children that is based on scientific knowledge of child development and human relationships. Here, in one text, a complementary student activity guide, and an instructor's manual, exists an efficient, effective, complete program for teaching and applying the integrated concepts. Thus, it should be no problem for students to acquire the needed knowledge and skills to practice the approach themselves.

This book is, as nearly as is possible, a prescription for filling the needs of the field of education regarding child socialization and child development. In *Guiding Children's Social Development*, the authors have created a whole course, not merely a textbook. Most exciting of all, the principles and skills espoused by the authors are generic skills, readily adapted to any setting in which adults care for and about children. If taken as seriously as it should be by all educators and care providers, this break- through book could change the whole field of child development, much to the benefit of us all.

Louise Guerney
The Pennsylvania State University
University Park, Pennsylvania

PREFACE

Our purpose in writing *Guiding Children's Social Development* is to do something to improve the quality of life for children and their families and to contribute to the professional development of practitioners in training. We believe that helping professionals have a primary role in providing emotional support and guidance to the youngsters with whom they work. This includes helping children develop positive feelings about themselves, increasing their ability to interact effectively with others, and teaching them socially acceptable means of behavior. We have also come to know that this type of learning is facilitated when children view the adult as a wellspring of comfort and encouragement as well as a source of behavioral guidance. How proficiently adults perform these roles is affected by the extent to which they understand child development, their ability to establish positive relationships with children, and their grasp of principles related to behavior management. Therefore, it is our premise that helping professionals must first learn about children's social development and then become adept in relationship-enhancement skills and behavior-management techniques.

Unfortunately, in the literature and in practice, a dichotomy often is assumed between relationship enhancement and behavior management. For example, approaches that focus on the former teach students how to demonstrate warmth and respect, acceptance and empathy, but leave them to their own devices in figuring out how to deal with typical childhood behaviors such as spitting, hitting, teasing, or making friends. Conversely, approaches that focus on behavior control address the latter circumstances but often neglect to teach students how to build rapport with children, how to help children develop coping strategies, or how to assist them in better understanding themselves and others.

We have decided to tackle these issues by including research, information, and skills associated with both relationship enhancement and behavior management. We have pulled together a unique blend of organismic and mechanistic theory and practice that establishes common ground between the two while maintaining the integrity of each. In doing so, we demonstrate that there is a factual knowledge base that can be brought to bear on how aspiring professionals think about children's social development and how they respond to it.

Additionally, too often, we have encountered students and practitioners who treat their interactions with children as wholly intuitive. They rely on "gut-level" responses, adhering to no explicit or comprehensive principles. These adults frequently view child guidance as a series of tricks that they use indiscriminately to meet short-range objectives, such as getting a child to stop interrupting. They have no purposeful or integrated set of strategies that address long-range goals, such as teaching a child to delay gratification. Other adults have more knowledge about broad principles regarding relationship building and behavior management but have difficulty integrating those principles into a systematic, consistent plan of action. Most distressing to us are those adults whose lack of training leads them to conclude that the normal behaviors children exhibit as they engage in the socialization process somehow are abnormal or malicious. These people also fail to recognize the impact of their own behavior on their interactions with children. As a result, when children do not comply with their expectations, they view condemnation, rather than teaching, as appropriate for the situation.

Our purpose has been to write a book that addresses these shortcomings. It is our goal to eliminate much of the guesswork and frustration experienced by professionals in the field as well as to improve the conditions under which children are socialized in formal group settings. To accomplish this, we have provided a solid foundation of child-development information. In addition, we have shown how to translate that information into related skills and procedures that support children's social development.

Presentation

Taken altogether, the chapters in this book comprise a thorough picture of children's social development. We have been careful to include traditional areas of study such as self-esteem, aggression, routines, rules, and consequences. We also have addressed more current topics of interest such as infant communication, stress, friendship, and prosocial behavior. Considered individually, each chapter offers an in-depth literature review in which findings from many fields have been integrated (psychology, physiology, education, medicine, sociology, home economics, personnel management, interior design). Thus, even within the confines of a single subject, there is breadth. The sequence of chapters also has been thoughtfully planned so that each serves as a foundation for the next—simple concepts and/or skills precede more complex ones; chapters that focus on relationship enhancement come before those that discuss behavior management.

Throughout the text, we have tried to establish a lucid, straightforward style, which we hope makes the book easy to read and interesting. Although many research findings have been cited, we have purposely used parenthetical notation rather than constantly referring to the researchers by name. We want students to remember the *concepts* those findings represent rather than to simply memorize names and dates. In addition, we have made liberal use of real-life examples to illustrate concepts and related skills. This is to assist students in making the connection between what they read and "flesh-and-blood" children. Furthermore, we

have described many different settings in which adults find themselves working with children so that regardless of their professional intents, students can relate to what we have written. Another reason for multiple-setting scenarios is to demonstrate that the content is not situation bound and that the knowledge and skills can be generalized from one setting to another.

Our scope of study encompasses the social development of children from birth to twelve years of age. We have targeted this period of childhood because it is during the formative years that the foundation for all socialization takes place. Furthermore, the skills taught have been specially designed to take into account the cognitive structures and social abilities particular to children of this age.

Because children live and develop within the context of a family, a community, a nation, and a world, they are constantly influenced by, and in turn affect, the people and events around them. Thus, our perspective is an ecological one in which children are viewed as dynamic, ever-changing components in an equally dynamic, ever-changing milieu. This ecological perspective is incorporated into each chapter in the literature review and in many of the examples provided. Additionally, in most chapters, at least one and sometimes more of the discussion questions raise these issues for students to think about.

It has been our experience that students learn professional behavior best when they are given clear, succinct directions for how to carry out a procedure. Defining a procedure, offering examples, and giving a rationale for its use are necessary, but not sufficient. Thus, our approach to skill training is to point out to the student research-based strategies related to chapter content. We then break those strategies down into a series of discrete, observable skills that students can implement. We have been direct, rather than circumspect, in articulating the specific steps involved. This forthrightness should not be taken to imply that our directions are immutable or that there is no room for students to use the skills creatively. Rather, we anticipate that students will internalize and modify skills according to their own needs, personality, interaction style, and circumstance once they have learned them. In addition, we recognize that an important component of using skills correctly is determining which alternatives from the entire available array are best suited for a given situation. Hence, knowing when to use a particular skill and when to refrain from using it is as important as knowing how to use it. For this reason, we discuss these issues throughout each chapter, both in the body of the text and in the pitfalls section at the end. We also have incorporated specific guidelines for how the skills can be adapted for use with youngsters of varying ages and differing cultural backgrounds. Finally, Chapter 16, Making Judgments, has been included to further help students make these decisions.

Supplementary Materials

In addition to the textbook, a student activity guide has been developed to augment students' understanding of the information and skills presented. We have also designed an instructor's manual and a variety of audiovisual materials as additional aids for the instructor.

Student aids. A student activity guide is available to help students understand and master the skills presented in the textbook. The guide includes modules that correspond to each chapter in the textbook. Every module contains performance objectives, a rationale for the skills, an outline of key points regarding skill performance, paper-and-pencil exercises, suggested field assignments, and a self-check review at the end. The guide enables students to practice and apply, in both hypothetical and real situations, skills they have learned. Skills are broken down into manageable segments and are presented in a sequence ranging from simple to more complex. In addition, students can gauge their own progress via an answer key. All of these features

increase students' ability to incorporate the skills into their professional behavior. Note that a prototype of the student activity guide has been extensively field tested with college students and practitioners (Kostelnik, 1978, 1983; Peters and Kostelnik, 1981). Data from those studies show that students who complete the guide significantly increase their ability to use the skills and to maintain them over time. Moreover, many of the items that have been included in this guide are ones that students have recommended.

Instructor items. A comprehensive instructor's manual further supplements the textbook. In it, we describe how to organize a course using the textbook and student activity guide; how to search out, select, and maintain appropriate field placements for students; how to model skills for students to imitate; and how to provide feedback to students assigned to field placements. In addition, we have included a series of rehearsal exercises, which are role-play activities meant to be carried out in class. They are aimed at acquainting students with how to use particular skills prior to implementing them with children and at clarifying basic concepts as they emerge during discussion or interaction. An extensive test bank also has been developed as part of the instructor's manual. Multiple-choice, true-false, short-answer, and essay questions are presented on a chapter-by-chapter basis. Finally, the instructor's manual contains a criterion-referenced observational tool, the PSI (professional skills inventory). This is a unique feature of our instructional package. It can be used by instructors and/or practitioners to evaluate the degree to which students demonstrate the skills taught.

To aid instructors in presenting content specifically related to the skills described herein, a series of 11 filmstrips and accompanying audiotapes is available for rent or purchase from the Instructional Media Center, Michigan State University, East Lansing, Michigan 48824. The series is entitled "Communication and Positive

Guidance Skills for Teachers of Young Children.'' There are filmstrips and tapes to correspond to Chapters 3, 4, 5, 7, 8, 12, and 16. There are two units for Chapter 7 as well as one that provides practice in reflecting and another that provides practice in limit setting.

The comprehensive instructional program described here minimizes instructor preparation time by providing a complete array of related materials and detailed information regarding course organization, suggested grading practices, procurement and maintenance of field placements, items for quizzes and exams, homework assignments, and a tool for measuring student performance in the field. The package maximizes instructor flexibility by:

Providing variations of how a course could be organized using the materials proposed.

Describing ways to include or exclude field placements as part of the course structure.

Presenting information and skills that are relevant to students in a variety of majors.

Providing opportunities for instructors to primarily stress knowledge acquisition by using the textbook alone or to combine knowledge and application by using the textbook and activity guide together.

Presenting knowledge and skills that can be applied to children of varying ages and that can be adapted to a variety of professional settings.

Learning Aids

This book incorporates a number of features aimed at enhancing student learning:

Each chapter is introduced by a statement of objectives, which tells students what they should know on completion of that segment of the book. This alerts them to the major foci of that chapter.

All chapters open with a discussion of theory and research related to a particular social-development topic. Implications of the research for both children and adults also are described.

A major portion of each chapter is devoted to presenting the professional skills relevant to the topic under discussion. Each skill is broken down into a series of observable behaviors that students can learn and instructors can evaluate directly. This section also makes extensive use of examples to further illustrate the skills under consideration.

Near the end of each chapter is a description of pitfalls or common mistakes students make when first learning to use the skills. Suggestions for how to avoid these difficulties are provided.

All chapters conclude with a summary that gives a brief overview of the material presented. This is a useful synopsis for student review of important concepts.

An added feature of each chapter is a listing of topics for discussion. These are thought-provoking questions aimed at helping students synthesize and apply, through conversations with classmates, what they have read.

To the Student

This book will give you a foundation of knowledge and skills necessary for guiding children's social development in professional practice. We hope it will contribute to your enthusiasm about the field and to your confidence in working with young children and their families. Although what you read here will not encompass everything you will need to know, it will serve as a secure base from which you can begin to develop your own professional style.

You will have the advantage of learning, in one course, a myriad of information and strategies that otherwise might take many years to discover. Through examples, you will be able to accumulate a background of experience that you may not yet have had a chance to develop or learn by other means. Finally, you will be reading a book authored by people with extensive practical experience in working with children, engaging in research, and teaching this content to learners much like yourselves. As a result, we are well aware of the issues related to children's social development that are important to students, and we have focused on those. We also have anticipated some of the questions you might ask and some of the difficulties you might encounter in working with this material. Consequently, we have made a conscious effort to discuss these in relevant places throughout the book.

Hints for Using the Materials

1. Read each chapter of the textbook carefully. Plan to read them more than once. Use the first reading to gain a broad grasp of the subject matter; then, read a second time, paying particular attention to the normative sequence of development presented. Identify major concepts regarding adult behavior, and focus on the actual procedures related to each skill. Use subsequent readings to recall the material in more detail.
2. Jot notes in the margin and underline points you wish to remember.
3. Go beyond simply memorizing terminology. Concentrate on how you might recognize the concepts you are studying in real children's behavior and how you might apply this knowledge in your interactions with children. Not only will this expand your understanding of the material, but both levels of information are likely to appear on quizzes and exams.
4. Work through each module of the student activity guide only after you have read the corresponding textbook chapter.
5. Ask questions. Share with classmates and the instructor your experiences in using the material. Participate fully in class discussions and role-play exercises.

6. Try out what you are learning with children. If you are in a field placement, are volunteering, or are employed in a program, take full advantage of that opportunity. Do not hesitate to practice your skills simply because they are new to you and you are not sure how well you will perform them. Persist in spite of your awkwardness or mistakes, and make note of what you might do to improve. Focus on your successes and your increasing skill, not just on things that don't go perfectly. Allow yourself to enjoy the children even as you are learning from them.

Acknowledgments

We would like to thank the following persons for their contributions to our work:

Louise F. Guerney, The Pennsylvania State University, was a major source of information regarding the philosophy and skills presented here. In addition, she contributed substantially to the general discussion of making judgments and to the section on extreme behaviors in Chapter 16.

The work of Steven J. Danish, Commonwealth University of Virginia; Anthony R. D'Augelli, The Pennsylvania State University; and Allen L. Hauer, Department of Health and Social Services, State of Wisconsin, provided the structure on which the student activity guide was based.

Stephen R. Jorgensen, Texas Tech University, our consulting editor, offered numerous suggestions and citations, which we have incorporated throughout the book.

A recent course taught by Alice Sterling Honig, Syracuse University, was the source for the theoretical underpinnings of Chapter 2.

Our colleagues at Michigan State University generously assisted us:

Lillian A. Phenice expanded our understanding of children's emotional development from a multicultural perspective and offered valuable insights into issues of ethnicity.

Verna Hildebrand gave numerous suggestions during the initial phases of this project.

Roshni Kulkarni provided sensitive insights into the impact death has on children and families.

Donna R. Howe contributed materials to the chapters on friendship and prosocial behavior.

Sharon Shay offered substantive research data and advice regarding child abuse.

Linda Nelson and Jean Schlater made available important material regarding values and decision making.

Nancy Corl contributed to the topic of corporal punishment in the schools; Helen Hagens, to the chapter on children's aggression; Sue Grossman, to the discussions on self-esteem; and Fran Wilson, to chapters relating to children's friendship, the verbal environment, and aggression.

Finally, over the years, we have worked with many students whose enthusiasm and excitement have invigorated us. Simultaneously, we have been privileged to know hundreds of children during their formative years. From them we have gained insight and the motivation to pursue this project. To them this book is dedicated.

CHAPTER 1
Professional Involvement with Young Children

SOURCE: Photo by David Kostelnik

OBJECTIVES:

On completion of this chapter, you will be able to describe:

1. Factors related to social competence.

2. Basic principles of human development.

3. How children learn.

4. An ecological view of children and the value of maintaining such a view.

5. Why families are important and how they function.

6. How formal group settings influence children's development.

7. What it means to be a helping professional.

8. The overall structure and format of this book.

Humans are social beings. From the moment we are born, we begin a lifetime of interdependence. Social interactions fulfill our intrinsic need for companionship, stimulation, feedback, and a sense of belonging. So crucial is this aspect of our lives that infants who receive adequate physical care, but who are deprived of social relationships, sometimes die (Spitz, 1949). In fact, in most cultures, isolation from others is considered the severest form of punishment, short of death.

It is through social exchanges that we develop a sense of self, acquire knowledge and skills regarding human relationships, and learn the rules and values of the society in which we live. Much of this learning occurs during childhood. Indeed, it is during the early years that children develop the social foundation on which they will build for the rest of their lives.

SOCIAL COMPETENCE

To operate effectively in the social world, children must learn to recognize, interpret, and respond to social situations (Hendrick, 1984). How well and how appropriately they do this is a measure of their social competence. Thus, Art, who notices that Gary is unhappy and attempts to comfort him, is more socially adept than Ralph, who walks by, oblivious to his peer's distress. Moreover, Debby, who habitually blurts out whatever is on her mind the instant it occurs to her, is less socially mature than if she were to wait without interrupting. Similarly, when Chip fails to turn in his homework on time, he is demonstrating less social competence than classmates who fulfill their assignments. There is strong evidence that in this society, children are viewed as more socially competent when they are responsible rather than irresponsible; independent versus suggestible; friendly, not hostile; cooperative instead of resistive; purposive rather than aimless; and self-controlled, not impulsive (Baumrind,

1970). In addition, children demonstrate greater social competence as they learn both to give and to receive emotional support (Bloom, Hastings, and Madaus, 1971).

Social competence is acquired over time and is influenced by developmental as well as experiential factors. As children mature, developmental changes occur in the structure of their thinking that increase their effective social capacity. Thus, social development becomes more complex and sophisticated as children's linguistic, memory, cognitive, and physical abilities expand. This progression is illustrated by the role that development plays in the strategies children use in eliciting caregiving behaviors in the first few years of life (Bowlby, 1969). Initially, it is the infant's reflexes that contribute most to closeness with the caregiver—grasping, sucking, and rooting are all automatic, unconscious actions that draw the adult near. Gradually, as infants' cognitive structures change and the use of their bodies comes more into conscious control, they have a greater range of eliciting behaviors at their disposal. Soon, they vocalize, smile, and reach as ways of gaining adult attention and affection. Once babies become mobile, their expanded physical development allows them to actively seek out their caregivers, crawling after them, clinging to them, and scrambling into their laps. Older children, whose language and reasoning are more developed, quickly take advantage of such strategies as asking for a story to be read, to have one more drink of water, or to participate in a game as ways to be close to adults.

Practice and experience go hand in hand with development to expand children's social competence. Youngsters practice relevant skills, such as collaboration or more precise communication, through numerous interactions with others. Each minute episode gives the child information about which behaviors to maintain, which to avoid, and which to try instead (Boneau, 1974). In this way, children learn social behaviors based on whether the outcomes of their interactions are rewarding or costly for them (Thibault and Kelley, 1959). Rewards result from interactions that are satisfying to children's needs; costs stem from negative, aversive social exchanges. Hence, interactions that lead to acceptance, positive feedback, encouragement, or clarification are highly rewarding and those that culminate in rejection, avoidance, or misinterpretation are costly. Children who experience predominantly rewarding interactions and few costly ones feel better about themselves and become more socially competent than children for whom the reverse is true (Chaikin and Derlega, 1974). For this reason, adults who work with children play a major role in their social development. Such adult influences can be either beneficial or harmful. To ensure that their influence is beneficial, adults should know how children's ideas about self and others change over time, how youngsters acquire social behaviors, and in what context these processes take place. Additionally, adults must learn ways of interacting with children that will enhance their social competence. Basic to this understanding is knowledge of how children develop and learn.

PRINCIPLES OF DEVELOPMENT

Each child who comes into this world is a unique being, the result of a combination of tens of thousands of genes inherited from his or her parents. Every child has a distinctive voiceprint, fingerprint, lip print, and footprint and a natural odor distinctive enough for a bloodhound to follow. Even the size, shape, and operation of a child's brain structure, glands, organs, and body systems are slightly different from those of all other children. Additionally, the singularity of an infant's temperament, which is a precursor to later personality, can be noted immediately in the way the infant reacts to the environment and the people in it. Yet, despite all these differences, children's development the

world over seems to adhere to the following principles, which have been derived from both research and theory (Smart and Smart, 1977).

Cognitive, Physiological, and Social Development Are Interrelated

There are numerous threads of development that interweave and exist simultaneously. No one facet of development occurs independently of the others. For instance, children's ability to make friends is considered a social skill, but is also affected by other developmental processes. Language, memory, cognition, self-esteem, and physical prowess influence what approach they use, how they adapt to social situations, and how they feel about the encounters they experience.

All Development Follows a Normative Sequence

Development is sequential, and behavior patterns mature in an orderly manner. This sequence is the same for everyone and therefore is relatively predictable. For example, in order to eventually move from place to place, a child first learns to lift the head, then sit up, then stand, then crawl, then walk, then run. Similarly, children's language develops from babbling to holophrases, to telegraphic speech, then to the addition of adverbs and adjectives in phrases, then to sentences. Although children spend differing amounts of time on each step and sometimes seem to skip some of them altogether, the increments emerge in the same order.

There Is a Variation in the Rate of Development Within the Same Person and Between Persons

For all individuals, the different developmental threads are dominant at different times. For instance, height and weight increase at a fast rate during infancy, moderately during the pre-school years, and slowly in middle childhood. During adolescence, the rate of growth again proceeds rapidly. On the other hand, expressive language development accelerates between the ages of two and five and then proceeds more slowly, although somewhat steadily. These are examples of *intrapersonal* variations. Variations in developmental rates also occur *interpersonally*. Although the principle of normative sequence still applies, the pace at which individuals go through the sequence differs. This explains why one child utters her first word at one year of age and another does not start talking until eighteen months of age. Both are exhibiting normal development, but at different points in time. Some of these variations are explained by children's individual timing and some by gender differences. For example, among pre-school children, girls are generally more physically mature than their male counterparts (Smart and Smart, 1977). Also, there is growing evidence that brain structure may be more mature in five-year-old girls than in five-year-old boys (Epstein, 1978). Later, boys will catch up.

There Are Optimal Periods of Growth and Development

There are certain limited times during the developmental process when children can most beneficially interact with their environment. Outside those parameters, it is of little value to push children toward physical, emotional, or cognitive functioning that structure does not allow. Conversely, if a child is not permitted the kinds of experiences that will enhance development at a critical stage, she or he may be unmotivated or unable to reach potential later on without expending an inordinate amount of energy. For instance, there are particular prenatal and postnatal periods during which the brain is actively growing and there is increasingly complex networking between neurons.

This allows the organism to develop more complex levels of thought. It is during these periods that the brain is most receptive to stimulation. As another example, children in early elementary grades are willing to practice specific motor skills such as skipping, hopping, and jumping that they can later combine in more complex skills; however, they are unwilling to practice these basic activities in later elementary grades, when most children have developed such skills. This makes the early elementary years an optimal period for the development of fundamental motor skills.

Development Proceeds Toward Optimal Tendency

A developing organism seeks to achieve its maximum potential in both structure and function, searching for substantive sources of satisfaction if the usual ones are not available. Thus, children find alternate ways of satisfying their needs when ordinary paths are blocked—a child with poor eyesight makes use of other senses to gain information, or a youngster becomes strongly attached to other children when deprived of adult affection.

There Is Continual Differentiation and Integration of Development

Behaviors first exhibit themselves in large, global patterns. From these, smaller, more specific behaviors emerge. This is the process of *differentiation*. Later, when integration occurs, these specific, smaller sub-patterns combine into new, larger, and more complicated configurations. For instance, infants initially greet others with thrashing limbs, wiggling body, and general vocalization. Out of this broad, undifferentiated array of behaviors, children gradually develop such specific actions as smiling, saying "Hello," or reaching out. At first, these behaviors may be displayed on separate occasions. Eventually, preschool youngsters put them all together when they run to another, laughing and shouting their greeting. School-age children display an even more sophisticated integration of greeting behaviors when they make judgments about whom to approach and what to say.

Development Is Epigenic in Nature

All development is based on a foundation; past, present, and future are related and continuous. Any aspect of development exhibited at any point in time must be considered in terms of what went on before. For instance, an infant cannot grasp an object deliberately until he or she has lost the grasping reflex and has learned to let go. Additionally, it is widely believed that children are unable to develop a sense of independence if they have not first developed an adequate sense of trust (Erikson, 1950). Likewise, the ability to understand the emotions of another is predicated on first recognizing feelings in oneself (Forbes, 1978).

There Are Developmental Tasks Throughout Life

At different points in time, people work through different developmental issues (Havighurst, 1954). For example, one task that all individuals must deal with over the life span is that of achieving autonomy or an appropriate dependence-independence pattern. In infancy (birth to age two), this simply means beginning the establishment of self-awareness as a separate person. In early childhood (ages two to seven), the child becomes more physically independent, learning to eat, dress, and use the bathroom alone, and in later childhood (age seven to puberty), the child's task is to free himself or herself from primary identification with adults and move toward greater interaction with a peer group.

The periods for accomplishing these tasks are not discrete. They often overlap, and there are variations in how dominant a particular issue is at a given time. Hence, behaviors

characteristic of a new life task begin to appear as the preceeding life task still is being resolved. Gradually, a person's effort and energy shift from the first task to the second until the latter is more dominant. Even so, vestiges of the first may still remain. People also may regress when they are under stress, manifesting characteristics of an earlier period. Thus, a child who has long since achieved bladder control at night might begin wetting the bed if very nervous or frightened.

Developmental Implications

The goal of development in individuals is to adapt to the changing conditions of life and to make the most of their human, physical, and psychological potential. Abraham Maslow (1954) termed this "self-actualization" and maintained that the high-order needs, such as "belongingness needs and esteem needs," can only be addressed after primary needs for safety, food, and shelter have been met satisfactorily. Thus, a child who comes to school hungry or worried about being abused by a parent may not be able to attend to a spelling or reading activity; a child who has not experienced feelings of secure ownership will not be inclined to share with others; and a child who has not been able to form a strong attachment to a significant adult very likely will have problems in forming future attachments.

Through the development of intellectual flexibility, language, sex-role establishment, and increasingly complex interactions with objects and people, children gradually become aware of themselves as distinct persons and become sensitive to the roles they can effectively play in an expanding environment (Smart and Smart, 1977). Moreover, as children become able to harmonize their own needs and desires with demands from significant others and the outside world, they develop the self-concept, internal control, and character that will allow them to internalize rules, become better able to distinguish right from wrong, and develop the will to do the right thing even when outside controls are absent. Changes in behavior also will occur as a consequence of experience. These changes are influenced by children's learning.

HOW CHILDREN LEARN

Children are expected to learn a variety of social behaviors, such as to say "Excuse me" when they bump into someone, to cross a street at a corner, and to derive pleasure from sharing with a friend. True learning, in each of these instances, occurs only when children make a change in their behavior that they retain over time and that cannot simply be attributed to the process of growth (Gagné, 1977). Thus, children who remember a telephone number for five minutes and then forget it have not truly learned.

Social learning takes time; it is not necessarily acquired in a single interaction. It may take a child 80 tries to learn how to appropriately comfort someone in distress, or twice that number to learn that the rule is "walk, don't run." It may take another child far fewer or even more attempts to gain these same milestones. Two factors affect this variation in rates. One factor entails the personal characteristics the child brings to the situation (temperament, past learning and experience, intelligence, gender). The second involves the conditions under which the learning occurs.

Conditions of Learning

Children learn best when they feel comfortable and secure. Youngsters who are exhausted, frightened, or suspicious are not likely to absorb information or lessons directed toward them. Children also are more receptive to learning new things when they are in the company of people they trust and like, when they know that mistakes are tolerated, when they feel supported in their efforts to improve, and when they are free of strong biological urges such as

hunger or the need to go to the bathroom. In addition, opportunities for actual experience with the concept being addressed lead to more tangible and long-lasting results than when children are simply told about it. It is for this reason that children become more adept at sharing when they are given many chances to see people share, to be shared with, and to share. Lectures alone are less fruitful.

Further, children are most open to learning things that are important to them at the time. Such opportunities are sometimes referred to as "teachable moments." They explain why a youngster who wants a turn with the jump rope may be more willing to take in information about how to negotiate for it than she would have been were she less anxious to jump. Even when the information has been presented and the child has had an opportunity to use bargaining skills, it cannot be assumed that she has "learned" to negotiate. Instead, this one instance must be viewed as a practice episode, which should be repeated on other occasions in both similar and somewhat different circumstances. It will take many such experiences before the child will be able to demonstrate effective negotiation skills on her own.

Adults can do much to ensure that such practice occasions are made available. However, simply giving children access to these opportunities, either through planned activities or by taking advantage of spontaneous events, is not enough. Adults also must monitor such situations to make sure they are manageable for children. A youngster who is overwhelmed may be unable to understand or apply knowledge gained regardless of how potentially useful it may be. On the other hand, children who experience no challenge also may fail to progress in their understanding or abilities. Thus, positive social learning is most likely to occur when children feel both stimulated and successful.

It is caring adults who create the kind of environment that supports children's development and learning. Children's families have the

FIGURE 1-1 Children's high interest signals that this is a teachable moment.
SOURCE: H. Armstrong Roberts

first and most long-lasting influences on them. Eventually, youngsters move beyond the family into contact with professionals whose job it is to provide them some specific service. These people too have an impact on what children learn. In order to fully appreciate what each child experiences, one must recognize the interrelationships among all the environments of which the child is a part.

AN ECOLOGICAL VIEW OF CHILDREN

Children do not live in a vacuum. Rather, they are part of a number of social systems that in-

fluence how they develop and learn and that, concurrently, are influenced by them (Bronfenbrenner, 1981).

The most basic social system is the *microsystem*, which includes the entire array of activities, roles, and interpersonal relationships experienced by children in an immediate setting such as home or classroom. The primary microsystem for infants is the family. Older youngsters might participate at any time in the microsystem of the classroom, the microsystem of the neighborhood, or the microsystem of the 4-H group.

A *mesosystem* is a combination of microsystems. For a child, this might include relations among home, day-care center, and neighborhood playmates.

An *exosystem* involves one or more settings that do not involve a person as an active participant, but in which events occur that affect, or are affected by, what happens in the microsystem. Thus, one exosystem for children includes the parent's place of work. Certainly, what happens to Mom or Dad on the job affects the child via the parent's mood, level of stress, material resources gained, and time available for the child. In turn, the child may influence this same portion of the exosystem by affecting the parent's motivation, level of concentration, or health.

The largest, most comprehensive systems that affect the child are *macrosystems*. They consist of broad, institutional patterns in the child's culture, such as the legal, economic, religious, social, educational, and political systems.

These four categories of systems represent a holistic, ecological environment in which microsystems are seen as embedded within mesosystems, mesosystems contained within exosystems, and exosystems subsumed within the macrosystem. This nested, ecological environment is depicted in Figure 1-2 (Bronfenbrenner, 1981; Bubolz, Eicher, and Sontag, 1979; Hill, 1985).

Ecological Principles

Some generalizations can be made regarding how both the people and the systems of which they are a part function within a human ecological framework. The first premise is that people are not passive receivers of information and experience. Rather, they are constantly growing and changing and are actively involved with the systems.

Second, individuals and social systems have the capacity to change (Newman and Newman, 1978). This process is described as adaptation. *Adaptation* occurs when individuals and/or systems react to novel or stressful events with new actions or new organizational structures

(Moos, 1976). How systems change is illustrated by how the family microsystem adjusts to a variety of novel circumstances—a child's illness, parental unemployment, a son or daughter getting a driver's license, a grandparent moving into the household. This microsystem also must adapt to changes in the exosystem and macrosystem, such as variations in the inflation rate, international conflict, and public pressure for zero population growth. Thus, family microsystems often are strengthened or weakened by changes that occur in the economic, political, biomedical, and social systems surrounding them. Moreover, because adaptation is two way, families also affect the exosystems and macrosystems, demanding changes in laws and community organizations to support their changing needs.

It is assumed that both the individual and the system are modified as a result of their interaction. Hence, not only will the family as a whole change as a consequence of Grandma moving in, but individual family members will be affected as well. This dynamic view of people and systems maintains that one cannot be altered without the other also undergoing some transformation.

A third principle, that of *interdependence*, implies that individuals and systems are mutually reliant. For instance, children depend on their families for nurturance, physical sustenance, and protection. They depend on the community for education, recreation, and safety. They rely on the legal system to protect their rights and to make decisions in their best interests (Newman and Newman, 1978). In turn, parents may depend on the child for affection, stimulation, and enjoyment. Institutions within the community depend on children to be their clients or to influence family members to buy certain products. Members of the legal system may need children's rights as a forum to become known or to gain influence and power.

Finally, all systems have boundaries. *Boundaries* involve the mechanisms by which systems

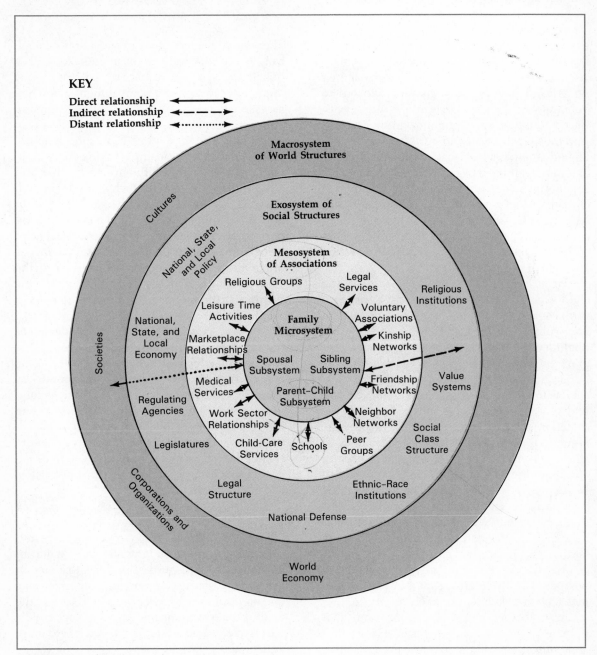

FIGURE 1-2 The interdependent ecological systems that directly and indirectly influence the development of children.

monitor the intake and output of information and resources. Resources may include tangible items, such as energy, food, and clothing, or psychological support, such as stimulation, affection, and respect (Newman and Newman, 1978). Boundaries are described in terms of their *permeability*, that is, how much is allowed to penetrate in either direction. Systems with closed boundaries allow minimal input and output; those with open boundaries permit an unlimited amount of information and resources to enter and exit the system. Some systems have semipermeable boundaries, which means that certain types or amounts of information and resources are allowed to go in or out. Such systems have *gatekeeping mechanisms* that monitor which inputs are used by the system and which outputs leave it.

For instance, in the microsystem of the child's classroom, the teacher is a primary gatekeeper. If the boundaries of this system were completely open, the teacher and children might feel compelled to repeatedly change program direction in response to such inputs as public concern over personal safety, the latest achievement test scores, magazine articles on hydrocarbon fuels, changes in the weather, the donation of 32 pairs of tap shoes, or parents' requests for lessons in manners. Obviously, if all these were viewed as having equal priority and requiring adaptation by the system, chaos would reign. On the other hand, were the boundaries to be entirely closed to all these inputs, the system would miss opportunities to benefit via appropriate adjustments. When the teacher as gatekeeper checks the flow of inputs by deciding which to discard, which to postpone, and which to respond to at the moment, class members are likely to profit.

From this example, it can be seen that human systems with semipermeable boundaries are more likely to enhance positive development and learning than those in which boundaries are completely open or closed.

The Value of Maintaining an Ecological Perspective

The primary benefit of viewing children ecologically is that one sees them in context. With a holistic perspective, a helping professional is more likely to consider many dimensions when assessing children's behavior and determining appropriate methods of intervention. This way of thinking also highlights the reciprocal nature of the helping relationship, making it clear that both adult and child influence each other and that it is not only the child whose behavior will change over time, but also the adult's. In addition, intervention with the child will have an impact on the other microsystems to which she or he belongs, such as the family. Also, what goes on in those microsystems will influence the child's behavior in the setting in which the helping professional sees him or her on a regular basis.

The ecological approach further underscores the importance of communication among the systems in which the child is included. This means that no one system can operate as though the others did not exist. Not only is communication vital, but so is the understanding that the influences of the microsystem, mesosystem, exosystem, and macrosystem are unique for each child. Therefore, it is to be expected that each child is unique and so must be considered individually.

Finally, adults who work with children often serve as gatekeepers to the microsystem in which they operate professionally. As a result, they have to make judgments about what information and resources to allow to enter or leave the system. In addition, they must take into account the nature of the boundaries of the various microsystems that make up each child's mesosystems and adapt their behaviors to those variabilities.

Keeping this framework in mind, we now turn to the two primary microsystems in which children are members—the family and the formal group setting. Together with other informal settings, these dominate the mesosystems of most children between birth and twelve years of age.

CHILDREN AND THEIR FAMILIES_____

The majority of children in this country grow up in families, and there is no doubt that this microsystem has the primary influence on their social development. A family usually is made up of individuals related to one another by strong reciprocal affections and loyalties, comprising a permanent household that persists over time. Members enter through birth, adoption, or marriage, and leave only by death (Carter and McGoldrick, 1980). Even when divorce or separation cause family members to be less available or to live in different places, they still are the child's family. Although families differ in configuration, size, life-style, available resources, history, traditions, and values, all families perform the same basic functions.

Family Functions

Many of the functions the family once performed, such as educating the young, passing on religious faith, maintaining health, providing protection, and ensuring the economic survival of its members, have been altered considerably. Other institutions have taken over major responsibility for those functions: the educational system; the religious system; the health-care system; and welfare, legislative, and police agencies.

Beyond the family functions of procreation and provision for actual physical needs, the primary tasks of today's family have come to be the nurturance and socialization of its members. Just as individuals have developmental tasks to perform over the life span, the family as a group has tasks it must accomplish in order to exist and have its members live in reasonable harmony (Havighurst, 1954). Some of the more important tasks for families with children from infancy to adolescence are the following:

1. Preserving the couple relationship during the demanding years of child rearing.
2. Meeting the changing needs of growing children for privacy, activities, friends, and wider social relationships.
3. Helping prepare children to make transitions to new roles.
4. Providing for parents' needs for privacy and quiet.
5. Continuing to establish basic values in a world that is continually changing.
6. Meeting expanded costs.
7. Maintaining the morale of the family.
8. Creating and maintaining adequate communication in the family.
9. Working out ways of sharing tasks and responsibilities.
10. Fitting into community life as a family and as persons.

How well the family performs these developmental tasks will predict the quality of environmental support within the family system.

Factors That Influence Family Environments

In order to make family life more predictable and to better meet family needs, most beginning families very early form what become relatively enduring patterns of how members make decisions, communicate with one another, and show affection. Some families conform closely to the kinds of roles that were traditionally played out in their families of origin, and other families construct role behaviors that seem to fit the emerging life-styles of the dual-employed, single-parent, blended, never-married, and extended-family forms.

Over time, all families encounter turning points (Neugarten, 1976). Examples of turning points are the birth of children, the beginning and ending of formal schooling of children, the entry of other members through marriage, a member entering a new career or losing a job, or a crisis such as substance abuse by a member. These changes include both normative (expected) and nonnormative events and require adjustment by the family in terms of identity and member self-concept. Family systems, like other complex systems, do not change smoothly but rather in discontinuous transformations or "leaps" in response to pressures from the surrounding environment. In other words, for at least one member of the family, the old patterns are not working any longer. The family system is then forced to alter its patterns, allowing new options and possibilities to emerge (Carter and McGoldrick, 1980). During these periods of disruption, two characteristics determine how well the family will "ride out" the disturbance: family cohesion (members providing emotional support for one another) and adaptability.

Families who have a high tolerance for member problems, and who provide both psychological and material support during periods of disruption, tend to function more effectively and with more self-satisfaction than those who are nonsupportive of one another. Similarly, families who are less adaptable have fewer options available to them when they encounter internal and external demands. Moreover, the attempt of one part of the system to restore balance may cause disequilibrium in another part of the system. Thus, a parent reacting to one child's poor report card may establish a rule about limited television viewing during the week. If this is a rule that all family members are expected to observe, it may be viewed by other family members as a "hardship" they

don't deserve, causing disruption elsewhere in the system.

On the other hand, families who are able to incorporate new social and emotional roles are better able to adapt and therefore regain stability. How adaptable a family is has much to do with the degree to which family boundaries are permeable. In the family system, members serve as the gatekeepers, screening and interpreting information, energy, and material inputs and outputs that serve as interchanges both within the microsystem and between it and others. Boundaries that are too rigid may deprive the family of necessary information or support; conversely, a family system that is too open may become disorganized and incapable of carrying out necessary functions to support the growth and development of its members. Optimally, families function best when they have clearly defined, semipermeable boundaries that remain flexible enough to allow change to occur while still maintaining a predictable, growth-enhancing environment.

What Is an Ideal Family?

Each of us has a differing personal concept of what the ideal family might look like. We draw that ideal from remembered experiences within our own family of origin and from what we know about the families of our colleagues, friends, and neighbors. We also have become acquainted with "media" families, few of which realistically depict the wide variations possible in family life.

Competent helping professionals are those who avoid judging family worth based on stereotypical or familiar personal constructs. For instance, in the past several years, it has become popular to assume that intact family systems automatically function better than those in which not all adult family members are present (Boss, 1980). Yet, family members can be physically present but psychologically absent. For example, a parent may be so consumed with a work role or with personal problems that she or he is truly unavailable to a child, despite the fact that they both physically reside together. Conversely, a parent can be physically absent but play such a dominant role that he or she is a tremendously important psychological presence in the child's life. In addition, one cannot assume that families with multiple children are the same as those with one child, or that families experiencing crises such as the death or chronic illness of a member, divorce, or loss of a job function in the same way as families not experiencing these events. Nor can we expect families who have a wealth of resources to behave in the same way as families who are experiencing scarcity. Because there is no one "correct" family form, value system, tradition, or life-style, it is best to remain flexible as to what constitutes normal family behavior and to perceive both children and their families within an ecological perspective.

From this discussion, it can be concluded that the family is the most significant microsystem in children's lives. As youngsters' mesosystems expand, they also become involved in the microsystems of any number of formal group settings.

FORMAL GROUP SETTINGS

Formal group settings are microsystems in which children participate in organized programs of service for some portion of the day. Although some children receive these services in their own households, the majority do not. Common settings include those that provide informal education in the community, such as 4-H, YMCA, YMHA, and Scouts; those that offer formal education, such as public and private schools, preschools, Head Start programs, Chapter I programs, and Home Start programs; those that supply health services, such as hospi-

FIGURE 1-3 Formal group settings vary, but the characteristics of organization and leadership do not.
SOURCE: Photo by David Kostelnik

tals, outpatient clinics, and therapeutic nursery schools; those that offer recreational programs, such as camps, parks, and recreational centers; and those that involve residential care, such as group foster homes and residential treatment centers. Although each of these settings is different in its primary focus, all have a defined purpose and a predetermined structure and require specialized leadership. They often involve physical settings that contain materials purposely designed for use with children. Also, formal group settings all support the basic functions of the family but are, in fact, tangential to it. Many services frequently are delivered without adult family members being present. For example, in a child-care center, parents give and receive information about their children at arrival and pick-up and through other formal contacts, but the child-care provider cares for the children without the parents most of the time. Even in a cooperative nursery, in which parents work with the professional caregiver on a scheduled basis, an individual parent is absent more often than present as other parents participate in their rotation of duty. Thus, adults who work in these settings have continual responsibility for the children in their care and must repeatedly make program-related decisions regarding their welfare.

The formalized structure described here becomes evident when comparing an informal setting, such as a family household, with a formal setting, such as a family day-care home. In the informal setting, children might come and go as they please, play inside or out, and frequently play without adult supervision. The choice of activities is largely up to them, and family members often are occupied with household tasks. In the formal setting, however, the provider expects to receive and release children and know where they are at all times. Children are never unsupervised, and they participate in planned activities. The adult's primary function is to watch and interact with the children rather than become involved in tasks for maintaining the household. There are no licenses or contracts in the informal setting, but both may be present in the formal situation. These same kinds of comparisons could be made between informal and formal settings in the educational, recreational, and medical fields as well.

The Atmosphere of the Formal Group Setting

Formal group settings consist of more than the organizational structures just described. In each setting, the interpersonal relations that exist among adults and children also are important and determine what is referred to as program *climate* or *atmosphere* (Gazda, 1977). People talk about this dimension when they depict a program as being friendly or unfriendly, chaotic or busy, relaxed or uptight, pleasant or unpleasant, caring or impersonal. All these terms describe an emotional tone that may either promote or inhibit children's learning.

It is the adults in the setting who dictate its atmosphere (Anderson and Brewer, 1945; Withall and Lewis, 1963). Their attitudes about the children with whom they work, what they say to them, and how they act toward them all determine the overall aura that prevails. For example, there is a noticeable difference between the climate that characterizes the Girl Scout troop at Adams School and the one at Springfield Elementary School. In the former, the leaders make it clear that "fooling around" will not be tolerated and that the troop members are there for one purpose: to earn their badges. For the candle-making project, the goal is for all candles to look exactly alike. Children are told which materials they must use and the precise sequence of steps they are to follow. Youngsters are expected to work on their own, neither giving nor receiving help from friends. The room is generally silent as the leaders stand at the front calling out instructions. When Madeleine has difficulty unmolding her candle, she is admonished to be less clumsy in her work. When Carrie asks a question, an adult sighs in exasperation and tells her to pay more attention next time. Two other girls whose final products are lopsided and somewhat askew are told to melt their candles down and try again until they get it right.

A very different atmosphere exists at Springfield. The troop's project for the day also is candles. Youngsters are given a wide array of materials from which to choose. They are told that each girl should decorate her candle in her own special way. They may either work by themselves or with a partner and are encouraged to lend assistance as necessary. The leaders circulate among the girls, praising their work and offering on-the-spot assistance. The room reverberates with laughter and chatter. When all the projects are finished, the adults urge everyone to applaud a job well done.

There is little doubt that the climate in the Springfield Scout program is more conducive to learning than the one at Adams School. At Springfield, children are comfortable and happy. Although youngsters are involved in a common activity, their individuality also is valued. They feel respected as human beings because the leaders treat them as competent and important. As a result, the girls view the adults as both supportive and capable of giving them clear guidelines for how to be successful. The Springfield Scouts feel good about themselves and their participation in the troop. This is not so for the Adams School Scouts. A tension pervades the setting that is a direct result of the adults' disparaging remarks and their obvious impatience with the girls. The children learn that their best efforts are not good enough and that failure is more likely than success. They also find that the adults are not sources of guidance. Rather, they are authorities to be avoided. These scouts come away each week feeling bad about themselves and their abilities.

Climatic outcomes. Program atmosphere has a major influence on children's opinions about themselves. In addition, it affects the social behaviors children acquire in the setting. Whether they learn to be cooperative or resistant, friendly or unfriendly, controlled or impulsive has much to do with how they are treated by the helping adults with whom they come in contact. For instance, poor social learning occurs when adults shame children, shout at them, coerce them, or physically hurt them. All too often, youngsters subjected to such conditions become destructive, hostile, and aggressive (Hoffman, 1983). They learn to be covert in their actions, continually looking for ways to avoid responsibility (Parke, 1977). In an effort to protect themselves, these children also become self-centered and have difficulty considering the needs of others. As a result, they are less likely to be helpful, cooperative, or kind. On the other hand, adults who convey respect for children through actions and words, and who provide constructive guidelines for how children can succeed, generate a positive social climate.

Children in such an environment are most apt to be responsive to others' feelings, cooperative, friendly, and eager to learn the rules of society.

Obviously, adults who work with children in settings such as these have a tremendous impact on social development. Such individuals are called helping professionals.

What Is a Helping Professional?

For the purpose of this book, *helping professionals* are defined as people employed by families to provide services to children. Services rendered are those that families may find too specialized, too time consuming, too cumbersome, or too expensive to provide directly themselves.

Regardless of whether the helping professional's title is teacher, counselor, caregiver, leader, social worker, or childlife specialist, certain characteristics differentiate the professional from the nonprofessional. One major distinction is that professionals have access to a body of knowledge and skills not available to the general public. People who do not have this background cannot perform the services as skillfully or support the development of children as well as those who have it, although in some settings they may be employed to do so.

Another means of distinguishing professionals from lay persons is that the former have to demonstrate competencies related to their field in order to enter it. The most formalized evidence of mastery requires earning a license or certification, which usually is governed by state or national standards. Slightly less formal monitoring involves having to take tests or pass certain courses as testimony to one's knowledge and understanding. Currently, most fields also require an internship or other experiential training. All these take place under the supervision of qualified professionals.

Professionalism also implies certain ethical standards to which each individual must conform. Specific codes govern professionals whose work involves children. Although the particulars may vary, such codes all aim toward ensuring confidentiality, providing safe and wholesome experiences, and treating people appropriately regardless of sex, race, or religion. Adults may have strong personal convictions, but as professionals, they cannot necessarily act on them. For example, an adult may have particular religious or political beliefs, yet in the professional setting, it is inappropriate to refer to children of different religious persuasions as heathens or to try to convert them or their families to a particular way of thinking. Further, professionals may have personal knowledge about children and their families, but must refrain from gossiping about them. Only in child-abuse cases, for which states mandate reporting, is the confidentiality rule waived. Thus, professionals are obliged to protect the interests of children and their families regardless of personal biases.

Fundamentally, it is expected that helping professionals will act in ways that enhance the development of children and maintain standards of acceptable behavior. Thus, groups of professionals monitor the behavior of their own practitioners in order to ensure high-quality service. This monitoring system is not available to lay persons.

The Role of the Helping Professional in Relation to Children's Social Development

Although helping professionals in different settings may concentrate on particular developmental domains, such as physical well-being or intellectual accomplishments, they invariably also must support children's social and emotional development. For instance, children in hospitals are there for specific health reasons. Yet, no matter how ill they might be, their needs cannot be met by medical intervention alone. Nurturance, information, and communication continue to be important social dimensions that cannot be ignored if optimal health is to be achieved. For this reason, all helping profes-

sionals must be prepared to support their young clients emotionally as well as carry out the procedures dictated by their professional role. Thus, helping has two dimensions: facilitation and action (Gazda, 1977).

The facilitation dimension. The basis of all helping is emotional supportiveness (Katz, 1972). The recipient of intended help cannot accept it from someone with whom he or she has no relationship. In addition, social learning is facilitated when youngsters view the helping professional as a source of comfort and encouragement (Baumrind, 1977; Katz, 1977).

Emotional supportiveness has four components: empathy, acceptance, respect, and warmth (Coletta, 1977; Gazda, 1977; Rogers, 1961). *Empathy* has been identified as the single most important element of the helping process (Carkhuff, 1969a). It refers to the ability to recognize and understand the perspective of another. An empathic person responds to another's *affective,* or *emotional, state* by experiencing some of that same emotion (Gordon, 1975). In common parlance, this is described as "walking in someone's shoes," or "seeing the world through another's eyes." Thus, empathy involves the cognitive process of examining and knowing, as well as the affective process of feeling.

Closely related to empathy is the concept of *acceptance* or unconditional positive regard. Acceptance refers to every human being's need to gain self-confirmation from others. Without this, constructive growth is impossible (Rogers, 1961). To be accepted unconditionally means to be valued fully with no strings attached. Adults who demonstrate unconditional positive regard toward children care about them regardless of their personal attributes, family background, or behavior. They do not require children to earn their caring through good grades, compliance, charm, or beauty. Rather, they believe that all chilren are worthy of acceptance simply because they are human. Thus, acceptance is a neutral act that implies the absence of any level of evaluation (Bessell, 1970).

Unfortunately, acceptance is the component of facilitation that has been most widely misunderstood. Often, it has been assumed that in order to accept children, one must condone and acquiesce to all behaviors, including antisocial acts. As you will discover throughout this text, there are ways to guide children into using more appropriate behavior while at the same time communicating support and concern. This is exemplified by the attitude illustrated in the following well-worn phrase: ''I care about you, but I don't like the way you are acting right now.''

Respect involves having faith in children's ability to eventually learn the information, behavior, and skills they will need to constructively function on their own. Thus, having respect for children implies believing that they are capable of changing their behavior and of making self-judgments. Helping professionals manifest respect when they allow children to think for themselves, make decisions, work toward their own solutions, and communicate their ideas. Lack of respect is evident when adults tell children how to think and feel, when they ignore children's points of view, or when they disregard children altogether.

Warmth refers to the manner in which people conduct themselves in social interactions. It entails showing an interest in others, being friendly toward them, and being responsive to them. People who are characterized as warm are those who make others feel comfortable, supported, and valued.

All four of these components—empathy, acceptance, respect, and warmth—contribute to the relationship-building process and provide the foundation from which action can be taken. The cardinal rule in helping is to refrain from moving into the action dimension until one has earned the right to do so by building a facilitative base (Gazda, 1977). Even if one has only a few moments, facilitation should always precede action.

The action dimension. The action phase of helping focuses on teaching children new knowledge and skills. To do this, one must provide children with appropriate behavioral *cues.* These are verbal or nonverbal expressions, direct physical acts, or a combination of these aimed at helping children maintain or change their behavior. It has been found that children receive and learn from some types of cues better than others (Hoffman, 1983). Also, certain cueing strategies are more effective than others in helping children learn productive ways of behaving (Gnagey, 1975). Effective cueing is dependent on two factors: concreteness and technical proficiency. Adults are *concrete* when they pinpoint and accurately label emotions, experiences, and behaviors relevant to the child and to themselves. This means they are specific and use techniques that make children fully aware of what is expected. *Technical proficiency* is achieved when adults know when to use particular strategies and how to carry them out.

Expert practitioners blend the facilitative and action dimensions. They understand when and how to use each component and are skilled in effectively implementing them. At this point, one might ask how such knowledge and skill can be attained by the aspiring helping professional.

Becoming a Helping Professional

That Jenny Taylor just has a gift for working with children. She's a natural.

He must be good with children. He comes from a large family.

Well, working with children might wear you out, but they're so young you don't have to know much.

Comments such as these often are aimed at people who indicate a desire to work with children on a professional basis. Such comments imply that effective helping professionals are born, not made, that productive helping behavior is a product of personality, and that, although working with children may be physically and emotionally demanding, it offers little intellectual challenge. Such notions are false. They are as erroneous as thinking that jet pilots fly solely on intuition or maintain good safety records based on their charm, or that all that is required to be a pilot is a love of airplanes. Certainly, when passengers buckle up for takeoff, they expect the pilot to have more than good looks, instinct, or the desire to get them safely to their destination.

Although some people do have qualities and abilities that enhance their potential for success in a particular profession, all professions have specialized knowledge that must be learned and certain competencies that must be acquired. This is no less true for professions that focus on helping children.

Knowledge and skills. The knowledge base from which helping professionals work is derived from a combination of theories and empirical research related to child development and human intervention. It delineates relevant terminology, facts, principles, and concepts aimed at explaining why children behave as they do and providing clues as to helpful and nonhelpful modes of intervention. Although the knowledge base of any field is constantly changing as new information becomes available through research, the information that currently exists provides a framework from which to operate. Professionals cannot approach their work haphazardly; they cannot simply react to children. Rather, they must respond rationally and purposefully, using theoretical and empirical information to guide their actions. Such knowledge also provides professionals working in widely divergent settings a common foundation from which to communicate with one another and work toward shared goals.

Once gained, knowledge must be translated into practice. It is not enough to simply recite textbook philosophy: one must also learn how to act in ways that accurately support and con-

vey that philosophy. Thus, professionals must learn certain behaviors that represent effective helping (D'Augelli, et al., 1980; Egan, 1975; Kostelnik, 1978). These learned behaviors are called skills.

Skills consist of observable actions that, when used in combination, represent mastery of a given technique or communicate general attitudes. Thus, they can be seen, learned, and evaluated. For instance, a person who wants to convey the facilitative characteristic of warmth toward children will smile at them, establish eye contact, and stoop down to their level. All of these behaviors can be readily observed and identified.

In addition, a person who does not smile much can be taught to smile more; an individual who avoids eye contact can be trained to look at people's faces; someone who tends to tower over children can learn to bend or squat. Finally, it is possible to assess how often these behaviors are exhibited and how appropriately they are utilized. Because smiling, establishing eye contact, and stooping are observable, learnable, and assessable, they are skills.

Some skills, such as these, are simple to understand and easy to learn; others are more complex and difficult. It all cases, skill mastery requires the learner to know what to do, why to do it, and how to do it. Yet, even when all this is accomplished, true mastery is not attained until the learner uses the skill in the setting for which it was intended. Thus, it is not sufficient only to realize the importance of smiling, or even to smile appropriately during a role-playing situation in a college class. One must also smile at children in the center, on the playground, or in the playroom. This transfer of training from practice situations to real-life encounters is the goal of skill learning.

CHAPTER STRUCTURE

Based on the previous discussion, it is apparent that both knowledge and practice are essential elements in the training of helping professionals. Consequently, the following chapters each contain sections representing the information and skills related to a particular facet of social development. A statement of objectives precedes the chapter text and tells you what you should know after completing the chapter. This list also helps make clear the progression from knowledge to practice for that unit.

The objectives are followed by a discussion of the latest empirical findings and the theory pertinent to the topic of the chapter. This constitutes the knowledge base for the chapter. The skills section that follows describes specific techniques related to the topic. Also included is a chronicle of common pitfalls you may experience when first adopting the skills in your own interactions with children. All chapters conclude with a summary, which provides a brief overview of the topic just presented. Discussion questions also have been developed to help you better assess your understanding of the material.

CHAPTER SEQUENCE _____

The next 15 chapters are presented in a specific sequence, with chapters that focus on relationship-building skills appearing prior to those that involve behavioral cueing skills. The sequence is based on the premise that adult attempts to maintain or change children's behavior are most successful only after bonds of trust and caring have been developed. For this reason, the chapters build on one another: skills covered in earlier chapters lead to those that follow.

This initial chapter introduced the basic premises around which the rest of the book is structured. Included was rudimentary information about how children develop and how they learn, as well as how adults influence these processes. Throughout this discussion, we have emphasized the interdependent nature of

children and the environment. Finally, those characteristics that set helping professionals apart from lay people, as well as how helping professionals should function in guiding children's social development, were identified.

Because social relationships begin at birth, Chapter 2 discusses infant development and the methods by which adults can relate to even the youngest child. Although positive communication goals are fundamentally the same throughout the life span, techniques that are effective with children younger than two years of age are somewhat different from those utilized with older youngsters. Thus, Chapter 2 focuses entirely on the earliest period of childhood. All the following chapters deal primarily with children between the ages of two and twelve.

With this in mind, Chapter 3 discusses the nonverbal aspects of communication. How toddlers, preschoolers, and school-age children communicate nonverbally and how they interpret the nonverbal communication of adults are discussed. Ways in which adults manifest empathy, acceptance, respect, and warmth through voice and action are also explained.

In Chapter 4, the emphasis turns to verbal communication. This chapter describes how adult words affect children's self-awareness and self-judgments about their competence and worth. Specific skills are introduced that, when implemented, positively influence children's development in these areas. A component of self-awareness involves recognizing and understanding emotions. Therefore, how children develop emotionally and what adults should do to enhance this domain is the subject of Chapter 5.

Chapter 6 deals with children's play. Why children play, how they play, and what role adults should take in enhancing play are discussed. This is the last chapter that focuses exclusively on the facilitative dimension of the helping role.

The next several chapters move into the action dimension of helping. Chapters 7, 8, and 9 focus on discipline. Factors that contribute to the development of self-discipline in children are described in Chapter 7, and ways to formulate appropriate rules are presented. Chapter 8 continues this theme by underscoring the developmental reasons why self-control is not automatic, as well as how adults can utilize consequences to enable children to take more responsibility for regulating their own behavior. One of the most difficult behaviors for children to learn to control is their aggressiveness. For this reason, Chapter 9 is entirely devoted to this subject. Why children are aggressive, variations in aggressive behavior, and how aggression changes with age are outlined. Tactics adults should avoid and those they should pursue are presented.

On a slightly different track, Chapters 10 through 14 concentrate on enhancing children's quality of life by helping them build a repertoire of social skills that go beyond rules and consequences. Chapter 10 deals with children and stress. Symptoms of stress, factors that contribute to stress in young people, and specific techniques children can learn to reduce such stress are described. How to handle children's burgeoning sexuality, racial awareness, and experiences with people who have handicaps are the subjects of Chapter 11. In Chapter 12, attention is turned to the influence of the physical environment on children's social development. In particular, techniques are emphasized that enhance children's ability to work independently and make decisions. To achieve this end, the process by which adults make decisions also is highlighted. Chapter 13 describes the value of children's friendships to them and how children's concepts of friendship change over time. This content provides a base from which particular strategies are derived for helping children initiate and maintain peer relationships. Chapter 14 then defines what is meant by prosocial behavior and describes the evolving nature of such behavior throughout childhood. Techniques for teaching children kindness, both informally and through more structured experiences, are presented.

The last two chapters of the book should enable you to integrate all the content and skills presented thus far. Chapter 15 focuses on working with parents. In it are discussed ways in which helping professionals can better relate to the other important people in children's lives, and why they should do so. In addition, guidelines are provided for how best to communicate with parents. The final chapter emphasizes how to match the skills you have learned to the situations for which they are best suited. This chapter also discusses the circumstances in which one should seek outside intervention or consultation in dealing with children and their families.

STUDENT OBJECTIVES_____

When used as a whole, the knowledge and skills presented in this book will provide aspiring and current helping professionals with comprehensive and systematic guidelines for promoting children's social development. When you have completed the book, you will know more about how to do the following:

1. Articulate the role of the helping professional in enhancing children's social development.
2. Integrate factual information with practical strategies for interacting with children individually and in groups.
3. Adjust your behavior with children to accommodate cultural and developmental differences.
4. Respond to children in a manner that the children interpret as supportive and predictable.
5. Identify the child's perspective within varying interpersonal and situational circumstances.
6. Talk to children in ways that promote positive adult-child relationships.
7. Extend children's understanding of their own emotions and the emotions of others.

8. Express your own emotions clearly and precisely to children.
9. Utilize rules and consequences that further self-discipline in children.
10. Help children develop specific coping skills for a variety of situations.
11. Facilitate growth-enhancing play among children.
12. Arrange children's environments to promote independence, decision making, and harmonious relationships.
13. Help children learn specific strategies to enhance their relationships with peers.
14. Assist children in developing specific proso-cial behaviors such as helping and cooperating.
15. Work cooperatively with families to enhance children's social growth and development.
16. Identify multiple issues to be considered in adult-child interactions.
17. Provide child-development-related ration-ales for choosing specific strategies when working with children and families.
18. Determine when children's behavior war-rants additional consultation and referrals to other helping professionals.

SUMMARY

Social competence refers to a person's ability to recognize, interpret, and respond to social situations in ways deemed appropriate by society. The acquisition of social competence begins in childhood and occurs as a result of both developmental and experiential factors. As children develop greater linguistic, memory, cognitive, and physical abilities, their capacity for social competence increases. This capacity also is affected by what children learn and how they learn it.

Social learning takes place within an interdependent network of systems—the microsystem, the mesosystem, the exosystem, and the macrosystem. Each system influences children and is in turn influenced by them. In addition, both the individual and the system are modified by the interaction. What comes into any system and what goes out of it is determined by the types of boundaries the system has. The understanding of all these concepts taken together contributes to what is called an ecological perspective. It is beneficial to maintain such a perspective because it enables one to see children and respond to their needs in context.

The most basic system within the ecological framework is the family. Families play a primary role in socializing the young. This function is effectively carried out by families whose structure and values differ widely. Thus, no one family form is considered preferable. As children mature, other systems, including formal group settings, play an ever-increasing role in their lives. In these settings, children receive a particular service from trained individuals. Such adults not only teach, counsel, lead, or supervise children, but also create a program atmosphere that can make children feel good or bad about themselves. Because these adults focus on helping children achieve positive growth, they are called helping professionals.

Because the basis of all helping is emotional supportiveness, professionals who work with children must learn to demonstrate empathy, acceptance, respect, and warmth. Only after these skills have been established can adults effectively help children change their behavior in ways that will increase their social competence. Becoming a helping professional requires both knowledge and skills. The structure of this book and the sequence of chapters within it are aimed toward teaching both in a systematic and comprehensive manner. In this way, adults can learn to guide children's social development.

DISCUSSION QUESTIONS

1. Define social competence. Discuss behaviors that could be described as evidence of social competence and those that illustrate lack of social competence.
2. With a partner, describe the microsystem in which you currently work with children.
3. With a partner, describe the mesosystems and exosystems of which each of you are a part. Discuss how they overlap and how they differ.
4. Talk about the factors that influence a person's social learning. Give an example from your own life.
5. Pretend you are entering a children's group setting for the first time. Discuss the clues you could use to judge whether the atmosphere supports or inhibits children's social development.
6. Discuss the ''gatekeeper'' role of the teacher in the classroom. Use the examples given in the text and assess what effect admitting each of those elements might have on the classroom microsystem.
7. Discuss the similarities and differences of formal and informal group settings. Choose two settings with which you are familiar to use as examples.
8. Describe the facilitative and action dimensions in terms of children's social development. Discuss their relationship.
9. Discuss the role of the helping professional in children's social development.
10. In a small group of three or four, discuss your aspirations as a helping professional.

CHAPTER 2
Initiating Social Relationships in Infancy

OBJECTIVES:

On completion of this chapter, you will be able to describe:

1. The behavioral states of infants and how to soothe a crying infant.

2. The sensory abilities of infants and how these relate to social behavior.

3. The role of motor development in social interaction.

4. The relationship of temperament to social interaction.

5. The sequential steps of individuation, or becoming a separate person.

6. The capacity of an infant for social interaction with peers and adults.

7. Strategies that adults can use to support healthy social-emotional development.

8. Pitfalls to avoid in interacting with infants.

SOURCE: H. Armstrong Roberts

23

Now, don't spoil the baby.

Please shut that baby up!

Oh, babies are no trouble to me!

In a few years, you may be working professionally with infants and their families in a newborn nursery of a hospital, in a child-care center, or in a community-based infant development program. How social development begins and how it changes as the infant matures will be important information for you to know. You may even be asked to teach others how to provide the responsive, loving care that infants need in order to thrive.

When a baby is born, it immediately is a member of a social group; a family, who lives in a community, which is contained within a larger culture. Although infants essentially are not social in the beginning, in two short years they will participate as full partners in social interactions within the family and with others as they encounter people outside the home.

The primary caregiver is central to the normal development of the infant. Although the primary caregiver usually is the mother in our society, others may fulfill this function. The relationship that develops between the primary caregiver and child during the first two years of life is the foundation on which all later development is based. Fortunately, other family members, friends, and helping professionals often participate in the early child rearing in ways that can support and enhance the efforts of parents.

This chapter focuses on abilities of newborns that enable them to become true social partners, typical behaviors that caregivers can expect during the first year, and the skills adults can learn to maximize infant social development.

INFANT COMPETENCIES

What does an infant look like? Newborns have large heads and trunks with relatively smaller limbs. They may or may not have much hair, but their heads smell nice. Their skin, in the beginning, may be discolored and wrinkly, but is always soft, and soon fills out. Eyes are large in a face that may be quite flat; rounded cheeks are characteristic of the first year. This cherubic appearance makes the infant cute and appealing to adults.

Newborns are small but grow rapidly during the first year, gaining in both length and weight so that a one-year-old seems heavy in comparison. Newborns are fairly still, or sedentary, but by the sixth or seventh month of age, they become intrepid travelers. Thus, rapid change is the hallmark of infancy.

There have been two widely held views about the nature of infants. The first, and earliest, is that infants are not yet "real people," are largely unaware of their environment, and have few resources for interacting with it. The second view, based on later research and parental experience, is that the human infant is remarkably competent and is able to respond socially quite early in life. These views are illustrated by the behavior of Mrs. Roberts and Mrs. James, two women who shared a hospital room after giving birth for the first time. Mrs. Roberts kept her newborn with her, watching her baby's hands and feet move about while quietly talking to her. She told the baby how glad she was to have her, about her family, and what her room at home was like.

Mrs. James looked at Mrs. Roberts in surprise and asked, "Don't you know she can't talk? She can't do anything for a long time." Her own infant was brought in for feedings and promptly returned to the nursery.

Mrs. Roberts thought of her newborn as a person already capable of engaging in social interaction, whereas Mrs. James expected her infant to become a real person at some later date.

Behavioral States

Infants do not behave in the same way all the time. The usual behavior alternatives are known as behavioral states (Wolff, 1966). The infant's current *behavioral state* influences how he or she perceives the world and responds to social encounters. For example, an infant who is sleeping or crying vigorously obviously is less able to attend to the environment than one who is quiet and watching what is happening nearby. There are seven different behavioral states, each of which is characterized by differences in respiration, muscle tone, motor activity, and alertness (Wolff, 1966; Dittrichova and Paul, 1971; Ashton, 1973; Papousek and Papousek, 1977). Newborns change states rapidly and irregularly and may not establish a routine pattern for several weeks. As infants mature, however, changes in state become more regular and infants establish their own routine *rhythm*, or predictable pattern of behavior. Adults who learn to recognize each of these states are better able to receive clues for responding to even the youngest child (Korner, 1974). The behavioral states of infants are summarized in Table 2-1.

Sleep states. Infants who are in any of the four sleep states should not be interrupted or stimulated. Only the infant who is waking up slowly from a long sleep and is still drowsy should be picked up. Infants should not be awakened to be changed, fed, or engaged in social interaction. For this reason, schedules fixed by the clock for adult conveniences rather than by the infant's cues are not appropriate.

Newborns spend much of their time sleeping (about 16 to 17 hours a day), with frequent episodes of wakefulness for feeding (Parmelee, Wenner, and Schultz, 1964). The total amount of time the newborn sleeps drops off rapidly in the first few days and then declines more gradually; babies sleep about 12 hours a day at six months of age.

Aroused states. In the quiet alert or alert inactive state, the infant may appear to stare and is more likely to be responsive to stimulation and social contact. States of quiet alert are both brief and rare initially, but increase noticeably over the first few months (Berg and Berg, 1979).

Caregivers should take advantage of moments when infants are displaying alert inactivity by talking to them, touching them, and presenting objects for them to enjoy. Caregivers should not conclude that quiet infants will entertain themselves or do not require stimulation just because they are not obviously demanding attention. However, if the amount of stimulation is too great, the infant will increase its activity or go to sleep as a way to avoid overstimulation (Lewis, 1972).

Newborns spend most of their waking time being fed, changed, dressed, or bathed. As the amount of time spent in sleep decreases, a corresponding amount of time is available in the quiet alert and waking activity states for social encounters.

Crying and Soothing

Adults spend much time and energy in responding to infant cries, trying to determine what the infant needs, and soothing the infant.

Although individual infants have recognizable voices, they also have characteristic cries for hunger, pain, and anger, which can be distinguished from one another by the pattern of pauses between bursts of crying, the duration of the cry, and by noticeable tonal characteristics (Wolff, 1967, 1969; Vuorenkoski, et al., 1969, 1971). The pain cry, for example, is a long, piercing wail. This cry is a peremptory signal that something is wrong and must be changed. It is quite different from speech sounds and is extremely effective as a communication signal in getting the attention of the caregiver (Lenneberg, 1964; Tonkova-Yampolskaya, 1962). Caregivers familiar with individual infants learn to identify and respond appropriately to these cries.

Infants also may cry for a variety of other reasons, such as fright caused by a loud noise

TABLE 2-1 Infant Behavioral States and Appropriate Adult Responses

	RESPIRATION	FACIAL EXPRESSION	ACTION	ADULT RESPONSE
Regular Sleep	Regular; 36 per minute	Eyes closed and still; face relaxed	Little movement; fingers slightly curled, thumbs extended	Do not disturb
Irregular Sleep	Uneven, faster; 48 per minute	Eyes closed, occasional rapid eye movement; smiles and grimaces	Gentle movement	Do not disturb
Periodic Sleep		(Alternates between regular and irregular sleep)		
Drowsiness	Even	Eyes open and close or remain halfway open; eyes dull/glazed	Less movement than in irregular sleep; hands open and relaxed, fingers extended	Pick up if drowsiness follows sleeping; do not disturb if drowsiness follows awake periods
Alert Inactivity	Constant; faster than in regular sleep	Bright eyes, fully open; face relaxed	Slight activity; hands open, fingers extended, arms bent at elbow; stares	Talk to infant; present objects; perform any assessment
Waking Activity	Irregular	Face flushed; less able to focus eyes than in alert inactivity	Extremities and body move; vocalizes, makes noises	Interact with infant; provide basic care
Crying		Red skin; facial grimaces; eyes partially or fully open	Vigorous activity; crying vocalizations; fists are clenched	Pick up immediately; try to identify source of discomfort and remedy it; soothe infant

or a sudden change in light, exposure to cold, or other physical discomforts, not just because of hunger or a wet diaper (Wolff, 1966). Infants around four months of age may cry because they have not been placed in the preferred sleeping position. Others in the second half of the first year may cry from rage or boredom. Once the source of distress is identified and attended to, the infant usually can be soothed and the crying stopped.

Normal, healthy infants may spend between 5 and 20 percent of their time crying (Berg, Adkinson, and Strock, 1973; Korner, et al., 1974). Infants cry more during the first three months of life, gradually becoming able to exert a little control. For example, a hungry four-month-old may stop crying when picked up and held while the caregiver gets the bottle ready. However, if put back down, this young infant may not be able to hold back the crying. A hungry six- or seven-month-old whose needs usually have been attended to promptly may stop crying when the caregiver is seen or heard approaching.

Occasionally, parents or other caregivers have tried to train very young infants not to cry by ignoring them, hoping that the crying will stop. This does not work (Bell and Ainsworth, 1972). Often, a newborn cannot control the crying because it has a physiological cause (Wolff, 1966). In general, the longer the infant has been crying, the longer and more difficult is the soothing time.

The most effective way to calm infants is to pick then up and hold them upright at your shoulder (Korner and Thoman, 1970). Infants also can be soothed by any stimulation that is continuous and unchanging for some minutes (Brackbill, 1979). Swaddling, or wrapping a young infant firmly in a blanket, also is effective (Stone and Church, 1973). In fact, the more senses that receive continuous stimulation, the calmer babies become (Brackbill, 1979). Thus, picking up crying babies, swaddling them, walking or rocking them, and singing lullabies continue to be effective.

Infants whose caregivers are most responsive to cries in the first few months of life cry least. These children also become more effective in noncrying communication later (Bell and Ainsworth, 1972). When adults use these strategies, infants learn that the environment is predictable and the caregiver can be counted on to respond to their signals of distress (Lamb, 1981, 1981). This is an important element of trust that is developed early in life (Erikson, 1963).

Sensory Ability and Social Interaction

Is it really possible to establish a social relationship with an infant? A social relationship requires the participation of at least two persons. Although the participation between an adult and a child is decidedly unequal and mostly dependent on the adult, babies are born with the capacity to receive information from the environment and to respond, although in a limited way. Thus, the foundations for social relationships exist from birth and are built up as the caregiver develops patterns of response to infant cues such as those discussed in the previous section.

When infants are in the alert inactive state, they are ready to interact with their environment. During the first two months, they usually are being held when they are in this state. Their first information about the world is based on sensations they receive while being handled. They smell the adult's hands, hair, and body. They taste his or her skin. They see the adult's face when being fed, bathed, clothed, and changed. They feel the caregiver's body directly as they are held close, so they sense muscular tension or relaxation as well as the rhythm of movement. Caregivers who are comfortable with their own bodies and can accept infants' ways of knowing about them through body exploration have taken the first step in establishing a relationship.

Perceptual abilities present at birth undergo a sequence of developmental changes during the first year of life (Lamb and Campos, 1982).

Piaget (1962) has described how these processes are essential to cognitive development. Perceptual capacities also are critical to social development as the avenue through which babies come to know what it means to be a person.

An infant may be competent to use a sensory ability, but may not perform a specific task (Chomsky, 1957; Flavell and Wohlwill, 1969). This distinction is important because caregivers sometimes think that an infant cannot do something simply because he or she did not do it when expected. One should not conclude that babies cannot see the pattern on the bumper guard simply because they do not look at it very often when the caregiver is at hand. For this reason, it is important for adults to understand the basic competencies that infants possess.

Touch. The sense of touch is clearly present at birth, and may be almost completely developed at that time. It is perhaps the least studied of the senses. We do know that touch triggers many infant reflexes, such as sucking and grasping. In addition, extremes of temperature cause distress in babies. Infants can be comforted by being swaddled, having a hand placed on the abdomen, or being held (Macfarlane, 1977). When caregivers are both firm and gentle during feeding, bathing, and diapering, silent messages of comfort, approval, and affection are conveyed. Rough or painful handling causes distress and may influence the infant's view of the environment as a risky place.

Infants also learn to identify objects through touch by the age of ten months (Soroka, Corter, and Abramovitch, 1979). This is why they may develop preferences for stuffed animals, blankets, or other objects. Preferred objects may assist older babies in controlling their crying or in soothing themselves when drowsy or distressed. Caregivers should recognize such attempts at self-regulation and show respect for infants' preferences by allowing them to keep such objects close at hand.

Smell and taste. Newborns have a well-developed sense of smell and can distinguish between pleasant and unpleasant odors (Engen and Lipsitt, 1965) as well as among certain food odors (Steiner, 1979).

Infants also have a keen sense of taste, preferring sweeter flavors than are preferred by adolescents or adults (Desor, Maller, and Green, 1977). Nevertheless, caregivers must consider the nutritional needs of the infant as paramount and not offer sweetened water or other sweetened drinks to infants, even if they like them. Additionally, it should be noted that infants and young children are not able to distinguish a poison by its taste or smell and have been known to consume noxious, lethal substances. Caregivers must make sure such substances are not available.

Hearing. Hearing is possible before birth, and newborns may be able to distinguish their own mother's voice from the voice of another female, even when most of their time has been spent in a nursery (Bernard and Sontag, 1947; DeCasper and Fifer, 1980). Also, most newborns will turn their heads in the direction of a shaking rattle (Muir and Field, 1979).

Very young infants are sensitive to speech sounds. When the caregiver speaks to them, they will turn toward the sound. Between three and five months of age, infants can imitate the changes of pitch in an adult's voice, and when they are sung to, they can "sing" back (Kessen, Levine and Wendrich, 1979).

Between three and six months of age, there is a sharp decrease in the child's auditory threshold, making infants much more sensitive to sounds around them (Hoversten and Moncur, 1969). This means they may startle at noises previously ignored. By the sixth month, infants recognize their parents or other caregivers by the sound of their voices alone. By eight months of age, infants recognize a variety of familiar sounds such as music boxes and sound toys.

FIGURE 2-1 This caregiver understands that intense communication is conveyed by sight, sound, touch, and smell.
SOURCE: Mimi Forsyth/Monkmeyer Press Photo Service

Vision. Newborns do not see as well as adults. They achieve visual clarity around six months of age (Dayton, et al., 1964) and develop the full range of visual competence at about twelve months (Cohen, De Loache, and Strauss, 1979). Initially, infants focus on objects between eight and ten inches away from them. Coincidentally, this is the approximate distance between an adult's face and that of a baby being held for feeding (Wickelgren, 1967). By the sixth week, babies appear to look directly at the faces of the caregivers, with eye brightening and eye widening, and by three months, infants can distinguish photographs of their parents from same-sexed strangers (Wolff, 1963; Maurer and Heroux, 1980). Infants prefer to look at people rather than objects during the first year (Sherrod, 1981) and, by six months of age, recognize all the people with whom they have regular contact.

Using each of the senses independently, infants are able to recognize the important people in their lives. Using the senses together, they go further, establishing basic social relationships such as attachment to their parents and preferences for particular caregivers.

Motor Control and Social Interaction

With the gradual increase in control of the head, arms, and shoulders, infants are able to manipulate the amount of stimulation they receive. By three months of age, they use their head position and gaze as a means of influencing communication with the caregiver. Three early gaze directions are possible. In the face-to-face position, infants are fully engaged in gazing at their caregivers. When infants turn their heads slightly, they maintain contact but signal that the play may be too fast or too slow. When the head is fully turned and the gaze lowered, contact is completely broken off (Beebe and Stern, 1977). When infants are completely overwhelmed by interactions that are too intense, they go to sleep, cry, or go limp. This behavior often is seen when infants are greeted by overly enthusiastic relatives. A summary of infant behaviors relating to head, gaze, and facial expression and corresponding typical meanings to the caregiver is presented in Table 2-2.

By the third month, infants are capable of tracking people as they move around the room. They stare at other people for long periods and, as they get older, will shift into a better position to watch what others are doing. For many sensitive caregivers, this is an invitation to conversion or play.

Once infants can sit up, between seven and ten months of age, they develop greater eye-hand coordination skills and a corresponding increase of interest in objects. They also may turn completely away from the caregiver to focus on an object. This is not a rejection of the caregiver, but is the exploration of the environment made possible by a comfortable relationship with a trustworthy adult.

TABLE 2-2 Infant Gaze and Social Meaning to Caregivers

POSITION AND EXPRESSION	TYPICAL INTERPRETATION
Face to face, sober	Fully engaged, intent
Face to face, smiling	Pleased, interested
Head turned slightly away	Maintaining interest; interaction too fast or too slow
Complete head rotation	Disinterested; stop for a while
Head lowered	Stop!
Rapid head rotation	Dislikes something
Glances away, tilts head up; partial head aversion	Stop or change strategy
Head lowered, body limp	Has given up fighting off overstimulation

Temperament —disposition_____

Infants are not all alike. Temperamental differences are evident from earliest life and are thought to affect personality development (Thomas and Chess, 1977). Also, characteristics of the child's temperament influence interaction with the caregiver right from the beginning.

An infant may be timid or intrepid, quick tempered or slow to anger, passive or actively curious, rhythmic or irregular. Some infants respond to every event, while others ignore loud noises, bright lights, and other sensations. *Temperamental differences*, then, are differences in the degree, or intensity, of emotional behavior and in timing and duration of responses. Individual differences in temperament influence the organization of the child's personality and social relationships.

Other factors may affect infant behavior, such as drugs administered to the mother just before birth or given to the infant, malnourishment, or parents' interpretation of their child's personality (Brackbill, 1979; Murray et al., 1981; Osofsky and Conners, 1981). However, all these factors can be changed by appropriate intervention, whereas temperamental differences are thought to be biologically based.

Influence of Temperament on Social Relationships

Several kinds of individual differences in temperament have been identified as well as their influence on the social relationship of the caregiver and infant. Emotionality, activity, sociability, impulsivity (Buss and Plomin, 1975), rhythmicity, approach-withdrawal, adaptability, intensity, distractabililty, attention span and persistence, and activity level all are dimensions that have been attributed to temperament (Thomas and Chess, 1977). The way these attributes are combined make the infant easy or difficult to care for and more or less pleasant and interesting to play with, and they influence the amount and quality of social interaction that the infant is likely to receive.

Adults often find building a supportive relationship with some infants natural, easy, and satisfying. Establishing a similar relationship with another infant whose temperament is different requires self-discipline, patience, and perseverance (Klein, 1980; Soderman, 1985).

For example, two children who differ markedly in activity and impulsiveness elicit different responses from adults. Mike moves slowly, watches what is going on, seldom cries, and plays in his crib contentedly for long periods of time after awakening. Todd, on the other hand, is distracted by every movement or noise; moves quickly from one part of the room to another; always seems to be underfoot; cries vigorously, long, and frequently; and rarely is content to play in his crib after awakening. Both boys are eight months old. Mr. McIntyre, who takes care of them, interacts less frequently with Mike but finds him satisfying and restful, if slightly boring, to play with. Todd gets much more attention, although Mr. McIntyre frequently feels irritated with him. The only time Todd seems to settle down is when he plays with him. Mr. McIntyre is aware of his tendency to ignore Mike and pursue Todd, so he carefully remembers to check on Mike regularly and involve him in play.

As patterns of interaction between adults and children emerge and become habitual, each child's social context becomes unique, influencing the organization of personality. "Goodness of fit" between adult and child is important because both parties to the relationship have temperaments. The experience of an infant like Mike, who is somewhat inactive and not very sociable, with an adult who is impulsive, impatient, and expects quick social responses from him would be very different from his experience with an easygoing, patient adult who is willing to wait for him to respond in his own good time.

The goodness of fit between the infant, the caregiver's temperament and expectations, and the infant's general living environment may be more important to the long-term outcome for the child than temperament alone. Even infants with difficult temperaments can be happy and successful if their caregivers are easygoing, if the caregivers' expectations for the child are clear and suitable for the child's age, and if caregivers use skills that enable them to be sensitive and responsive.

SOCIALIZATION AND INDIVIDUATION

Two functions of social development begin to operate during the first year of life. *Socialization* is the process that includes one's capacity to cooperate in a group, to regulate one's behavior according to society, and, in general, to get along with others. *Individuation* is the process by which the self or personal identity is developed and one's individual place in the social order is acquired. Individuation integrates the emerging perceptual, memory, cognitive, and emotional capacities to form a unified personality or self-identity in the young child. Both of these functions operate at the same time throughout childhood, and both are absolutely essential to successful adaptation to life.

The processes of socialization and individuation have long been of interest. Much of the work completed thus far focuses on how these processes operate and how they influence the behavior of children. Behavior can be observed, but the processes themselves are internal and must be inferred. For this reason, theories have been developed that help to explain the process and the outcome for the child.

The process of becoming a person and then becoming a member of a group begins in infancy. It occurs over a long time in a sequential manner and is dependent on a relationship between the infant and a loving adult. This adult may be either parent, a grandparent, a foster parent, or a helping professional. What happens in infancy forms the foundation for later

social-emotional development. It also influences all other aspects of the child's behavior. For infants to develop a sense of self, their physical needs must be met and they must enjoy a stable emotional climate (Erikson, 1950, 1963; Mahler, Pine, and Berbman, 1975; Bowlby, 1969; Ainsworth, 1973).

Becoming a Separate Person Within a Social Group

Individuation differentiates the self from others, and takes place in a social context. Individuation must occur if *attachment*, or preference for specific adults, is to take place. Table 2-3 summarizes the process of individuation, including infant capabilities; social actions that stem from these capabilities, and appropriate adult responses that support individuation.

Phase I. The infant does not psychologically differentiate self from parent and has no sense of time and place in the first phase of the process of individuation. He or she uses sucking, grasping, visual tracking, and cuddling to maintain contact with the parent. The infant's behavior is primarily reflexive or accidental in response to external stimulation. For example, grasping and bringing objects to the mouth, smiling, and simple thumb-sucking all are unintentional acts.

Phase II. The second phase is characterized by the infant's internal notion of parent and self as one omnipotent unit (Mahler, Pine, and Bergman, 1975). Young infants are likely to be alert and ready to pay attention and learn information when they are picked up (Korner and Thoman, 1970, 1972). Because the caregiver is the most noticeable feature in the environment, infants are likely to learn first about people, particularly the parents, through their senses. Also, adults tend to act in response to infant behaviors. In this way, there is a beginning differentiation between self and objects, such as the blanket, bottle or toy, as well as between

TABLE 2-3 The Individuation Process and Appropriate Adult Responses

PHASE	AGE OF ONSET IN MONTHS	INFANT CAPABILITIES	SOCIAL OUTCOME	FUNCTION IN INDIVIDUATION PROCESS	ADULT BEHAVIORS THAT SUPPORT INDIVIDUATION
I	0	Sucking; visual tracking; grasping; cuddling	Reflexes	Proximity to mother	Observation of states; prompt basic care
II	1–2	More time quietly alert; sensory learning about people and objects; molding to caregiver's body; continues interesting activities	Mother-infant pair perceived as a unit; beginning social responsiveness; mutual cueing; gazing	Begins differentiation between self and objects; more ways of maintaining proximity	Provide objects; engage in turn-taking play; give prompt basic care; respond sensitively to different states
III	4–8	Sits, grasps; creeps; increased interest in objects; sensory learning: mouthing, manipulating, examining, banging, etc.	Recognizes familiar people; shows clear preferences among people; intentionality limited to previously learned actions; playful; social smile, laughter	No self-awareness; beginnings of social expectations; stranger fear; maintains proximity by following, checking back on caregiver after short excursions	Provide a safe environment for floor exploration; establish limits for child; respond predictably
IV	9–12	Walking, climbing, running; joyful exploration; curious, excited; beginning use of language and gesture; person and object permanence becoming clearer; trial-and-error problem solving; intentions conveyed by language, gesture, and action; makes requests	Strong desire for approval, inclined to comply; self-willed; increased self-control; variety of emotions; social play with adults; interest in events	Beginning to recognize that mother is not part of self; maintains proximity by following and calling mother; strong preferences for particular people; protests separation; uses mother as a "base of operations" and moves outward	Protect from hazards (child has mobility without judgment); respond promptly to communicative acts; set and maintain routines and limits; provide opportunity for independence; use language to comfort, explain; leave child with familiar adults; have patience
V	15–24	Increase of all motor tasks; skillful exploration of objects, events; rapid increase in language and nonverbal communication skills; likely to carry objects to preferred adults; object permanence achieved at end of phase V	Is likely to cling, then run away; plays "mother chase me!"; self-willed: "No" before compliance; considerable amount of self-control; self-comforting; may show sudden fear after departure from mother; may cry from relief at her return	Realizes mother's goals are not own goals; may be ambivalent about dependence/independence; can play happily in absence of preferred person; uses "gifts" of toys in seeking proximity, more language	Verbalize about departures, reassure; tolerate rapid changes in approach and withdrawal; use language to discuss events, relationships, objects, etc.; allow child to control some holding on, letting go; make social expectations clear over and over; have patience
VI	24–30	Good understanding of ordinary language; intentionality well developed; mental problem solving; ability to ask for help based on need; goal-directed behavior	Increasing interest in other children; peer play and communication stronger; mutually regulated social interactions; pretend play	Realistic sense of self and others; uses a wide array of techniques to maintain proximity (helping, conversation, play, stories); can cope well with separations	Continue to reassure, support, and provide affection; praise efforts at self-control and independent behavior; provide experience with another toddler

parent and objects, although not between parent and self. During this phase, the infant molds to the parent's body when held, engages in mutual cueing with the parent, is most easily soothed by the preferred adult, and responds to signals contingently with another. Contingent responses are like a conversation with turn taking, but using only gesture, facial expressions, touching, or playing, often with vocalizing.

In addition, infants eventually discover how to make interesting events last, and the beginnings of intentional behavior thereby emerge (Piaget, 1952). Even though infants cannot discover new ways to engage in social exchange or physical activity, such as getting a mobile going, they are capable of continuing an action that was discovered by accident (Frye, 1981).

Phase III. During the third phase of the individuation process, the preference for the primary caregiver (usually the mother) is clear, but the infant still has no self-awareness. Behaviors such as arching the back away from the parent, creeping away, focusing on objects, but regularly checking back on the parent are common (Mahler, Pine, and Bergman, 1975).

By this time, the infant has learned about social expectations. The distress-relief sequence contains all the components necessary for the infant to accomplish the following (Lamb, 1981:159):

1. Learn that distress predictably elicits an intervention that brings relief.
2. Recognize the person responsible for facilitating the transition from displeasure to pleasure.
3. Develop an integrated, multimodal (complex) concept of the caregiver.
4. Associate the person's features with the pleasurable outcome that he or she produces.

It is from these simple, everyday interactions that the infant develops the ability to engage in an affectively positive relationship, to generate expectations concerning the parent's responses, and to acquire a sense of power. Apparently, the more promptly parents respond, the more likely infants will learn associations between their own and another person's behavior. They are capable of learning and remembering positive social behavior from six months of age and are likely to show surprise if their caregivers behave unexpectedly (Tronic, et al., 1978). Infants in the third phase of individuation are able to use behaviors that they have previously learned in order to pursue a goal. They creep after the parent when she or he leaves the room; they may cry in order to bring the parent close. Intentionality, however, is limited in that only previously learned behaviors can be used to bring about the desired end (Frye, 1981).

Fear or wariness toward adult strangers may appear around seven months of age. The age at which "stranger anxiety" occurs and the duration and intensity of the fear vary considerably among infants (Emde, Gaensbaur, and Harmon, 1976). Infants show less anxiety in the presence of the parent, in familiar surroundings, and when adult strangers give infants enough time before approaching closely or attempting to touch them (Trause, 1977; Sroufe, 1977). Some infants may show no noticeable stranger anxiety, and infants usually exhibit no fear of other children.

Phase IV. The accomplishment of separation from the primary caregiver, or the capacity to recognize that another human being is not a part of the self, is gradually acquired during the fourth phase of individuation. This ability becomes the basis for learning about others. To succeed, infants must understand that a person continues to exist when not in their presence.

During this phase, the infant is joyfully and actively engaged in exploration, using the parent as a secure base of operations. Starting from and returning to the parent, the infant investigates objects and events. The infant is practicing being a separate person and having a will, and is beginning to develop a sense of autonomy. Creeping and walking enables these older infants to experiment with new ways to achieve some desired goals. For this reason, this phase has been called "practicing" (Mahler, Pine, and Bergman 1975), and the child has been described as having a "love affair with the world" (Kaplan, 1978).

The exploits of this period require persistence and patience in adults. Barriers that previously protected children from falls are surmounted. Climbing makes forbidden objects high on shelves accessible. Saying "No!" is common at the end of this phase and is a means to exert self-will. The emergence of self-will is accompanied by the gradual development of enough physical self-control to enable the child to act, to do.

The child must learn when to hold on and when to let go (Erikson, 1963). From the necessity of controlling body movements emerges the sense of autonomy. Children feel that if they can control their own bodies, then they can exert their will over their own actions. However, children who are not permitted to exert control over their own movement will feel doubt about their ability to do so. This is probably why floor freedom and appropriate independence have been found to be related to the ability to internalize self-control (Stayton, Hogan, and Ainsworth, 1971). Playpens, which well-meaning adults use to control the movement of babies, may interfere with the related long-term goal of self-control if overused.

Children learn by imitating people important to them. Direct imitation of the routines of dressing, eating, eliminating body wastes, locomotion, and speech are primitive at first. Adults should expect mistakes as new skills are learned and not shame or scold the child for approximations of success.

During the fourth phase, infants have preferences for individuals and are capable of intentional behavior. They express a variety of emotions, including anger, rage, sadness, and despair. Seeking proximity to preferred adults,

particularly parents, by crying, calling, pointing, and following can be expected. Parents can handle separations best by first allowing the child to become familiar with an alternative adult, then explaining that the parent is leaving soon, having the familiar adult help the child to start an activity, then quickly departing. Helping professionals must, of course, provide comfort and reassurance and support the child in exploration as soon as possible. Practices such as lying to or deceiving the child, encouraging parents to sneak out, or pulling a screaming infant from the parent's arms are to be avoided because the infant is quite capable of associating these terrifying and painful experiences with the caregiver as a person.

Phase V. Near the end of the second year, children begin to realize that their parents' goals and desires may be in conflict with their own. Having begun to think of themselves as separate persons, they begin to realize that parents are persons, too. No longer is the parent-infant pair one omnipotent being. Wanting to be self-willed and independent, children often are frightened by the accompanying sense of separateness and aloneness. This ambivalence of feelings often is observed in behavior: a child might cling one minute and dart away the next; he or she may show a toy or show off and then turn abruptly away.

Because older infants have developed a considerable amount of self-control and can maintain a mental image of the absent parent, they might be able to tolerate several hours of separation. However, because holding back crying still is difficult, they might burst into tears at the moment of return. Parents may need help to understand that the child contained the desire to cry as long as possible and that this behavior should not be misinterpreted as the infant not wanting the parent (Mahler, Pine, and Bergman, 1975).

Phase VI. During the last phase of individuation, toddlers engage in mutually regulated conversation, conveying their intentions and understanding well the verbalized intentions of others. They cope well with the loneliness and distress of separation and are capable of using a variety of behaviors to achieve closeness to preferred adults. Language plays an important role as they begin to attend to adult verbal reasoning as a guide to behavior. Goal-directed partnerships with adults are possible (Frye, 1981).

The presence and reassurance of the parent continues to be important. As the child reaches out into the neighborhood and community and meets the challenge of interacting with peers, behaviors seen in earlier phases are likely to reappear and be worked through again.

When children are away from parents for substantial periods of time, or when parents are under such stress that they are emotionally unavailable to the child, a helping professional may become the child's primary nurturer. The attachment figure can be anyone, but it must be *someone* if healthy development is to occur. Therefore, caregivers should act as if they were the preferred adult with all their young charges. Children prefer a parent when exposed to several caring adults, so this does not entail competing with the family for the child's affection and loyalty.

The process of individuation is never really finished. The development of self-control, identity, and the place of the individual within the group continue to challenge each person as he or she is socialized as a member of the culture.

Individual Differences in Outcome

Developing a wholesome sense of trust is central to the process of individuation (Erikson, 1963). If feelings from the sensory world are typically pleasant, the infant will develop a sense of trust. However, if sensory stimulation is harsh, the child will develop a sense of mistrust, or a sense that the world is a dangerous place. The discomforts infants experience from hunger, gas, wet diapers, cold or excessive heat are typical, as are the pleasures of being dry and warm and being fed, cuddled, or played with. Trust and mistrust are the endpoints of a continuum, with each child needing some of both.

Complete trust is as maladaptive as complete mistrust. On one hand, a completely trusting child may be oblivious to the real dangers of the world, such as rapidly moving cars, because of the inappropriate expectation that she or he will always be taken care of. On the other hand, a completely mistrustful child may be unable to interact with the world because nothing but pain and danger are expected.

The ideal is to have children on the trusting end of the continuum so that they can risk exploration and learn to tolerate frustration and delay gratification. Such children expect to be safe and comfortable most of the time, and their view of the world is hopeful. Trust is acquired through communication with the caregiver. The interaction between the infant's behavior and the caregiver's response is the basis of affective bonds, security, and the confidence on the part of the infant (Bishop, 1977; Sroufe, 1977; Lamb, 1981). The consistent responsiveness of the caregiver to the child and the type of relationship that develops between them are important factors in determining the degree to which children thrive (Rutter, 1971).

Another outcome of the process of socialization and individuation is the child's self-concept. If adults are available, responsive, and loving, children perceive themselves as endearing, worthy, and lovable. However, if adults are inaccessible, unresponsive, or unloving, infants perceive themselves as disgusting, unworthy, or unlovable. The adult's general pattern of expressing affection and rejection will influence how well a baby's strong need for affection and comfort are met (Tracy and Ainsworth, 1981). Most infants' world views and self-perceptions are a blend of these continua (endearing, disgusting; worthy, unworthy; lovable, unlovable).

FIGURE 2-2 Professionals who care for children must be alert to the overtrusting child.

From this discussion, it can be seen that no two infants emerge from the early individuation process alike. Differences in temperament, daily relationships with the parents and other caregivers, and the comparative amounts of pleasant or unpleasant experiences they accrue influence the degree of trust, the quality of attachment, and the perception of self they develop.

Friendliness

Adults may not think of babies as being friendly with one another, but as more infants are experiencing group care, more of them have the opportunity for true peer interaction. It seems that infants acquire social styles and an endur-

ing orientation toward other people from their parents (Lamb and Campos, 1982).

Like other aspects of development, social interaction with age-mates changes rapidly during the first year as the child's cognitive, motor, emotional, and linguistic abilities become increasingly complex (Campos, et al., 1983).

As mentioned earlier, babies show more interest than fear when strange babies approach. Prior experience with other infants helps when strange age-mates are encountered. Babies initiate more interactions and more complex interactions with familiar peers (Field and Ignatoff, 1980). They cannot engage in complex play with more than one other child at a time, however.

Toys attract children and bring babies together, but they also may draw attention away from the other player (Mueller and Lucas, 1975). Babies usually can start a friendly approach, but they have difficulty keeping the interaction going. Those under eight months of age are not really capable of the intentional behavior necessary for more than a cursory friendly gesture (Frye, 1981). Typical early peer behavior is summarized in Table 2-4.

COMMUNICATION

Social relationships are based on communication between people. Misunderstandings occur when a message is misinterpreted. The social relationship between an infant and caregiver is no different in this regard. However, the adult participant must bear the burden of interpreting all the meaning from the array of signals that infants produce during the first year. At one time, it was thought that interpreting infant communication "came naturally" or was based on "maternal instinct." We now know that interpreting infant signals can be learned by anyone, and it is based on observation of infants and information about how infants gradually acquire adult communication skills.

Making Contact

As mentioned earlier, looking toward a sound, gazing into another's face, and visual tracking indicate attentiveness. Other signaling behaviors such as crying, smiling, cooing, and babbling have the effect of drawing the caregiver closer. Following brings the infant closer to the caregiver. Although these signals are not intentional, they are part of the attachment system, which tends to ensure that an adult is present to provide for the basic needs of the infant (Bowlby, 1969).

In addition to communicating the need for proximity, infants effectively communicate emotional content (Sroufe, 1979). The pain cry of the newborn alerts every adult within hearing distance. Contentment is accompanied by silence or by grunting noises.

Very young infants respond to human speech, showing a preference for vocalization over instrumental music, and respond to the rhythms of speech with their own body movements (Butterfield and Siperstein, 1972). Thus, infants learn elements of language early in life, although speech occurs much later.

Between three and six months of age, babies expand their array of communication skills.

TABLE 2-4 Peer Relationships in Infancy

AGE	INFANT BEHAVIOR
0–2 months	Contagious peer crying; intense visual regard between familiar infants
2–6 months	Mutual touching
6–9 months	Smiling; approaching and following
9–12 months	Giving and accepting toys; simple games: "chase," "peekaboo"
12–15 months	Vocal exchanges with turn taking; social imitation; conflicts over toys

Pleasure is expressed by smiling, and active laughter indicates delight. They seem to enjoy simple games such as "tug the blanket." Infants cry in rage when disappointed. When angry, the infant's eyes are open and vigilant and the facial expression reflects anger. Adults can easily distinguish rage from distress because the infant's eyes are closed during the distress cry (Izard, 1981). A baby may express wariness, a mild form of fear, by looking away, knitting the brows, and having a sober facial expression.

When control of the head and torso is achieved, infants become better able to signal when they want to engage or disengage in social interaction. They may turn their backs toward someone when they would rather focus on something else. An infant who is playing with a toy may glance at the caregiver and turn away to concentrate on the toy (Stern, 1977). This behavior should not be interpreted as dislike of the caregiver. Instead, it can be explained by the fact that infants cannot concentrate on several things at the same time. The focus is either on the adult or on the object.

Maintaining Contact

Once contact is made, infants influence whether the communication proceeds by using a variety of options in gaze, head and body orientation, spatial positioning, distance from the adult, and posture. Caregivers can observe these behaviors and interact when the message is clear that the baby is ready for social activity. Forcing interaction when the infant is otherwise involved may lead to anger or fussiness.

Between five and seven months of age, babies babble, producing sounds common to their native language and omitting other sounds. When caregivers reply to the infant's "talk" in a conversational manner, infants tend to increase the amount of their vocalization (Kagen, 1971). Babbling, which is a part of this kind of conversation, is different from the vocalizations heard when infants are alone or when they are in the same room with caregivers but not "talking" to them (Beckwith, 1971; Jones and Moss, 1971).

By the last quarter of the first year of life, infants have developed some alternative ways of handling certain emotions. They might appraise a new situation before responding to it instead of responding immediately. One means of evaluating a situation is called *social referencing*. In this process, the infant observes the caregiver's face and if the expression is neutral or smiling, the infant will respond by exploratory behavior. On the other hand, if the caregiver appears fearful or upset, the infant is likely to behave warily (Klinnert, 1981).

The effective use of social referencing means that infants can observe and interpret some of their caregiver's nonverbal messages and are likely to act on the messages that come from a loving adult. The caregiver's tone of voice, muscular tension, and facial expression convey feelings of affection, anger, fear, and interest, which infants use as a guide to behavior.

Caregivers also begin to label infants' feelings and act according to these interpretations, although the infants are not yet likely to understand these labels (Lewis and Michalson, 1982). Words and gestures have meaning for infants well before they begin to speak. The outstretched, open arms of a smiling adult, with a simple command, "Come here," and the offered cookie usually are understood well before the child talks.

Real speech begins early in the second year. Babies may imitate words such as "Haaaaachooo" and repeat them in a manner similar to repetitive babbling as early as eleven months of age. Words used by the baby are "holophrasic": one word is used to communicate a complex idea. Adults use the context of the situation to interpret the meaning. Much shared experience with a specific baby is necessary to interpret the one-year-old's words. The words may have a unique meaning and may be composed of easily produced sounds, such as "Piti" for "That's interesting" (McNiel, 1970). Words such as

"Mama" and "Dada" appear early and also are composed of easily produced sounds.

Beginning word use usually is accompanied by gestures that enhance the expression of the baby's intent, desire, or goal. When the baby says "Meh!" and points to the refrigerator, you can easily determine that hunger is being expressed, but whether the baby wants milk or a whole meal must be interpreted from your knowledge of that child's routine.

Early real words are about objects, actions, and locations (Bloom, Lifter, and Brazelton, 1981), with rapid increases in vocabulary occurring during the remainder of the second year. As babies develop a small vocabulary, they tend to overextend their word use. "Dada" may be applied to all male adults indiscriminately. However, when adults use only the correct names for objects and actions, babies soon learn to correct words (Gruendel, 1977). "Dada" will be applied to one important male adult and "Bompa" to the grandfather. Some sounds are more difficult to produce than others, and the baby will substitute sounds as necessary until

skill in articulation is acquired. When adults consistently use precise words for objects or actions, that is, use "walk" or "run" instead of the more general word "go," babies will also use precise words by the end of the second year.

Between eighteen and twenty-four months of age, the infant learns to use both referential speech and expressive speech. *Referential speech* is about concrete objects, actions, and locations. *Expressive speech* is about emotional content, feelings, and social experiences. Less dependent on gestures to convey feelings, the baby uses words that express possession ("Mine"), negation or defiance ("No!"), and goals ("Want down"). Two-word sentences appear.

With the increased competence of the baby to send and receive messages that can be understood by anyone, and the ability to mentally formulate intentions, the baby achieves a milestone in social relationships. By the end of the second year, the infant can function as a social partner and can communicate intentionally to influence the behavior of adults or other children.

SKILLS FOR INITIATING POSITIVE SOCIAL RELATIONSHIPS IN INFANCY

You have read about the importance of being a responsive, loving adult in the lives of infants. Feelings of concern, affection, and attraction for infants seem to come naturally to many adults, but the skills to help infants grow and develop must be learned. Many of the skills first presented here will be more fully developed for older children in later chapters. All the skills focus on the quality of sensitivity.

How do people demonstrate sensitivity? Lamb and Easterbrooks (1981) have identified four sequential acts that, when used together, comprise sensitive behavior: perceiving the infant's signal or need; interpreting it correctly; selecting an appropriate response; and implementing it effectively. In addition, sensitive adults provide contingent, appropriate, and consistent responses to infants' needs.

Provide Prompt Basic Care

1. Respond promptly to infants' bids for aid. When an infant six months of age or younger cries, pick up the infant quickly and attend to his or her needs. Older infants have an increased ability to wait and will respond to speech and other signs of attention while waiting for care, but their patience is limited. No child under a year of age should wait long for routine care such as feeding, diapering, or being put to bed for a nap. Infants who cry a great deal, and conversely, infants whose caregivers do not wait for them to cry, do not associate their communication behavior with the caregiver's response. This leads to increased feelings of helplessness (Suomi, 1981). The pattern of prompt response to infant cries enables the infant to learn that adult help is an outcome of their distress signals.

2. Establish a regular pattern in giving care when responding to infant signals. Timing is important, so is developing a particular pattern of picking up, talking, soothing, changing diapers, feeding, or holding the infant. Consistent adult behavior allows children to learn through the adult's repetitious acts to expect a particular kind of response to their bids for aid. Although some general consistencies in common procedure among caregivers in the child-care center are highly desirable, infants are able to distinguish among potential caregivers with whom they are familiar and can develop preferences for specific individuals by six months of age.

3. Confer with parents about the child's routine. Exact duplication of the parents' caregiving style is not necessary, but undue stress can be avoided if the caregiver knows the child's particular pattern of sleeping, playing, and eating. In addition, caregivers should inquire about the preferred sleeping position and the preferred soothing strategy for infants over four months old. Ask simple, direct questions: "What do you usually do to sooth Terry when he cries?" or "Show me how you usually place Terry on the bed for sleeping."

4. Handle infants gently but firmly, moving them so they can see your face or other interesting sights. Infants will not "break" and should be held securely, with the head supported during the first weeks until head control is attained. Place them at your shoulder when walking so they can see the environment. Support them in the crook of your arm for feeding so they can gaze into your face. Carry older infants at your side with their backs supported so that when they pull away from your body, they will not fall backward out of your arms. At the end of the first year, some infants may protest at being carried at all. In such a case, if for any reason you must carry the child, hold her or him closely and firmly to your body, wrapping the arms and legs with your arms so the child does not strike you in the process of protesting. When held, an infant should be safe and secure, and should not experience falling, being squeezed too tightly, or other discomfort.

5. Ensure that infants experience tactile comfort.

a. Change wet clothing promptly. Babies who urinate several times before being changed get a painful rash. Some disposable diapers are designed to absorb substantial amounts of fluid before appearing wet; therefore, change diapers when damp.

b. Pat gently when burping the baby; a thump is not required.

c. Use caution when securing diaper pins. Place your hand under the diaper next to the skin to avoid pricking the skin. Place the pin so that it points across the abdomen. The baby then can bend without being jabbed with the closed head of the pin.

d. Wash the baby's skin as needed. Smeared food, feces, and mucus from the nose irritate the skin and should be promptly removed.

e. Caress the infant whenever opportunities arise. Loving touches are pleasurable to them. Back rubs or massage also may be effective in helping infants to relax.

Detect Individual Needs

1. Use all your senses to gain information about the children.
Scan all the infants under your supervision regularly. Look for signs of drowsiness, level of activity, degree of involvement with objects, potential opportunities for social engagement, and possible safety hazards. Listen to their vocalizations as well as their cries. Sometimes you can smell that an infant needs a diaper change or has spit up. Observing in detail is not enough because perception requires that you make some sense of what you see.

2. Use your knowledge of development and the infant's typical behavior to interpret behavior.
Your knowledge of all these can help you understand what children's behaviors mean. For example, Juan, four months old, awakened quietly and has been staring blank faced into distant space for the last ten minutes. Saba, at eight months of age, has tossed all her toys onto the floor and is looking at them with an angry expression, waving her arms and vocalizing loudly. Alexis, ten months old, is rapidly crawling toward the discarded toys. Bridget, only one month old, is sleeping restlessly.

Miss Zimmerman knows that Juan usually takes a long time to become interested in exploration after he wakes up. She promptly removes Saba from the crib, offers a toy, and changes her diapers. Attending to another child, Miss Zimmerman did not know the reason for Saba's displeasure. Bridget's need obviously is to be left alone, and Alexis is clearly attending to his own needs to move in space and to explore objects. Finished with diapering Saba, Miss Zimmerman places her on the floor near Alexis, offers her a plastic bowl and balls, and moves to speak to Juan. This example demonstrates how knowledge of child development in general and of individual children in particular can enable adults to respond with greater sensitivity and skill.

3. Take into account the temperament and experience of all the children in your care.
Be sure to provide adequate stimulation for the very quiet child as well as the fussy baby. If you are more comfortable with peaceful babies, do not ignore the frequent crying of infants whose responses are less satisfying

to you. In working with infants, preferences are almost always inevitable. These feelings are legitimate, but should not alter your standards of professional practice. As a caregiver, you will have to exert self-control and self-discipline. You must distribute your attention among all the infants under your supervision.

4. Keep pace with the changing needs of children as they mature. During the first year of life, infants' abilities and interests change rapidly, and a response appropriate to an infant only a short time ago now may be somewhat outdated. Turning the head away when a new food is offered and promptly spitting it out is not unusual for an infant between four and six months of age who is just learning to eat pureed foods. The appropriate response is to continue offering the food if at the beginning of a feeding or discontinue if the child is at the end of a feeding. However, when the infant is only a few months older, head-turning, arm-waving interference, and spitting may signal the infant's emerging motor competencies, and offering a curved-handled spoon for the infant's participation in the feeding process might be messier but more appropriate.

5. Permit older infants to participate in their own care. Adults can do practically anything faster and easier themselves, and infant participation usually is inefficient and messier. The purpose of participation is to support the infant's emerging concept of the self as an actor: a person who can do something and is not always done unto. For instance, an infant who can sit can participate in diaper changes, altering his or her body and leg position as necessary; one who can sit, reach, grasp, and let go can put at least one object into a storage container; an older infant who has sufficient eye and hand coordination to easily move objects to the mouth and who can sit independently may be ready to hold a bottle and later, a spoon.

Once basic finger control is achieved, undressing is possible. The removal of socks and shoes is common at about twelve months of age with other articles of clothing coming within the motor-skill range of the older toddler. Children need to learn the appropriate time and place to remove clothing, as they are likely to practice this interesting skill indiscriminately. Putting clothing back on usually is more difficult.

6. Report new skills and abilities to parents as soon as they are observed. This is particularly important to parents who are away from the infant all day. Parents may have little time with the infant while he or she is awake and may not have the opportunity to observe the new abilities as soon as the caregiver can.

Establish and Maintain Effective Communication

1. Respond to infants' signals in a way that is consistent with your interpretation of the meaning and appropriate for the developmental level of the child. If a young infant is in the quiet alert state, provide something to look at. If the same child becomes drowsy after a period of wakefulness, settle him or her for a nap. Immediately respond to a crying infant less than six months old. However, if a child nineteen months old cries in similar circumstances, she or he may be signaling for your attention and wanting to play. The need of the older child for social interaction is also legitimate, but can be delayed for a few minutes while the younger child's needs are attended to. The older child is capable of intentional behavior; the younger one is not. This means that the younger child is crying due to discomfort and the older one to attract attention. Explain your behavior to the older child: "It seems that you want to play, Hanna. I will come as soon as I change Billy's diaper."

The behavioral state the infant is in, the nonverbal cues of facial expression, pointing, and vocalization, and the typical behavior of the child are useful in determining appropriate responses.

2. Talk to all babies of all ages. Words are never wasted on infants. Maintain a face-to-face position and eye contact while speaking. Use short, simple sentences or phrases. Use a higher pitched voice, emphasizing vowel sounds, and allow time for the infant to respond. This language is sometimes called "Motherese" because of its notable differences from speech between adults. Imitate the infant's vocalizations, facial expressions, and gestures in playlike conversations. Once you begin to converse with a baby, she or he will respond with coos, smiles, laughter, babbling, and attentiveness, depending on the baby's age.

Pause for the child to respond in much the same way that you would carry on an adult conversation. Allow older infants enough time to respond to your speech with words or gestures.

3. Talk during routine care about objects, positions, or actions that concern the infant and are immediately observable. Use specific vocabulary. The following script is based on an interaction between a three-month-old and his caregiver.

Charlie begins to cry and Ms. Nu approaches. "Charlie, are you hungry? The bottle is warming." (She picks the infant up and walks toward the changing table.) "I'll bet you are wet . . . a diaper, yes . . ." (Charlie has stopped crying and appears to be watching her hands.) "Lay you down . . . now, unfasten this diaper . . . take it off, oo000ff, ooooff." (She smiles and looks into Charlie's face as he wiggles his body and moves his arms.) Ms. Nu continues to tell Charlie what she is doing as she completes the diaper change, puts him in an infant seat near the sink, and washes her hands.

4. Slow down or discontinue the interaction if the infant looks away for a few seconds, lowers the head, or cries. A child who looks away, lowers the head, or cries may be experiencing overstimulation. Going to sleep or shutting the eyes is another means for younger infants to terminate an interaction. Older babies may simply crawl or walk away.

5. Use language to respond to older infants' gestures. When a toddler points to a cookie, say, "Cookie?" Or, when an older infant bangs the cup after drinking juice, say, "Looks like you're finished." Name actions that the child is doing. For example, when Jeff was bobbing up and down while music was playing, his caregiver smiled and said, "Gee, Jeff, you're dancing!" Simple, short, direct statements are best.

6. Wait for a physical response to key phrases for babies who don't talk yet. Before toddlers begin to talk, they understand several words and phrases such as "Bye, bye," "So high," or "All gone." They may, however, take a little time to respond before waving the hand, putting the arms up, or looking into the cup.

7. Repeat and expand toddler utterances. At the end of the first year, infants may begin to say their first words. Simply use their word in a way that seems to make sense: "Mama!" exclaims Diedra.

Her caregiver responds, "Mama's gone to work."

Sometimes a baby's word is not readily recognized by people outside the family; parents must be consulted if the word is used regularly.

"Manky" may mean a particular blanket; "Doe" may mean "Look at that." In either case, respond with words such as "Do you want your blanket?" or "Blanket?" This skill is further developed in Chapter 4.

Encourage Exploration and Learning

1. Provide play materials and interaction experiences that encourage infants to explore the environment. Allow young infants to explore your body. Provide toys and materials that are within children's developmental range but that challenge their awakening interest in objects. Demonstrate how toys work, such as how a pull toy chimes when dragged across the floor. Place toys and materials where older infants can reach them. Periodically remove the clutter of toys on the floor and replace two or three so that children can more readily perceive them.

2. Praise each success. Rejoice in the infant's accomplishments. Finding a toy that has rolled behind a box is a significant achievement for a eight-month-old. Getting food from the plate onto the spoon and into the mouth is a feat for a one-year-old. The first time to sit, to crawl, or to walk is the result of concentration, effort, and practice for the developing infant. Let children know you are proud of their successes. Laugh with them. Hug them. Talk to them. Let them know how glad you are that they can do something new.

3. Encourage exploration by being physically available to children during play. Infants not asleep or engaged in other routine care should be on the floor for play. Stay in close proximity as infants move out into the world of objects. Do not walk away as soon as they are engaged or leave them alone in a strange environment or with strange people without giving them a chance to accustom themselves to the new situation. Timid infants especially need patient support because to them, the world may appear to be a frightening, dangerous place. Be aware that older infants can "read" your fear, pleasure, anger, or joy from the tone of your voice, your facial expression, and your body tension. This social referencing helps the exploring baby to deter-

mine if he or she should cry after a fall or other painful event.

Help Infants Comply with Adult Requests

1. Use simple, common verbs to make requests of older infants. Say things like "Come here," "Look," and "Show me." A baby can understand and comply with these requests sometime between eight and ten months of age. Use a warm tone of voice that is relaxed and in your usual pitch and make requests or suggestions in a conversational volume, and children will be more likely to comply. Harsh voices and physical force are less effective. *stop, hot, walk*

2. Show infants what to do. Demonstrate the action that you wish the infant to perform. At the same time, describe it in words. For example, if you want an infant to place a toy in a storage box, then sit on the floor, pick up a toy, place it in the box, offer another toy to the infant, and, pointing to the box, ask him or her to put it in. Infants learn by imitation. They are likely to do what they see others doing. Do not expect infants to already "know how to behave." They are just beginning to learn social behavior and must experience many appropriate interactions with adults who patiently demonstrate what is to be done.

3. Repeat suggestions or requests. Babies need to hear directions and see demonstrations more than once. Infants generally comply with requests for behaviors that are made with a warm voice by an adult who has taken into account their needs and interests (Honig, 1985). Children under the age of two cannot really stop an action in progress on their own, but a simple repetition of the request with a few moments' delay is likely to be effective.

Sometimes older infants respond with "No!" when asked to do something. Wait a moment or so and repeat the request. This assertion of self is not the same as defiance, and many toddlers will happily comply a minute or so later.

4. Distract an infant's attention by offering a substitute action or object. Getting the child's attention is the first step. This usually is done by offering an alternative object or pointing something out that might be of interest. An exploring infant may readily give up a pair of glasses if offered an appealing toy. Use simple substitution; infants often let go of what they are holding in order to get something else. Verbal demands and pulling objects out of the infants' hands are less effective and lead to angry confrontations that need not occur.

Use *proactive controls* such as engaging the infant's attention, distracting her or him from less appropriate actions or objects, making suggestions about what to do, and showing how to do it. These will avoid power struggles and are likely to achieve compliant behavior.

5. Physically pick up and move an infant who does not comply with your requests when safety or orderly function is at stake. Never delay action when safety is involved! Simple, firm, friendly physical removal with appropriate redirection of the child's interest is both appropriate and effective. Quietly voiced explanations, such as "It's not safe for you outside all by yourself" or "You can play in the tub of water when it's out, not the toilet," should accompany the removal and be followed by helping the child into another exploratory experience.

Support the Beginnings of Peer Relationships

1. Arrange social experiences between infants when they are comfortable and alert. Place small infants in seats so they can see other children. Provide opportunities for creeping infants to explore objects in the same area. Usually, any social overtures between infants

occur when there are only two children in close proximity and when each child is comfortable and unafraid. Even then, infants in the first 12 months of life will not be able to maintain an interaction for very long (Eckerman, 1978). Peer play skills are slowly acquired in the second year of life.

2. Provide adequate space and material for older infants to use while playing together. Toddlers are unable to stop quickly and often have poor balance as they acquire locomotor skills and therefore are likely to inadvertently lurch into other children. They should have enough uncluttered space to avoid getting into one another's way.

Duplicate play materials are useful in minimizing conflict over toys and for increasing social play. Sharing toys is unrealistic before the age of three. Older infants are just beginning to act on their own goals and are unable to comprehend that others also have goals.

Quick action that prevents interpersonal stress between infants supports the eventual development of more positive relationships.

Be Available to Interact with Infants

Even though you know what to do and how to do it, there inevitably will be times when you are unavailable to respond promptly. You will experience time and energy constraints. Infants whose caregivers usually respond sensitively receive the beneficial effects of developing expectations of adults, acquiring a sense of effectiveness, and associating their own actions with the outcome. Being available is not always the same as being present.

1. Do housekeeping chores when infants are asleep or when another caregiver is available to interact with the children. Any task that diminishes your attentiveness to the children makes you unavailable.

2. Limit the frequency and duration of adult-to-adult conversations. People who are unfamiliar with infants sometimes consider them unsocial or uncommunicative and seek to engage other caregivers in conversation to meet their own affiliative needs. Helping professionals must focus their attention on the children and meet their own affiliative needs in other social contexts. Telephone conversations should be limited to short, essential messages and emergencies.

3. Use techniques of efficient body movement to minimize fatigue.   Squat on the floor, bring a child toward your body, and then stand up rather than bending over to pick up a baby. This shifts the stress from the back to the stronger leg muscles. Adjust the mattress level of cribs so that lifting is minimized, ensuring that older infants who can sit or stand are still protected. Lifting tiny infants from a low crib is unnecessarily exhausting. Use a changing table or counter of comfortable height for diapering rather than a crib, bed, or low counter. The repeated bending of the upper body necessary for changing several infants at a low height numerous times each day causes excessive fatigue for the caregiver. Select a comfortable rocking chair with arms to use when giving infants bottles and rocking them. The strain on the muscle of the upper arm and shoulder caused by using a chair without arms all day with a group of infants is likely to induce the inappropriate practice of propping bottles in cribs. A better alternative is to stack pillows on the floor to support the arm holding the infant. Caring for one infant is hard physical work; caring for several can create such fatigue and muscular aching that, if appropriate furnishings and efficient movement techniques are not used, the caregiver becomes effectively unavailable at the end of the day.

4. Limit the number of infants cared for by one adult.   The adult-to-child ratio should be established after taking into account the age distribution of the infants in the group, the skill of the caregivers, the physical setting, and other resources. For all practical purposes, an adult-to-child ratio of 1:3 or 1:4 would be needed to implement the skills previously described. Ratios as high as 1:8 are not recommended (Scarr, 1984).

When an adult is involved with one infant, he or she is essentially unavailable to all the others. The probability of giving adequate, sensitive, supportive nurturance necessary for healthy social and emotional development decreases as the number of infants for each caregiver increases.

PITFALLS TO AVOID

Regardless of whether you are working with infants individually or in groups, informally or in structured activities, there are certain pitfalls you should avoid.

Heeding the myths that urge the ignoring of infant cries.   Such notions as "Let him cry it out" or "Crying exercises their lungs" or "You'll spoil the baby if you pick her up when she cries" are not true and do not work. The infant continues to cry because crying is the only signal for pain, hunger, or distress that is available. Infants cannot be spoiled in the first six months of life (White, 1975). Providing quick, responsive, sensitive care to infants is likely to produce a compliant, cooperative, competent infant rather than one with unacceptable behavior.

Attributing intentionality to infants' behavior before age two.   Infants don't cry to make you run; they cry because of some discomfort. Infants don't get into things to annoy you; they are exploring the environment and are mentally incapable of planning to aggravate an adult. In the second half of the first year, intentional behavior begins when the child notes the effects of his or her behavior on adults. Children stumble on these behaviors through trial and error, so ignoring whining or screeching and suggesting another alternative to get your attention is fine.

Attributing moral characteristics to infants. There are infants who are easy to take care of and infants who are very difficult or challenging to care for. These babies are neither "good" nor "bad." Sometimes, adults project their feelings onto a baby. An infant is born with a temperament not of his or her choosing. Colic is a painful condition that makes life as difficult for the infant as for the caregiver. A sunny, happy temperament does not make an infant an "angel," nor does an intestinal complaint make a baby a "perfect devil." The ability to make choices based on a value system is not acquired for several years. *Avoid the trap of "good child–bad child" by focusing on actual infant behavior and emerging competencies.*

Focusing all your attention only on the attractive, cuddly, or responsive infants. Distribute attention to all children and be sure that infants who are slow to warm up or who are not cuddlers get reasonable and appropriate care. The more passive, less demanding infant should not be left alone in the crib for more than 15 minutes after awakening. Give this child the encouragement to explore and to socialize even if she or he appears content to do nothing at all.

Assuming that nonspeakers cannot communicate. Communication includes a wide range of verbal and nonverbal behaviors that allow us to send and receive messages. Speech is universally understood, but infants have an array of abilities to both send and receive information long before they develop speech.

SUMMARY

Infants are born with the sensory systems that equip them to become independent members of society. Having the capacity to communicate their emotions and degree of alertness, they interact with caregivers and the environment from early life. All development is very rapid during the first two years.

Skills that will enable you to become a sensitive, responsive adult who can support the child's individuation process were presented so that children in your care may establish a system of maintaining proximity to you, of exploring the environment, of establishing an identity, and of beginning social relationships with adults and other children.

Using these skills, you can recognize individual differences among children and quickly perceive their needs, accurately interpret their signals, and select appropriate alternatives for action.

Integrating social interaction into the basic care of infants and using an array of communication skills will help you to nurture the infant's development of basic social relationships. Strategies for managing the environment to ensure true availability of caregivers, combined with strategies for influencing infant compliance, work together in establishing a harmonious relationship between you and the infants in your care.

Now that you understand some of the foundations of building a social relationship during the earliest part of life, you are ready to concentrate on building and maintaining positive relationships with children as they mature. You will begin by examining the role of nonverbal communication in the next chapter.

DISCUSSION QUESTIONS

1. Why is it important for helping professionals who are concerned with social development to be able to distinguish the behavioral states of infants?
2. Describe the techniques that are most effective in soothing a crying infant.
3. How do the newborn's sensory capabilities influence the course of social interaction?
4. Describe how children with temperaments differing markedly in rhythmicity and activity might influence the same caregiver. What impact, if any, do you think this would have on the development of the child?
5. How does the way in which basic care is given to an infant influence the course of the child's development?
6. What are the typical infant behaviors in each phase of the gradual individuation process in infancy?
7. What peer relationships can be expected of infants between nine and twelve months of age? Would you say that they could react to an experience as a group or simply as a collection of individuals? Why?
8. Describe how infants six, nine, twelve, and eighteen months of age are likely to communicate. How are they similar, how different?
9. Steven has toddled over to the window where the poinsettia plant is sitting and is reaching out to grab it. What should you do first? How could this have been prevented?
10. Mary has just taken her first step from the table into the center of the room. Should you do anything? What?

CHAPTER 3
Building Positive Relationships Through Nonverbal Communication

SOURCE: Sybil Shackman/Monkmeyer Press Photo Service

OBJECTIVES:

On completion of this chapter, you will be able to describe:

1. The channels of nonverbal communication.

2. Cultural differences in nonverbal communication.

3. The function of nonverbal communication in working with children.

4. Adult abuses of nonverbal behavior.

5. The means by which children acquire nonverbal skills.

6. How nonverbal behaviors communicate messages about relationships between adults and children.

7. Specific adult skills related to nonverbal behavior.

8. Pitfalls to avoid in interacting nonverbally with children.

Don't look at me in that tone of voice!

Shari, age five, clearly understood the message conveyed by her mother, who stood stiffly with feet apart, hands on hips, scowling from the doorway as she viewed a clutter of baking supplies spilled on the counters and shelves where Shari was playing. Like most children, Shari could quickly interpret the meaning of her mother's stance and facial expression.

Such nonverbal messages rarely are discussed but usually are understood by people sharing the same culture. Unlike spoken language, in which words are explicitly defined, nonverbal codes are implicit, with the meaning derived from the context of the situation and the flow of the interaction. For this reason, nonverbal messages may be ambiguous or confusing. However, they are a common way for people to convey their feelings.

Nonverbal communication is composed of actions rather than words. It includes facial expressions, hand and arm gestures, postures, positions in space, and various movements of the body, legs, and feet. In addition, nonverbal communication includes paralinguistic, or vocal, behaviors such as the frequency range of the voice, its intensity range, speech errors or pauses, speech rate, and speech duration (Mehrabian, 1971).

FUNCTIONS OF NONVERBAL COMMUNICATION _____

Some of the functions of implicit behavior have been described by Ekman and Friesen (1969). Gestures such as a handshake, nodding the head, or waving the hand are used as *emblems*. Such gestures can be directly translated into words but are efficient, meaningful signals by themselves.

Usually, emotional or evaluative content is conveyed nonverbally, and is transmitted more

accurately in this way than by verbal means. Feelings of pleasure, surprise, happiness, anger, interest, disgust, sadness, and fear are expressed in interactions, and may be demonstrated with or without accompanying speech. However, words alone cannot convey the depth of meaning present in a verbal message enriched by nonverbal cues. For example, compare a written note with a telephone conversation, which has both words and intonations, and then with an interpersonal experience, in which words, intonations, and visual information are available simultaneously. The amount of meaning that can be derived from a message increases as the number of nonverbal behavioral cues increases. Words alone may be the result of careful thought and may offer more possibilities for concealment or distortion. Maintaining a deception across all nonverbal channels is extremely difficult, however, so true feelings are likely to be revealed in face-to-face interactions.

Nonverbal communication acts as a regulator of social interaction. For example, turn taking in a conversation is indicated by changes in eye contact, voice pitch, and body position. Nonverbal cues may serve a *metacommunication* function, that is, may communicate about the message itself (Leathers, 1976). For example, facial expressions can convey a notion about the way the total message is to be interpreted, such as, ''I'm only kidding'' or ''Now, seriously speaking.'' Some nonverbal behaviors also may serve an adaptive need rather than function as a communication signal. For example, a person may scratch the scalp because the skin is dry and it itches, or the gesture may indicate bewilderment or confusion. Some actions related to satisfying body needs would, in other circumstances, indicate an emotional state. Nonetheless, unintended signals may have communicative potential if they are misinterpreted by the receiver, who may ascribe affective or social meaning to them.

Nonverbal cues represent the most suitable vehicle for suggestion (Leathers, 1976). Because nonverbal cues are not explicit and can potentially be misinterpreted, they also may be denied. Adults use them to minimize psychological risks in interpersonal relationships or to enhance their image. Clothing can be selected to suggest that an individual is a professional, a student, or a potential sexual partner. Older children who have learned to use nonverbal cues as suggestions may adopt an amazing look of innocence when a misdeed has been discovered. The "Who, me?" expression is not usually considered to be a falsehood, as a verbal denial would be.

A clear relationship exists between the level of development of an individual's social skills and his or her successful use and interpretation of nonverbal behavior (Feldman, White, and Lobato, 1982). Children become adept at nonverbal communication by interacting with skillful adults. In addition, children are more likely to learn from people who show them acceptance, genuineness, warmth, and respect and who show sincere interest in them. All of these attitudes are made tangible to children by nonverbal means.

CHANNELS OF NONVERBAL COMMUNICATION

A *channel* of communication is one of the modes or types of nonverbal communication. For example, the tone of voice itself is one mode, or channel; posture and position in space are others. Each channel of nonverbal communication may function independently and may or may not be congruent with the verbal message sent. Under ordinary circumstances, nonverbal messages are not likely to be under conscious control.

Nonverbal communication is a major medium of communication in everyday life (Henley, 1977). In interpersonal interactions, people may choose not to speak, but they still send and receive nonverbal cues. These cues influence the flow and outcome of human interactions. For example, a person may "look daggers" at another, "deliberately ignore" some-

one, or perhaps give the appearance of mental abstraction or boredom that is sometimes called "woolgathering" or being "out to lunch." On a more subtle level, the relationships of people interacting in a group can be discerned by observation of nonverbal cues. The leader or speaker usually can be identified by noting the body orientations, head tilt, and arm gestures of all the group members. For example, in a group of children on the other side of the playground, one could pick out the leader by watching the children interact. One child is gesturing; her head is tilted up and she is looking at the others in sequence. The others in the group are looking and nodding in response to her gesturing. There is little doubt as to which child is the center of attention, even though the conversation cannot be heard.

In the following section, selected components of nonverbal behavior will be described as they relate to the helping professional's ability to deliberately send and receive messages while working with children.

Position in Space

"Personal space," radiating from the center of the body, has specific boundaries. Comfortable distances for interacting with others are from 0 to 1½ feet for personal contact, from 4 to 10 feet for social or consultive contact, and 10 feet or more for public interaction (Hall, 1966).

Another, more recent, description of personal space places the boundaries in relation to body parts or functions (Machotka and Spiegel, 1982). *Internal space* is the area between the inner core of the body and the skin and is the most intimate and personal of all spaces. Openings to the body, such as the mouth, ears, nostrils, anus, vagina, and urethra, all represent access to internal space. Internal space also is entered when the skin is broken in injury or when a hypodermic needle is inserted. *Proximal space* is the area between the body and its covering of clothing, hair, or ornament. Uncovered body parts, such as the face, are not physically restricted but are psychologically restricted. Casual acquaintances do not touch one another's arms, legs, or face, even though those parts are not covered by clothing. Some uncovered sections of proximal space, such as the hands, are freely accessible to entry unless otherwise protected by countermoves in axial space, such as crossing the arms or turning away. This means that, ordinarily, people do not touch portions of another's body that are clothed and limit touching the skin of others except when invited, as in shaking hands or giving a hug. *Axial space* is bounded by the full extension of the arms and legs in all directions. Invitation to enter the axial space is indicated by open arms, in contrast to crossed arms or legs. Internal space, proximal space, and axial space also correspond to Hall's (1966) concept of intimate and personal space. *Distal space* is located between the axial boundary and the outer limits that the eye or ear can scan. The knowable world, the impersonal world, exists in distal space.

It is important for professionals to understand the implicit rules of interpersonal space for three reasons. First, violation of personal space generates negative feelings (Hall, 1966). These negative feelings may be only mild irritation, such as that experienced in overcrowded church pews or elevators. Adults in these situations carefully refrain from inadvertently touching one another. Children, however, may poke or shove, violating both the axial space and the proximal space of another. Negative feelings increase as successive boundaries of personal space are crossed. Defense against a perceived attack, avoidance of the attacker, or a counter-attack on the person who violated proximal space can be expected from young children. Rage and violent protest are common when internal space is entered without permission. Medical personnel can expect to meet with severe protest when patients have not accepted that nurses and doctors have special roles that permit them in invade internal space. People prefer to have only their most intimate companions, the ones they prefer the most, to have any access to internal space. In fact, this is why children want their mothers or preferred caregivers to take care of them when they are sick. Extrusions (feces or vomit) from internal space also are considered to be intimate.

The second reason for understanding the rules of personal space is that a message is considered more remote, impersonal, or inapplicable as the distance between the communicators increases (Machotka and Spiegel, 1982). For example, Phillip, a college student, entered a theater and saw someone across the wide expanse looking in his direction and beckoning. He looked around, noted numerous other people in his general vicinity, and ignored the signal, which he assumed was not meant for him. Similarly, Sally, age seven, was stirring the water in a mud puddle on the playground with the toe of her shoe. She looked up to see the playground attendant shaking her head and shouting "No!" while looking in her direction. Sally was aware that a lot of children were in her vicinity and ignored the signal. However, when the attendant walked up to her and suggested that she use a stick for playing in the water rather than her shoe, Sally willingly complied because she then knew the message was meant for her. The power or potency of a message is greater at lesser distances and more remote and impersonal at greater distances.

The third reason for understanding the concepts of personal space is that the definitions of intimate space, personal space, and general social or public space vary by culture and subculture. Children learn the rules of interpersonal space from their parents, and helping professionals must recognize cultural differences as they interpret children's behaviors. The observed behavior may well be appropriate from the child's point of view, yet different from that expected by the adult. Although cultural differences exist for all channels of nonverbal communication, variations in the distance factor may be the most apparent. For example, a child who stands very close to an adult, speaks

FIGURE 3-1 Communication is enhanced when people talk face to face.
SOURCE: © Joel Gordon 1983

in a slightly louder voice than is usual, orients the body in a face-to-face position, and maintains eye contact longer than expected may be considered by an American teacher to be pushy, brassy, or aggressive, when the behavior actually is rather typical for an Arabic male child. Another child, who also stands close to the adult while conversing, but maintains less eye contact than expected and speaks in a softer voice, may inaccurately be considered clingy or dependent. Such behavior reflects simple courtesy in Asian cultures.

Body Motion

People don't remain stationary. They move through space toward or away from others. An approach into one's axial space may be met by accepting it, either by standing still or by extending the hands or arms. An approach may be reinforced by a mutual approach, with each person moving toward the other. However, an approach may be refused by moving away slightly, by simply avoiding the person approaching, or by closing the axial space by folding the arms.

An unwanted approach into another's axial space may be enforced by grasping the person, who may respond by acquiescing to the undesired contact, remaining immobile and passive. There is no reciprocity in this passive resistance. The alternative is averting the grasp by throwing it off, shaking it off, or pushing the person away.

When unfamiliar adults make contact, the asserting and accepting movements usually are ritualized, such as a handshake, a salutation, or other formal introduction or greeting. Frequently, adults are much less polite to children, particularly when the children are in a group. Children may experience being shoved into a line by a strange adult or may be patted on the head, pinched on the cheek, or chucked under the chin. Often, children correctly interpret these as hostile invasions of proximal space and attempt to avoid the approach or avert the contact as best they can. Then, the child is sometimes chastised for improper behavior!

A termination of interaction may be met by accepting the separation and moving away simultaneously or by one person moving while the other remains still. On the other hand, a separation may be refused by advancing while the other retreats. When a separation is refused, expulsive movements sometimes are used to push the person away. To avert a separation, a person may slow down his or her retreat, turn and stand, or show defiance against the other's intentions by facial expression or posture. Sometimes, forced separations are accepted by a rapid retreat.

Difficulties in separation often are seen as parents leave their very young children with caregivers. This particular situation was discussed in the preceding chapter. Older children frequently experience exclusion from other children. For example, Mike, age six, was listening to older boys talk about their marbles. Mike had some marbles, too; so, when the others decided to play a game, he bent down to join them. They told him that he was too little and didn't know how to play. Mike stood up, in the way of the other players. One of them pushed him slightly. Mike moved a step back. The older boys formed a circle with Mike on the outside. Mike took a step back and watched for a while before going to join other children on the climber. In this case, Mike tried to refuse the separation, then accepted it.

Body Orientation

The position of the front of the body in relation to the front of the body of another conveys meaningful information. The face-to-face position is the most confronting body orientation. This is the position used in greeting, comforting, fighting, and conversing intimately. Avoidance of this position usually indicates evasion or the desire to conceal. When people are facing the backs of others, they are proceeding in turn, following, or chasing. The side-by-side position implies companionship, togetherness, or a united front. The back-to-back position is associated with disengagement that is not simple separation, that is, hostility, or protection in a hostile situation. Rotating the body around is simply a display. Slight turns of the body usually are a transition from one position to another, but may convey disinterest or distrust or indicate impending separation (Machotka and Spiegel, 1982).

The relationship between body orientations of people who are interacting also has a vertical dimension. The term *one-upmanship* is descriptive both visually and in meaning. The position of being higher, or on the top, denotes status, authority, or power. The position of being lower denotes incapacity, humility, or servility. In the natural course of things, adults are big and powerful and children are small and weak. Movement to diminish the vertical space between adults and children signals that an important message is about to be conveyed. This leveling can be done by squatting to the child's level or by lifting the child into a face-to-face position with the adult, as is commonly done with babies and very young toddlers. Between adults, leveling may be accomplished by sitting down, as height differentials among adults are usually in the legs. This movement may indicate friendliness or a willingness to interact on a cooperative basis (Machotka and Spiegel, 1982).

Body orientation also has other dimensions. Leaning toward another implies interest or

FIGURE 3-2 This child knows that the teacher is interested in his activity because she is at his level and is focused on his behavior.
SOURCE: Photo by David Kostelnik

regard, and leaning away suggests interpersonal distancing, offense, or disinterest. An *inclusion*, in which the axial space of a person is surrounded by another, usually is either an emotionally positive experience, such as an embrace, or a negative one, such as a struggle. Professionals who work with children use inclusion in giving affection or comfort or when they use their bodies to keep children from harming themselves or others. The intersecting of the axial spaces of two persons indicates togetherness or friendship, but also occurs in fighting. When two children are angry with each other, one child approaching the other within two child-sized arm lengths usually indicates that physical battle is about to begin.

Gesture

Movements of the hands, arms, and body accompany speech and may be used to illustrate a word, such as moving the hands apart to show how large a fish was; to emphasize a statement, such as bringing the fist down on the table; and to replace speech, such as pointing to where the missing truck went. Gestures may be used as insults such as in raising the middle finger from a clenched fist, or as terms of endearment, such as a caress (Lee and Charlton, 1980). Most gestures occur in the axial space of the sender and may be made without speech at all. For example, Steffan slumped his shoulders, lowered his head so his face couldn't be seen, and inched along, scuffing the toes of his shoes on the sidewalk. Clearly, this child's gestures alone communicated his dejection.

People in lower social positions gesture more, and more vividly, than people of higher social status in all cultural groups. There are, however, distinct differences between ethnic groups in the amount and expansiveness of the gestures commonly used. The English probably use the fewest and the least expansive gestures, and people from southern Europe use larger gestures and use them more frequently (Lee and Charlton, 1980).

Touch

Situations in which touching occurs may be the most intimate, loving experiences, or the most hostile, angry, or hurtful ones. Situations in which touching is least likely to occur also are the most emotionally neutral. The probability of touch occurring is implied in the discussions of position in space (nearness to one another) and body orientation (face-to-face encounters). The skin is both a communication sender and receiver (Geldhard, 1960: Brown, 1974). The role of touch in soothing and stimulating infants was discussed in Chapter 2. Other affective messages also can be conveyed. Feelings related to mothering, fear, detachment, anger, and playfulness can be conveyed between adults by touch alone (Smith, 1970). Although little research has been done with children, gentle strokes, cuddling, caresses, and pats of affection are associated with nurturance or mothering. Games of walking fingers up a child's arm or "buzzing the bee to the tummy" illustrate playful touches. Slaps, kicks, pinches, and pokes that hurt are clearly understood by even young children as being hostile.

Two factors influence the quality of tactile communication: the quantity (how much touching takes place) and the region of the body where one is touched (Leathers, 1976). People touch and are touched by friends and family more than by casual acquaintances. People tend to touch peers or younger persons more than those older than themselves. Touching is more likely to occur in less formal situations and when the person touching is dominant in the interaction (Henley, 1977). The accessibility of the body to touch is limited by age, relationship, and gender. Obviously, infants must be changed, fed, and otherwise handled extensively by caregivers of either sex. As children mature, direct touch of the skin between the chest and the knees is taboo. In adulthood, most direct touching of the skin is limited to the hands, arms, neck, and face for parents and same-sexed friends (Jourard, 1966). Mothers, followed by other close relatives, are more likely to touch children than are other people. However, caregivers who have established a relationship with a child also have more freedom to touch or be touched by a child. Touching the clothed body of a child in an appropriate public situation is acceptable for caregivers of either sex. For example, lifting a child so that a climber can be reached, putting an arm around a child who has suffered a mishap, or cleaning a cut are acceptable regard-less of the age and sex of child or adult. Men initiate touching more frequently than do women, such as backslapping and handshaking, but the regions of the body that are acceptable to touch are more limited (Henley, 1977).

Touch is an important means for establishing personal regard. The concept of "being touched" by a story implies emotional involvement. Being "close" to someone implies being close enough to touch, as well as having strong affectionate bonds.

Facial Expression

Facial expression is the most obvious component of body language. It also is the component most readily brought under conscious control and, therefore, may be confusing or used for deception.

Many dimensions of meaning can be communicated by facial expression (Leathers, 1976). The face communicates evaluative judgments, the degree of interest in the environment, and the intensity or degree of involvement in a situation through pleasant and unpleasant expressions. Although the face can clearly convey specific emotions, such as happiness, surprise, fear, anger, sadness, disgust, contempt, and interest, it is very mobile, and combinations of affect also may be displayed (Ekman, Friesen, and Ellsworth, 1972). Children display affect through facial expressions from early infancy onward. Pouting is a well-known expression of displeasure, and sticking out the tongue is a widely known expression of insult in Western cultures. Wrinkling of the nose when smelling an unpleasant odor and the disgust displayed when children taste new or different foods are readily understood. More subtle expressions, such as surprise quickly followed by interest or anger, sometimes are more difficult to detect.

The smile is one of the earliest facial expressions acquired. The simple smile, the broad, open smile, and the grin convey different meanings and use different muscles (Key, 1975).

FIGURE 3-3 Some messages have no need for words.
SOURCE: H. Armstrong Roberts

When the smile is broad and lines form at the corners of the eyes, the person is amused or very pleased. A grin frequently is associated with mischief, and may also indicate pleasure with oneself. A simple smile sometimes called a *social smile,* is the gesture of slight pleasure, greeting, and appeasement (Henley, 1977). It may be used to avert aggression or to indicate submissiveness. The simple smile with an otherwise neutral expression is called a *mask smile* (Key, 1975) because it is used to hide unpleasant or unacceptable feelings. The mask smile often has been described as being ''painted on the face'' or ''plastered on'' and has a rather immobile quality.

Some middle-class women have been socialized to perform a traditional role that is warm, compliant, and submissive, so the smile may be situationally or role defined rather than an indicator of true feelings. The combination of a mask smile and either very serious or emotionally negative verbal content is particularly offensive to children (Bugental, Love, and Gianetto, 1971; Bugental, et al., 1970). Adults who have developed this pattern of behavior in other social contexts will have to alter their typical pattern so that they smile genuinely when giving praise, when amused, or when making a friendly gesture toward a child and do not smile at all when they are very serious or angry.

The cultural meaning of the smile varies. For example, children of western European descent traditionally smile when greeting another person, and Japanese children offer greetings with a sober face. As with other nonverbal communications, cultural variations in the use of the smile are modified as children interact in the context of the larger society (Klineberg, 1935).

Use of the *mask face*, or the face with no expression at all, makes communication with children more difficult. This expression, sometimes called the corporate face or poker face, conceals feelings, as any student who has used it while attending lectures well knows. The nonexpressive face, if used with children, may be interpreted as disinterest, lack of caring, or phoniness, and may become a serious hindrance to real communication.

Finally, adults must be careful in interpreting children's facial expressions as well as in using their own expressiveness to highlight the message they intend to convey. For example, a young child may smile when a person slips on the ice and falls because the movements of the arms and legs are unusual, not because the child is amused that someone has been hurt.

Eye contact. Eye contact between two persons is a special kind of communication that can rapidly move an interaction to a personal or intimate level even though considerable physical space may separate the communicators. The *eye lock,* or prolonged gaze, implies a more intimate holding or communication. The very long gaze between an infant and an adult is normal communication, but a similarly long eye lock between an older child and an adult is a glare and may be interpreted as hostility or aggression (Key, 1975).

The glance also holds meaning between persons who know each other well. A shared moment of eye contact may mean anything from "Have you ever seen anything so ridiculous?" to "Let's go!"

Eye aversion also is used to indicate turn taking in normal conversation. In Western cultures, people tend to look more when listening than when speaking (Kenden, 1967). Speakers glance away briefly at the end of an utterance, then return the gaze to the other (Kenden, 1967); they expect the listener to be looking at them at this point. This pattern is essentially reversed in African cultures and modified in mixed racial interaction (La France and Mayo, 1976). In mixed racial interaction, black listeners gaze less at the speaker than do white listeners. In fact, in black culture, eye-to-eye gazing is considered rude, a put-down, or a confrontation (Scheflen, 1972). The pattern of looking down to show respect also is common to Japanese, Puerto Ricans, and Mexican-Americans (Johnson, 1971). Unfortunately, adults sometimes become very angry when a child violates the rules of establishing rapport through eye contact and may not recognize that the child is behaving correctly within a different set of culturally defined rules.

Paralinguistics

Nonlexical sounds, or sounds that are not words, are produced by everyone and can serve all the functions of nonverbal speech. Physiological acts such as coughing, clearing the throat, sneezing, spitting, belching, sucking the teeth, hiccuping, swallowing, choking, yawning, and sighing can be used solely as adaptive mechanisms or to demonstrate affect. For example, the cough, besides clearing the throat, may be used to communicate tension, anxiety, criticism, doubt, surprise, a prompting to pay attention, or recognition of one's own lies while talking (Feldman, Jenkins, and Popoola, 1979). Several familiar sounds are used as emblems, in place of words, such as "Uh uh" (no), "Ah, ah'' (warning), ''Mmhmm'' (yes), ''Mmmmm-mmm'' (good!), ''Psst'' (look here), and ''Ugh!'' (how unpleasant!). Intonation is used to denote the end of a sentence, an exclamation, or a question and serves as an indicator in conversational turn taking.

In addition, much of the affective content of a message is conveyed by particular vocal qualities expressed simultaneously with speech. These include rhythmicity, intensity, volume, pitch, and tone (Ostwald, 1963).

The rhythm of speech is composed of differential stress on words, the length of time sounds are held while speaking, and pauses. The stress given to each part of a sentence can determine its meaning. For example, when different words are stressed in the following sentence, the meaning of the pure lexical, or word, content is altered. ''*Philip* is sharing the book with Harriet'' implies that it is truly Philip, not someone else, who is interacting with Harriet. However, ''Philip is sharing the *book* with Harriet'' indicates that the book is the focus of attention.

In the English language, the lengthening of consonants gives a terrifying or dramatic effect. ''*Runnnnnnn*!'' is a serious, urgent, frightened demand for haste. Adults are likely to lengthen consonant sounds for dramatic appeal when reading stories to children. Variations in the lengths of vowel sounds, though, simply may reflect dialectal patterns.

Hesitations, or pauses in speech, allow the speaker to retain the floor or a speaking turn while gathering the next thought. People may pause for mental deliberation when they have been interrupted or as a reaction to an external disturbance such as a slamming door. Pauses may be filled with verbalizations such as ''Er,'' ''Um,'' or ''Ah,'' nonlexical sounds such as a cough or nonverbal expressions such as swallowing. Major pauses in children's speech to adults usually occur because the child needs time to organize his or her thoughts. The tempo of a child's speech may be fast or slow, and the total rhythm smooth, jerky, or abrupt.

Adults should allow plenty of time for children to complete their thoughts, should refrain from jumping in to finish the sentence for them, and should suppress the urge to take a talking turn prematurely. Such restraint shows respect for the child.

An increase in intensity, the force and volume with which something is said, usually is associated with strong feelings such as excitement, joy, eager anticipation, terror, rage, and coercion. However, how loud is ''too loud'' in normal speaking usually is situationally and culturally determined. For example, speaking intensely and loudly may be perfectly appropriate in a gym or on the street, but speech of the same volume would be inappropriate in a classroom or movie theater. High-volume speech in situations that call for moderate-to-low volume is considered by adults to be boorish, inappropriate, and annoying.

Whispering or simply mouthing words may be interpreted as attempts at secrecy or intimacy. When a voiced utterance dwindles to a whisper, embarrassment may be being expressed (Key, 1975). In any case because a whisper lacks pitch and volume, a listener must attend to it more intently than to regular speech to receive the message.

Silence, the absence of sound when sound is expected, also is a powerful communicator. Deliberate silence in response to a question may be an insult or a provocation or may indicate resistance. Silence also stresses the utterance following it, making the message stand out as being of extreme importance.

Variations in pitch and tone convey a variety of emotional messages. High-pitched voices are associated with strong emotions such as great excitement or panic. Fluctuations in pitch are characteristic of the angry tone of voice. The pitch and tone of the voice are difficult to control; therefore, subtle interpersonal attitudes and emotions can ''leak through'' (Bugental, Caporael, and Shennum, 1980; Weitz, 1972; Zuckerman, et al., 1981). Voice quality can be described as follows (Key, 1975:61):

raspy	heavy	gruff
shrill	dull	full
resonant	gravelly	reedy
squeaky	soft	moaning
deep	rough	thin
harsh	smooth	breaking
guttural	groaning	singing

In an emergency situation, an adult who is distraught may speak rapidly in a shrill, fluctuating tone. Such speech is not likely to instill confidence in his or her ability to handle the problem. On the other hand, an adult's voice that is within the normal range of speech tone and volume enhances the message that the adult can cope with the circumstances (Mehrabian, 1972).

ADULT ABUSES OF NONVERBAL BEHAVIOR

There are some forms of paralinguistics, body motion, and gesture that are not appropriate for adults who work professionally with children. The use of these behaviors communicates that the adults cannot be trusted or that they do not like or care for the child.

Baby Talk

Baby talk, a stylized form of adult speech, does not imitate any developmental stage of infant speech. It is used to establish an intimate relationship, a status relationship, or a nurturant relationship or is used to control behavior. It is produced by puckering the lips, which alters the sounds of the words, and using either a falsetto voice, a high pitch, or an unusually low pitch. Use of the diminutive form of words is common (doggie, dolly, horsie), as are sound substitutions (''twain'' instead of train). The plural first-person pronoun is used improperly. For example, a nurse might say: ''How are we today?'' or ''Did we shower yet?'' Other pronouns either are not used or are used improperly: ''Is you going bye-bye?'' (Are you going outside?); ''Let teacher carry Davie'' (Let me carry you) (Key, 1975).

Adults often use baby talk when talking to pets, children, persons considered inferior in status, mentally incompetent persons, and sick persons. Professionals should not use baby talk in interacting with children because it is insulting to the child and confuses meaning. For example, the statement ''We must put away the toys'' can legitimately be interpreted to include the adult speaker. Particularly offensive is the habit of adults to fix diminutives on personal names, such as ''Ralphie'' instead of Ralph or ''Annie'' instead of Ann, particularly when the family uses the regular form.

Yells

Screams, shouts, roars, howls, bellows, squeals, shrieks, or screeches have unique qualities of volume, pitch, and tone that demand attention (Key, 1975). Adults who work with children may hear these frequently in the course of play as children express their exuberance. However, adults should not scream or yell at children. Shouting across a room for children to be quiet, although common, is particularly ineffective and inappropriate. When these unique paralinguistic forms are used by an adult, children surmise that the adult has lost self-control and is potentially dangerous or, at best, ineffectual.

Hurtful Touching

Adults should never physically injure children. Yanking children by the arms, dragging them by the legs, pulling their hair, twisting their arms or wrists, biting, pinching, kicking, or even chucking them under the chin, or otherwise causing the child bodily pain or injury, are always inappropriate. In many states, such behavior is illegal. Because adults provide guidance and support to children, they should never abuse the authority they have.

COMMUNICATING ABOUT THE RELATIONSHIP

People communicate specific messages nonverbally in the course of everyday interaction. In addition, through a combination of various nonverbal channels, people convey impressions about their overall relationships with others. Messages that communicate authority, warmth, and caring, or the relative importance of another person, are mostly nonverbal.

Time

young children don't have a sense of time

Many social expectations are based on the shared meaning of time. Helping professionals must be aware of their own concept of time so that they can more easily understand their responses to children's behavior. In addition, they must learn how others, particularly people of different cultural backgrounds, interpret time. Otherwise, misunderstandings about time between adults and children will be inevitable. An adult may interpret that an eight-year-old is late for a Cub Scout meeting because the child arrived several minutes after the scheduled meeting time. However, the child may consider himself "on time" because he arrived before the major activities that were important to him had begun.

Children must learn a complex set of rules for the use of time in American culture. Children from Native American and Hispanic cultures perceive clock time as less important than subjective time, which may cause additional misunderstanding (Hall, 1981). *Subjective time,* in contrast to clock time, is ambiguous. It is based on an internal feeling of the people using it. Native American adults attending a powwow may know the dancing will be done on a particular weekend, but it may be at any hour during that period.

Americans treat time as a material resource: it can be bought, saved, wasted, and segmented. Time is future oriented, but very short.

Our focus is on the minutes, hours, and days, not on months, seasons, or generations. The control of time is an indicator of status. This means that adults are likely to become angry with children who are slow, who dawdle, or who use what the adult perceives as too much time for a task. On the other hand, adults get angry with children who are impatient and do not wait for them for "just a minute." In American culture, being fast is equated with being intelligent or being good. For example, a seven-year-old announced that she had finished her sentences before the others. Her paper had a period on each of the lines but no words on the page. Clearly, she had understood that speed was important, and she had, indeed, put on the finishing touch!

Adults who take the time to listen to a child demonstrate that the child is important and the conversation is interesting. Adults who interrupt children, who are obviously ready to leave the interaction at the first opportunity, or who are excessively distracted by the events around them demonstrate disinterest. Attending to children promptly, keeping appointments or commitments, and taking the time to observe the child's work or play communicate to the child that she or he is important. On the other hand, adults must keep in mind that although children understand these cues in others, they are just learning to adopt such actions in their own behavior. As a result, their own use of time to convey respect and interest is not fully developed.

Warmth

How do children know that you like them? Only a small portion of the message of liking a child is conveyed by words; much more of the message is communicated by vocal characteristics and most by facial expression (Mehrabian, 1972). Warmth is communicated entirely nonverbally (Gazda, Childers, and Walters, 1982). Adults who want to communicate caring and concern are more likely to approach the child and interact in axial space. They will maintain frequent but not continuous eye contact and will face the child directly, keeping their head at about the same level as the child's. They may lean or reach toward the child while gesturing or speaking. Smiling and a relaxed facial expression and body also indicate warmth and interest. Speech is at normal pitch, speed, and volume, and the tone is relaxed and melodious. The overall impression is smooth, comfortable, and relaxed.

Coolness, aloofness, or the absence of warmth is communicated by fidgeting, turning away, a mask expression, a sharp tone of voice, or maintaining vertical and horizontal distance. Maximum coldness can be communicated by crossing the arms or legs and either staring or failing to maintain normal conversational eye contact. The overall impression is either tense or carelessly offhand. Unfortunately, adults who are unsure of themselves or who are afraid of doing the wrong thing also may behave in this manner. Children and other adults may misinterpret this behavior as uncaring and disinterested.

Power

Fortunately, adults have the legitimate power, or authority, to provide for the safety, security, and well-being of the children in their care. Obviously, adults control the resources needed for survival such as food, clothing, shelter, and medicine. Perhaps less obvious is the fact that adults also provide for the order, safety, and feeling of security that children need. Much of this sense of authority is conveyed to children nonverbally. Adults demonstrate their *assertiveness* when they interact in close physical proximity, maintain eye contact, and use a firm, even, confident tone of voice. They may need to grasp a child firmly to prevent an injury to the child or someone else. *Aggressiveness* implies the addition of excessive force or hostile feelings

to assertive behavior. *Nonassertiveness* implies lack of control of the situation or unwillingness to act responsibly. Both of these are communicated nonverbally, and even very young children can detect the fluctuating, intense, loud voice of anger and the weak, waivering, hesitant voice of nonassertiveness. As a result, they are likely to respond to these aspects of the adult message rather than to the words that are used.

The normal nonverbal behaviors of adult males also are the noverbal behaviors of power (Henley, 1977). This may present problems to adults who work with older children, particularly ten- to twelve-year olds. In adopting the correct "male behavior," boys also adopt assertive behavior. This often is considered a "discipline problem" when their interaction is with adult women. General behaviors considered "tough," "all boy," "smart-alecky," or belligerent usually are of this type and should be distinguished from actual disobedience. Many women are infuriated when their legitimate authority is challenged in this way by a child. The problem is especially difficult because normal feminine nonverbal behavior is submissive. Women need to assert authority when necessary. To do so, they must distinguish between true infractions of expectations, such as direct noncompliance with stated directions or breaking of group rules, and an inappropriate use of assertive behavior. In older boys, this might be throwing the head back and rolling the eyes when asked to comply, or swaggering and grinning at the adult when complying. The boy may comply, but the adult is likely to feel angry. The adult should focus on the actual act or behavior rather than the way it is carried out.

THE IMPACT OF MIXED MESSAGES

Unspoken messages are transmitted by one or all channels of nonverbal communication. In addition, it is possible to communicate one message in one channel of communication, such as facial expression, while communicating something quite different in another channel, such as the tone of voice. Neither of these may correspond to the meaning of the actual words spoken. For instance, an adult may smile and say, "Sure, have another helping," at the same time display a rigid posture, a tense voice tone, and a clenched hand, which clearly demonstrate disapproval.

There is evidence that, by nine months of age, infants can both interpret discrepant affect and apply its meaning to a social context (Blanck and Rosenthal, 1982). Children of preschool age are sensitive to and wary of naturally presented discrepant social messages that involve facial expression and tone of voice (Volkmar and Siegel, 1982). When modalities are discrepant, young children tend to respond more to the auditory channel than the visual channel (Blanck and Rosenthal, 1982). Children as young as one year of age are capable of weighing and interpreting discrepant affective messages. Research supports the folk wisdom that little children seem to know who really likes them and who does not.

As children get older, they show greater accuracy in decoding facial expression, and youngsters between five and sixteen years of age become increasingly competent in detecting and interpreting discrepant social messages (Blanck and Rosenthal, 1982). The dominance of the voice channel for younger children (with interpretation of body movement also important) shifts with age to increased reliance on the visual channel, especially facial expression. In general, the relative dominance of nonverbal over verbal cues increases with age as the child's competence in decoding increases (Bugental, et al., 1970; Volkmar and Siegel, 1982).

Sarcasm combines negative lexical content and a scathing tone of voice with a pleasant facial expression. Adults perceive this markedly incongruent message as funny or a joke. Young children are disturbed by it because the words

and tone of voice are both strongly negative, and these are the cues they rely on to interpret the affective meaning of a message. Preadolescents interpret such humor as negative in tone or a bad joke (Blanck and Rosenthal, 1982; Bugental, et al., 1970; Bugental, 1974). Even between parent and child, sarcastic "joking" by the adult is perceived as ridicule by the child (Bugental, Kaswan, and Love, 1970).

CHILDREN'S ACQUISITION OF NONVERBAL COMMUNICATION SKILLS

Nonverbal communication skills in childhood are mostly caught, not taught. Children tend to imitate the patterns of behavior of the adults with whom they interact. This means that youngsters who interact with skillful, expressive adults also will eventually become skilled in nonverbal communication. Also, children who have a cultural experience at home that differs from that of their mesosystem will modify their behavior when they encounter the larger culture at school or in other community settings. They become nonverbally bilingual.

Some rules of nonverbal behavior are pointed out by admonition. When adults see a child doing something that "everyone" finds inappropriate, like spitting on the floor, they respond with a strong statement such as "Don't you ever do that again." Formal traditions are learned when a child makes an error and is corrected. Americans have firm rules about nudity and all interactions with internal space. Children simply cannot urinate in public! Rarely are these nonverbal rules formally explained.

A third way children learn nonverbal behavior is through instruction. Adults may give children suggestions on how to "be friendly" or how to stand up for their rights. This is relatively rare, however.

The pattern of the development of nonverbal language is very similar to that of speech. Children become increasingly skillful as they get older. Their messages become more complex and come increasingly under their control. Understanding of discrepant messages becomes easier with age and experience, although children cannot send mixed messages (lies) that are undetectable by an adult until the age of eleven or twelve. Comprehension precedes expression, and children shift from reliance on the verbal channel to the adult pattern of major reliance on facial expression between seven and ten years of age.

Communication of emotional content also is influenced by social learning. Boys are less likely to spontaneously express their feelings as they get older, and girls are less likely to be aggressive or show an achievement orientation (Buck, 1982). Girls also are more likely to be tolerant of mixed messages or "white lies" than are boys (Blanck and Rosenthal, 1982).

GUIDING CHILDREN WITH ADULT NONVERBAL BEHAVIOR

When adults use nonverbal communication that repeats, complements, or accents the lexical meaning of their messages to children, they clarify the total meaning of the message. Thus, children are more likely to understand and respond to what is being said. People usually display subtle differences in their styles of nonverbal communication, and an individual may communicate differently in varying circumstances. These differences in communication style also influence the flow of communication with children and affect the probability of them responding appropriately. The following guidelines will help you increase the effectiveness and accuracy of your nonverbal communication.

SKILLS FOR BUILDING POSITIVE RELATIONSHIPS THROUGH NONVERBAL COMMUNICATION

1. Observe the nonverbal behavior of the children in your care. Observing your typical interactions with a child, those between the child and other children, and those between the child and other adults will help you acquire information about the meaning of various movements and gestures for that particular child. For example, Anne Janette's teacher checked for a fever when the child had been playing quietly by herself at the puzzle table. Ordinarily, Anne Janette was noisy, boisterous, social, and physically active. Her temperature was over 100°F. The teacher was alert to the *change* in the child's typical behavior.

2. Recognize cultural and family variations in children's nonverbal behavior. With so many variations among cultural groups, only direct observation within an appropriate context will provide enough information to understand the meanings of particular behaviors. Does the child usually look toward the speaker or away from the speaker when listening? Does the quiet wriggling of a three-year-old when listening to a story mean that the child is uncomfortable, is bored, or has to go to the bathroom? Be alert for consistent sequences of behavior in individual children so you can eventually learn what these cues mean. Respect children's nonverbal indications of violations of personal space.

3. Maintain the integrity of children's proximal space. Pat children on the back; shake their hands; give them congratulatory hugs. Avoid absent-minded fondling or patting children on the head or buttocks. These gestures communicate patronization or disrespect.

4. Use nonverbal signals to gain the attention of a group of children who are engaged in an activity or who are dispersed in space. Indoors, signals such as playing a chord on a piano, flicking the lights on and off, singing a specific tune, clapping your hands, or other signals are effective in getting the attention of the children. Then, you may signal for silence by putting a finger over your pursed lips or beckoning the children nearer with your hand. Outdoors, signals such as whistling, waving a hand or flag, holding an arm high with flattened palm toward the children, ringing a bell, or blowing a whistle are effective for getting children's attention.

Children cannot be expected to receive and understand spoken messages if they don't know that you are trying to communicate with them. You can tell that they have received a signal if they turn toward you or begin to quiet down. Your spoken message should begin after you have gained their attention. Very young children will need to be taught the meaning of nonverbal signals such as those mentioned in the preceding paragraph, as they are seldom used by families: "When I turn the lights on and off like this (demonstrate), stop what you are doing, stop talking, and look at me. Let's practice it once."

5. Walk up to children with whom you want to communicate and orient yourself in a face-to-face position. Move your body into the axial space of the child to get the child's attention before trying to deliver a message. For example, Paul was concentrating on gluing together a model airplane. The recreation leader, standing about ten feet away from him, said: "Put newspaper down on the table before gluing. That stuff won't wash off." Paul continued with his task, completely unaware that someone had spoken to him. The message would have been effective if the adult had walked over, stooped down, and looked directly at Paul when speaking to him.

Thus, when children are engaged in activities, move from child to child and speak to them individually. *You will have to squat down to achieve face-to-face communication with small children.* Children should be able to see your face. Verbal messages can otherwise go literally "over their heads"! Facial expressions that reinforce your words help children to understand what you are saying.

6. Keep all channels of communication consistent when communicating about your feelings. When expressing your feelings to a child, your words should match your behavior. During the course of working with children, you are likely to experience a variety of feelings such as joy, amusement, annoyance, anger, surprise, puzzlement, and interest. Communications that are consistent across all channels are authentic, genuine, and honest. You can achieve clarity and understanding by using all channels to convey one message. Multiple feelings can be expressed in rapid sequence and still be genuine. When adults try to suppress, mask, or simulate feelings, they are not being authentic, genuine, or honest. If you are angry, you should look and sound angry; if you are happy, your face, body and voice should reflect your joy.

7. Touch the child. The younger the child, the more likely it is that he or she will find physical touching acceptable. Frequently, boys over eight years of age resent being touched. The adult must, of course, respect

the child's preference. However, when trust has been established, touching or patting a child in a friendly or congratulatory manner is acceptable regardless of age. When used appropriately, touch is soothing, comforting, and emotionally healing because it is a tangible link between you and the child. Something as simple as a nurse holding a child's hand while someone else is drawing a blood sample can reduce the child's anxiety.

How to Show Warmth and Caring

1. Stand, sit, or squat close to the child, not more than an arm's length away. Don't allow furniture or materials to act as a barrier between you and the child.

2. Sit or stand so that your head is at the same level as the child's. This avoids the appearance of talking down to the child.

3. Maintain frequent but not continuous eye contact. This is normal listening behavior and demonstrates your interest in the child.

4. Face the child so that your shoulders and the child's are parallel. When your upper body is at an angle to another's you are in an unstable position that usually implies that you are going to move. Therefore, your upper body as well as your face should be in a front-to-front position with the child.

5. Lean slightly toward the child. Leaning toward the child communicates interest and also helps you hear what the child is saying. Maintain a relaxed body posture. Slouching or rigidity do not convey interest or concern. Your body should not appear "ready to leave immediately." The arms and legs should be open, not tightly closed or crossed.

Use movements that convey alertness. Nodding the head or using other gestures to indicate your understanding are appropriate. This should not be confused with fidgeting, which usually indicates disinterest or boredom. Feet should be unobtrusive, not moving about. Mannerisms (hair flicking, lint picking, or table tapping) should be unobtrusive or absent. None of your movements should compete with the child's words for attention.

6. Convey a generally positive facial expression in neutral situations. Smile when greeting the child. Relax and enjoy everyday interactions with the child.

7. Respond as quickly as possible when spoken to, and take the time to listen. Taking time to really listen to a child is sometimes very difficult to do. If you don't have time to listen to what a child has to say, let the child know that you are interested and will be able to attend more fully later. Then, be sure to do so. For example, Mr. Wardlich had begun reading a story aloud to the class when Carrie announced that she was going to Florida during spring break. Mr. Wardlich told her that she could tell him about it when the children were working on their penmanship, but that now it was time to read a story.

8. Use voice tones that are normal to soft in loudness and normal to low in pitch, and a voice quality that is relaxed, serious, and concerned. Your voice should be clear, audible, and free of many filled pauses such as "Ah" or "Um." The speech should be regular and even in tempo, not impatient or excessively slow. Your speech should be fluent when answering simple questions or commenting on a topic rather than staccato or full of hesitations.

How to Demonstrate Authority and Security

1. Maintain a tone of voice that is firm, warm, and confident. The pitch should be even and the volume normal. Tonal quality should be open (sound is full and melodious) and the speed steady. The desired tonal quality can be achieved by dropping the jaw, relaxing the throat, and projecting through the mouth rather than the nose. Variations in pitch during a sentence or very rapid speech give the impression of uncertainty. A weak, distant, wavering, or very soft voice is nonassertive and may convey the message "I am telling you to do this, but I don't think you will. And if you don't, I won't follow through." Adults whose normal voices are very soft or very high may need to add extra depth or intensity to their very important messages in order to be taken seriously.

2. Look directly at the child when speaking and maintain regular eye contact. Eye contact may be maintained for longer periods while speaking firmly to a child than is typical of usual conversation, but staring or glaring at a child usually is not necessary. A steady, firm look at a child who is misbehaving sometimes is sufficient to remind the child to redirect the behavior in question. Aversion of eye contact or a pleading look are nonassertive.

Because some adults are shorter than tall eleven- and twelve-year-olds, serious messages will be more effective if both child and adult are seated. Differences in height are usually differences in leg length. When a child towers over an adult, assertive messages are unusually difficult to deliver. Face-to-face interaction is more effective.

3. Relax, maintain close physical proximity, and maintain arms and legs in either an open or semi-open position. You are in a naturally authoritative position in regard to small children. It is unnecessary to display aggressiveness, as demonstrated by hands on hips, feet apart, and a tense body, to achieve compliance. However, having a stooped or dejected-looking posture or leaning on something for support certainly is not assertive and children may not comply with requests when they detect a nonassertive stance.

4. Use your hands to gesture appropriately or if necessary, to grasp the child until the communication is complete. Little children are quite capable of darting away when they don't want to hear what you have to say. They may also twist about, turn their backs toward you, or put their hands over their ears. The child can be held firmly and steadily without pinching or excessive force until the message is completed.

Gestures that enumerate points, that describe the meanings of the words used, or that indicate position in space are appropriate. Fidgeting, restless hands, or even "clammy" hands are nonassertive.

PITFALLS TO AVOID

Regardless of whether you are using nonverbal communication techniques with children individually or in groups, informally or in structured activities, there are certain pitfalls you should avoid.

Giving inconsistent nonverbal messages or nonverbal messages inconsistent with the verbal content. Don't smile when you are angry, stating a rule, or trying to convey an admonition or your displeasure. Don't use a loving tone of voice while giving an admonition, or use a cold, distant tone while expressing approval or affection. These classic double-bind messages result in confusion or distrust on the part of children.

Hurting children. Some nonverbal means of getting attention, such as rapping children on the head with a pencil, yanking them to get into line, or using excessive force to hold them in place so you can talk, are aggressive and inappropriate.

Using baby talk. Parents and intimates may use baby talk as a form of affection. Professionals who work with children must establish clearer communication based on respect for the child.

Interrupting children. Allow children the chance to speak. Don't complete sentences for them even if you think you know what they mean. Don't try to fill the normal hesitations of a child's speech with your own words. Allowing children time to speak their own thoughts shows respect. Interrupting children and finishing sentences for them is intrusive, patronizing, and disrespectful. Let children choose the words to use, and don't hurry them along. This demonstrates good listening skills, providing a positive example for children to follow.

Shouting, bellowing, shrieking, or screaming at children. More effective ways have been described for getting the attention of children. In addition, loud or shrill voices can be frightening. Such behavior in adults usually indicates that the adult has lost self-control.

Calling to children across the room. In neutral or positive situations, adults usually remember to walk over to children and speak to them directly. However, in emergencies or when danger threatens, this procedure often is forgotten. In such a situation, you may attempt to regulate a child by calling out a warning. Unfortunately, this usually is ineffective because children do not always know the message is directed toward them. In addition, they may startle and thereby get hurt. Take a few seconds and move toward the child to deliver the message.

SUMMARY

People use nonverbal behaviors to efficiently and subtly communicate their feelings about a relationship as well as about the substance of the verbal message they are sending. Nonverbal messages usually are implicit and often fleeting and therefore can be denied or misinterpreted.

Each of the channels, or modes, of nonverbal communication can work independently of the others and can complement or contradict the lexical message. Messages that are consistent across all channels are more easily understood; in addition, the speaker sends the general message of honesty, genuineness, and integrity. Mixed messages—those that are not consistent across channels—are confusing to children, convey a general sense of deception or disinterest, cause children to distrust the adult, and are less likely to elicit the desired response.

Children learn to interpret nonverbal messages before they learn to deliberately send them. Most of their learning is based on imitation. Therefore, children exposed to effective communicators will themselves become more effective communicators. Infants are able to detect mixed messages, and they rely substantially on the paralinguistic features of the message. As children get older, they become more skillful in understanding and sending nonverbal messages. They also tend to rely more on facial expressions in decoding messages, except when they detect deception.

Adults who understand the meanings of nonverbal messages can deliberately use them to enhance their effectiveness in communication. Skills have been presented that will increase your ability to nonverbally convey warmth and concern as well as authority. Using these skills will help you to communicate clearly and develop positive relationships with children built on respect and concern.

Pitfalls have been identified that should be avoided. These will, in the long run, either prove ineffective or interfere with building positive relationships with children.

Now that you understand some of the most basic components of communication with children, you are ready to explore ways in which these can be combined with verbal communication skills to facilitate the development of positive, growth-enhancing relationships with children.

DISCUSSION QUESTIONS

1. Describe the functions of nonverbal communication and how each is used in ordinary interactions.
2. How does nonverbal communication regulate social interaction?
3. Why is it necessary to describe how the different channels of nonverbal communication operate when discussing building relationships with young children?
4. Imagine watching two ten-year-olds in a face-to-face situation in which one is thrusting a stick at the other. What would be your interpretation of this event if the children were 12 feet apart; 3 feet apart; quite close together? Why would you interpret these differently?
5. Answer Question #4 in relation to internal, proximal, axial, and distal space.
6. Why is it important to know something about the cultural heritage of children when interpreting the meaning of their nonverbal behaviors?
7. How do age, relationship, and gender affect nonverbal communication behaviors? Give examples.

8. Why should helping professionals use congruent verbal and nonverbal communications with children and strictly avoid incongruent messages?
9. Nonverbal communication, unlike language arts, is not taught in school. How do children learn about it?
10. How does your use of time in interactions with other people denote your social relationship to them?
11. Which nonverbal behaviors are most likely to convey warmth?
12. Which nonverbal behaviors are most likely to convey assertiveness?
13. How do the nonverbal communications of adults contribute to building positive relationships with children?

CHAPTER 4
Promoting Children's Self-Awareness and Self-Esteem Through Verbal Communication

SOURCE: © Ulrike Welsch

OBJECTIVES:

On completion of this chapter, you will be able to describe:

1. Self-awareness.

2. How children develop a concept of self over time.

3. What constitutes self-esteem.

4. The origins of self-esteem.

5. Characteristics of a negative verbal environment.

6. Characteristics of a positive verbal environment.

7. Adult communication strategies associated with a positive verbal environment.

8. Pitfalls to avoid in communicating verbally with children.

If asked to respond to the question, "Who am I?" depending on his or her age, a child might answer:

"I am a boy with red hair."
"I live on Elm Street."
"I like to play baseball."
"I play the clarinet better than my brother."
"I am a member of Student Council."

Statements like these describe how children perceive themselves and how they distinguish themselves from those around them. The aggregate of perceptions a person has about himself or herself is referred to as *self-concept*, that is, the sense of being a distinct individual who possesses a combination of attributes, values, and behaviors that are unique (Shaffer, 1985). A person's notion of self goes beyond the physical entity bounded by her or his skin; it is a psychological construct in which the concepts of "me" and "not me" are defined (Maccoby, 1980). These distinctions emerge gradually, having rudimentary beginnings in infancy, and continue to evolve throughout adulthood.

THE CHILD'S EVOLVING CONCEPT OF SELF

Self-awareness comes about through children's interactions with objects and people and is inextricably linked to their cognitive development. Experience provides the context within which self-knowledge is generated. Children's cognitive structures influence what information they select and how they integrate it into their definition of self.

It is widely believed that newborns do not distinguish themselves from the surrounding environment and that psychologically they merge themselves with their mother, not knowing where one person begins and the other ends. Hence, it can be said that babies begin life with no real concept of self (Mahler, Pine, and Bergman, 1975).

Gradually, as the process of individuation takes place, the beginnings of self-awareness appear. By about twenty months of age, children differentiate between themselves and others and can identify their own face in the mirror (Lewis and Brooks-Gunn, 1979; Bertentahl and Fischer, 1978; Harter, 1983). Part of this self-understanding involves recognizing that they have unique attributes that can be named and described with words (Clarke-Stewart, Friedman, and Koch, 1985). Thus, toddlers (20–30 months of age), realizing they are distinct from other people, are quick to verbalize "Mine" when claiming a favored possession and "Me" when referring to their image in a looking glass or photograph. They also are able to use personal pronouns such as "you," "he," and "she" when referring to others.

Throughout the preschool years, children think of themselves primarily in terms of physical attributes—whether they are boy or girl, their age, what they look like, what they possess, and where they live (Broughton, 1978; Livesley and Bromley, 1973; Selman, 1980). Somewhat later, more of their self-definitions will focus on their attributes in comparison with another person (I am taller than she is; I have more computer games than he does). These differentiations and eventual comparisons are quite logical when one considers that children younger than seven years of age focus much of their attention on organizing their world. Readily observable features such as age, gender, and material goods are convenient categories for grouping "me" and "not me." In addition, preschoolers concentrate on the here and now, making few references to past or future personal states (Mohr, 1978). Abstract notions such as continuity in time, as well as nonobservable psychological traits such as intelligence and ambition are more difficult for them to think about. During this period, children do respond to questions about the "self," thereby acknowledging its existence. However, they combine the notions of self and body and make little distinction between the two (Selman, 1980).

Five- and six-year-olds extend the idea of the physical self to include activities as part of self-concept (I take gymnastics; I walk to the center) (Keller, Ford, Meachum, 1978). This seems to indicate that once children have explored the physical boundaries of self, their interests and capabilities become noticeable to them. Although still observable, these attributes are less concrete and more abstract than those identified by younger children. Physical activities continue to be an important aspect of self-concept for several years, although the manner in which children think about them changes over time. Five-year-olds say, ''I roller-skate''; nine-year-olds announce, ''I roller-skate better than my cousin'' (Secord and Peevers, 1974). Just as with physical attributes, children initially describe what they themselves can do and then later make comparisons with others.

Children's thinking about the self becomes even more abstract as they move into the period of concrete operations around age seven. Their answers to the question ''Who am I?'' now encompass both visible characteristics (I am a boy; I run fast) and psychological traits (I am dependable; I know a lot about baseball; I don't like liver) (Livesley and Bromley, 1973). For the first time, youngsters conceive of the self as including internal states such as feelings, thoughts, and knowledge. By the sixth grade, most youngsters no longer rely on the concrete, physical descriptors of the earlier years. Instead, their self-definitions focus almost entirely on those internal states that they consider most characteristic of them (Mohr, 1978). This more sophisticated view also is more complex than before because their perceptions are influenced by what they have done in the past as well as by what they might do or be like in the future. Such descriptions often refer to patterns of behavior that have been established over time and that children perceive will continue (I am smart; I am shy; I am a hard worker). Thinking of the self in these terms represents a more abstract orientation, which has become possible via the child's increased experience and more advanced cognitive powers. At this point, youngsters perceive the self to be a purely psychological construct. Hence, they enter adolescence with much greater self-awareness than was possible at the beginning of life.

Self-Esteem

As children gain self-knowledge, they begin to evaluate that knowledge, making positive and negative judgments about their self-worth. For instance:

I am good looking.	I am not very good looking.
I am someone people like.	I am not someone people like much.
I am smart.	I am not very smart.
I can do things well.	I can't do many things well.
I am agile.	I am clumsy.
I like myself.	I don't like myself.

This evaluative component of the self is called *self-esteem* (Openshaw, 1978). Self-esteem has two dimensions: competence and worth. *Competence* involves the belief that one has the wherewithall to accomplish tasks and influence events that affect one's life. The extent to which people value and like themselves is a measure of their *worth*. People who judge their competence and worth in positive terms are said to have high self-esteem, and those whose self-evaluations are generally poor are described as having low self-esteem (Gecas, Colonico, and Thomas, 1974). Whether people's self-esteem is high or low has a tremendous impact on their ability to derive joy and satisfaction from life. It affects how they feel about themselves, how they anticipate that others will respond to them, and what they think they can accomplish (Gecas, 1971).

Youngsters whose self-esteem is high feel good about themselves. They consider themselves to be likable and competent. In social interactions, they anticipate that their encounters with others will be rewarding and that they will have a positive influence on the outcome of the exchange (Coopersmith, 1967). These optimistic feelings make it easier for them both to give and to receive love (Fromm, 1956). Such children also have confidence in their own judgments. As a result, they are able to express and defend ideas they believe in, even when faced with opposition from others. When confronted with obstacles, they draw on positive feelings from the past to help them get through difficult times. In addition, they tend to appraise their abilities and limitations realistically and can separate weaknesses in one area from successes in others (Rosenberg, 1965). For these reasons, high self-esteem is related to positive life satisfaction and happiness.

Low self-esteem, on the other hand, is associated with depression, anxiety, and maladjustment (Damon, 1983). Children whose estimations of self-worth are negative experience feelings of inadequacy and incompetence and fear rejection (Openshaw, 1978). They also are less likely to be objective about their capabilities. Theirs is not a balanced view but one that focuses primarily on failings. Such youngsters have little hope of influencing others and anticipate that most interactions will be costly for them. Consequently, they hesitate to express their opinions, lack independence, and tend to feel isolated or alone (Coopersmith, 1967). This pessimistic outlook often leads them to build elaborate defenses as a way to protect their fragile egos or ward off anticipated rebuffs (Dreikurs, 1972). Typical means of self-protection include denigrating themselves, keeping all associates at a distance, or building themselves up by tearing others down (Kaplan and Pokorny, 1969). Because of these outcomes, low self-esteem detracts from one's quality of life and makes a happy existence difficult to achieve.

Influences on self-esteem. Children continually gather information about their value as people through interactions with the significant people in their lives—family members, helping professionals, and other children (Coopersmith, 1967; Swayze, 1980). Such persons serve as the mirror through which children see themselves and then judge what they see (Maccoby, 1980). If what is reflected is good, children will make a positive evaluation of self. If the image is negative, children will deduce that they have little worth. Children are sensitive to the attitudes people have toward them and often adopt those opinions as their own (Openshaw, 1978). Beginning at birth, children build a history of experience that forms the basis for future self-evaluation; the earliest images they have of themselves tend to influence how subsequent experiences are perceived (Mischel, 1976). Thus, experience has a cumulative impact on self-esteem.

This explains why two children who seem very similar to an outsider may, in fact, differ considerably in their self-judgments. Take the case of Chuck and David. Both are nine-year-old boys in the same class at Marble School and have similar socioeconomic and cultural backgrounds. In a recent teacher-led discussion, time ran out before either boy was called on to express his ideas. Both were disappointed. Chuck reasoned that the teacher might not have seen his hand waving in the air; David assumed that the teacher deliberately ignored him because nothing he had to say would have been important anyway. Initially, one might wonder why the boys' reactions were so different. An analysis of their past experience would yield some clues.

The majority of Chuck's interactions with his parents and teachers tend to be positive. They listen to what he has to say and often point out the merit of his observations. The message he receives is that he is a competent, valued person. David's experiences tend to be more negative; frequently, he is cut off before he has finished speaking or told to be quiet. On numerous occasions, adults have dismissed his ideas as silly. His self-esteem mirrors the poor opinion others have of him. Based on what he has learned to expect, each child perceived the situation in a way that fit what he had already come to believe about himself. This incident also was added to their store of self-knowledge and will be used to interpret future social encounters.

The differences between Chuck and David are, in part, due to their interactions with adults who may approach their relationships with children quite differently. However, because people are contributors to their own microsystems, the boys also influence the milieu that is created. Thus, Chuck may promote the favorable reaction he receives by thinking before he speaks, by waiting for others to make their point, and by acknowledging the value of other people's opinions. Some of David's aversive interactions may result from his impulsive outbursts, which frequently have little relation to the topic; his constant interruptions; and his refusal to consider that others may have valuable ideas to share. From this, it can be seen that self-esteem is a product of one's social interactions and that both others and the person involved contribute to the final image that is projected and perceived.

The evolution of self-esteem. Just as the development of self-concept follows a normative sequence, so, too, does self-esteem. Toddlers and preschoolers tend to make assessments about their self-worth that are all-encompassing. That is, they evaluate themselves holistically and tend not to distinguish success in one area of their lives from failure in another. Because their self-concept is rooted in the here and now, they think of themselves as completely good or completely bad. These assessments change as circumstances change. For instance, three-year-old Jessica, who has mastered opening and closing the screen door entirely on her own, may feel quite pleased with her newfound prowess. Yet, moments later, she may be plunged into tears when her older brother says she's too little to join him in a game on the playground. Her self-evaluation at that point

may be "I can't do anything." Gradually, as Jessica broadens her range of experience, it will seem to her that she has either mostly positive or mostly negative social encounters.

School-age children begin to compartmentalize their notions of self-worth by making different evaluations of the self in different realms—social, physical, and intellectual (Harter, 1982). Hence, a child may have positive feelings about himself or herself in relation to physical activities, such as sports, while simultaneously feeling inadequate academically. The relative weight of both positive and negative self-evaluations in these areas then contributes to an overall estimation of self-esteem. It is at about eight or nine years of age that children develop a general index of their value as a person that is predominately favorable or unfavorable. From then on, this same pervasive view remains relatively constant throughout life (Coopersmith, 1967).

How Adult Practices Relate to Children's Self-Esteem

Earlier, it was noted that adults serve as the mirror through which children make assessments regarding their own worth and competence. The reflections children perceive are manifested through the adult's behavior toward them. Certain adult actions are known to promote positive self-judgments in children, and others clearly contribute to negative ones. These key adult behaviors can be grouped into two major categories: guidance and nurturance. *Guidance* involves the disciplinary approach adults use; *nurturance* refers to the types of relationships they establish with children.

The guidance dimension. In general, it can be said that adults who have high standards for children's behavior, who consistently enforce reasonable rules, and who allow children to participate in developing some of those rules contribute to the development of positive self-esteem in children. Adults who are harsh or who employ unreasonable rules and those who enforce no rules at all contribute to children's negative self-judgments (Coopersmith, 1967). Exactly why this is so and what it means to helping professionals is fully explained in Chapters 7 and 8. For now, we turn our attention to the nurturance dimension.

The nurturance dimension. Adults who demonstrate warmth, respect, acceptance, and empathy are most likely to foster self-judgments of competence and worth in children (Gecas, 1971; Gecas, Colonico, and Thomas, 1974). You will remember that these are the very qualities that mark the facilitative dimension of the helping relationship and that have been identified as the primary components of positive adult-child relationships. Adults exhibit these qualities when they show affection to youngsters, when they take an interest in what children are doing, and when they become actively involved with them (Coopersmith, 1967).

On the other hand, children whose contacts are primarily with rejecting, disinterested, insensitive adults find it hard to feel good about themselves (Coopersmith, 1967; Rosenberg, 1965). Adults manifest these attitudes when they ignore children or when they are aloof, impatient, discourteous, or acerbic toward them. If adults act in these ways, youngsters often conclude that because the authority figure finds them unworthy and incompetent, it must be so. This is exemplified in the extreme by abused children who perceive that their failings justify the treatment they receive from their parents.

Relating nurturance to adult talk. Whether adults convey esteem-enhancing or esteem-damaging attitudes frequently is determined by what they say to children and how they say it. In fact, adult verbalizations are a key factor in the degree to which children develop either high or low self-esteem (Rosenberg, 1965; Coopersmith, 1967). Consider the following scenario.

SITUATION: You are invited to visit a program for children. When you arrive, you are asked to wait until the youngsters return from a field trip. As you survey your surroundings, you notice brightly colored furniture comfortably arranged, sunlight softly streaming through the windows, children's artwork pleasingly displayed, attractive materials that look well cared for, green plants placed about the room, and a large, well-stocked aquarium bubbling in a corner. You think to yourself, "What a pleasant place for children!"

Just then, a child bursts into the room crying. She is followed by an adult who snaps: "Rose, you're being a big baby. Now, hush." As the other youngsters file in, you hear another child say, "Look what I found outside!" An adult replies: "Can't you see I'm busy? Show it to me later." After a while, you overhear a child ask, "When do we get to take these home?" He is told, "If you'd been listening earlier, you'd know."

Your favorable impression is shattered. Despite the lovely surroundings, the ways in which adults have responded to children have been so negative that the setting no longer seems pleasant. Adult comments have caused you to question whether it is possible for children to feel good about themselves in this program and whether the adult-child relationships can be anything but distant and unfavorable. What you have overheard has made you privy to an invisible but keenly felt component of every program—the verbal environment.

THE VERBAL ENVIRONMENT

The *verbal environment* encompasses all of the verbal exchanges that take place within a given setting. Its elements include words and silence—how much is said, what is said, how it is stated, who talks, and who listens. The manner in which these elements are used and combined dictates whether the environment is one in which children's estimations of their self-worth are favorable or unfavorable. Thus, verbal environments can be characterized as being either positive or negative.

The Negative Verbal Environment

Verbal environments that are negative are those in which adult-child intractions engender social costs to children as a result of what adults say to them. It is likely that you could readily identify the most extreme illustrations of these. Adults screaming at children, ridiculing them, cursing at them, or subjecting them to ethnic slurs are blatant examples. Less obvious adult behaviors that contribute to a negative verbal environment, and hence detract from children's self-esteem, are summarized as follows:

1. Adults ignore children, showing no interest in their activities. They walk by children without making any comments or even acknowledging their presence. When they do station themselves near a child, they do not engage the child in conversation and respond only grudgingly to a child's attempts to initiate an interaction.
2. Adults misuse times designated for adult-child interaction by talking more with their peers than with the youngsters themselves. Rather than paying attention to children, they chat with other adults about matters of personal interest.
3. Adults pay superficial attention to what children have to say. Instead of listening attentively, they are absorbed in other thoughts. They communicate their preoccupation by asking irrelevant questions, responding inappropriately, failing to maintain eye contact, or cutting the child off in order to follow through on whatever was on their mind.
4. Adults are discourteous when speaking with children. They interrupt the child who is speaking to them as well as youngsters who are talking to each other. They expect children to respond to their requests immediately and do not allow them to finish what they are doing or saying. Their voice tone may be demanding, impatient, or belligerent, and they neglect such social niceties as saying, "Excuse me," "Please," and "Thank you."
5. Adults discourage children from expressing themselves. When children approach them with something to talk about, they say: "Hush," "Not now," or "Tell me about it later." The "later" often never comes.
6. Adults use sarcasm in talking with children. The negative impression conveyed has as much to do with the adult's voice tone as with the actual words they use. Their remarks often make children the butt of a group joke or otherwise establish the adult's superiority ("Hey everybody, listen to this! Erica thinks she's so smart she doesn't need to read page twelve. She already knows the answers").
7. Adults use judgmental vocabulary in describing children to themselves and to others. Typical demeaning remarks include "He's such a brat"; "She's so spoiled"; "You're always acting like a baby"; "She'll never learn"; "Well, Edgar, here, is not too bright. He tries hard, but he just doesn't get it." These comments sometimes are said directly to the child and sometimes to another person within the child's hearing. In either case, youngsters are treated as though they have no feelings or as if they were invisible or deaf.
8. Adults denigrate children's interests in order to pursue their own. They do this in either of two ways. One is to come right out and tell the children that what they are doing or saying is uninteresting or unimportant and that they should be doing or talking about something else instead. Thus, youngsters hear admonishments like: "I'm sick of hearing about your new bike; find something else to talk about," or "You've

had plenty of time to examine that butterfly; now come over here and help me pass out the books.'' Another tactic is for adults to pretend they did not hear what a child asked or said, pursuing their own agenda instead.

9. Adults rely on giving orders and making demands as their primary means of relating to children. Their verbalizations consist mostly of directions (''Sit in your chair,'' ''Turn to page five,'' ''Do your spelling first, and then begin the math assignment'') and admonishments (''No fighting,'' ''Everybody get your coats off and settle down for lunch,'' ''Only one person in the bathroom at a time''). Questions addressed to children are aimed at testing their powers of memorization, not at eliciting their opinions or ideas. Neither are the questions meant to inquire into children's well-being or personal interests (''Daryl, how many paper towels are you allowed to have?''; ''Who remembers where we put our projects when we're through?''). Children who respond or make comments are treated as transgressors of the program code. This is the epitome of one-way communication—adults talking, children listening.

All of the preceding verbal behaviors convey to children adult attitudes of aloofness, disrespect, lack of acceptance, and insensitivity. They cause the program setting to be dominated by adult talk and make it clear to youngsters that adult agendas take precedence over their own. In addition, children quickly learn that their ideas, thoughts, and concerns are not valued, nor are the children important enough as persons to be afforded the courtesy and respect one would anticipate if held in high regard. The aversive encounters that occur in a negative verbal environment tend to make children feel inadequate, confused, or angry (Hoffman, 1963). If interactions such as these become the norm, then children's self-esteem is likely to suffer. A

different set of circumstances exists in programs characterized by a positive verbal environment.

The Positive Verbal Environment

In a positive verbal environment, children experience socially rewarding interactions with the adults present. Adult verbalizations are aimed at satisfying children's needs and making the children feel valued. At all times, when speaking to children, adults concern themselves not only with the informational content of their words, but with the affective impact their speech will have as well. Adults create a positive verbal environment by adhering to the following principles in their verbal exchanges with children:

1. Adults use words to show affection for children and sincere interest in them. They take the time to become engaged in children's activities and to respond to their queries as well as to make remarks showing

FIGURE 4-1 A positive verbal environment is one in which children feel safe to express their ideas.
SOURCE: Photo by David Kostelnik

children they care about them and are aware of what they are doing ("You've been really working hard to get the dinosaur puzzle together"; "You look like you're enjoying that 'Brain Teaser' "). When children invite adults to participate with them, the adults accept the invitation enthusiastically ("That sounds like fun"; "Oh, good; now I'll have a chance to work with you").

2. Adults treat children's verbalizations as important. This means they really listen to what children have to say and concentrate on the child's words. In addition, they respond in an accepting and sensitive manner, not by refuting, criticizing, or brushing aside the child's remarks.

3. Adults speak courteously to children. They refrain from interrupting children and allow them to finish what they are saying, either to the adult or to another person. The voice tone used by adults is patient and friendly, and social amenities such as "Please," "Thank you," and "Excuse me" are part of their conversation.

4. Adults use words to show that they take pleasure in the child's company. They laugh with children, respond to their humor, invite children to join them, and tell them that they enjoy being with them.

5. Adults use children's interests as a basis for conversation. They converse with them about the things youngsters want to talk about. This is manifested in two ways. First, they follow the child's lead in conversations. Second, they bring up subjects known to be of interest to a particular child based on past experience.

6. Adults plan or take advantage of spontaneous opportunities to talk with each child informally. Every day, children have opportunities to talk with the adults about matters that interest or concern them.

7. Adults avoid making judgmental comments about children either to them or within their hearing. Children are treated as sensitive,

aware human beings whose feelings are respected. Discussions about children's problems or family situations are held in private between the appropriate parties.

The importance of establishing a positive verbal environment. Positive verbal environments are beneficial to both the adults and children who participate in them. The principles outlined here provide concrete ways for adults to communicate warmth, respect, acceptance, and empathy to children. This makes it more likely that youngsters will view adults as sources of comfort and encouragement. Demonstration of such attitudes also creates the facilitative base from which adults can more confidently take appropriate future action. Simultaneously, children gain because there are people in the program with whom they feel comfortable and secure. In addition, the adult-child interaction patterns enable children to learn more about themselves and to feel good about the self they come to know. Thus, a positive verbal environment is associated favorably with self-awareness and self-esteem.

Positive verbal environments do not happen by chance, nor do they occur automatically just because adults have children's best interests at heart. Rather, their creation is purposeful. Adults must pay careful attention to the principles just described and incorporate, as part of their daily interactions, such simple but telling behaviors as greeting children, addressing them by name, inviting children to talk to them, speaking courteously to children, and listening attentively to what children have to say. These basic actions convey fundamental attitudes of affection, interest, and involvement. Another technique helping professionals can utilize to further communicate these same qualities is the behavior reflection.

Behavior Reflections

Behavior reflections are nonjudgmental statements made to children regarding some aspect of their behavior or person. The adult observes a child and then directs a comment to the child related to her or his attributes or activities. Such statements are devoid of opinion or evaluation, consisting only of the exact features or behavior the adult sees.

SITUATION: A child is coming down a slide on his stomach.

Adult: You're sliding down the slide. (Or, either of the following: You found a new way to come down; You're sliding head first.)

SITUATION: Joe and Melissa are drawing a mural together.

Adult: You two are working together. (Or: Each of you has figured out a way to contribute to the mural; You're concentrating on what you are doing; That's a very involved project you're working on.)

SITUATION: A child arrives at a day-care center.

Adult: You're wearing your tennis shoes today. (Or: You look all ready to go; That bag you're carrying looks like a heavy load.)

The value to children of using behavior reflections. Behavior reflections are fundamental verbal tools for demonstrating interest in children. When adults reflect what children are doing, they talk about actions and experiences that have the most meaning for youngsters—those in which they themselves are involved. Verbal observations such as these increase children's self-awareness and make them feel valued because the adult notices them and takes the time to note aloud something they have done.

As a result, children learn that their everyday actions are important enough to be noticed and that extreme behavior is not needed to gain appropriate attention. This is an important concept for children to understand because they sometimes assume that adults will only notice behavior that is out of the ordinary (Dreikurs and Cassel, 1972). Youngsters' interpretations of "out of the ordinary" might include excelling in a particular area, or acting out. Such conclusions are not surprising because in many group settings, one has to be the birthday child, the one who gets all A's, or the child who pinches a lot in order to receive individual attention from adults. By reflecting, adults instead make note of such commonplace events as:

> "You're sharing the paint with Wally."
> "You're trying hard to tie your shoes."
> "You noticed our math books are brand new."

Simple comments such as these say to the child, "You are important." Because each takes only a few seconds to say, these comments are particularly useful to helping professionals who must work with more than one child at a time. Thus, while helping Nakita with her coat, the caregiver also can attend to Micah and Leon by saying: "Micah, you have almost every single button done," "Leon, you wore your brown coat today," and to Nakita, "You figured out which arm to put in first." This spreads the attention around and helps Micah and Leon as well as Nakita feel that the adult has taken them into account.

Because reflections are nonevaluative, children learn not to feel threatened by adult attention. The nonevaluative nature of the reflection enables adults to actively and concretely demonstrate acceptance of children; youngsters interpret reflections as tangible efforts by adults to understand them better (Kostelnik and Kurtz, 1986).

Further, when used appropriately, behavior reflections enable the adult to enter the child's world by becoming cognizant of that child's perspective within an interaction. Understanding what is important to a child about a particular activity by seeing it through the child's eyes sets the stage for adults to be more empathic in

FIGURE 4-2 ''You look like you're having fun'' captures the *children's* perception of their game.
SOURCE: Photo by David Kostelnik

their responses to children (Rogers, 1957, 1961). Also, observing closely and taking cues from the children makes it more likely that youngsters feel good about the interactions that take place. Thus, an adult watching children dancing in a conga line might reflect: ''You formed a really long conga line,'' or ''Everybody's figured out a way to hang on,'' or ''Everyone's smiling. You look like you're having fun.'' These are child-centered remarks that correspond to the youngsters' agenda in that situation rather than the adult's. All too often, adults in group settings feel more comfortable supervising children than actually interacting with them. Within this mode, their remarks might have been: ''What's that you're doing?'', ''That's a hopscotch

outline, not a conga pattern,'' or ''You forgot to put the kickstep in. It goes like this.'' Even if these observations were meant to show adult interest, they do not match the children's perception of what is important in their game. Such comments only disrupt the activity and tell children that the adult knows better. Neither outcome promotes favorable self-judgments in children or positive adult-child relationships.

Besides enabling adults to indicate interest in, acceptance of, and empathy toward children, behavior reflections offer a means by which children can increase their receptive language skills. This is because children derive word meanings from hearing the words used in context in relation to their immediate experiences (Mattick, 1972). This type of contextual learning occurs when youngsters hear new words and new ways of putting words together to describe day-to-day events. For instance, young children who hear the day-care provider observe on different occasions:

''You are walking to the door.''
''You and Jeremy walked into the coatroom together.''
''We were walking along and found a ladybug.''

will begin to comprehend the meanings of different verb forms based on their own direct involvement in each situation. Similarly, words children already have in their repertoire help them deduce the definitions of new words they hear (DiVesta, 1974). Thus, a child may surmise that ''gargantuan'' means ''big'' because a helping professional reflects, ''You found the most gargantuan dinosaur of all'' as the child points to an Apatosaurus, which he already considers a large animal. New words add to children's store of knowledge about themselves and the world around them. Becoming better able to understand the words directed toward them contributes to positive self-esteem.

An added benefit of using behavior reflections is that they may serve as an opening for children to talk to adults if they wish. Often, youngsters respond to the adult's reflections with comments of their own. Thus, a verbal exchange may develop that is centered around the child's interests. On the other hand, children do not feel compelled to answer every reflection they hear (Guerney, 1980). For this reason, reflecting does not interrupt children's activities or make them stop what they are doing in order to respond to an adult query. Even when youngsters remain silent, they benefit by being made aware of the adult's interest in them.

When to use behavior reflections. Behavior reflections can be used singly, in succession, and with other skills you will learn about in later chapters. When interacting with toddlers, preschoolers, youngsters whose primary language is not English, and children whose receptive language development has been delayed, it is appropriate to use a series of behavior reflections. For example, in a ten-minute interaction at the water table, the teacher might say: "You're pouring the water down the hose and watching it come out the other end," "You found a funnel to use," "You all remembered to put your smocks on," "Lucy, you're churning the water with an eggbeater," "Mimi, you're getting the water to move with your hands." Such remarks could be addressed to one child, to more than one child, or to the group as a whole. Regardless of whether or not they answer, children of this age and ability appreciate knowing the adult is nearby and attentive.

School-age children, on the other hand, may feel self-conscious having that many remarks directed their way. For them, a single behavior reflection acts as an appropriate signal that the adult is interested in them and is available for further involvement if they wish it. Thus, out on the playground, children would consider it a friendly overture for an adult to say: "That was some catch!" or "You figured out the rules all by yourselves." In each case, if the child were to reply, the adult would have a clear in-

vitation to continue the interaction. Were children to remain engrossed in their activity or direct remarks to others, this would be a cue to the adult that a prolonged interaction was not desired at that time.

Both children and adults benefit when helping professionals utilize behavior reflections in their repertoire of communication techniques. Most importantly, behavior reflections afford adults an excellent means to show children they care about them and are interested in their activities. Behavior reflections are particularly effective with young children, children who are just learning to speak English, and children who are mentally impaired and as an entree to more involved interactions with older youngsters. Yet, to build relationships with children over time, it is necessary to implement additional skills that eventually will lead to more prolonged verbal exchanges.

Demonstrating Affection, Interest, and Involvement via Conversation

One of the most basic ways for adults to manifest their concern for children and their desire to become involved in their activities is to converse with them. Adult-child conversations contribute to children's positive feelings about themselves. When adults are attentive and respond meaningfully, they are demonstrating interest in the youngsters with whom they interact. Because adults represent authority figures, this clear sign of the adult's respect, caring, and acceptance conveys a powerful message to children about their value (Danish and Hauer, 1973). Attitudes such as these increase children's self-respect and self-acceptance.

In addition, conversations that center around topics in which children are interested are more likely to produce spontaneous and lengthy discussions than those focusing on adult topics. In such an atmosphere, youngsters begin to feel more confident about expressing their own thoughts, ideas, and feelings. As adults become actively involved with children in this manner, children come to view them as people worthy of receiving their trust and as potential sources of information and guidance. Thus, the foundations for positive adult-child relationships are extended and built on.

Unfortunately, many adults inadvertently discourage conversations because they have difficulty engaging in the give-and-take necessary for communication to occur. Instead, they feel compelled to take charge of the exchange rather than allow the child to dictate its direction. They see their role as instructor or admonisher, not listener (Hendrick, 1984). This is manifested in any one of several ways.

Conversation Stoppers

Adults communicate disinterest, disdain, and intolerance for children when they:

> Brush aside children's comments.
> Interrupt children to correct their speech.
> Immediately supply a fact or render an opinion.
> Ask too many questions.

All of these tactics inhibit conversation, inhibit self-awareness, and contribute to feelings of low self-esteem. In addition, they are barriers to the development of positive adult-child relationships.

Missing children's conversational cues. At times, children make comments that, to an adult, seem irrelevant or only remotely related to the topic at hand. Sometimes, when this happens, adults are tempted to circumvent the child's overture in order to stick more closely to their original vision of the topic. For instance, several kindergarteners and Mr. Yakely, their teacher, found a robin's nest that contained an egg and began to examine it. As the teacher was pointing out characteristics of the egg, one child piped up: "I had eggs for breakfast. Mine were scrambled." Immediately, the others chimed in

with comments about breakfast. Mr. Yakely ignored what he considered to be an interruption and continued his discourse on robins and their nests. (A variation on the teacher's disregard of the remark would have been for him to say, "That's nice" and then continue his own train of thought.)

Mr. Yakely missed an opportunity for a positive interaction with his pupils by passing over their remarks. The children had, in fact, found a way to connect the finding of the nest with something relevant to them. By his verbal behavior, Mr. Yakely demonstrated to the children that the bird's nest was a more significant topic of conversation than any the children could initiate. The children felt brushed aside and unimportant because they did not have a chance to explain their own ideas.

Correcting grammar. In their attempts to convey ideas, children may make grammatical errors. In response, adults sometimes ignore the content of the child's speech and interrupt them by making them repeat the phrase correctly. This is ill advised. Most children do not change their grammar when corrected in this manner and, in the process, may be offended. They feel usurped, lose track of what they are saying, and have difficulty associating the correction with their actual words (DiVesta, 1974). None of these sensations are conducive to positive adult-child relations or feelings of high self-esteem. Rephrasing the child's message appropriately and conversationally is a better approach (Cazden, 1972). If LaDonna says, "I holded the record real careful," she would feel more accepted and heard and, incidentally, would learn more about grammatical sentence structure were the adult to reflect, "You held it very carefully so it wouldn't break" instead of admonishing, "Don't say 'holded,' say 'held' " (Nelson, 1977). In addition, LaDonna would be more likely to express her feelings to this adult in the future without fear of criticism. This could lead to a more constructive relationship between the two individuals.

Supplying facts and rendering opinions. Adults sometimes stifle conversation by evaluating the content of the child's message rather than simply responding to it. Consider the following dialogues.

Carly: I bet Michael Jackson would love my dad's pumpkin pie. He would jump right out of the T.V. and get some.

Adult: Now, you know that can never happen. He's not really in the T.V.

Carly: (Walks away)

Carly: I bet Michael Jackson would love my dad's pumpkin pie. He would jump right out of the T.V. and get some.

Adult: Your dad must make great pumpkin pie.

Carly: Yeah, it's all orange and yummy and has whipped cream on top.

Adult: Mm-m! No wonder Michael would want some.

Carly: He would eat one whole pie all by himself.

In the first example, Carly's attempts at conversation were hindered by the adult's preoccupation with getting the facts straight. In the second, the adult used Carly's ideas and interests as a basis for prolonging the verbal exchange. The latter was more conducive to positive relationship building because the adult's verbalizations helped Carly to feel interesting and important.

Advising. When children approach older persons with a problem, it is natural for adults to try to help by offering solutions and advice. If this is done before the child has had sufficient time to talk out his or her ideas, two problems may result. First, the real issue may never be defined, so the solution that is proferred may not suit the actual dilemma. Second, whenever an authority figure makes a pronouncement about what is best, it is difficult for the conversation to continue because children are often uncomfortable about questioning their elders' judgments or indicating that the adult's favored solution is unpalatable. In either case, further elaboration by the child is unlikely (Gazda, 1977; Gordon, 1975). This prevents children from exploring ideas or increasing their own problem-solving abilities.

Inappropriate questioning. A common strategy adults use in conversing with children is to ask them questions. When used judiciously, questions can be an effective way to indicate interest in children and to gain needed information from them. However, questioning is a strategy that is often abused, which can result in fewer and shorter responses (Dillon, 1978). For this reason, constant probing interferes with relationship building (Gazda, 1977; Kostelnik, 1978). Questioners become the dominant persons in conversations by taking the lead and dictating the direction the dialogue will go. This detracts from the respondent's feeling that she or he is a partner in the communication process. Moreover, a questioner may force a child into disclosing information that he or she prefers to keep private, at the same time giving the child no opportunity to say what he or she really wants to say (Dillon, 1981). This is illustrated by the child who is asked probing questions about his performance on a test and in the process reveals a low score he has hoped no one else would find out about. Time spent on this subject also preempts his opportunity to describe the weekend he spent with his cousins.

Another reason why questions are so often a poor conversational tool is that many queries are inquisitive in inflection only, not in intent (Parten, 1979; Holzman, 1972). Samples include: "What do you think you're doing?"; "Haven't you finished that project yet?"; "Don't you think you ought to get busy?"; "How do you expect us to be on time if you spend your whole day in front of the mirror?'' One study found that only 20 percent of the questions asked of children in group settings actually require them to think or to reply (Gall, 1971). In addition, adults may ask so many questions in such rapid sequence that children tune them out. For example, studies of teacher behavior indicate that, on the average, 60 percent of all adult-child interactions involved questions, with at least one question being asked every 72 seconds (Resnick, 1972). Some teachers asked as many as 150 questions in half an hour (Hyman, 1977). Other research has found that, on the average, children are allowed only 1 to 3 seconds to provide answers to questions (Rowe, 1974). As a result, approximately half of the questions that adults ask go unanswered and when children do respond, their answers tend to be brief. Most typically, answers consist of one word or a short phrase (Boggs, 1972). In fact, the more questions that are asked, the fewer words children use to answer them. This is particularly true when children are subjected to a series of questions (Boggs, 1972; Drake, 1972; Labov, 1970). Thus, when Enrico is at the easel and the adult asks:

> ''Why did you pick green paint?''
> ''Do you like green?''
> ''Is green your favorite color?''
> ''Can you think of anything that's green?''
> ''Are you going to use any other colors?''
> ''What's that shape you just made?''
> ''What other shapes can you make?''

It is probable that he will ignore most, if not all, of these queries. Additionally, the interaction that the helping professional hoped would be positive has turned into an unpleasant interrogation. Thus, when questions are used rhetorically, in succession, or too often, they are a poor means of prompting conversation and, hence, are poor relationship builders.

All of the preceding conversation stoppers should be avoided. Instead, adults can learn two techniques that are known to be effective ways to keep conversations going: paraphrase reflections and open-ended questions (Yinger, 1975).

Paraphrase Reflections

A *paraphrase reflection* is a restatement, in an adult's words, of something a child has said. The adult listens carefully to what the child is saying, then repeats the statement to the child in words slightly different from those she or he had originally used. As with behavior reflections, paraphrase reflections are nonjudgmental statements. They are not vehicles through which adults express personal opinions about what the child is trying to communicate. Rather, they are a tangible means of indicating that the adult is listening attentively. Examples might include:

Child: Teacher, see my new dress and shoes!

Adult: You have a new outfit on today. (Or either of the following: You wanted me to see your new clothes; You sound pleased about your new things.)

Child: (At lunch table) Oh no! Macaroni again.

Adult: You've had more macaroni than you can stand. (Or: Macaroni's not your favorite; You thought it was time to have something else.)

Child: Is it almost time for us to get going?

Adult: You think we should be leaving soon. (Or: You're wondering if it's time to go yet; You'd like to get started.)

In each of the preceding situations, the adult first listened to the child, then paraphrased the child's statement or inquiry. You will note that there was more than one appropriate way to reflect in each situation. Although paraphrase reflections are all similar in form, the content of each depends on the adult's interpretation of the child's message. Thus, there is no one reflection that is most correct in every situation.

Rather, any one of several alternate responses is possible.

Why paraphrase reflections benefit children. For true conversations to take place, it is important that adults listen to what children have to say. However, real listening involves more than simply remaining silent. It means responding to children's words with words of one's own that imply, "I hear you; I understand you" (Sayles and Strauss, 1981). Paraphrase reflections are an ideal way to get this message across. Sometimes called active, reflective, or empathic listening, paraphrase reflections are widely used in the helping professions to indicate positive regard and involvement. People who employ this technique often are perceived by those with whom they interact as sensitive, interested, and accurate listeners (Egan, 1975; Guerney, 1975). The result is that people talk more freely and that conversations are more rewarding for both participants. This favorable outcome occurs for several reasons (Ivancevich, Donnelly, and Gibson, 1983; Sayles and Strauss, 1981; Gordon, 1975):

FIGURE 4-3 Successful adult/child conversations focus on the child's point of view.
SOURCE: Photo by David Kostelnik

1. Paraphrasing gives the message sender the impression that the listener is carefully considering his or her ideas and is trying to understand the sender's frame of reference. Hence, although the listener may not always agree with the other person's point of view, he or she manifests an awareness and a comprehension of it. Such understanding is critical if miscommunication is to be avoided.

2. Paraphrasing helps the listener to be more empathic toward the message sender. In order to accurately paraphrase another person's words, one must not only heed them literally, but must take into account the underlying meaning they convey. When both aspects of the message are considered, the listener gains a better understanding of how the message sender is seeing and interpreting his or her world.

The ability to achieve this understanding is always beneficial, but is particularly critical when the listener and the message sender have different opinions or goals within the interaction.

3. Paraphrasing may cause the message sender to restate the original message if the listener has not quite grasped the point or to correct a mistaken reflection if the listener's interpretation was inaccurate. Additionally, senders have a chance to elaborate and provide further information that they think is important for the listener to know.

4. Paraphrasing highlights what the message sender really said. Often, people are surprised to hear what someone else has understood by their words and are

rewarded by a deeper insight into their own thoughts on hearing a reiteration of them.

5. Paraphrasing allows the message sender to control the direction of the conversation. She or he determines what to reveal and what channels to pursue. This is particularly advantageous to children because the nature of the instructional and socialization process often requires them to follow the adult's lead in a discussion rather than determining it themselves. Use of paraphrase reflections enables children to discuss topics adults might never think of or might consider too silly, too gory or too sensitive to talk about.

6. Paraphrasing children's queries often prompts them to answer some questions or solve some problems on their own. Children are more likely to rely on their own ideas if the adult helps them clarify the issue via a paraphrase reflection rather than immediately furnishing a fact or solution (Hendrick, 1984). How this can work is illustrated in the following:

Helene: Is it snack time yet?

Adult: You're not sure when we'll be having a snack.

Helene: Must be soon. There's the cups out already.

In this situation, Helene used the evidence available to her in the physical environment to determine that it was almost time for a snack. The adult's response prompted Helene to think more than if the question had been answered directly.

7. When used with children younger than seven years of age, paraphrase reflections can have a positive influence on their language development. This occurs when adults expand children's verbal messages. Between the ages of eighteen months and three years, simple expansions are best (Brown and Bellugi, 1964):

Child: Kitty sleep.

Adult: Yes, the kitty is sleeping.

Child: Me eat.

Adult: You are eating.

In each of these examples, the adult has expanded the child's telegraphic message to include appropriate connecting words in the same tense as the child's. This type of paraphrasing is slightly different from and more complex than the youngster's speech and has been shown to stimulate children to produce lengthier, more varied sentences (Cazden, 1972).

Children aged four and older profit from a more elaborate variation termed *recasting* (Nelson, 1977). Recasting refers to actually restructuring the child's sentence into a new grammatical form:

Child: The cat is sleeping.

Adult: Snowball is asleep on the windowsill.

Child: I'm eating my hot dog.

Adult: Soon, you'll have eaten your whole hot dog.

Recasting preserves the child's meaning, but rephrases it in a way that is moderately novel. Novelty can be introduced by changing the sentence structure, by adding auxiliary verbs, or by using relevant synonyms. This helps the child to notice the more complex grammatical form. Recasting works best when adults make modest changes in the child's words but do not alter them entirely. Overcomplication causes children to overlook the new grammatical structure, making it unlikely that they will use it themselves.

Using paraphrase reflections. Paraphrase reflections can be used any time a child addresses a comment to an adult. They may consist of a simple phrase or multiple statements. Sometimes, a simple verbal acknowledgement of something a child has said is all that is required:

Child: I'm up to page fifteen.

Adult: You've gotten pretty far in a short time. (Child resumes reading)

On other occasions, program pressures preclude the feasibility of involved adult-child interactions. Again, a single paraphrase can indicate interest in the child while minimally interrupting the flow of events.

However, when time permits, paraphrase reflections are also excellent conversation starters and may be used to prolong an interaction once it begins. Consider the following two conversations. The first involves Chris, who is five; the second, his six-year-old brother, Kyle. Both discussions were spontaneous.

Chris: We got a new dog over the weekend!

Adult: You sound excited. Tell me more.

Chris: Well, he's got a flat nose . . . well, ah . . . he's been biting a lot . . . and, he's ah, he's cute . . . you know, he's ugly and homely. He's cute . . . and, ah . . . he's in a biting mood . . . you know, he has to chew on something a lot of times, he's just, he's going to be . . . ah, October . . . um, August seventh was his birthday! Not his real birthday. His real birthday was . . . what was his real birthday? His real birthday . . . was February seventh, I think.

Adult: Ah, but you celebrated his birthday at a different time even though it wasn't his real one.

Chris: August, uh huh, August. He's only six months old. Six months . . . .

Adult: Oh, he's only six months old. He's just a small dog.

Chris: No, he's not a small dog. He's about, you know, from here to here (child spreads arms to indicate size) . . . you know . . . he's . . . .

Adult: Oh, he's a pretty large dog.

Chris: Yeah. He's pretty large, all right! He's got a fat stomach and tiny legs! (Laughs)

Adult: (Laughing) He sounds comical, with a flat nose too.

Chris: Yeah, and . . . you know, he has knots on his head . . . and he has a face like he's real sad, and . . . um . . . .

Adult: Sad-faced.

Chris: Uh huh.

Adult: Sad-faced dogs are really cute sometimes.

Chris: Yeah.

Kyle: Know what? Our dog's really cute, and . . . we keep him in one of those kinds of pens where you keep like babies when you want to keep them from falling down the steps or something. Well, we . . . we keep him in one of those. We keep him in our laundry room and, uh . . . we got him from North Carolina. My dad says that he was . . . he, his father, um, was registered as Nathan Hale. Well . . . he was the champion bulldog of the nation . . . and, uh . . . we got him for free, because we know the people, who know the owner of Nathan Hale.

Adult: Sounds like you were pretty lucky to get such a special dog.

Kyle: Yeah. We are. We got him from North Carolina.

Adult: He came from far away.

Kyle: Yeah. We, they took him . . . they took him on a trip for eight hours . . . and, he threw up about four times.

Adult: Four times, huh, in eight hours. That must have been a long trip.

Kyle: Yeah, when he got out, um . . . he just sorta layed there, and he was . . . he really looked sick, and um . . . this is the stage when he has long legs, but *you should see his stomach!*

Adult: It's really something else.

Kyle: Yeah.

As can be seen from the preceding conversations, youngsters may pursue the same topic in very different ways. Each child talked about the same dog, but chose a different feature to discuss. By paraphrasing, the adult was able to respond to Chris and Kyle individually. She also was able to key in on what interested them most. If she had led the conversation by asking a series of questions, such as:

"What kind of dog did you get?"
"How big is he?"
"What's his name?"
"What color is he:"
"Where did you get him?"

the two interactions would have been similar, rather than as unique as they were. In addition, it is unlikely that the adult would have thought to inquire about the knots on the dog's head or how many times it threw up, important considerations to the boys. Note, too, that Chris felt comfortable enough to correct an inaccurate response. This occurred when the adult's interpretation that a six-month-old dog was small (meaning "young") did not match what Chris wished to convey. Because paraphrase reflections are tentative statements of what the adult thinks she or he heard, children learn that the reflections are correctable.

Directing the conversation in these ways makes children feel important and worthwhile. Another strategy that contributes to similar feelings is the effective use of questions.

Effective Questioning

Earlier in this chapter, a strong case was made for limiting the use of questions in conversations with children. Questioning, however, is not entirely undesirable; but questions must be posed thoughtfully and skillfully. The kinds of questions adults ask dictate the quality of the answers they receive (Smith, 1979; Turner, 1980). Thus, to stimulate verbal exchanges, the best questions are those that draw people out and prompt them to elaborate (Yinger, 1975). These are sometimes called *open-ended* or *creative questions* (Hendrick, 1984; Schlichter, 1983). Open-ended questions are questions for which there are many possible answers and for which no one answer is correct. Their purpose is to get children to talk about their ideas, thoughts, and emotions, not to quiz them or test their powers of memorization. Using open-ended questions communicates acceptance of the child, thereby enhancing children's self-esteem and promoting positive adult-child relationships (Marion, 1981).

Conversations that begin with questions that do not meet these criteria ("Are you rooting for the Cubs?"; "Do you like grapes?"; "What kind of bird is this?") end when the response is given. Although the intent might have been to show interest in a subject presumably favored by the child, such probes give him or her little to work with in thinking of what else to say.

On the other hand, questions that require children to reason, predict, make decisions, or describe their reactions also encourage verbal interplay (Yinger, 1975). Samples include:

"How do you think this will turn out?"
"What do you think will happen when the sun comes out?"
"Why do you think the bridge fell down?"
"Where do you think this tunnel comes out?"
"Who do you think put this tunnel here?"
"How do you think we could make a bridge?"

"Where do you think we could make a bridge?"

"Where do you think we could find a caterpillar this time of year?"

"What do you think we can do now that the grinder doesn't work?"

All of these questions are open to a wide variety of answers.

A variety of techniques have been discussed that, when used in combination, contribute to the development of a positive verbal environment. These techniques have included fundamental strategies, such as greeting children and calling them by name, as well as the more complex skills of behavior reflections, paraphrase reflections, and open-ended questions. Let us now examine ways to formulate and adapt these skills.

SKILLS FOR PROMOTING CHILDREN'S SELF-AWARENESS AND SELF-ESTEEM THROUGH VERBAL COMMUNICATION

How to Formulate the Fundamental Skills Associated with a Positive Verbal Environment

1. Greet children when they arrive. Say "Hello" to youngsters at the beginning of the day and when they enter an activity in which you are participating. Show obvious pleasure in their presence through the nonverbal communication skills you learned in Chapter 3.

2. Address children by name. When speaking to children, insert their names into your remarks. This lets children know that you have remembered them from one day to the next; that you perceive them as individuals, unique from others in the group; and that your message is aimed especially at them. Take care to pronounce each child's name correctly; check with a family member or ask the child for the exact spelling and pronunciation if it is not known to you.

3. Extend invitations to children to interact with you. Use phrases such as: "We're making tuna melts. Come and join us," "There's a place for you right next to Sylvia," "Let's take a minute to talk. I wanted to find out more about your day," or "You look pretty upset. If you want to talk, I'm available." These remarks create openings for children to approach you or to join an activity and make it easier for shy or hesitant children to interact with you.

4. Speak politely to children. Allow children to finish talking before you begin your remarks. If you must interrupt a child who is speaking to you or to another person, remember to say, "Excuse me," 'Pardon me," or "I'm sorry to interrupt." Remember also to thank children when they are thoughtful or when they comply with your requests. If you are making a request, preface

it with, "Please." Use a conversational, friendly voice tone rather than one that is impatient and demanding.

5. Listen attentively to what children have to say. Show your interest through eye contact, smiling, nodding, and allowing children to talk uninterrupted. In addition, verbally indicate interest by periodically saying, "Mmm-hm," "Uh-huh," or "Yes." If the child has more to say than you can listen to at the moment, indicate a desire to hear more, explain why you cannot, and promise to get back to the child. Remember to keep your promise.

6. Invite children to elaborate on what they are saying. Prolong verbal exchanges with children by saying: "Tell me something about that," "Then what happened?", or "I'd like to hear more about what you did." Such comments make children feel interesting and valued.

7. Think of some conversation openers in advance. Prior to seeing the children each day, generate ideas for one or two topics that might interest them ("Tell me about last night's game", "How's that new brother of yours?", "I was really interested in your report on Martin Luther King. Tell me what you liked best about him"). Comments or questions like these can be answered in any number of ways and have no right or wrong answers; thus, they are easier for children to respond to and serve as "door openers" for further communication.

8. Remain silent long enough for children to gather their thoughts. Once you have asked a question or made a remark in response to something a child has said, pause. Children need time to think of what they are going to say next. This is particularly true if they have been listening carefully to what you were saying, because their attention was on your words, not on formulating their subsequent reply. Adults who feel uncomfortable with silence often rush into their next statement or question. This overwhelms children and gives them the impression that the adult has taken over completely rather than becoming involved with them in a more participatory way. A pause that lasts less than three seconds is too short. Listen to yourself. If your pauses are too brief, consciously wait (or even count silently to five) before continuing.

9. Take advantage of spontaneous opportunities to converse with children. Look for times when you can talk with children individually. Snack time, dressing, toileting, having lunch, waiting for the bus, settling down for a nap, wheeling a child to the x-ray room, or the time before the group is called to order afford excellent possibilities for communication. It is not necessary to wait for some special, planned time to initiate a conversation or respond to one.

10. Refrain from speaking when talk would destroy the mood of the interaction. Remember that silence is the other component of the verbal environment. Too much talk, inappropriate talk, or talk at the wrong time detracts from a positive verbal environment.

When you see children deeply absorbed in their activity or engrossed in their conversations with one another, allow the natural course of their interaction to continue. Keep quiet even if you think of a relevant remark. These are times when the entry of an adult into the picture could be disruptive or could change the entire tone of the interchange. Speak only when your comments would further the child's interests, not only your own.

In addition, there will be times when you find yourself interacting with a child in a comfortable silence. When this is the case, do not feel compelled to verbalize. The absence of talk in situations like these is a sign of warmth and respect.

How to Formulate Behavior Reflections

1. Describe some aspect of the child's person or behavior in a statement to the child. After observing a child carefully, select an attribute or behavior that seems important to him or her and remark on it. At all times, focus on the child's perspective of the situation, not your own. Thus, an appropriate behavior reflection to Manny, who is tying his shoes, would be any of the following:

"You're working on your left shoe."
"You know how to make a bow."
"Those are the new shoes Grandma bought you."

The following statements would not constitute behavior reflections:

"I wish you'd hurry up."
"I'm glad you're putting those on all by yourself."
"If you don't hurry, we'll be late."

Although the latter remarks may be accurate statements of what is important to the adult in the interaction, they do not mirror the child's point of view.

2. Phrase behavior reflections as statements. Reflections should not be phrased as questions. Rather, they should be constructed as declarative statements. Questions imply that children must respond; reflections do not. Because the goal of this skill is to enable adults to manifest interest in children without pressuring them to answer, the nonintrusive nature of behavior reflections must be preserved by phrasing each reflection in statement form.

3. Address behavior reflections directly to children. Use the word "you" somewhere in your statement so that the child recognizes that your reflection is aimed at her or him. This makes each reflection more personal.

4. Use descriptive vocabulary as part of your reflection. Including adverbs, adjectives, and specific object names as part of the reflection makes them more meaningful and valuable to children. Children's contextual learning is more favorably enhanced when you say, "You put the pencil on the widest shelf" than when you say, "You put it on the shelf."

5. Use nonjudgmental vocabulary when reflecting children's behavior. Reflect only what you see, not how you feel about it. It does not matter whether your evaluation is good or bad; reflections are not the appropriate vehicles through which to express opinions. Therefore, "You're using lots of colors in your painting" is a reflection; "What a nice picture" or "You used too much grey" is not. This is because evaluations represent the adult's point of view; the reflection represents the child's. A painting the adult likes may be one with which the child is dissatisfied; a picture with more grey than the adult would prefer may fit exactly the child's perception of the blur made by a herd of elephants rushing by.

How to Formulate Paraphrase Reflections

1. Listen actively to the child's words. Consciously decide to pay attention to the child's message. Actively involve yourself in this process by looking at the child and listening to his or her entire verbalization without interrupting. Concentrate. Momentarily set aside other thoughts; think more about what the child is saying than what you are going to say in response.

2. Restate in your own words what the child has said. Make sure that your rewording maintains the child's original intent. Neither introduce your own opinion nor add things you wish the child had included.

3. Rephrase erroneous reflections. At times, children give signs that your reflection was not in keeping with their intent. They may correct you directly by saying, "No" or "That's not what I meant." Other, more subtle cues are children repeating themselves, adding new information, or sighing in exasperation. Be alert for these and, if they occur, try a variation of your statement. Do this conversationally, with no implication that the child was at fault for communicating inaccurately. This is not the time to insist that *you heard* correctly based on the child's words. Instead, focus on more acutely perceiving the child's frame of reference.

4. Match your reflection to each child's ability to understand language. Use simple, short reflections with toddlers. Construct these by adding one or two connecting words to the child's telegraphic utterances. Go beyond simple expansions, however, when working with children aged four and older. Recast the child's message by adding auxiliary verbs or relevant synonym phrases. Periodically, use multiple-phrase reflections when working with school-age children:

Child: There's Webelos on Tuesday and all the guys are going. Me too. My mom's gonna drive.

Adult: Sounds like you've got a special meeting coming up. Lots of your friends are going.

These adaptations demonstrate respect for children's varying communication abilities and make your reflections more interesting and comprehensible to them.

5. Use a conversational tone when reflecting. Use an expressive voice tone when reflecting either children's behavior or language. Adults who reflect in a monotone or singsong voice sound condescending and disrespectful. Children do not respond well when they perceive these attitudes.

6. Summarize children's actions and words rather than reflect each individual behavior or idea expressed. Formulate reflections that tie together a series of actions or statements. For instance, if Malcolm is playing with colored blocks, do not say, "You have a red block. You have a green block. Now you're picking up a blue block." Do say, "You're using many colors in your building." Similarly, if Katie announces, "I got a bear and a cake and a dress for my birthday," do not say, "You received a bear and a cake and a dress for your birthday." Say, "You got lots of gifts for your birthday."

7. Select one idea at a time to paraphrase from the many a child may express. There will be times when children spend several minutes describing a particular event or expressing their thoughts, ideas, or concerns. It is neither feasible nor desirable to reflect everything, because this would take too much time from the child, who might be anxious to say more. Instead, pick one main idea that stands out to you and reflect that. If this is not the child's major focus, he or she will indicate this discrepancy by correcting you or by rechanneling the conversation in the favored direction. An example of this was evident in the adult conversation with Kyle about his dog. Initially, Kyle made several comments regarding where the dog was kept and how his family got it. Based on his building excitement when describing the dog's championship lineage, it was this part of the description the adult reflected. Had Kyle wanted to talk more about the laundry room, he might have said: "Yeah, he's special. We keep him in the laundry room" as a way to return to his main interest.

8. Add interest to your reflections by periodically phrasing them in a form opposite from that used by the child. Thus, if Sue says, "I want the door open," it would be appropriate to say, "You don't want the door closed." If Mark announces, "I want another helping of everything," you could say, "You don't want to miss anything." If Beth whispers: "I have a headache. I wish everybody would be quiet." You could reply, "You hope no one gets too loud."

9. Reflect first when children ask you a question. Reflect children's wonder, uncertainty, confusion, or interest prior to offering an answer or solution to their queries. This helps children clarify what it is they are really asking and gives them an opportunity to answer some questions themselves. If the child repeats the question, asks a second, more pointed question, or waits expectantly for an answer, provide it.

SITUATION: Miss Drobney is tenderizing meat with a meat pounder. Audrey approaches and asks, "What are you doing?" The adult reflects, "You noticed I'm using a special tool."

At this point, it is possible that Audrey might say, "It makes holes in meat." This provides an opportunity for Miss Drobney to reflect again. "You've figured out one thing this tool can do—it makes holes." This could be the beginning of a verbal exchange in which Audrey discovers for herself the various attributes of a meat pounder. On the other hand, it is also possible that when the adult reflects, "You noticed I'm using a special tool," Audrey would remain quiet, waiting for more, or would respond, "Yeah, what is that?" Miss Drobney would then have a choice of simply answering, "This is a meat pounder" or pointing out attributes of the tool that might help Audrey discover some of its characteristics on her own: "Look at the bumps on the end. See what they do when

I pound the meat,'' or ''See how it puts holes in the meat? That makes it easier to chew.''

How to Formulate Questions

1. Ask open-ended questions. Monitor the questions you ask. Determine when you are asking questions for which you have a predetermined answer in mind as well as ones for which only a yes-no answer will suffice. In either case, rephrase the question so it allows for a variety of answers.

2. Ask questions when you are truly perplexed. Some questions are genuine requests for information rather than conversation starters. Questions such as ''Who has to go to the bathroom?'', ''What time is your appointment?'', ''Who hasn't had a chance to bat yet?'' are legitimate inquiries. At the same time, they are not designed to prompt a conversation, so none should be expected. Also, avoid empty questions. If you really do not want to know what time the appointment is or whose turn it is at bat, do not ask.

3. Carefully choose when to ask open-ended questions. Consider both the time available and the circumstances under which the question is to be asked. Pick an unhurried time, giving children ample opportunity to respond. Youngsters become frustrated when adults make inquiries knowing that children's answers will have to be rushed or terminated prematurely. If you catch yourself saying, ''Okay, okay,'' ''Fine, fine, fine,'' ''That's enough,'' or ''I get the idea'' in the middle of a child's response, your question should have been saved for later.

Similarly, pose conversational questions during those parts of the day in which child-directed activities predominate rather than during activities that require a great deal of adult instruction or management. For instance, it would be inappropriate to initiate a prolonged conversation with a child while you are counting noses during a fire drill or proctoring a spelling test, or when the rest of the children are waiting for you to lead them in the next activity.

4. Emphasize quality over quantity in using questions in conversation with children. It is better to ask one or two open-ended questions than to pose several of the yes-no variety in which neither you nor the children have much interest. Measure the effectiveness of the questions you ask by listening to children's answers in regard to both content and tone. If responses become monosyllabic or the child sounds weary of answering, stop. If answers are lively and lead to elaboration, continue.

PITFALLS TO AVOID _____

Whether your words are aimed at demonstrating your interest in children, or whether you are using your speech to become more involved in children's activities, there are certain hazards to beware of.

Parroting. A common way in which adults paraphrase children is to respond by mirroring exactly the child's words and voice tone. Parroting is often offensive to children because it makes the adult sound insincere or condescending. Although parroting is a natural first step for people just learning how to paraphrase, adults should learn to vary their responses as quickly as possible. Several techniques can be used. One is to listen to children who are talking to one another and *silently* formulate paraphrases for statements they make. Although you are not actually saying anything, this provides good mental practice. A second tactic is to listen to children talking or remember things they have said throughout the day, and then later, write down several alternate paraphrases. Finally, students have reported that it is helpful to practice paraphrasing family members and friends. In many cases, this involves paraphrasing adults, which may prompt the student to work harder at sounding original because mimicing someone's words is not part of natural conversation.

Reflecting incessantly. It is a mistake to reflect everything children do or say. The purpose of behavior and paraphrase reflecting is to give adults opportunities to observe children, to listen to them, and to understand their point of view. None of these goals can be accomplished if adults are talking nonstop. Using summary reflections is a good way to avoid overpowering children with excessive verbiage.

Perfunctory reflecting. Reflecting without thinking is not appropriate; it is another form of parroting. Adults who find themselves simply "going through the motions" or responding absentmindedly to children just to have something to say should stop, then intensify their efforts at attending more closely to what children are really saying or indicating through their actions. A good reflection increases children's self-understanding rather than merely serving as a placeholder in a conversation. Another form of perfunctory reflecting occurs when adults reflect children's questions but neglect to follow up on them. For example, Ralph asks Mr. Wu, "When are we going to have music?" Mr. Wu responds, "You're wondering when we're going to have music," and then immediately turns to talk to Alicia. In this case, his response was not wholly correct, because he did not attend to the entirety of the child's message. He should have waited to determine if Ralph was going to answer the question himself, or if he needed additional information. The best way to avoid such a dilemma is to think while reflecting and to pay attention to how children react to the reflections.

Treating children as objects. There are many times when adults speak to children in the third person. That is, they make comments about the child that they intend the child to hear but that are not personally addressed to the child. For instance, Miss Long is playing with two-year-old Curtis in the block area. No one else is nearby. She says things like: "Curtis is building with square blocks. Curtis is making a tall tower. Oops, Curtis' tower fell." If other youngsters were close at hand, her remarks might be interpreted as information aimed at them. But, as the situation stands, her impersonal running commentary on his activity is not conversational and leaves no real openings for a response from Curtis should he choose to make one. Miss Long's remarks could be turned into reflections by the insertion of "you" in each one: "Curtis, you're building with square blocks. You're making a tall tower. Oops, your tower fell."

Turning reflections into questions. Phrases such as "aren't you?"; "didn't you?"; "don't you?"; "right?"; or "okay?" tacked to the end of a sentence transform reflections into questions. A similar result occurs when the adult allows his or her voice to rise at the end of a sentence. When adults slip into this habit, the nature of their verbal exchanges with children changes from unintrusive interest and involvement to a tone that is interruptive and demanding. This is one of the most common misuses of the reflecting technique and occurs because adults would like some confirmation regarding the accuracy of their reflection. They want some sign from the child that what they have said is right. Yet, rarely does one hear:

Child: I'm at the top.

Adult: You're excited to be so high, aren't you?

Child: You're right, Teacher.

The real confirmation of appropriate reflecting is that children continue their activity or conversation. If they stop or correct the adult, these are signs that the original reflection was not on target. Adults who find themselves questioning rather than reflecting must consciously work at eradicating this habit from their repertoire. If you notice that you have done this in conversation with a child, it helps to stop and repeat the reflection correctly.

Answering one's own questions rather than allowing children to answer. Adults frequently answer many of their own questions (Borg, 1969). For instance, Ms. Cooper asks, "Who remembered to bring their permission slips back?" Without a moment's hesitation, she says: "John, you've got one. Mary, you've got one, too." Later, she inquires, "Why do you think birds fly south for the winter?" Before children have a chance to even think about the question, she supplies an answer: "Usually, they're looking for food." In both instances, Ms. Cooper precluded children answering by responding too quickly herself. Unfortunately, as this becomes a pattern, Ms. Cooper may well conclude that children are incapable of answering her questions, while the youngsters translate her actions as disinterest in what they have to say. If you detect this habit in yourself, deliberately work to eliminate it. When you answer prematurely, verbally make note of it; then, repeat your question: "Oops. I didn't give you a chance to answer. What do you think about . . . ?"

Habitually answering children's questions with one's own. Sometimes, when children ask a question, adults automatically echo the question back to them:

Child: Where do bears sleep in the winter?

Adult: Where do you think they sleep?

Echoing causes children to form negative impressions of adults. The question sounds like a put-down; youngsters translate it to mean: "You're dumb. You should know that," "I know and I'm not going to tell you," or 'I'm going to let you make a fool of yourself by giving the wrong answer. Then, I'll tell you what the real answer is." Although this may not be the adult's intent, it is often the result. To avoid these unfavorable impressions, either supply the needed fact or reflect the children's questions and then help them discover the answer by working with them.

Interrupting children's activities. Reflecting or asking a question when a child is obviously engrossed in an activity or is absorbed in conversation is intrusive. At times like these, adults can exhibit interest in children by observing quietly nearby and responding with nonverbal signs such as smiles, nods, laughter at appropriate moments. When children are working very hard at something, an occasional reflection that corresponds to their point of view is appreciated; constant interruptions are not. Children who are speaking to someone else and give no indication of wanting to include the adult should not be reflected or questioned at all. If, for a legitimate reason, the adult must get the child's attention or enter the conversation, he or she should just say, "Excuse me."

Failing to vary one's responses. It is common when learning new skills to find a tactic with which one is comfortable and then to use that to the exclusion of all others. For instance, after reading this chapter, you might be tempted to use a behavior reflection in response to every situation that arises. This would be a mistake; certain skills meet certain needs. When one skill is developed to the exclusion of others, the benefits offered by the other skills will not be available to children. In addition, overuse of one form of verbal communication becomes monotonous and uninteresting for adults and children alike. For this reason, it is best to utilize all of the skills thus far presented rather than only one or two.

Hesitating to speak. Individuals new to the helping professions, as well as those who have worked with children before, may experience awkward moments in which they find themselves fumbling for the right words when trying to implement the skills presented in this chapter. By the time they think of a response, the opportunity may have slipped by or the words that come out may sound stilted. When this happens, some find it tempting to abandon these techniques and revert to old verbal habits. Others stop talking altogether. Both of these reactions arise from adult efforts to avoid embarrassment or discomfort with unfamiliar verbal skills. Such experiences are to be expected, and every student goes through these uncertain times. Yet, the key to attaining facility with reflections and appropriate questioning techniques is to use them frequently so that they become a more natural part of your everyday interactions. In fact, in the beginning, it is better to talk too much than to neglect practicing these skills. Once the mechanics are mastered, you can turn your attention to appropriate timing.

Sounding mechanical and unnatural while using the skills. Implementing reflections and open-ended questions feels awkward and uncomfortable at first. Beginners complain that they do not sound like themselves and that they have to think about what they are saying more

than they ever have in the past. They become discouraged when their responses sound repetitive and lack the warmth and spontaneity they have come to expect from themselves. Again, at this point some people give up, reverting to old verbal habits. As with any new skill, however, proficiency develops only after much practice.

Learning these techniques can be likened to learning to roller-skate. Beginning skaters have a hard time keeping their balance, shuffle along, and fall down periodically. They have enough trouble going forward, let alone going backward, doing turns, or making spins. Stopping also is a major hurdle. If people only roller-skate a few times, chances are they will continue to struggle and feel conspicuous. If these feelings cause them to give up skating, their progress is halted and they will never improve. However, should they keep on practicing, not only will their skill increase, but they will be able to get beyond the mechanics and develop an individualized style.

The process is the same for the skills taught in this chapter. When readers are willing to practice and continue working through the difficulties, noticeable improvement occurs. The artificial speech that marks the early stages of acquisition of verbal skills gradually gives way to more natural-sounding responses.

SUMMARY

The aggregate of perceptions people have of themselves makes up their self-concept. A person's notion of self begins in infancy and evolves gradually throughout adulthood as a result of both cognitive development and experience. When babies are born, they do not yet have a concept of self. As children mature and gain experience in the world, they come to realize their distinctness from others. At first, toddlers and preschoolers identify themselves only in terms of physical attributes; later, they include activities in their self-descriptions as

well. During the early elementary school years, youngsters incorporate psychological traits along with physical traits in their self-images, and by the sixth grade, they think of themselves entirely in terms of internal or psychological states.

Self-esteem is the evaluative component of the self and includes perceptions related to both competence and worth. Children who judge their competence and worth postively have high self-esteem; those who do not have low self-esteem. Individuals with high self-esteem lead happier lives than those whose self-judgments are negative. The development of self-esteem follows a normative sequence, evolving from assessing oneself in the here and now as a preschooler to a more compartmentalized view of the self as a young grade-schooler to a general index of one's value as a person by eight or nine years of age. This predominantly positive or negative index remains relatively constant throughout life.

Adult behaviors prompt children to make either positive or negative judgments about themselves. Self-judgments of competence and worth are likeliest in children who interact with adults who demonstrate warmth, respect, acceptance, and empathy. What adults say to children conveys these or the opposite messages to children and therefore is a key factor in the degree to which children develop high or low self-esteem.

The atmosphere adults create by their verbalizations to children is called the verbal environment. It can be either positive or negative. Continual exposure to a negative verbal environment diminishes children's self-esteem, whereas exposure to a positive verbal environment enhances children's self-awareness and perceptions of self-worth. Behavior reflections are a specific verbal strategy adults can use to help create a positive verbal environment. Behavior reflections are nonjudgmental statements made to children about some aspect of their behavior or person. Using behavior reflections increases children's self-awareness and self-esteem; it helps adults look at situations from children's perspectives; it demonstrates interest, acceptance, and empathy for children; and it helps children increase their receptive language skills.

Conversing with children is another way for adults to demonstrate affection, interest, and involvement. Perception of these attitudes increases children's self-respect and self-acceptance. However, certain common errors, such as missing children's cues, correcting grammar, supplying facts and rendering opinions prematurely, advising, and using unnecessary or unskillful questioning act as conversation stoppers. On the other hand, paraphrase reflections, restatements in the adult's own words of something the child has said, are effective conversation sustainers. Paraphrase reflections help clarify communication, help the listener to be more empathic toward the message sender, allow the message sender to control the direction of the conversation, provide the message sender an opportunity to solve his or her own problems, and have a positive influence on the language development of young children. In addition, appropriate use of open-ended or creative questioning also adds to the creation of a positive verbal environment.

Finally, certain pitfalls are to be avoided, such as parroting, reflecting incessantly or perfunctorily, treating childrens as objects, using inappropriate questioning methods, interrupting children, and failing to vary one's responses. Hesitating to speak and sounding mechanical at first also are common problems encountered by individuals who are just beginning to learn these skills.

DISCUSSION QUESTIONS

1. Describe the normative sequence of the development of self-concept in children from birth to early adolescence.
2. Describe an incident from your childhood that enhanced your self-esteem. Describe another that detracted from it.

3. Discuss various settings in which you have observed or interacted with children during the last year. See if classmates can categorize each setting as representing a negative or positive verbal environment.

4. Describe three ways in which you could improve the verbal environment of a setting in which you currently interact with children.

5. Describe an incident in which someone with whom you were conversing utilized one of the conversation stoppers presented in this chapter. Talk about its effect on you.

6. Describe at least four benefits of using behavior reflections with young children.

7. Describe how the adult's use of paraphrase reflections affects children's self-awareness and self-esteem.

8. Describe the characteristics of an open-ended question, and discuss how the use of this technique relates to self-awareness and self-esteem in children.

9. Describe a situation in which you used a behavior reflection, a paraphrase reflection, or an open-ended question with children. If you were able to relive the interaction, discuss what you would maintain and what you would change about your use of the skills.

10. Describe one pitfall you have encountered using the skills presented in this chapter. With classmates, plan ways to avoid it in the future.

CHAPTER 5
Responding to Children's Emotions

OBJECTIVES:

On completion of this chapter, you will be able to describe:

1. What emotions are and what functions they serve in people's lives.

2. How emotions develop and what prompts them.

3. The emotional tasks of childhood.

4. How children conceptualize their emotions.

5. Problems children experience in expressing their emotions.

6. How adult behavior influences children's emotional development.

7. Strategies for helping children cope more effectively with emotions.

8. Pitfalls to avoid in responding to children's emotions.

SOURCE: H. Armstrong Roberts

102

A butterfly lands on Sean's hand—his eyes widen in amazement.

Paulo proudly announces, ''I won honorable mention in the cooking contest!''

On her first day at the center, Maureen sobs as her mother attempts to leave.

Emily makes a diving catch and is elated to find the ball in her mitt.

Tony has a tantrum when the clown runs out of balloons before he gets his.

When Larry calls her stupid, Jennifer yells furiously, ''No, I'm not!''

Children experience hundreds of different emotions each day, ranging from happiness to anger and curiosity to despair. Emotions are inextricably linked to everything children do and are triggered by numerous happenings, both large and small. Emotions are what cause children to be affected by the people and events around them. Thus, they serve a significant function in children's lives.

Positive emotions give children a sense of safety and security; they help youngsters recognize that particular actions or relationships are beneficial to their well-being. Joy and affection, for instance, feel good. These emotions stimulate children to seek out or maintain contact with something or someone and prompt them to be receptive rather than resistant (Coleman and Hammen, 1974).

On the other hand, negative emotions feel bad and signal danger or discontent. They alert children to the fact that something is wrong, often inducing them to act to resolve their distress. Fear compels children to escape from, avoid, or protect themselves from something; anger activates them to surmount obstacles or to correct an injustice (Coleman and Hammen, 1974). For these reasons, all emotional experiences are important, adding to children's store of knowledge about themselves. They also serve as the foundation on which children base many of their actions.

What Emotions Are

People in all cultures experience emotions. Joy, sadness, disgust, and anger are universal (Ekman, 1973). Although these emotions differ, they do have certain attributes in common. Each is triggered by a particular situation or stimulus event that sends signals to the brain and central nervous system, resulting in arousal. As people are aroused, they begin to think about the situation. Their bodies respond to the eliciting cues with physiological changes generally referred to as emotional states, feelings, or sensations. Such feelings usually are accompanied by observable alterations in facial expression, posture, voice, and body movement. As these physiological changes occur, people interpret what they are experiencing. The same internal conditions can be interpreted differently depending on the individual's assessment of the circumstances at hand (Schacter and Singer, 1962). Perceptions are formed from an appraisal of the context in which the feeling is occurring and from past experience. Based on this interpretation, people take action (Lewis and Rosenblum, 1978; Plutchik, 1980).

Although scientists vary in their beliefs about the order in which physical sensations, thoughts, and interpretations occur, there is general agreement that all three factors play an important role in emotional life (Bower, 1981; Izard 1977; Leventhal, 1979). To illustrate one way in which these elements might work together, consider what happens when Kitty is called on to read her report aloud. The teacher speaking her name, the other children's silence, a giggle from the back all are eliciting cues received by Kitty's brain. Simultaneously, she thinks about past difficulties in front of an audience. Her mouth dries up, her heart beats faster, and her stomach contracts. Kitty interprets this as nervousness. On the other hand, had her thoughts focused on past public-speaking triumphs, she might have construed her response as one of keen anticipation. In either case, it is Kitty's interpretation that dictates her emotional reaction. Her notion of reality is based on this interpretation, and it may not necessarily match other people's interpretations. Even if others expect Kitty to do well, if she perceives the situation as threatening, she will be nervous. Thus, people's interpretations affect how they feel. Another contributing factor is their current stage of emotional development.

CHILDREN'S EMOTIONAL DEVELOPMENT

Emotional development in childhood is marked by sequential change. As children grow up, significant differences emerge in the emotional states they experience, in what prompts their emotional responses, in the nature of the emotional issues that are important to them, and in how they conceptualize what their emotions are.

How Emotions Develop

Are very young children capable of experiencing real emotions?

Do children's emotions remain constant, or do they change?

Is the same emotion always prompted by the same stimulus event?

To answer these questions, scientists have charted the emergence of emotions in children from birth through later childhood (Bridges, 1932; Murray, 1964; Sroufe, 1979). They have concluded that people are genetically programmed with *core emotions* (Campos, et al., 1983; Plutchik, 1980). Although the exact number of core emotions that exist still is being debated, it is agreed that joy, anger, sadness, and fear are among them. These are intense and relatively pure emotions from which, over time, other related but more differentiated clusters of emotions emerge. Basic anger, for instance, serves as a foundation for the eventual emergence of frustration, disgust, annoyance, jealousy, fury, and boredom. Combinations of these produce more complex emotional reactions, as when anger and disgust together lead to feelings of contempt. The core emotions and their corresponding emotional clusters are listed in Table 5-1.

In the first month of life, the core emotions manifest themselves not as true emotions but as simple, reflexive actions (Sroufe, 1979). When baby Jane is startled by a loud noise, her innate

TABLE 5-1 Core Emotions and Corresponding Emotional Clusters

JOY	SADNESS	ANGER	FEAR
Happiness	Dejection	Frustration	Wariness
Delight	Unhappiness	Jealousy	Anxiety
Contentment	Distress	Disgust	Suspicion
Satisfaction	Grief	Annoyance	Dread
Pleasure	Discouragement	Fury	Dismay
Elation	Shame	Boredom	Anguish
Pride	Guilt	Defiance	Panic

reflex to recoil is not true fear, but merely its forerunner; similarly, her occasional smile is the predecessor of joy (Jabs, 1985). Although these behaviors show that the capacity for emotional expression is present at birth, purposeful expression comes later.

When they do appear, the core emotions and their related clusters do not become evident all at once. Instead, they follow a developmental sequence equally as predictable as those associated with language and physical development. Just as six-month-olds say "Mama" and/or "Papa" and imitate the speech sounds they hear, so too will they express real anger around the fourth month and sadness sometime prior to their first birthday. Similarly, as creeping precedes walking, the expression of sadness precedes that of guilt.

Joy, the first real emotion to appear, occurs at about six weeks of age and is seen in the first social smile. This is an unmistakable sign of infant pleasure and is most often elicited by the face of the primary caregiver. Two to three months later, the smile erupts into laughter. At approximately sixteen weeks of age, anger comes on the scene. Anger at this age results from physical distress and is expressed through crying. Sadness is the next core emotion to become recognizable as a distinct state. It is most often precipitated by separation from the primary caregiver and usually is evident by eight or nine months of age. Signs of sadness are pouting, down-turned mouth, and sometimes crying or sobbing. From sadness evolves fear, another fundamental emotion. Fear usually is manifested by clinging or withdrawing behavior, as well as by crying, trembling, and cringing. Fear usually is elicited by unpredictable circumstances and incongruity between what the child expects and what actually occurs (Bronson, 1972).

Even as the later core emotions are surfacing, earlier ones are becoming more differentiated. Thus, by the end of the first year, a child's repertoire of emotions has moved beyond the basic four to include elation, disgust, frustration, and wariness (Murray, 1964). Further diversity and greater specificity of emotion is seen in the second year, with shame, pride, affection, jealousy, and defiance being added to the list. By three years of age, children also exhibit guilt, beginning signs of empathy, and a difference between their affection for children and that for adults (Murray, 1964; Hoffman, 1976). Numbers of emotions and finer discriminations between emotions continue to increase with age, as evidenced by older children's verbal descriptions of how they feel (Kostelnik, 1977; Lewis, Wolman, and King, 1972). The emergence of emotions in early childhood is represented in Figure 5-1.

Variations in Stimulus Events

There is an essential similarity in the stimulus events that prompt certain clusters of emotion over the life span. Joy is evoked by discovery, triumph, creative work, or the reduction of stress (Izard, 1977). Anger occurs when individuals are thwarted or prevented from pursuing their goals; when they are offended, interrupted, taken advantage of, or forced to act against their desires; when they are in pain or prolonged distress. Sadness comes about when people are separated from others. Isolation, rejection, and lack of caring all cause sadness (Clarke-Stewart, Friedman, and Koch, 1985). Fear is the emotional response to danger.

Although there is constancy in the types of stimuli that trigger certain emotions, cognitive maturity and experience affect an individual's interpretation of what constitutes discovery, being thwarted, being rejected, or being endangered. Thus, age-related variations in how children interpret events result in their experiencing the same emotion for different reasons, from birth to adolescence. To illustrate this concept, we will examine children's changing notions of what is threatening and, therefore, frightening.

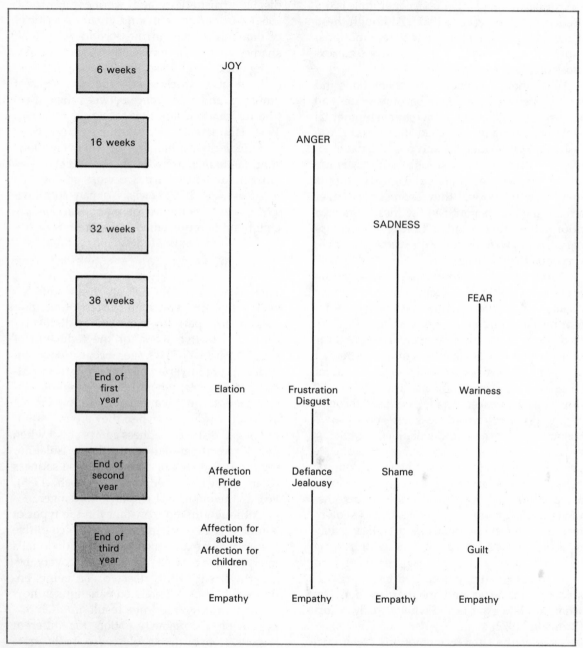

FIGURE 5-1 The emergence of children's emotions during the first three years of life.

Developmental changes in children's fears. Both younger children and older ones experience fear, but they are not necessarily afraid of the same things. For instance, toddlers have little comprehension of death, so they often are fearless in circumstances older children find dangerous, such as approaching a busy street. On the other hand, grade-schoolers are less apt to find loud noises or bright lights intimidating. They can reason that sounds cannot hurt them and have enough experience to know that this is so.

Certain fears typically appear as children reach differing stages of development. One of the earliest observed fears that may appear is the infant's demonstration of ''stranger anxiety.'' Wariness is apparent between four and six months of age and reaches a peak at approximately twelve months (Bronson, 1972; DeCarie, 1974). Such reactions occur only after infants have developed a schema for the familiar face of the caregiver. When confronted with a face they do not recognize, they become distressed. Gradually, as the child gains experience with each new adult, such fears decrease.

Fear of the dark and of being left alone emerge at about two and a half years of age and may continue well into childhood (Ostfeld, 1971). It is at this time that children's imaginations are beginning to develop, and they are able to mentally conjure up potential dangers (ghosts or bogeymen). Such fears are not possible in infants because they cannot produce vivid mental images.

Three-year-olds frequently report being afraid of animals, particularly dogs (Bauer, 1976; Miller, 1983). These youngsters recognize the very real danger of sharp claws and teeth and find the unpredictability of animal behavior threatening. Because they have a rudimentary knowledge of cause and effect and can envision potential happenings, they are able to foresee a possibly hazardous situation and so become afraid.

Nightmares are a common problem for children aged four through eight because they cannot separate thoughts and dreams from the physical things they represent (Piaget, 1969). Preschoolers think that their dreams are caused by some external force and that dreams actually take place outside of their bodies, in the room, right beside them. When they dream something unpleasant, they think it is real and that they have no control over the situation. Their reaction is to become frightened. Gradually, youngsters recognize that they are the source of their dreams, but they still do not understand that dreams are merely thoughts that occur while sleeping; they still believe that the frightening events are actually happening. It is not until the period of concrete operations (seven or eight years of age) that youngsters recognize that dreams are their own unreal imaginings over which they have some control.

At about seven years of age, youngsters become more concerned with potential physical harm and the unnerving prospects of unpleasant social situations (Scherer and Nakamura, 1968). Having been out in the world, children have had direct and indirect experiences with people being injured and humiliated. They are well able to project the misery of being hit by a car, being sent to the principal's office, or being chastised for not getting their homework done. They also are more cognizant of potentially life-threatening situations over which they have little or no control such as being kidnapped (Miller, 1983) or perishing in a nuclear blast (Croake, 1973). These, then, are the triggering stimuli for fear in the preadolescent.

The fact that children's imaginary fears (such as anxiety over events that may not be real to anyone but the child) gradually give way to more realistic fears (for example, fear of physical danger) demonstrates a developmental shift in children's thinking about their emotions (Bauer, 1976). A similarly pervasive chronological change occurs in the emotional tasks with which children are involved.

The Emotional Tasks of Childhood

Currently, it is widely believed that people work through a series of emotional tasks over the course of their lives. The person who has most influenced our understanding of what these tasks are is Erik Erikson (1950, 1968). He has identified eight emotional stages through which people progress, four of which take place during the childhood years. Each stage is characterized by positive and negative emotions as well as a central emotional task. This task is to resolve the conflict that arises between the two emotional extremes. Although all children experience a ratio between both poles of a given stage, optimal emotional development occurs when the proportion is weighted toward the positive. These stages build on one another, each serving as the foundation for the next.

Trust versus mistrust. The first stage of emotional development takes place during infancy and was described in detail in Chapter 2. The emotional conflict during this stage is whether children will develop self-confidence and trust in the world or feelings of hopelessness, uncertainty, and suspicion. Children who develop positive feelings in this stage learn, ''I am all right.''

Autonomy versus shame and doubt. Sometime during their second year, toddlers who have developed a strong sense of trust begin to move away from the total dependency of infancy toward the realization of having a mind and will of their own. Thus begins a struggle between feelings of self-assertion and helplessness. What is at stake throughout this period is whether the child will emerge with a sense of being an independent, self-directed human being, or one who has fundamental misgivings about self-worth. Autonomy begins with muscle control (holding on and letting go), then extends to the social life of the child. Autonomous children do what they can for themselves, whereas non-autonomous children do not act even when they and their caregiver believe that they should. Autonomous children also know that they can take advantage of help and guidance from others while still maintaining ideas of their own. Nonautonomous youngsters doubt their ability to control their world or themselves and so become overly dependent on other people. Children who develop a dominant sense of shame and doubt are those who have few opportunities to explore, to do for themselves, to experiment with objects in their environment, or to make decisions. Their attempts at exploration and and independence usually are met with impatience, harsh criticism, ridicule, physical restraint or resistance. In contrast, children who develop a healthy sense of autonomy are those who are given numerous opportunities for mastery, are permitted to make choices, and are given clear, nonpunitive messages regarding the boundaries of self-determination.

In order to promote a sense of autonomy, many adults working in programs for young children emphasize giving them choices, ranging from which activity to pursue to where to sit at group time. Likewise, youngsters are encouraged to pour their own juice, to dress themselves as much as possible, and to become actively involved in cleaning up after play. Although any of these activities could be more efficiently and skillfully accomplished by adults, the point is to give children opportunities to practice and to let them experience the exhilaration of accomplishment. Autonomy issues also explain the heavy focus in early-childhood education to encourage children to experiment with objects, to participate in ''hands-on'' activities, and to use their bodies to explore the environment. Opportunities for mastery are increased because activities are repeated numerous times and children have ample time to work with each material. Youngsters who successfully navigate this stage learn, ''I can make decisions; I can do some things on my own.''

Initiative versus guilt.   During their fourth or fifth year, children develop a new sense of energy. The emotional conflict during this stage is whether this energy will be directed constructively and be valued by others, or whether it will be nonproductive and rejected. Throughout the pre-school and early grade-school years, children have experiences with both initiative and guilt by:

Putting plans and ideas into action.
Attempting to master new skills and goals.
Striving to gain new information.
Exploring ideas through fantasy.
Experiencing the sensations of their bodies.
Figuring out ways to maintain their behavior within bounds considered appropriate by society.

Youngsters whose efforts fall short of their own expectations or what they perceive to be adult expectations develop a sense of guilt. It is also typical for children to feel guilty for simply thinking "bad" thoughts because they equate thinking with doing. Adults compound this sense of guilt when they make children feel that their motor activity is bad, that their fantasy play is silly, that their exaggerations are lies, that their tendency to begin projects but not complete them is irresponsible, and that their exploration of body and language is so objectionable that they are no longer acceptable persons (Tribe, 1982).

On the other hand, children who develop a strong sense of initiative take pleasure in their increasing competence and find ways to use their energy constructively. They become better able to cooperate and to accept help from others as well as more aware that they can work for the things they want without jeopardizing their developing sense of correct behavior.

It is this positive feeling of initiative that helping professionals in early-childhood programs try to facilitate when they give children an opportunity to explore their skills in a variety of ways. This is why children are given real tools with which to work—magnifying glasses, tape recorders, kitchen utensils, woodworking tools. It is also one reason why process rather than product is emphasized and why children are encouraged to create their own projects rather than to duplicate models provided by adults. Planning activities in which a number of solutions are possible takes into account children's needs for experimentation, as does the introduction of dramatic-play materials.

Finally, when children's transgressions are handled reasonably and sensitively, too great a sense of guilt is avoided. The optimal outcome of this stage is a child who thinks, "I can do, and I can make."

Industry versus inferiority.   The fourth stage of emotional development takes place throughout the middle childhood years (approximately six to twelve years of age). During this phase, children become preoccupied with producing things and with assuming more adultlike tasks. They also are more interested in joining with others to get things done and in contributing to the society as a whole. The central emotional issue is whether youngsters will come away feeling competent and able, or whether they will surmise that their best efforts are inadequate. Although all children at times are incapable of mastering what they set out to accomplish, some experience a pervasive sense of failure. This happens when adult, peer, or school standards are clearly beyond their abilities or when they themselves have an unrealistic view of what is possible to achieve. Strong feelings of inferiority also arise when a child is made to believe that mastery is only desirable in a few select areas in which he or she may not be skilled and that those other areas in which the child is accomplished are not worthwhile. Additional contributing factors include adult and peer use of shame or ridicule to influence children's behavior.

Industriousness is fostered when adults offer praise and recognition for children's success, when they encourage children to explore their competence in a variety of areas, when they help children set realistic goals, and when they set up tasks in such a way that children are able to experience mastery. Providing guidance and support to children when some efforts end in failure eases the pain and gives children the confidence to try again. In addition, this is an important time for adults to encourage children to work with one another in order to experience the satisfaction of working in a group as well as to learn the skills necessary to do so.

In our culture, this stage corresponds to the time when children are becoming deeply involved in formal learning. It also is a period when youngsters pursue extracurricular activities (4-H, Scouts, music lessons, athletics). Both types of experience can give children opportunities to learn the basic skills and knowledge they will need to advance in society. However, if feelings of industry are to outweigh those of inferiority, supervising adults must employ the strategies discussed here. When this occurs, children emerge into adolescence thinking, "I can learn, I can contribute, I can work with others."

In addition to working through the emotional tasks just described, children's thoughts about the nature of their feelings influence their emotional development.

Childrens Conceptualization of Emotion

Children's ideas about what emotions are and where they come from change significantly throughout childhood (Carroll and Steward, 1984; Harris, Olthof, and Terwogt, 1981; Harter, 1977). This change in affective development is directly linked to children's increasing cognitive maturity and expanding language skills (Shapiro and Weber, 1981). As with any developmental sequence, greater sophistication does not occur abruptly, nor are age norms rigidly representative of all children. Some youngsters display advanced thinking early, and vestiges of immature perceptions may be evident in adolescents. However, it is safe to say that emotional reasoning is more complex in older children than it is in younger ones.

Identifying the source of emotions. Children ten years of age and younger usually think of their emotions as consisting of just two parts (Harris, Olthof, and Terwogt, et al., 1981):

1. A situation, such as a birthday or an argument,
2. A physical reaction to that situation, such as laughing or shouting.

Children of this age view their emotional response as a result of physical sensations rather than as a product of their own thinking. As an outgrowth of this conceptualization, the youngest children describe their reactions as being triggered by physiological cues associated with biological needs. In other words, hunger, thirst, or sleepiness equal sadness, anger, or fear, and satisfaction of these needs equals joy (Wolman, Lewis, and King, 1971). As children become older, they begin to identify other physiological sensations as well: upset stomach, racing heartbeat, sweating palms, chills. Throughout this entire period, children most often describe their emotions as occurring within their trunk and limbs, treating physical states and emotions as one and the same. They have little awareness of the mental aspects of emotion. It is not until preadolescence that children associate emotions with what happens in their head and brain.

Ten- to thirteen-year-olds talk about emotions not only in terms of situations and reactions but also in terms of mental states that are internal and unobservable by others (Selman, 1981). They make a clear distinction between inner experiences and outward appearances and are aware that the two are not always congruent. Over time, they rely more and more on their inner, mental state than on their bodily response to tell them what they are feeling.

Emotional complexity. Children's understanding of how complex emotions can be undergoes a similar transformation. When they first become aware of their emotions, children believe people can experience only one at a time. The existence of one emotional state leaves no room for any other. Thus, children think that when people are angry, they are completely angry; when they are pleased, they are entirely pleased. If young children feel smart, they feel smart about everything; if they feel dumb, they think they cannot do anything right (Harter, 1977).

Around the age of five or six, youngsters begin to recognize that people can hold more than one feeling at a time, but they believe that contrasting feelings are directed toward different things (Selman, 1981). They do not think it is possible to be both happy and sad about the same event.

In the middle elementary-school years, children come to believe that multiple feelings toward the same event are feasible. They also perceive that this may involve conflicting emotions. However, they postulate that such feelings occur in succession, not all at the same time. One feeling replaces another rather than existing in tandem with it. Thus, they now think it is possible to be both happy and sad about the same event, but not at the same time.

It is not until about the fourth or fifth grade that youngsters are able to identify having simultaneous feelings about the same object or situation. At this point, children perceive that one feeling can blend into another. This blending of feeling often results in a state of mixed emotions that children label as "confusion." For this reason, youngsters who feel both happy and sad about something have difficulty sorting their feelings out. Instead, they tend to experience a general sense of anxiety over not having one clear-cut response.

The most mature thinking begins in late adolescence, when young people describe mixed feelings as producing new and different emotions. In this way, they may identify disap-pointment as a composite of anger, sadness, and regret. They now are able to analyze more accurately what all their emotions are. This analysis may occur internally or through conversations with others. The trends children exhibit in thinking about their own emotions parallel the ways in which they identify feelings in others.

Children's recognition of emotions in others. Children initially rely solely on behavioral reactions to tell them what someone else is feeling (Reichenbach and Masters, 1983). By three or four years of age, when presented with a representation of another person (pictures of facial expressions, videotapes, or live models), youngsters accurately identify facial expressions illustrating happiness, sadness, anger, and fear (Camras, 1977; Conn, 1968). Their assessment tends to focus more on how the person looks than on the context of the situation. The core emotions are consistently easier for children to identify than are emotions characterized by subtle external cues. Thus, feelings like contempt, disgust, mirth, and determination often cause confusion when youngsters are asked to identify outward portrayals of them (Thompson and Meltzer, 1964).

As children grow up, they more accurately recognize a wider range of emotional expression. In addition, they have a larger "feeling-word" vocabulary than younger children and are more likely to choose words that are a variation on the core emotions (Kostelnik, 1977). They also become more adept at projecting how another person might feel in a particular situation (Borke, 1971; Harter, 1979; Trabasso, Stein, and Johnson, 1981). To do this, youngsters first rely heavily on situational cues and then on their assessment of the person's probable mental state.

Predictably, the youngest of this group seldom suggest that a person might be feeling two emotions simultaneously (Harter, 1979). Over the years, children gradually become able to imagine others' feelings as a succession of emotions and finally become more accurate at identifying potentially mixed emotions (Selman, 1981).

In real-life situations, the perception children have of another person's feelings is influenced by more than just their intellectual capabilities. It also is affected by their own feelings at the time and their repertoire of past experiences. Anticipated interactions with individuals being observed and stereotypical attitudes toward some trait or characteristic of the individual also influence children's perceptions (Feshbach and Singer, 1957; Gage, 1952). How well children know the person, how comfortable they feel with him or her, and how predictable that individual's behavior has been in the past all determine how well children recognize that person's emotional state at a given time.

Yet, even when all conditions are favorable, children still may not be accurate in their assessments of another person's feelings. This is because similarities of behavior are not invariably predictive of the same feeling state for any one person or among groups of people. A slight smile might indicate amusement for one individual and embarrassment for another. Further, the same emotions may manifest themselves through different behaviors in varying situations. One day, the teacher may express annoyance with a frown and an impatient tone; another day, he or she may express the same feeling through sarcasm. To make matters even more complicated, the same stimulus event may elicit different responses from different people or from the same individual on separate occasions. Loud music may cause one person to respond exuberantly while making someone else feel overwhelmed. On another day, the exuberant respondent may react with irritation. All of these variations frequently are difficult for children to discern on their own. Thus, even when youngsters become able to discriminate someone else's emotions, other factors may affect their ability to do so. These variables are primarily social. How proficient youngsters eventually become at conceptualizing their own emotions and those of the people around them is dependent, in part, on the social learning they acquire over the years.

How social learning affects children's emotional conceptualization. Throughout their youth, children not only mature developmentally, but they also gradually accumulate a history of social experience that influences their conceptualization of emotion. The latter comes about through observing and interacting with others. Adults play a central role in this form of socialization by serving as models for children to imitate and by providing related instruction. The social knowledge children gain is threefold: First, children come to recognize which emotions their society honors and which it scorns. Second, they learn which forms of emotional expression are considered acceptable and which are not. Third, they learn to associate events with certain emotional states. Obviously, younger children and those who have had fewer opportunities for learning have a less sophisticated grasp of those concepts than do older and more experienced youngsters.

The emotions society values. Within the context of their ecological milieu, children develop an overall concept of whether or not emotions are a natural and acceptable part of living. Thus, they assimilate ideas about how much of the private self society deems appropriate for public exposure (Ekman, 1973). For instance, children who observe people exhibiting, talking about, and responding to a wide range of affective states get the message that emotions are normal and can be shared. These concepts are underscored when children's own feelings are accepted and when they are encouraged to bring them out into the open. On the other hand, youngsters who witness people habitually covering up or denying personal feelings, as well as ignoring or refuting those of others, quickly come to view emotions as unnatural.

They also learn that the way to deal with feelings is to keep them secret or to pretend that they do not exist. This perception is compounded when, in their own attempts to disclose emotions, children experience social costs.

In addition to this general conceptualization, children also learn that particular emotional states are either expected or forbidden. As a case in point, Japanese children learn to feel mutually dependent on other people. This is considered a core emotion in the Japanese culture and has been given a special name, *amae* (Kato, 1979). Similarly, American children as young as two years of age report having learned to discriminate between worry and fear, describing the former as acceptable within their society and the latter as less so (Kostelnik, 1977). They also report being conscious that feeling jealous or angry is taboo (Borton, 1970). American children describe differentiated affective codes for males and females. Both genders agree that it is more permissible for boys to feel angry than it is for girls and that girls are encouraged to experience feelings of tenderness and sadness, emotions frequently denied to boys (Lewis, Wolman, King, 1972).

Besides being taught broad principles, children often are instructed on how they should or should not feel in a particular circumstance:

> "You really hurt his feelings; you should feel sorry."
> "You shouldn't feel sorry for her. She had it coming."
> "People who make a mistake like the one you made are supposed to feel sorry."
> "You're sorry you lost his book, aren't you?"

In all of the ways described, society actively contributes to the mental image children form regarding the role of emotions in their lives. Which modes of emotional expression children perceive as available to them also are a product of social learning.

Cultural mores governing emotional expression. Worldwide, children are much more transparent about their emotions than are the adults with whom they live. Adults universally tend to be more covert about what they are feeling and more circumspect about how they react in emotional situations than are children. Cross-cultural studies support the idea that this is a learned phenomenon (Ekman, 1973).

To become successfully integrated into society, children must learn their culture's unique set of rules regarding which specific facial, body, and verbal expressions are acceptable and which are not. Hence, Chinese children must learn to smile to show respect when being scolded by an elder, and Mexican-American children must learn to look downcast to indicate deference. Likewise, Navaho children come to recognize that they should lower their voices to communicate anger, unlike Anglo youngsters who learn to raise theirs in order to get the same message across (Opler, 1967).

Children acquire such knowledge by watching how other people handle emotional circumstances and from the emotional episodes in which they themselves participate. For example, youngsters who see adults express affection through hugs and kisses learn to use the same gestures to communicate their own caring. Similarly, children who witness adults angrily pounding their fists in frustration may be seen at some later time doing the same thing.

Adults also provide feedback to children regarding the appropriateness of the ways they choose to express their emotions. For example, when a baby's smile is greeted with the excited voice of the caregiver, the adult's tone serves as a reward. If this happens often, the baby will smile more frequently. If the infant's smile is consistently ignored, his or her smiling behavior will decrease.

Adults also directly instruct children regarding standards of emotional expression. They do this when they point out appropriate and inappropriate reactions of others as well as by giving similar cues to youngsters:

> "Look at Sarah—she's being such a baby. She's too old to be carrying on like that."
>
> "John did a good job of speaking up for himself at the meeting. He was angry but he didn't lose control."
>
> "You shouldn't laugh at people in wheelchairs. It's not nice."
>
> "You just won first place. You should be smiling."

Rules such as these may be formal or informal and are enforced using a variety of social costs and rewards. Taken together, imitation, feedback, and instruction contribute to children's ideas about which emotion-based behaviors to retain and which to avoid.

Associating events with emotions. Children learn to associate certain events with particular physiological reactions and emotional states based on social experience. This learned interpretation actually dictates how they will feel in a given situation. For example, children sometimes develop persistent fears of particular events or situations. Earlier in this chapter, we discussed the normative sequence in which typical fears emerge. Those fears come about as a result of children's developing capabilities and understandings and as such are common to most youngsters. However, many children experience special fears that are unique to them and that are primarily learned (Schickedanz, Schickedanz, and Forsyth, 1982). Take, as an example, six-year-old Tessa's intense apprehension about visiting the dentist. Her fear may have arisen from actual experience (at an earlier visit, she had a tooth filled, and it hurt); she may have observed her mother becoming pale and anxious while settling into the dentist's chair and deduced that this was a frightening situa-

tion; or she may have been told directly, "If you're not good,, the dentist will have to pull out all your teeth," a horrifying thought. Most likely, she experienced a combination of these influences and encountered them on more than one occasion. In this way, she *learned* to be frightened of going to the dentist. Another child in her place might have put together a different interpretation as an outgrowth of his or her different experiential history.

In this portion of the chapter, we have focused on the many different variables that affect children's conceptualization of emotion. These have included both developmental and experiential components. The formulation of mature concepts evolves slowly and is still incomplete as children move into adolescence. As a result, children often experience understandable difficulty in dealing with emotions.

PROBLEMS CHILDREN ENCOUNTER WHEN DEALING WITH EMOTIONS

Martin is so excited about going to the zoo that he keeps interrupting his father, who is trying to get directions for the trip.

Andrea has been waiting a long time to use the kite. Frustrated, she grabs it from Barbara, then dashes to the other side of the playground.

Marsha is jealous of Anita. She constantly "puts her down" to her friends.

Fred is worried about what will happen when his mother goes into the hospital. Rather than letting anybody know his fears, he pretends he doesn't care.

None of these children are handling their emotions particularly well. That is, none of them are dealing with their emotions in a way that will lead to greater personal satisfaction, resolution of a dilemma, or increased interpersonal competence.

Difficulties Experienced by Children from Infancy Through Age Seven

Children are not born knowing how to manage their emotions. As a result, they often rely on strategies that are unproductive. Throughout the preschool years, one of the most common strategies children employ is to simply act out their feelings in the hope that someone will interpret them accurately and respond accordingly. There are several reasons why youngsters resort to this approach. First, since infancy, physical reactions have been their primary mode of communication. Crying elicits comfort; laughing prompts prolonged interaction; drawing away from a stranger often causes a reunification with the caregiver. Because these nonverbal messages have been effective in helping children achieve their goals, they continue to rely on them even when their messages become too complicated to be understood so easily. Second, even though words are a more precise way to convey meaning, children may not have the vocabulary to describe what they are feeling or the conceptual framework to know what their feelings are. Additionally, children's assessment that the site of their emotions is in their stomach and limbs leads them to persist in their use of physical reactions. As a result, they lash out when angry, huddle when frightened, and jump up an down when excited.

At times, this type of nonverbal communication works well. The crying of a child with a bruised knee is easily understood, and the remedy is obvious. However, behavioral cues are not always so evident. Consequently, children often are frustrated in their attempts to have others understand their emotional needs.

One difficulty children experience occurs when their nonverbal expression of feelings is misinterpreted, leading to a response that is not suited to their actual feelings. For instance, an adult may infer that a crying child is tired when fear really is the source of her anguish. Putting the child to bed will not address the real issue. In fact, it may make the situation worse because in the future, the child may pursue a line of action that is dysfunctional (Chaikin and Derlega, 1974). That is, the next time the child feels fearful, she may hide under the covers.

Another difficulty arises when peers or adults ignore emotions that are not blatantly obvious. Feelings of frustration, discouragement, wariness, anticipation, and curiosity often are signaled by subtle cues that do not stand out. Therefore, rapt attention from an observer is required if such emotions are to be recognized. Because such focused attention is not always forth-coming, these emotions may be overlooked. An added dilemma is that in the early elementary-school years, children who are experiencing mixed emotions may look either confused or blank. Focusing on external behavioral cues alone frequently does not give an observer enough information with which to respond appropriately. When this happens, youngsters are prevented from learning more about themselves because the insight to be gained from another person's response is lost. Thus, the opportunity to gain increased self-awareness is restricted (Jourard, 1971). In addition, youngsters may come to learn that only extreme emotions are likely to elicit a reaction, causing them to rely more heavily on radical affective expression.

Another common pitfall for youngsters two to seven years of age is that they often choose inappropriate actions to show how they feel. Their poor choice may be due to ignorance (they don't recognize an acceptable alternative) or to immature conceptualizations. The latter results from young children's tendency to recognize only one emotion at a time. Consequently, they feel each emotion intensely and totally. This is why they become angry with such a vengeance and affectionate with such a passion. Thus, the physical actions they choose to relay their feelings often are equally extreme. Such dramatic behaviors frequently are categorized as socially unacceptable.

Finally, because preoperational youngsters generally find it difficult to recognize another person's feelings without help, they may react in ways that are inappropriate for the situation. This problem is compounded by their limited repertoire of alternate social responses.

Difficulties Experienced by Children Aged Seven to Twelve

An additional source of difficulty emerges as children move into the later elementary-school years. Although children of this age are more aware of what their emotions are and how to use words to communicate them, they are less likely to do so than before. Instead, older youngsters may try to hide, minimize, or avoid their emotions altogether via withdrawal, regression, denial, repression, and projection (Lewis, Wolman, and King, 1972). Such reactions result from their belief that what goes on inside their heads is personal and so should be kept within. In addition, their increasing awareness of the social mores regarding acceptable and unacceptable emotions and responses prompts them to hold back if they anticipate that social costs will result from revealing an emotion. When children use such strategies, negative effects are heightened by the addition of emotional stress caused by the discrepancy between their real emotions and what they think those emotions should be (Jourard, 1971).

Unfortunately, when children hide their emotions, they have no opportunity to find out that they have emotional experiences in common with others. This leads to feelings of isolation, self-doubt, and inferiority (Adler, 1923; Sullivan, 1957). Youngsters in these circumstances come to think of their emotions as unnatural: different from anyone else's or the established norm. The more intense this perception, the more frantically the child may attempt to keep the feelings secret. Hence, a self-destructive cycle is established. In fact, some helping professionals maintain that many school-age youngsters channel more energy into concealing their emotions than would be necessary to develop constructive coping behaviors (Mowrer, 1971).

Finally, although preadolescent children are better able to recognize and respond to other peoples' emotions, they still lack the conceptual and social skills necessary to so unfailingly. Their confusion about multiple and conflicting emotions contributes to this dilemma, as does their awareness that people's true emotions may not be evident through their behavior.

The Negative Effects of Adult Behavior

The difficulties children naturally experience in handling their emotions sometimes are compounded by inappropriate adult responses. For example, several outcomes are possible when Paulo declares his pride in achieving recognition in the cooking contest. If an adult responds with a comment like "Neat!", or "You're really excited," or "Good for you," the acceptability of his proud feeling is confirmed, as is the appropriateness of his telling people about it. In contrast, the adult who ignores Paulo's enthusiasm by saying, "That's nice, but when are you going to finish your chores?" gives a clear indication that Paulo's feelings are unimportant and that he should not be talking about them. Moreover, if the adult were to retort: "You should be more modest. Remember, 'Pride goeth before the fall'," Paulo learns that feelings of pride and accomplishment are inappropriate. Because the last two responses could be interpreted by the child as meaning that his feelings are bad, he may evaluate himself negatively for having experienced them and may repeat this negative assessment the next time he feels proud. If this trend continues, Paulo may come to view a natural part of himself as unacceptable.

When children arrive at such conclusions, they often choose maladaptive ways of coping. Paulo may become boastful as a way of bolstering his sagging confidence; he may reject compliments in an effort to adhere to an expected code of conduct; he may stop trying to excel as a way to avoid pride and achievement; he may develop a headache or stomachache in response to situations in which he might otherwise feel proud; or, Paulo may turn into a child who continually disparages himself in an effort to look modest. All of these strategies are detrimental to Paulo's future happiness.

In addition to ignoring children's emotions or telling children that their feelings are not worth considering, there are three other ways of responding that are ineffective and potentially harmful. These include lying about emotional situations, denying children's feelings, and shaming children (Fraiberg, 1968; Gazda, 1977; Peake and Egli, 1982). All of these strategies not only cause damage at the time that they are used, but also eliminate the adult as a future source of emotional support on which children can rely.

Lying to children about emotional situations. Sometimes, in an effort to "protect" children from difficult emotional experiences, adults fail to tell the truth. For example, Arnie is afraid about having blood drawn, and the technician attempts to soothe him by saying, "This won't hurt a bit." Similarly, Mary Ellen expresses concern to an adult about going to the church picnic because of another child who often picks on her. The adult, knowing that the bullying child will be attending, attempts to smooth over the situation by saying, "I heard he wasn't coming." In neither case had the child been helped to prepare for what actually will happen. Furthermore, the adult's credibility has been seriously damaged. Bonds of trust, which take time to establish, have been destroyed.

Denying children's emotions. There are many ways in which adults deny children's emotions. Sometimes, adults actually forbid children to have certain feelings. Phrases like "Stop worrying," "Don't be angry," or "You shouldn't be so scared" are examples of this approach. At other times, adults dismiss the importance of the emotion being expressed, as when Lucas cried, "Look, there's blood on my finger," and the adult responded: "It's just a little cut. You won't die." On other occasions, adults tell children they don't really have the emotion they claim to be experiencing: "You know you aren't really mad at each other," "Let's see you smile," "No more tears!".

In every one of these situations, adults are not necessarily trying to debase children. They may be trying to avoid a scene or to comfort children by attempting to minimize the intensity of the moment. The message they are conveying, however, is that these emotions are wrong and that children are bad for experiencing them. As a result, an emotionally difficult situation for the child is made worse: not only do the original feelings remain, but the child now must cope with new feelings of inadequacy and inferiority for failing to meet the adult's standards.

Shaming children. Making fun of children or attempting to shame them out of their emotions is a destructive practice. Adults demoralize children when they say things like: "What are you crying for? I can't believe you're such a baby about this," "All the other kids are having a good time. Why are you being so difficult?", or "Manny isn't afraid. What makes you such a scaredy-cat?" As with lying and denying, shaming makes children feel doubtful, inferior, and inadequate. It certainly does not cause them to respond positively or make them feel better. For this reason, it has no place in a helping professional's verbal repertoire.

In lieu of these destructive practices, adults can learn productive ways of responding to children's emotions. These alternate strategies promote self-esteem in children and help them increase their interpersonal skills.

APPROPRIATE WAYS OF RESPONDING TO CHILDREN'S EMOTIONS

In order to help youngsters cope more effectively with their emotions, adults must act in supportive ways. Rather than trying to eliminate or restrict children's feelings, adults should accept them, even as they attempt to change the behaviors children use in emotional situations. Such acceptance is synonymous with the idea of acceptance or unconditional positive regard described in Chapters 1 and 4. Adults are better able to take on this role when they keep in mind the following tenets:

1. Children's emotions are real and legitimate to them.
2. There are no right or wrong emotions. Both positive and negative feelings stem from core emotions, which occur naturally.
3. Children cannot necessarily help how they feel, nor can they simply change their emotions on command.
4. Both positive and negative emotions serve useful functions in children's lives.

It can also be said that words are a satisfying, more precise way to express emotions and frequently are an appropriate substitute for physical action. Thus, in working with either preschool or school-age children, one obvious solution to the difficulties children experience in handling emotions is to teach them to talk more openly about what they are feeling.

Talking to Children About Their Emotions

The first step in encouraging children to talk about their emotions is to acquaint them with the vocabulary used to describe emotions (Peake and Egli, 1982). Because children learn most comprehensively within the context of their personal experience, they benefit when their emotions are named and described to them at the precise moments at which they occur. For instance, if Matt is angry and an adult identifies this emotion ("Matt, you look angry"), the child has a "hands-on" experience with the concept. Not only does he learn that his emotional state is describable, but he also has a relevant opportunity to take in both the internal and situational cues related to that state. This is a more total learning experience than simply having Matt identify emotions in hypothetical situations because it combines all three elements of mature emotional conceptualization—a situation, a body reaction, and a mental state. The strategy adults can use to name and describe children's emotions is called an *affective reflection*.

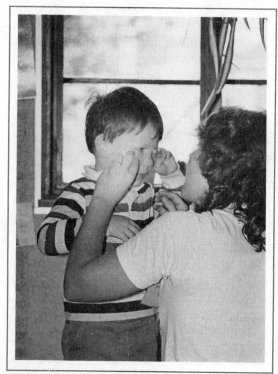

FIGURE 5-2 When children are distraught, offering comfort is the first and most important thing to do.
SOURCE: Photo by David Kostelnik

Affective Reflections

Affective reflections are similar in form and intent to the behavior and paraphrase reflections presented in Chapter 4. They involve recognizing the emotions a child may be experiencing in a given situation and then using a reflection to name the emotions.

SITUATION: Barry has climbed to the top of the jungle gym. With a big smile on his face, he announces, ''Hey, everybody, look at me!''

Adult: You're proud to have climbed so high. (Or, either of the following: It feels good to be at the top; You made it! that's exciting.)

SITUATION: Marlene complains that she had to clean up before her turn was over.

Adult: You wish you didn't have to clean up just yet. (Or: You didn't get to finish your turn; That's annoying; It's frustrating to be interrupted.)

SITUATION: Earl is embarrassed about having to take a shower with the other boys after gym class.

Adult: It makes you uncomfortable to take a shower in public. (Or: You wish you didn't have to take your clothes off in front of everybody; It really seems unbelievable to you that this is required.)

Affective reflections like these acknowledge and help to define children's emotions. In each situation, the adult's words and voice tone should match the emotional state being described, thus enhancing the completeness of the message.

Benefits to children of using affective reflections.   Labeling children's emotions via affective reflections makes abstract, internal states more tangible. The name for any phenomenon is intrinsically tied to one's understanding of it. Thus, naming something helps it to become more concrete (Bruner, 1966). In addition, the known is easier to comprehend than the unknown. Labels allow sensations to become more familiar. Because emotions cannot be touched or held and have elements that are not directly observable, labeling them is a particularly important strategy.

Verbal labels also are the primary means by which people recognize and recall past events (DiVesta and Rickards, 1971; Luria and Yudovich, 1959). Hence, an irritated child who has heard irritation described in the past is better able to identify her or his current emotional state. This recognition helps her or him draw from past experience to determine a possible course of action (Boneau, 1974).

Furthermore, language labels help to differentiate emotions that are perceptually similar but not entirely the same (DiVesta and Rickards, 1971). On hearing the words annoyed, disgusted, and enraged, one thinks of slightly different emotional states. All of these are variations on anger, yet are distinctive in their own right. Hearing different affective reflections enables children to be more precise in conceptualizing what they are feeling. Moreover, as youngsters hear alternate feeling words, they adopt many of them for their own use. The broader their vocabulary, the more satisfied youngsters are in using feeling words to express their emotions to others (Kostelnik, 1977). They also are likely to exhibit more varied emotional reactions. Annoyance, disgust, and rage for instance, may cause a child to envision different behavioral responses. Support for this line of reasoning comes from language research that shows that as people learn new words, their conceptualization of experience and the control of their behavior is increasingly regulated by speech (Bernstein, 1961; Luria and Yudovich, 1959; Meichenbaum and Goodman, 1971).

When adults acknowledge children's emotions using affective reflections, they exhibit sensitivity and caring in a way children can understand. This acknowledgement makes children feel heard and accepted (Rogers, 1961; Ginott, 1972). Not only do youngsters recognize that their emotions are respected by the adult, but as they hear their own and other people's emotions being described, they discover that their emotions are not so different from anyone else's (Bessell, 1970). This reduces the chances that they will view their own emotional experiences as abnormal. Affective reflections help children comprehend that all emotions, both good and bad, are an inevitable part of living.

The affective reflections just described are fundamental to enhancing children's emotional development. They can be used with children of all ages and in a wide array of circumstances. At times, the adult's purpose in using this skill is to focus more closely on the emotional aspects of an interaction. At other times, affective reflections are used to acknowledge the child's feelings while also dealing with other kinds of issues, such as making a rule or enforcing a consequence. Furthermore, use of this skill contributes to the construction of a positive verbal environment. Finally, as you progress through this book, you will see that affective reflections are a foundation on which many other skills are built.

Helping Children Express
Their Emotions to Others

There are additional strategies adults can use in concert with affective reflections to enhance children's emotional development. Among the most important are those that prompt children to talk about their emotions and to deal more constructively with the negative emotions they experience.

Children who are able to verbally describe their emotions make it easier for others to identify the emotions and increase the likelihood that they will receive a relevant response. This type of emotional sharing is often referred to as *self-disclosure* and is considered a basic interpersonal skill (Chaikin and Derlega, 1974; Levinger and Snoek, 1973). Interaction theories that stress open and honest communication all describe skills similar to, or synonymous with, this concept (Danish and Hauer, 1973; Gazda, 1977; Guerney, 1975; Rogers, 1961). This is because there is strong evidence that the degree to which people are able to express their emotions to others influences their ability to maintain close personal ties (Allman and Taylor, 1973). Also, when children learn to use words, they are less likely to resort to physical means to express negative feelings.

Children become skilled at describing their emotions when adults provide appropriate information about what another person is feeling and why, rather than expecting children to know already (Hendrick, 1984). Younger children benefit from information related to situational cues, and older children profit from data related to people's internal affective states. Additionally, children increase their interpersonal skills by learning actual phrases and scripts to use in emotional situations (Spivack and Shure, 1974).

Youngsters in difficult emotional circumstances become more adept at coping when, in addition to helping them acknowledge their own feelings, adults instruct them in how to make such situations more manageable. This can be accomplished either by teaching a child a specific skill or by remaining supportive to children who are working out these issues for themselves. The following section describes ways to implement such strategies.

SKILLS FOR RESPONDING TO CHILDREN'S EMOTIONS

How to Formulate Affective Reflections

1. Observe children carefully before saying anything. The context of a situation is important to its meaning. Pay close attention to children's facial expressions, voice tone, and posture as well as their actual words. If no words are spoken, you will have to rely on body cues alone. Because younger children tend to be more open about what they are feeling, the behaviors they display may be easier to interpret than those exhibited by older children. The emotions of grade-schoolers, who have been socialized to respond in certain ways, or who have learned to hide their emotions, may be more difficult to decipher. With these children, you must pay particular attention to nonverbal cues. A child who is talking "happy" but looking "distressed" most likely is distressed.

2. Be sensitive to the wide range of emotions children exhibit. Children manifest numerous emotions. Some are extreme, some are more moderate; some are positive, some are negative. All of their emotions are important. If you only take the time to notice intense emotions, or focus solely on the negative ones, children soon learn that these are the only emotions worth expressing. They get a broader perspective when all sorts of emotions are noticed and described.

3. Make a nonjudgmental assessment of what the child is experiencing. Form your impression of the child's feelings using only evidence about which you are certain. Avoid jumping to conclusions about why children feel the way they do. For instance, you may observe Paul entering the room crying. It is obvious that he is either sad or angry, but why he is so distressed may not be evident. Although you may assume that he is missing his mother, he might really be upset about having to wear his orange sweater to school. Because you cannot be sure what is bothering him, an appropriate affective reflection would be "You look sad," rather than "You're sad because you miss your mom." Opening the interaction with the first statement is potentially more accurate than using the latter.

4. Make a brief statement to the child describing the emotion you observed. Keep your reflection simple. Do not try to cram everything you have noticed about the child's emotional state into one response. Young children understand short sentences best. This also is true for youngsters who do not speak English well, or those who are mentally impaired. Older children will appreciate longer sentences or combinations of phrases, but will resent being overwhelmed with a plethora of adult talk.

5. Use a variety of feeling words over time. Employ many different words to describe children's emotions. This emphasis on diversity expands children's vocabulary of feeling words and makes your responses more interesting to them. Begin by using words to describe the core emotions (happy, mad, sad, afraid). Gradually, branch out to include related words that make finer distinctions (variations of happy, such as delighted, pleased, contented, overjoyed). Once you have reached the latter point, think in advance of two or three words you have not used recently and plan to employ them on a given day. Each time a situation arises for which one of your words is suited, use it. Repeat this process with different words on different days.

Finally, when you reflect using one of the more common feeling words in your vocabulary, follow it with a second reflection using a slightly different word ("You seem sad. It sounds like you're disappointed the model didn't fly").

6. Acknowledge children's emotions even when you do not approve of them. At times, children express emotions adults find unreasonable, unfathomable, or loathsome. For instance, Shavette comes to the recreation center, furious. Snarling through clenched teeth, she hisses, "I hate that teacher. All she knows how to do is give homework, and there's no time for anything else." At this point, it might be tempting to:

Lecture. "Shavette, I've told you never to say 'hate.' That's not a nice way to feel about anyone."

Rationalize. "Well, she really has to do that so you'll learn your math."

Deny. "You couldn't hate anybody, could you?"

Ignore. "Well, enough of that. Go pick out a board game to play."

Unfortunately, all of these responses communicate an insensitivity to the situation from Shavette's perspective and make it unlikely that she will share her feelings with you in the future. Additionally, responses such as these cause her to react defensively or resort to more extreme measures to make her true emotions known. Moreover, her impression probably will not be changed, and she has not learned constructive ways of handling her rage. A better response would be: "It doesn't seem fair to have to do so much homework," or "It sounds like you had a rotten day at school." Affective reflections like these are not only desirable but imperative. They force you to get beyond your own emotions and make you recognize a viewpoint very different from your own. This must be accomplished if children are to trust you and give you access to their private selves.

7. Revise inaccurate reflections. Affective reflections are tentative statements of your perceptions of the child's emotional state. If you reflect, "You seem worried," and the child says something like "No" or "I'm just thinking," accept the correction gracefully: "Oh, I misunderstood you," or "I'm sorry. I didn't mean to interrupt."

Common Questions About Formulating Affective Reflections

The mechanics of formulating an affective reflection are not difficult. However, when adults begin to practice affective reflections, questions often come up regarding their implementation in real-life situations. We have identified the most common of these questions and have provided answers that should enhance your ability to use this skill more effectively.

1. Do children really correct inaccurate affective reflections? Expect that there will be times when your interpretation of a child's emotional state does not exactly match the child's perception. Initially, children may not know enough about their emotions to correct you. However, it is likely that there will be other times when your reflection is accurate. As children come to identify both the internal and situational cues that match the label you have applied, they will become more sensitive to your occasional inaccuracies. Once this happens, most children will not hesitate to correct a mislabeled emotion.

Correcting inaccurate reflections will come more easily to children once they become more familiar with your use of reflective responses and recognize that all reflections are tentative statements. You reiterate this point when you say "You seem pleased" or "You look sad" rather than "You must be pleased" or "I know you are sad."

2. How do I introduce feeling words that I'm not sure children already know? One way to help children understand new feeling words is to use your body, face, and voice to illustrate the affective state to which you are referring. For example, if Annice seems to be frustrated, say, "You look very frustrated," and accompany the words with a serious tone, a frown, and a shrug of the shoulders.

A second approach is to tell Annice what it is about her behavior that leads you to believe she is frustrated: "You seem frustrated. Your body is very tense and you are frowning."

Another effective strategy is to use the unfamiliar word in a short reflection and then follow it with a second sentence defining the word you have used: "You seem frustrated. It can be discouraging to work and work and still the pieces don't fit," or "You're disappointed. You wish we didn't have to stay inside because of the rain."

3. Why use an affective reflection, rather than just ask children about their feelings? At times it may seem easier to simply inquire: "How are you feeling" or "Are you feeling sad?" or "Why are you so angry?" Well-meaning questions such as these sometimes are answered, but many times they are not (Kostelnik, 1977). When you are involved in emotional situations, remember that children are not always sure what they are feeling or why. Also, they may not be ready to give you the answer you are seeking. In either case, children's discomfort may be increased by an inquiry directed at them. It is more supportive to first give children an indication that you are simply trying to recognize their emotional state. This is best communicated through an affective reflection, to which the child does not have to respond, and which is correctable. Children are more likely to answer questions after you have reflected first. Thus, it is appropriate to say:

"You look sad. What happened?" In this situation, the child has the option of accepting your help or not. Regardless of which is chosen, the child knows you are available.

4. What if, after I reflect, the child still doesn't want to talk to me? Adults sometimes are nonplussed when they try to demonstrate their empathy through an affective reflection and the child remains unresponsive. For instance, you might reflect: "That looks like fun. You seem excited," or "You weren't expecting him to say that. You look upset," and the child does not acknowledge your comment. At times like these, it helps to remember that the purpose of any reflection is to indicate your interest in children without intruding on them. Once children come to understand this purpose, they frequently say nothing. Thus, lack of response may indicate that you are using the skill well. Moreover, if your reflection is accurate, there is no need for youngsters to confirm your interpretation. It is not likely that you will hear: "You noticed that I'm excited. Yes, I'm having a wonderful time!" or "You're right," or "Yes, I am." Children often do not talk because they are absorbed in what they are experiencing and prefer to focus on that, rather than on you. Yet, even in circumstances such as these, they have the opportunity to hear their feelings defined and to know that you are interested in what is happening to them. Both of these factors have a positive influence on children's emotional development. When children obviously are distressed but do not want to talk about it, it can be very effective to say: "You seem pretty angry. It looks like you don't want to talk about it right now. I'll be around if you want to talk later," or "I'll check back with you to see if you change your mind."

5. Do I always have to reflect before I take action? Some adults mistakenly presume that reflecting must always precede or take the place of action. They envision themselves having to have a long conversation with a child prior to intervening in a problem situation. This is an erroneous assumption. For instance, Billy comes in from the playground and says, "Teacher, teacher, Margo cut her knee!" The adult could easily respond to Billy, "You're worried about Margo's knee. Let's take a look," while hurrying over to the playground. Likewise, if two children are hitting each other, the adult should quickly grasp their hands while reflecting, "You two are very angry with each other." This affective reflection sets the stage for further action and explanations.

6. What do I do if children use inappropriate behaviors to express their emotions? Although children's behavior may be unacceptable, their feelings still must be acknowledged. Occasionally, this acknowledgement will be sufficient to satisfy the child's emotional needs. For instance, Mallory spits to demonstrate her anger. If the anger is recognized with an affective reflection, Mallory may no longer think it is necessary to spit to get her point across. The conditions are now set for the adult to assist the child in figuring out more acceptable ways to communicate anger. Even if Mallory were to continue spitting and the adult had to employ more extensive discipline strategies (many of which will be discussed later in this book), an affective reflection is the first step toward changing the child's behavior. What you must make clear to the child is that although all emotions are acceptable, all behaviors are not.

7. What if I can't tell what the child is feeling? Emotions that are not extreme sometimes are difficult to interpret. Additionally, some children are less expressive than others. Both of these circumstances may impede your ability to immediately recognize what a child is feeling. As you get to know indi-

vidual children, you will become more adept at identifying the behaviors they use when they are experiencing certain emotions. Iris flexes her fingers rapidly when she is nervous; Phil makes long pauses between his words when confused; Justin becomes belligerent when frightened. If you do not know the child well, or there are no outward signs to guide you, use a behavior or paraphrase reflection as an entree to the interaction. Wait, and use an affective reflection after you have ascertained, via words and gestures, what the child may be feeling. If no such opportunity arises, ask children directly; they may or may not be willing or able to tell you. If none of these strategies have worked, continue to observe and remain supportive, but do not force children to pursue a conversation.

How to Increase Children's Verbal Expressions of Emotion

1. Set an example for talking about emotions by bringing them up yourself. Include emotions in your casual conversations. Talk about how everyday events affect you ("What a great day. I'm so happy to see the sun out," or "I hate it when this plumbing keeps backing up"). Discuss events in terms of how they will affect people's feelings ("It sounds like if we don't have macaroni for lunch, everyone will be disappointed," or "If we were to leave without telling Ms. Jones, she might be worried"). Ask children how they might feel about particular events as they arise ("Oh, it's raining. Who here likes rain? Who here doesn't like rain?" or "Today, we're going to hear a poem about trees. Everyone think of one way they feel when they look at a tree"). Discuss emotions experienced by people children know or people they have heard about in the news ("Mr. Sanchez, our principal, feels really good

FIGURE 5-3 Effective helping professionals respond to the entire range of children's emotions—not only to the extreme ones.
SOURCE: Irene Bayer/Monkmeyer Press Photo Service

today. He became a grandfather," or "It was scary for the people along Spring Creek when the flood came"). Point out emotions experienced by characters in stories. Any kind of story can serve as a prompt for this type of discussion, not only "official" feeling stories ("Goldilocks was pretty frightened," or "Laura Ingalls felt excited about going to town with her pa").

2. Explain to children who are involved in emotional situations that they can tell their emotions to the other person. Children often mistakenly believe that what they are feeling is obvious to everyone around them. Tell children this is not always true (''You're disappointed that Melinda didn't help you as she'd promised. She doesn't know that's how you are feeling. Tell her so she'll know,'' or ''You didn't want Claudia to take the hammer just yet. Say that to her'').

3. Assist children in describing their emotions to others if they cannot do so entirely on their own. Sometimes, children fail to express their emotions verbally because either they lack the words or they are too emotionally involved to think of them. If this happens, do one of the following:

a. Suggest words to the child that fit the situation. This is, in essence, a verbal script (Kathy could be advised to say: ''Claudia, I wasn't finished with the hammer,'' or ''Claudia, I don't like it when you grab''). Younger or less experienced children benefit when given brief phrases to consider. Older or more experienced youngsters are better able to consider longer sentences and more than one alternate approach. Once children become more comfortable and adept at using the scripts you provide, help them think of some of their own (''You're upset with Claudia. Tell me words you could use to let her know that'').

b. Ask children questions that prompt them to describe how they feel. Begin by using simple yes-no questions (''Marco took your pliers. Did you like it when he did that?''). Over time, advance to more open-ended inquiries (''Marco took your pliers. How did that make you feel?'').

4. Help children decipher behavioral cues that tell how another person is feeling. Children are not always aware of what other people are feeling, nor are they completely accurate in their interpretations. Point out specific signs of people's emotional expression to toddlers and less experienced preschoolers (''Pearl is crying. That means she is unhappy''). Prompt older, more experienced youngsters to notice these cues for themselves (''Look at Pearl. Tell me what she is doing and what she might be feeling''). If a relevant answer is not forthcoming, provide the appropriate information yourself.

5. Draw children's attention to situational cues that contribute to people's emotions. Tell toddlers and preschoolers what features of a situation triggered an emotion (''Julie and Chris both wanted the last banana cupcake. They decided to split it. They're pretty happy. People feel good when they can work things out,'' or ''Garland, you had been waiting a long time to use the easel, and now it's all drippy. You look disappointed about that''). Ask older children to tell you what it was about a situation that they thought prompted the emotional reaction. This strategy can be applied both to situations in which the child is an observer and to those in which the child is directly involved. In addition, point out similarities and differences in children's reactions to the same event (''You both saw the same movie, and it sounds like each of you enjoyed it,'' or ''You both saw the same movie. Emma, it sounds like you really thought it was funny. Janice, you're not so sure'').

How to Help Children Cope with Difficult Emotions

1. Acknowledge children's negative emotions and forbid destructive actions. Do this using an affective reflection followed by a statement such as: ''It's all right to be angry. It is *not* OK to hit.'' (More about this type of intervention will be presented in later Chapters).

2. Comfort children who are sad or afraid. Offer physical and verbal consolation. In this way, you provide a safe, secure refuge for children in distress. It is from this secure base that they eventually may be able to face the cause of their feelings.

3. Help children sort out mixed emotions. Begin by listening to the child describe the situation. Acknowledge each of the emotions you hear or observe when multiple emotions are evident. Tell children that it is normal to have different feelings at the same time. Also, point out discrepancies between the child's words and what he or she might be expressing in nonverbal ways ("You're telling me everything is fine, but you look miserable").

4. Provide children with information that may enlarge their perception of a situation. One way to modify negative emotions is to introduce new information. Point out to children facts about the situation they may have missed ("You thought Andrew was making fun of you, but he was laughing at a joke he just heard").

When children are afraid, what they might imagine is often worse than reality. Again, information is useful. Tell children what to expect in new situations. Describe possible outcomes, both pleasant and unpleasant. Offer explanations for events as children experience them.

Under no circumstance must you expect rationales alone to change children's emotions. Probably, explanations will have to be offered many times.

5. Provide opportunities for children to observe how others cope in a situation they fear. Encourage youngsters to watch peers who are unafraid in situations that are anxiety provoking for them. For instance, children who are afraid of the water often feel less fearful after watching other age-mates play safely at the water's edge. Refrain from chastising fearful children if they do not immediately follow suit. Instead, allow them to observe, or even not observe, as long as they wish.

6. Allow children to approach a feared situation gradually. Help children work their way to a point at which the fear becomes manageable. For example, a child who is afraid of dogs could benefit from going through the following steps:

a. Looking at pictures of dogs.
b. Playing with a stuffed toy dog.
c. Observing other children playing with dogs.
d. Observing a puppy being held in the lap of an adult.
e. Touching a puppy being held by an adult.
f. Holding a sleeping puppy on his or her lap.

There is no one right way to carry out such a process. Adults should be sensitive to the cues children exhibit and introduce a new, harder step only after a child has comfortably mastered the current one. Youngsters vary in how long the process takes and how elaborate it must be. Adult impatience only adds to their anxiety and negates the potential benefits that may be derived.

7. Help children think of new strategies or learn new skills as a way to deal with difficult emotions. Talk over possible ways to better cope. Brainstorm a wide variety of ideas for how children can prepare themselves for similar situations in the future or how they can respond to an ongoing problem. Here are ideas children have come up with to master a personal crisis:

A child who was easily angered imagined his foe as having three funny heads.
A youngster who was frightened about going to a new school drew a map showing the way from the main office to her room.

An anxious fourth-grader brought his teddy bear to camp and cuddled it under the covers whenever he needed to.

A child who felt awkward at games decided to practice kicking the ball every day for fifteen minutes.

If children cannot think of any ideas themselves, offer several suggestions of your own for them to consider. Accept their choice, even if it involves no choice being made.

PITFALLS TO AVOID

Regardless of whether you are responding to children's emotions individually or in groups, informally or in structured activities, there are certain pitfalls you should avoid.

Sounding "all knowing."

"You must be feeling sad."
"I know you're feeling sad."
"You're feeling sad, aren't you?"

All of these phrases make you sound all knowing. Their use makes it more difficult for children to correct a mistaken reflection. Because reflections are supposed to be tentative and correctable, phrases such as these should not be used.

Accusing children.
Words like vicious, stubborn, uncooperative, nasty, greedy, manipulative, and belligerent are not feeling words, even when used in the form of an affective reflection. They are accusatory terms based on adult evaluations of child behavior rather than accurate interpretations of children's emotions, and so should not be used. For instance, a child who wants all of something may feel justified, wishful, or entitled, but certainly not greedy, which implies getting more than one deserves. Likewise, a youngster who remains fixed on doing something a certain way may feel determined, but would not identify his or her feelings as stubborn, meaning unreasonably obstinate. If you find yourself employing such a term, stop. Observe what the child is really trying to communicate, and then restate your reflection nonjudgmentally.

Trying to diffuse children's emotions too quickly.
When children are involved in highly emotional situations, adults may feel compelled to dilute or modify what the children are feeling. They attempt to move children along to an affective state that is less intense or more comfortable for the adult to deal with. As a result, they may try to cajole children out of unhappiness, jolly them out of anger, or distract their attention from what they are feeling. Unfortunately, these tactics often do more harm than good. Children get the idea that they'd better "snap out of it" or risk the adult's disapproval. Also, they learn no constructive way to deal with their true emotions. A better approach is to make use of the strategies described in this chapter by acknowledging children's emotions and allowing them to talk about them. This may take place in one sitting or in several. Only after children have recognized what their feelings are is it appropriate to help them think of coping strategies.

Coercing children into talking about their emotions.
In an effort to show concern, adults may probe into children's emotional states, ignoring signs that such inquiries are frustrating for the child or unwelcome. With preschoolers, repeated questions such as "Are you disappointed?" or "Why are you so upset?" may be beyond the child's ability to answer, thus creating pressure that children find stressful. Similarly, older children may find these probes

intrusive, preferring to keep their reactions to themselves. The best way to avoid such negative circumstances is to remain alert to actions by children indicating they are not ready to talk. Turning away, pulling back, vague answers, mumbled replies, increased agitation, and verbal statements such as ''I don't know'' or ''Leave me alone'' should be respected.

Forcing children to face frightening situations. In the mistaken belief that children will overcome a fear by facing it directly, some adults force children into confrontations with what they fear most. Rarely does this alleviate the child's fear. Instead, the fear often is intensified and, in some cases, may last a lifetime. For instance, all of us know people who were forced to ''sink or swim'' as a child and who now hate the water. Coercing children also betrays their sense of trust. A better technique is to acknowledge children's fears and allow them to overcome them gradually.

SUMMARY

Emotions are an intrinsic part of children's lives. Positive emotions, such as joy and affection, feel good. They encourage children to reach out and to be receptive to people and experiences. Negative emotions, such as fear and anger, feel bad, inducing children to avoid, escape from, or surmount difficulties. Emotions are universal. They are triggered by particular events to which the body responds. People interpret what they are experiencing and take action based on their interpretation.

Emotions develop in a normative sequence and arise from such core emotions as joy, anger, sadness, and fear. Clusters of related emotions and combinations of them emerge over time to form more complex emotional reactions. The stimulus events that prompt particular clusters of emotion are essentially similar over the life span. Cognitive maturity and experience affect an individual's interpretation of these stimulus events. How children experience fear as they grow up is an example of this developmental change.

People are thought to work through a series of emotional tasks over the course of their lives. Optimal growth occurs when the balance is toward the positive of the opposite poles in each stage. The developmental stages during which children work through emotional tasks are known as trust versus mistrust, autonomy versus shame and doubt, initiative versus guilt, and industry versus inferiority. In addition, changes in how children think about their emotions as they mature influence their emotional development. Children move from thinking that their emotions consist of a situation and a body reaction (under ten years of age) to the added recognition of an associated mental state. The youngest children believe that only one emotion can be experienced at a time; five- and six-year-olds begin to recognize that two emotions can be experienced simultaneously (but about different things); and ten- to twelve-year-olds begin to identify multiple reactions to the same event. Children's recognition of emotions in others follows a similar trend. However, even older children may not be accurate interpreters of others' emotions because similar behavioral cues may represent different feelings, and the same stimulus may provoke varying responses among different people or within the same individual at different times. Children's learning also affects their conceptualization of emotion. Adults are the most significant teachers of what emotions society values, cultural mores regarding emotional expression, and the interpretation of feelings and events as emotions.

Children encounter difficulties dealing with their emotions. They often rely heavily on others recognizing their nonverbal cues, which may be overlooked or misinterpreted; they may choose inappropriate actions to show how they feel; and they may try to hide, minimize, or avoid their emotions. Inappropriate adult responses compound these problems. Adults sometimes resort to lying, denying children's emotions, or shaming children. It is more supportive and helpful to talk to children about their emotions by using affective reflections. Affective reflections involve recognizing the emotions a child may be experiencing in a particular situation, then using a reflection to name them.

Affective reflections make abstract, internal states more tangible. Verbally labeling emotions helps children recall past events, helps them to differentiate emotions that are similar but not identical, allows adults to demonstrate caring and understanding, and contributes to a positive verbal environment. Other ways of helping children cope with their emotions are to use strategies that prompt them to talk with others about their emotions.

DISCUSSION QUESTIONS

1. Discuss the role of both positive and negative emotions in children's lives. Give examples based on your own childhood, or on your observation of young children, as to how this process actually works.
2. Malcolm is three years old and his brother, William, is ten. Discuss how each of them probably thinks about his own emotions and to what extent he is likely to be aware of his brother's emotional reactions.
3. Describe each of the emotional tasks of childhood and identify children's behaviors that would be characteristic of each stage.
4. Describe the developmental and learned aspects of children's fear. Discuss these in relation to your own fearful childhood experiences or the experiences of children you know.
5. Phyllis' mother tells you that she has scheduled Phyllis for an eye appointment. For some reason, the child seems very upset by this and has had a stomachache for a week.
   a. Discuss possible reasons for Phyllis' anxiety.
   b. For each of these, discuss approaches that would likely increase her fear and approaches that would be helpful to her.
6. Describe at least three ways in which affective reflections benefit children's emotional development.
7. Discuss specific ways in which you could make your own affective reflections more effective.
8. In each of the following situations, describe:
   a. What emotions the children involved might be experiencing.
   b. How you would use the strategies presented in this chapter to help the children become more aware of their own feelings and the feelings of others, and how you would help them cope effectively with the situation.

   SITUATION A Calvin and George are playing in the sandbox. Calvin wants George's pail, so he takes it. George begins to cry, but Calvin continues to play, unperturbed. George comes running to you, saying, "He took my pail!"

   SITUATION B Sandy has been standing watching the others jump rope. It seems as if she'd like to join in, yet she makes no move to do so.

   SITUATION C Curtis is in a quandary. He was just invited to a barbecue at Steven's house, but his best friend, Travis, has not been asked to come.

9. Describe four problems children experience in dealing with their emotions. Identify corresponding strategies adults can employ to help youngsters cope more effectively.
10. Describe one pitfall you have encountered using the skills presented in this chapter. Brainstorm ideas with classmates about how to deal with the problem in the future.

CHAPTER 6
Enhancing Children's Play

OBJECTIVES:

On completion of this chapter, you will be able to describe:

1. The function of play.

2. Various types of play.

3. Developmental trends in various types of play.

4. The role of the adult in facilitating children's play.

5. Pitfalls to avoid in facilitating children's play.

SOURCE: © Ulrike Welsch

132

SITUATION: Two children are playing family roles of husband and wife.

Anne: (Looking at rocking horse) Gotta go.

Phillip: Go?

Anne: Gotta go to work.

Phillip: No, you cook.

Anne: Can't cook, gotta go to work. (Climbs on the horse and begins to rock)

Phillip: No, you cook and stuff. I'll go to work. (Holds the reigns of the rocking horse)

Anne: Gonna be late for work. You stay and cook.

Phillip: Don't you know? *You* cook and *I* go to work.

Anne: (Trying unsuccessfully to rock) Drop you off on my way to work.

Phillip: (Mounts the horse behind her)

The play of these two children nearly floundered for lack of a shared meaning for the roles that they were playing. Fortunately, they were able to agree on the notion of both riding the horse to work even though they did not fully realize the difficulty of their differing perceptions of the roles of wives. Anne's mother had been employed throughout Anne's four years of life, and Phillip's mother was a full-time homemaker.

Adults who work with young children frequently observe play that demands conceptual shifts of the participants. Play is both common and complex. Frequently, adults take it for granted, referring to this exciting activity of childhood as ''just play.'' Although play is a predominant social activity of early childhood, it continues to provide common ground for informal social exchange as children mature. Therefore, adults who guide the social development of children need to understand the nature and function of play.

THE NATURE OF PLAY

Any definition of play must take into account the gleeful game of chase a toddler plays while running from his mother, the intense dramatization of an irate father played out in the nursery school, the boisterous and rough horsing about of young boys on the playground, the concentrated practice of a ten-year-old as she shoots basket after basket in the gym, the chanting cadence of the jump-rope rhyme, and the patience and strategy of the school-age child accumulating wealth in a Monopoly game.

Play, although not easily defined, has certain definitive characteristics (Garvey, 1977). Play is essentially pleasurable or enjoyable; although players may not be actively laughing, play still is highly valued. Play is intrinsically motivated; there are no extrinsic goals. It is essentially an unproductive activity in which the process is more important than the ends. Play is voluntary; to be play, the activity must be freely chosen by the child. Play also involves activity; the player is actively engaged in the process. In addition to these universal characteristics, play has certain systematic relationships to other aspects of development: cognition, language, knowledge about the world, perceptual and motor development, and social and emotional development.

Adults sometimes contrast play with other concepts. The opposite of play is reality, or seriousness, rather than work. People can play at their work, enjoying it thoroughly, and may work hard at developing play skills necessary for a sport. Therefore, work and play are not necessarily opposites.

Play is determined as play by the players. This means that the player may begin, end, or alter the activity in progress without consulting anyone but the other players. Play is fun, or at least pleasurable. Adults do not order children about in play. Such behavior would make the episode unplayful.

Helping professionals may be asked why they allow children to play and what benefits play provides for the child. Therefore, the relationship of "play" to "nonplay" aspects of development will be briefly described. These relationships are graphically illustrated in Figure 6-1.

Genetic Foundations

Play is a species behavior (Fagen, 1981; Ellis, 1973). This means that all humans play. However, as with other behaviors, there may be individual differences. The characteristics of adaptability and behavioral flexibility have had great survival value for humans and are practiced and enhanced throughout play. Other species also play. The most familiar forms of animal play are *play fighting* and *play chasing*, which are the nonthreatening chasing, wrestling, and hitting seen in the friendly tussles of puppies and kittens (Fagen, 1981). This play in animals has its own distinct communication signals and social conventions. Similar play-fighting and play-chasing behaviors are common among children as well (Blurton-Jones, 1976).

Cognition

The relationship of play to cognitive development has been the focus of many scholars (Piaget, 1962; Levenstein, 1976; Saltz and Brodie, 1982). Children tend to play in ways that are consistent with their cognitive development and, through play, construct ideas about the world around them (Piaget, 1962). For example, play with objects enhances the problem-solving abilities of preschool children when they use the objects in a task (Sylva, Bruner, and Genova, 1976). Probably one of the greatest achievements of early childhood is understanding that an object and the word representing it are distinct. This ability to distinguish an object from its name is demonstrated when a child names an object something else, such as calling a stick a spoon in play (El' Konin, 1976). Of

course, this achievement is an indicator of abstract thought, and requires mental flexibility.

Language

Language is used systematically in play, and can be the subject of play. Almost all levels of organization of language are potential play material (Garvey, 1977). Children play with sounds and make up words, joke with the meanings of words, and use all aspects of speech such as noises, intonation, and pauses as they play. Certain occurrences, such as a group of four-year-olds chanting "Delicious, nutritious, delectable juice" with great glee and accenting the syllables by pounding the table with cups or hands when faced with the detested apricot nectar, are a playful variation of the adult's words. Humor, especially in school-age children, often is based on multiple meanings of words and altered speech forms.

The language used in play is far more complex than that used in regular conversations. Children use more adjectives and adverbs, and the utterances are longer (Cathrine Hutt, as quoted by Chance, 1979). In fact, the general level of cognitive functioning in self-directed play may be far above the level expected of the same children in academic subjects in school (Chance, 1979).

New Information Skills

Play and learning have a complex relationship, with new learnings being utilized and practiced in play. Play may not be an activity in which concepts are acquired, but it surely is where they are reinforced, where parameters are explored, and where competence is acquired. As children become more competent, the complexity of their play alters, creating a play-learning spiral. For example, young children do not understand the principles that determine which materials will float and which will sink. However, with opportunities for water play and

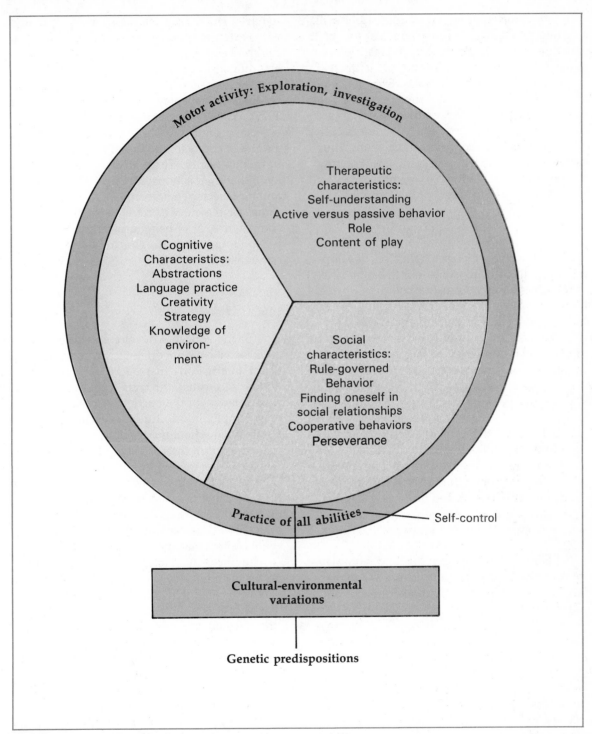

FIGURE 6-1 The integrative function of play.

a variety of materials to play with, children will begin to predict which things are best for constructing boats: the flat-bottomed plastic butter tub is selected over the glass bowl, the flat leaf over a crumpled one with holes. Experience in making play boats provides the opportunity to determine which characteristics of materials are likely to provide better results. As children continue to construct boats and float them, they become increasingly proficient in selecting materials and estimating the weight a particular boat will be able to carry without sinking.

Perceptual-Motor Development

The relationship of play to physical development usually is the most obvious to adults. Skill in movement and coordination comes as a result of maturation and experience. Grasping rattles, building block towers, making mud pies, playing tug-of-war, running races, and other vigorous play contribute to the organization of motor behavior and perceptual development.

Emotional Development

Since the days of Freud, the relationships of play to wish fulfillment and to the mastery of experiences have been explored. Life among adults, who are powerful, is filled with frustrations, and children are too powerless to rebel. They can, however, suspend the rules and alter the outcomes through fantasy play (Peller, 1971).

Children who enjoy playing, and who play more, seem to be happier than those who play less. They are fun to be with and are the preferred playmates or are more popular than less skillful players (Chance, 1979). Fantasy play allows for the personal integration of temperament, experience, and concepts that help the child understand the all-important question, "Who am I?" and thereby become a mentally healthy person (Newman and Newman, 1978). When Dr. Brian Sutton-Smith was asked by a mother whether her young son would be likely

to have mental health problems if he continued in his extensive fantasy play, he responded that the child was in greater danger of being an outstanding artist or scientist, as research showed that these people engaged in a lot of play, including fantasy play, when young (Chance, 1979). When children pretend, they manipulate objects, events, and actions, which gives them a sense of competence, an important ingredient in mental health. Through play, children also learn that their actions have an effect on others and on objects. The direct feedback from playthings or playmates provides for the sense of competence, or of being an actor or doer, that is so important in the development of self-concept.

Social Development

One of the concepts developed earlier in this book is that children do not learn everything by direct instruction. Instead, they learn many things indirectly through experiencing the consequences of their actions (Coleman, 1976). For example, in one study, preschool children who played school made an easier adjustment to kindergarten than did other children (Sarah Smilansky, as quoted by Chance, 1979). These children had acquired a notion of the rules prior to entry. Their play served to focus attention on the salient behaviors that would be expected of them and to demonstrate that they could affect events somewhat themselves.

The ability to make eye contact is learned partly through play. Another skill learned in play is the ability to empathize, or to be sensitive to others' emotions. This skill is demonstrated when children portray a variety of emotions in pretend play. Turntaking is learned in toddlerhood with simple games like peekaboo or rolling a ball back and forth. This is, of course, a primitive form of cooperation, which becomes elaborated as children share, engage in pretend play, and participate in team play. Children also may learn about competition, struggling toward arbitrary goals, rules, and aggression as they play.

Sex roles. Sometimes, new information is acquired as children try out roles that will be helpful as they gain experience in the larger society. The episode at the beginning of the chapter illustrated the differing ways a familiar role like "wife" can be played. Recently, studies of *sex-role* development have focused on early play behavior for insight into the different outcomes for girls and boys.

Boys and girls differ in their play, which may be accounted for by parents' differential treatment (Etaugh, 1983). In fact, even for toddlers, toys and furnishings are differentiated by sex (Rheingold and Cook, 1975). Parents and peers often reward sex-appropriate play and punish cross-sex play (Fagot, 1977, 1978), although they may find it more acceptable for girls to play with materials traditionally thought of as "boyish" than for boys to play with "feminine" toys. Preschool children have no difficulty in discriminating sex-stereotyped toys for boys and girls, even though they may not choose to restrict themselves to the toys intended for their gender (Eisenberg, 1983).

In general, girls' play activities generate rule learning, imitation, task persistence, bids for recognition, compliance, remaining close to adults, and help-seeking behaviors, whereas boys' play activities force them into creative problem-solving behaviors, exploration, and the restructuring of prior learning (Block, 1979). These behaviors usually are considered by society to be typical for the sex role of the children.

Categories of social participation. Social participation is important if children are to practice interacting with other children. Interacting with other children is more difficult than interacting with a parent or other adult. Clearly, watching others play is easier than coordinating one's behavior with one or more other players. The types of social participation described in the following list once were thought to represent increasing degrees of ability, but it is now recognized that, although acquired in sequence, each type of participation has independent, important characteristics (Parten, 1932; Smith, 1978):

1. *Unoccupied behavior.* The child is not engaged in any task or social participation. She or he spends most of the time looking around or wandering around, but is occupied with no specific task.
2. *Onlooker.* The child watches other children and sometimes talks with them. The child is actively engaged in observing specific activities.
3. *Solitary play.* The child plays with toys alone and independently, without interacting with others.
4. *Parallel activity.* The child plays independently, but the chosen activity brings him or her among other children who are engaged in the same activity. Two children putting puzzles together on the same table is typical of this type of play.
5. *Associative play.* The child plays with other children and interacts with them around a similar, but not identical activity. For example, Niki rides his truck back and forth near a block construction where Dennis and Mark are working together. Occasionally, he stops to comment and then continues his "deliveries."
6. *Cooperative or organized supplementary play.* The child plays in a group that is organized to make some material product or to strive for some common goal. A simple game of ring-around-a-rosy is cooperative play, as is the previously mentioned play of Dennis and Mark, who are engaged in building.

Solitary play and group play are not hierarchic categories for children between two and five years of age (Smith, 1978; Moore, Everton, and Brophy, 1974; Rubin, MaConi, and Hornung, 1976): Certain levels of maturity are required for each type of play, and most preschool children participate in both types, depending on the situation. Solitary play is not necessarily an immature form of play. In fact, it has been suggested that solitary play fosters the formation of novel behavior patterns and exercises creativity, while social play serves to enhance the bonds between individuals (Dolgin, 1981).

Solitary play is the most common form of play for toddlers, partly because they lack experience in interacting with peers and partly because there is a point in their development at which toddlers switch from treating peers as objects to treating them as people. Obviously, it is more complex to interact with an unpredictable peer than to roll a ball. Midway through the second year, toddlers are capable of mutual involvement, turntaking, and repetition in playful activities between two children (Hay, Ross, and Goldman, 1979).

Overall, the adult may see various forms of social participation in play. For example, the onlooker, although not socially involved, may be acquiring the knowledge that later will enable him or her to participate more directly. Some children may need time to wander through the play setting to see what their choices are before making a decision. Therefore, each kind of social participation has something to contribute to the child's development.

Social status. When children play together, they invariably learn about status in the group, dominance roles, and other power relationships. Their play provides a safe way to explore their own position in the group and also to indirectly comment on the existence of power relationships (Swartzman, 1979). For example, Toby, who faces Jeanette and announces, ''Let's play house,'' is communicating her desire to play but also is excluding Marie, on whom she has turned her back. This message is equally clear to all concerned. Toby has established her role of leader by initiating the play activity and may continue by defining the ongoing play.

TYPES OF PLAY

Exploratory Behavior

The manipulation and examination of objects often has been lumped into the category of play, although in some ways it differs from true play. Children engaging in exploratory behavior are scanning the environment, scrutinizing, feeling, smelling, mouthing, shaking, hefting, moving, operating, probing, or otherwise investigating the nature of the object at hand. The questions being addressed are: What can this do? How does it work? What is the nature of this object or situation? Exploratory behavior of novel objects precedes true play behavior (Hutt, 1971). Investigative exploration also is the first step in learning about objects and in solving problems.

Adults who take into account the tendency of children to explore objects and materials in the environment allow time for this behavior, even such problem-solving activities as using a microscope to look at a drop of water. Children who have the opportunity to examine the changes in focus, the use of the various lenses, and the glass slides before beginning the planned experiment will have a clearer understanding of the microscope and its uses than children who move from microscope to microscope glancing at each prepared view.

The need for exploratory behavior in the very young child is related to the behavior of infants and toddlers described earlier in this book. Every object is new; every event is novel; independent movement is a new event to be explored. This is why young children seem so busy, getting into one thing after another, and why safety is such a concern, as very young children are as likely to mouth or bite an electrical cord as they are a new food.

As children mature, more objects become familiar, or similar to familiar objects, and may take less time to explore. The toddler may notice that cubes used to make a pattern on a card are similar to the blocks he or she played with as a baby, differing only in color and size. Exploration time still is needed, but it may be less than a minute or two.

During the preschool years, children explore paste by tasting, smelling, and smearing before using it to adhere pieces of paper. Water and sand are poured, patted, tasted, and smelled. Paper is crumpled, torn, cut, and chewed. All of these are simple exploratory behaviors. Exploration becomes play when the child shifts from the question, "What does this object do?" to a slightly different question, "What can I do with this object?" The object itself ceases to be the major focus of concern as the child incorporates the object into play in which meanings and goals are assigned by the player.

Children shift from exploration to play repeatedly during a single episode of using an object (Hutt, 1971). For example, Renzell, age four, picked up a stethoscope, blew into the bell, looked at the earpieces, put the earpieces in his ears, tapped the bell, then walked over to a doll and announced that he was a doctor. He played out this role with several dolls, listening to their bodies all over. When Michael walked into the area, Renzell said, "I think you are sick," and began to listen to Michael's arm. Michael told him, "Listen right here," pointing to his chest. Renzell listened to Michael's chest and said the thing didn't work. He then listened to Michael's chest in different places, asking, "Can you hear that?" every now and then. He also listened to the radiator, to the hamster, and to other children, momentarily forgetting his doctor role.

Play with Objects

Children use a variety of toys, materials, and other objects in their play. The *novelty* of an object attracts attention and stimulates exploration. However, the *complexity* of an object is more important in sustaining interest. This is true of all objects for all ages (Weilbacher, 1981).

Children will play with anything: utensils, furnishings, leaves and sticks, stones, animals, and toys. Play behavior can occur anywhere: in the car, yard, playground, nursery school, living room, classroom, or hallway. Adults frequently admonish children to "quit playing around with that." Because play with some objects, such as a burning match, a real stove, glass containers, or knives is potentially dangerous, models of real objects and specialized objects called *toys* have been constructed to channel play to preferred objects.

Aspects of toys. Some assumptions about toys have been made by researchers investigating other areas of development (McBride, 1981). The first assumption is that toys are *attractive*, that they will lure children into exploration and independent behavior or engender a sense of security because of familiarity. The second assumption is that toys are *stimulating*, that they heighten sensory-perceptual arousal and provide feedback and information. It is also assumed that the stimulating quality of toys will strengthen motor responses and elicit language production and cognitive and social behavior. The third assumption is that toys are *symbolic*, that they transmit cultural values, model sex-role behavior, represent family relationships, and symbolically represent the child's own personality or self-concept. Adults who support children's play should keep these assumptions in mind and select toys that are likely to meet one or more of them. Of the alternatives available in the marketplace, some toys won't meet any of the assumptions, and others are likely to meet several. A ball, for example, is likely to strengthen motor responses and to elicit social behavior for a school-age child. A puzzle, on the other hand, is more likely to stimulate sensory-perceptual responses and problem solving.

Complexity. Another aspect of objects is the number of ways in which they can be used. This may be influenced by the responsiveness of the material or object itself. For example, play dough or clay is more responsive than plaster of Paris, which hardens rapidly. The level of complexity may increase if the pieces come apart and can be combined in a variety of ways.

The presence of more equipment on playgrounds seems to encourage individual behavior and more movement, and less equipment tends to encourage more social contacts and more aggression. On the other hand, movable equipment tends to elicit a greater variety of pretend play than would the same pieces if immobile. Children use the immobile equipment with a greater variety of movements and are more likely to initiate group games unrelated to the equipment (Weilbacher, 1981).

Spatial arrangements. In indoor play in a preschool setting, activities in which there are materials or space for only one player are more likely to elicit antisocial behavior than are activities in which materials and space are designed for more than one. In multiple-niche play spaces, such as when playing with a large set of blocks, children socialize more and engage in more helping and sharing behavior than they do in single-niche play spaces, such as when playing with a single box of Lincoln Logs (Doyle, 1981).

Design. Some playthings are realistic, and others are more abstract. Toddlers need realistic materials to pursue a play theme. They simply do not have enough experience or knowledge of what to do with abstract pieces. However, school-age children will play longer and engage in more complex play with abstract toys (Fein, 1979). Children between two and six years of age play with less structured materials like sand, water, blocks, and dough for substantial periods of time, but seem to need more realistic props for complicated dramatic play.

There are basically two aspects of play with objects. The first involves characteristics of the objects that are likely to influence the quality of play. Complexity, degree of structure, attractiveness, sensory-perceptual qualities, and symbolic value have been briefly discussed. However, characteristics of the child determine the nature of the actions that can be brought into play with objects. Children are limited by their motor competence, cognitive functioning, and social skills. Once some of the basic competencies of early childhood have been achieved, play becomes more refined, more challenging, and more elaborate.

Developmental Changes in the Use of Objects

Object play in infancy shifts from repeated motor behavior, such as banging the top of the table with the hand, to repetitious action on objects, such as dropping the spoon to the floor over and over. In the last quarter of the first year, babies begin to explore objects and, by the end of the first year, to use them functionally. For example, drinking motions are used with a cup. This is followed by exploring longer and beginning to combine objects and actions, such as putting the cup on a saucer or pretending to stir in it with a spoon. By the end of the second year, toddlers use longer sequences of action related to the functions of the objects, such as stirring in a cup with a spoon, feeding a doll, combing its hair, and putting it to bed. By the time the child reaches the third year, he or she can assign to the doll the role of actor. In other words, the doll is made to "pick up the spoon" and "eat" (Lowe, 1975).

The shift from simple manipulation of objects to dramatic play is made during the second year. Children learn to make this shift from the literal use of objects to pretend play as a result of their interactions with adults (Smilansky, 1968; Eiferman, 1971). In subsistence cultures, and in cultural groups in which people work more with objects than with abstractions, the shift to pretend play may occur in middle childhood or may not occur at all (Swartzman, 1978).

What general sequences occur? The following list is a sequential summary of the play behaviors that occur as the very young child develops play with objects.

1. Repetitive motor behavior, mouthing.
2. Systematic exploration of objects.
3. Actions begin to be appropriate for objects.
4. Objects that have functional relationships are combined.
5. Action patterns are combined to form larger sequences.
6. Action patterns are applied to self (may be simple pretending).
7. Action patterns are applied to others or to replicas (doll ''eats'').
8. The ability to act is attributed to replicas (doll ''feeds'' teddy bear).
9. Objects that are not present but are needed to complete a logical sequence are ''invented'' (pretends a spoon to stir with).
10. Objects are transformed for use in sequences (uses pencil for spoon).

The term *transform* means to substitute one object for another. For example, a three-year-old might use a pencil, a stick, a tongue depressor, or a screwdriver in the absence of a spoon to stir a drink or to feed a doll.

The first six behavior patterns are sometimes combined and practiced in order to gain mastery over an object. Mastery play or practice play is repetitious, but may have slight variations until the properties of the object and what it can do have been thoroughly mastered. One two-year-old manipulated a set of seven nesting cubes in 30 different ways. Each cube was combined with one, two, and three other cubes, in addition to the full set. She also tried stacking the cubes. Mastery play, as well as exploratory behavior, is common when people of any age encounter objects that are novel and complex. Ten-year-olds engage in similar play with computers.

Individual differences. Some children respond to the symbolic potential of objects more readily than others. Their play style has been called the *dramatist* style. However, other children respond to other attributes of objects; they are more interested in the color, texture, shape, form, and other physical characteristics of the materials. They are the *patterners*. They differ in their approach to materials in that between the ages of two and three, these children communicate meaning by the spatial location of objects. For example, Gieshala poked holes into a wad of tissue paper to represent eyes for her snowman, who needed to see. The dramatist simply would have pretended the eyes. By three years of age, patterners tend to communicate meaning mostly by spatial location. They also are concerned with design elements and the functions of the structures or arrangements that they make. A child who is a patterner may use all the trucks and arrange them by size, color, function, or other criteria. Adults who do not recognize this style of play sometimes expect the child to give up some of the trucks to other players, who could be satisfied with using one in the dramatic style. However, the removal of several units of the design would totally disrupt the purpose of the play. For the patterner, the objects themselves are the significant elements of the play. Children's play style appears to develop early and to carry on as a preferred mode of play throughout childhood (Shotwell, Wolf, and Gardner, 1979).

Between two and three years of age, both patterners and dramatists will build with blocks in horizontal and vertical axes. The dramatist, however, builds more simply, just enough to construct the house or store where the people live and shop. The patterner of the same age combines blocks in larger, more complex, more elaborate structures, experimenting with line and balance.

Dramatic Play

Dramatic play, or *pretend play*, probably is one of the most apparent forms of play seen in young children. In middle-class families, dramatic play begins at around one year of age, and the amount of time spent at it peaks between the ages of five and six (Smilansky, 1968). Older children also participate in pretend play, but school and group games take more of their time. Children from less advantaged circumstances may develop pretend play skills later, and participate in pretend play more around the age of ten (Eiferman, 1971). Pretend play is learned from adults who coach children in using symbols with words, actions, situations, and objects. Middle-class families tend to do this without thinking about it, and less advantaged families tend not to think of doing it at all.

Object substitution. Children need to develop several skills before they can easily pretend play with other children. First, they need to be able to substitute one object for another, or transform one object into another. The closer the substituted object resembles the object needed for the dramatization, the more likely the child will be to use it. A shell can be substituted for a cup, but not for a bat. Between two and three years of age, children can substitute one object in their play, but not two. For example, an abstract wooden object might be used for a horse and a cup for a drinking trough, but the play breaks down if the child is given the abstract wooden object and a shell. In the third year, children will substitute a cup for any container: potty-chair, bowl, hat, or dish. Adults know the child is substituting because the object is renamed or because the action with the object is clearly an action appropriate for the object being substituted for. However, four-year-olds tend to use objects more realistically (Fein, 1979). They are more likely to engage in group pretend play, or *sociodramatic play*, in which all the players must agree on the meaning of each pretend object. There are obvious complications in having many substituted objects in group play.

Object invention. Next, children need to be able to invent an object, to imitate its use through actions even when no object is at hand.

This is simple pantomime, and in its simplest form, only one pretend object at a time is used. A child may use a stirring action above a bowl to invent a spoon, or twirl an arm above the head to symbolize a rope. Younger children find it very difficult to mime without a placeholder object, but between three and four years of age, this is more common. School-age children do it readily.

Children who have not learned how to pretend may approach toys in an exploratory mode and then respond to them as if they were real. In one preschool room, Emily entered the housekeeping area and examined the model stove, turning the knobs, gingerly touching the burners, and opening the oven to peer inside. Then, she pulled the stove from the wall and examined the back. Putting her hands on her hips in great disgust, she addressed the teacher, "This damned stove won't work!" She was upset when the adult responded that the toy stove was not supposed to work like a real stove.

Changes of time and place. Children also learn to transform time and settings. They might substitute a climber for a spaceship in flight or pretend that the sandbox is a beach during the period when prehistoric animals lived. Players are very aware of this convention and tend to play consistently with it. For example, Mia, the "baby," climbed out of her bed to iron on the ironing board. Her "mother" admonished her that babies can't iron or they'll get burned. Mia climbed back into her bed, said: "Grow, grow, grow. I'm the big sister now," and returned to the ironing board, condensing many years into a few seconds. Time and place have no restrictions except in the information of the players. In addition, children who have no knowledge or experience of objects such as buses and airplanes are quite unable to initiate play situations involving them.

Role playing. The young player must learn to take on a role. The simplest kind of role is the *functional role* or *behavioral role* (Watson and Fisher, 1980): the child becomes a person who is driving a truck. This role does not contain a permanent identity or personality, but is defined by the person in the present situation. A child taking on a *character role*, however, engages in many behavioral sequences appropriate for the part. Character roles include family roles (mother, father, sister), occupational roles (fire fighter, doctor), and fictional roles (Wonder Woman, witch). Family roles are played with much more detail than the others. Younger children tend to limit themselves to roles with which they have had direct experience (baby, parent), but older preschoolers are more likely to act out roles that they have observed (husband, wife) and try more occupational roles. Lastly, preschool children are able to portray multiple roles. One thirty-month-old girl was observed playing "mother" to "baby" and "wife" to "husband" while coaching "husband" in how to perform the role of "father" (Miller and Garvey, 1984). Role and action representations initially are affected by the availability of realistic props.

Cultural and experiential differences in children. Children bring to the play experience their cultural background and life-style as sources of information. Considerable variety can be expected. For example, one child tried to bounce an orange. He had never eaten an orange, but had played with balls. Because of the orange's roundness, he treated it as a ball. This is not a situation for a reprimand, but for information.

Some children play out life experiences that are completely foreign to their teachers, such as being evicted, gang fighting, family violence, and burglaries, as well as explicitly sexual activities. Privacy in some households is limited, and children may have observed adult behavior that is kept more private in other households. On one hand, adults may not want this play in the group, but on the other, children may need to play out their experiences. Children may be

redirected into other aspects of role behavior such as going to work or cleaning house. They should not be scolded or shamed about theme or role depiction.

Play behavior is built on variations of nonplay behavior, then repeated, combined in a number of ways, reduced to unimportance through humor, or magnified through play ritual. Children, of course, must use what they know, regardless of content. As in all other behavior, experience is important in determining how children play with objects and participate in dramatic play.

Peer communication about play. The term *metacommunication* means a communication about communication (Bateson, 1971). Metacommunications about play may indicate what is "play" and what is "not play." Four-year-olds can understand the meaning of the paradox in "Let's pretend this fire is real!" Metacommunications may be nonverbal, such as beginning to "shovel snow" in the middle of the summer, or they may be verbal. These messages *frame* play so that it is socially defined as play and is not, therefore, "for real." To maintain play, some messages must be said "out of frame" in order to share information so that the play can continue.

Metacommunications begin and end play, but also are used in planning and negotiating the content and direction of play and in coordinating role enactment. Helping professionals support and promote skill development when they demonstrate or suggest typical metacommunication devices to children who are less skillful.

Some statements are procedural, such as "Do you want to play house?" or "It's my turn." Other statements that serve to initiate play are statements about role, objects, or setting, or about planning the theme (Garvey, 1977; Garvey and Berndt, 1977). Children mention another's role ("You can be the daddy"), their own role ("I'll be the nurse"), or a joint role ("We can be neighbors").

Children mention objects, transforming them into something else ("This is the car," while arranging four chairs in a square) or inventing an object ("Here is the menu. What do you want?" while handing a pretend menu to a patron).

Children transform settings ("This here [pointing to some blocks] is the boat on the ocean") and also invent settings ("We are lost kids in the forest," while standing in the middle of the play yard).

Children make plans about the behavior or feelings of another character ("Pretend you are lost and scared"), about their own actions ("I gotta go shopping and I'm in a hurry"), or about joint plans ("We better build a big house so the monster won't get us").

Some statements terminate the play. These statements can be about the role ("I'm not the daddy anymore"), about actions ("I'm not chasing you"), about props ("This isn't a boat anymore"), or about settings ("We are not in the forest").

Influencing the direction of the play. Preschool children tend not to expose their pretend illusion unnecessarily. If possible, they keep their communications "within frame," but metacommunications lie on a continuum from deeply within frame to completely out of frame (Griffin, 1984). As suggested by Griffin (1984), there are several ways in which the content of the play can be redirected.

Children use *ulterior conversations*, which might appear to be role enactment but do alter the course of the play. The query "Is it night-time?" from the "baby" effectively initiates a caregiving sequence from the "mother."

Underscoring provides information to other players (for example, "I'll get the dinner now," spoken in character voice). Underscoring also is used to "magic" something: "Grow, grow, grow. Now I am big." Another common example is "Wash, wash, wash" for dishes or laundry. This making of "magic" is done in a rhythmic, singsong voice.

Storytelling frequently is couched in the past tense and often is spoken in cadence. It allows for the development of more elaborate plots: "Let's say this spaceship went up, way up . . . and the computer went out . . . and the moon wasn't there."

Prompting is a technique in which one player instructs another on how to act or what to say, often in a stage whisper or a softer voice: "I'm ready for breakfast now; . . . (whispering) no, you have to cook the eggs first before I eat."

Formal pretend proposals sometimes are embedded into ongoing play, as in "Let's pretend the family goes to the beach." The suggestion for play variation usually is used when the play scenario is becoming repetitive or falling apart. Usually, the more indirect methods are preferred once a play sequence is begun.

When children pretend using small figures and blocks or a doll house, nearly all of the story line is provided by narrative rather than by action of the dolls. When children themselves are the actors, however, they are more able to use nonverbal communicators as well to supply the content of the play.

Role selection. The social relationships in a group of children are reflected in their play (Swartzman, 1978). High-status children can join ongoing play by peremptorily adopting a role or defining an activity ("I'll be the aunt, coming to visit"). Lower-status children must ask permission to join the play ("Can I be the sister?") and may be restricted to particular roles. Often, higher status children will assign lower status children to the roles they may play ("You can be Grandma, who's sick"). The roles assigned may reflect actual status in the group. Play leaders also use rejection statements ("You can't play here" and counter-defining statements ("We aren't in a forest—we're in a jungle").

The role play of children is very complex. They must participate as writer-directors of their make-believe play from outside the play frame and enact make-believe roles and events within the play frame.

Children tend to resist certain kinds of make-believe. They are much more willing to change generations than to change gender. Boys prefer male roles, whether they are baby or grandparent roles, and will not readily take mother roles.

High-status children tend to resist taking a lower status in the make-believe play, preferring to be the parent rather than the baby, the captain rather than the seaman, and so on. When one player refuses to play an unsatisfactory role, she or he usually is incorporated into the more desirable role. For example, a child unwilling to be the victim becomes one of two monsters, and the victim is invented.

Children resist interrupting pretend play with reality. For example, if a child trips and falls down, he or she is likely to pretend a hospital-doctor sequence rather than interrupt the flow of the play to seek help from an adult. The child simply incorporates the event into the play if at all possible.

Once children have become skillful players, between the ages of five and seven, they modify and extend their pretend play, improvising nonsense or acting out a storybook theme or television show. By nine or ten years of age, they may engage in improvisational contests and develop their own plays.

Construction Play

Children play with objects for the purposes of pretend, but they also play with them for the purposes of manipulating them based on their physical properties alone. Some aspects of this have previously been described as children's handling of objects as dramatists or as patterners.

Young children. During the second half of the first year of life, children can bang on objects and twist, turn, push, pull, open, and shut them. Between one and two years of age, children acquire the abilities to empty and fill objects, to hammer a peg into a peg board, and to separate play dough. Real construction begins during the second year when the child learns to connect objects together (such as threading beads or attaching the pieces of a train) and develops the corresponding ability to disjoin objects (such as snap beads). Children also learn to stack and knock down blocks and to build both vertically and horizontally with them.

Between two and three years of age, children make constructions and name them "houses" and may combine various construction materials, such as mixing blocks with cars or toys. This often is done for the purpose of initiating pretend play. Given the guidance of supporting adults, they also will learn the use of tools, such as knives and rollers for clay, cookie cutters, scissors, and hammers and nails. At this age, children's constructions are very simple; they are more interested in the process than the product.

By the time children are four, their constructions become more detailed and elaborate. They might construct a house of blankets and boxes and blocks, or a toy world with miniature dolls, trucks, and soldiers. They also make music in time, particularly with percussion instruments. They begin to show interest in their paintings as products and to cut paper designs.

Between five and seven years of age, children have sufficient small-muscle control to plan and make a variety of things. They can do simple sewing and weaving; they can use pot holders and cook simple dishes. At this time, they also begin to make costumes or other supplementary props for their pretend play.

Older children. Children in elementary school may be interested in model construction, handicrafts, weaving, woodworking, metalworking, bookbinding, basketry, carving, and a variety of other projects. They also construct some of their own games and do creative writing. Skillful pretend players also build sets, make costumes, and put on their own plays; the planning of script, actors, action, props, and sets may take hours, days, or weeks, whereas the production itself may be less than ten minutes long. This also is the period of collecting and hobbies (Sutton-Smith and Sutton-Smith, 1974).

Play with Movement

Adults are familiar with the joyous running, jumping, and laughing of children coming outside for recess. Physical educators have extensively studied the motor development of older children, and recently have focused on the development of the fundamental motor skills of early childhood: walking, running, jumping, hopping, skipping, and striking (Seefeldt and Haubenstricker, 1982).

Most physical games are composed of these skills in combinations designed to improve strength, endurance, balance, and coordination. The scope of this chapter, however, is limited to the informal play of younger children and to situations in which a physical educator is unlikely to be working.

Babies express pleasure in motion itself. Piaget (1962) noticed that babies repeated a movement sequence over and over, getting more enjoyment out of the experience each time and paying decreasing attention to the outcome. The fun was in the movement. Babies are soothed by walking and laugh when they are held high or experience vertigo with a trusted adult. Once in motion, they are intrepid travelers, enjoying mightily the movement itself as well as the new experiences it brings.

The feeling of sheer splendor experienced by a preschooler racing down a hill, feet thudding on turf, wind blowing through the hair and on the skin; the careful placement of each step as a timid child threads a way up to the top of the climber; the amazingly empty feeling in the stomach of a child on a zooming sled: these all involve play with motion itself. The children may or may not laugh, but they are exquisitely satisfied and pleased with their performance.

Play with movement begins in infancy and continues throughout adulthood, as is evidenced in the popularity of swimming pools, ski resorts, and bowling alleys. Helping professionals, themselves players, usually are sensitive to the more mature forms of play with movement. Four aspects of movement play will be addressed that will illuminate the safe supervision of children's play: practice play, challenge, risk taking, and rough-and-tumble play.

Respecting repetitious activity. Practice play begins in infancy and continues throughout childhood (Eiferman, 1971). Quite simply, it is a behavior repeated over and over. For example, Esther, age five, wanted to try the high slide in the park. An adult went with her and offered to catch her the first time. Hesitant and timid at first, Esther went up the slide and down with growing satisfaction and pleasure. She took twenty-one turns on the slide without ever repeating exactly her previous performance. She varied the placement of hands and feet; went down on belly, bottom, and back; climbed up the slide forward and backward; went down feet first and head first. The adult observed her, commented on her performance, and stood close to the slide when concerned for Esther's safety. This child, who began hesitantly, left the experience with satisfaction and greater confidence in her ability.

From infancy to adolescence, what the child practices varies but the process remains much the same. In the second year, toddlers walk, run, march, throw, climb, and dance. Between two and three years of age, they jump from low heights, hop on one foot, balance on a beam, and hang by their arms. Between the ages of three and four, they begin to catch balls, climb jungle gyms, and ride tricycles. Between four and five years of age, they roller-skate, swim, ride scooters and other vehicles, dance to music, bounce balls, and play catch. Between five and seven years of age, they can use stilts, swing and pump the swing, and jump rope. Older children are likely to practice for specific sports.

Maintaining interest in movement play. The selection of a play activity usually is based on its potential *challenge* for the child. The challenges undertaken are those that require slightly greater skill than the child already possesses. Usually, the child observes the action, tests his or her ability to do it, seeks instruction or help if necessary, and then practices the skill until it has been mastered. Because play is not ''for real,'' children are free to drop a task that is too difficult for them without loss of self-respect. Sometimes, this is verbalized as ''just playing around.''

Interest in the action remains high until mastery is completed. If a mastered skill, such as dribbling a ball, can be varied and incorporated into other skills, such as evading and running, interest may remain with the activity for long periods of time. In this sense, challenge comes from within the players and is a test of their own skills. This self-challenge should not be confused with a challenge from another player, such as ''I can run faster than you,'' which then turns the movement play into a game. At its best, challenging play helps children to understand themselves and their competencies and to recognize their own accomplishments against the background of previous behavior.

Understanding risk. There frequently is some *risk* in play with motion. Skiing is definitely more risky than running. Some youngsters seem like monkeys, climbing high into trees; others of the same age are frightened of simple climbing frames with padded mats beneath. Temperament and previous experience play a part in the willingness of children to take risks in play. Toddlers have little sense of potentially dangerous situations and must be protected by adults. Preschool children, however, should be provided many opportunities to try out appropriate developmental skills in supervised play so that they can learn just how competent they are.

By the age of seven, most children can judge for themselves the risk involved in any activity and are unlikely to go beyond their limits unless urged by peers and adults to do so. For example, Gwendolyn was well coordinated for a seven-year-old, was an excellent swimmer, and could ride a two-wheel bike. Jeff, only two weeks younger, moved easily enough but couldn't swim or do gymnastics. He spent more of his time at indoor activities. When the children were playing together outside, Gwendolyn climbed a tree and invited Jeff up. After being urged and called a scaredy-cat, Jeff attempted the climb. He fell three times because he couldn't catch the branch with his hands and pull himself up by his arms as Gwendolyn could. Bruised and shaken, he clung to the trunk once Gwendolyn had pulled him up. Apparently realizing that the tree was too risky for Jeff, Gwendolyn swung down and procured a ladder to help him in his descent. Children frequently assume that an activity that is easy for them will be easy for an age-mate and may need guidance in recognizing the difference between being supportive to peers and challenging them to potentially dangerous activities. Children rarely attempt feats that are beyond their abilities unless pressured to do so.

Supporting social and physical testing. Many children participate in rough motor play, which increases both the challenge and the risk. At a high pitch of activity, children run, hop, jump, fall over, chase, flee, wrestle, hit at, laugh, and make faces. Usually played in a group, *rough-and-tumble play* differs from aggression, which includes such behaviors as pushing, taking things, grabbing, frowning, and staring down another (Blurton-Jones, 1972, 1976).

Play fighting is similar to rough-and-tumble play in that the participants know it's not real (Aldis, 1975). Play fighting is carried out in interrupted sequences or in incomplete actions. For example, a child will say ''Bam!'' while striking at another but without following through with physical contact. Play fighting has clear metacommunication signals to let the participants know that it is play and not aggression. For example, one third-grade child passed a note to another girl, making her intentions quite clear (see Figure 6-2).

All preschool children engage in rough-and-tumble play, although boys do so more often than girls. Boys tend to play in this way in larger groups at the perimeter of the play yard and girls are more likely to carry out rough-and-tumble play near equipment and in a more restricted area. This play nearly always is accompanied by shrieks, shouting, howling, and laughter. Rough-and-tumble play at this age frequently is combined with character roles of super heroes (Kostelnik, Whiren, and Stein, 1986). Usually, young children spend more time watching this kind of play than participating in it.

School-age children usually play with children of the same sex, unless the play specifically requires a member of the opposite sex. One game, called "kiss or kill," requires one player to chase another of the opposite sex, get him or her down, say, "Kiss or kill?", and proceed with the kiss or the "strike" as the downed player prefers. Rough-and-tumble play is most likely to occur after the children have been engaged in set tasks or when they are just coming outdoors for recess.

Helping professionals must be able to discriminate between real aggression and rough-and-tumble play or play fighting. The differences often are apparent only in facial expression, such as a smile, a silly face, or a frown. Laughter and noisemaking (such as "monster sounds") often signify that an activity is playful. Other play signals also are used to indicate the intent to play rough-and-tumble, such as "Let's play chase!" The adult's task is to help children indicate to peers whether or not they want to play ("Don't chase me—I'm not the dragon anymore," or "I'm not playing"). Often, safety zones must be established to avoid inadvertent involvement of unwilling players.

FIGURE 6-2 A written play signal for rough-and-tumble play that was passed between two nine-year-olds in school

Adults usually want to squelch rough-and-tumble play, perceiving it as aggression. It is, however, a form of play typical of many species (Fagen, 1981; Aldis, 1975) and may well serve the overall development of children in ways not yet understood. Experienced helping professionals note that children not allowed rough-and-tumble play in one setting (school yards, recreational settings) do so in others (bus, neighborhood, backyards). It is better to supervise this play to minimize the risks to children's safety.

Games

Games involve other players, and are eminently social. Games develop gradually as children's social skills mature, from the simple turn taking of toddlers to the complex games of older children. Older preschool children can play hide and seek or any number of games with a central person, like follow the leader or "duck, duck, goose." They are able to take turns if the wait isn't too long. With more experience, they become able to change roles, playing various versions of hide and seek such as kick the can, or hide and seek combined with tag. Between five and seven years of age, children play games of acceptance and rejection, such as "farmer in the dell," and of attack and defense, such as snowball fighting. Seven- to nine-year-olds add games of dominance and submission such as "Mother may I," card and board games, and sandlot sports such as modified forms of softball and kick ball. Older children, more concerned with outcomes, enjoy intellectual games such as charades or trivia and are more likely to participate in organized teams. The roles older children take in games are likely to depend on special skills they may have, such as playing guard in a basketball game.

Games may be based on *chance* (most dice games), *skill* (baseball), or *strategy* (checkers). Most American children have experience with all three types of games. Games of skill are most directly linked to movement play. Many games of skill have become sports in which the play is administered and directed by adults, such as Little League coaches, rather than by the children. In this book, we will focus on the informal games in which children can follow, make, or change the rules themselves.

Adults who guide the social development of children should understand that young children do not approach a game in the same way that adults and older children might. Young preschool children play games in much the same fashion that they participate in movement play. They observe a particular way to move and imitate it. They are, in fact, frequently confused. In the game of tag, for example, a young child will run to avoid getting caught, but is likely to have difficulties if tagged and declared to be "it." At this point, a very young child may refuse to play or may just stand there. If older players are willing, they may allow the little one to tag them so the game can go on.

Older preschool children frequently perceive rules as an interesting example of how to play rather than a required behavior. When playing together, they sometimes have difficulties regulating sequential turn taking. Nor are they concerned with what other players do; they simply are interested in their own actions. Each player is on his or her own. This is not the same as cheating, although adults observing young children playing a simple board game might interpret it as such.

Seven- and eight-year-olds begin to be concerned with problems of mutual control, winning, and losing. They are likely to discuss the rules before play but may have conflicting notions on what the "real" rules are. Conflicts may break out; these can be handled as discussed in Chapter 13. Children of this age often regard rules as sacred and untouchable, emanating from adults and lasting forever (Sutton-Smith and Sutton-Smith, 1974; Piaget, 1976).

Rules may vary for some games, especially those that are passed on verbally by children themselves. Adults should observe the play and ask older or more skillful players about the rules before arbitrating the play. Children develop skill in negotiation as they decide among themselves what the rules are to be.

Games are varied and are combined with many other forms of play. There are singing and dancing games, games using a variety of objects, movement games, games associated with dramatics (Dungeons and Dragons or charades), language games (Scrabble), and games that involve construction (Bug). Fortunately, most public libraries have good collections of books on games suitable for children to play in groups or individually.

Humor

Adults usually do not find the humor of young children very amusing, if they even recognize that the child is trying to joke. Children's humor is limited by their experience and their cognitive development, so what they perceive as funny is altogether too obvious for the adult. Children are not likely to find adult humor funny, either, especially if they do not get the point of the joke. Understanding the development of children's use of incongruity for humor will help adults appreciate attempts at humor by the very young (McGhee, 1979).

Incongruity in children's humor. When an arrangement of ideas, social expectations, or objects is incompatible with the normal or expected pattern of events, it is *incongruous.* Although incongruity is not the only ingredient in humor, it may be the most common element in children's humor. Incongruity does not always elicit amusement, however. Children may react with interest, curiosity, anxiety, fear, or amusement. Humor, like other play forms, is framed by clear play signals. The younger the child, the clearer the play signals need to be— laughter or a traditional joke opening such as "knock, knock"—if the incongruous statement is to be treated as humor. Otherwise, the child will ignore it or treat it with curiosity. Something too outrageous might be frightening; Halloween costumes sometimes have this effect on three-year-olds.

Laughter and smiling have many causes. They denote pleasure in infancy, but not humor. Humor is dependent on the ability of the child to pretend and to have a playful orientation toward the situation in which humor occurs (Singer, 1973). If children do not have a playful orientation, they may enjoy the incongruity but not find it funny.

Humor also is social. Children laugh longer in a group than when alone. They also try to share their jokes with people with whom they already have a close bond. Playful attitudes or moods are more easily maintained in a social group than when alone, as well. Parents often are the ones selected to hear a joke, as Chukovsky (1976:601) reports:

> One day in the twenty-third month of her existence, my daughter came to me, looking mischievous and embarrassed at the same time—as if she were up to some intrigue . . . . She cried to me even when she was still at some distance from where I sat: "Daddy, oggie-miaow" . . . . And she burst out into somewhat encouraging, somewhat artificial laughter, inviting me too to laugh at this invention.

Developmental trends in children's humor. Incongruity humor, like other aspects of development, proceeds sequentially (McGhee, 1979). The child first experiences humor while engaged in object play during the second year. The child simply uses an object in a way known to be inappropriate. For example, picking up a parent's shoe and using it as a telephone might lead to laughter if the child is in a playful frame of mind. The fantasy is known to be at odds with reality.

The second stage of the development of children's humor frequently overlaps with the first as language is used to create the incongruity with an object or event. Children simply give names to objects or events that they know to be incorrect. For example, young children delight in calling a cat a dog or an eye a foot. In initiating this type of humor, however, adults should remember that the confidence of very young children in the naming of objects is not great; if a joke is made without clear play signals, a two-year-old may think that new information is being presented.

In the third stage, between the ages of three and four, children delight in conceptual incongruity. For example, drawings of a cat with no ears, or a dog with such long ears that they trail on the ground, are seen as funny. The distortion must be clear, but enough normal elements must be present for the child to recognize the familiar object. Another form of humor typical of this stage is to call someone by the wrong name. Older preschoolers who have mastered gender-related concepts may find it funny to call a girl a boy. However, this is threatening to some children and may be taken as an insult.

Preschoolers are perceptually oriented. A drawing of a bicycle with square wheels or stories of a "backwards day" or an elephant sitting on a nest all are perceived as funny. In the same way, young children are likely to laugh at people with disproportionate facial features, disfigurements, or noticeable handicapping conditions. They also laugh when someone falls in a funny way. Because of their cognitive limitations, very young children are unable to empathize, and although their amusement may appear cruel, it is not intended to be.

This period also is the beginning of producing nonsense words from regular words: "Doggie, loggie, moggie," "Lyssa, missa, rissa," "Hamburger, samburger, ramburger." Inventing new nonsense words also is amusing at this age. For example, children might set out to capture a "torkel" with great glee.

The fourth stage in the development of humor, when children understand multiple meanings of words, starts at about age seven. This is the beginning of humor that is most similar to adult humor. Puns or simple play with the meaning of words begins, such as: "Why are ghosts like newspapers?" "Because they appear in sheets." Incongruous actions also are incorporated into the question-format joke: "What goes 'Zzub! Zzub!'?" "A bee flying backwards." Jokes dealing with "what is it" questions and "knock, knock" jokes also appear:

What's black and white and red all over?
A sunburned zebra. (older children)
A newspaper. (younger children)

Knock, knock.	*Knock, knock.*
Who's there?	*Who's there?*
Ether.	*Stella.*
Ether who?	*Stella who?*
Ether Bunny.	*Stella 'nother Ether Bunny.*

FIGURE 6-3 Playing with language meaning in riddles, jokes, puns, and other word games reaches a high level in elementary school children.
SOURCE: Photo by David Kostelnik

Older school-age children, having well-developed cognitive abilities, are able to enjoy humor based on illogical behavior, such as a person buying a cat when they don't like cats so they can use up the cat shampoo that they got on sale.

Younger children imitate older ones in attempts to generate humor. However, they frequently forget the punch line or substitute a logical answer to the question, thereby "destroying" the joke.

Humor also may be used as a means for gratifying sexual aggression, or inappropriate desires. For example, young children often use words related to bowel or bladder functions shortly after control has been established. Helping professionals usually have witnessed young children saying, ''Pooh, pooh,'' ''Pee,'' or ''Doo, doo,'' to the merriment of their peers.

Valuing children's humor. Children's humor can be encouraged by adults who understand the developing child's attempts at humor, listen attentively, and at least smile at the jokes. Admonishing children to stop being silly or quit fooling around inhibits the development of humor. In addition, children imitate humor from adults and older children.

Humor is a social experience for children. It can be used to help define the child as a member of a group, enhance the member's position in the group, or increase morale. As an aspect of play, humor also is supported by those adult behaviors that support play in general.

By knowing how humor develops, adults can recognize and support children's development of a sense of humor. In the early phases, children's humor isn't recognizable to many adults, who may then ignore, suppress, or even reprimand children for attempts at humor. Although the content of humor changes as the individual matures, the skill and confidence that children develop in this area enables them to participate successfully in a variety of social situations.

Even though each type of play has its own sequence of development in childhood, all require the support and guidance of caring adults if the quality of the play is to become optimal for each child.

SKILLS FOR SUPPORTING, ENHANCING, AND EXPANDING CHILDREN'S PLAY

How to Set the Stage for Children's Play

1. Establish the necessary conditions for play. Plan for play when children are not excessively tired or hungry. Provide snacks during play and comfortable nooks where children can rest or sleep. Quality play, in which the players use their full array of skills, rarely occurs when children are experiencing stress. If children are experiencing physical pain, fear, or extreme anger, follow the guidelines in Chapter 5 for responding to children's emotions. Quality play is not possible until these more pressing concerns are addressed.

2. Say to yourself, "It's OK to play, to laugh, to have fun." Accept the playfulness in yourself and in the children.

3. Stand or sit near children at play. Keep children in view from a little distance—from one to six feet away from the play space for younger children. Be outside the play area, but adjacent to it for children of all ages. Hovering over children stifles their play. However, do not stand at one end of the play yard while children are dispersed 30 feet or more from you. This great distance communicates disinterest and may not provide adequate supervision of children's activities.

4. Pay attention to what the children are playing and what they say and do. Observe carefully; concentrate. Listen, and begin to remember the play preferences and styles of individuals within the group. Begin enjoying their play behavior.

5. Schedule playtime in segments that are long enough for play concepts to be developed. For example, in a nursery school, an hour or more usually is devoted to activities in which children can choose either to play or to engage in other experiences. If time is segmented for the group in 10- to 15-minute intervals, children spend most of their time waiting or in transition and cannot develop a play theme. On the other hand, elementary-school children can engage in movement play during a 15-minute recess, although well-developed fantasy play or extended group games take much longer. Older elementary-school children may work in interrupted shifts preparing a drama that they have created themselves. The preparation time (including related play) may be spread over several days and may amount to an hour or two for the final 10-minute production. The amount of time needed depends on the age, experience, skill, and interests of the group of children. Children of all ages need time to develop high-quality play.

6. Provide adequate space for the number of children playing. Match the number of children and the quantity of play materials to the given area. A board game for four players requires enough space for the children to play without interruption or congestion. In addition, a sense of privacy is essential if children are to develop quality dramatic play.

7. Provide quality playthings for all types of play. Children will play with anything, and some of the most interesting playthings, such as sand, water, and mud are not toys. Provide materials for construction, such as bristle blocks, unit blocks, paints of various types, paper, musical instruments, clay, and dough. Children of all ages love to take on roles; make available props that promote pretend play for occupations such as community helpers, for family roles, and for fictional characters. Give young children realistic props; offer older children less realistic materials. Movement-and-skill play may require jump ropes, balls of various sizes, and other appropriate materials such as tricycles, ice skates, or basketball hoops. See that these are at hand. Provide different types of games: those that require cooperation (lifting one child in a parachute); those that encourage competition; some that are played in small groups indoors, such as checkers; and others that are played in larger groups outdoors, such as volleyball.

How to Maximize the Play Potential of the Materials Available

1. Mix unrelated toys together. Put water or play dough in the housekeeping area. Place the furnishings of the dollhouse in a box in the block area. Fasten butcher paper onto the wall of the building outdoors where children usually ride tricycles, and provide paints. Put Lego blocks and other small construction toys into a pretend play area set up as an office or hospital. Don't be limited by these suggestions: think of all the possible, then the not-so-possible recombinations of materials. Materials need not have any obvious relationship. The point is to stimulate the creative potential of the children.

2. Introduce novel toys and materials slowly. Avoid putting out all the new things at the same time. The stimulus value of each one competes with the others, and all become stale too soon. One teacher made the mistake of thinking that new toys would engage the children so well that they would be engrossed during playtime for the entire week. Much to her surprise, the children dashed from toy to toy, attempting to get at everything and really playing with nothing. They explored, but did not develop their play. Because of their high mobility level, they also experienced many more conflicts. A different approach was used by Miss Davison, who set up a housekeeping area for a group of four-year-olds in a day-care center. It had dishes, pots and pans, stove, refrigerator, table and chairs, and sink. On the second day, she added dolls, a doll bed, and a rocking chair. On the third day, she put a bowl of uncooked macaroni on the table. On the fourth day, she put out a small clothes rack containing shirts and dresses on hangers. On the fifth day, she put hats for men and women in a box nearby and adult shoes under the rack. The following week, she did nothing for two days, but then removed the macaroni and put a pail of water near the sink.

3. Rotate playthings. Remove some play materials. When brought out again, they will generate increased interest. For example, a first-grade teacher had both Candy Land and Raggedy Ann board games. The games required about the same skills. She would leave one game out in the children's play area and put the other in the cupboard for a month or two, then switch them.

Similar to simple rotation is the practice of having a special set of toys that are used only in the late afternoon in daycare. The "new" materials, although similar to those used in the morning, generate much better play than would the same materials played with earlier.

4. Arrange the materials to encourage interaction between children. Set out two sets of Lego blocks instead of one. Place several puzzles on a large table rather than one on a small table. Have enough dress-up clothes for several children to play. When too many children want to play in the housekeeping area, suggest that some of them construct a home next door so that they can play neighbors. Other children are by far the most novel, interesting, and complex resources for play; children should be encouraged to play with one another.

Older children enjoy many of the new games that emphasize cooperation and working together. As children mature, they are able to play in larger groups, and materials such as cards and board games can be played with as many as six players. Make materials for such activities available and arrange them so that several children can play at once.

How to Help Children Acquire Skills Through Your Direct Involvement as a Player

1. Play with materials. Children love to see adults smear the finger paint, work with a paintbrush on an easel with drippy paint, or build in the sandbox. Comment on your play, saying things like: "I'm smearing my paint all over," or "I'm glad the sand is wet so my house stays up." Then, wait for children to comment on what they are doing. When modeling, respect your own play. Bring your play to some closure: flatten the sand castle, finish the painting, or announce that you are through. Children should not expect you to give way to them automatically when they want to play or when they just grab your materials. Simply tell them, "I'm nearly finished, and then you can have this place," as you complete whatever you are doing.

2. Take a role to encourage pretend play. Select either a behavioral role, such as saying "Varoom, varoom" as you "drive" a truck down a block highway, or a character role, such as becoming the parent, the baby, or the spaceship captain. Use a variety of techniques to influence the direction of the play, such as engaging in ulterior conversations or storytelling. Respond to the role cues of other children, and remain in character while in the play frame. Remember that you can't get out of the play frame to give directions without some clear signal that you are not playing any more. Gradually take a less active part until you can exit the play frame altogether.

3. Demonstrate movements as necessary. If you should see a two-year-old attempting to jump down a step but walking it instead, the most playful thing to do is to jump yourself, with feet together, landing with knees slightly bent and using your arms for balance. A simple demonstration of jumping, hopping on one foot, or striking with a bat or hockey stick provides information, and if briefly and playfully done, it can be a part of the ongoing play. Prompting, such as saying "Bend your knees when you land," then resuming the game or movement play, also is acceptable.

4. Participate fully in the game. Play by the rules as you understand them and participate fully, taking turns, running, or whatever is required. Children learn some games, especially games of strategy, only by observing a better player. Chinese checkers is like this, as are Risk, chess, and Monopoly. Discuss the play as other players do, pointing out what you did and why, if appropriate. Be careful not to become so engrossed in your play that you forget that your goal is to support the play of the children.

How to Help Individual Children Change the Level of Social Participation in Play

1. Observe the child for cues that the present level of participation is inadequate. Cues indicating that children may need help in increasing their level of participation might be: prolonged observation of a group at play (more than ten minutes); following more skillful players from one activity to another; forceful crossing of the play boundaries, or disruption of others' group play; crying, complaining, or stating that they want to play too.

Children who appear to be satisfied with their level of participation should be allowed to continue to function at a comfortable level. They usually appear to be relaxed, happy, and fully involved in what they are doing.

Sometimes, talented and bright children play alone, not because they cannot play with others, but because they do not have any real peers in the group. Shifting them into more social experiences requires identifying an aspect of development that is most like that of other children in the group. For example, a child with outstanding musical ability might best pursue that area independently and be matched with another player with similar motor abilities for movement play.

2. Match the activity to the child's level of skill. Observe children carefully so you know what level of skill is typical for them. Allow children to practice playing alone or in parallel play until they are comfortable with this level. Notice when individuals shift from parallel play to short episodes of greater social interaction. Usually, parallel play is unstable and will shift into more direct interaction or solitary play (Bakeman and Brownlee, 1980). Again, select a potential playmate based on similar levels of competence in a particular area.

3. Play with the child yourself. Less skilled players perform more easily with a predictable, responsive adult than with other children. Give clear play signals and use a variety of metacommunications.

4. Invite the child and a second, less skilled player to play with you, then ease yourself out of the situation. Do not try to match the best player or the most popular child with the least skilled player. The disparities in skill may be too great for the play to continue. Remember that children are sensitive to social status in developing their play role.

How to Escalate the Level of Play Gradually by Varying Your Play Performance or by Giving Cues Through Play Signals or Metacommunications

1. Extend object play by imitating what the child is doing, then vary the activity a little.

Incorporate the child's ideas into your modeling. This may be accomplished by using the same object in a slightly different way, such as tapping a maraca with your hand instead of shaking it, or talking to a doll in an emotionally expressive tone of voice instead of a normal tone or monotone.

2. Suggest that children use specific play signals to initiate or sustain play. Tell the least skillful player what to say to indicate the play: ''Tell James, 'I'll be a policeman.' '' This active approach is more likely to lead to success than the more general question, ''Do you want to play?''

Select the type of play signal that is commonly used by other players in the group. Consider ulterior conversations, underscoring, storytelling, prompting, or formal pretend proposals. The less skillful player will then have your prompting as well as opportunities to observe other children as a means of improving his or her skills. For example, when one player seems exasperated with the inability of another to play a role correctly, lean over the props and stage-whisper directions: ''Whisper to the mail carrier that she is supposed to give the letters to other people, not read them herself.'' Or perhaps if the play theme seems to be floundering, note the materials of interest and suggest the storytelling approach to one of the players: ''Think what would happen if there were an earthquake and the city had to be rebuilt. Tell the story.''

Demonstrate how to use nonverbal play signals when they would facilitate the play, especially if they will enable less skilled players to enhance their skills. For instance, show a child how to ''fall ill'' just outside the pretend hospital by making moans and holding a part of the body as if in pain. Show a child how to portray being a sad ''baby'' outside the housekeeping area as a way to get a response from other players. Some children may need much more support and direction than others, but play skills can be learned and enhanced.

3. *Withdraw from the play and resume the role of observer once the play is well under way.* Think of a way to exit the game gracefully ("Let's pretend that I am teacher and I have to go to work now") or step out of the play and state clearly that you aren't playing anymore. If you have a central role, such as pitcher in a softball game, you might just say that your turn is up, and ask who would like to pitch.

How to Coach Children Occasionally from Outside the Play Frame

1. *Suggest a related theme.* If children are playing house and the play is disintegrating, extend the theme by suggesting that they go on a picnic, move, go on vacation, or engage in some other family-related activity.

2. *Add a necessary prop.* Children "going on a vacation" need a suitcase, and the play may break down without it. When you observe this occurring, go to the storage area, get the suitcase, and place it near the play area. Obviously, you should not leave children unsupervised for long periods of time while you search for materials, but when possible, make such impromptu additions to enhance their play.

3. *Introduce new players from outside the play frame.* One way to introduce a new player is to indicate that she or he would like to join the ongoing activity. Say something simple and direct, like "Mary has been watching you play and would like to play, too." The children participating in the play may or may not accept Mary. It's their choice. Should they not want Mary to play at this time, help Mary find another place to play, providing several alternatives. Small group games and pretend play are much more difficult to enter than are activities such as artwork or block construction, because the children in play with an ongoing theme have already established roles and relationships. Don't force acceptance of another player; the play may completely disintegrate if established roles, themes, and relationships are disrupted. Play, by definition, is child directed and voluntary.

A second approach is to offer a new character role for a player joining the group ("Here is the grandmother, coming to visit"). Additions of mail carriers, meter readers, relatives, guests to a party, and so on, can be incorporated into the ongoing play. Do not give the entering child a role that overshadows the other players, such as a space person landing in the yard. The new player is likely to be "killed off" or rejected.

4. *Teach players to use a clear signal when leaving the play frame.* Clear communication probably is most important when children are engaged in rough-and-tumble play. Say: "Tell Sarah you don't want to be the monster anymore," or "John doesn't know you don't want to chase him. Tell him that." Such suggestions will allow children to exit the play and will reduce the likelihood of the nonplaying child responding to rough-and-tumble play with aggression.

5. *Make suggestions to further the goals of children, such as pointing out a problem or restating game rules.* Offer specific help when it is needed to keep a game going. For example, if a child's block construction is wobbling, point out the area where the problem is occurring if the child does not see it. If children are confused about how a game should proceed, restate the relevant rules.

6. *Teach children games when necessary.* Children between the ages of three and seven may not have had the opportunity to learn games from the older children and so must be taught by an adult. Have all materials set up, and know the rules yourself. Invite the children to participate. Then, give brief directions, one at a time. For example, in the game of "duck, duck, goose," say, "Take hands" (to form a circle). You may have to help by giving more specific directions, such as, "Jacob, hold Susan's hand." When the children are in a shoulder-to-shoulder circle, ask them to sit down. Once they are all seated, stand up and announce that you will be "it" the first time. Walk around the circle, tapping heads and saying "Duck, duck, duck, *goose!*" When the word "goose" is said, direct the child to chase you, then run around the circle, sitting in the child's empty space. Then, direct the standing child to be "it." With very young children, go with the child who is "it" for the first time as he or she taps heads and says, "Duck, duck, . . . , goose," and then run with the child to the empty space of the new person who is "it." Give directions and demonstrate in alternating patterns. With young children, don't give all the directions at once.

Allow the children to play until all have had a turn or their interest diminishes. Repeat the directions as necessary each time you play the game until the children can play it by themselves.

How to Become Directly Involved in Children's Playfulness

1. Demonstrate a nonliteral approach to resources. Playfully respond to the environment and to commonplace situations. For example, Mr. Phipps used to sing little songs or make up verses about ordinary things as they occurred during the day: the rain on the windowsill, blocks falling down, parents going to work, or children not wanting naps. He did this quite unconsciously to amuse the children. No one noticed until parents commented that their children could make up songs and poetry by themselves and wondered what the school was doing to promote such creativity.

Another way to do this is to propose impossible conditions: "I wonder what if . . . ?" What would happen if so much snow fell that the houses were covered? What would happen if all the girls grew wings and could fly? Encourage children to be expansive and to try to imagine all the possibilities. This often generates a lot of laughter. Show your interest in each child's contribution regardless of how silly it is.

2. Be accepting of young children's humor. Smile and show interest even if you do not have the least idea of what the joke is. When group glee strikes, with every child laughing uproariously, laugh along with them. They will quiet themselves down eventually. It is not at all unusual for the children not to know what they are laughing at either.

3. Explain that a child was only joking when someone misinterprets the meaning of what was said or did not recognize a play signal. It is especially important that play signals be recognized when some members of the group are older or more mature than other members. For example, to call a boy a girl is a serious insult, except in a joke, which would be common for older preschool or kindergarten children. Nonsense names or other names used to address people may be very distressing to children not in on the joke or too young to understand it.

4. Use affective reflections when preschool children laugh at disfigurement, falls, or handicapping conditions; then, provide brief but accurate information. Preschool children are not mature enough to take another's perspective and do not intend to hurt another person's feelings with their laughter, although this is often the result. Say, for example: "You thought Mr. North walked very funny. He cannot help that because one leg is shorter than the other. People who cannot help the way they walk feel sad when other people laugh at them."

How to Demonstrate Awareness of Individual Differences

1. Accept the young child's approach to games with rules. Little children are not cheating or committing a moral error if they don't play precisely by the rules. Simply restate the rule in question and go on with the game. Children learn to play games with rules by playing with better players who know the rules.

2. Match the play activity to the skills of the players. Children from less advantaged circumstances may not be as skilled in taking roles as are much younger children from middle-class families. Therefore, they will need the opportunity to participate in pretend play well into the grade-school years. They also will need to have more adult interventions so that their skills will improve. Play skills are developed by experience. All children should begin with simple games, roles, and constructions and move on toward more challenging activities as their skills develop. Use the developmental information provided in this chapter to help you match the level of play to the skills of the players.

3. Accept the child's play style preferences. Both patterners and dramatists engage in high-quality play. It is hoped that all children will experience both construction and role-taking play, but if children have a clear style, let them develop in their preferred mode.

4. Provide support for younger boys when girls outperform them in movement play. Girls' motor skills often develop faster than do boys' until the later elementary grades, when the trend is reversed. Boys may be vulnerable to feelings of failure when the girls run faster, jump farther, and ride bikes earlier. Reassure them that they too will be able to do all of these things soon.

5. Support children in their choice of play activities; do not limit play to sex-stereotyped choices. Boys frequently are teased if they choose to play jacks or jump rope because these are "girl games." Such teasing should be treated as you would any other form of verbal aggression. Sometimes, girls are called "tomboys," or parents become concerned with their rough-and-tumble play, which they perceive as inappropriate for girls but acceptable for boys. Allow young boys to take nurturing roles as well. Children need opportunities to try out all kinds of activities, and they benefit from the varied experience. Play, after all, is not serious, and it allows children the opportunity to develop other perspectives.

Older children frequently exclude the opposite sex in their free play. Choices of playmates should be respected whenever possible as both boys and girls develop sex-role-related skills in their play. However, when you organize games, avoid assigning children to teams based on gender. Pitting the boys against girls is not fair. It would be better to count out the teams so that they are evenly balanced.

6. Respect cultural and experiential differences in children. Allow children to explore play themes that might be unfamiliar to you. Encourage children to freely express their ideas and emotions in their play.

PITFALLS TO AVOID

Sometimes, when people are trying to use the skills described here, certain attitudes and behaviors may interfere with their ability to carry them out in a truly playful spirit.

Believing that children learn only what they are taught. Learning is something that children do for themselves. Adults may structure the learning, but the information learned by direct instruction is limited compared with the information children acquire from the environment, from their families and friends, and at play. Adults can facilitate children's learning to play, but they should not require children to perform to specification. Facilitation requires that the adult truly believes that the children have the capacity to learn, to perform, and to be competent within themselves.

Organizing play to meet academic ends. Children learn from all of their play experiences. Adults should not try to limit the songs they sing to number songs and alphabet ditties. These activities are designed by well-intentioned adults who use children's play interests to meet other ends. Play is only play when it belongs to the children, is voluntary, and is fun. If children choose to put together an alphabet puzzle, fine; however, a clown puzzle is just as good from a playful perspective.

Watching for mistakes. Play is not serious, so mistakes in play simply do not count. By all means, assist a child when asked to do so, but never point out mistakes to a playing child. Let the child discover the error independently. Many interesting products were invented out of mistakes that someone played with.

Making demands for specific responses. Children do need to learn specific information about their world and these tasks are organized into lessons. Lessons about materials, for example, should not be substituted for play with materials. For example, adults may present a lesson on the effects of mixing paint colors and ask the child to predict the color to be produced. The scientific approach to light and color has its place. However, it should be separated from the creative activity of painting a picture, in which some colors might become mixed. Answer questions if asked; otherwise, leave the child alone to manage the situation without giving instruction. The distinction between curious investigation from a scientific perspective and playful exploration often is not clear. The best criterion to help distinguish between the two is to determine who has control of the situation. If the child does, and the adult only responds to inquiries, then the adult is behaving appropriately. However, if the child is passive and the adult is talking quite a bit, requiring answers from the child, or giving a series of directions, then this is a lesson, not play.

Setting too many restrictions. Children cannot play if they are expected to maintain silence, not move, create no disorder, never touch one another, remain clean and tidy, and never create a mess. Play requires action. Action inevitably leads to disorder, messes, noise, joy, conversation, and, usually, jostling about. When adults set unreasonable restrictions on play, they simply are trying to prohibit play altogether. Of course, even the youngest player can be expected to clean up after the play, but that is a task in social responsibility, not play itself.

Squelching the creative use of materials. Consider whether there actually are reasons of safety or economics that restrict the use of a particular material. For example, poker chips make better money to carry in purses than do puzzle pieces, and most children would rather use them; and puzzles are ruined if pieces are missing. However, the same thing does not apply to macaroni, strings, Lego blocks, or other small items that might be used in role play. The challenge is in planning to manage the proper return of the items once play is finished for the day.

One teacher maintained a pail for small items, and children deposited them there whenever they were found. Later, they were returned to the appropriate storage area.

Having no constraints at all. Play is planned disorder, or organized, rule-governed interactions that do not fit adult predetermined conceptions. Play simply does not flourish when there are no rules or means of controlling its scope or parameters. Rules regarding safety, rights and feelings of others, and other necessities of group living are essential prerequisites of quality play. Children who do not have limits spend most of their time in social testing to see just where the boundaries of acceptable behavior are rather than in productive play. You will learn about setting limits in Chapters 7, 8 and 9.

Ignoring play. Given the right conditions, play probably will develop without adult prodding. However, quality play, that which stretches the imagination and the social and cognitive abilities of the player, does not develop in a vacuum.

Amusing yourself with materials without responding to children's play. Adults who do not focus on what children are doing sometimes play with materials in a fashion that is disconnected to the children's activities. To expand play, the adult's behavior must be based on observed child behavior and varied in some way.

Encouraging premature competition. Children under eight years of age do not understand games with rules well enough to engage in competitive games in which winning and losing is stressed. They may want to bat balls thrown to them or catch and toss balls, all of which is movement play. Most sandlot games do not have the two-team, win-and-lose system; turns usually are rotated so that each player plays for the fun of the process. Sometimes, adults

misinterpret this play as competitive sport and take over, making it competitive.

Directing play or games too soon. Children learn from the process of deciding on rules or setting up a fantasy play situation. It may take longer to do these tasks than adults think is necessary. Unfortunately, adults often move in too soon and usurp the planning and organizational functions. Unless children ask for help, or unless conflict erupts that the children are unable to resolve themselves, adults should show interest but remain uninvolved.

Asking children to explain their humor. Asking for an explanation quickly kills all the fun of a joke. If one does not "get it," using a social smile, social laughter, or a simple pleasurable expression is an appropriate response.

Admonishing children to be quiet or to quit being silly when engaged in humor. Sometimes, adults are annoyed by children's laughter, especially if it occurs in the wrong time and place. In such cases, let children know you understand their merriment ("You kids are having a great time telling jokes"), then explain why their humor is inappropriate ("I'm concerned that I won't be able to drive safely in this traffic with all the distraction"). Don't just set limits on children's humor in a general, disapproving way.

Becoming too involved in the play. You may find yourself having so much fun playing that you forget that the purpose of participation is to stimulate children's high-quality play. Play should go on nicely once you have ceased to be so active. If it does not, you might have been dominating the play, the activity might have been above the children's level, or the role you had chosen might have been so central to the theme that the play cannot continue without it. Facilitate rather than dominate.

SUMMARY

Play is a normal part of childhood, allowing children to practice skills in motor coordination, language, reasoning, social behavior, and in learning to cope with emotionally challenging problems. It is pleasurable, voluntary, and valued for the process of play from the players' perspective rather than for any useful product.

There are several types of play: play with movement and objects, construction play, and fantasy play. Within each play form, sequences of development were suggested through which children pass before they become skillful players. Most of these sequences occur in early childhood, with older children using early skills in new combinations for more complex forms of play.

The role of the adult is to facilitate play. This means that the adult must establish an atmosphere conducive to play, provide appropriate materials and facilities, and guide the skill development of the children toward increasing levels of performance. Responsiveness to children's observed behaviors is essential to this role.

Several pitfalls were identified so that you can avoid them as you begin to support children's play.

DISCUSSION QUESTIONS

1. Is it likely that play can ever be eliminated as a human behavior? Why or why not?
2. What is the function of play in the overall development of children?
3. Describe the characteristics of play and give examples of playful and nonplayful behavior.
4. Why aren't the concepts of work and play opposites? Why is it more accurate to contrast play with seriousness than with work? Use your own life experience to elaborate on this.
5. List the skills needed for children to participate in dramatic play. Give examples of each one.
6. What does metacommunication mean? Describe play signals that are nonverbal and those that are spoken.
7. When adults observe a child engaged in repetitious play, should they stop it? Why?
8. Select a simple game with which you are familiar. Write out sequentially everything you would say or do to teach it to a group of children.
9. When a young child starts to tell a joke but forgets the punch line and then laughs, how should you respond?
10. When a group of school-age children of mixed ages are playing softball and are not following the Little League rules on their own, how should you respond?
11. When older children are fully involved in play and everything is running smoothly, what should you do?

CHAPTER 7
Fostering Self-Discipline in Children: Expressing Appropriate Expectations for Their Behavior

SOURCE: H. Armstrong Roberts

OBJECTIVES:

On completion of this chapter, you will be able to describe:

1. Emotional, developmental, and experiential factors that contribute to the development of self-discipline in children.

2. Variations in the degree to which people display self-regulated behavior.

3. How different adult discipline styles affect children's behavior and personality.

4. What a personal message is and when to use it.

5. How using a personal message enhances the development of self-discipline in children.

6. Guidelines for formulating each part of the personal message.

7. Pitfalls to avoid in formulating and using personal messages.

Cross at the light.

Cover your mouth when you sneeze.

Keep your eyes on your own paper.

These are some of the rules children must learn in order to fit into our society. Although no code of behavior is universal, all cultures devise rules that members must obey if they are to remain in good standing (Kagan, 1977; Shaffer, 1985). It is adults who are primarily responsible for transmitting this code to the next generation (Honig, 1985; Turiel, 1978). They often refer to this responsibility as "teaching children to behave." Thus, adults instruct children to refrain from acting in ways considered offensive, such as spitting on the sidewalk, hurting someone else's feelings, or taking all the chocolate-covered cherries for themselves. They also train children to engage in behaviors they interpret as socially desirable, including sharing, answering politely, and telling the truth.

Initially, adults expect to spend much of their time monitoring the degree to which children conform to their expectations. However, they hope that eventually youngsters will assume greater responsibility for regulating their own behavior by acting in accordance with these ideals even when an authority figure is not present. Hence, their ultimate goal is for children to become self-disciplined.

WHAT IS SELF-DISCIPLINE?

Self-discipline is the capacity to regulate one's actions to match personal values and societal expectations rather than depending on others to enforce compliance (Kopp, 1982). It comprises several behaviors, all of which involve inhibiting or initiating particular acts on one's own.

One of these is curbing initial impulses that could be damaging to self or others (Fabes, 1984; Fraiberg, 1977). A child who refrains from striking out in anger or who suppresses the urge to taunt a clumsy classmate is demonstrating impulse control. Resisting the temptation to do something that is appealing but inappropriate also is important and is exemplified when a child turns in a found wallet rather than keeping it or continues working quietly rather than talking with a friend when the teacher leaves the room (Mischel, 1978). A third behavior related to inhibition is postponing immediate rewards in order to achieve a long-range goal or to help another person (Flavell, 1977; Rohwer, 1970). Giving up recess to practice for the school play or waiting for everyone to have a turn before taking another are situations that illustrate delay of gratification.

Another facet of self-discipline involves being able to initiate and implement plans of action (Jensen and Hughston, 1979). Such plans entail making judgments about what ought to be done, what can be done, and how to coordinate personal behaviors in order to follow through on these intents (Rest, 1983). The development and execution of a typical plan is demonstrated when a child wants possession of an object, is able to generate a strategy for getting it (like trading), and then tries to negotiate for it. Self-discipline also is manifested when children initiate appropriate behaviors in social situations regardless of their preference at the time (Fabes, 1984; Kopp, 1982). A child who shares a favorite possession, or one who tells the truth at the risk of negative personal consequences, exemplifies this capacity. Thus, self-disciplined children are those who, independent of adult or peer monitoring, inhibit potentially harmful impulses, resist temptation, delay gratification, make and carry out plans, and initiate positive social actions.

There are three variables that affect children's ability to achieve self-discipline: emotions, developmental processes, and experience.

Emotional Components of Self-Discipline

The emotions contributing to self-discipline serve a "stop-and-go" function, signaling children that particular behaviors are either inappropriate or acceptable (Newman and Newman, 1978). These feelings are guilt and empathy (Erikson, 1950; Freud, 1938). Guilt feelings warn children of the undesirability of a current, planned, or past action. There is evidence that children as young as three or four years of age experience guilt when they are unable to resist temptation or when they violate a known rule. At this age, children feel guilty because they recognize a discrepancy between their own behavior and an external standard (Sears, 1960). Personal or true guilt evolves only after they can distinguish themselves from others and recognize that their behavior may be the source of someone else's distress (Hoffman, 1967). Thus, over time, children begin to experience guilt based on their failure to meet personal expectations rather than the expectations of others. This contributes to the inner control necessary for self-regulation. Although the ability to feel guilt or empathy is very important, this capacity alone does not ensure that a person will internalize a particular code of ethics. Other factors also play a role.

The beginnings of empathy also seem to be present at about three or four years of age (Borke, 1973). It occurs when children identify another person's emotion and feel it themselves. This often prompts them to engage in some definite behavior as a way to deal with their feelings, as when a toddler watches a playmate fall and then promptly begins to cry. Kindergarteners are more likely to act to help a person or to feel remorse if they are the source of the unhappiness (Hoffman, 1967). Eventually, school-age children and adults feel empathy and guilt even when they are not the perpetrator but perceive that they could have done something to avert or counteract an unpleasant episode.

Developmental Processes That Influence Self-Discipline

Scientists and helping professionals alike have observed that children become more capable of self-discipline as they mature. This is due, in part, to a variety of changes in children's development. For instance, there is evidence that children's ability to make judgments about what is right and wrong emerges in concert with cognitive maturation and experience (Damon, 1978; Kohlberg, 1964; Piaget, [1932] 1965). Toddlers and preschoolers use rewards and punishments as their main criteria for determining good and bad. Actions that result in social rewards are interpreted as desirable, and those that result in costs are undesirable. This is true even if the behavior is actually viewed differently by society. For instance, a child who observes another child "get his way" by whining might interpret this action as "good" because the complainer was, in fact, rewarded. Older children use more sophisticated reasoning. They recognize that many factors must be considered, such as intentions, personal consequences, and effects on others. They are able to think more abstractly about psychological influences of particular actions. This means that older children are better able to accurately evaluate appropriate and inappropriate behavior in the models to which they are exposed and in themselves.

Perspective taking. Another component of self-discipline is the ability to view a situation from perspectives other than one's own. This ability is at its most primitive in children under the age of five. The difficulty young children have in putting themselves in another person's place is a direct result of being unable to comprehend or predict the thoughts of others (Forbes, 1978; Weston and Turiel, 1980).

Youngsters between six and eight years of age begin to recognize that someone else's interpretation of a situation may be different from their own (Selman, 1976; Selman and Byrne,

1974). However, they cannot always recognize what the differences are and assume that differences occur simply because each person has received different information.

Nine- and ten-year-olds recognize that their own thoughts and the thoughts of another person are different, and may even be contradictory. They understand that two people can react to the same data in opposite ways, or that the same person can have a mixed reaction (Forbes, 1978). However, they are only able to think about their own view and another person's view alternately.

Older grade-school children are able to simultaneously consider their own perspective and that of another person (Selman, 1976; Shantz, 1975). They also can speculate about what other people currently are thinking or what they might think in the future. These abilities help children determine how to behave in an increasingly varied number of situations.

Impulsivity.   Children become less impulsive with age. Although impulsivity is a primary issue of toddlerhood, children's capacity to inhibit damaging impulses steadily improves, with the most dramatic change taking place around age six (Sroufe and Ward, 1980; Toner, Halstein, and Hetherington, 1977). Hence, grade-schoolers exhibit fewer fits of rage, are more adept at delaying gratification, and can handle greater levels of frustration (Maccoby, 1984). This comes about because of their increasing attention span and because of their broader repertoire of social skills (Lane and Pearson, 1982). In addition, as they mature, children develop more autonomy, thereby becoming more goal directed and eager to learn ways to control their own behavior.

Language and memory.   The phenomenal rate of language acquisition during the childhood years also contributes to the development of internal behavior controls. As children learn to use language more effectively, they become more successful at telling others what they

want. As a result, they resort to less physical, more controlled means of expression. Simultaneously, they become better equipped to understand and respond to the verbal instructions, requests, explanations, and reasoning used by others as guides for behavior (Maccoby, 1984; Marion, 1983). Children also use private speech to control their own behavior. That is, they learn to talk aloud to themselves as a way to postpone gratification, reduce frustration, or remind themselves of instructions previously given (Luria, 1961; Mischel, Ebbesen, and Zeiss, 1972). In this way, children eventually use communication skills to help themselves execute expected standards of behavior.

Memory is another variable that influences self-discipline. Although scientists have not yet determined whether memory actually increases from one year to the next, it does seem that as children grow older, they become better able to use the information they have stored in their memory as a resource for determining future behavior (Maccoby, 1984). Consequently, they become less dependent on others to show or tell them how to respond to each new situation. Instead, they use remembered information to guide their actions (Boneau, 1974).

As children's memory increases, so does their ability to recognize linkages among behaviors, events, and consequences. Children aged two through six think of social incidents as totally separate events rather than comprehending connections among them. Older children become better able to mentally group like actions or happenings and to identify interrelationships that may exist. Thus, a preschooler may see no connection between the act of hitting and the act of pinching, whereas a grade-schooler would recognize both as "hurtful" actions.

Cause and effect.   Another developmental change that contributes to self-discipline involves children's increased understanding of cause and effect. Preschoolers are not very accurate reasoners about what makes some things happen. They often attribute specific outcomes to magical, personal, or otherwise erroneous factors (Clarke-Stewart, 1983; Fraiberg, 1977). Increasing sophistication of thought leads to the awareness of an actual relationship between an action and its outcome. However, such ideas are not fully realized until adolescence (Smart and Smart, 1977).

VARIATIONS IN CONDUCT AND MOTIVATION

Because children naturally develop so many capabilities, it might seem that self-discipline is an inevitable by-product of maturation. However, adults display varying degrees of discipline, ranging from total lack of self-regulation to primary reliance on internal standards. Numerous theorists have tried to explain these variations (Hoffman, 1970; Kelman, 1958; Peck and Havighurst, 1962). Although there are differences among the theories that currently enjoy popular support, there are major points on which they all concur. These include three general categories of personal behavior: adherence, identification, and internalization.

Adherence

Adherence is the most superficial level of compliance and occurs when people follow a rule or custom solely to gain a reward or to avoid a punishment (Hoffman, 1970; Kohlberg, 1976). For instance, a child demonstrating adherence will share, but only as a way to gain praise or to escape a reprimand. This behavior is entirely self-serving and shows little regard for other people's welfare. Children whose thinking falls in this category have little understanding of why sharing is good and, as a result, perform the required behaviors only under direct supervision (Kelman, 1958; Stengel, 1982). In the absence of a punishing or rewarding adult, they have no rationale for following the rule on their own

and may resort to hitting or grabbing to get what they want whenever the adult is out of sight. While children remain at this level of development, adults must continually monitor their activities rather than relying on them to exercise self-regulation. The longer children depend on adults to reward or punish their actions, the more they become conditioned to expect this control. As a result, children fail to develop the ability to generalize standards and behaviors and to apply them in unfamiliar situations (Stengel, 1982). Furthermore, they have no tools for weighing or evaluating conflicting societal demands once they leave the direct supervision of a particular authority figure.

Identification

Another reason why people comply is because they *identify* with a person who advocates a particular code of conduct. That is, children follow specific rules not because they analyze their content or comprehend their social justification, but because they wish to establish and/or preserve a satisfying relationship with a particular person (Erikson, 1950; Freud, 1938). Identification leads to the emulation of the behaviors or standards of the admired one in order to gain praise and approval (Hawley and Hawley, 1981; Hoffman, 1970). Therefore, children who share because of identification do not recognize that sharing is valuable in relation to its impact on those with whom they share. Instead, they use sharing as a way to further their own aims— pleasing an authority figure who advocates sharing.

The persons with whom youngsters identify are nurturing, powerful people, usually adults or older children (Bandura, 1977). In all cases, they are individuals with whom children have strong affectionate ties rather than those with whom they have negative or neutral relationships (Parke, 1969; Prescott, 1965). Compliance is maintained as long as the relationship lasts, but may give way if the ties become less intense.

Internalization

Internalization is the most advanced basis for self-discipline; it represents achievement of an internal code of ethics. Internalization results from a person's idea that behaving in a certain way is an extension of his or her own beliefs and is consistent with personally established values (Hoffman, 1970; Kelman, 1958; Peck and Havighurst, 1962). In each case, children behave in certain ways to avert self-condemnation rather than seeking approval or avoiding disapproval from others. Thus, long-lasting behavior change is related to the internalization of standards and cannot be expected before this has occurred (Lepper, 1983).

Internalization of standards and values often is referred to as conscience, meaning that the person feels a moral commitment to a line of action and experiences guilt when he or she deviates from it. The reasoning employed in such decisions takes into account not only how compliance will affect the doer but how it will affect someone else. Based on their ability to reason in this way, children become able to behave appropriately regardless of whether or not an adult is present. At one time, it was thought that young children were incapable of moving beyond adherence and that internalization only could be achieved in late adolescence. More recent evidence suggests that even preschoolers can use higher order reasoning in particular situations (Irwin and Moore, 1971; Bandura, Ross, and Ross, 1963).

Onlookers cannot always discern the motivation behind a particular act carried out by a child. The same behavior could be prompted by that child's desire for a reward, for approval from a significant adult, or as a result of a personal belief that dictated it. Thus, it is motivation that differentiates internalization from adherence and identification. Internalization is evident when children sustain their actions in situations in which they are tempted to transgress and that afford slight chance of discovery, punishment, or reward (Thomas, 1985).

All people beyond toddlerhood are likely, at some time, to exhibit behaviors that represent adherence, identification, and internalization (Cairns, 1979). The same individual will cross with the light in order to avoid getting a ticket, will wear clothes in the same style as an admired friend, and will avoid cheating in a game because it just would not feel right. In the behavior of adults, one of these patterns tends to dominate (Peck and Havighurst, 1962). Thus, some people exhibit primarily external morality based either on reward and punishment or the opinions of others, and others are more self-regulated. Because self-discipline is so important, it is important to ask why such differences occur.

HOW EXPERIENCE INFLUENCES SELF-DISCIPLINE

Because most young people experience the developmental changes described previously and thus acquire some of the basics for internalization, the reasons for variation can best be attributed to differences in experiences. Children learn the rules of society from others through direct instruction, observation, reinforcement, and punishment (Bandura, 1977). Infants and preschoolers are chiefly responsive to parents and other adults with whom they have a positive relationship; grade-school children are also influenced by peers (Smith, 1982).

Direct Instruction

Throughout childhood, adults regulate children's behavior using physical and verbal controls. At first, they rely mainly on bodily intervention to keep youngsters safe and help them get along. Adults separate squabbling siblings, remove dangerous objects from reach, extract forbidden items from children's grasps and restrain them from dashing across busy streets. These actions usually are accompanied by brief verbal commands such as "Stop," "No," "Give me that," or "Wait for me." Gradually, physical intervention gives way to greater reliance on verbal directions and warnings, to which children become increasingly responsive (Lytton, 1979; Maccoby, 1984).

Typical adult instructions usually fall into the categories outlined in Table 7-1.

Verbal instruction are the quickest way to let children know what the appropriate, inappropriate, and alternate behaviors are. They are particularly effective when combined with another technique known as modeling.

Modeling

Adults *model* a code of conduct through their own actions (Bandura, 1977). Returning library books on time, helping an injured animal, or resisting the urge to eat a candy bar before supper all convey messages to children about desirable behaviors.

Thus, setting a good example is an important way of teaching children right from wrong. However, although it is true that children imitate much of what they see, modeling is most effective when the model's behavior is pointed out to them (Meichenbaum, 1977). This helps children to recognize important details that they otherwise might not notice. Thus, if the object is to demonstrate gentle handling of animals, it is useful to say, "See, I'm picking up the chicks very gently so I don't hurt them or crush their feathers. Look at how loosely I'm bending my fingers." Simply showing children the proper procedure without direct explanation may not cause them to imitate the appropriate behavior themselves at a later time (Meichenbaum, 1977).

Verbal descriptions of modeled behaviors are especially valuable when the adult hopes children will recognize that a person they are watching is resisting temptation or delaying gratification (Toner, Parke, and Yussen, 1978). Children may not recognize what the person is doing unless told. Statements such as the following assist children in recognizing someone's efforts to delay gratification: "Raymond really wants to use the unabridged dictionary, even though the college dictionary is available now. He has decided to wait until Karen has finished with it so he can use it next." Children also benefit when an adult model clearly states a rule he or she is following and the rationale for not committing a certain act (Grusec, et al., 1979). For example, explaining that the guinea pigs are eating and that it is important to let them finish before picking them up illustrates this technique. Children who watch a model delay action and understand what they are seeing are better able to postpone gratification in subsequent situations themselves (Bandura and Mischel, 1965).

Unfortunately, modeling not only accentuates positive actions; children also learn from the negative models they observe. Youngsters who see others act aggressively with no negative consequences learn powerful lessons. These actions frequently are duplicated in their own behavior (Stein, 1967; Bandura and Walters, 1963).

Reward and Punishment

In addition to instructing children about how to act and modeling particular behaviors themselves, adults reinforce desirable deeds and punish those they consider unacceptable. *Reinforcement* involves providing some consequence to a behavior that increases the likelihood the child will reproduce that behavior in similar situations. *Punishments* are consequences that reduce the probability of a particular behavior being repeated (Becker, Engelmann, and Thomas, 1971). Although the principles of reinforcement and punishment are relatively straightforward, appropriate enactment is complex. For this reason, Chapter 8 is devoted entirely to this subject. For now, it is important merely to recognize that children experience

TABLE 7-1 Modes of Adult Instruction

Telling children what is right and what is wrong

"It isn't nice to pull the cat's tail."
"Share your toys."
"Stealing is bad."

Informing children of expected standards

"Pet the cat gently."
"Put your toys away."
"Give Grandma a kiss."

Restricting certain behaviors

"Five more minutes on the swing."
"No painting until you put on a smock."
"Don't wipe your nose on your sleeve."

Advising children about how to meet the standards they set

"You could stack all the big plates on one side and the little plates on the other, like this."
"You could use the ball together or you could take turns."
"If you think about something else, that will make the waiting go faster."

Redirecting children's behavior

"Don't bounce that ball inside. Go outdoors instead."
"That spoon is too big. Try this one."
"You can tell him you're angry. Don't bite."

Providing children with information about how their actions affect themselves and others

"He hit you because you hit him."
"Every time you tease her, she cries."
"Mr. Martin really appreciated your helping him rake the leaves."

Giving children information about how their behavior looks to others

"Comb your hair. People will think I don't take good care of you."
"When you don't say 'Hi' back, he thinks you don't like him."
"When you forget to say 'Thank you,' people don't know you appreciated what they did."

both rewards and penalties as a result of their behavior and that these play a major role in their acquisition of self-discipline.

Integrating Emotions, Development, and Experience

The individual interactions children experience each day help them create a unique internalized map of the social environment (Boneau, 1974). That is, children mentally chart their experiences and make note of which behaviors make them feel guilty, which make them feel good, which are rewarded and which are not, and under what circumstances those conditions apply. Gradually, this map grows in breadth and complexity. Over time, children catalogue a growing number of experiences and make finer discriminations among events. They draw on information gleaned from these episodes to fit their behavior to situational demands rather than depending on other people to direct them at that moment. In addition, their increased developmental competence enables them to interpret more accurately the cues they receive and to envision more varied responses to those cues. As a result, they become progressively more successful in monitoring their own behavior.

Gradually, other children also contribute data to children's understanding of what constitutes desirable and undesirable behavior. The combined experiences with adults and agemates lead to greater self-discipline. Interactions with adults teach children about obligations, responsibility, and respect, and peer relations give children firsthand experience with cooperation and justice (Youniss, 1980). This difference in perspective is a result of children's general interpretation that positive behavior with adults means obedience, and positive behavior with peers involves reciprocal actions such as sharing or taking turns. This chapter and the next concentrate on the adult's role in helping children achieve self-discipline. Chapter 13,

Supporting Children's Friendships, describes how peers influence this process as well.

HOW ADULT BEHAVIOR AFFECTS CHILDREN'S BEHAVIOR

All adults rely on instruction, modeling, rewards, and punishments to teach children how to behave. However, the combination of techniques they use and the way in which they apply them differ.

Much research has been devoted to studying these variations. It has been found that the manner in which adults exert control, as well as the strategies they use, have a major impact on children's behavior and subsequent personality development (Baumrind, 1967, 1971; Hoffman, 1970, 1983). Also, certain discipline strategies are more effective than others in helping children assume responsibility for their own behavior. Although most research has focused on the parent-child relationship, other adult-child interactions also have been examined with similar results.

To date, three major discipline styles have been identified. These can be described as *authoritarian*, *permissive*, and *authoritative* (Baumrind, 1967, 1973, 1977). Each is characterized by particular adult attitudes and practices related to the child-rearing dimensions of control, clarity of communication, maturity demands, and nurturance. *Control* refers to the manner and degree to which adults enforce compliance with their expectations. The amount of information offered to children regarding behavior practices constitutes the *communication* component. *Maturity demands* involve the level at which expectations are set. *Nurturance* refers to the extent to which adults express caring and concern for children.

Differences among the three styles of discipline are reflected in differing combinations of these dimensions. Authoritarian adults are high in control, low in clarity of communication, high in maturity demands, and low in nurturance. Permissive adults are low in control, high in clarity of communication, low in maturity demands, and high in nurturance. Adults high in all four dimensions are described as "authoritative." Although no adult utilizes only the few strategies representative of a particular category, behaviors do tend to cluster according to one pattern or another.

The Authoritarian Parenting Style

Authoritarian parents are harsh and detached in their relationships with their offspring, seldom showing affection or giving praise. They have high expectations for children's behavior and tend to focus on children's failure to meet these standards (Baumrind, 1967, 1973, 1977).

Authoritarian parents value children's unquestioning obedience above all qualities. Their rules are absolute. The standard rationale for why children should obey is "Because I said so," and transgressions are swiftly and forcefully punished. The stock discipline techniques are physical punishment, shame, and ridicule. This approach, sometimes described as power-assertive discipline, keeps children dependent on adults to dictate right from wrong (Hoffman, 1983). Thus, children maintain an external moral orientation and remain at the adherence level of self-regulation.

Children who grow up under these conditions are withdrawn, unfriendly, suspicious, resentful, and unhappy. They avoid their peers and new situations (Baumrind, 1967). Both boys and girls exhibit little self-control and often have difficulty adapting to the demands of society. Additionally, daughters react by being low achievers, and sons tend to be hostile (Lamb and Baumrind, 1978). It should therefore come as no surprise that children of authoritarian parents have low self-esteem and little awareness of the needs of others (Openshaw, 1978).

The Permissive Parenting Style

At the other extreme is the permissive parenting style. Permissive parents generally are affectionate and tolerant of their child's behavior. They avoid control either because they do not believe in authority or because they are not sure how to exert it. Such parents have low expectations for children's achievement, few rules, and low standards of compliance and delegate little responsibility. On the rare occasions when they do institute consequences for misbehavior, they depend on love withdrawal ("I won't like you if. . . .") rather than physical punishment or reasoning. This approach leads to only limited changes in children's overt behavior and does not result in the adoption of beliefs children can maintain on their own (Hoffman, 1967; Hoffman and Saltzstein, 1967). Youngsters who are the product of this parenting style are strikingly similar to the children of authoritarian parents; immature, withdrawn, and unhappy. They exhibit the lowest levels of independence and self-control of all three parenting styles (Baumrind, 1967).

The Authoritative Parenting Style

Authoriatitive parents are friendly and affectionate. They set high standards for children's behavior, but gear their expectations to match children's changing needs and abilities. Although they do set firm limits on inappropriate behaviors, they rely primarily on explanations, demonstrations, and other-oriented reasoning to teach children how to behave (Hoffman, 1970; White and Watts, 1973). This nonpunitive form of behavior regulation often is referred to as *inductive discipline.* That is, parents induce children to anticipate the effects of their behavior on others while helping them recognize appropriate alternative actions to pursue.

Children of authoritative parents see themselves as competent because they know what is expected of them and how to comply (Katz, 1977). They are sensitive to others' feelings and are cooperative, happy, resistant to temptation, and socially responsible (Parke and Walters, 1967; Parke, 1977). Their behavior is the most self-reliant and self-controlled of the three patterns discussed here and represents an internalized mode of self-discipline.

Similar findings have been documented in teacher-child relationships. Moreover, the additional factor of productivity has been explored and found to be affected by teacher style. As might be expected, children under authoritarian leadership are productive as long as the teacher monitors them directly. However, productivity suffers dramatically when the adult is not available for continual supervision. Also, children whose teachers display this style exhibit increased instances of misconduct and are more extreme in their use of inappropriate behaviors. The permissive style results in low productivity regardless of adult presence. Children who are supervised by an authoritative adult are above-average producers and maintain the same level of output without constant surveillance. They are better able to independently initiate tasks, can delay gratification, are more cooperative with their peers, and are more constructive in their attempts to satisfy teacher demands (Beller, 1969, 1971; Prescott, 1965).

Implications

As evidenced by the behavioral outcomes associated with the three dominant patterns of adult supervision, each has a profound impact on children's immediate and long-term development. Heavy-handed discipline produces children who are compliant, afraid, dependent, and angry (Becker, 1964). Coercive tactics, such as physical force, shame, and dictatorial demands cause youngsters to act out of fear or blind obedience, not out of empathy or concern for others (Raffini, 1980). This interferes with

their ability to develop the reasoning and caring that is necessary for internalization (Hoffman, 1967). Thus, control exerted without explanation or affection does not help children become self-disciplined.

Likewise, internalization does not occur when adults are affectionate but fail to provide children with direction or predictable expectations. In these situations, children have few opportunities to receive accurate feedback about how other people perceive them and how their behavior affects others. With so few cues about what is socially appropriate, they are unable to create a realistic foundation of experience to serve as a guide for future behavior. For them, the world often is unfriendly because other adults and peers who do not share the same permissive standards find their unrestrained behavior unacceptable. The resulting rejection contributes to feelings of anxiety and low self-esteem. Unfortunately, such children also are less likely to develop feelings of empathy for others (Hoffman, 1983; Damon, 1978). These omissions add up to a dismal prognosis for youngsters who are the product of a permissive discipline style.

Obviously, the adult behavior pattern that is most likely to lead to internalization is the authoritative style. Authoritative adults effectively address all three factors contributing to self-discipline: emotions, cognition, and experience.

When adults are able to convey acceptance to children while at the same time making it clear that they have expectations for their conduct, children feel secure knowing that they are cared about and that they have a resource for determining how to behave. Discipline encounters provide an opportunity for discussions about guilt and empathy, two emotions not easily acknowledged by a child who is defensive or hostile as a result of power assertion or concerned over love withdrawal (Hoffman, 1970).

Reasoning with children also contributes to their cognitive development because they are exposed to moral judgments that are beyond their own. This strategy has been shown to be an important element in developing higher levels of thinking about what is right and what is wrong. In addition, children acquire precise information about which behaviors to choose again, which to avoid, and which alternatives to select. This increases the breadth and depth of their cognitive map of the social environment. Such younsters are most likely to maximize the potential successes available to them because they have learned to satisfy their needs within guidelines established by adults.

Becoming Authoritative

Exhibiting an authoritative style is not simply a matter of personality or temperament, but of skills. Adults must pay attention to how they establish relationships with children and to how they make children aware of their expectations (Clarke-Stewart and Koch, 1983; Kostelnik, 1978). Skills presented in previous chapters have focused on relationship enhancement. Thus, you have already learned one major component of the authoritative approach. The skills presented in this chapter will focus on making children aware of adult expectations.

STATING BEHAVIORAL EXPECTATIONS_____

Adults can best express their behavioral expectations for children through a personal message. A *personal message* consists of three parts. The first is a reflection in which the child's point of view is acknowledged. In the second portion, the adult articulates his or her emotions about the child's behavior, names which specific action prompted those feelings, and explains why. The third segment, used only in situations in which behavior change is desired, involves describing an alternate behavior for the child to pursue. This last step is, in fact, a statement of

a rule that the child is expected to follow for that situation.

The ultimate aim of using personal messages is to give children the information they need for both current and future reference. Personal messages help children better understand how their actions affect others and provide them with cues about desirable and undesirable behaviors.

In favorable circumstances, personal messages tell children what they are doing right so they can repeat the behavior in subsequent interactions. For instance, an adult who values cooperation may acknowledge two children's efforts to share by saying: "You're working together. It makes me feel happy to see you sharing. Sharing is a good way of cooperating."

In problem situations, personal messages set the stage either for children to comply on their own or for the adult to impose consequences when children fail to obey. For example, adults who want to redirect a child's anger away from hitting and toward talking could say: "You're angry. It upsets me when you hit. Hitting hurts. Tell Stuart what he did that made you so mad." For now, we will turn our attention to personal messages aimed at changing problem behaviors; later, we will consider how to use them in positive situations.

Knowing When Behavior Change Is Called For

Every day, adults are faced with situations in which they must decide whether or not a child's behavior is appropriate. If a behavior is not acceptable, they must also determine what conduct would be more suitable. In order to make these decisions, the following questions must be asked:

1. Is the child's behavior unsafe either for self or others?
2. Is the child's behavior destructive?
3. Does the child's behavior infringe on the rights of someone else?

If the answer to any of these questions is yes, it is a clear sign that the adult should intervene (DiCaprio, 1974; Galambos-Stone, 1976; Hildebrand, 1985). If the response is no, then demands for behavior change are unnecessary.

For example, concern about *safety* is the reason why children are stopped from running with scissors, prevented from dashing across a busy street, or kept from playing with matches. Similarly, the sanctions adults impose on writing graffiti or writing in library books are aimed at *protecting property*. When children are rebuked for copying from someone else's paper

FIGURE 7-1 Adult intervention is necessary when safety is at risk.
SOURCE: Photo by David Kostelnik

or for bullying a timid classmate, adults are making an effort to teach children *respect for others*. In all of these situations, there are legitimate grounds for trying to alter children's behavior.

On the other hand, adults are not justified when they insist that children behave in certain ways simply because it is traditional or more convenient. Hence, requiring children to take their seats on the bus in alphabetical order rather than sitting with their friends is an example of unnecessary and inappropriate adult intervention.

Finally, adults also must decide whether a problem behavior is important enough to warrant persistent attention. This can be described as the principle of importance. In other words, is the behavior serious enough to deal with each and every time it happens? When a behavior meets these criteria, a personal message is in order. For example, when Mr. Smith sees children throwing rocks on the playground, he takes action to stop it regardless of when he sees it or how tired or preoccupied he is. Because rock throwing is so dangerous, preventing it is a top priority for Mr. Smith. In this case, a personal message that forbids rock throwing is appropriate.

On the other hand, it annoys Mr. Smith when children scuff the toes of their shoes on the cement. Sometimes, he tries hard to get them to lift their feet when they walk. However, if he has a headache or has put in a long day and a child scuffs her shoes, Mr. Smith pretends not to see it rather than dealing with the problem. The intermittent nature of Mr. Smith's attention to this behavior is a sign that the standard is not important enough, at least for now, to warrant a personal message.

The standards of safety, property, and people's rights are simple and all encompassing. They provide basic guidelines by which to judge children's behavior. However, it should be noted that because adults differ, their interpretations vary as to what constitutes a dangerous situation or a potential threat to another's self-esteem. People's personal standards are uniquely influenced by past experience, family, community, and culture. This means that no two adults' standards match exactly. However, when adults relate the standards they set to at least one of the principles just described, they minimize major variations, which are confusing to children.

An assessment regarding all of these criteria must be made prior to making one's standards known. With so many factors to consider, adults may wonder if prompt action can ever be taken. Experienced professionals consider all these points quickly and intervene in a timely fashion. It may take the novice slightly longer to decide if a personal message is appropriate.

Part One of the Personal Message

In order to successfully teach children how to achieve their aims appropriately, adults must first understand what children are trying to accomplish. Once this has been established, it is easier to determine an acceptable alternate behavior that will satisfy both the adult and the child. Based on this rationale, the first step of the personal message is to recognize and acknowledge the child's perspective using a behavior, paraphrase, or affective reflection.

There are several reasons why a personal message begins with a reflection. First, in problem situations, adults and children often have very different points of view. For example, when four-year-old Allison lifts her dress up over her head in the supermarket to show off her new panties, she feels proud, but her mother is mortified. At times like these, adults wish children would act differently, so it is common for them to center on this desire and forget that children's emotions are legitimate, although contrary to their own. Reflecting helps adults avoid this pitfall. It compels them to remember that each child has a unique perception that must be considered prior to subsequent action.

Another advantage of reflecting first is that it serves as a clear signal to the child that the adult is actively attempting to understand his or her position. Children are more willing to listen to adult messages when they think their own messages have been heard. Even when children have chosen a physical means to express their desires, knowledge of adult awareness reduces their need to escalate the behavior in order to make their feelings known. For instance, if Sam is angry, he may be ready to fling a book across the room to make his point. When the adult reflects, "Something happened that really upset you," Sam may not feel so compelled to throw the book to show his anger because someone has already acknowledged it.

A third value of reflecting first is that it is a way to mentally count to ten before committing oneself to a particular line of action. If offers a moment in which adults can sort out their emotions, organize their thoughts, or readjust their approach. It reduces the risk of overreacting or responding precipitously. For instance, from across the room, Ms. Romano notices Danny painting a picture with tempera dripping all over the floor. Her first reaction is one of annoyance. She hurries to the easel, a reprimand on her lips. However, as she approaches, she becomes aware of Danny's obvious pride in his work and his total absorption in his painting. By reflecting, "You're really excited about your painting," she is able to put a check on her initial response. Instead of blurting out, "How many times have we talked about keeping the paint on the paper," she is able calmly to provide him with important information. "Some paint dripped on the floor. I'm worried someone might slip and get hurt. Get a sponge and we'll clean it up." In this way, the reflection served as a reasoned entry into what could have been an emotionally charged situation.

Finally, reflecting is a way for adults to show their respect and caring for children. This demonstration of positive regard must continue, particularly when disciplinary action is in order. When used in conjunction with the other portions of the personal message, reflecting unites the two components of the authoritative style: affection and clear behavioral expectations.

To summarize, in problem situations, the child has one perspective, the adult another. In order for a resolution to take place, each must accurately and correctly take into account the other's attitudes. This mutual understanding forms the basis for a shared response that will join the two separate lines of thought (Goffman, 1967). The reflection represents the adult's effort to assess the child's attitude; the second portion of the personal message is aimed at helping the child recognize that of the adult.

Part Two of the Personal Message

The second portion of the personal message describes the adult's emotions, identifies the child's behavior that led to those feelings, and gives a reason for why this is so:

> "I feel annoyed when you hit. Hitting hurts."
> "It upsets me when you interrupt. I keep losing my place."

Why adults should talk about their emotions. Helping professionals often have an emotional reaction to children's behavior. They feel pleased when children cooperate, distressed when they fight, annoyed when they procrastinate. Emotions are just as natural for adults as they are for children (Chernow and Chernow, 1981).

Experienced practitioners learn to use their own emotions as a guide to interacting more effectively with children. They do this by talking about the emotions as they arise (Mead, 1976). When adults disclose their emotions to children, they illustrate the universality of feelings. They demonstrate that at different times, everyone feels unhappy, pleased, frustrated, worried, proud, satisfied, or angry. This helps children realize that all human beings experience emotions and, as a result, makes them more will-

ing to accept feelings in themselves and to recognize them in others (Hendrick, 1984). Talking about emotions also aids children in learning that people have different reactions to the same situation. They find out that what makes them happy may prompt sadness in others, or that an event that causes them anxiety is welcomed by someone else. Children do not automatically know this and, instead, often assume that their current feelings are shared by everyone else. As they hear more about other people's emotions, they gradually become aware that this is not always the case. Another advantage is that adults serve as a model for using words to express emotional states. Children discover that people can have a variety of reactions and still be capable of verbalizing how they feel. Eventually, children find that emotions can be put into words and that words offer a satisfying way to communicate with other people.

Adults who wish to maintain positive relationships with children also should keep in mind that sharing their feelings with children promotes closer ties. People who are able to talk honestly about their emotions are considered more trustworthy and helpful by the persons with whom they interact than are those who avoid such conversations (McCarthy and Betz, 1978). When adults risk revealing something personal about themselves, it is seen by children as a demonstration of the regard in which they are held (Raffini, 1980). In addition, when such revelations are the norm, children find it less threatening to reveal their own emotions. This leads to mutual understanding and respect.

Finally, children are interested in how the significant adults in their lives react to what they say and do. They care about how adults feel and are responsive to their emotions. In fact, adults who describe their own disappointment or disapproval regarding a particular child's behavior place that child in an optimal state of arousal for receiving the rest of the information contained in their message (Hoffman, 1983). Without this type of sanction, children will not be induced to seriously consider the adult's reasoning. On the other hand, adults who depend on power assertion or love withdrawal as a way to communicate their concern provoke such strong reactions in children that they are unable to attend to the specific content of the message. Thus, when children refrain from hitting because it would upset their teacher, or when they share materials because the caregiver has advocated cooperation, they are demonstrating identification. It is from this base that they eventually will begin to internalize some of the behavioral expectations adults think are important.

Focusing on children's behavior. Once adults have described their emotions, it is important that they tell the child which behavior has caused them to react. This means identifying by name the undesirable behavior that the child is displaying. This designation is imperative because it helps children pinpoint actions to avoid (Baumrind, 1972; Clarizio, 1980; Hawley and Hawley, 1981). For example, a personal message that includes the statement "It bothers me when you keep jumping out of your seat" tells the child what behavior prompted the adult's irritation and describes an issue that can be resolved. On the other hand, remarks such as "It annoys me that you're showing off" or "I get upset when you're such a slob" are accusations that attack a child's personality and do not further mutual respect and understanding (Chernow and Chernow, 1981).

Behaviors are actions one can see. Taking turns, hitting, kicking, handing over, and coming on time are all visible. Using specific behavior names is an objective rather than a subjective way of describing how people act. On the other hand, descriptors such as lazy, uncooperative, hyperactive, vindictive, greedy, hostile, nasty, and surly are all subjective and accusatory labels. They make children feel defensive without giving them clear cues as to which specific actions are being discussed. Youngsters who are under attack are not likely to be receptive to adult desires for compliance.

Instead, they may become hostile or think that satisfying the adult is beyond their capability. In either case, effective behavior change is more difficult to achieve. To avoid such adverse reactions, adults must use objective behavior names rather than subjective labels.

The importance of giving children reasons. Children are better able to understand and respond to adult expectations when those expectations are accompanied by reasons (Baumrind, 1972; Parke, 1977). This is why the second portion of the personal message also includes giving children an explanation for the adult's reaction.

Why are adults upset when children hit? Because hitting hurts. Why are they frustrated when children dawdle? Because they may be late for something important. Why do they become annoyed when children interrupt a story over and over again? Because interrupting interferes with their train of thought, or it makes it difficult for others to concentrate. Although such conclusions may be perfectly clear to adults, they are not so obvious to many children.

When adults give children reasons for their expectations, they help them to recognize that behavior standards have a rational rather than an arbitrary base. Reasons also help children see the logic of expectations that they might not discover on their own. In addition, reasons offer children information about the effect their behavior has on others. This increases their understanding of interpersonal causality, that is, the relationship between their own acts and the physical and psychological well-being of another person (Damon, 1978).

Reasons make the connections among actions clearer. Although adults easily identify common attributes among those actions they consider undesirable as well as among positive ones, children may not automatically perceive the same linkages. For instance, a child who has learned that hitting is not allowed because it is hurtful may not conclude that scratching and biting are equally inappropriate until an adult explains their negative effects as well. When such explanations are offered over and over again, children eventually use them as guidelines for making their own judgments about what is right and what is wrong (Parke, 1972). A child who says to himself, "I shouldn't eat a candy bar before supper because it will spoil my appetite," is relying on reasons he has heard previously as a way to control current behavior.

Reasoning is the hallmark of the authoritative adult. It has been shown to be more important than any other single factor related to helping children achieve self-control (Parke, 1977). Youngsters who see adults model reasoning as a way to resolve problem situations demonstrate more self-discipline and less aggression than do children for whom such models are not available (Slaby and Parke, 1968). Children can only internalize standards that make sense to them and that help them to predict the possible aftermath of the things they do or say. Thus, reasoning leads to the establishment of long-term behavioral controls.

Matching reasons to children's understanding. A child's current developmental level has an impact on what types of reasons will make the most sense to him or her. For instance, preschoolers are most responsive to demonstrable, object-oriented rationales, such as "Be careful with the magnifying glass. It's fragile and it might break" (Parke, 1974, 1977). They also understand reasons that emphasize the direct physical effects of their actions: "If you keep pushing him, he'll fall down and cry" (Hoffman, 1983). Young children are less able to comprehend explanations that focus on ownership or the rights of others, such as "Don't touch the magnifying glass, because it belongs to Timmy."

On the other hand, children six years of age and older are more receptive to reasoning that focuses on the rights, privileges, and emotions of other people. The most effective reasons at this age emphasize the psychological effects of children's actions ("He feels sad because he was proud of his tower an you knocked it down") as well as explanations that focus on the fairness of the child's actions in terms of someone else's motives ("Don't yell at him—he was only trying to help") (Hoffman, 1983).

Variations in part two of the personal message. As we have discussed, the second portion of the personal message consists of a statement of the adult's emotion, a reference to the child's behavior, and a reason for this reaction. These three components can be arranged in any order after the reflection. Adults should always reflect first and then proceed with the second part in a way that seems most comfortable for them. There is no one correct order. For example, in the case of Allison, who was lifting her dress over her head in a proud display of her underwear, more than one response is appropriate:

1. "Allison, you're proud of your new panties. Underwear is very personal clothing. It's not meant for everyone to see. It upsets me when you lift your dress so high."
2. "Allison, you're proud of your new panties. It upsets me when you lift your dress over your head. Underwear is very personal clothing and is not meant for everyone to see."

How adults decide to articulate the second part of the personal message will depend on what they think of first and on their own individual style. What matters is that all the components be accounted for.

In addition, individuals are not all alike in their reactions. Some adults may have felt amused at Allison's performance, some would be indignant, and others might be embarrassed. Personal messages are ideally suited to account for these variations. They enable adults to respond to each situation individually based on their own impressions, without having to second-guess how someone else might respond in their place. Instead, the adult's emotions serve as a guide for how they will proceed. In the situation just discussed, if the adult is amused, she or he may do nothing but smile; if the adult is indignant or embarrassed, she or he probably will tell Allison to put her dress down. In the latter case, depending on which emotion is involved, explanations for why the child is required to assume a more modest demeanor will differ somewhat, thus enabling each adult to express personal views.

Finally, if the adult uses a behavior reflection as an introduction to the personal message, the behavior does not have to be mentioned again in the second portion. For instance: ''Allison, you're lifting your dress up over your head. That upsets me. Underwear is very personal clothing, so it is not something everyone should see.'' In this case, the reflection specified the behavior in question, making it unnecessary to repeat.

Part Three of the Personal Message

Telling children an appropriate course of action for a particular circumstance is the function of the third portion of the personal message. Because preadolescents have a limited rather than comprehensive perception of events, they often focus on one particular approach in trying to achieve their aims. They also have difficulty attending to all the important facets of a problem (Flavell, 1977; Jackson, Robinson, and Dale, 1977). This phenomenon, referred to as *centration*, explains why youngsters may try the same unsuccessful strategy over and over again. Although they may recognize that what they are doing is wrong, they often are unable to generate suitable alternative actions. For this reason, it is not enough to tell children which behaviors are unacceptable; they must also be told what to try instead (Mendler and Curwin, 1983). This designation of an appropriate substitute behavior serves as a rule for children to follow. Thus, the ''rule'' portion of the personal

message is a guide for behavior—it tells children what to do (Brophy and Putnam, 1979; Chernow and Chernow, 1981). Some examples are:

''Walk, don't run.''
''Keep your dress down.''
''Turn your homework in as soon as you get to school.''
''Share the jump ropes.''
''Talk quietly in the lunchroom.''

Rules make the world more predictable because they help children recognize what they can and cannot do. This knowledge enables them to be more successful in interacting with both peers and adults (Gordon, 1975; Hendrick, 1984). When children are not sure what the rules are, they are less likely to know how to get what they want in ways that enhance rather than interfere with their relationships with others (Moore and Olson, 1969). In addition, if the rules they must follow are arbitrary, unreasonable, or inappropriate for their developmental level, youngsters may be unable or unwilling to comply (Krasner and Krasner, 1972; Raffini, 1980). Thus, how rules are set has much to do with how well children are able to follow them (Beller, 1971; Gnagey, 1975). Therefore, it pays for adults to learn the specific attributes that characterize good rules.

Rules must be reasonable. Reasonable rules are rules children are capable of following. Being capable means having both the ability and the knowledge necessary to carry out the desired behavior. To create reasonable rules, adults must take into account children's development, their past experiences, their current abilities, and the type of task required (Brophy and Putnam, 1979; Clarizio, 1980). For example, if a child is expected to put the Cuisenaire rods back in the box according to shape and color, it must first be determined whether he or she has the skills necessary to perform the task. In this case, a child would have to be able to manipulate the rods, distinguish color, know that like pieces go together, and also know that all of the rods should lie flat and in the same direction. If the child lacked know-how in any of these areas, the expectation would have to be revised to correspond to what the child could do. This might mean telling the child to simply gather the rods, or to pile them into the box randomly, or to work with another person to collect the materials.

In addition, rules must have long-term positive effects that benefit the child, not just the adult (Krasner and Krasner, 1972). Hence, adults must decide whether a rule enhances a child's development or hinders it. Development is enhanced when expectations promote significant increases in children's interpersonal, academic, or life skills (Clarizio, 1980; Kostelnik and Kurtz, 1986). Development is hindered when adults fail to take into account children's individual needs and abilities or when they prohibit children from engaging in constructive activities. Such instances occur when adults set standards capriciously or solely for their own convenience. Thus, forbidding all the children in a mixed-age group from climbing on the high monkey bars because the youngest ones are afraid, preventing a crying child from clutching a blanket for comfort because the adult thinks it is high time she grew up, forbidding a boy from using a loom because the leader sees weaving as too feminine, or demanding that children be silent during lunchtime because the principal wants to make sure they don't yell across the table are all growth-inhibiting measures because they deprive children of potentially beneficial experiences.

Adults avoid such problems when they recognize that each child is an individual and that although some standards are appropriate for a group (such as walking rather than running inside), others are best applied on a child-by-child basis. For instance, because physical mastery is important for everyone, younger children could be encouraged to tackle a low climber, while older youngsters could attempt a more challenging apparatus. Moreover, adults

FIGURE 7-2 Enforcing a rule that would limit the ability of these children to develop physical mastery at this time would be growth inhibiting.
SOURCE: © Joel Gordon 1982

should examine their own attitudes for biases that curtail children's exposure to a wide range of opportunities. Intolerance and sexism, as illustrated in the preceding blanket and loom incidents, are examples of these. Additionally, in an effort to deal with definite problem behaviors, such as shouting during lunch, adults must be careful not to exact a standard that is unnecessarily extreme. Because children benefit from peer interaction, they should be encouraged to talk informally with classmates. Teaching youngsters to monitor the volume of their voices is a better approach to the problem of too much noise than eliminating conversation altogether.

Finally, adults must continually re-examine their rules in an effort to keep them up to date. A rule that is appropriate for a child of four may be inhibiting at age six.

Rules must be definable. Rules are definable when both the adult and the child have the same understanding of what the rule means (Brown, 1979; Krasner and Krasner, 1972). Good rules specify the *exact* behavior that adults value and find acceptable. It is confusing to children when adults use language that is open to may interpretations or that requires abstract reasoning (Jackson, Robinson, and Dale, 1977). This is exemplified when adults tell children to "behave," "act nice," "be good," or "act like a lady." Such phrases mean different things to different people. The child may construe these generalizations in one way, the adult in another. Youngsters who make genuine attempts to carry out the instructions become frustrated when their efforts fall short of the expected standard. For example, the teacher's notion of "nice" might mean sitting quietly with hands in lap, while the fidgeting child thought that he was complying by refraining from spitting at a teasing classmate.

Problems also arise when adults devise and rely on pat phrases to tell youngsters how to behave. Unfortunately, the meaning of such phrases often is ambiguous to children and does not give them a clear idea of what the adult expects. Some examples of ambiguous phrases appear in Table 7-2.

Often, the difficulty is compounded when adults assume that because they use the same phrases over and over, children *must* know what they mean. For instance, a teacher tried to stop two children from fighting. She said:

"You're angry. I get upset when you fight. Someone could get hurt. Use your words." Following her directions, one child said to the other, "Okay. You @#$@!" The adult did a quick double take . . . she certainly didn't mean *those* words! Adults who want children to use words to express their emotions, who want children to cooperate, or who want children to stop acting up must tell them a specific way to accomplish these things.

Rules must be positive. Children are most successful at following rules that tell them what to do rather than what not to do or what to stop doing (Clarizio, 1980; Hoffman, 1970; Parke, 1972). In other words, it is easier for children to respond appropriately when they are told "Put your hands in your pockets" rather than "Stop pushing"; "Walk" rather than "Don't run"; and "Eat your food" rather than "Don't play with your food."

One reason why preschoolers are slow to respond to inhibiting commands is that they don't pay much attention to the words "don't" and "stop." Rather, they focus on the verb in each directive as a guide for what to do (Luria, 1961). Thus, the child who is told, "Don't play with your food," hears "Play with your food." This problem is intensified when the adult speaks forcefully because children respond to the tone or physical energy of the message and actually are stimulated to continue. Also, although school-age children are more aware of the importance of listening to all the words of

TABLE 7-2 Undefined Adult Phrases

What Adults Say	What Adults Mean
Use your inside voice	Talk quietly
Walk like a shadow	Walk, don't run
Use your words	Say "I'm angry" rather than hitting

an instruction, it is not unusual for them to miss the "don't" or the "stop" in unfamiliar or highly emotional situations (Ginott, 1973; Gordon, 1975).

In addition, toddlers and preschoolers do not routinely mentally reverse actions they initiate physically (Flavell, 1977; Tribe, 1982). This means they are not always proficient at thinking of an opposite action. They also have difficulty spontaneously interrupting an ongoing behavior. A case in point is Jennifer, a three-year-old, who was busy gluing dry macaroni to her collage. In her effort to get to the bottom of the glue bottle, she tipped it upside down, and the glue ran all over. The caregiver said, "Stop tipping the bottle so far." Jennifer continued gluing, and the glue kept on dripping. When the adult called out, "Don't tip the bottle," she assumed Jennifer knew how to reverse that action mentally. In other words, she expected the child to think of how to hold the bottle with the open end up. To the adult, it was obvious that returning the jar to an upright position was the reverse of holding it upside down. However, she should not have anticipated that Jennifer would know this. Young children do not have enough experience to picture in their minds how to transpose a physical action. For this reason, adults must help children reverse an inappropriate act by showing them or telling them how to do it.

Articulating the Entire Personal Message

The following situations illustrate the integration of all three parts of the personal message:

SITUATION 1: A child is poking Mr. Kee in order to get him to listen to her story.

Adult: You're anxious to tell me something. I don't like it when you poke me to get my attention. Call my name or tap my shoulder lightly.

SITUATION 2: Several youngsters have left their gym towels scattered about the locker room.

Adult: You're in a hurry to get back to class. It bothers me when you leave your dirty towels all over the locker room because then I have to pick them up. Put them in the laundry basket before you leave.

SITUATION 3: It is a hot, humid day. The class is restless, and children are beginning to fidget and whisper while a classmate is reporting on the life of Sojourner Truth.

Adult: You're hot and uncomfortable. It's distracting to Karl when you whisper while he's giving his report. I'm concerned his feelings will be hurt. He worked hard to find this information. Sit quietly until he is finished.

Messages such as these can be given to individual children or to groups. In addition to being used to correct children's behavior, personal messages should also be implemented as a way to reinforce appropriate actions.

Positive Personal Messages

A positive personal message contains only parts one and two of the format just described, and therefore is a variation on the basic skill. Previous emphasis on problems should not be taken to mean that one can expect primarily negative behavior on the part of children. In reality, the evidence is to the contrary. Children often strive to comply with adult expectations and, in fact, frequently initiate constructive actions on their own (Green, Forehand, and MacMahon, 1979; Lytton, 1979). As a result, not all of the emotions prompted by children's behavior are ones of anger or concern. For this reason, personal messages should be used to identify adult's positive reactions as well. Adults must "catch" children being "good"—displaying behaviors that please them—and tell children what those behaviors are: "You're all working together. It makes me feel good to see you negotiating to take turns using the keyboard. You get a lot more done when you work it out rather than arguing" or "You waited until I came back to start the tape. Thank you. I wanted to hear it, too" or "You cleaned up all the art scraps without anybody reminding you. I'm delighted. Now, this table is reading for making popcorn."

A message used in this way is a personal form of praise. Adults go beyond telling children that they have done a "good job" or "great work." Instead, they are saying that the child's specific behavior had special meaning for them. Research has shown that this type of praise is most effective because it describes the impact a particular behavior has had on the person offering the praise (Chernow and Chernow, 1981). General terms such as "good," "nice," or "pretty" soon lose their meaning for both children and adults if they are used over and over again or applied indiscriminately. Moreover, effusive praise that glorifies children rather than their behavior often is viewed as insincere or "too gushy." Thus, it is more effective to say: "You worked hard on your essay. I really liked it. It made me want to know more about Molly Pitcher" than to say, "You are a born writer." In the same vein, children learn more about their behavior from a statement such as "You're trying to comfort Andrew. It makes me feel good that you noticed he was so sad. He needs a friend right now" than from a comment like "You're a terrific kid."

When adults identify behavior they are pleased to see children display and tell them why, they encourage youngsters to repeat those actions another time. All too often, adults take children's proactive behaviors or compliance for granted; they simply expect children to do as they are told or to automatically behave in an appropriate fashion. When this happens, adults have failed to recognize that it takes effort for children to achieve these productive outcomes.

Formulating positive personal messages. Positive personal messages begin with a reflection. This step clarifies the situation from the child's point of view and alerts children that the adult has noticed what they are doing. Next, the adult identifies a personal emotion regarding the child's action and gives a reason for it. In addition, the specific behavior that prompted the adult's emotional reaction is described. This may seem like a lot of verbiage when a simple "Thank you" or "Good" would do. However, the purpose of a positive personal message is to teach children which behaviors they should retain for future use. Thus, the positive personal message is a teaching tool aimed at helping children internalize the constructive behaviors they display. Again, the emphasis is on helping children move from adherence to higher levels of social conduct. Children need reasons for why they should behave in certain ways as much as they need to know why they should not engage in particular actions. They also need to know that the adults with whom they identify are sources of approval as well as correction.

At this point, you have learned about parts one, two, and three of the personal message. Rationales for each component have been offered and suggestions made for how to use personal messages in both positive and negative situations. Following are specific guidelines for how to carry out effective personal messages.

SKILLS FOR EXPRESSING EXPECTATIONS FOR CHILDREN'S BEHAVIOR

How to Reflect in Problem Situations

1. Observe children carefully before reflecting. Enter a problem situation by first considering what the child may be trying to achieve and why.

2. Formulate reflections that accurately describe the child's perspective. Maintain a nonjudgmental stance. This means avoiding thinly veiled accusations, such as "You just don't want to cooperate today" or "You thought you could pull a fast one." These statements represent adult bias and are not real reflections.

3. Remind yourself to describe the child's point of view before your own. At times, because of haste, indignation over a child's behavior, or surprise, you may launch immediately into an expression of your own feelings. One way to avoid this self-centered reaction is to develop the habit of taking a deep breath prior to speaking. That breath can serve as a cue that the reflection comes first. If you catch yourself skipping the reflection, stop and begin again. Later, think of alternate reflections you might use should the situation arise another time. This type of mental practice will help you in future encounters.

4. Pay attention to children's age when deciding which type of reflection to use. Affective reflections generally are most effective in satisfying children under eight. For instance, if two first-graders have come to blows over who will get the next turn at bat, it would be accurate to say, "You're hitting," and then proceed with the rest of the personal message. However, it would be nearer the mark to reflect: "You're really angry. You each thought it was your turn next." This acknowledges what the children consider to be the real problem (the dispute over turns) and

provides a more helpful introduction to the subsequent message.

On the other hand, older children may resent the adult's interpretation of their feelings in front of others. It seems too personal an approach. In such a case, the more neutral behavior reflection or paraphrase reflection would be more appropriate.

5. Avoid using "but" as a way to connect the reflection to the rest of the personal message. The word "but" means "on the contrary." When it is used to connect two phrases, the second phrase contradicts the first. For example, if a friend were to meet you on the street and say, "You look wonderful, but . . . ," you would know that the initial praise was a perfunctory introduction to what the person thought was really important. The same is true when it comes to the personal message. Adults who say, "You wish the story would end, but I want to finish it" are telling children that their feelings do not count. This betrays the true spirit of the reflection.

How to Express Emotion to Children

1. Identify the emotions you experience. State your emotions clearly to the child. Do not rely on nonverbal cues alone. Adults sometimes tap their fingers to show irritation, wrinkle their nose to convey disgust, or sigh to indicate exasperation. Children often misinterpret these signs or miss them altogether. They do not automatically know how you feel and, in fact, are often surprised to find that your feelings may be quite different from their own. Subtle hints will not get your message across. Children benefit from the explicit communication that words provide. Words are specific and to the point. They help children know how you feel and why you feel that way:

"I feel pleased . . ."
"It makes me angry . . ."
"I'm annoyed . . ."
"It's important to me . . ."
"I wish . . ."

2. *Become sensitive to your own array of internal cues that signal a particular emotional state.* Perhaps your cheeks get hot when you start to feel angry, your stomach gets jumpy when you are anxious, or your head seems heavy when you are overwhelmed. At first, it will be the more extreme emotions, like anger, fear, or excitement that will be the easiest to discern and express. Eventually, you will become better able to recognize and talk about more moderate emotions such as contentment, irritation, discomfort, or confusion.

3. *Use a wide range of feeling words of differing intensities.* Purposely select an assortment of feeling words. The greater the vocabulary at your disposal, the more likely you are to be attuned to the gamut of emotions these words represent. If you find yourself using the same few words over and over, look up or discuss possible variations to use in the future.

How to Pinpoint Behaviors

1. *Name the behavior that is affecting you.* Be specific. Describe actions you can see or hear. Avoid generalities that clump several behaviors together or that are open to misinterpretation. Rather than saying, "I get upset when you are mean," say: "I get upset when you (hit me; throw things; tease Jacquie; punch Frank"). Both you and the child must know exactly what you find acceptable or unacceptable.

2. *Describe the behavior, not the child.* It is inappropriate to tell children that they are not nice, bad, nasty, a hard case, "hyper," incorrigible, that they should be ashamed, or that they should know better. All of these descriptions malign children as persons and should not be used.

How to Formulate Reasons

1. *Give children specific reasons for why you approve or disapprove of their behavior.* This means providing children with information that helps them see what will happen if they carry out the behavior in question, either for their own safety and happiness or to protect the rights and safety of others. Rationales such as "Because I said so," "Because I want you to," "Because it's important," "Because it's not nice," "Because I'm bigger than you," "Because that's the rule," or "Because that's how we do things around here" are not real reasons. They do not clearly relate to any of the criteria for deciding when behavior change is appropriate. Phrases like these often are employed when adults cannot think of anything else to say or when they are demanding blind obedience rather than rational compliance. If you cannot think of a legitimate reason for your reaction, reexamine the situation to determine whether your expectations really are appropriate.

2. *Phrase reasons in terms children understand.* Use familiar language and short, simple sentences. Focus on one main point rather than offering an explanation that incorporates several ideas.

3. *Give a reason every time you attempt to change a child's behavior.* Do not assume that, because you gave an explanation yesterday for why running is prohibited, the children will remember today. Children often forget the rationale or may not realize that the reason still is legitimate after a lengthy time lapse (Parke and Murray, 1971). They must hear the same explanations repeatedly before they are able to generalize from one situation to another.

How to Formulate Rules

1. Study child-development norms. Learn what behaviors and understandings might realistically be expected for children of a particular age. Become familiar with the knowledge and skills of children younger and older than those with whom you are working so you will have an understanding of the wide range of children's abilities that are apt to be represented in the group. This also will help you realize what sequence of skills and concepts children must master to move from one point to the next. Identify actions and concepts that are clearly beyond the capability of most of your children.

2. Get to know the children in your group as individuals. Recognize differences in interaction style, reactions to new situations, mood, level of involvement, tolerance for frustration, and attention span. Identify specific abilities exhibited by each child as well as those concepts and skills they have yet to master.

3. Think about what combination of knowledge and action children must carry out to successfully follow a given rule. Analyze your rules and determine exactly what they entail.

4. Only implement legitimate rules. Use the criteria of safety, protection of property, and respect for others and the principle of importance in determining whether a rule must be set. If the child's behavior cannot be linked to any of these, reconsider the validity of the rule.

5. Tell children what the rules are. Rules should be explicit rather than implicit. Do not assume that children know a rule just because you know it, or that they remember it from past experience. Remind children of what the rules are at a time when the rules are not at issue. Calm, rational discussions of why certain rules are in force help children understand the value of and reasons for specific expectations. Also, remind children of the rules in situations in which those rules apply. For instance, it is more effective to say, "Remember to walk in the classroom," when a child is caught running than to say, "How many times have I told you about running indoors?" This last generalization assumes that the child knows that the actual rule is "walk." Although the child may recognize that running is not allowed, there is no guarantee that he or she remembers the rule that specifies what to do instead.

6. Reward children's approximations of the rule. Do not expect children to comply perfectly with all rules each and every time. Recognize behaviors that show that children are attempting to follow the rule, although they may not be totally successful. For instance, if the rule is that children must raise their hands and wait to be called on in order to talk in a group, you should not expect perfect silence as you survey the waving hands before you. That would be too much for children to accomplish all at once. At first, it is likely that raised hands would be accompanied by excited vocalization as children attempt to gain your attention. Rather than focusing on the infraction of talking, it would be better to praise them for remembering to raise their hands. Gradually, with time and many reminders, fewer children will call out when they raise their hands to speak.

7. Revise unreasonable rules. If you become aware that a child is not able to follow a rule as you have formulated it, do not press on in the mistaken notion that rules must be absolute. It is better to revamp the rule at a level at which the child is able to comply. In the preceding example, this would mean changing the rule from "Everyone must raise his or her hand and wait quietly to be called on before speaking" to "Everyone must raise his or her hand in order to be called on." The "wait quietly" portion of the rule should be added only after most children have demonstrated the ability to raise their hand.

8. Use language that is clear and to the point. Identify a specific behavior that you wish the child to enact. *Avoid generalizations*, such as "be nice," "don't be mean," "don't act up," "act your age," "make me proud of you," "behave yourself," "be good at school," "don't make me ashamed of you," or "mind your manners,"

9. Ascertain whether children have the same understanding of the rule that you do. Ask children to repeat the rule in their own words, or get them to demonstrate their comprehension in some manner. At other times, you will depend on more subjective evaluations, such as considering children's facial expressions or the "look in their eyes."

10. When in doubt, assume that children have not understood, rather than concluding that they are deliberately breaking the rule. If children have not understood your rule, you will have to do something to make your rule more clear. Some things you can try are:

a. Repeating your words more slowly and articulating more clearly.

b. Rephrasing your message in simpler, more familiar language and emphasizing key words.

c. Restating your message using a combination of gestures and words.

d. Taking the child to an area where there is less interference from noise and other distractions.

e. Emphasizing your message using physical prompts such as pictures or objects in combination with gestures.

f. Demonstrating what you want by doing it yourself.

11. Practice thinking about what you want children to do as well as what you wish they *would refrain from doing.* Anticipate potential problem situations and the positive actions children could take to avoid or remedy them.

12. Catch yourself saying "No" or "Stop." Rephrase your negative instruction as a positive statement. This may mean interrupting yourself in the middle of a sentence. Also, couple negative instructions with positive ones, such as saying: "Don't run. Walk."

13. Tell younger and less experienced children what the alternatives are. Let older or more experienced children generate alternatives for themselves. If a young child is pushing to get out the door, you could say: "You're anxious to get outside. I'm worried that when you push, someone will get hurt. Take a giant step back away from the door and we'll try again." The message to an older child might be: "You're anxious to get outside. I'm worried that when you push, someone will get hurt. Let's think of a way everyone can get outside safely."

Selection of one response or the other will be determined by the adult's estimation of children's previous experience and their potential readiness to negotiate. Two-year-olds, a fifth-grade class that has come together for the first time, or a group of youngsters frenzied with excitement probably will have neither the skill, the patience, nor the trust necessary to work out a compromise. However, youngsters who have had lots of practice generating ideas and alternatives and who are calm usually will rise to the challenge.

14. Talk and act simultaneously. Immediately stop children's actions that may be harmful to themselves or others. Use physical intervention if necessary. For example, if two children are fighting, stop the hitting by grasping their hands or separating them. If a child is about to jump off a too-high step, move quickly to restrain him or her. If children are using the saw inappropriately, gain control of it. Once the dangerous situation has been neutralized, youngsters are bet- ter able to hear what you have to say. It is at this point that personal messages have their greatest impact.

PITFALLS TO AVOID

Regardless of whether you are fostering children's self-discipline individually or in groups, informally or in structured activities, there are certain pitfalls you should avoid.

Talking in paragraphs. Effective personal messages are brief and to the point. However, beginners who are struggling to include all of the parts may inadvertantly add extra words or sentences. An awkward example would be: ''You seem really unhappy about not getting a turn. I'm sorry you didn't get a turn but you are hitting Tanya with a stick. When you hit her with a stick, I'm afraid she could get hurt. I'd like you to hand the stick to me.'' This mouthful of words probably will have a discouraging outcome for several reasons. First, children cannot distinguish the main point, and may have forgotten what was stated in the beginning. Laborious personal messages are those children are the most likely to ignore. They get tired of listening and tune out.

When first learning this skill, talking too much is better than forgetting an important element. If adults find themselves delivering a particularly long personal message, they should think afterward of a more concise way of expressing it. For instance, the preceding example could have been condensed to: ''You're upset. It worries me that if you hit Tanya with a stick, you could hurt her. Hand the stick to me.''

Failing to initiate the personal message for fear of making a mistake. Adults may become tongue tied at moments when a personal message would be appropriate. They dread stumbling over the words, getting the order wrong, or forgetting parts. Unfortunately, the more adults remain quiet, the less practice they get, and so improvement and comfort with the skill does not develop. The only remedy is to make fledgling attempts whenever the opportunity arises. It often is easier to begin with positive personal messages because there is less risk involved. Once these flow smoothly, corrective messages seem less difficult.

Talking about personal feelings only in problem situations. Some adults have a tendency to focus primarily on children's mistakes. They are quick to express their dissatisfaction, and tend to see their role as one of admonishing children who fall short of their expectations. This outlook fails to recognize that behavior change is not solely a product of telling children what they are doing wrong, but is also a function of strengthening those positive behaviors children already display. Thus, in order for children to keep certain behaviors in their repertoire, they must hear that adults feel pleased, excited, amused, appreciative, comforted, or supported by their actions.

Children do not always wait patiently to hear an entire corrective personal message. They may turn their heads or simply walk away. Sometimes when this happens, adults become flustered and give up. A better approach is to use the nonverbal strategies presented in Chapter 3. Adults should lightly hold onto a disinterested child and should pursue youngsters who dash off in an attempt to avoid confrontation. This does not entail jerking children around or forcing them to establish eye contact. It does mean trying to gain the child's attention for the entire duration of the message.

It also is important for children to be told that adults become annoyed when children do not listen. A personal message such as the following would be in order: "You don't want to hear what I'm telling you. It upsets me when you walk away while I'm talking. Stand still and listen."

Focusing on short-term rather than long-term goals. In problem situations, adults sometimes find it easier to simply say "No" or "We don't do that here." Occasionally, these shortcuts have the desired effect: children stop what they are doing. Unfortunately, such success usually is temporary because it does not prompt children's internalization of the rule. Instead, adults have to repeat their admonitions over and over again. Moreover, children may not comply without direct supervision. Personal messages are worth the time they take because they contribute to increased self-discipline.

Making expectations known from a distance. When adults see children in threatening situations, their first impulse is to shout a warning: "Look out! You'll drop the fish tank" or "Watch it! The floor is slippery." In cases such as these, children frequently ignore the message because they do not realize it is directed at them. The adult's loud voice may cause alarm or stimulate children to become louder or more active themselves. In either case, the adult's message is not received adequately. A better approach is to move quickly over to the child and state expectations in a face-to-face interaction. The benefits of such a direct approach outweigh the seconds lost to achieve it.

Waiting too long to express emotions. In an effort to avoid committing themselves to a line of action, some adults refrain from expressing less intense emotions and allow their emotions to build up over time. When they do react, it is often when they they have reached the limit of their endurance. Then, their irritation explodes into fury, concern blossoms into real anxiety,

or confusion escalates into panic. None of these are constructive responses because they are so intense that rational action becomes difficult. In addition, children usually are shocked at such extreme reactions and are genuinely uncertain as to what led to the eruption. Adults who rely on this approach also model that only extreme emotions are worth expressing. They should not be surprised when children copy their example. This pitfall can be forestalled by discussing one's emotions when first aware of them.

Attempting to disguise expectations. Adults who feel nervous about telling children what to do often disguise their rules. They do this in any number of ways. The most common tactic is to phrase the rule as a question. Instead of saying, "It's time to clean up," they cajole: "Don't you want to clean up, now?"; "Clean up, okay?"; "You wouldn't want us to have a messy room, would you?"; or "We want a clean room, right?"

In every case, adults are hoping children will see things their way. Yet, children usually interpret these messages not as rules, which they are obligated to follow, but as questions, which are optional and that can be answered with either "Yes" or "No." Adults who are unwilling to hear "No" eliminate ambiguity when they phrase their rules as statements: "Start cleaning up"; "It's time to clean up."

Another way adults camouflage rules it to tell children that they "need to" or that the adult "needs them to" do something rather than saying children "have to" or adults "want them to." This confuses children because "needs" relate to basic physical and psychological necessities, such as food, sleep, love, and shelter (Maslow, 1954). Sitting down together does not fall into this category. The adult does not "need" the child to sit down; the adult *wants* the child to sit down, and for very good reasons: so others can see, so the child can get information, so the teacher is not distracted. Children as young as two years of age talk about what they want and have an understanding of this concept. They also understand the notion of "have to" ("I have to go to the bathroom," "Mommy has to go to the store," "We have to eat supper now"). The concept of "need" is much more nebulous and less precise. It is more accurate to use the words "want" and "have to."

A final error that obscures a behavioral requirement is for adults to include themselves in the rule when they have no real intention of following it. For instance, adults say, "Let's wipe our bottom until it is clean," when what they mean is, "Wipe your bottom," or they say, "Let's brush our teeth," rather than "Brush your teeth." Adults who do this imply that children should look to them as a model of the behavior in question. When this does not mirror reality, the statement is confusing.

Adults who use disguising tactics limit children's chances to be successful. They do a disservice to youngsters who are trying to discover what the real rules are and how to obey them. Thus, rules should be phrased as statements rather than questions, using words with precise, rather than ambiguous, meanings, and in a way that leaves no doubt as to who is expected to follow them.

SUMMARY

All children must learn to behave in accordance with the expectations of their culture if they are to be accepted by society. Adults are responsible for teaching children what those expectations are, and they spend much of their time engaged in this role. Their ultimate aim is not only to teach children specific standards but to help them develop the ability to regulate their own behavior.

Self-discipline is composed of several capabilities: curbing initial impulses that might be damaging to self or others; resisting temptation; postponing gratification; implementing plans of action; and initiating appropriate social behaviors. How children feel about their behavior, how they think about it, and their previous experiences affect children's ability to achieve self-discipline. Guilt and empathy are emotional factors influencing this capacity. The development of moral reasoning, role-taking abilities, impulse control, desire for independence, language, memory, and understanding of how events are associated are cognitive processes that influence children's achievement of self-control.

It is generally agreed that children become more self-disciplined as they grow older; however, even in adulthood, people exhibit a wide range of behavior ranging from no self-control to much self-discipline. Adherence, identification, and internalization are terms used to describe these variations. Adherence is the most primitive form of compliance; internalization is the most sophisticated. Individuals' behaviors generally fall into one or another of these categories, although it should be noted that everyone at different times and in different circumstances may display any of them.

Because most people experience the developmental and emotional changes previously described, thus acquiring some basis for internalization, the reasons for variation can best be attributed to individuals' experiences. Children learn the values of society through direct instruction, observation, and reward and punishment. Adults tell and show children what is expected of them—explicitly in words and implicitly by their own behavior. Different parenting styles, authoritarian, permissive, and authoritative, have been linked to emotional and behavioral outcomes in children. The authoritative mode produces children who feel good about themselves and are most likely to internalize standards of behavior. Therefore, it is the style of interaction most desirable for adults to adopt.

Authoritative adults can express their expectations through a personal message. This consists of a reflection acknowledging the child's point of view, a statement to the child that describes the adult's response to a specific behavior of the child and the reason for the reaction, and, finally, an alternative, desirable behavior in which the child is to engage. This last step is used only in situations focusing on behavior change and serves as a rule that governs the child's behavior for that situation.

Circumstances under which rules are appropriate deal with safety, protection of property, and the rights of others. The rule portion of the personal message must be reasonable, definable, and positive. Personal messages also should be used to reinforce existing constructive behavior. Difficulties students encounter when first learning how to formulate personal messages can be overcome by paying close attention to the rationale for this particular skill.

DISCUSSION QUESTIONS

1. Define self-discipline and describe its component parts.
2. Jamal is a preschooler. His older brother Ahmed is ten. Discuss how guilt and empathy would figure into each child's thinking.
3. It has been shown that children become more capable of self-discipline as they mature. Explain the developmental changes that contribute to this increased capacity.
4. Define adherence, identification, and internalization. Then, discuss which behavioral cues tell you when a person is operating at any one of these levels.
5. Name three rules you had to follow as a child. Talk about whether your compliance with each rule was at the adherence, identification, or internalization level.
6. Describe all of the things you could do in relation to instruction and modeling to teach a child how to handle guinea pigs safely. Make sure you take into account children's varying levels of maturity.
7. Think about a teacher you had while growing up. Describe that person to someone else, keeping in mind the three discipline styles discussed in this chapter. See if the listener can categorize the teacher's behavior based on your description. Then, discuss the effect that style had on your learning.
8. Describe what changes you might have to make in your own interaction style to make it more authoritative.
9. With classmates, identify the three parts of the personal message and provide no less than three reasons per part why each is included.
10. Describe a situation in which your use of a personal message was effective, both from your point of view and the child's. Next, describe a situation in which your use of a personal message was ineffective. Analyze what went wrong and how your response could be improved in the future.

CHAPTER 8
Fostering Self-Discipline in Children: Implementing Consequences

SOURCE: © Ulrike Welsch

OBJECTIVES:

On completion of this chapter, you will be able to describe:

1. Typical reasons why children misbehave.

2. Ways adults can change their behavior to make children's compliance more likely.

3. Four different kinds of consequences.

4. The difference between consequences and punishment.

5. Effective ways of implementing consequences.

6. How to combine personal messages and consequences to enforce limits on children's behavior.

7. Time-out.

8. Pitfalls to avoid in implementing consequences.

In the previous chapter, you learned about personal messages. This skill provided a mechanism for establishing rules in formal group settings. Now, we turn our attention to enforcing such rules through the use of consequences.

Adult: You're enjoying the easel. It's time to clean up. I'd like some help because there is a lot to put away. Please cap the paints or tag the projects that are already dry.

Child 1: No.

Child 2: You can't make me.

Child 3: I don't want to.

Child 4: I cleaned up last time. It's someone else's turn today.

As everyone knows, there are times when children do not listen, when they misbehave, and when they disobey. In fact, it is no secret that many people leave the helping professions because of problems enforcing rules (Madsen and Madsen, 1981).

When children act unacceptably, some adults attribute their behavior to familial, cultural, social, or economic conditions, thereby concluding that there is little that helping professionals can do to change their behavior. Others surmise that youngsters just want to misbehave. Both assumptions are faulty. First, although a variety of ecological factors do influence how children behave away from home, helping professionals *can* teach children how to conduct themselves more appropriately in the formal group setting. Moreover, there is strong evidence that most children want to comply with adult expectations (Lytton, 1977; Green, Forehand, and MacMahon, 1979).

Yet, at one time or another, all children digress from behavior considered correct. When this happens, it could be for any one of several reasons:

1. They cannot identify appropriate alternate behaviors to substitute for unacceptable actions.
2. They are unaware of the rule or are uncertain about what behaviors are demanded.
3. They are not capable of meeting the standards set.
4. They do not know how to control impulsive behavior.
5. They have developed faulty perceptions about how to gain acceptance.
6. They have been taught by other significant adults, siblings, or peers to use behaviors that differ from those espoused by the helping professional.
7. They have concluded that the rule is unwarranted.
8. They have learned that certain behaviors labeled unacceptable actually are rewarded, or that the rule makes no difference in what happens to them.
9. They are trying to determine the boundaries of the situation and whether the adult will maintain them over time.

Any one or a combination of these reasons may be why children misbehave in most instances. Such difficulties often are amenable to improvement when adults make particular changes in their own behavior.

Behavior Problems and Their Solutions

Problem 1: children's inability to determine appropriate actions to replace inappropriate ones,

Problem 2: children's uncertainty about what the rules are and which behaviors are required to satisfy them,

Problem 3: inappropriate adult standards for children's behavior. The first three reasons cited for children's misbehavior are a result of the inappropriate ways adults sometimes make rules (Hawley and Hawley, 1981; Flavell, 1977). In each case, transgressions come about because children are incapable of following the rule rather than unwilling to do so. In essence, the way the adults structure the rule predetermines failure. If this experience is repeated frequently, children may cease trying to comply, convinced that their efforts are hopeless. What began as a problem related to inappropriate rule setting may escalate into one of children disobeying because they assume that is the best they can do.

Solution. As described in Chapter 7, adults must tell children what alternative behaviors to substitute for the inappropriate ones in which they are engaged. They do this by stating explicit rules that are reasonable, definable, and positive. When adults adhere to these guidelines, children are less likely to misbehave.

Problem 4: acting on impulse. Many times, children act without thinking: an idea or desire pops into their heads, and they are in motion; they see something they want and grab for it; they think something and blurt it out (Kagen, 1966; Rohwer, 1970). Earlier, it was pointed out that impulsivity decreases with age and that by six years of age, most children can inhibit their impulses relatively well. However, there are youngsters who remain impulsive because that is their cognitive style. These children continue to act immediately on their desires, in contrast to their more reflective age-mates, whose cognitive approach is to respond more thoughtfully (Harrison and Nadelman, 1972).

Solution. Recent evidence shows that children as young as three years of age, as well as older youngsters described as impulsive, can be taught specific tactics to help them learn to wait and respond more carefully (Ritchie and Toner, 1985; Toner, Moore, and Emmons, 1980). For

example, children who hear themselves described as patient eventually become more so and become better able to delay gratification. This happens because when adults tell children they are patient, children incorporate a notion of self-control into their self-concept and try to live up to that image.

In addition, young people can be taught self-instructional strategies as a way to inhibit impulses and resist temptation (Mischel and Patterson, 1976). For instance, children who are taught to say to themselves "It is good if I wait" will find it easier to hold back than youngsters who do not have such training. The same is true when adults tell children to repeat pertinent rules to themselves, such as "I shouldn't touch the stereo" (Mischel and Patterson, 1976). Moreover, children are less impulsive when they talk to themselves about the task in which they are involved rather than focus on a possible reward for their behavior (Fabes, 1984). Thus, it is more effective to teach them to say "I am putting away the books" rather than "When I'm through, I'll get to go outside."

Problem 5: children's faulty perceptions. Some children engage in unacceptable behavior because they have an erroneous perception of how to achieve group status. There are three common perceptual errors. Certain children mistakenly believe that the only time they are valued is when they are the center of attention. Others are sure they must have power over peers and adults in order to be important. Still others conclude that they never will be special to anyone and so devote much of their energy convincing people that they are as unlikeable or as helpless as they imagine themselves to be (Dreikurs and Soltz, 1964). These children can be described in turn as attention seekers, power seekers, and hopeless children. Regardless of which perception prompts their behavior, such youngsters are unable to consider the needs of those with whom they interact and are incapable of recognizing the destructive impact of their actions. As a result, they tend to perpetuate negative interaction patterns that support their erroneous conclusions.

For instance, attention seekers demand constant, undue notice by playing the clown, bragging, badgering, engaging in games of one-upmanship, demanding continual praise, and deliberately breaking known rules in order to elicit a reaction. Adults inadvertently encourage these problem behaviors by responding to inappropriate demands for attention and/or by failing to recognize appropriate behaviors.

Power seekers either do so blatantly, via brute force, or more subtly by resisting other's requests. This often results in power struggles in which the child's goal is to outwit the adult. Children who have no legitimate power over their lives are those most likely to succumb to this maladaptive pattern.

Hopeless children are those who have given up all prospects of gaining attention or power. They may feel so completely rejected that their only gratification comes from hurting others, thereby eliciting a response (Dreikurs, 1972). Children in this state of mind sometimes are violent or vengeful. They make it their business to discover the vulnerability of the people with whom they come in contact and take advantage of this knowledge. This counterproductive approach gains them the notoriety they seek.

Not all hopeless children resort to hurtful behavior, however. Some act completely helpless in an effort to discourage anyone from expecting too much of them (Dreikurs and Soltz, 1964). They avoid any situation in which there is a chance for failure. Their perception of absolute inadequacy is reinforced when adults focus primarily on their mistakes or take over rather than allowing them to do things for themselves (Mead, 1976).

Solution. Changing children's perceptions is no easy matter; yet, in situations such as these, it is the key to making permanent improve-

ments in their behavior. Adults must first recognize and acknowledge misconceptions, then make a conscious effort to help children learn alternative ways of establishing their self-worth (Mead, 1976).

Attention seekers. The positive behaviors of the attention seekers should be rewarded by personal messages and praise. When the child engages in inappropriate actions, the adult can choose either of two options. The first is to ignore minor eruptions and wait for the child to choose a more appropriate action before giving attention (Patterson, 1977). The second option better suited to more severe bids for notice, involves reflecting the child's desire for attention, explaining that it will not be given until he or she demonstrates more desirable behavior, then following through with this plan.

Power seekers. Power-seeking youngsters should have an opportunity to experience legitimate power. Giving children choices, allowing them to make decisions, and requesting their participation in planning are effective and appropriate ways to achieve this. When power struggles occur, the key to defusing them is to remain calm, to refrain from fighting, and to refuse to give in (Dreikurs and Cassel, 1972). The exact ways in which adults can extricate themselves from these entanglements will be described later in this chapter.

Hopeless children. When children feel hopeless, it is critical for adults to recognize that this is the basis of their antisocial or apathetic behavior. Such youngsters are the ones who most need to experience nurturing relationships with adults to boost their self-esteem. It is particularly important that adults not demonstrate agreement with children's dismal assessments of their capacities by becoming punitive or detached. Instead, they must see through children's defenses and show the children that there are some things about them that are likable and worthy. It often takes imagination and effort to identify such qualities, but it is obvious that if adults cannot see them, children never will.

Problem 6: contradictory rules. It is not at all unusual for the influential people in children's lives to have differing ideas about how children should behave. As a result, they may actively espouse conflicting codes of conduct (Shanab and Yahya, 1977). For instance, school personnel may tell children to settle disagreements peacefully, but family members may encourage them to "fight it out." In this situation, the school's main focus is on teaching children harmonious group living, and parents are interested in teaching them self-defense skills. Both goals have merit, but are different. This puts children in a dilemma. In an effort to obey one set of expectations, they may have to violate another.

Solution. Helping professionals must remember that their expectations are not the only appropriate ones, nor are they the only ones with which children are expected to comply. Consequently, they must work with the other members of children's mesosystems to minimize the dilemmas youngsters face. How this can best be accomplished is the subject of Chapter 15, Working with Parents, and also is described in Chapter 16, Making Judgments.

Furthermore, when adults use personal messages, they help children realize that adults have differing reactions to their behavior. This enables helping professionals to stress that certain standards may be situation specific: "You're upset. At home you don't have to pick up. It bothers me when the puzzles are all over the floor. We could lose the pieces. Here at school everybody helps. There is a puzzle for you to put away."

Problem 7: controversial rules. Children often reject rules that seem capricious or unwarranted (Rich, 1984). Although most youngsters see the value of moral guidelines (such as those

advocating honesty and justice), they are less inclined to treat social conventions (such as answering politely or eating with a certain fork) in the same way (Damon, 1978; Turiel, 1978). Hence, they may conclude that a rule is "stupid" and feel no inclination to comply.

Solution. Adults minimize children's rejection of rules when they explain why the rules have been set. Moreover, children are most willing to adopt a code of behavior in which they have some say (Rich, 1984). Children as young as three years of age can participate in discussions about why rules are important to groups of people living and working together and what rules should be observed (Glasser, 1969; Kostelnik and Stein, 1986). When children have opportunities to make up some of the rules that govern their lives, they come to recognize those rules as social agreements of which they are a part.

Problem 8: mixed messages. Even when a rule is appropriately stated to children, adult actions may undermine it. This happens when adults fail to reward compliance, ignore broken rules, or give in to noncompliance (Parke and Duer, 1972; Shanab and Yahya, 1977). Such acts create an unpredictable environment in which children cannot be sure what the real expectations are. For example, at Roosevelt Elementary School, the rule is that children should eat their lunch at a moderate pace. Youngsters are understandably confused when, on the days they eat slowly, no one notices. Additionally, on some days they are scolded for gobbling their food, but on other days, they are urged to eat faster (adults are running late), and on still other days they are ignored when they wolf down their sandwiches (adults are too tired to cope). Adult actions have made enforcement of the rule arbitrary. Over time, youngsters will conclude that the rule has no real meaning and so will not feel obliged to uphold it.

Have to be consistent

Problem 9: testing the limits. Children constantly try to determine what constitutes inbounds and out-of-bounds behavior. The only way they can discover these differences is to test them out by repeated trial and error. Moreover, because adults vary in their willingness to obtain compliance, children test each adult with whom they come in contact to ascertain that person's limits. Both forms of testing frequently result in children engaging in inappropriate behavior.

Solution. The way to resolve behavior problems related to mixed messages and limit testing is to enforce rules consistently through the use of consequences. The following portion of this chapter will focus on this important skill.

CONSEQUENCES

Consequences are events that make a particular behavior more or less likely to happen in the future. Positive consequences increase the chances that behaviors will be repeated, and inhibiting consequences reduce them.

Positive Consequences

Positive consequences are those that reward children for maintaining a rule. One of the most common, and most effective, is to praise children with a positive personal message (Gordon, 1975; Mendler and Curwin, 1983). When adults affirm children's compliance using this skill, children are likely to comply again in the future. This is because a positive personal message reminds children of the rule and its rationale at a time when they have demonstrable proof that they are able to follow it. For instance, the adult who says: "Leroy, you remembered to raise your hand before talking. I'm pleased. That gave me a chance to finish what I was saying" is highlighting the child's appropriate behavior in a way that will make an impression on him. In addition, it acknowledges that following the rule took effort. This type of confirmation works well with children of all ages.

Positive consequences also can take the form of earned privileges. For instance, if the rule is "handle library books carefully," children might be told that when they demonstrate this skill they can use the books without adult assistance. This type of reward actually formalizes the natural aftermath of their positive behavior. It also emphasizes the positive outcomes that will accrue from their actions. When this information is articulated, the linkages between behavior and outcome become more evident.

Similarly, when adults acknowledge the accumulated benefits of following a rule over time, they promote children's feelings of self-satisfaction and pride in their own performance. For instance, if the rule were "practice the piano every day," the adult might say: "You were a big hit at the recital. All of your practicing really paid off."

Inhibiting Consequences

Behavioral scientists commonly refer to all inhibiting consequences as punishments (Baumrind, 1977; Becker, 1964; Hoffman, 1970; Parke, 1974). However, data have been generated that show that some uses of punishment are effective in promoting self-discipline, and others are not. In order to clearly distinguish between the two, we will label strategies that enhance self-control as *negative consequences* and strategies that detract from self-control as *punishments*. There are significant differences between the two. These are summarized in Table 8-1.

Punishments. Punishments are harsh, unreasonable actions taken against children whose conduct is disapproved. They depend on the use of power or force to change behavior and often occur when adults lose self-control. As a result, adults respond in haste, in anger, or without thinking (Sheppard and Willoughby, 1975). As described in Table 8-1, punishments

TABLE 8-1 Differences Between Negative
Consequences and Punishments

Do it because I say so. is wrong

NEGATIVE CONSEQUENCES	PUNISHMENTS
Suggest that the children are accepted, although their behavior is not	Imply that children themselves have been rejected
Are instructive—they teach children how to correct problem behaviors by having them approximate acceptable behaviors or restore the situation to a more positive condition	Are not instructive—they merely inform children that an infraction has occurred, but do not teach them how to correct it
Have a clear and easily discernible relationship to the unacceptable behavior based on content or timing	Have no relationship to the behavior to be changed
Are thoughtfully imposed	Are capricious and demeaning
Communicate that children have the power to correct their own behavior	Communicate the personal power of the adult
Enable children eventually to change their own behavior	Force adults to assume the entire responsibility for behavior change
Focus on prevention of future infractions	Focus on retaliation for current infractions
Are applied matter-of-factly	Are applied with obvious resentment
Imply that misbehavior is a product of the situation	Imply that misbehavior is due to the "badness" of the child
Are levied in direct proportion to the magnitude of the transgression	Are severe and exceed the magnitude of the infraction
Require adults and children to reason together and correct problem situations	Require adults to use coercion to correct problem behaviors

Sources: R. Dreikurs and P. Cassel, *Discipline Without Tears* (New York: Hawthorn Books, 1972); A.N. Mendler and R.L. Curwin, *Taking Charge in the Classroom* (Reston, Virginia: Reston Publishing Company, 1983); J.P. Raffini, *Discipline: Negotiating Conflicts with Today's Kids* (Englewood Cliffs, New Jersey: Prentice-Hall, 1980).

are a form of retribution, the goal of which is to make perpetrators pay for their misbehavior (Mendler and Curwin, 1983). Adults who resort to punishments assume that children have little capacity to reason; they believe youngsters respond only to conditioning. Based on this premise, they think children will avoid misbehaving for fear of being punished. In reality, youngsters learn to avoid the punishing agent and spend much of their time figuring out how to escape being caught (Becker, Engelmann, and Thomas, 1971; Parke, 1977). In addition, although punishments serve to mollify the adult, they often promote fear and hostility in the child (Hoffman, 1983). Neither of these emotions enhances the probability of future cooperation.

Another characteristic of punishments is that although they serve as sanctions against certain behaviors, they do not emphasize the desirable alternatives. Thus, children may come to learn that particular actions are disapproved, but gain no information on how to correct them. Moreover, because punishments are so intensely negative, children become so emotionally involved that they are incapable of carrying out the cognitive reasoning necessary to correct their behavior on their own (Hoffman, 1983).

Finally, adults who rely on punishments fail to model calm, rational approaches to problem situations (Caldwell, 1977; Feshbach, 1970). Instead, they display the very actions they may be trying to curb in children. This type of behavior keeps children at an adherence level because it gives them none of the tools necessary for internalization.

Negative consequences. Negative consequences are constructive actions aimed at helping children recognize the impact their behavior has on themselves and others. They are founded on the idea that reason is the basis for behavior change, and they are implemented with the long-term goal of teaching children self-discipline. Negative consequences help children learn acceptable conduct from the experience of being corrected (Mendler and Curwin, 1983). They enable children to approximate the desired acts. These serve as practice for the future and make it more likely that children will succeed in repeating the behaviors (Wolff, Levin, and Longobardi, 1972). When properly applied, negative consequences also encourage children to think about characteristics of problem situations, which may be useful to them in future encounters. For example, what prompted the episode, how and why did people react to the child's behavior, and what acceptable alternatives were suggested? This self-analysis is possible because negative consequences do not elicit intense feelings of fear or shame, which interfere with children's ability to reason.

Another attribute of such consequences is that they make the children's world more predictable; they know exactly what will happen when a rule is broken. Infractions are dealt with matter-of-factly and consistently, no matter who the perpetrators are or how often they have broken the rule before. In this way, negative consequences serve as the logical outcome of particular actions. They have nothing to do with personality, favoritism, or vengeance.

Types of Negative Consequences

Negative consequences come in three varieties: natural, logical, and unrelated.

Natural consequences. Natural consequences happen without intervention (Dinkmeyer and McKay, 1976). They show children that their actions are significant and do influence what happens to them (Hawley and Hawley, 1981). For instance, children who come late for lunch may suffer the natural consequence of eating cold food or eating alone because everyone else is finished. Children who talk while the homework is being assigned may miss the page numbers. Children who fail to put their sneakers in the locker may lose them. These repercussions all are a direct result of circumstance rather than of adult manipulation of the environment. Hence, there are times when adults do not have to create a consequence because the outcome follows directly from the child's action. Children will learn to come on time for lunch if they dislike eating cold food or eating by themselves; they will learn to listen when directions are being given if they value their grades; and they will remember to put their shoes away if they expect to find them quickly.

Natural consequences are very effective in teaching children what to do and what not to do and are well suited for many situations. However, they cannot be relied on when children's safety is jeopardized. For instance, the natural consequence of letting a child run in the street or drink cleaning fluid would result in serious injury, an outcome no adult would permit. In these types of situations, logical consequences are more appropriate.

Logical consequences. Logical consequences are directly related to the rule. This means there is an obvious connection between the child's behavior and the resulting disciplinary action (Clarizio, 1980; Hawley and Hawley, 1981).

Penalties of this type help children either approximate the desired behavior or correct problem situations. For example, if Rudy is running down the corridor, the logical consequence would be to have him go back and walk. The act of walking serves as a more vivid reminder of the rule than would simply scolding him or making him sit out for several minutes. Having children practice rules to be remembered increases their chances for future success (Wolff, Levin, and Longobardi, 1972).

At times, such approximations are less feasible, and so rectification is more appropriate. For instance, if children throw food on the floor, it would be logical to insist that they clean it up prior to getting anything else to eat. This type of action restores the situation to a more acceptable state and shows children that the unacceptable act of throwing food will not be tolerated.

Forbidding children to play outside for a week is not a logical consequence for fighting with peers over the ball. Although this approach temporarily halts the dispute, it does not teach children how to deal with the issue more effectively in the future. A better solution would be to tell children they must take turns if they wish to continue to play, and then help them carry out this plan if they are unable to do so on their own. This proposal teaches children that sharing can be a viable solution. The same is true if Maranda spills the paint seemingly on purpose. It would be more logical to have her wipe it up than to send her out of the room or to relegate her to a desk in the corner for some portion of the day.

Another benefit of using logical consequences is that they teach children behaviors that are incompatible with the noncompliant behaviors (Richards and Siegel, 1978). As these incompatible responses are strengthened through practice and positive consequences, the less desirable behaviors that they replace are weakened. For instance, children who must go back and walk each time they run down the hospital corridor are rehearsing walking in the specific situation in which it is called for. This rehearsal makes it more likely that they will remember to walk on their own once in a while. If such instances are noted and praised, eventually youngsters learn to replace the disallowed behavior (running) with the more desired behavior (walking).

Unrelated consequences. The third type of negative consequence is the unrelated consequence. As the name implies, these consequences are not the natural outgrowth of a child's behavior, nor do they enable children to approximate desired behaviors or rectify less desirable ones. Instead, they are outcomes manufactured by the adult in response to children's misbehavior. Examples might include forbidding Lisa to watch television until she brushes her teeth or to choose a work station until she hangs up her coat. Brushing teeth has nothing to do with watching television, so denial of television neither teaches Lisa how to brush her teeth nor corrects her unclean mouth. However, if Lisa really values her time in front of the set, she will quickly learn that watching television is contingent on tooth brushing. The same is true regarding the coat. Forbidding Lisa to choose a work station neither approximates hanging up her coat nor rectifies neglecting it. What it does do is create an aversive situation that the child can make more positive by doing what is required.

Most unrelated consequences involve loss of a privilege or introduction of a penalty. Because they have such little relation to the broken rule, adults must take particular care to enforce these in the true spirit of consequences, not punishments. Furthermore, the most beneficial unrelated consequences are those that, although dissimilar in content, are linked in time to the infraction. It is more effective to withhold the next event in a sequence than one far in the future. Therefore, it is better to deprive Lisa of participating in some portion of the free-choice period for forgetting to hang up her coat than to keep her in from recess several hours hence.

Deciding Which Negative Consequences to Use

Negative consequences are important instructional tools that have the power to teach children to discern right from wrong, to help them distinguish appropriate from inappropriate behavior, and to demonstrate to them the potential impact of their behavior on themselves and on others. With so many valuable lessons to offer, they cannot be carelessly applied. Rather, adults must thoughtfully formulate the consequences they use. The three types of negative consequences should be considered in order, from natural to logical to unrelated.

Step one. It is best to consider first what natural consequences pertain to the situation and to determine if it is acceptable to let them happen. It should be noted that acceptability is an idea that varies from adult to adult. What might be permissible to one adult might be unthinkable to another. As mentioned earlier, the natural consequence for children who arrive late for a meal is to have cold food or eat alone. Some caregivers might view these outcomes as reasonable; others could not bring themselves to maintain them. Instead, they would find themselves reheating the meal or keeping the child company. If the latter is true, and adults can predict that they will be unable to sustain a hands-off policy, the natural consequence is not the consequence of choice; in fact, no negative consequence would occur for the child. In this case, a logical or unrelated consequence would be more suitable. The decision to use one of these instead of a natural consequence also is mandated in situations in which nonintervention obviously would lead to injury or property damage.

Step two. If the adult has contemplated the natural consequences and found them unacceptable or difficult to maintain, logical consequences should be considered next. These can be tailored to fit any situation. Adults should think about ways in which the rule could be re-enacted (such as repeating an action correctly or carrying out the behavior with adult help) or ways in which a problem situation might be redressed. Although logical consequences take more imagination than stock favorites such as sitting in a chair in the corner, going to detention, or being sent to the principal's office, they are much more effective in helping children learn appropriate alternate behaviors (Clarizio, 1980; Lundell, 1982; Walker, 1979).

Step three. As a last resort, unrelated consequences should be implemented. Although they are effective, they must be used sparingly because their primary value is in curtailing behavior for the moment (Clarizio, 1980). For long-term change to occur, children must learn acceptable substitutes for which logical consequences are preferable. Unrelated consequences should be implemented only when no logical consequence is available.

Implementing Negative Consequences

When children are engaged in potential problem situations, adults should first remind them of the rule in a serious, firm tone (Lundell, 1982; Charles, 1983). Within the sequence of skills presented in this book, the rule portion of the personal message serves as this reminder. Often, such prompting is all that is needed for children to comply. If at this point, children obey, they should be praised. However, if they continue to disregard the rule, the adult must implement an appropriate negative consequence.

The consequence is first stated to the child in the form of a warning (Raffini, 1980; Mendler

FIGURE 8-1 The professional may have to hold on to the child while giving the warning.
SOURCE: Photo by David Kostelnik

colors on your own, or I will help you find a way.''

In each case, the warning gives children an opportunity and an incentive to change their behavior in accordance with adult expectations. It also notifies children that this is the last chance for them to control the situation prior to the adult taking over.

The warning is not intended to be frightening, abusive, or retaliatory. Rather, it is a plain statement of fact. This means adults must warn children calmly. They should not scream at children, shake them, wave a fist in their face, or incorporate threats such as ''Just you wait'' or ''I'll show you'' as part of their statement.

Once the warning has been given, the adult pauses to give children an opportunity to comply. Children's reaction times are somewhat slower than adults sometimes wish. Adults have to take care not to jump in before the child has had time to respond. For instance, when Alex is told to wait his turn or go to the end of the line, he make take several seconds deciding what to do. His delay poses no real threat to those around him, and so it can be tolerated. On the other hand, there are times when safety is jeopardized. These circumstances call for immediate physical intervention, even as the warning is being stated. For example, if Amy is about to throw a stone, the adult should quickly catch her hand while saying, ''You can either put the stone down yourself, or I will take it from you.'' Even here, a moment's pause is necessary to give Amy a chance to drop the rock herself. The adult should maintain a grasp on Amy's hand and try to sense her intention, based on whether she remains tense or begins to relax as well as by what she might be saying. If Amy were capable of releasing the stone herself, she would be displaying a modicum of self-control. If she were not, the adult would exert the maximum external control by taking the stone away from her. This last step is a follow-through on the stated consequence and is very important.

and Curwin, 1983). The *warning* is phrased as an either-or statement that repeats the rule and then tells the child what will happen if he or she does not follow it. For example, if the rule is ''wait your turn to get a drink,'' the warning could be ''Either wait your turn, or you will have to go back to the end of the line.'' If the rule is ''share the watercolors,'' a warning might be ''Either find a way to share the water-

Following Through on Negative Consequences

It is not enough simply to tell youngsters what the negative consequences will be. Adults must enforce them if children do not comply (Canter and Canter, 1983; Charles, 1983). This is called *following through*. The follow-through is a critical part of the discipline process because it involves the enactment of the negative consequence. Because appropriate negative consequences are instructional in nature, this step provides children with valuable information about how to redirect inappropriate behavior. It also demonstrates quite clearly that adults mean what they say and that there is a limit to the amount of out-of-bounds behavior they will tolerate. It is from discipline encounters such as these that children begin to build an accurate picture of their effect on the world and its reaction to them (Hoffman, 1983).

When adults find themselves in situations that demand a follow-through, there are certain things they must say so that the reasoning behind their actions is made clear to the child. It is important for children to recognize that negative consequences are a result of their own behavior; they are not arbitrary or vindictive actions on the part of the adult.

The follow-through begins with a brief reflection that summarizes the situation from the child's point of view. Next is a sentence that restates the warning. This often is prefaced by the words "Remember, I told you. . . ." Then, the adult repeats the consequence as a statement of what will happen next as a result of the child's behavior. This statement often begins with the word "now." Thus, a typical follow-through would sound like this: "You're still anxious to get ahead in line. Remember, I told you, either wait your turn or go to the back. Now, go to the back." While this is being said, the adult might have to escort the child to the back of the line as a way to physically affirm what was stated.

When to Implement Negative Consequences

Two key factors influence how well children learn from the consequences they experience: consistency and timing. *Consistency* involves how often the rule is enforced. *Timing* refers to the period between when the rule is broken and enforcement is initiated.

Rule enforcement must be consistent (Canter and Canter, 1983; Lundell, 1982). Every time the rule is broken, the adult must be prepared to enact appropriate negative consequences to ensure compliance. Rules that are administered one day and neglected the next are ineffective (Parke and Duer, 1972). Because children cannot be sure whether or not the rule is in operation, they are not likely to follow it. As a result, youngsters who experience erratic rule enforcement tend to demonstrate more incidents of deviant behavior than do children whose experience has been more regular (McCord, McCord, and Howard, 1961; Parke and Duer, 1972). Because consistency is so important, adults are cautioned to insist on only a few rules at a time. It is better to unwaveringly enforce one or two important rules than to halfheartedly attempt many rules.

In addition to being consistent, rule enforcement must be immediate. Long delays between the moment when the child breaks the rule and the moment when the follow-through takes place weaken the impact of the consequence (Parke and Duer, 1972; Marion, 1983). Thus, statements such as "Wait 'til your father comes home" or "I'll have the head teacher deal with you when she gets back" are nonproductive. Children must have an opportunity to associate their inappropriate behavior with the resulting consequence. The further removed the consequence is in time from the act itself, the more difficult it is for children to make a connection. For the same reasons, consistency and immediacy are important to the implementation of positive consequences as well.

COMBINING THE WARNING AND FOLLOW-THROUGH WITH THE PERSONAL MESSAGE_____

Up to this point, we have focused on the appropriate use of both positive and negative consequences. Yet, consequences do not stand alone. Rather, the follow-through stage of rule enforcement represents the final step in a sequence of skills aimed at enhancing children's development of self-control. This sequence consists of a personal message succeeded by a warning, and then, if necessary, a follow-through. The sequence is illustrated in the following situation:

SITUATION: Mr. Howard, a student teacher, enters the bathroom to find Allen stuffing several paper towels down the toilet. Water and towels are all over the floor. The child does not see the adult come in.

Personal message. Mr. Howard quickly approaches Alan and stands close to him. He catches Alan's hand just as the child reaches for another towel. Mr. Howard says, "Alan, you're having fun. I'm worried that with this water all over the floor, someone will slip and get hurt. Start cleaning up this mess." Mr. Howard pauses a moment and waits for Alan to comply. Instead, Alan tries to edge toward the door. Mr. Howard stops him.

Warning. You'd rather not clean up. Either you figure out where to start cleaning, or I'll tell you where to start.

Again, Mr. Howard waits a few seconds in the hope that Alan will begin. The child just stands there. Mr. Howard calmly hands Alan a bucket and a sponge.

Follow-through. "You didn't make a choice. Remember, I said either you choose, or I'd choose. You can start in this corner." Mr. Howard places the sponge in Alan's hand and bodily edges him toward the puddle.

Skill-Sequence Rationale

By combining a personal message with a warning and follow-through, Mr. Howard was using a step-by-step sequence designed, in the short run, to change Alan's unacceptable behavior. Its long-range objective is to provide a structure through which Alan eventually learns to regulate his own behavior.

Short-term benefits. The immediate advantages to both Mr. Howard and Alan of the sequential use of a personal message, warning, and follow-through are outlined in Table 8-2.

Long-term benefits. The skill just described offers short-term advantages to adults and children, but it also provides long-term benefits as well. Combining a personal message, a warning, and a follow-through helps adults deal with children's problem behaviors consistently, both for the same child over time and among different children. This consistency enables helping professionals to establish an authoritative patten of interaction with youngsters in the formal group setting. In addition, the time adults initially invest in using the sequence with children pays off later in fewer future incidents (Stein and Kostelnik, 1984).

Children also profit when their confrontations with adults are eventually reduced. They feel more successful and better able to satisfy their needs in ways that result in social rewards rather than social costs. The resulting positive self-appraisal enhances their feelings of self-esteem. Moreover, as children experience this sequence on a variety of occasions, they gradually shift from complete dependence on external, adult control, as embodied in the follow-through, to greater internal control, as prompted by the personal message and warning.

When the sequence is first introduced, most youngsters will test the adult's predictability and resolve by proceeding all the way to the

TABLE 8-2 Short-Term Benefits of the Sequential Use of a Personal Message, Warning, and Follow-Through

	Short-Term Benefits for Mr. Howard	**Short-Term Benefits for Alan**
Step 1a: Personal Message	Has a way to enter the situation calmly and rationally Has a means of communicating respect and acceptance of the child, but disapproval of the behavior Has a blueprint for what kinds of information to provide the child initially	Is treated with respect and acceptance Is alerted that his behavior is inappropriate and is told why Is informed via the rule of what to do instead (clean up the mess)
Step 1b: Pause	Has a chance to see if Alan can comply before he exerts further external control Has a moment to think of an appropriate consequence to use if necessary	Is given a chance to change the inappropriate behavior on his own, thereby exercising internal control
Step 2a: Warning	Has a constructive way to exert increased external control over Alan's behavior Establishes a legitimate foundation for carrying out the follow-through if necessary	Is reminded of the rule Gains a clear understanding of what will happen if he does not comply
Step 2b: Pause	Has a chance to see if Alan can comply before he exerts further external control	Is given a chance to change the inappropriate behavior on his own, thereby exercising internal control
Step 3: Follow-Through	Has an authoritative way to resolve the situation without becoming abusive or giving in Has been able to stop the negative behavior as well as remedy the problem situation Has had an opportunity to demonstrate that he means what he says, increasing his predictability in the eyes of the child	Is able to rehearse an acceptable behavior he was not able to carry out on his own Has evidence that the adult means what he says and is predictable in his actions

follow-through. As children become more familiar with both the adult and the sequence of steps described here, they often respond to the warning without having to experience the follow-through directly. This happens because they have learned that the adult means what he or she says and that a warning indicates that a follow-through is forthcoming unless the behavior is changed. Behavior change at this point shows that children are beginning to exercise some self-regulation, albeit at the adherence level in order to avoid a consequence or gain the benefits of compliance.

Eventually, children reach a point at which a personal message is all that is needed to guide their actions. In this way, they begin to exert greater control over their behavior, while the adult exerts less. Initially, this change occurs because children respond to the emotions of the adult with whom they identify. Gradually, however, they take into account the reasoning behind the expectation and, as a result, consider the effects their actions have on those around them. Such reasoning ultimately leads to internalization. As this occurs, it is the child who assumes the greatest responsibility for his or her conduct, not the adult. Thus, the adult's use of the skill sequence in any given situation will match the child's ability to exercise inner control. If the child is able to comply based on the reasoning of the personal message, further intervention is unnecessary. However, should a youngster need more support, it is provided.

Successive Use of the Skill Sequence

It is not unusual for children to resist complying by attempting to divert the adult's attention from the issue at hand. Shouting, protesting, escalating the problem behavior, or running away are common strategies. All of these tactics are aimed at getting the adult to forget about enforcement, allowing the child to escape consequences. Unfortunately, if adults throw up their hands and say, ''I can't do anything with this child,'' they are teaching him or her that these tactics work. As a result, children begin to rely on inappropriate strategies more and more frequently. This dilemma must be avoided at all costs because the more ingrained an inappropriate behavior becomes, the more difficult it is to change. The best way to deal with such situations is to defuse them right at the start. This means always following through once a warning has been stated and the child has failed to demonstrate compliance. For example, if the warning is ''Either walk, or I will help you,'' that is exactly what must happen. If Ginger runs away, she must be retrieved; if Camille flails her arms, they must be grasped; if Vince curses, it is best to ignore his words; if Saul become stiff or goes limp, his feet should be shuffled along. Even a few steps is enough to make the point.

In addition, there are times when one problem behavior will lead to another. For instance, four-year-old Linda climbs to the top of the bookcase as part of her Wonder Woman play. The helping professional approaches and goes through the sequence to the warning, which is ''Either come down by yourself, or I will take you down.'' Linda laughs and shouts, ''You can't get me!'' Grasping the child's foot, the adult begins to follow through. As she takes the child into her arms, Linda starts to kick. Kicking represents a new problem behavior and is treated as such. The adult initiates the sequence again. This time, the warning is ''Either stop kicking, or I will hold your feet until you do.'' The adult then follows through until Linda becomes less agitated. In this way, the adult has demonstrated that he or she will follow through over and over again until no negative behaviors are evident. When adults enforce their rules as illustrated here, they create a predictable, stable environment for children and leave no doubt in children's minds as to what will happen when rules are followed or broken. This type of consistency is absolutely necessary if children are to learn that there is no ultimate behavior they can display to which the adult is unable to respond rationally and firmly.

TIME-OUT: THE ULTIMATE CONSEQUENCE

The types of consequences presented thus far are applicable in the majority of discipline encounters you will face. However, there will be times when a child engages in a problem behavior that is so intense or so objectionable that a specialized consequence, time-out, is called for. Time-out involves isolating a child from the group for a designated period of time. This consequence is appropriate only when children have a temper tantrum or when they demonstrate habituated antisocial behavior.

Temper Tantrums

Most people know a temper tantrum when they see one. There is no mistaking the physical signs: red face, flailing arms and legs, screaming, and crying. Although such behavior can be disconcerting to adults, it is important to remember that a temper tantrum is such an intense emotional and physical response that children's normal thought processes are no longer available to them. This means that the impassioned child cannot hear or respond to adult directions or efforts to comfort; cannot think out a logical, more socially appropriate sequence of actions; and can no longer gauge the effect his or her behavior has on self or others. Any child, at any time, may become involved in a tantrum, and although such behavior is most common in toddlers, older preschoolers as well as school-age children may, on occasion, resort to these volcanic outbursts.

Children have tantrums for several reasons. Tantrums initially appear when urgent wants are not immediately gratified. Later, tantrums usually occur because adults have previously given in to children's tantrums, because children are fatigued, because they receive little attention for positive behavior, because they are continually subjected to unrealistic adult demands, or because rule enforcement is unpredictable (Brooks, 1981).

The best way to avoid temper tantrums is to acknowledge children's feelings before they become intense, to teach children alternative ways to express their desires, to respond positively when children behave in appropriate ways, and to make reasonable rules and enforce them consistently. Yet, children occasionally will resort to temper tantrums in spite of all these precautions. When this happens, the goal is to help them regain their self-control. In the case of toddlers, whose outbursts are extreme but short lived, the best way to restore calm is to ignore their outrageous behavior and let them quiet down in their own way and time. Older children, whose emotional states are longer lasting, benefit from the logical consequence: time-out.

Habituated Antisocial Behavior

At times, all children engage in some antisocial behaviors, such as kicking, hitting, or biting. These occasional bouts of misbehavior are best dealt with using personal messages and the consequences described earlier. For some children, however, reliance on such actions becomes habitual—they engage in these negative behaviors again and again because they have learned that punching, pushing, or pinching gets them the attention they want, intimidates others to give in, or enhances their prestige with some members of the group by allowing them to gain power over others. Another type of habituated antisocial behavior is displayed when children unthinkingly rely on unacceptable actions as their primary method of interacting with others. When adults recognize that this is happening, they must work at stopping the problem behavior as well as interrupting the pattern of positive reinforcement that has allowed it to continue. Here again, time-out is the consequence of choice.

FIGURE 8-2 State the follow-through clearly and calmly. Demonstrate firmness by using appropriate nonverbal behaviors.
SOURCE: H. Armstrong Roberts

Time-Out

Time-out is a technique in which the adult removes the child from an environment where reinforcers for undesirable behavior are available to an environment where such reinforcers are absent (Becker, Engelmann, and Thomas, 1971; Sheppard and Willoughby, 1975). In most cases, this means taking the child from the group setting for a specified period of time, during which all possibilities of gaining rewards for inappropriate behavior are cut off. In this way, time-out serves three functions:

1. It acts as a clear signal to children that they have behaved unacceptably (Patterson, 1977).
2. It interrupts a sequence of naturally occurring events that have served to reinforce a negative behavior (Crary, 1980).
3. It provides out-of-control children with a cooling-off period during which they can regain their composure privately (Kostelnik and Kurtz, 1986).

Consequently, time-out serves as a logical consequence directly related to the problem behavior. With children who are out of control, time-out offers a means of regaining control; with children who are receiving rewards for negative behavior, the reward is temporarily removed.

Time-out has been used with children in a variety of settings and is an effective way to change behavior (Crary, 1980; Harris, 1980). However, helping professionals are cautioned that the technique is viable only when it is used judiciously, compassionately, and correctly (Martin, 1975; Walker, 1979). The procedure begins with the selection of an appropriate time-out area.

Establishing the time-out area. The time-out area must be decided on in advance. It is impossible to select one while carrying a kicking, screaming child, and it takes away from the immediacy of the consequence if the adult must spend five minutes deciding where the time-out will be held.

The major concerns in designating a place for time-out are safety and convenience. Minimizing distractions, removing equipment, and eliminating anything sharp or breakable are essential. Many helping professionals have found that providing a chair structures the space, offering a specific place for the child to sit. The best time-out area is immediately adjacent to, but not within, the group setting itself. This may be a separate room, the hallway, or an alcove. Having a separate area for time-out is least disturbing to the group, ensures that the child taking a time-out will not receive attention from others, and helps the adult who is managing the time-out to focus on that process rather than being distracted by whatever else is going on. In addition, the privacy offered by such a locale makes it easier for the child to re-enter the group once he or she has settled down. This is an important aspect of time-out because peers may avoid, tease, or otherwise react negatively to a child who they feel has made a spectacle of himself or herself. Obviously, choosing a time-out area outside the main room means that at least two adults must be available to properly supervise both the child in time-out and the remaining children in the group. This is most easily arranged in team situations, but sole adults in adjacent rooms also can plan to help one another. In either case, adults should discuss ahead of time what they will do to maintain the ongoing group activity should one of them become involved in a time-out.

It may not be possible to designate a time-out area outside the group setting due to lack of space or other supporting adults. Under these circumstances, it is better to select a time-out place within the room rather than to not have one at all. The same guidelines previously described should be followed as closely as possible. The time-out place should be away from general activity, but where the adult can keep an eye on both the child and the group. If at all possible, it should not be in a place where children go for other reasons, such as the book corner or the child's cubby. Any way of partially screening the area off from curious onlookers also should be explored. Regardless of whether time-out occurs within or away from the group setting, the time-out place should never be so cramped, enclosed, or dark that it will frighten a child who is put there (Clarizio, 1980).

Preparing the group for time-out. Talking about time-out with a group should take place after the adult has begun to develop a relationship with them. The presentation could be an outgrowth of talking about emotions and how people express them in different ways. Adults can say things like:

There are times when people become so angry, or so excited, or so sad that they use their whole body to let other people know what their feelings are. Sometimes, when people use their bodies in this way, there is a danger that they will hurt themselves or someone else. If this happens in our group and I am worried that someone could be hurt, I will have a time-out with the child who is upset. Time-out means time away from the group in a safe, quiet place. It is a chance for the person who is very upset to calm down. If you need a time-out, I will be with you in the time-out area to make sure you are safe. I will not be talking to you, because that may make it harder for you to think about what's on your mind. Once you feel more relaxed and comfortable, you can return to the group. Then we can talk, if you would like.

Depending on the circumstances, the adult could also say: "If I have a time-out with a child, the other children will be expected to continue their seat work until we are finished," or "Ms. Lindstrom will stay with the other children until the time-out is over." Once time-out has been described, show younger children where the time-out area is. Older children can help select an appropriate spot.

Throughout the discussion, adults are reminded to use the words "time-out" in their description. It is important that children learn that time-out is a particular procedure, with specific steps and goals that are implemented in response to predesignated behaviors. Time-out is not the same as "quiet time," "sitting in the chair," "thinking time," or "sitting in the cubby." All of those labels have connotations that differ from the meaning of time-out.

Preparing an individual for time-out. Time-out for children whose antisocial behavior has become habituated is very similar to the procedure described for temper tantrums. The major difference is that adults must first establish that the problem behavior is habitual. The behavior is then identified privately to the child during a time when the misconduct is not actually present. At this point, the use of time-out as a consequence for future misbehavior also is described: "Lila, there are many times during the day when you pinch. Pinching hurts. You must stop. Every time you pinch, you will have time-out for five minutes. Time-out means time away from the group in a quiet place. There is no talking and no playing in time-out." Note that when time-out is used to correct this type

of behavior, the adult states in advance under what conditions time-out will occur and how long it will last. Implementation should take place each and every time the problem behavior happens.

Implementing time-out. A specific sequence of steps must be followed in order to implement time-out correctly:

1. The child is warned, and if the behavior continues, he or she is removed to the time-out area.

   a. When a child is in the midst of a tantrum, the adult first warns him or her of the consequences of such behavior: "You're very upset. I can't talk to you when you're screaming (kicking or biting) like this. Please stop. Either calm down here or we will have a time-out." If the child continues the tantrum, the adult follows through by saying, "Now, we will have a time-out," and then leads the child to the time-out place. This often is easier said than done. The adult may have to bodily remove the child by using a firm grasp and possibly lifting the child and carrying him or her. Children should never be jerked, pulled, or shoved as the adult attempts to move them along. One effective method of physically handling a struggling child is for the adult to position himself or herself behind the child, crossing the child's arms across the body and holding on. Simultaneously, the adult spreads his or her legs so that the child's kicks will not be harmful. In this position, the adult then sidles out of the room. This is a safe approach regardless of the child's size or physical movement.

   b. In the case of a child who demonstrates habitual antisocial behavior, the adult already has warned the child that time-out will take place if the behavior is repeated. If it is, time-out is immediately

(Handwritten margin note, left side:) If tantrum, don't start the time-out. Start the time for time-out until they're quiet it gets worse when u put them in time-out.

initiated by saying: "Lila, you pinched. Time-out." The child then is led to the time-out area. If the child resists, proceed as in step 1a.

2. Once in the time-out area, the adult reflects the child's feelings and provides basic information so that he or she will know what to expect: "You're still very angry. When you're quiet for one minute we can talk about what's bothering you," or "You pinched. You will have time-out for five minutes."

3. The adult holds to the stated time limit before allowing the child to leave the time-out area. One to two minutes usually is appropriate for children between the ages of three and six; five minutes is satisfactory for older school-age youngsters. This means a prescribed period of calm. Any time the child spends screaming is not included.

4. The adult places the child in the time-out chair. It is acceptable for the child to leave the chair but not the area. If the child tries to run out of the area before the time is up, he or she should be returned to it.

5. Throughout the time-out process, the adult must remain silent. Talking only aggravates the situation. First, it may prolong the time-out because the child may not yet be at a point at which she or he is able to focus on what is being said. Second, talking teaches the child that one way to get undivided adult attention is to engage in unacceptable behavior.

6. It should be noted that the child's extreme behavior probably will escalate during time-out. Adults are urged to ignore misbehavior as best they can by busying themselves with something at hand: reading a magazine, tidying shelves, correcting tests, writing in a notebook.

7. Any attempts to harm the adult must be stopped immediately. Hurting an adult can lead to later feelings of guilt and fear that the child may find hard to overcome. In addition, adults will find it extremely difficult to react rationally and calmly if they have been injured. One way to prevent injury is to physically restrain the child. The child can be held facing away from the adult. A good precaution is for the adult to put one hand between the back of the child's head and the adult's face. This prevents injury to the adult's nose or teeth should the child rear back. Restraint calms some children and further incites others. Unfortunately, one does not always know in advance how a child will react. If an adult learns that holding a child will add to his or her distress, physical restraint should be avoided, if possible. If the situation seems potentially unsafe, it helps to say: "You don't want me to hold you. I will only hold you if it looks like you could get hurt. If not, I will stand here, but I won't touch you."

8. If peers seem curious about what is going on, an adult should reflect their concerns, remind them about time-out, and assure them that the child is unharmed and will be returning to the group when calm.

9. The child is led from time-out once the conditions have been satisfied and then is given an opportunity to discuss the incident that led to the time-out. This discussion should not take place in the time-out area; in this way, the child will learn that problems can be solved in the regular group setting rather than only in a special place. Some children will not want to discuss the incident at this time. If that is the case, the child should be allowed to resume his or her place in the group without being forced into conversation.

10. A child who has completed time-out as the result of a tantrum should be praised for the hard work he or she put into calming down.

11. Later in the day, the adult who implemented time-out should have a pleasant contact with the child to reassure him or her of the adult's continuing affection. When

adults maintain a nurturing relationship with the child, she or he becomes better able to exercise control in subsequent situations (Parke and Walters, 1967).

After the child leaves time-out. One question often asked is whether children who have just been through time-out should be required to comply with the adult demand that may have triggered it. In other words, should Cecily have to put away the materials she didn't want to put away earlier, or should Harley be made to finish all the problems on page 2? For children who have resorted to a tantrum, it must be remembered that time-out was implemented as a consequence for out-of-control behavior, not as a consequence for failing to clean up or for not finishing an assignment. Self-control is a prerequisite to achieving the other desired behaviors. If self-control has been regained, the child has learned a big lesson. It is up to the adult to decide whether the child will benefit from attention to the secondary goals at this point. However, adults should never become so enmeshed in their own immediate desires (cleanup rules, completed assignments) that they lose sight of their long-term goals for children.

When youngsters have gone through a time-out for habituated antisocial behavior, a good follow-up is to have them perform an act of kindness for their victim sometime during the day. This does not mean making the child apologize; rather, it involves some positive behavior, such as helping the victim do something (Schickedanz, Schickedanz, and Forsyth, 1982). Restitution reduces the chances of the victim feeling a need to retaliate, and helps teach the erring child a substitute form of interaction.

Another question that arises is how long time-out will take. Although this naturally varies from child to child, there is evidence that the acting-out behavior that goes with the first use of time-out can last from 30 minutes to two hours (Becker, Engelmann, and Thomas, 1971). Documentation shows that if adults do not give in or abandon time-out, subsequent episodes with the same child are much shorter in duration (Whaley and Malott, 1971).

SKILLS FOR IMPLEMENTING CONSEQUENCES

1. Anticipate consequences that fit the rules you make. Generate in advance some possible consequences for common rules you expect to make. For example, if you are working with preschoolers, think about consequences you will use to enforce rules about sharing, sitting though group time, independence in dressing, and keeping quiet at nap time. If the children in your group are older, decide on consequences for resolving playground conflicts with peers and to enforce rules for paying attention, turning assignments in on time, and doing one's own work. These are all typical situations in which rule enforcement may be necessary. Think first of the natural consequences you might use. Then, plan out possible logical consequences. Consider unrelated consequences as a last resort. Generate ideas for positive consequences as well; consider forms of praise as well as earned privileges.

2. Give children opportunities to generate their own ideas for consequences. Just as children benefit from formulating some of the rules that govern their lives, so, too, do they learn from helping to generate potential consequences. This approach can be utilized with children as young as four years of age and continues to be effective throughout childhood (Hawley and Hawley, 1981). Introduce potential problem situations at a time when an infraction is not an issue, and help children consider open-ended questions such as ''What should we do when people knock down others' blocks?'' or ''What should we do when people keep wandering around the room and interrupting those who are working?'' or ''What should we do when people push ahead in line without waiting their turn?'' When youngsters weigh out the value of the rule and what action might lead to better compliance, they are directly experiencing the causal relationship between behavior

and outcome. They also have an opportunity to explore why the rule is important and to discuss the role of consequences. It is not unusual for such talks to begin with children suggesting lurid, cruel, or totally unfeasible penalties. Do not reject these outright, but include them for analysis along with the other suggestions. Experience has shown that once the novelty of such outrageous notions has dissipated, children settle down to serious discussion.

3. Articulate consequences in the form of a warning. Link the rule and the consequence in an either-or statement to the child: ''Either choose your own place in the circle, or I will help you choose one,'' ''Either put that puzzle together, or you won't be allowed to get another off the shelf,'' ''Either stop whispering, or I'll have to separate you.''

4. Give warnings privately. Children who are preoccupied with saving face as a result of public humiliation are not inclined to comply with rules. When giving warnings, move close to the child. Use a firm, quiet voice in explaining what will happen should the misbehavior continue. Remember to use the child's name.

5. Point out the natural consequences of children's actions. Provide information to children about the natural consequences of their behavior in a matter-of-fact, nonjudgmental tone. Children benefit from factual information such as, ''When you shared the paste with Tim, he was willing to share the glitter with you'' or ''When you forgot to feed the fish, it meant they went hungry all day.'' Children tune out when they catch a hint of ''I told you so'' in your words or demeanor. Resist the temptation to tell children how smart you were all along. They will learn more from supportive explanations of the facts. Thus, instead of saying: ''See.

Those were never intended to go every which way in the box,'' say, ''You've discovered that when the pieces go every which way, they don't fit in the box.''

6. Use the personal message, warning, and follow-through in order. Do not vary this sequence or skip parts of it. To do so invalidates both the short-term and long-term benefits described earlier in this chapter.

7. Allow children enough time to respond to each step of the sequence. Approach discipline encounters with the idea of spending at least a few minutes. At each phase of the sequence, wait at least several seconds so children have time to comply if they are able. In situations you consider dangerous, stop the action physically and watch for signs that the youngster will obey. In less pressured circumstances, a time lapse of a few minutes between personal message and warning, then warning and follow-through may not be too long. For instance, Mr. Gomez, the social worker, has decided it is time for LouEllen to choose a work station rather than flitting in and out, disrupting everyone. He says: ''LouEllen, you haven't found an activity that really interests you yet. It bothers me when you wander around because it is distracting. Pick one spot where you would like to work. I'll check on you in a minute or two to see which you decide on.'' Three minutes later, Mr. Gomez checks and finds that LouEllen still is unoccupied. Approaching her, he says: ''LouEllen, you're still looking for something to do. You can either select a station, now, or I'll pick one for you.'' He stands by the child for 30 seconds or so. She does not move. At this point, Mr. Gomez enforces the rule by stating: ''You still can't decide. Remember, I said you choose, or I'd choose. Now, we'll try bird calls.'' Mr. Gomez takes LouEllen by the hand and heads in the direction of the bird-call station.

Notice that in the prolonged interaction, a reflection prefaced each portion of the se-

quence. Reflecting helped to reclarify the situation each time and provided continuity from one step to the next.

Helping professionals who work in a team should be alert to fellow team members who are caught up in a limit-setting situation. When this occurs, other adults should provide supervision to the group until the follow-through has been completed. Professionals who work alone may have to follow through while simultaneously maintaining a global view of the room throughout the procedure. In addition, they should be prepared to tell other children in the group what to do until the situation is resolved. (''Dolores and I have to work this out. Review Chapter 4 until we are through'').

8. Finish the follow-through once you begin it. Although it is important to give children enough time to respond, it also is critical to enforce rules once you progress to the follow-through phase of the sequence. If you have begun to say, ''Remember, I told you . . . ,'' and the child vows never to do it again or says, ''Okay, okay, I'll do it,'' continue to implement the consequence calmly and firmly. Do not get sidetracked at this phase by other issues. Reflect the child's concern or promise, thereby acknowledging it, and then point out that the consequence is for current behavior, not future actions.

9. Communicate with other adults regarding rule enforcement. Sometimes, children push the limits with one adult and then move on to someone else when a follow-through is forthcoming. In this way, the same child may engage in problem behavior all over the room with no real enforcement. Prevent this from happening by alerting other adults about the warning you have given a certain child. Do this within the child's hearing so that she or he is aware that the warning remains in effect even though the location has changed. Be receptive when other adults advise you of their warnings. Follow through on their warning if necessary. For example, if Kathleen has been warned that if she pushes another child on the playground one more time, she will have to sit on the side for five minutes, tell other adults that this is the case. Thus, anyone seeing Kathleen push again can enforce the consequence. This creates a much more predictable environment for Kathleen in which she will learn that pushing is unacceptable.

10. Avoid power struggles.

Adult: Yes, you will.

Child: No, I won't.

Adult: Yes, you will.

Child: No, I won't.

This is the common language of a power struggle. It typically occurs when adults try to implement consequences and children refuse to comply (Mendler and Curwin, 1983; Dreikurs and Cassel, 1972). The situation escalates when both become more adamant about their positions. Power struggles usually involve a verbal battle and often happen in front of an audience. Unfortunately, there are no winners—both parties stand to lose something. The adult may gain temporary adherence, but may well have lost the respect of the child. On the other hand, if the child gains superiority for the moment by having the adult back down, he or she likely will suffer future repercussions from an adult who feels thwarted or ridiculed. There are a number of strategies you can use to circumvent this quandary:

a. Avoid making unnecessary rules.
b. Do not embarrass children in public—keep all communication between you and the child private.
c. Remain calm.
d. Avoid contradicting children's assertions. For instance, if the warning is

"Either take a drink without snorting, or I will take your straw" and the child snorts, reach for the straw. If the child says, "But I didn't mean it," do not debate the purposefulness of the act. Instead, acknowledge the child's contention with the words, "That may be . . .," and continue to implement the consequences: "You didn't snort on purpose. That may be. Remember, I told you, any more animal sounds and I would take the straw away. Now, I'm taking the straw."

e. Stick to the main issue. Do not allow yourself to become involved in an argument over extraneous details.
f. Discuss the power struggle privately with the child. This strategy is particularly effective with older children who have learned some attributes of compromise. Tell the child directly that a power struggle seems to be developing and that you would like to work out the issue in another way.
g. Avoid entrapment. When children begin to argue, refuse to become involved. You can do this either by quietly repeating the rule and the consequences and then resuming your normal activity, or by telling the child that you would be willing to discuss it later when you both are more calm.

11. Teach children self-instructional strategies. Help impulsive children exert greater self-control by teaching them to tell themselves "I can wait," "I am patient," "I am picking up the books, one at a time." Support youngsters' attempts at self-regulation with reflections of your own: "You waited very patiently," "You're picking up the books, one at a time."

12. Actively attempt to alter children's faulty perceptions. Give attention seekers appropriate attention. Provide power seekers with legitimate power. Confer on hopeless children your affirmation of their worth. Refer to the earlier portions of this chapter for ideas on how to accomplish these goals.

13. Prepare in advance to use time-out. Review the steps for time-out presented in this chapter so that when you have to use this consequence, you will know what to do. If you are working in a team, discuss time-out with your colleagues and come to some agreement about how the procedure will be conducted and how the classroom will function when a time-out is in progress.

14. Use time-out only with children who are having a temper tantrum or who exhibit habituated antisocial behavior. Remember that time-out is the ultimate consequence you have at your disposal. Avoid implementing it indiscriminately. Do not use it when another, logical consequence could better teach the child how to follow the rule. For instance, if Benny forgets to raise his hand before blurting out an answer, it would be better to tell him that he won't be called on until he does raise his hand than to send him into the hall for time-out. Arbitrary overuse of time-out weakens its effectiveness.

PITFALLS TO AVOID_____

Regardless of whether you are fostering children's self-discipline individually or in groups, informally or in structured activities, there are certain pitfalls you should avoid.

Reluctance to follow through.

Jonathan, you're having a good time up there. I'm worried you might fall. Climb down, please.

Jonathan, I mean it: climb down.

Jonathan, I really mean it this time.

Jonathan, how many times do I have to tell you to climb down?

Jonathan, am I going to have to get angry?

Jonathan, I'm getting mad.

O.K. Jonathan, I'm really mad now—climb down.

Jonathan, that's it! I'm going to carry you down.

This scenario illustrates a common problem for many adults: their reluctance to follow through on the limits they set. In an effort to avoid a confrontation, they may find themselves repeating a warning or some variation of it numerous times. They do this out of a mistaken desire to give children another chance to comply. In reality, adults undermine the predictability of the children's world when they vacillate in this way, giving them no way of knowing at what point the adult will no longer be willing to wait for compliance. In this situation, will that point be reached after the third warning, the fifth, or the sixth? Perhaps yesterday, the adult waited until the fifth warning; tomorrow, he or she may stop at the second. Children are not mind readers and can only predict an adult reaction by testing it out. The one way to avoid this situation is always to follow through after you give the first warning. In this way, children learn that the description of the consequence is a cue for them either to change their behavior or to expect the consequence.

Relying on convenient or familiar consequences rather than finding one best suited to the situation.
It is natural for adults to feel frustrated or unsure when first implementing consequences. In an effort to ease this discomfort, they may utilize the same consequence over and over. Frequently, they choose an unrelated

consequence, such as removing children from a situation or having them lose a particular privilege. Although such consequences may stop the behavior for the moment, they do not teach an appropriate alternative for children to use in future situations. Over time, children may learn to anticipate the consequence and may decide that certain misbehaviors are worth it. This problem can be avoided by varying consequences to fit the situation at hand.

Ignoring natural consequences. Sometimes, adults fail to recognize that a natural consequence has taken place and so institute additional, unnecessary consequences. For instance, Peggy accidentally stepped on her guinea pig. She was terribly distressed over the possible injury and attempted to soothe the animal. Her distress was the natural consequence of her error. The 4-H leader completely missed the importance of the natural consequence and proceeded to scold Peggy for being so careless, then told her she was not to hold the guinea pig for the next hour, even though the child already had recognized the negative results of her actions. Because the purpose of a consequence is to make children aware of the impact of their behavior, no further penalty was called for. Instead, the adult could have talked with Peggy about ways to avoid future injuries. Unfortunately, many adults do not think the natural aftermath of a child's mistake is enough. They cannot resist the desire to drive the point home by lecturing, moralizing, or instituting more drastic consequences (Mead, 1976). However, children who feel victimized are less able to change their behavior. Adults who ignore natural consequences by intervening either prematurely or unnecessarily fail to provide children with opportunities to learn from their own actions. The best way to avoid this pitfall is to survey the situation carefully and note any natural consequences that may have occurred. If these are evident, no further consequences should be imposed.

Demanding cheerful compliance. When adults follow through with a consequence, they should not expect children to comply cheerfully. This means that a child may pout, complain, mutter, or stomp as he or she adheres to the rule. Adults must keep in mind that the aim of the follow-through is to enforce the consequence. It would be too much to insist that a child also put a smile on his or her face when doing something he or she really does not want to do. Adults create unnecessary confrontations when they insist that youngsters obey with pleasure. Although it may be annoying when children show their obvious distaste for the rule, attitude is not something over which adults have control, and so it should not become a major issue in adult-child interactions.

Harboring grudges. After imposing a consequence, the adult's motto should be ''forgive and forget''. It is counterproductive to allow feelings of anger, resentment, or hostility for past actions to color present interactions. Once a consequence has been imposed, that is the end of it. Treat each new day as a fresh start. Furthermore, if on a particular day, one adult has had continual confrontations with the same child or is feeling frustrated or overwhelmed, she or he should take a break, or, in a team-teaching situation, ask someone else to deal with the child for a while.

Insisting that children apologize. Frequently, adults think that if they can just get children to say they are sorry, the problem is rectified. Unfortunately, some children conclude that apologizing takes care of everything, enabling them to engage in any behavior they like so long as they are prepared to express their regret at the end. Sorrow and remorse are emotions. One *cannot* make children experience these emotions on demand. Children *can*, however, be taught to make restitution for a wrong they have committed. This can involve having the child soothe the victim, get a wet cloth to wash the victim's bruised knee, or repair a broken object. Research has shown that children definitely grasp the concept of restitution prior to understanding the true significance of an apology (Irwin and Moore, 1971; Hendrick, 1984). As a result, concrete reparations have the most meaning for children.

Avoiding time-out to save time. In an effort to shorten the time-out period, adults may try to avoid enforcing a time-out when it is obviously necessary or may try to coax an out-of-control child into calmer behavior. Such approaches rarely help the child regain control. Instead, the youngster usually has recurrent difficulties throughout the day. Ultimately, adults who had hoped to save valuable minutes spend more time in repeated confrontations with the child than they would have spent in working out the problem in the first place. A subsequent disadvantage is that children who have numerous negative interactions each day begin to lose self-esteem. This frequently leads to further misbehavior because children who feel bad about themselves are not likely to behave in positive ways.

Talking too much in time-out. Adults sometimes forget that the real purpose of time-out is to help children regain control or to interrupt a negative chain of rewarding circumstances. In a mistaken effort to hurry children along, they attempt to engage them in conversation. Conversation in the time-out area nullifies its neutrality. Remarks aimed at distracting, cajoling, or bribing children into being quiet are, in fact, perceived by them as rewards: they have the adult's undivided attention for an unlimited period of time. Children should be rewarded for returning to the group, not for being separated from it. Talk during time-out should focus on explaining to children why they are in time-out and what they must do for time-out to be over. Other conversation is unnecessary and detracts from this process.

Misjudging the length of time-out. Children vary in how long it takes them to regain their composure sufficiently to return to the group. A child who is still sobbing and hiccuping, grinding his or her teeth, or clenching and unclenching his or her fists is not ready to leave time-out. Wait until the child seems more relaxed or says calmly that he or she is ready. Time-out should not be terminated prematurely, nor should it be prolonged beyond the period that it is useful for the child to remain in the area. This means that once children have regained their composure, they should be permitted to re-enter the mainstream of activity.

Using time-out for inappropriate reasons. Time-out is not simply a convenient way of eliminating unruly children from the group. Adults who put children into time-out and then forget they are there, or who force children to stay in time-out after it has ceased to be beneficial, are misusing the technique. It also is inappropriate to implement time-out as a consequence for behavior that is not extreme. Time-out should only be used when a logical consequence or a less severe, unrelated consequence is impossible.

Expecting too much, too soon. Adults sometimes are nonplussed when they begin to implement consequences and children react by sassing, ridiculing their new way of talking, registering indifference to their feelings, or looking incredulous at what they are hearing. It is not unusual for children to say:

"So what?"
"I don't care how you feel."
"You talk funny."
"Don't try that stuff on me."

Such reactions are common among older children who may suspect helping professionals' motives; from children with whom adults have been working a long time and who become wary of the changes they perceive in the adult's manner; and from youngsters with whom such reasoning has seldom been used before. With children who are unfamiliar with the adult or who are inexperienced with this type of reasoning, the best tactic is to continue trying to build rapport and to keep using the skills so they become more commonplace. For children who are dubious about a changed style, it often is beneficial to tell them what one is trying to accomplish. Such youngsters become more tolerant when better informed: ''I'm try-ing to find a better way to communicate and work with you. I'm still new at this and hope to improve so that I don't sound so stiff or funny.'' In any case, children's derision should not prompt one to abandon the technique pre-maturely. Continue the sequence to the follow-through, regardless of its reception. This shows children that adults mean what they say and that they will not be thwarted in their efforts to elicit appropriate behavior change. As adults become more adept, children will become more cooperative.

SUMMARY

There are times when children do not follow the rules set by adults. They may misbehave because they lack the capability or the under-standing to follow the rules, because adults have given mixed or unclear messages as to which behaviors are desired, or because they believe the rule to be unwarranted. On other occasions, youngsters misbehave because they are impulsive or because they have developed faulty self-perceptions. Adults can avoid or counteract these problems by making rules that take into account children's development, by clarifying or rephrasing their expectations, and by helping children develop positive, ap-propriate alternative behaviors. In addition, adults can monitor their own behavior so that their words are congruent with their actions, of-fer explanations for rules, and provide oppor-tunities for children to become part of the rule-making process.

Adults enforce rules through the use of positive or negative consequences, which are aimed at helping children recognize the impact of their behavior on self and others. Positive consequences are instructive, have a clear relationship to the undesirable behavior, are based on a rational approach by both child and adult, and are humanely and matter-of-factly administered. Negative consequences for rule infractions are categorized as natural, logical, or unrelated. Natural consequences happen without adult intervention, logical conse-quences are directly related to the rule, and unrelated consequences (to be used only when the others are not possible) are manufactured by adults. The latter should be linked, at least in time, to the rule infraction. Adults must care-fully weigh many factors in deciding which consequences to use in particular situations.

Adults implement negative consequences by reminding children of the rule, and then, if com-pliance is not forthcoming, repeating the rule and articulating a warning as an either-or state-ment. Adults pause long enough to give children an opportunity to correct their behavior on their own. If they do not, adults follow through with the consequence. All conse-quences should be implemented consistently and immediately.

Personal messages combined with the warn-ing and follow-through allow adults to help children to learn to regulate their own behavior. As children become more accustomed to this process, they learn to respond to earlier phases, decreasing the necessity for adults to go through the entire sequence. At times, when one problem behavior leads to another, adults must exercise patience and implement appropriate consequences for each problem behavior.

The ultimate logical consequence, time-out, is used for children who are out of control or who exhibit habituated antisocial behavior. In this technique, the child is removed from the environment in which the behavior is occurring to a predetermined, secluded spot. There are special considerations to take into account when choosing a time-out area, when preparing children for time-out, and when carrying out this procedure.

DISCUSSION QUESTIONS

1. Describe six reasons why children misbehave and their corresponding solutions.
2. Discuss the faulty perceptions that may prompt children's misbehavior. Describe (without naming) a child you have observed whose behavior might indicate that such a perception was in operation. Explore strategies that might be employed to alter the child's perception.
3. Discuss the similarities and differences between positive consequences, negative consequences, and punishments.
4. Generate ideas for positive consequences and for natural, logical, and unrelated consequences for the following rules:
   a. Walk, don't run, down the hall.
   b. Throw the ball, don't kick it.
   c. Only use your own gym towel.
   d. Handle the computer keyboard gently.
   e. Walk on the sidewalk, not in the flower bed.
   f. Tell someone when you need help.
   g. Call people by their real names, rather than mocking their names.
5. Discuss the importance of following through on consequences as well as the results of not doing so.
6. Discuss how the personal message, warning, and follow-through tie together. Enumerate the advantages both adults and children experience when the sequence is used. Relate this discussion to your own personal experience in working with children.
7. How would you respond to another helping professional who said: "The sequence takes too long. Besides, children can't respond to so much talking. Just tell them what's not allowed and be done with it"?
8. Identify any difficulties you have had in implementing the skill sequence described in this chapter. With classmates, brainstorm ways to improve.
9. Describe a time-out you have observed. Discuss why it is done, how it was done, and what its effect was.
10. Pretend you have been assigned to describe your center's use of time-out to a group of parents. Give a five-minute presentation to a group of your classmates. Then, generate a list of questions parents might ask and discuss how you would respond.

CHAPTER 9
Handling Children's Aggressive Behavior

SOURCE: © Ulrike Welsch

OBJECTIVES:

On completion of this chapter, you will be able to describe:

1. The four types of aggression.

2. Differences between assertion and aggression.

3. Factors that contribute to aggressive behavior.

4. Adult actions that increase children's aggressive behaviors.

5. Techniques that reduce children's aggression.

6. A model for on-the-spot conflict resolution.

7. Pitfalls to avoid in mediating children's conflicts.

Frog face.

Wart nose.

Take that back!

No, I won't. You take it back!

Slam! Bang! Hit! Sock! . . .

Mrs. Phillips comes running across the playground. Leroy and Robert are at it again, fists flying. She wades into the fray.

Inevitably, anyone working with children will be faced with such a scene. At these moments, helping professionals wonder why children act so aggressively, whether aggression is a natural part of growing up, and why some children are more aggressive than others. Most of all, they want to know what can be done about children's violent behavior.

WHAT AGGRESSION IS

Aggression is any behavior that results in physical or emotional injury to a person or animal, or one that leads to property damage or destruction. It can be either verbal or physical (Bandura, 1973; Berkowitz, 1973; Caldwell, 1977). Slapping, grabbing, pinching, kicking, spitting, biting, threatening, degrading, shaming, gossiping, attacking, reviling, teasing, breaking, and demolishing are all examples of aggressive actions (Marion, 1981). Although each of these behaviors has hurtful results, children engage in them for different reasons.

Types of Aggression

Psychologists have identified four distinct types of aggression. These are accidental aggression, expressive aggression, instrumental aggression, and hostile aggression (Feshbach and Feshbach, 1976; Orlick, 1978).

Accidental aggression. Often, children unintentionally hurt others in the process of their play. When this occurs, it is called accidental aggression. Stepping on someone's fingers while climbing the monkey bars, tagging a friend too hard in a game of hide and seek, telling a joke that unexpectedly hurts someone's feelings, or crushing a butterfly in an effort to keep it from flying away are all circumstances in which there is no conflict and the aggression happens by chance.

Expressive aggression. Expressive aggression is a sensory experience for the aggressor. It occurs when a child derives pleasure from a physical action that inadvertently hurts someone or interferes with their rights (Orlick, 1978). The aggressor's goal is not to elicit a reaction from the victim or to destroy something; instead, he or she is preoccupied with the physical sensation of the experience. For instance, when Roger knocks down Sammy's building, he feels satisfaction in a well-placed karate chop; when Elizabeth unexpectedly bites Tulana, it is because it feels good; when Marvin rams his bike into the back of Jack's wagon, it is because he likes the sudden jolt he receives. Expressive aggression is marked by the absence of angry, frustrated, or hostile emotions. It is a playful or exploratory act that causes unintentional unhappiness in another.

Instrumental aggression. Children often engage in instrumental aggression to further their goals. They resort to force as a way of establishing who will get the next turn or who will sit with whom on the bus, and so forth. In addition, children commonly fall back on hitting, grabbing, pushing, or biting when their desires are thwarted. Their purpose is not to hurt someone, but to get what they want. Therefore, the spontaneous physical encounters that result from disputes over rights, privileges, or possessions are by-products of each interaction rather than their ultimate aim. This lack of purposefulness and premeditation distinguishes instrumental aggression from more deliberate attempts to hurt people or reduce their self-esteem.

Hostile aggression. Children who display hostile aggression experience satisfaction based solely on someone else's physical or psychological pain (Caldwell, 1977; Feshbach, 1970). Their hurtful actions are purposeful attacks that serve as retaliation for prior insults or injuries or as a way to get a victim to do what they want. Due to its deliberate nature, hostile aggression is different from all other types of aggression.

Children use hostile aggression to make themselves feel more powerful when they are threatened with loss of face or security or when they think someone is purposely trying to sabotage what they are doing.

SITUATION: Several fourth-graders are rushing to get to their lockers before the bell rings. In her effort to get in and out on time, Jean inadvertently knocks Claudia down. Before anyone can respond, Claudia, red faced, jumps up and runs into the classroom. Later, as the children line up at the water fountain, Claudia shoves Jean and says, "There, see how *you* like it."

Initially, Jean's behavior was an example of accidental aggression. However, Claudia interpreted it as a deliberate blow to her ego, which required her to pay Jean back at the fountain later in the day. By pushing Jean, Claudia felt they were "even," and her honor was restored. Unfortunately, this may begin a cycle of retaliation between the two girls that could escalate over time.

Assertion Versus Aggression

Clearly, aggression shows itself in many forms. Yet, not every child who attempts to assert her or his will is necessarily being aggressive. The distinction between aggression and assertion is that assertion definitely does not include any intent to injure, but is, instead, a positive, purposeful, goal-directed action that serves the healthy function of self-protection (Craig, 1979; Haswell, Hock, and Wenar, 1982). Unlike aggressive children, assertive youngsters do not respond in generalized frustration. Rather, they utilize forthright, direct behaviors such as resisting what they consider to be unreasonable demands ("No, I won't give you the eraser. I still need it"); accepting logical disagreements ("Okay, I see what you mean"); and suggesting solutions to conflict ("You can have it in a minute" or "I'll use it again when you're through")(Stocking, Arezzo, and Leavitt, 1980).

Assertion is related to children's emerging sense of autonomy. You will remember from earlier discussions that children develop positive feelings about their own abilities when they can express themselves and when they can exert some control and influence over others. They can also benefit from having opportunities to make some of their own decisions without always conforming to other's wishes. Toddlers are expressing their need to assert their will when they say "Me," "Mine," and "No" (Smith, 1982). It is not by chance that these words are among the first that children learn and use.

Preschoolers who hope to extend their influence also try out many strategies to accomplish this aim. Their widening circle of contacts gives them more frequent social opportunities that include both cooperation and confrontation. Because young children have not yet mastered all the social skills necessary for harmonious interactions, assertion often initially takes the form of aggression. Through observation, instruction, feedback, and practice, children learn the more constructive, socially acceptable behaviors that are associated with positive assertion. The early years therefore mark a critical period for children to learn to be assertive rather than aggressive (Marcus, 1979). Youngsters in grade school who fail to shift from aggression to assertion tend to be rejected by their peers and disliked by adults (Rubin, 1980). Such reactions contribute to a reduction of self-esteem in aggressors and limit their opportunities to practice other, more acceptable approaches. This increases the likelihood of hostile, angry feelings, which lead to further aggression. When such a pattern develops, it is difficult to break.

Hence, it is important for children to learn to substitute assertion for aggression right from the start. How this can best be accomplished is more easily understood if one first knows why and how aggression develops.

WHY CHILDREN ARE AGGRESSIVE _____

In explaining the roots of aggression, scientists do not agree on how much can be attributed to biology and how much is a result of learning (Lorenz, 1966; Moyer, 1971; Patterson, Cobb, and Ray, 1973). However, there is general accord that, from infancy onward, children's aggressive behavior is shaped by both factors. Thus, there is no single cause of aggression.

Biology

Some scientists believe that aggression is an instinctive component of human nature (Lorenz, 1966). According to this hypothesis, children are genetically programmed to be aggressive, particularly when safety or other basic needs are threatened. In addition, the presence of high levels of androgen and testosterone (male sex hormones) have been linked to aggressive impulses (Olweus, et al., 1980). This may explain, in part, why boys generally are more aggressive than girls and why boys who have higher concentrations of these hormones generally are more aggressive than boys with lower levels. Clearly, biology contributes in some measure to children's aggression, but it is not the only factor involved.

The Frustration-Aggression Hypothesis

For a long time, it was widely believed that frustration was the source of all aggression

(Dollard, 1939). Over the years, the link between aggression and frustration has gained much support. However, we now know that other variables, such as biology and learning, also prompt aggressive impulses. Moreover, one can respond to frustration in ways that are noninjurious. For instance, children may react to frustrating experiences by trying harder, requesting help, simplifying the task, giving up, or taking a break.

Imitation

Another explanation for why children behave aggressively is that they learn how to be aggressive by watching others (Bandura, 1973; Patterson, Littman, and Bucker, 1967). For instance, they see television programs in which disputes are settled by violence; they observe Aunt Martha shake Tony in order to make her point; they watch peers and siblings use physical power as a successful means to get what they want. Children experience aggression directly when they are smacked, pulled along, or shoved as punishments for misbehavior.

All of these examples illustrate to children that aggression is an effective way to assert one's will. They also break down any inhibitions children may have regarding the use of force (Bandura, Ross, and Ross, 1963; Marion, 1981). It makes little difference that adults frequently admonish youngsters not to resort to violence or advise them to "act nice." Instead, for children, seeing is believing, so adults must realize that the old maxim "Do as I say and not as I do" is totally ineffective. Moreover, children are most likely to imitate notable or outstanding behaviors in others. Due to its violent nature, aggression stands out, generally overshadowing neutral or less dramatic prosocial behaviors. Unfortunately, the problem is further compounded because children exposed to aggressive models retain the effects long after a particular incident is over. They remember what they see and hear and are able to imitate it months later (Hicks, 1965). All of these factors contribute to the enormous influence aggressive modeling has on children's lives.

Direct Instruction

In many cases, adults actually tell children to use aggression to resolve a problem situation. Children who balk at such demands are faced with subsequent adult disappointment, derision, or disapproval. Therefore, children sometimes are aggressive in an effort to obey adult commands. Such direct instruction has a powerful effect on children's behavior. For example, in an experiment involving children six to sixteen years of age, 75 percent of the children carried out an aggressive action in order to comply with adult expectations (Shanab and Yahya, 1977; Staub, 1971). "Hit her back," "Stick up for yourself," "Don't be a sissy," and "Prove you're a man" are common examples of such commands.

Reinforcement

There are many ways in which children are rewarded for aggressive behaviors. One involves the reinforcement they receive when they hit, bite, scratch, taunt, or threaten in order to assert their will, and other children give way by withdrawing from the conflict, crying, or yielding to their wishes (Patterson, Littman, and Bucker, 1967). Success in one situation prompts the aggressor to repeat the behavior toward the same victim in the future. For instance, if Mary Jane teases Viola to the point that Viola gives up her place in line, it is likely that Mary Jane will try the same tactic the next time she wants something from Viola. As her rate of success increases, Mary Jane may generalize this approach to other children as well.

In addition, many aggressive children have low self-esteem and feel they are incapable of eliciting positive reactions from others. They report a pattern of interactions with adults and peers that is characterized by rejection, disapproval, humiliation, lack of affection, isolation,

and retaliation (Feshbach and Feshbach, 1976). Such children fall back on the one sure way to get attention—to be aggressive. The problem is exacerbated when adults generally ignore children, paying attention to them only when their behavior is aggressive (Clarke-Stewart and Koch, 1983). To these young people, the negative attention of a scolding, or worse, is infinitely better than no attention at all. They quickly learn that it is aggression that elicits notice and so adapt to this requirement.

Another instance of reinforcement occurs when a child's aggressive act prompts a reciprocal aggressive act from someone else. Over time, the aggressor comes to anticipate this predictable response and so is able to elicit it at will. In this way, an aggressive pattern is established (Sheppard and Willoughby, 1975). For instance, ten-year-old Shavette knows how to get a rise out of her younger brother, Chad. All she has to do is chant "Chad is a baby, Chad is a baby" over and over. Before long, Chad will cry and rush at her in an effort to bowl her over. Laughing, Shavette can hold him at arm's length as he kicks and flails helplessly. This chain of events bolsters her feelings of power and induces her to continue over time.

Finally, aggression may be one of the few strategies available to children for creating a little excitement in an otherwise boring environment (Roedell, Slaby, and Robinson, 1976). Children are rewarded by the stir that ensues from their actions. For instance, during a story he had already heard 20 times, Carl began poking his neighbor as a way to liven up the afternoon. This type of innocuous beginning often sets the stage for retaliation and an escalation of the negative behavior, and, as such, becomes a predictable way to relieve the tedium.

THE EMERGENCE OF AGGRESSION_____

The causes of aggression are varied and complex. Any one or a combination of the factors just described may result in antisocial behaviors.

The particular form in which aggression is manifested also depends on differing personal variables such as maturity, experience, and gender.

Maturity and Experience

How children express aggression changes with their cognitive maturation and experience. Most aggression exhibited by children aged two through six is instrumental, and the aggression of older children is more likely to be hostile (Hartup, 1974). These variations occur for several reasons.

Toddlers and preschoolers are impulsive. When they want something, they are likely to go after it directly. Their limited communication skills and minimal knowledge of acceptable alternatives often cause them to use coercive strategies. Similarly, the fact that they are egocentric and have difficulty envisioning someone else's needs makes it less likely that they will willingly give up something in response to another child's requests. For both reasons, conflict is likely to occur when children have differing interpretations of who should have control over a particular object or right.

Interestingly, when preschoolers fight, they center on their own desires within the confrontation rather than focusing on the intention or motivation of the person with whom they are struggling. Once their desires have been satisfied, they are able to resume their play almost as if nothing had happened. As far as they are concerned, the episode is over. They do not see conflict as a challenge to their honor, so no retaliation is necessary. Thus, conflicts among very young children, although highly emotional, tend to blow over quickly (Smith, 1982).

Instrumental aggression reaches its peak during the preschool years. Disagreements of this sort are so common that they comprise the largest number of aggressive encounters a child will experience during his or her entire lifetime (Hartup, 1974).

The greater cognitive and language skills of school-age children lead to a reduction in instrumental aggression. Yet, these same, more advanced abilities contribute to an increase in hostile aggression. This is because grade-school children more clearly recognize the negative motives others have toward them and have memory skills that are well enough developed that they can remember angry encounters long after they are over (Flavell, 1963). Because these children are more aware of the reciprocal nature of relationships, they also are more likely to value "getting even" (Hewitt, 1975; Johnson, 1972). This is particularly true of six-, seven-, and eight-year-olds, who, when aggression is aimed at them, have great difficulty differentiating accidental from intentional acts. Consequently, they respond to any hurtful behavior as if it were purposeful, regardless of whether it actually was (Shantz and Voydanoff, 1973). During the later elementary-school years, youngsters begin to make these distinctions and respond less aggressively if it is clear to them that an instance of aggression was not deliberate.

Due to their past experience, older children also shift from physical to verbal strategies because they know that adults disapprove of physical conflict (Feshbach, 1970). Their increased facility with language makes the verbal taunt a satisfying weapon that leaves no visible traces. Also, the probability for hostile aggression intensifies as rivalry among peers increases. Children between the ages of six and twelve spend much of their time comparing themselves with age-mates. Consequently, it becomes more common for them to feel threatened by the accomplishments of peers and to try to build themselves up by tearing others down (Moskowitz and McClintock, 1977). As a result, physical fighting diminishes during the elementary-school years, but verbal disputes increase. Minor disagreements or misunderstandings can quickly escalate to expressions of hostile aggressions through insults, baiting, and rejection (Smith, 1982).

Gender Differences in Aggression

One question often asked is whether there are differences in aggressive behaviors between boys and girls. A number of studies have shown that boys are more aggressive than girls and that these differences are apparent in children as young as two years of age (Hyde, 1984). Males are more physical and blatant in their expressions of aggression, and females tend to use aggressive strategies that are covert, indirect, and verbal (Marion, 1981; Siegal and Kohn, 1970).

Some researchers suggest that the male's greater concentration of androgen and testosterone, as well as his greater physical strength and more vigorous motor impulses, are the biological reasons for this difference (Feshbach, 1970). Others point out that learning also is a factor because aggressive behavior is more approved for boys than it is for girls (Maccoby and Jacklin, 1974, 1980). Girls who rely on physical aggression tend to be rejected by peers and disliked by adults (Levitan and Chananie, 1972). It is more socially acceptable for girls to scold, gossip, resist, reject, and argue than it is for them to punch and kick. In addition, although both boys and girls frequently are reprimanded for physical aggression, boys tend to be more successful than girls in achieving reinforcement for physical violence. When little boys hit, adults say "Boys will be boys"; when little girls hit, they are admonished for acting like roughnecks. On the other hand, boys who engage in verbal aggression are treated with scorn and labeled as sissies; girls who practice the same techniques are tolerated. In this way, the stereotypes of the "tough guy" and the "bitter-tongued female" are perpetuated.

There also is evidence that because of societal pressures, female aggression declines over time, whereas aggressive behavior in males remains relatively stable from toddlerhood through the college years (Kagen and Moss, 1962). It is interesting to note, however, that when adult research subjects perceived aggression to be justified, or when they could remain anonymous, males and females were equally aggressive (Frodi, Macaulay, and Thome, 1977). Thus, it would seem that boys and girls alike have the potential to be aggressive.

As the previous discussion illustrates, most children will at times exhibit aggressive behavior—some more, some less. Although aggression may seem inevitable, it is possible and desirable to reduce the amount of hurtful behaviors children display. In large measure, how well children learn alternatives to aggression depends on adult intervention. Most adults agree that this is an important responsibility for them to assume, but often are at a loss about what to do. As a result, they may unwittingly choose strategies that stimulate or prompt aggression rather than diminish it. Thus, helping professionals must learn not only which strategies are useful, but which ones to consciously avoid. Fortunately, there are substantial research data that clearly differentiate effective techniques from those that are detrimental. We will explore each of these, beginning with those that should be discarded.

INEFFECTIVE STRATEGIES ADULTS USE TO REDUCE CHILDREN'S AGGRESSIVE BEHAVIOR

Physical Punishment

Many adults adhere to the old adage "Spare the rod and spoil the child." Their response to children's misbehavior, including those instances when youngsters exhibit aggression, is to resort to aggression themselves via physical punishment. The premise that guides their actions is that children will learn to adapt their behavior to adult standards in order to avoid the pain of a spanking (Dobson, 1970). However, these ideas are not borne out by research data (Caldwell, 1977).

A wealth of evidence shows that physical punishment actually increases, rather than limits, children's use of aggression (Azrin and Holz, 1966; Berkowitz, 1973). There also is documentation that such effects are long lasting. The more frequently and the more severely children experience physical punishment when they are young, the more aggressive they are as adolescents (Welsh, 1976). Several factors contribute to these outcomes.

First, when adults rely on spanking, slapping, shoving, pinching, shaking, or pulling children roughly, they stand out as aggressive models for youngsters to imitate. Their actions demonstrate the power of aggression as a means of asserting one's will (Feshbach, 1970). From such episodes, children quickly discover that "might makes right" and that aggressive solutions are viable ones (Caldwell, 1977).

SITUATION: Miss Chang had tried everything to get four-year-old Rose to stop pinching. She had talked to Rose, made her sit out, scolded her, and warned her that other children would not want to play with her, but Rose continued to pinch. Miss Chang felt stymied. Finally, in exasperation, she said: "Rose, you don't seem to understand how much pinching hurts. . . . There!" (pinching Rose). "Now, you see what I mean."

Miss Chang hoped that by pinching Rose, the child would learn her lesson. Although Rose did learn a lesson, it was not the one Miss Chang intended. Rose found out that being pinched was painful, but she also noted that Miss Chang used pinching to make her point. The youngster therefore concluded that to get away with pinching one simply had to be bigger, stronger, or older than the victim. She resolved to limit her pinching to younger, smaller children in the future.

Even if Rose had recognized that pinching was a poor choice, she had little notion of what to do instead. Miss Chang's failure to model a nonaggressive alternative represents a second reason why physical punishment does little to decrease children's hurtful actions. Youngsters who routinely are physically punished see few nonviolent modes of problem solving. Consequently, they can conceive of no substitute for their own aggression.

A third problem related to physical punishment is that children come to view it as a form of retaliation by adults for transgressions. This conceptualization often causes them to adopt the same retaliatory thinking in their own behaviors with peers (Staub, 1971). Such a mind set contributes to increased incidents of hostile aggression. The negative aspects of this situation are exacerbated because when children are punished physically, they focus primarily on their own discomfort, not on the impact their misbehavior may have had on another person. Thus, Rose, who is pinched for pinching others, concentrates on her own pain, not on the pain of her victims. This egocentric focus adds to the difficulty of dealing with the child's hostile aggression because hostility can be reduced only when children begin to feel empathy or concern for others.

Finally, although a sharp pinch interrupts Rose's negative behaviors for the time being, her compliance is at the adherence level. Continual surveillance by the adult will be required if Rose's obedience is to be maintained. Miss Chang's action did not help Rose internalize values that are inconsistent with aggression. If children are to move beyond the adherence level, adults must implement consequences that contribute to children's abilities to reason and to understand how their behavior affects others.

The undesirable effects just cited make a strong case against the practice of physical punishment. Unfortunately, even though few helping professionals advocate striking children in anger, adult aggression is practiced and even mandated in many formal group settings under the rubric "corporal punishment."

Effects on children of corporal punishment. Corporal punishment is commonly practiced in elementary, middle, and high schools throughout this country as a response to discipline problems with students. Paddling has been declared constitutional by the United States Supreme Court (Baker v. Owen, 1975; Ingraham v. Wright, 1976), and most states permit school personnel to use "reasonable" force against children as a way to maintain discipline (Flygare, 1978). This formalized approach to physical punishment often is accompanied by numerous regulations regarding the circumstances under which it is to be administered. School boards and administrators spend much time deciding what constitutes grounds for paddling, how many swats are appropriate for children of varying ages and what type of witnessing procedures must be followed. In addition, the majority of schools that permit spanking require written permission from a child's parents prior to corporal punishment being used with that child. Interestingly, a significant number of parents provide this consent. With so much support from government, schools, and parents, one might conclude that corporal punishment must be an effective strategy for controlling children's behavior in formal group settings. Nothing could be further from the truth.

No research has ever indicated that corporal punishment provides any positive effects. The consensus of medical, psychological, and educational researchers is that corporal punishment is neither necessary nor useful and is, in fact, counterproductive (Michigan Association for the Education of Young Children, correspondence, June 4, 1986). The National Center for the Study of Corporal Punishment and Alternatives in Schools reports that paddling does not lead to fewer discipline problems for teachers and principals (Hyman and D'Alessandro, 1984). Nor does it lead to orderliness and cooperativeness among children and faculty or an increased commitment to learning as its proponents claim. Instead, a review of research indicates that children subjected to corporal punishment in school become more aggressive, coercive, and destructive over time (Bongiovanni, 1977). Corporal punishment also is

associated with increased vandalism and delinquency (Welsh, 1976). Possible explanations for such trends include the obvious fact that, regardless of how the situation is structured, the person administering corporal punishment is modeling aggressive behavior as a way to deal with another human being. This has several likely outcomes:

1. Children whose behavior already is out of bounds will not learn alternatives to aggression from methods so closely resembling their own idea that the way to approach a problem situation is through force (Clarizio, 1980).
2. Youngsters can become so accustomed to physical pain that such pain is no longer important to them, and therefore it becomes useless as a deterrent to future violence (Maurer, 1978). In addition, habitual offenders may interpret their ability to withstand the paddling without flinching as a badge of honor. This increases their status with peers, causing offenders to repeat their provocative behavior.
3. The use of corporal punishment often serves as a stimulus for counterattacks by the child in the future (Long, 1981).

Findings such as these indicate that corporal punishment benefits neither its recipients nor the adults who carry it out. Furthermore, paddling has undesirable long-term side effects for children. Why, then, is corporal punishment still common practice? The answer involves a complex amalgamation of politics, societal beliefs regarding the value of so-called old-fashioned discipline, and lack of awareness of how else to control children's behaviors (Hyman and D'Alessandro, 1984).

The latter issue is of particular significance because people can learn nonviolent alternatives. There *are* school districts, even in states in which corporal punishment is legal, that prohibit its use. It has been found that teachers and

FIGURE 9-1 A positive school climate is created when children are treated with respect, expectations are clearly stated, and school policies support their social development.
SOURCE: Paul Conklin/Monkmeyer Press Photo Service

children are able to function effectively in such settings regardless of whether they are in rural, suburban, or urban areas (Clarizio, 1981). Although each of these schools has its own approach to positive discipline, there are certain tenets to which they all subscribe. First, school personnel make the basic assumption that each child has the capacity to solve problems. Consequently, they believe that children can learn appropriate behaviors if they know what to expect and if rules and consequences are enacted in an authoritative rather than authoritarian manner. A second principle is that the best way to improve school discipline is to improve school climate. Taking a preventive rather than a remedial stance to discipline is a third point of agreement. Some of the specific ways in which these principles have been implemented across the country include the following (Clarizio, 1981; Hyman and D'Alessandro, 1984):

Providing a clear orientation to pupils and parents about school programs, school rules, grading systems, and special services.

Developing school rules that are reasonable rather than arbitrary.

Explaining the reasons behind school rules both to students and their parents.

Training teachers and administrators in positive classroom management techniques.

Making the curriculum relevant to pupils.

Providing feedback to students about their behavior.

Teaching children how to express emotions appropriately.

Creating a positive verbal environment.

Effectively implementing rewards and consequences.

Using democratic procedures for solving classroom problems.

Using therapeutic approaches for some behavioral problems.

Other effective techniques that preclude paddling involve the development of well-planned alternative-school programs, in-school suspension, the appropriate use of time-out, and peer and cross-age counseling.

From this discussion, it can be seen that there are many alternatives to corporal punishment. The pursuit of these is critical because not only does spanking have the potential for hurting young children, it does not promote the development of self-respect or teach them substitute behaviors—two primary building blocks of self-control. There is little doubt that physical punishment increases, rather than decreases, behavior problems in children. For this reason, we have taken the stand that corporal punishment is unacceptable in the formal group setting. We contend that there is no justifiable reason for helping professionals to slap, spank, or otherwise inflict physical pain on children in an effort to control their behavior.

Ignoring Aggression

Sometimes, adults ignore children's aggressive acts in the hope that these behaviors eventually will go away. This is a mistake. Numerous studies have shown that when children played in the vicinity of an adult who ignored their aggressive behavior, aggression increased (Caldwell, 1977; Lefkowitz, 1977). Children assumed that adults who could stop the aggression but did not were, in fact, condoning it (Becker, 1964; Patterson, 1967). Inaction by an adult encourages an aggressor to persist and prompts victims to yield (Smith and Green, 1975). This creates a permissive atmosphere in which both the aggressor and victim learn that aggression has its rewards (Caldwell, 1977). Aggressive children continue unabated, and children who cannot depend on a protective adult eventually begin to counterattack. As children's counterattacks become more successful and they are less frequently victimized, they begin to initiate aggressive acts towards others (Patterson, Littman, and Bucker, 1967). In this way, unchecked aggression in a group setting not only perpetuates itself, but escalates.

Catharsis

A popular myth that should be laid to rest is that children are purged of their violent tendencies by participating in aggressive play. Research evidence shows that acting out aggression, or experiencing it vicariously by watching others commit antisocial acts, encourages rather than discourages aggressive behaviors. For instance, children exhibited a significant increase in verbal and physical attacks after playing with aggressive toys such as guns. However, aggression did not rise when children played with neutral materials (Feshbach, 1970). Moreover, children who saw violence demonstrated on film imitated the violence in their play (Bandura,

Ross, and Ross, 1963; Murray, 1980). These youngsters also were less likely to consider violence inappropriate (Comstock, 1980; Drabman and Thomas, 1975). It has been hypothesized that this occurred because the play actually served to instruct children in how to be aggressive and that the aggression felt good, providing reinforcement (Yarrow, 1983). In either case, it is clear that children who play at aggression tend to be more aggressive than children who do not.

Displacement

Some people believe that the way to deal with children who are aggressive as a result of being upset is to have them displace their angry emotions from the original object to some unrelated target. For instance, they would encourage a youngster who was frustrated with a playmate to leave that situation and pound some clay, punch a pillow, or smack a Bobo doll instead as a way to vent his or her feelings. Once these actions were carried out, the adult would assume that the child's anger was resolved and that his or her need to be aggressive had been satisfied. The evidence is to the contrary.

Children who are taught that displacement is the ultimate means of handling angry feelings continue to believe that aggression is an effective response to problems (Bergan and Henderson, 1979). They do not learn how to deal with the real source of their emotions (such as lack of cooperation from a peer) and so fail to develop strategies for confronting problems constructively or for preventing problems in the future. It is not surprising that such children eventually become frustrated at never having an opportunity for direct resolution and so become increasingly hostile.

Additionally, as children mature, they may shift the "safe target" chosen by an adult to one of their own choosing, such as a child down the street, a family pet, or a younger sibling. Although displacement of angry feelings from a person or animal to an inanimate object is an appropriate first step in teaching some children how to cope with their emotions, it is not an adequate solution in and of itself (Wolfgang, 1977).

Inconsistency

A fifth ineffective means of dealing with children's aggressive behavior is to be inconsistent. Adults who are haphazard in their approach promote increased aggression (Hom and Hom, 1980; Parke and Duer, 1972). "Coming down hard" on one child while avoiding confrontation with another, or sticking with the rules today and ignoring them tomorrow, leads to confusion and frustration for children (Stein and Kostelnik, 1984). In addition, this sets up a pattern of intermittent reinforcement for the aggression. Intermittent reinforcement means that rewards (when a victim yields, when the child gets a predictable rise out of an adult, when adults overlook violent transgressions) do not follow a predictable pattern, and so children never know whether or not a reward is forthcoming. The only way to find out is to try it. Even if punishment is the result now, there still is no guarantee that such will be the case later. Children therefore persist in seeking undesirable rewards. This, then, is a potent pattern of reinforcement, which leads to continued aggression (Becker, Engelmann, and Thomas, 1971).

It is obvious that physical punishment, permissiveness, catharsis, displacement, and inconsistency all contribute to, rather than reduce, aggressive behavior in children. These methods fail because they allow the aggression to continue and/or because they fail to provide children the opportunity to learn acceptable alternatives for future use.

EFFECTIVE STRATEGIES ADULTS USE TO REDUCE CHILDREN'S AGGRESSIVE BEHAVIOR

Strategies found to be effective in decreasing children's aggression are those that teach children how to exert their will nonaggressively as well as how to respond assertively to the aggression of others. Just as children learn to be aggressive through modeling, reinforcement, and instruction, so, too, can they learn to be nonaggressive through these same channels. Such learning takes place whether a child is in the role of aggressor or victim. In all cases, the key to reducing children's aggressive behavior is to help them internalize values and methods of interacting that are incompatible with violence (Grusec and Arnason, 1982; Katz, 1984).

Modeling

There are two ways adults can influence what behaviors children imitate. First, they can model nonaggression through their own behavior. For instance, when children see adults talking about problems, reasoning with others, and making compromises, they are likely to view these approaches as desirable alternatives to aggression (Bandura, 1973). Moreover, when adults treat children calmly and rationally regardless of the situation, youngsters gain firsthand experience by watching someone utilize a nonaggressive solution to a problem. In both cases, adult modeling provides a standard of peaceful conduct for children to emulate.

Besides serving as appropriate models themselves, adults can screen out some of the aggressive models to which children are exposed. Toys, games, films, books, pictures, television programs, and live demonstrations that depict aggression are powerful, pervasive teachers. It has been shown that when these aggressive models are reduced, children's aggressive acts become fewer (Bandura, 1973; Comstock, 1977;

Yarrow, 1983). Although helping professionals cannot eliminate all of the aggressive influences in children's lives, they can limit aggressive models within the formal group setting and help children find satisfaction in nonaggressive play. Thus, ray guns, light sabers, plastic bazookas, punching bags, and slingshots have no place in child-care centers or schools. Nor do posters, books, or films that portray violence as a way to solve problems.

Reinforcement

As with any other behavior, children are more likely to repeat nonaggressive strategies for making their desires known when those strategies are rewarded. One type of reinforcement occurs when adults acknowledge children's efforts with positive personal messages. Adult praise gives youngsters the important information that their peaceful behavior is both appropriate and appreciated. Another way children find such behavior rewarding is when it helps them to successfully reach their goals. Hence, Pablo, who asks for a turn with the kite rather than grabbing it, and who ultimately gets a chance to use it, is likely to incorporate asking into his future repertoire of social behaviors. Even though he occasionally is turned down, if, over time, his requests are honored more often than not, he will learn that asking is a useful approach.

Direct Instruction

The following are a number of instructional techniques adults can use to minimize children's aggressive behavior.

Reducing the frustration in children's lives. Because frustration makes aggression more likely to occur, its reduction leads to fewer aggressive incidents. When adults stress cooperation rather than competition, structure the environment to avoid potential conflict, keep rules to a minimum, explain the reasons for rules, warn children in advance about changes in the daily routine, and modify each child's expectations to match his or her current level of ability, children have more opportunities for success and will have less reason to resort to aggression (Hendrick, 1984).

Helping children feel more competent. Children who feel they have some control over their lives are less likely to resort to aggression as a way to establish power. When adults give children choices, help them to develop their skills, and avoid insisting on perfection, they influence children to be less aggressive (Hendrick, 1984; May, 1972).

Teaching children prosocial behaviors. Kindness, helpfulness, and cooperation are incompatible with aggression. When adults actively teach children these behaviors, aggression diminishes (Marion, 1981; Caldwell, 1977). Because this is such a powerful strategy, all of Chapter 14 is devoted to it.

Helping children recognize instances of accidental aggression. Frequently, victims of accidental aggression react as though the aggression were intentional. Providing accurate information changes the child's view of the purposefulness of the act and reduces the necessity for retaliation (Berkowitz, 1973; Mallick and McCandless, 1966). Adults defuse the situation when they identify the victim's feelings and clarify the accidental nature of the incident ("You were surprised to get hit. It hurt. He wasn't trying to hurt you; he was trying to keep the ball from going out of bounds" or "You look upset. She didn't mean to snap at you. She isn't feeling well today").

This kind of information does not excuse the aggression but rather attempts to explain its unintentional nature. Added benefits occur when adults point out to the aggressor the impact that the action had on the victim, and,

when possible, enlist the aggressor's aid in repairing the damage: "When you jumped for the ball, you knocked Jesse over. His knee is scraped. Come with us and we'll fix it up together" (Schickedanz, Schickedanz, and Forsyth, 1982). Using this approach helps both victim and aggressor to better understand the context of the incident and circumvents the establishment of a vicious cycle in which each aggressive act prompts another in return.

Rechanneling children's expressive aggression. When carried out safely, kicking, pounding, throwing, and knocking down are appropriate physical activities for children. Youngsters derive satisfaction from mastering the environment and their bodies by kicking or throwing a ball as hard as they can, from pounding at the workbench, or from crashing down something they've built.

Problems arise when children go beyond these safe situations to gain pleasure from ones that are potentially damaging to people or property. Thus, Rodney may become so engrossed in his play that he fails to notice that the ball he is throwing is interfering with other children's games or that the blocks he is pushing over are someone else's prized construction. Likewise, when he chases Joel, he may assume that Joel, in spite of his protests, is experiencing the same thrill that he is. Because of their potentially destructive outcomes, these circumstances represent expressive aggression, thereby requiring adult intervention. The focus of that intervention should be on allowing the child to continue the pleasureable physical movement while structuring the situation so it becomes harmless. This is accomplished through substitution. *Substitution* consists of replacing the unacceptable target of the child's expressive aggression with one that is more suitable. Rodney could be redirected to throw the ball away from the group, to tumble only his own block tower, or to chase a more willing playmate. The substitution cited here is related to the child's desire to gain satisfaction through physical mastery. Rodney is still allowed to throw the ball or crash the blocks, albeit in a different way. Thus, the support offered by the adult is congruent with the child's needs within the situation.

At this point, you may notice some similarities in form between substitution and the ineffective strategy of displacement discussed earlier in this chapter. Displacement strategies are not congruent with teaching children what they need to learn from particular situations: how to deal with the cause of their anger and frustration. Instead, the adult attempts to divert the child's attention from the original source of his or her frustration to some unrelated activity. For instance, if Rodney were chasing Joel because Joel had done something to upset him, the displacement technique of telling Rodney to "work out" his anger by pounding the clay would be ignoring his need to confront Joel directly.

Helping children de-escalate potentially aggressive play. Frequently, play episodes that begin as positive social interactions escalate at a rate and in a manner children do not intend or expect (Caldwell, 1977). This may lead to accidental aggression, which, in turn, may develop into an angry confrontation. Adults can head off the development of purposeful aggression by keeping an eye on children as they play and by watching for early signs of difficulty. When youngsters stop laughing, when their voices become strident or complaining, when their facial expressions show fear, anger, or distress, and when verbalization moves out of the realm of pretend into real-life menace, aggression is imminent (Kostelnik, Whiren, and Stein, 1986). If such signs become apparent, adults should intervene immediately by redirecting the play or by becoming involved in the play themselves. For example, in a game of chase, if a child shows signs of angrily turning on her pursuers, the helping professional could dissipate potential

problems by laughingly becoming the object of the chase.

Similarly, there are times when children's solitary play escalates into aggression due to frustration prompted by circumstance. Children become angry when a toy does not work, when they are unable to produce the picture they envision, or when something interferes with the accomplishment of a goal they have in mind. At times like these, children often lash out, throw something, or explode in fury. Alert adults can de-escalate aggression by helping children to cope directly with the source of their frustration rather than simply criticizing them for acting inappropriately: "You're upset! That model keeps falling apart. The glue you're using works better on paper than it does on plastic. Let's look for some better glue."

Such intervention may involve giving children information, offering assistance, helping them re-evaluate their goals, breaking the task into more manageable steps, or offering a means by which they can take a break before resuming the project.

Making it clear that aggression is unacceptable. When physical or verbal aggression occurs, adults must intervene before children experience the satisfaction of getting what they want through negative means (Sherman and Bushell, 1975). Interrupting aggression takes away the reward of such behavior and provides a perfect opportunity for adults to help children identify and carry out appropriate alternative actions to achieve their aims.

When helping professionals make it clear that aggressive behavior will not be tolerated and when they reason with children and point out the harmful effects of aggression, violence diminishes, even when the adults are not immediately present (Baumrind, 1966; Berkowitz, 1973).

Teaching children to generate potential responses to the aggression of others. Many children become frustrated because they do not know what to do when someone teases them, hurts them, or calls them names. They may either yield to the aggressor or counterattack. Neither strategy is desirable because both lead to further aggression. Adults who do not discount children's complaints of aggression, but who instead intervene directly or model appropriate ways of handling problem situations, contribute to a reduction in the aggressive behavior of younger children.

With older children, on the other hand, direct intervention may lead to later reprisals by the aggressor. Indirect approaches, such as discussing possible motives behind the aggressor's behavior or brainstorming with children about the potential advantages and disadvantages of various responses, are more effective (Smith, 1982). Some children also appreciate having an opportunity to rehearse what they are going to say or do prior to actually trying it out.

It also is useful to help identify other children with whom a victim of continued aggression could establish a relationship. Perpetual victims tend to feel isolated and so are likely to tolerate continued aggression directed at them, thus reinforcing it. It is especially common for young children not to recognize alternate playmates but instead to center on maintaining their interaction with the aggressor. Helping them to recognize others as potential choices breaks this nonproductive cycle. Finally, the comfort and information offered by a caring adult goes a long way toward helping children feel that they do indeed have some power within the situation.

Teaching alternatives to aggression through planned activities. One major source of aggressive behavior is children's inability to generate alternate solutions to conflict situations (Schickedanz, Schickedanz, and Forsyth, 1982). Children who depend on only a few ways to get their point across tend to think that the fastest, surest approach is through some kind of attack (Smith, 1982). On the other hand, children who can envision a wide range of possibilities are less apt to resort to violence (Spivack, Platt, and

Shure, 1976). Fortunately, there is growing evidence that even very young children can increase their repertoire of appropriate options through planned activities (Ridley and Vaughn, 1984; Spivack and Shure, 1974). One approach is to have group discussions with children. These can center around effects of aggression, nonviolent ways to get what they want, how to resolve problem situations, and how to respond to the aggression of others. Another strategy involves teaching children specific skills related to assertiveness and negotiation (Hendrick, 1984; Marion, 1981). Adults can use puppets, stories, flannel boards, skits, or open-ended vignettes to illustrate the skills and stimulate debate.

Helping professionals who use these techniques on a regular basis report that children improve in their ability to identify, describe, and suggest socially appropriate alternatives to aggression (Bessell and Palomares, 1979; Dinkmeyer, 1970; Ridley and Vaughn, 1984). This indicates that planned activities serve as an appropriate introduction for teaching children how to substitute positive behaviors for aggressive ones. However, although discussions and skits are effective, children also must directly experience the process by which nonviolent solutions are derived in order for behavior change to occur.

Taking advantage of conflicts to teach alternatives to aggression. Even when youngsters are able to talk about sharing and taking turns in planned activities, they may sometimes forget and resort to instrumental aggression in the heat of real confrontations (Bryan and Walbek, 1970). These occasions can be turned into learning opportunities by having youngsters practice those conflict-resolution behaviors with peers in real-life situations. The arguments and conflicts that are a natural part of everyday living provide a golden opportunity for this to occur. Children who disagree with their peers quickly find out that not everyone thinks alike—an important discovery for egocentric children. They also have a chance to engage in the give and take of compromise while receiving feedback regarding the effectiveness of the approaches they try (Schultz, 1979). Perhaps most importantly, when children attempt to defend their own position, they learn either to use nonviolent conflict-resolution techniques or to depend on force as their primary mode for interaction. It is significant that the resolution pattern children develop while they are young stays with them throughout middle childhood and adolescence (Marcus, 1979). For this reason, adults must be willing to allow children to argue out their differences so long as their actions do not turn to violence. If aggression does occur, the adult must stop the hurtful behavior and then support children as they negotiate a resolution. Because children learn by watching others, when they observe adults acting as models in the problem-solving process, they identify potential conflict-resolution strategies for their own future use (Bandura, 1977; Bandura and Walters, 1963). At the same time, an adult who assists children in progressing through the steps necessary for reconciliation helps them to develop positive attitudes toward mutual consideration and compromise (Newman and Newman, 1978). Those youngsters who do eventually learn how to assert their will without harming another person have built a foundation that will enable them to sustain positive relationships throughout their lives (Bach and Goldberg, 1974).

Next, we will focus on a practical, systematic way for adults to mediate children's disputes while teaching them appropriate conflict-resolution skills.

A MODEL FOR CONFLICT MEDIATION

From the far end of the yard, Mrs. Woznawski, the after-school supervisor, hears Sarah shout, "Give me that pogo stick—I need it!" Bianca screams back: "Use something else! I'm not

done." Alerted to the difficulty, the adult watches from a distance as the children continue their argument. However, as the dispute heats up, the children begin to grab and pull on the pogo stick. The time is ripe for Mrs. Woznawski to begin conflict mediation.

Step One: Initiating the Mediation Process

The first step in approaching a conflict situation is for the adult to assume the role of mediator. This is accomplished by stopping the aggressive behavior, separating the combatants, and defining the problem: "You both want the pogo stick at the same time. It looks like you each have different ideas about what to do." The adult may have to position himself or herself between the children as he or she helps them focus on the mutual problem rather than on the object or territory they are defending. It is helpful to neutralize the object of contention by temporarily gaining control of it and assuring the children that it will be safe until the conflict is resolved: "I will hold the pogo stick until we can decide together what to do." This procedure stops the children from continuing to hit or grab, helps them to hear the adult and each other, and sets the stage for them to approach a highly emotional situation in a more objective manner.

Step Two: Clarifying Each Child's Perspective

Clarifying the conflict based on the children's perspective is the primary focus of the second step. The adult solicits from each child in turn a statement of the situation from his or her point of view. It is important to allow each child ample opportunity, without interruption, to state his or her ultimate desire with regard to the conflict, such as possession of the toy or getting a turn. Some sample statements might include: "You both seem very angry. Sarah, you can tell

FIGURE 9-2 For conflict mediation to work, children must be assured that both sides in an argument will be heard.
SOURCE: Photo by David Kostelnik

me what you want. Bianca, you can tell me what you think when Sarah is finished." This step is critical. In order for the adult to be an effective mediator, the children must trust him or her not to make an arbitrary decision in favor of one child or the other. The adult establishes neutrality by withholding any evaluation of the merits of either position. Paraphrasing each child's view to the other child is another important tool to be used in this step. It ensures that the adult correctly perceives each child's point of view and helps the children to clarify both positions. Children who are very upset or reticent may require several opportunities to describe their position. It must be emphasized that, depending on the level of the children's distress, this step may take several minutes. Children may need help from the adult in articulating their desires, and the adult should try to be as ac-

curate as possible in paraphrasing, checking back with the children at each turn.

Step Three: Summing Up

The third step occurs when the adult has elicited enough information to understand each child's perception of the encounter. The adult then defines the problem in mutual terms, implying that each child has a responsibility for both the problem and its solution: "Sarah and Bianca, you each want to play with the pogo stick all by yourself. We have a problem. It is important that we find a solution that will satisfy each of you." In other words, the adult states that a problem exists and that a solution must be found.

Step Four: Generating Alternatives

Generating several possible alternative solutions is the aim of the fourth stage of the mediation process. Suggestions may be offered by the adversaries themselves or may be volunteered by bystanders. Each time a possible solution is offered, the mediator paraphrases it to the children directly involved: "Jonathan says you could share." At this point, each child is asked to evaluate the merits of the recommendation: "What do you think, Sarah? What do you think, Bianca?" The mediator elicits as many divergent ideas as possible and should have no stake in which solution is eventually selected. Caregivers should be cautioned that each child should be a willing participant in the outcome and that no alternative should be forced on any child. It is typical during this procedure for children to reject certain possibilities that they may later find acceptable. Therefore, when a suggestion is repeated, the mediator should present it rather than assume it will be rejected again. If the children are not able to originate alternatives, the adult should help them out by saying something like: "Sometimes when people have this problem, they decide to use it together, take turns, or trade toys back and forth. What do you think?''

Step Five: Agreeing on a Solution

Children will reject certain suggestions outright and will indicate that others seem more palatable. The ultimate aim of the fifth step is to get the children to agree on a plan of action that is mutually satisfying. The role of the mediator at this point is to help the children explore the possibilities that seem most acceptable to them. The plan should not include any alternatives that either child vehemently opposes. The final agreement usually involves some concessions on the part of each child and so may not represent the action the child would take if she or he did not have to consider another person's point of view. Eventually, the children will exhibit behaviors that indicate that each can find a way to accept one or a combination of ideas. The mediation process continues until the possibilities have been narrowed down to a workable solution. When this finally occurs, it is important for the mediator to identify that a resolution has been achieved. For example: ''You think you can use the stick together. It sounds like you've solved the problem! Try out your idea.''

Step Six: Reinforcing the Problem-Solving Process

The purpose of the sixth stage of the mediation process is to praise the children for developing a mutually beneficial solution. The message to be conveyed is that the process of reaching the solution is as important as the solution itself. The way the mediator achieves this is to acknowledge the emotional investment each child had in the original conflict and the hard work involved in reaching an agreement: ''It was important to each of you to have the pogo stick. You worked hard at figuring out how to do that without hurting each other.''

Step Seven: Following Through

The conclusion of the mediation process involves helping the children to carry out the terms of the agreement. This is accomplished by reminding the children what the terms were and, if necessary, physically assisting or demonstrating how to comply. At this point, adults should remain in the vicinity to determine the degree to which children carry out the agreement. If the plan begins to falter, the children should be brought together again to discuss possible revisions.

Conflict Mediation in Action

The following is a transcript of an actual conflict between two children, both five years old, in which the helping professional utilized the model just described.

Step one.

Angela: Mr. Lewin, Evan and Aaron are fighting.

Adult: Aaron and Evan, you're both trying to put on that stethoscope. (Restrains the two children, who are pulling on the stethoscope, crouches to the children's level, and turns each child to face him) I'll hold it while we're deciding what to do about it. I'll hold it. I'll make sure it's safe. I'll hold on to it. (Removes the stethoscope from the children's grasp and holds it in front of him)

Step two.

Aaron: I wanted that!

Adult: You wanted the stethoscope. How about you, Evan?

Evan: I want it.

Adult: You wanted the stethoscope, too. (Another child offers a stethoscope)

Evan: I don't like that kind.

Aaron: I want it.

Adult: Aaron says he really wants that stethoscope. What about you, Evan?

Evan: I want it!

Step three.

Adult: You want it, too. Evan and Aaron both want to play with one stethoscope. We have a problem. What can we do about it? Anybody have any ideas?

Step four.

Aaron: He can have Angela's.

Adult: You think he can have Angela's. It looks like Angela still wants hers. (Angela backs away).

Evan: I still want mine, too.

Adult: Evan, you want yours, too. Sometimes when we have a problem like this, we can figure out a solution. Sometimes we share it, sometimes we take turns. Anybody have any ideas?

Another child: Share it.

Adult: Shanna thinks you can share it. What do you think Aaron?

Aaron: Take turns.

Adult: Aaron thinks we should take turns. What do you think, Evan?

Evan: Unh uh. (Shaking his head from side to side).

Adult: You don't think we should take turns.

Evan: Then I just want it.

Adult: Then you just really want it, hmm. That's still a problem.

Aaron: I want it.

Adult: You really want a turn with it. How about you, Evan? What do you think?

Step five.

Evan: No. Aaron can have one turn.

Adult: You think Aaron can have one turn.

Evan: Yes, guess so.

Step six.

Adult: Thank you, Evan.

Evan: Not a long turn.

Adult: Not a long turn. You want to make sure that you get it back. Aaron, Evan said you could have one turn, and then you'll give it back to him.

Evan: A short turn.

Adult: A short turn. Aaron, you may have a short turn. Thank you very much, Evan. That was really hard to do.

Step seven.

Adult: It's about five minutes till it's cleanup time. So Aaron can have a two-minute turn, and you can have a two-minute turn.

Adult: (Two minutes later) Aaron, two minutes are up. Now, it is time for Evan's turn. Thank you, Aaron. You kept your part of the bargain, and Evan kept his.

Solutions Children Choose

Conflict mediation can be used with some children as young as three years of age and is effective well into junior high school. The nature of the solutions that children prefer is determined in large measure by how they perceive conflict in general. Children's conceptualization of conflict resolution evolves as their understanding of relationships becomes more sophisticated. Initially, very young children usually suggest either force or withdrawal as the most likely way to approach a disagreement (Selman, 1980). This simplistic view can be summed up as "fight or flight." As they mature, children "view conflict essentially as a problem that is felt by one party and caused by the actions of the other" (Selman, 1980:170). Grade-schoolers expect interactions to be balanced (Hewitt, 1975; Johnson, 1972). The aggression of one person toward another creates an imbalance, which must be rectified. In their view, the most common equalizer is for the victim to return the aggression in kind. It is important to note that although children consider aggression as a justified response to mistreatment, even five-year-olds disapprove of indiscriminate aggression or violence for personal gain (Berndt, 1974; Hewitt, 1975). This idea contributes to the feeling that victims must get some restitution from the offending party. Therefore, further resolution often depends on the transgressor taking responsibility for restoring harmony. This can take the form of an apology or some action to reverse the hurtful words or deeds (Youniss, 1980). For instance, it is common to hear children shout "Say you're sorry" or "You take that back!" as evidence of this level of thinking.

Eventually, children's reasoning evolves to a point at which they recognize that both participants bear some responsibility for the conflict and will benefit from a mutually satisfying settlement (Selman, 1980). Arrival at this notion depends on cognitive maturation and experience. The mediation model presented here helps children move in this direction: they have an opportunity to observe problem solving in action and experience the consequences of nonviolent resolution while benefiting from the guidance of a supportive adult.

When this model was used with preschoolers, most suggested some form of alternative action as a solution. Taking turns, trading objects, replacing one object with another, and dividing the materials were the most common solutions offered. Only older children were able to decide to use material simultaneously or to select an altogether new material. Older children also were willing to forego their claim to a right or possession if the other child gave way by acknowledging the error of his or her aggressive approach (Stein and Kostelnik, 1984; Kostelnik and Stein, 1986).

Does Conflict Mediation Work?

At this point, you may be wondering whether using the model just described actually reduces children's aggression and expands their ability to resolve conflicts on their own. Studies do indeed show that children who participate in conflict mediation on a regular basis improve in their ability to engage in that process. Over time, children increase the number and variety of solutions they suggest and decrease the amount of time they need to negotiate a settlement (Stein and Kostelnik, 1984). In addition, as the negotiation process becomes more familiar, the number of onlookers increases. These children, along with the disputants, become more actively involved in suggesting ideas and reasons for a particular course of action. As a result, during none of some five hundred documented conflicts did a second conflict erupt elsewhere in the room while mediation was going on (Kostelnik and Stein, 1986; Stein and Kostelnik, 1984). Finally, there is promising evidence that in groups in which mediation has been used, not only does aggression diminish, but positive, prosocial behaviors increase (Kostelnik and Stein, 1986). This type of instruction, combined with the other strategies suggested in this chapter, will go a long way toward decreasing children's aggressive social interactions.

SKILLS FOR HANDLING CHILDREN'S AGGRESSIVE BEHAVIOR

How to Deal with Aggression in the Formal Group Setting

1. Model nonaggressive behavior. Utilize the skills you have learned thus far to present a calm, rational demeanor for children to imitate. Even when confronting children or adults whose behavior angers or frustrates you, keep your voice level and firm, your movements controlled, and your gaze directed at them. Do not scream or make threatening gestures.

2. Eliminate aggressive materials from your setting. Forbid children to bring aggressive toys to the program. If youngsters arrive with toy weapons, slingshots, or BB guns, temporarily confiscate them and send them home with the child at the end of the day. Inform parents of this policy. In addition, monitor books, pictures, filmstrips, films, and other instructional aids. Avoid those that depict aggression as a preferred means of solving problems. Do not assume that materials are suitable just because they have won awards or are recommended by a friend.

3. Anticipate and rectify situations in which children may be unduly frustrated. Check equipment to make sure that it works. Ascertain whether materials are appropriate for the children's developmental stage. If they are not, revise them. Materials that are too simple or too challenging often are a source of frustration to children. If a piece of equipment does not function, repair it or replace it with something else. Have enough materials that youngsters do not have to wait for long periods of time to gain access to them. Simultaneously, allow children to have things long enough so that they feel satisfied. If there are too few items for either of these to happen, supplement the materials in some

way. Reintroduce familiar materials on a regular basis so children can have repeated experience with them and expand on their skills.

Alert children to upcoming changes in routine so they are not taken by surprise when such changes occur. Warn them prior to transitions between activities so they can finish what they are doing before going on to the next thing. Keep rules to a minimum, and explain their purposes with personal messages. Provide options throughout the day so that children do not feel regimented and can gain a sense of autonomy. Periodically, present new things for youngsters to work with or revamp old activities so children perceive the program as interesting.

4. Remain alert to children for whom frustration is building. Watch children for signs of frustration. When it is evident that a child is becoming distressed, intervene. Offer comfort, support, information, or guidance as befits the situation.

5. Point out instances of accidental aggression when they occur. Explain the unintentional nature of the aggressor's actions to the victim. Use phrases like "It was an accident," "He (or she) didn't mean it," or "It wasn't on purpose." When appropriate, assist the aggressor in finding ways to make restitution.

6. Use substitution in response to children's expressive aggression. When working with toddlers, acknowledge the aggressor's perspective. Point out firmly the inappropriateness of the behavior and provide a substitute object for his or her use: "Geoffrey, it's fun to crash blocks. Those are Brian's—here are some you can play with." Move the aggressor away from the victim to focus his or her attention on the substitute object. Comfort the victim and help him or her repair the damage.

When working with older children, include the aggressor in the reparations before offering the substitution. Help the victim articulate a reaction to the aggressive act as a way of making the perpetrator more aware of the inadvertent impact of his or her violent behavior.

7. Set consistent limits on children's aggressive behavior. Stop an aggressive behavior, relying on physical intervention if necessary. Acknowledge the aggressor's emotions, express your concern, and explain why the behavior is unacceptable. Suggest specific alternative behaviors for younger children to pursue; help older children generate their own ideas for a solution to the problem. Clearly state the consequences for continued aggression, and follow through immediately should children persist. This approach can be employed in response to accidental, expressive, and instrumental aggression as well as those incidents of hostile aggression that obviously have been provoked by another child's actions. Given a case of accidental aggression, if the aggressor fails to desist after being told the victim's acts were unintentional, use the personal message, warning, and follow-through skills you have learned. Do the same if a child engaged in expressive aggression does not accept the preferred substitute. Implement similar strategies in response to cases of instrumental aggression in which children are developmentally unable to negotiate or there is no time to do so. Use the same tactic when you observe children using hostile aggression as a way to "save face." For example, children who shove in reaction to being jostled themselves, or those who get into a teasing interchange, are exhibiting signs of having been provoked and will benefit from having their point of view acknowledged while at the same time hearing that their behavior is forbidden.

8. Respond to children's unprovoked hostile aggression using parts two and three of the personal message only. When children engage in deliberate acts of cruelty that have no obvious connection to personal efforts to maintain self-esteem, do not reflect. Instead, move immediately into a statement that outlines your emotion and the reason for your reaction, identifies the specific behavior that has prompted your ire, and directs the child to stop. Look directly at the child and deliver your message in a calm, matter-of-fact tone. For example, when Mary deliberately trips Justine for no apparent reason, you might say: "It really bothers me that you tripped her. She could get hurt. Don't do that again." Similarly, when Mark calls William "four eyes" to embarrass him in front of a group, you could say: "It makes me angry when you taunt people. That's unkind. Stop." In both cases, if the behavior continues, proceed immediately to the warning and follow-through. Your goal in situations such as these is to limit the aggression without further embarrassing the victim or prompting unnecessary escalation of the incident.

Note that this is one of the few times in which a reflection is not advised. When a child is capriciously trying to damage another person's self-esteem, injure them, or destroy their property, their emotions are often unfathomable to the adult. Thus, either an affective or behavior reflection may sound accusatory, and a paraphrase reflection may inadvertently reinforce the negative features of the behavior.

9. Attend to the victims of aggression. Comfort the victim in front of the aggressor, and help the child generate ideas for how to respond to similar aggressive acts in the future. "You're upset. Jeanna hit you. The next time she tries that, put up your hand and say, 'Stop'." In addition, whenever possible, involve the aggressor in helping the victim as well. Avoid humiliating the aggressor or coercing her or him to apologize in your attempt to assuage the victim's distress.

10. Rechannel group play in which children are pretending to kill one another. When you observe children pretending to use blocks, Tinker Toys, or their fingers as weapons, step in immediately and redirect the play. Say something like: ''You're having fun. You're using the Tinker Toy as a gun. It upsets me when you pretend to shoot someone else. Use the Tinker Toy to build with. You may not use it as a weapon.'' Do not be sidetracked by children's protestations that they were ''just pretending.'' Reflect their assertion: ''You weren't shooting each other for real. That may be. It makes me feel sad when children even play at hurting others. There are better games to play. Let's figure one out.''

11. Praise children when they attempt nonaggressive solutions to difficult situations. Use positive personal messages when you observe children settling a potential dispute, refraining from hitting to resolve a conflict, or coming to the aid of a victim of hostile aggression. Compliment children's efforts to be nonviolent even if their approach has been rebuffed by others. Offer comfort and suggestions for how their performance could improve in the future.

12. Mediate children's conflicts. When incidents of instrumental aggression occur, utilize the conflict-mediation model described in this chapter. Carry out each step in order:
  a. Initiate the mediation process.
  b. Clarify each child's perspective.
  c. Sum up the situation.
  d. Assist children in generating alternatives.
  e. Help children agree on a solution.
  f. Reinforce the problem-solving process.
  g. Aid children in following through on their agreement.

Make sure you allow yourself enough time to work through the entire process. If you have less than five minutes available to you, do not begin negotiation. Rather, implement the strategies of the personal message and negative consequence presented in Chapters 7 and 8.

13. Use planned activities to increase children's awareness of alternatives to aggression. Plan discussions and formulate activities to highlight the differences between assertion and aggression and to develop nonaggressive solutions to everyday problems. Consult curriculum guides in early childhood education for ideas. Refer to Chapters 13 and 14 to learn more specific skills related to skits and planned activities.

14. Explore alternatives to corporal punishment if it is practiced in your setting. Most schools and centers do not require that all helping professionals use corporal punishment, even though some on the staff may. Prior to accepting a position, ascertain whether you will be expected to paddle children. If this is a requirement of the job, consider seeking another. If it is not, discuss with your supervisor ways in which you can use your disciplinary approach within the confines of the system.

15. Communicate to parents how you intend to deal with aggression in the formal group setting. Explain what you will do as well as what you will not do. Provide a rationale for your choices. Do not try to coerce parents into adopting your methods for themselves, but do make it clear that in your setting, certain adult practices are acceptable and others are inappropriate. If parents tell you to spank their children if they misbehave, say something like: ''You're really anxious for your child to behave at school. That's important to me, too. I will be making it clear to children what the rules are, and I will be using consequences to enforce them. However, paddling is not one of my consequences.'' Briefly describe a sample disciplinary encounter, using the skills you have learned, to demonstrate what you mean.

How to Help Children Deal with Aggression Beyond the Formal Group Setting

1. Provide accurate information when children assume that, because society condones aggression in one arena, it is permissible in all arenas. Children often try to justify their own aggressive behavior by likening it to behaviors they attribute to sports figures, the police, or the military. For instance, a child might say that he or she was acting like a particular boxer when responding to an insult with a swift uppercut. If children fall back on arguments such as these, point out that the child's use of violence was outside the bounds society considers appropriate. The aggressive action of the boxer is confined to the boxing ring, is governed by rules, and requires special equipment and training. Moreover, although society permits a person to fight under these constraints, fighting in day-to-day interactions is not acceptable. Use similar reasoning regarding police or military use of force. Explanations such as these are more likely to garner children's attention than are absolute condemnations. Whether or not you personally agree with these forms of violence, they do exist, and children are exposed to them. Your job as a helping professional is to assist children in understanding the constraints society places on certain forms of violence.

2. Point out to children that individuals can choose nonaggressive solutions to problems. Children who see violence on television, read about it, and are exposed to it in their daily lives may assume that there is no alternative to aggression. Take advantage of group discussions and private conversations to explain that people can choose many different ways to solve problems; some are hurtful, and some are not. One reason people resort to the former is that they do not always know nonhurtful alternatives. Tell children that you would like them to learn nonaggressive solutions and will work with them to discover what some of these might be.

3. Help children formulate ways to cope with aggressors beyond your jurisdiction. Listen sympathetically when children talk about aggression to which they have been subjected in other settings. Reflect their concern, anger, frustration, or fear. Brain-storm with the child alternatives that would be both acceptable and feasible for her or him to implement. Allow the child to rehearse a chosen tactic with you prior to trying it out. Ask the child to let you know the eventual outcome. If more planning and practice are needed, offer it. For instance, if a child is being victimized by a bully, some alternative strategies to consider might include avoiding the bully, talking back, assuming an air of indifference to taunts, finding allies whose presence will make being singled out less likely, and improving his or her skill in the area that is the subject of derision.

PITFALLS TO AVOID

The major pitfalls in handling children's aggressive behavior have already been covered in the section on ineffective strategies. Hence, the following section focuses on the common mistakes adults make when mediating children's conflicts.

Failing to lay the groundwork. Prior to initiating conflict mediation, the adult must have established himself or herself in the children's eyes as someone who cares about them, who will keep them safe, and who is predictable in reacting to children's actions. It is on these primary elements of adult-child relationships that the model is predicated. Failure to establish these conditions undermines the spirit of the process. Therefore, the mediation model is most effectively implemented only after children are comfortable and familiar with their caregivers, the surroundings, and the daily routines.

Ignoring developmental considerations. In order to successfully participate in conflict mediation, children must be able to indicate acceptance or rejection of proposed alternatives. Children whose age or development has not reached the point at which they can state their desires, or children who do not speak the same language as the mediator, are not yet ready to engage in this model. Children can communicate verbally or by using an effective substitute such as signing.

In addition, adults who try conflict mediation are cautioned to remain sensitive to children's tolerance for frustration. Not all children are ready to go through all of the steps at once. Most children calm down as mediation proceeds. Those whose behavior becomes increasingly agitated are demonstrating a lack of readiness. At that point, the procedure should be terminated, with the adult enforcing a limit to resolve the original conflict: "You both want

the stethoscope. I can't let you hurt each other as a way to decide who gets it, so I will have to decide. Evan, you can have the stethoscope for two minutes, and then Aaron, you can have a two-minute turn." At the same time, children should be praised for their hard work up to that point: "Evan and Aaron, you worked hard at telling me what you wanted. That helped a lot." Gradually, children will be able to proceed further in the process.

Mandating rather than mediating. Adults often neglect to use conflict mediation properly because they feel uncomfortable taking their attention away from an entire group in order to focus on only one or two children. They worry that the mediation process requires more time than they can spare. Instead, they may separate children, remove the disputed toy, and dictate an expedient solution. This approach undoubtedly works in the short run. However, it does not provide an opportunity for children to practice problem-solving strategies. As a result, over time, the adult continues to bear the primary responsibility for conflict resolution rather than gradually transferring this responsibility to the children.

It is important to consider the fact that mediation takes place where the conflict occurs; disputing children are not removed from the group. As a result, children who are not directly involved in the conflict frequently participate as observers or advisors. In this way, the teaching that is taking place affects several children at once. Also, because children become so engrossed in the process, another conflict rarely erupts elsewhere in the room during this time.

Denying children's legitimate claims. In his or her zeal to reach a compromise, a helping professional may inadvertently deny a child's legitimate right to maintain possession of a desired object. The mediator may hear such statements as "I had it first," or "She took it from me." When this occurs, the focus then shifts to helping the perpetrator generate appropriate strategies, such as asking, trading, or bargaining, to achieve his or her goal. There also will be times when a child has used an acceptable strategy for obtaining the object and the child in possession refuses. When this occurs, the mediator can help the children develop a suitable time frame for the exchange to take place. If the mediator does not know who has the legitimate claim, this can be stated in a personal message that also stresses the inappropriateness of *any* violent solution to a difference of opinion.

Affixing blame. Sometimes, when adults hear a commotion, their first impulse is to say: "Okay, who started it?" or "Haven't I told you not to fight?" Children's responses to these queries frequently take the form of denial or accusation, neither of which leads to clarification or constructive problem solving. It is better to approach the conflict saying "You both seem very upset" or "It looks like you both want the stethoscope at the same time." These statements focus on the problem that exists between the children rather than attributing sole responsibility to either child.

Taking sides. In order to establish credibility and be accepted as a mediator, the adult must be perceived as impartial. For this reason, she or he should avoid indicating initial agreement or disagreement with any position that is stated. This means strictly avoiding giving nonverbal cues such as nodding, frowning, and finger tapping as well as refraining from verbal indications of support, sympathy, disdain, or revulsion.

Denying a child's perspective. There will be times during conflict mediation when a child expresses a point of view that seems ludicrous or untrue. In those circumstances, it is tempting for the adult to try to correct the child's perception: "You know you really don't hate John,"

or "You shouldn't be so upset about having to wait your turn," or "You should feel pleased that John wants to play with you at all after the way you've been acting." Although any one of these statements may seem accurate to the adult, they do not correspond to the child's perception of the situation. As a result, what began as mutual problem solving will end in fruitless argument. As hard as it may be, it is the adult's responsibility to exercise patience and allow children to work through their own feelings about the problem under discussion.

Masterminding. It is natural for adults to want to resolve conflicts quickly. Sometimes, to accelerate the mediation process, they step in with their own solution rather than permitting children to work out the problem themselves. A related tactic is to force children toward a preconceived conclusion by asking such questions as "Don't you think . . . ?" or "Doesn't it seem that you should . . . ?" or "Wouldn't it be nice if we . . . ?" If the teacher has chosen to initiate the mediation process, he or she should allow it to proceed to a mutual resolution. Otherwise, children become frustrated at being led to believe that they are responsible for reaching a decision when in reality, they must acquiese to the teacher's conclusion. When this occurs, the chances for continued conflict are high because children do not feel a real commitment to an approach that is dictated to them. In addition, coercive strategies do not help children to practice the problem-solving skills they will need to reconcile future disagreements. Finally, the use of such autocratic techniques seriously jeopardizes the adult's credibility in subsequent attempts to mediate children's conflicts.

Ignoring ripple effects. There is a normal tendency for the adult to center his or her attention only on the children directly involved in the dispute, missing the effect the conflict has on other children in the vicinity. When children fight, it is common for a general sense of tension to pervade the group. Children on the periphery feel quite relieved when the adult steps in to mediate, and they should be allowed to watch the process as it unfolds. In this way, they have an opportunity to see that disagreements can be resolved in safe, supportive ways. It is important to note that even when the conflict has been settled to the satisfaction of the two adversaries, other children may be reluctant to play with either of them or to enter the area in which the conflict occurred. The adult can remedy this situation by announcing, for example: ''Evan and Aaron have figured out a way to share the stethoscope. They are going to take turns. There is plenty of room in this hospital for other children who would like to play.'' This proclamation provides a signal that the conflict is officially over and playful interactions may resume.

SUMMARY

Aggression is any verbal or physical behavior that injures, damages, or destroys. Four types of aggression have been identified: accidental, expressive, instrumental, and hostile. The first three categories are unintentional by-products of an interaction; hostile aggression is a purposeful act. Assertiveness and aggressiveness are two different things. Although both involve exerting influence over others, assertion does not include any intent to injure or demean. There is no one factor that causes violent behavior in children. Current research shows that aggression is influenced by biology and is learned through imitation, direct instruction, and reinforcement as well. The way children express aggression changes over time due to cognitive maturation and experience. Hostile aggression becomes more evident as children mature. Both boys and girls demonstrate aggressive behavior, although the tactics they use are somewhat different. Males tend to be more direct and physically abusive, and females rely on indirect, verbal strategies. It has been difficult to ascertain whether these patterns depend more on biology or culture.

Adults have tried different ways to reduce children's aggression. Physical punishment, ignoring aggression, catharsis, displacement and inconsistency actually increase children's antisocial behavior and should not be used. Effective preventive techniques include serving as a model of self-control and limiting the aggressive toys, films, books, pictures, or television programs to which children are exposed in the formal group setting. Helping children to recognize their own competence while reducing the frustration in their lives also is beneficial. When adults teach children prosocial behaviors and praise them for nonaggressive action, aggression is replaced with more appropriate conduct. When children do exhibit aggression, adults can assist them in changing their behavior by explaining instances of accidental aggression, by using substitution to rechannel expressive aggression, and by intervening to de-escalate aggressive play. At the same time, it is important for adults to create an environment in which children know that aggression is unacceptable. Setting limits on hurtful behavior and following through on those limits is an important tactic for accomplishing this aim. Children also benefit when they have an opportunity to explore potential responses to the aggression of others. It is difficult for some children to shift from violent to peaceful strategies all at once. Adults must gradually introduce a logical sequence of steps to help children move in this direction. Children can learn alternatives to aggression through planned activities. In addition, they can be taught to negotiate their differences through on-the-spot conflict mediation.

DISCUSSION QUESTIONS

1. Describe the four types of aggression. Discuss behaviors that differentiate them from one another. Present examples of behavior you have witnessed that fit into a particular category.

2. Describe an interaction in which you have observed either a child or an adult being aggressive. Discuss what changes would have to have occurred in that person's behavior for it to have been assertive instead.

3. Based on your knowledge of child development and biology and on information presented in this chapter, discuss physiological factors that contribute to the development of aggression in children.

4. Choose a fictional character or a public figure you consider aggressive. In a small group, identify some of that person's characteristics. Apply your knowledge of learned aggression to offer some explanation for the person's behavior.

5. Describe the emergence of aggression in children. Discuss how maturity and experience influence the types of aggression children display at different ages.

6. In this book, we have taken a strong stand against corporal punishment. Discuss your reactions to that position.

7. Describe the differences between catharsis, displacement, and substitution. Identify instances from your own experience in which you have seen these techniques used. Talk about the outcomes you observed.

8. Describe an aggressive behavior exhibited by a child without revealing the child's identity to the group. Use the strategies and skills outlined in this chapter to assist you in formulating a plan for reducing the unwanted behavior.

9. Of all the effective strategies described in this chapter, select the one you most often rely on. Explain why, and offer examples of the strategy in action.

10. Share with the group your experience in attempting the conflict-mediation model presented in this chapter. Describe children's reactions, your own reactions, and the eventual outcome. Brainstorm with classmates ways to improve your technique.

CHAPTER 10
Helping Children Cope with Stress

SOURCE: © The Boston Globe
Photo: Ulrike Welsch

OBJECTIVES:

On completion of this chapter, you will be able to describe:

1. The nature of stress.

2. Sources of children's stress.

3. Children's physical, psychological, and behavioral reactions to stress.

4. Strategies for helping children cope more effectively when they are under stress.

5. Pitfalls to avoid in dealing with stressed children.

David is entering Hambly Junior High. He's never experienced a school as large as Hambly and is worried about remembering his locker combination, finding all of his classrooms, and undressing in front of everyone for gym. Lately, he feels dizzy and shaky and wonders if everyone else knows how he's feeling inside.

Three-year-old Karen has begun following her mother closely and crying inconsolably whenever they are separated. She often thinks of the violent fights her mother and father have been having and the fact that her father doesn't come home anymore. She wonders if her mother will go away, too.

Kevin, who is six, has come to dread going to school and especially fears reading time. He has a hard time doing what his teacher wants him to do—he would do the work if he could, but he can't. He wonders how other kids can make sense of the letters and words in the reader. His stomachaches are becoming frequent.

Although David, Karen, and Kevin differ with respect to sex, age, family situation, and many other characteristics, they do have one thing in common: childhood stress.

Many professionals are concerned that the task of growing up in today's world is getting tougher. Although not all children are experiencing difficulty, increasing numbers apparently have fewer sources of adult support, affirmation, and love than in the recent past, and many are being pressured to grow up faster (Brenner, 1984; Elkind, 1981). Childhood tensions cited range from the normative stresses of growing up in one-, two-, and multiple-parent families to the extremely painful and damaging stress experienced by children who are physically and sexually abused. It has also been suggested that children are viewed more frequently today as obstacles to adult fulfillment and careers; children also are seen as economic burdens (Packard, 1983).

In addition, the American Academy of Pediatricians has indicated concern about the growing numbers of chronically unhappy, hyperactive, or lethargic and unmotivated children now being seen by clinicians; these youngsters are inclined toward school failure, psychosomatic problems, and early involvement in delinquency and drugs (Elkind, 1981). Such children have been described as "unwilling, unintended victims of overwhelming stress . . . borne of rapid, bewildering social change and constantly rising expectations" (Elkind, 1981:3).

THE NATURE OF STRESS

Stress is unavoidable. Daily, we are surrounded by loud noises, pollution, and changes in the temperature. We become oblivious to the strains induced by artificial lighting, noxious smells, crowds, hurried schedules, and poor nutrition. Constant decision making, juggling of commitments, balancing newly learned facts with previous interpretations, lack of physical exercise, pain, disease, and injuries also contribute to the pressures we feel on a day-to-day basis. Most stressful, however, can be the demands that result from our relationships with others.

Adults, with all of their experience to draw on, sometimes find these demands overwhelming. It is easy to forget that children also face such demands and are called on daily to make an extraordinary number of adaptations—at home, in the classroom or day-care setting, and in the peer group—frequently, with severely limited resources and experience.

Defining Stress

Stress, in and of itself, is neither positive nor negative but rather is "an integral element in the biological scheme of any living organism. All living things are designed with innate stress-alarm reactions which enable them to cope effectively with their environments. Without stress, there would be little constructive energy or positive change" (Pelletier, 1981:1) Hans Selye, a Canadian physician, was an important pioneer in helping us understand the potentially damaging effects of stress. He referred to stress as the rate of wear and tear on the body and also as a nonspecific biological response that involuntarily results whenever the human organism perceives a demand of some sort (1974:14). This *demand* can range from increased stimulation in response to something pleasant to anxiety over the perception of real or imagined danger. Perception of a stressor is extremely important, for it is only when individuals perceive that their resources to handle a situation may fall short of what is demanded that they become "stressed." For example, a child who has been frequently abused by adults may perceive an adult's movement toward her as threatening when no threat is intended. Another child who has not experienced such abuse will perceive the event entirely differently and, as a result, the event will produce two entirely different physical, psychological, and behavioral responses in the children. The child who does not feel threatened simply assimilates the adult's movement into the general scheme of things; the child who feels threatened, however, is involuntarily moved to behave in some way, perhaps by flinching, moving away, or shuddering. This external movement by the child is preceded by an internal response to the perceived threat.

Human Adaptation to Stress

Whether the source of a perceived demand is positive or negative, the adaptation response in the human organism follows a predictable, three-stage sequence; Selye labeled this process the "General Adaptation Syndrome" (G.A.S.). Pelletier (1981) describes it as follows:

1. In response to any perceived threat, the body reacts with increased alertness as adrenocortical reactions rise significantly. This is sometimes referred to as an "adrenalin rush." The heart speeds up, pumping blood toward the brain and the skeletal muscles, and the lungs draw in more oxygen. The liver is mobilized, producing glucose for quick energy. Noradrenalin also is produced, constricting the arteries and raising the blood pressure.

2. In the second stage, adrenocortical action decreases. Resources such as blood, oxygen, and so on, are concentrated on a particular organ or system that is designated to resist the stressor; thus, resources are diverted away from other organs and systems, which then "shut down" their activity. This process can be seen when digestive activity is shut down during a period of high stress, resulting in a stomachache, constipation, or diarrhea. Because the immune system is one of the systems so affected, it is believed that, under prolonged or intense stress, an individual's general resistance to disease declines.

3. In the final phase of the G.A.S., the exhaustion phase, the organ or system designated to resist the stressor can no longer perform effectively and becomes worn out or breaks down. When this happens and stress is still present, the body will shift the burden of resistance to another organ or system by moving again to the "alert" stage, allowing the worn organ a rebuilding or restoration period. This cycling cannot go on indefinitely, however; eventually, total exhaustion of the organ or system occurs, rendering it unrecoverable. It is at this point that the body becomes vulnerable to the "diseases of stress."

Why Be Concerned?

There are two reasons to be concerned about childhood stress:

1. We have become more knowledgeable about both the short-term and long-term effects of stress, and evidence suggests that undischarged stress that is prolonged and/or especially intense leads ultimately to disease.

2. It is believed that a child's stress-coping responses are learned early in life through watching how "significant others" (parents, siblings, extended-family members, teachers, and peers) cope when under pressure. These behaviors then become ingrained through habitual practice. When learned coping patterns are negative, they serve only to increase the demand in a child's life, making the child more vulnerable to stress.

Thus, a preventive approach must be twofold: eliminating or modifying undue stress early in children's lives, and teaching children positive stress-management techniques before they learn negative coping patterns—and before the effects of stress have begun to take their physical and psychological tolls.

SOURCES OF CHILDREN'S STRESS

The Child's Own Personality

Why some children "march to the left while almost everyone else seems to be moving to the right" is a question that puzzles many who interact on a regular basis with young children. These are the children who do not appear to be comfortable in any program, no matter how wide the range of offerings. They have noticeable trouble getting along with their parents, peers, siblings, and people in general. As they grow older, they often continue to struggle with poorly developed social skills, difficult personal interactions, and low self-esteem. Whether such children are "just born that way" or whether their personalities develop as a result of poor socialization techniques on the part of the significant adults in their lives is receiving considerable attention from researchers in the field of personality development.

A pioneering work in the individuality of temperament was that of Thomas, Chess and Birch (1968), who studied 136 children from infancy to preadolescence. On the basis of interviews with parents and direct observation, the researchers delineated nine characteristics of temperament: activity level, rhythmicity of biological functioning, approach and withdrawal, adaptability, intensity of reaction, threshold of responsiveness, quality of mood, attention span and persistence, and distractibility. These components were then clustered into three general types of temperament (Gardner, 1981):

1. Forty percent of the sample were classified as "easy" children—those who were moderately low in intensity and who were adaptable, approachable, predictable with respect to bodily function, and positive in mood.
2. Ten percent were termed "difficult" children. These children often were negative in mood, demonstrated slow adaptability to change, were unpredictable with respect to biological functioning, and were given to intense reactions when stressed. They also had a tendency to withdraw when confronted with unfamiliar people, activities, or stimuli.
3. Fifteen percent of the sample were termed "slow-to-warm-up" children. Although they took considerably longer to adapt than did "easy" children, they eventually were responsive, although they demonstrated low activity levels and low intensity levels.

Of the sample, 35 percent did not appear to fit into any of the three categories.

Given the particular characteristics of the "difficult" temperament, such as negative mood, high intensity, slow adaptability, and erratic rhythmicity, it may be that these are the children who later make up our "type A" personality populations (Friedman and Rosenman, 1974). "Type A" people are highly competitive, aggressive, time oriented, and hostile, and they apparently are predisposed to suffer stress-related diseases later in life. These individuals believe they are "mastering" their environments, coping with situations at maximum efficiency, and actively overcoming difficulties, when in fact their aggressive-defensive behavior patterns cause continual psychological and neurophysiological strain (Pelletier, 1981).

Some scientists question the desirability of labeling children "difficult," maintaining that such identification may not be valid and may, in fact, be damaging, given the caregivers' resulting expectations for such children (Rothbart, 1981). Reality reminds us, however, that although serious issues continue to surround valid assessment of difficult temperament, there is no question that certain children *are* more difficult to deal with than others (Soderman, 1985). Moreover, children today are ingrained members of a hurried society (Elkind, 1981). Those who cannot fit easily into tight schedules, tight curricula, and a decidedly faster pace—are children who are going to be in trouble. Whether their difficulties are a reflection of their own constitutional characteristics, disturbed caregiver-child interactions, or other environmental stressors, the fact remains that difficult traits do appear early in young children. Equally important is our knowledge that difficult behavior may be modified or intensified by life experiences. The child, as an active agent in his or her own socialization, plays an important part in flavoring those experiences. The other important people in a child's life also play ongoing roles in the dynamic unfolding of his or her individual personality.

This concept of mutual influence is important. When children are difficult to handle, less confident caregivers often develop self-doubts, feelings of guilt, and anxiety over what the future holds for the child and their relationship with the child. Unless difficult behaviors, or caregivers' perceptions of those behaviors, can be satisfactorily modified, a sense of helplessness often begins to pervade all interactions with the child. Dreams of being a competent parent or teacher may yield to the hard reality

that the child is unhappy, out of control, and moving in a negative direction developmentally. Attitudes toward the difficult behavior may move swiftly from early amusement or pride over a child's "assertiveness" to disapproval and even rejection by the adult. Adult responses, in turn, have a marked effect on whether additional stress will be imposed on the child or whether the child will be guided successfully toward developing more positive coping behaviors (Soderman, 1985).

Intrafamilial Stressors

Family life, which often serves as a buffer for children, also can be a source of stress for them. The ordinary aspects of family life may pile up to create demands for children that can range from mildly stressful to overwhelming. The birth of a sibling, the death of a pet, breaking a favorite toy, getting caught stealing or lying, carelessly spilling milk, losing a grandparent, or bringing home a bad report card all can be either opportunities for growth or highly negative experiences, depending on the responses of significant adults.

Death. Death of a family member is recognized as a major stressor for both adults and children (Holmes and Rahe, 1967; Elkind, 1981). Although all children older than seven months of age will tend to show some distress when separated from a parent by death (Brenner, 1984), the amount of trauma will depend on the child's age, the child's understanding of the event, and how the loss affects the child personally, both presently and in the future. Also important is the strength of the child's psychological attachment to the deceased person.

Research currently available indicates that there are developmental stages through which children progress in their understanding of death. These stages are directly related to cognitive maturation (Nagy, 1948; Safier, 1964; Koocher, 1973; Maurer, 1966). Although there

FIGURE 10-1 Children's understanding of death's finality varies based on their development.
SOURCE: H. Armstrong Roberts

is some disagreement about the age at which children move from one level of thinking to another, the consensus is that the factors that influence this process include children's egocentric thinking, as well as the degree to which they grasp the concepts of time and cause and effect.

There are three stages through which children proceed before achieving a realistic view of death. The stages overlap, and children may develop the outlined concepts earlier or later, depending on their personal experiences and cognitive maturity. Also, as the concepts in one stage become more fully understood, children may already have developed increased awareness, although not complete understanding of concepts in the subsequent stage.

Stage one (three to six years of age). Children in the first stage of conceptualizing death do not believe that death is final. They think of it as temporary and reversible. They also believe that life and death are in a state of constant flux. That

is, life as well as death comes and goes over a period of time (Safier, 1964). People who are dead can become alive again, just as someone who is sleeping can wake up or someone who is away on a trip can return. Some children think that death is a continuation of life on a restricted scale: people who are dead still eat, sleep, and walk around, although not very well (Kastenbaum, 1981). It also is common for youngsters to equate death, which is unknown, with sleep or separation, which are familiar experiences.

Young children may not react immediately to a loss, or may not express grief in adult terms. Adults may mistakenly view the child as taking the event ''exceptionally well.'' Adults frequently are misled in their judgments of the depth of children's misery by the fact that young children can tolerate only short outbursts of grief and, because they are easily distracted, they may appear to be finished with mourning before they actually are (Brenner, 1984). There may be *little* crying, and the child may seem almost untouched by the event. This response also may occur when children are not able to grasp what the event truly means, that is, the permanence of the loss and the extent of the loss.

Young children are not fully able to perceive the kinds of future demands the event may set in place: the permanent loss of an important source of support, love, and companionship, as well as the potential emotional, financial, and social disruption for all of the family. This kind of understanding may come later; if a child is very young when the event occurs, full understanding may come even years later. When this happens, the stress may appear later, either physically or psychologically. Unfortunately, the later stress may be difficult to link to the earlier event, which may have long since been mourned and ''taken care of'' by adults. Because children are in the process of developing their cognitive structures, they may be temporarily thrown off balance psychologically when rethinking an earlier, critical life event.

[handwritten: They may experience grief later & you might not know it. You might not know why either]

The possibility should always be considered that a seemingly unexplainable stressor for the child is not necessarily something that currently exists, but may be something that remains as "unfinished business" in the child's past experience.

The combination of what young children know and do not know about death leads to an active effort on their part to find out more (Nagy, 1948). Hence, children demonstrate great curiosity about the concrete details of death: the funeral, the coffin, the burial, the wake. Their interest at this point focuses more on what happens once death has occurred than on what led to the death or how the death might have been prevented. This is a logical focus for children, based on their view that death is semi-permanent. They are anxious to know how burial rites may affect the person's future state and his or her ability to return.

Stage two (four to ten years of age).   A major advance in children's thinking occurs in the second stage as they become increasingly aware that all living things eventually die. As children work through this stage, they develop an initial understanding that death is final and irrevocable. Although there is some disagreement about the age at which this realization occurs, researchers agree that older children have a better grasp of this concept than do younger children. Although children begin to accept that other living things will die, at this stage they do not recognize their *own* mortality (National Institute for Mental Health, 1979). Children in the second stage tend to attribute death to an outside agent (Safier, 1964). That is, life is given and taken away by an external force whose role is to make life "go" and "stop." Within this interpretation, children may personify death in the form of a bogeyman, a skeleton, a ghost, or the angel of death. Although these personifications have humanlike characteristics, they also represent mystical power (Kastenbaum, 1981). Because death is a person, it can be eluded if one is careful and clever (Nagy, 1948).

Children also typically confront their image of death by games in which killing plays a major role (Eddy and Alles, 1983). It is not uncommon for children to extend this confrontation to their dreams, which at times results in nightmares (National Institute for Mental Health, 1979).

Stage three (nine years of age and older).   The third stage represents the development of the realistic notion that death is personal, universal, inevitable, and final. Those in this stage understand that all living things must die, including themselves. Rather than imagining life and death as being controlled by an external agent, children recognize the internal forces involved (Safier, 1964). As preadolescents come to accept the inevitability of death, they also become intrigued with the meaning of life. It is at this point that they develop philosophical views about both life and death.

For children who more fully understand the meaning of the death of someone they love, the stress may be intensified if they receive little support in working through the disequilibrium that will naturally result. Grief may be intense, and since children's experience with loss is so limited, they may feel that their overwhelming feelings of sadness and the urge to cry will never end. Adults need to help children realize that unhappy times have ends as well as beginnings (Balaban, 1985). Other intense feelings may include guilt, anger, and resentment, and children may be cut off from expressing these feelings if adults appear uncomfortable with or unaccepting of such expression. Children who realize that their visible hurt may be causing discomfort in adults may tend to hide their feelings. *[handwritten: encourage them to talk about it.]*

Separation and divorce.   For some children, the rupture of family life due to separation and divorce may be every bit as stressful as loss through death. Over 1 million children a year (40 percent of all children born after 1970) will experience the pain of seeing their parents divorce (Wallerstein and Kelly, 1980). Because 70 percent of divorced spouses remarry within a three- to five-year period and 42 percent of them will again divorce, many children move in and out of a variety of family structures.

Accompanying these changes are all the problems associated with the breakdown, breakup, and restructuring of the relationships involved: loneliness; poor coping skills on the part of the adults; fractured ties with siblings, peers, neighbors, schools, churches, and extended-family members; and greater complexity in the maintenance of significant relationships (Soderman, 1985).

Two myths seem to persist about children's views of their parents' divorce: that they probably are just as relieved to see the end of a bad marriage as are their parents; and that so many of their friends' parents are divorcing that the trauma probably has been reduced considerably. However, preschool children are unable to intellectualize the event. Their focus tends to be on their own families, not on the record high numbers of families "out there" whose foundations are crumbling. Although seeing their parents argue is tremendously stressful for children, being separated from a parent ranks even higher as a stressor, particularly before the age of five.

Because attachments at early ages often are intense, fear of abandonment may cause a child to cling to the remaining parent. The child may throw an unexpected tantrum about going to school or to the day-care center and may begin tagging after the custodial parent, not wanting to allow him or her out of sight (Gardner, 1977).

Much of this tension in children is caused by their uncertainty about what the separation or divorce means with respect to their own security. Will they get up in the morning and find the other parent gone, too? Does the separation mean that they will have to move to another neighborhood or go to a different school? Will the parent who left come back and take the dog? Did the parent leave because she or he is mad at the child? Parents add to children's stress when they fail to sit down with their children and explain, as much as possible, the changes that are in store for the family because of the change in the spousal relationship.

Also, because children's thinking at early stages tends to be egocentric and "magical" in nature, children younger than six years of age tend to feel somewhat guilty about certain events that happen in family life. Some children believe they may have caused their parents' separation or divorce by something *they* did—because of naughty behavior or wishing a parent away for one reason or another.

Children's problems are intensified when parents are unable to successfully restructure family life following divorce. Parents may continue to hurl insults at each other whenever possible, using their children as an audience. Ex-spouses who are unable to resolve their angry feelings may later use their only link with each other—their children—to vent their hostilities or to maintain some sort of control over each other. Children may be used as hostages to obtain child-support payments, as spies to find out what the ex-spouse is doing, or as messengers to carry information back and forth. Confusion may ride high for young children who are forced to adjust to the different lifestyles and parenting approaches they encounter on the weekend as well as those they live with during the week with the custodial parent. Additional pressure is felt by both the parent and child who may want the visit to go perfectly. Neither may feel comfortable about "just hanging around" with each other, as ordinarily happens in intact families. A feeling often exists that, in order to maintain the relationship, the time spent must be "high quality" because there now is so little of it.

Tension also can be created by what "can't be talked about." Children wrestle with the dilemma of feeling disloyal to one parent if they appear loyal to the other. When a parent is openly hostile about the other parent, discusses the "sins" of that parent with the child in an attempt to vent some of their own feelings, or asks the child to keep certain information from the other parent, he or she induces additional stress as the child is forced to deal with the worry and guilt of handling adult-sized problems.

Even more stressful for some children, however, is the lack of opportunity to see the noncustodial parent or related grandparents because of continued hostility on the part of the custodial parent or severed affection by noncustodial family members. Adults who terminate relationships in an attempt to reduce their own pain can seriously add to a child's loss of self-esteem and support networks.

The transition time needed for most families to equilibrate following divorce is at least two years (Heatherington, 1979). A child's ability to handle tension will depend greatly on the way parents are able to resolve their relationship problems. Many children, however, even those whose parents handle the transition well, manifest some signs of disequilibrium. For this reason, divorce has been targeted as the single largest cause of childhood depression. Boys tend to take the event harder than girls, and the most painful years for a child of divorcing parents range from fifteen months to 15 years of age (Packard, 1983). Thus not many children escape without some signs of distress.

Wallerstein and Kelly (1980) found that children's concerns, feelings, and behavioral responses to parental divorce regularly fell into categories by age and development. These are summarized in Table 10-1.

Single-parent families. Largely because of separation and divorce, but also because of more out-of-wedlock births, the proportion of children living in single-parent families has grown significantly in the past decade. In 1983, 22 percent of all children lived in single-parent households, which numbered 6.3 million and represented 30 percent of all families with dependent children at home. It is estimated that 46 percent of all Black children and 15 percent of all White children reside in single-parent households (Glick, 1984).

The stress a child encounters while living in a single-parent family has less to do with the marital status of the parent than with the resources available to the family. Most of these families are headed by women, and three out of five fall below the poverty line. Poverty, a growing problem for children in the United States, has serious consequences. The world of the poor child is a "world of aching teeth without dentists to fill them, of untreated ear infections that result in permanent deafness. It is a world wherein a child easily learns to be ashamed of the way he or she lives" (Keniston, 1975:6).

Problems can be compounded when the child is not only poor, but black and poor, as evidenced by Dick Gregory's (1964) vivid account of his own experiences (Segal and Yahraes, 1979:263):

> *The teacher thought I was stupid. Couldn't spell, couldn't read, couldn't do arithmetic. Just stupid. Teachers were never interested in finding out that you couldn't concentrate because you were hungry, because you hadn't had any breakfast. All you could think about was noontime, would it ever come? Maybe you could sneak into the cloakroom and steal a bit of some kid's lunch out of a coat pocket. A bit of something. Paste. You can't really make a meal of paste or put it on bread for a sandwich, but sometimes I'd scoop a few spoonfuls of the paste jar in the back of the room. Pregnant people get strange tastes. I was pregnant with poverty. Pregnant with dirt and pregnant with smells that made people turn away, pregnant with cold and pregnant with shoes that were never bought for me, pregnant with five people in my bed and no Daddy in the next room, and pregnant with hunger. Paste doesn't taste too bad when you're hungry.*

The strains commonly felt by almost all single parents—economic difficulty, role strain, loneliness, depression, and the need to rebuild self-esteem—also become strains for the

TABLE 10-1 Children's Reactions to Divorce

Three to Five Years of Age

Marked silence during play

Fear of abandonment

Bewilderment and sadness

Worry about causing the divorce

Clinging behavior; reluctance to leave custodial parent

Anxious behavior, especially at bedtime

Regressive behavior

Six to Eight Years of Age

Better ability to grasp cause and effect of situation

Pervasive sadness

Crying (especially in boys)

Disorganized behavior

Unrealistic fantasies

Denial

Marked rise in or inhibition of aggressive behavior

Guilt

Hunger for affection and physical contact with adults

Increase in mastery play

Feelings of deprivation (seen in behaviors relating to food, toys, etc.)

Yearning for departed parent

Inhibition of anger at departed parent

Anger with custodial parent (mostly in boys)

Denial of feelings of responsibility in causing divorce

Fantasy about reconciliation of parents

Loyalty conflicts

Nine to Twelve Years of Age

Increased external show of poise, courage

Diffuse feelings of anxiety

Realistic perception of family disruption

Constant body motion

Shame over what is happening

Covering up of feelings

Mastery of feelings through activity and play

Anger at the parent who they blame for the divorce

Shaken sense of identity

Somatic symptoms (headaches, stomachaches, etc.)

Alignment with one parent

TABLE 10-1 *(continued)*

Thirteen to Eighteen Years of Age

Premature independence from parents; decreased participation in family

Worry about sex and marriage

Mourning (profound sense of loss)

Anger (at both parents, at parents' new partners)

Perceptions of parents as fallen idols or instant ''saints''

Temporary or prolonged delay of entrance into adolescence

Pseudo-adolescent behavior (sexual acting out)

Loyalty conflicts

children of these parents. One mother, describing her mounting frustration in dealing with a full-time job and total responsibility for rearing her child, noted that she came very close to child abuse. She became unreasonably angry when her son procrastinated at bedtime, thereby infringing on the small amount of time left to her (Weiss, 1979).

Often, the care that is provided for children in single-parent families may be less than adequate because of financial strain. Some parents are forced to accept somewhat undesirable day-care arrangements for their children when working to keep food on the table, which becomes a higher priority than providing for their child's emotional needs.

Of the approximately 13.7 million children under the age of eighteen who are living with single parents, some will suffer little stress. They are the children of parents who have the necessary resources to cope effectively with single parenthood—positive self-esteem, financial security, a supportive network of family and friends, parenting skills, and, in many cases, a workable relationship with their ex-spouse. Other children will feel the effects of living with parents who are struggling to do the best they can for their children. Sometimes, their best will not be enough.

Blended families. It has been estimated that of marriages that occur each year in the United States, 500,000 involve at least one partner with children from a previous marriage (Visher and Visher, 1983). Today 20 percent of all children, or 6.5 million, are living in a step family, and it is believed that the blended or reconstituted (bi-nuclear) family quickly is becoming the most common family form in the United States. Often, because dependent children are involved, there may be fantasies that the new marriage will provide a normal and natural family life. Such expectations rarely are fully realized (Gardner, 1977). Multiple problems that predictably beset such new families include those connected with weakened sexual taboos, biological ties that predate the new spousal ties, different life histories, difficulty in deciphering roles, competition between natural and stepparents and between step siblings, and matters of loyalty and affection.

These families often do not have the luxury of time to develop attachments between non-biological parents and children. Occasionally, children can be blunt about seeing the stepparent as an intruder. Stepparents, on the other hand, often view stepchildren in much the same way—as driving a wedge into the marital relationship.

Major stressors that children encounter in a step-family situation have to do with feelings of insecurity and jealousy that crop up between them and other members of the newly formed family. The child who has formed an overly close relationship with a single parent may resent having to share that parent with a stepparent and/or step sibling. He or she may view the stepparent as having contributed to the breakup of their parents' marriage (which may or may not be the case). They may constantly compare the stepparent with the biological parent who has been "lost" through death or divorce. Often, this parent is idealized to such a degree that only time and a reorganized perspective on the child's part can allow the child to accept anyone else.

Children may feel that their identity in a family is gone. For example, the oldest child may no longer be the oldest or the youngest child no longer the youngest. An "only child" may instantly have two or three siblings with whom he or she must now share the parent's attention (Visher and Visher, 1983). Resentment over a stepparent's efforts to discipline a child can be fierce, both by the child and the biological parent.

Stepparents can add pressure to the situation when their expectations of a stepchild are unrealistic or incompatible with previous expectations. Sometimes, expectations are based on experience with their own children's personalities and abilities; a stepchild's inability to be responsive may be viewed as insubordinate and uncooperative behavior when the child simply is at a loss about what the stepparent wants.

Barriers to open communication about natural parents can be highly damaging. For example, Roy, who had just returned from seeing his natural mother, innocently began telling his stepmother about the garage sale his mother was planning. He was startled at the fury in his stepmother's voice as she told him: "I'm sick and tired of hearing about your mother's financial problems. She probably told you that she has to have a garage sale in order to eat this week, didn't she? We don't want to hear *anything* about what she's doing. Just keep it to yourself."

Life in a bi-nuclear family also brings with it the demand of maintaining a complex network of primary relationships for children. Keeping up with all of them can be overwhelming. For example, three-year-old Lissa wondered how the Easter Bunny could carry all those baskets! She had received one at home, another at her father and stepmother's, two others when she visited her maternal and paternal grandparents, and still another when she was introduced to her "new" grandmother and grandfather—her stepmother's parents.

Working parents. Whether children live in intact families, single-parent families, or blended families, an additional stressor today is the trend toward greater involvement in the work force by parents. Currently, 60 percent of married mothers work outside the home, compared with 37 percent in 1970 (U.S. Census Bureau, 1985). By 1990, 75 percent of all mothers will be working, and 10.4 million children will need substitute child care (Smith, 1979). The fastest growing group of women entering the labor force are those with children under six years of age. Because these children have higher dependency needs and can be greatly stressed when those needs are not met effectively, demands are growing for early-childhood professionals, parents, and business, and community leaders to work together to be responsive to and responsible about the needs of these children.

Frantic juggling of family and work responsibilities often leaves parents feeling exhausted, anxious, and guilty. The phrase "It isn't the quantity of time that parents spend with their children, but the quality, that counts" has become a tired cliche when one objectively considers the hurriedness of family life today.

Four-year-old Cameron and his nineteen-month-old sister, Amy, probably aren't articulate enough to express their feelings about the quality-versus-quantity issue. They have become somewhat accustomed to the rushed exits in the morning and the noise and confusion in the less than adequate day-care setting where, from infancy, they have spent their days separated for long periods from their parents and from each other. They endure, sometimes not very graciously, the equally rushed times when they are picked up at 6:00 p.m. to make the trip home, often with stops at the supermarket, drugstore, and cleaners. By 8:00, both children are in bed. Cameron and Amy's parents are genuinely concerned about the quality issue; in fact, it's one of the things that causes *them* a great deal of stress. Their commitment to quality, however, constantly is usurped by the need to take care of such routine daily demands as laundry, the report that has to be ready for a client the next day, a Tuesday-night meeting at their church, a retirement dinner for someone at work, a flooded basement, and cleaning the bathroom.

Next door to Cameron and Amy, another family wrestles with the dilemma of fitting family life into demanding work schedules. They have decided this year that, rather than contending with the hassle of finding someone to come in before and after school, they will experiment with leaving six-year-old Sammy by himself until they arrive home at 5:30. Sammy has found that he becomes afraid only occasionally in the morning after his parents leave and before he leaves for school; however, he has come to really dread the after-school period. Rather than tell his parents about his fears, he has begun a ritual of turning on all the lights and the television set as soon as he arrives home. He fantasizes about what he would do if a "burglar got in" and how he could escape.

It is difficult to evaluate the long-range effects of the stress children such as Sammy experience on a day-to-day basis. In many communities, efforts are expanding rapidly to offer before- and after-school care for these children. In addition, where such resources are unavail-

able, or for children who prefer to go home after school, community and school professionals are providing information to children about self-help and safety procedures in case of emergency, hoping that such dialogue will minimize some of the strain children are feeling.

Abusive and neglectful treatment of children. The personal transitions that many adults face today, when coupled with the strains of parenting, can have devastating effects on children. Garbarino and Gilliam (1980:3) describe such a situation:

> *Joan Higgins is a 23-year-old mother of three children, ages 5, 3, and 1. Her life is a bleak procession of work and children, which she must face alone. She no longer lives with the children's father. She has few friends and none who are doing much better than she is coping with day-to-day life. Her money goes for rent, cigarettes, beer, and whatever food she buys for her family. Each of her children show signs of neglect. Often unattended, they have the dull eyes of children whose emotional and physical diet is inadequate. They do not see a doctor regularly and have little contact with anyone outside the family. Joan often feels like giving up and she sometimes does. On one such occasion, a neighbor called the police when the three children were left alone overnight with no food in the house. Much of the time, she is lonely and apathetic. Sometimes she is angry. This is nothing new. Her life has been this way as long as she can remember.*

The quality of care any child receives today is determined by a combination of social stress on the family and the adults' level of skill in caring for the child (McClelland, 1973). These two variables intermix to shape the transactions that occur. Effectiveness of skill in an adult depends on that person's previous opportunity to rehearse the role of caregiver (for example, with a pet or younger sibling) and whether he or she had effective models of caregiving during his or her own development. Also important are having a realistic rather than idealistic understanding of children's development and being able to prioritize parenting responsibilities over self-gratification. When any of these abilities are absent, there is great potential for high stress in a caregiver. This, then, sets the climate for abuse or maltreatment of children, including excessive use of force, sexual abuse, emotional rejection, or inadequate provision of essential nurturance (Garbarino and Gilliam, 1980). This problem is so far reaching, and the helping professional's role in dealing with it is so critical, that much of Chapter 16 is devoted to it. What should be noted at this point is that abuse and neglect may be a major source of stress for children.

Extrafamilial Stressors

Obviously, not all the stressors children encounter today come from within the family. Although we have concentrated thus far on factors within families that contribute to tension in young children, most families are highly successful in doing what families do better than any other system—nurturing children.

As children move outward from the relative security of their family into the family's social networks, the neighborhood, the day-care center, and formal school systems, stressors naturally will increase. In addition to familial stressors, children will encounter additional demands in the form of rules, expectations, and interaction patterns that are significantly different from those in their own family. Other persons with whom children must interact frequently may not accept them as readily as their family does, resulting in decreased self-esteem and confidence.

In moving between family and extrafamilial settings, children must adapt to differences between home and societal values, peer cultures, and the continuous pressure of exchanging the relative security of the family microsystem for the less secure realm of the outside world. And, there is evidence that children are having to make these adjustments at earlier and earlier ages.

Unsatisfactory day care. Many studies have examined the stressful effects of maternal employment and day care on children (Belsky and Steinberg, 1978; Kagan, 1977; Bronfenbrenner, 1979; Peters and Belsky, 1982). Researchers have looked at such issues as attachment, delinquency, academic performance, responsibility, cognitive development, and parent-child relationships. To date, we have little evidence that there are significant differences between children whose parents work and those who have a full-time parent at home, if the care those children receive is developmentally sound. That is, the care they receive must fall into one of the following categories:

1. Comprehensive child-development programs that provide for all, or nearly all, the needs of growing children and their families —educational, nutritional, and health, as well as parenting instruction in child development and family counseling.
2. Developmental day care, which provides children with experiences that promote social and educational development.

These programs are staffed by trained professionals; learning resources, such as books and toys, are varied and in good condition; nutritional requirements are met; and medical care is offered. Moreover, a national day-care study indicated that children function best when interacting in small groups (no more than 14) and when adults are trained in early-childhood education, special education, or developmental psychology (Irwin, 1979).

Few day-care programs in this country fit these descriptions. Most can be categorized as custodial child care, offering little more than supervision. Children may spend a great deal of their time in the care of untrained or poorly trained staff who promote activities such as

FIGURE 10-2 Day care that is responsive to children's developmental needs can provide a nurturing environment for growth.
SOURCE: Paul Conklin/Monkmeyer Press Photo Service

television viewing for large parts of the day (Papalia and Olds, 1981). Children from high-risk environments (that is, those characterized by family violence or instability) who are enrolled in such day-care arrangements prior to their first birthday experience negative effects (Peters and Belsky, 1982). What seems unclear is how much such children's emotional health has been affected by already weak attachments to parents and how much it is affected by the unstable day-care experience.

Most research on child care has been primarily restricted to high-quality, university-based programs rather than on a random sample of community programs. What must be examined further is what happens to the millions of children who are receiving less than adequate care: infants who have their needs met by any number of adults rather than a primary caregiver; children who become addicted to constant stimulation and rushing; children who spend 10 to 14 hours a day in crowded, noisy, and punitive environments—all potentially stressful situations. Also needing further attention are the stressful effects of limited family interaction: siblings growing up separated from one another and children and parents consistently spending little focused time with one another on a daily basis.

Stress in formal school settings. Once children begin their formal education, most will spend

6 hours per day, 180 days per year for 13 years in educational settings. This amounts to roughly 14,000 hours for the 71 percent who will finish school. Although a few children function poorly in school because of the stress they bring with them from home or because they have lower than average intelligence, many more simply are not ready developmentally for what is expected of them academically. Such youngsters experience high levels of stress because they lack the intellectual, physical, or emotional resources they need to perform the tasks given them in the classroom. All too often, this mismatch between a child's ability and curricular expectations is blamed on a deficiency in the child rather than in the system. Although both boys and girls are affected, the problem appears to be far more serious for boys, who later are overrepresented in resource rooms for nonreaders and the emotionally impaired (Soderman and Phillips, 1986).

Across the nation, a kindergarten "crisis" has developed. We have rushed to hurry children into activities (such as reading) that require interneuronal development between the two halves of the brain. Often, when children struggle or fail because their development is not advanced enough to allow them to meet these demands, we move to "remediation" with them. Because we experience success with some children who are on the advanced end of the normal cognitive continuum, we have come to believe that all children can achieve the same success if they can only learn to "crack the code." Instead, it is the children who have begun to crack under pressure.

How brain growth relates to stress. Research on brain growth may provide a basis for understanding why so many kindergarten children today are failing and, apparently, are being set up for failure (Toepfer, 1981). The human brain, which weighs approximately one pound at birth, increases by another pound before the child reaches one year of age. Following that period until approximately age sixteen, a third

pound of weight is added to the brain. Although some scholars believe this growth is fairly continuous, there may be periods of little brain growth (plateau periods) and others in which brain growth is significant (acceleration periods) (see Figure 10-3).

Approximately 85 percent of all individuals experience a significant spurt in brain growth (as much as 40 months of cognitive growth) at some time during the age spans between three and ten months, two and four years, six and eight years, ten and twelve years, and fourteen and sixteen years of age (Epstein, 1978). During these acceleration periods, myelinization (formation of the insulation around nerve fibers that allows the passage of electrical and chemical impulses) and axon and dendrite growth in the brain is significant, enabling millions of new connections to form between neurons (see Figure 10-4). There also is sequential myelinization of increasing areas of the corpus callosum. This is the bundle of nerve fibers connecting the right and left halves of the brain. As these connections occur, the structure of the brain changes, allowing the individual to attain new levels of thought or develop new modes of thought. Consequently, spurt periods signal the time when children are most capable of accommodating new knowledge and concepts.

Plateaus occur from birth to about three months and between ten months and two years, four and six years, eight and ten years, and twelve and fourteen years of age. During plateau periods, there can be as little as seven months' worth of cognitive growth; much of the developing organism's energy instead is directed toward biological growth and/or stabilization as well as toward practicing newly learned skills. As a result, plateau periods are a time when children do better at synthesizing already established knowledge than at taking in completely new information and concepts. Unfortunately, it is precisely during a plateau period that our society introduces children to formal schooling for the first time. Stress often results during these periods when youngsters

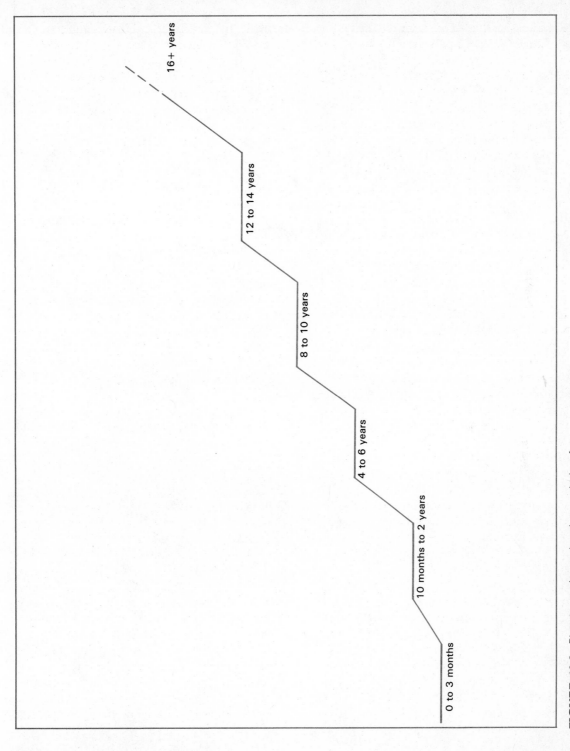

FIGURE 10-3 Plateau and acceleration periods of brain growth according to Epstein (1978)

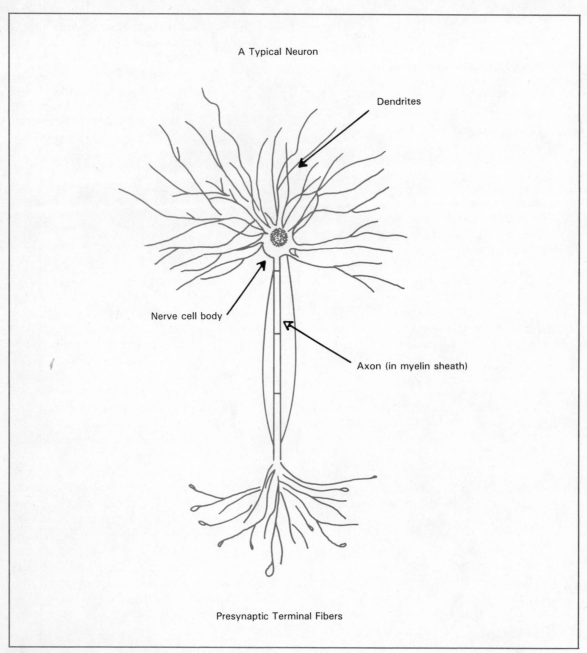

FIGURE 10-4 One of 100 billion neurons in the human brain that branch and connect to form the neural network necessary for intellectual functioning

are forced to cope with information that is ''beyond'' them.

School difficulties. Every fall, at least 10 percent of children entering school are not ready for what awaits them. Because physical and intellectual growth is more uneven in the early years than later, there are wider differences among children in the preprimary and primary years than will be found as this group of children moves into secondary schools. As children enter formal learning settings, these early differences may become more problematic when:

1. A child is significantly younger than the other children. Although chronological age by itself is not a reliable indicator of a child's school readiness, probably 80 percent of children experience similar patterns of development within a span of two years. Because boys are likely to be anywhere from 6 to 18 months behind girls developmentally in the early years and have less mature eye development, they are more likely to experience problems when entering school too early.
2. A child has not made the intellectual shifts (brain maturation) to reach new levels of learning that are required for formal schooling. This does not necessarily mean that a child will experience learning difficulties in the future. The child simply is not ready at this particular point in development and, and long as she or he is not pushed prematurely into a stressful learning experience, the child will catch up in the later years. Some even bypass their more ready peers in the future.
3. A child is emotionally unready for the pressure of moving into a large-group situation with unfamiliar adults and children. There may be too strong an attachment to a parent or fewer experiences than normal with people outside the family. The child may be experiencing unsettling family difficulties such as parental divorce or death.

Any of these could temporarily undermine a child's emotional stability and security.
4. A child has some organic condition that will require special education for at least a period of time. Many of these conditions, including learning disabilities and other problems, are not discovered until a child enters a formal learning environment.
5. The kindergarten curriculum is so demanding that only the brightest and most mature kindergarteners achieve success.

Although young children may experience stress in adapting to the demands of formal education, children entering middle school also experience their share of distress. They must move from the more protective environment of the elementary school to one that demands increased independence, responsibility, and competence on the child's part. There may be concerns about very basic needs such as locating classrooms and lockers. The child may harbor fears about the use of the rest rooms, being picked on by older students, keeping personal possessions safe, and undressing in front of others in physical-education classes. Belonging to a group, making at least one close friend, and learning to interact comfortably with the opposite sex become tremendously important as well as stressful (Soderman, 1984).

Children at this age benefit greatly from empathic parents and teachers who recognize the potential insecurities of venturing out further toward independence. Providing the child with specific information about new expectations, locations, rules, regulations, and schedules can help to reduce anxiety. Adults also can provide positive reassurance that transitions sometimes are hard but can be weathered pretty well, given some time and experience.

Other Assaults

Childhood historians believe we may be moving into a period in which children are less valued than in the past and distinctions between adulthood and childhood are becoming dangerously blurred. They remind us that in bygone centuries, adults held naive, even cruel, views regarding children and tended to ignore their needs (Postman, 1982). Pearsall (1983:2) says that today we see children as "safe little Peter Pans [who are somehow immune from our] fast-paced, high-geared, McDonalized society." Evidence, of course, is to the contrary.

There are numerous assaults on children today, including the kinds of food we are feeding them, the amount of television to which they are exposed, the usurping of play by adult-directed extracurricular activities, and the continuous and ominous "forced blooming" that is taking place (Elkind, 1981). Many children today don't go to camp as a place to interact casually with their peers; they go to gain computer skills, athletic skills, or preprofessional skills. Additionally, they are encouraged to copy adults in dress and behavior, so many of the "markers" that indicated passage from childhood to adulthood are missing. Elkind has remarked that we have not stolen away children's innocence; they are still innocent, but very confused and stressed innocents.

CHILDREN'S REACTIONS TO STRESS

Like adults who become overwhelmed when they are overloaded, understimulated, or faced with too much change, fear, or uncertainty, children exhibit individual responses when stressed. Personality characteristics, feelings of self-worth, learned coping skills, and the child's perception of how personally threatening any particular stressor is will affect each child's reaction when under pressure.

Physical Reactions

Highly stressed children often *look* stressed. When compared with other children, they fre-

quently exhibit slumped posture or a noticeably rigid body carriage. There may be observable activation or demobilization, so that the child appears to be "charged up" (one or more body parts in constant motion) or peculiarly passive. Breathing is concentrated predominantly in the upper chest rather than in the lower abdomen. The voice may have an explosive or shrill quality, and speech may be accelerated. In children who have experienced prolonged or intense stress, the hair often is dull, and there may be dark circles under the eyes (not usually seen in children). Frequency and/or urgency of urination may increase significantly, as do the numbers of somatic complaints such as headaches, stomachaches, and earaches (Pearsall, 1983). Appetite may increase or decrease dramatically, with accompanying gain or loss in weight. There may be vomiting, diarrhea, difficulty in swallowing, unexplained rashes on the face or other parts of the body, and frequent wheezing and/or coughing (Crow, 1978). The child may be particularly susceptible to colds, flu, and other viral infections.

Additional somatic and motor reactions to stress often include flushing, perspiring, dry mouth, chest tightness, heart palpitations, feelings of fatigue or weakness, muscular tightness, tremors or tics, incoordination, and startled reactions (Cotler and Guerra, 1975).

Psychological Reactions

When individuals are under prolonged or intense pressure, a common psychological reaction is lessened ability to attend to relevant stimuli. There also is a marked inability to internalize information available in the environment or to make the best use of that information. It becomes more difficult to make decisions. Those of us who have ever found ourselves in a group setting in which we felt upset, inferior, or unprepared can understand this. We probably found ourselves unable to attend to the activity going on around us, or tremendously anxious and tense. Most likely, we had little to offer that was relevant to what was going on because our psychic energy was directed toward our own equilibrium. There is little reason to believe that young children feel any differently, although it often is difficult for them to articulate how they are feeling.

How Children Cope with Stress

Coping with disturbing amounts of stress calls into play two different coping strategies: facing the stressor and adapting to it, or avoiding it. The latter usually is an initial response to something that bothers us. In order to reduce the tension we feel, we employ *defense mechanisms*, strategies that allow us to temporarily regain a sense of balance. There often are both advantages and disadvantages in using any of them. Brenner (1984:5–6) describes four broad categories of evasive actions (flight responses) typically used by children:

Denial. When using denial, children act as though the stress does not exist. For example, a preschooler goes on playing with her toys while being told that her father has died. Denial serves to alleviate pain and thus can help children preserve their equilibrium. Youngsters may also deny by using fantasy to obliterate reality. They may conjure up imaginary friends to keep them company or rely on magical beliefs to protect themselves and their loved ones.

Regression. When children act younger than their years and engage in earlier behaviors, they are using regression. They become dependent and demanding. As a result, they may receive more physical comforting and affection than usual, thus easing the existing stress.

Withdrawal. In withdrawal, children take themselves physically or mentally out of the picture. They run from the stressful environment or become quiet and almost invisible. They concentrate their attention on pets and

inanimate objects or lose themselves in daydreams to escape mentally when they cannot escape physically. Their efforts bring them respite from tension for the time being.

Impulsive acting out. Children act impulsively and often flamboyantly to avoid thinking either of the past or of the consequences of their current actions. They conceal their misery by making others angry at them. They seek quick and easy ways to stop their pain. In the process, they draw attention to themselves and find ways of momentarily easing their feelings of stress. However, in the long run, this coping strategy (and others, listed above) is almost guaranteed to be self-destructive.

When these strategies fail to reduce the psychological disequilibrium being experienced, a child may manifest other symptoms, such as panic, increased irritability, depression, agitation, dread, forgetfulness, distractibility, and sleep disturbances (including frequent nightmares).

More serious symptoms of emotional distress may include children pulling out their hair, repeatedly inflicting pain on themselves or others (including animals), frequently annoying others to draw attention away from themselves, having severe temper tantrums, running away, defying authority often, stealing repeatedly, and expressing excessive or indiscriminate affection toward adults. Children in even more severe trouble may express the feeling that they are no good, hear voices or see things that are not there, often think people are trying to hurt them, have many unusual fears, or be preoccupied with death. They may refuse to respond when others talk to them and refuse to play with their peers (Crow, 1978).

Kuczen (1982) has developed a listing of common childhood stress signals (see Table 10-2). She suggests that it is normal for children to demonstrate a few of these characteristics during childhood. These signs can be symptomatic of typical growing pains or of the process of wrestling with a temporarily troublesome problem. However, multiple signals, lasting for a period of time and evident even when there is no apparent cause, may be a signal that undue stress is threatening the well-being of the child.

Stress Coping as a Learned Behavior

People are not born with coping skills. Some of us were lucky enough to have had important adults around us—parents, teachers, or someone else we liked a lot—who modeled effective coping skills when they were under pressure. We watched what they did when things weren't going so well for them or when things were going *extremely* well for them, and we sorted out those behaviors that seemed to yield the best payoffs in certain situations.

Some children rarely see effective coping strategies being used. They are reared in authoritarian settings in which power and striking out pays off, at least in the short run. Others spend their days in laissez-faire settings in which no one really cares what they do so long as they are not bothering someone, or in overprotective environments in which they learn to become extremely vulnerable to peer pressures or to the exploitive behaviors of others.

Children frequently are reared in confusing environments in which parents and/or teachers react to them according to the adult's mood at that particular moment. If things are going well, the children are treated permissively; if things aren't so rosy, the atmosphere becomes more threatening. These children try to become good at "reading" the given moment. They also have a tendency to become exploitive and lean toward a great deal of "testing-out" behavior when they aren't quite sure where they stand.

One of the most critical elements in a child's ability to deal positively with strain and pressure is his or her self-concept. This develops in tandem with stress-coping abilities. It is the children who spend a great deal of their time

with supportive and authoritative adults who develop both high self-esteem and the best coping strategies. This is because they become aware that the way their life goes has a great deal to do with some of the choices *they* make and that there are consequences attached to those choices. They also learn that some consequences are more unpleasant than others and that those caring adults are a little cooler toward them when reasonable expectations have not been met. They discover that outcomes are not necessarily always in their control, but tend to be generally more positive when they have observed the limits set for them by others. They learn to see other people as predictable and are able to see strengths and weaknesses in both themselves and others.

These "styles of coping" do not happen randomly. They are the cumulative results of children's continuous observation, reflection, action, and interaction with other important people in their lives—people who ultimately have tremendous influence on how each child will approach life's events (Soderman, 1985).

Caring adults need to recognize that today's bombardment of choices, temptations, and pressures are as distressing for children as for adults (Kuczen, 1982). Because of the increased incidence of stress-related disorders among children, it is important for helping professionals to both model and teach effective skills for withstanding undue stress.

What Adults Can Do to Help Children Manage Stress

In order for adults to be effective in helping stressed children, they need a combination of knowledge, appreciation, skill, and self-awareness (Brenner, 1984). They must learn as much as possible about the variety of demands children face, their typical ways of responding, and the likely effects of both the stressors and the responses on the children and their families. Helping professionals also need to become familiar with the legal issues related to any

[handwritten margin notes top: eat alot — or not very much / hair turns dull looking / dark circles under eyes]

TABLE 10-2 Warning Signs of Childhood Stress

[handwritten margin note right: attention span shortened]

Bed-wetting	Increased number of minor spills, falls, and other accidents
Boasts of superiority	Irritability
Complaints of feeling afraid or upset without being able to identify the source	Listlessness or lack of enthusiasm
Complaints of neck or back pains	Loss of interest in activities usually approached with vigor
Complaints of pounding heart	Lying
Complaints of stomach upset, queasiness, or vomiting	Nightmares or night terrors
Compulsive cleanliness	Nervous laughter
Compulsive ear tugging, hair pulling, or eyebrow plucking	Nervous tics, twitches, or muscle spasms
Cruel behavior toward people or pets	Obvious attention seeking
Decline in school achievement	Overeating
Defiance	Poor concentration
Demand for constant perfection	Poor eating or sleeping
Depression	Use of alcohol, drugs, cigarettes
Dirtying pants	Psychosomatic illnesses
Dislike of school	Stealing
Downgrading of self	Stuttering
Easily startled by unexpected sounds	Teeth grinding (sometimes during sleep)
Explosive crying	Thumb sucking
Extreme nervousness	Uncontrollable urge to run and hide, social withdrawal
Extreme worry	Unusual difficulty in getting along with friends; shyness
Frequent daydreaming and retreat from reality	Unusual jealousy of close friends or siblings
Frequent urination or diarrhea	Unusual sexual behavior, such as spying or exhibitionism
Headaches	
Hyperactivity or excessive tension or alertness	

Source: Adapted from B. Kuczen, *Childhood Stress: Don't Let Your Child Become a Victim* (New York: Delacorte Press, 1982), pp. 13–14.

action they might take on behalf of a child and/or family and the kinds of resources that are available in the community.

Appreciation involves respecting children's viewpoints as well as their coping modalities, including any negative strategies they currently employ in lieu of something more positive. This is where empathy becomes important, enabling the adult to see the stressor through the child's eyes. Moreover, a holistic look at the stressor in terms of what other demands the child and family are facing is necessary in order to avoid simplistic "solutions."

Skill in approaching children about the way they are responding to a stressor is of paramount importance in allowing both the adult and the child to progress toward stress reduction. This requires that adults respond to children in warm, nonthreatening, friendly, and helpful ways.

Caregivers must honestly examine their own biases and belief systems in regard to each kind of stressor and each kind of child and family (Brenner, 1984). No matter how adept children become at coping with stress, it never is possible for them to be completely successful, to avoid all negative consequences, and to be able to take everything that comes. Children cannot cope with stress on a daily basis without help and support from at least one caring adult. For some children, a day-care center or school may be the only place where they can find such help.

The process of helping children begins when the helping professional "recognizes the child's 'loss of wholeness' or 'togetherness,' be it evidenced by fear and withdrawal, anxiety, inability to read or pay attention (or complete a task). It blossoms when the teacher is committed to furthering the overall goal of helping, which is to promote more useful behavior by students. It unfolds when the teacher carefully and skillfully uses his or her attending and responding skills to promote increased self-exploration and self-understanding on the part of the child" (Schultz and Heuchert, 1983:86). In addition, helpful caregivers also create a safe environment for children and actively develop stress-coping skills in the children with whom they are working. Working cooperatively with parents is another necessary element in the process of childhood stress reduction. The following are suggestions for supporting the development of positive stress-management strategies in children.

SKILLS FOR HELPING CHILDREN COPE WITH STRESS

General Stress-Reduction Skills

1. Use nonverbal attending skills. Focus on the child's feelings as much as on what the child is saying in situations in which children obviously are experiencing difficulty. Carefully observe changes in posture, expression, tone of voice, and other paralinguistic characteristics, as these communicate affect. Use you own body language to demonstrate interest and concern. Keep your own emotions and behavior under control. Don't jump to conclusions or try for a ''quick fix'' when you don't fully understand the situation. Accept the fact that a child's stress can be very distressing for you as well as for the child. The child's greatest need, at first, is to know that someone understands and cares.

2. Use effective responding skills. Let the child know that you are earnestly involved in helping and also in guiding him or her toward more effective coping. Use reflections to encourage adequate self-disclosure. Verbalize your perceptions of the situations to check for accuracy. Communicate clearly and directly, using the skills learned in Chapters 4 and 5. Do not tell the child that he or she will ''outgrow'' the problem or that the problem is essentially insignificant. If it is stressful for the child, the problem is important from his or her perspective.

How to Create a Safe, Growth-Enhancing Environment

1. Intervene immediately in aggressive encounters. Make sure that children feel safe. At no time should they feel threatened with physical or emotional harm from other children or adults. Do not allow children to express tension by harming others. Use the skills outlined in Chapter 9. Develop rules that promote an esprit de corps or a sense of ''we-ness'' whenever possible by encouraging prosocial behavior. Praise children's efforts when they demonstrate respect for one another and when they behave empathically.

2. Promote self-esteem in all children. Take advantage of every opportunity to help children feel competent and worthwhile. Use appropriate nonverbal behaviors and reflective listening. Praise children who use prosocial behaviors. The following example illustrates the application of these skills in a stressful encounter. Juan had rebuffed his teacher's attempts to talk with him about his many conflicts with other children by holding his hands firmly over his ears. One morning, following a shouting match with another child, Juan was alone with his teacher. As she sat down next to him, she noted aloud that he still looked pretty angry. Although Juan sat sullenly with his arms locked tightly across his chest, for the first time he did not put his hands over his ears. His teacher was quiet for a moment and then added softly: ''You're angry, Juan . . . but you're also listening. I appreciate that very, very much.''

3. Make every child the object of daily focused attention. The younger the child, the more important it is to have a particular caregiver working consistently on a one-to-one basis with the child. Children never outgrow their need for individualized attention, however brief it may be. Keep a daily journal that you fill out after the children leave for the day. Briefly record your thoughts about the children with whom you recall having encounters. Reread the journal after multiple entries have been made. Evaluate your pattern of comments on children; determine if there are some children who rarely are mentioned. (This often happens to the best professionals.) Make additional efforts to attend to those children; observe their behavior more assiduously. Another way to evaluate your performance is to go over a list of the children's names and mentally describe some aspect of their development such as motor skills or the ability to maintain peer relationships. If you cannot spontaneously recall information about a particular child, pay more consistent attention to that child.

4. Give children opportunities to work out their feelings through play. Accept the child's choice of a play theme. Do not try to direct play or determine how the details of play should be carried out. Play allows children to gain a sense of control when they are feeling fearful or uncertain. In the context of play, children can reduce their problems to manageable size and work at understanding them and themselves. For example, children commonly play "hospital" when they have just experienced hospitalization. Rarely are these children interested in being the patient. Instead, they prefer to play the role of doctor, making sure they are "in control" of the situation.

It also is common for children to play at death: falling down "dead," "zapping" a playmate, telling spooky stories, or pretending to be in a casket. Play is a safe and appropriate avenue through which death can be explored. Do not intervene when you see this kind of play even though you may feel it is morbid or unhealthy. In fact, playing out difficult concepts and situations is the child's way of making them manageable.

5. Eliminate unnecessary competition. Opportunities to learn about absolute standards of performance permeate our society. Adolescents are better prepared to evaluate their performance with their peers in absolute standards than are children under the age of thirteen, especially if they have had many op-

portunities for involvement, participation, and cooperation.

Protect preschool children, who are especially vulnerable to competitive activities that may appear to adults as acceptable. For example, "musical chairs," a game that may be highly enjoyed by eight-year-olds, creates distress for younger, egocentric children.

Select cooperatively based group activities for grade-school children whenever possible. Focus on the group achievement rather than on individual performance. In one instance, a fifth-grade music teacher held competitions for the spring performance. Although all the songs were to be chorus numbers, with a few speaking parts, she eliminated all but a few singers from the chorus. One child, who loved to sing and who was not chosen, cried nightly during the selection process and, according to his parents, would not sing on any occasion, including birthday parties, for the next three years! Prevent unnecessary stress whenever possible.

6. Build relaxation breaks into the program. Plan for periodic relaxation breaks in which everyone takes part in activities such as the stretching, tensing, and relaxing of muscle groups, aerobic exercise, or exercises designed to relax breathing. Children who participate in these activities are better able to concentrate and spend more time on assigned tasks. Take children on "fantasy vacations." Ask them to close their eyes and depart together on an imaginary journey. Use sensory vocabulary to encourage more elaborate imagery. Sometimes, ask children to pretend that they are going to attempt a challenging task, and ask them to pretend each step while breathing deeply. Help them to envision themselves as an actor, a doer, one who can face the challenge.

7. Allow children to participate in decision making and conflict resolution. Children should be included in the solving of real, genuine problems. This skill is developed fully in Chapter 12.

8. Use teaching materials, strategies, and resources that promote divergent as well as convergent thought. Promote the consideration of alternative solutions to problems by saying: "How else do you think we could use these materials?" or "If we use these another way, the end result may be very different. Let's try it!"

Choose textbooks or other curricular materials that depict males and females doing a variety of tasks. Select materials that depict variations in family structures and situation without implying that one family form or another is somehow deviant. A variety of cultural and racial groups should be depicted in positive terms.

9. Plan how to modify individual differences that cause children problems in their interaction with others. Although every effort should be made to respect individual differences, behaviors that are destructive to the child's own growth and/or destructive to others should be modified, if possible. Support the child while she or he is learning new behaviors. Say: "I know this is hard for you. I'll be right here to help." Acknowledge even the smallest effort at self-modification. Praise each modest success. If destructive behaviors are significantly difficult for you to change even after consistent effort, seek advice and/or assistance from other professionals who are more highly skilled.

How to Develop Preventive Stress-Coping Behaviors in Children

Teach children how to cope with stress before they find themselves in a highly stressful situation. Behaviors that develop habits of exercise and good nutrition, when combined with self-understanding and good coping strategies, enhance children's abilities to deal with short-term and long-term stressors.

1. Teach children about nutrition. Provide children with opportunities to learn about appropriate diet choices. Demonstrate careful planning of diet in the selection of snacks and in the menus offered at the day-care center or school. Invite knowledgeable resource people to speak to the class, and ask them how diets high in sugar, salt, and fat affect the health of children. Involve children in planning snacks that are appropriate for them.

2. Expand children's vocabulary to facilitate communication of troubling feelings and thoughts. Read children's books that depict stressful situations for the characters, or suggest titles for independent readers. Use precise vocabulary when making affective reflections ("You're so enthusiastic today!" or "I sense that you're pretty disappointed"). Help children formulate descriptions of what they are feeling when under stress. Remember, stress can be produced by a very happy event, such as a party, as well as an unhappy event, such as the death of a pet.

3. Increase children's sensitivity to their own body sensations when they feel angry, sad, tense, joyful, and so on. Be specific in your reflections: "I can tell you're angry because your hands are in such tight fists." Provide information: "You're so excited that you seem just ready to jump. Every muscle seems ready to go."

4. Allow children to experience the positive and negative consequences of their decisions unless doing so would endanger their safety or physical or emotional health. Tell children that mistakes are one useful way to discover better ways of doing something. Ask them to generate other alternatives that might have led to different consequences. Do not intervene unless there is a clear risk to the child.

5. *Provide opportunities for vigorous daily exercise.* Teach children that regular exercise reduces the natural stress on the body and maintains health. Do not assume that children are getting enough exercise; this frequently is not true. Children and adults need at least 20 minutes of vigorous activity each day. Demonstrate the relationship of stress and activity: ''I was feeling 'logy' because I've had such a hard day. Now that I've had a chance to do aerobics, I feel better! How do you feel?''

6. *Teach children specific relaxation techniques.* Encourage children to practice exercises such as deep muscle relaxation and relaxed breathing daily so they become habitual. Have children do some just before going home so they do not arrive there tense. One teacher asked children to investigate their own bodies to find out where all their ''hinges'' were (neck, elbow, wrist, waist, pelvis, knees, ankles). She had the children practice ''bending'' these hinges, then ''locking them up'' to develop an awareness of how their bodies felt when tense and when loose. She taught them to ''turn themselves into Raggedy Ann and Andy dolls'' who become increasingly limp as they unlocked one hinge after another. This game, and others she developed, allowed children to contrast tense and relaxed feelings. One of the best breathing-and-relaxation exercises appears in *The Relaxation Response* (Benson, 1975). Practice these exercises yourself on a regular basis before using them with children.

7. *Teach children to practice positive self-talk in tense situations.* Teach children to tell themselves to take it easy or calm down, and to sit quietly before responding to a situation. Young children may need to say these things out loud: ''I am in control,'' ''I can

stay calm,'' ''I'm scared, but I can handle this,'' ''I can breathe in and out very slowly to help myself stay calm.'' In contrast, discourage children from saying how stupid, incompetent, or helpless they are when in the middle of a stressful situation.

Children cannot control their feelings, but they can learn to control their behavior. First, they must believe that they have control. Help them to develop self-talk that is appropriate to the particular problems that they experience: ''I can get really mad, but I don't have to hit,'' ''I can choose to yell instead of hitting,'' ''I can tell them what they did that made me so angry.'' Self-talk contributes to self-control and decreases impulsiveness, which sometimes escalates a stressful event.

8. *Use encouraging responses to help children feel better about themselves.* When children have developed the habit of focusing verbally or mentally on the negative aspects of an experience (''I'm *so* dumb,'' ''I knew everyone would laugh at me,'' ''I can never remember anything!''), positive behavior changes can be facilitated by offering encouraging statements that verbalize positive aspects. These encouraging statements should not deny children's feelings (''You shouldn't feel that way,'' ''It's not *that* bad''). Rather, they should be used to point out the potential benefits or good in a situation. For instance, after missing the word ''chaotic'' in a spelling bee, Chris sits down, saying, ''I'm not any good at spelling anyway.'' At this point, you could say: ''You're disappointed that you missed a word. You lasted for five rounds. That's pretty good.''

9. *Help children practice imagery.* Children who have very limited skills in a particular area or poor self-esteem often foresee themselves as performing poorly in a particular situation before they even begin. This tends to decrease their potential for performing at

least adequately, if not well. Suggest that children pretend that they are going to perform very well the particular task that worries them. Tell them to begin the task in their minds and go through it step by step until it is successfully "completed." Have the children pretend with all their senses; for example, they might imagine themselves preparing for an oral presentation, reading, writing note cards, walking to the front of the group, and seeing classmates listening attentively. Encourage them to envision success and competence for this potentially threatening experience. Tell children to use this technique whenever they have to do something that worries or frightens them.

10. *Use ordinary experiences and daily activities to discuss feelings, thoughts, and behaviors that people can use when they are afraid, uncertain, faced with change, or overwhelmed by what is happening to them.* Discuss current events seen in newspapers, television shows that children watch, and experiences others share with the class. Highlight the coping techniques that were used. Explain to younger children how difficult the experience was for the person who went through it. For example, if a residence caught fire in the area, children will talk about it. Use this opportunity to discuss how frightening it was for the family and what they or their neighbors did to help. Stories also can be used as opportunities to play out some dramatic event. Do not deliberately try to frighten children; focus instead on positive steps they can take in similar situations.

11. *Collaborate with parents to reduce childhood stress.* Establish a positive relationship with parents and share ideas about ways each of you can most effectively support the child's needs. Use frank, open communication that is nonthreatening and nonjudgmental. Provide information on development and on stressors through parent newsletters and seminars. Listen with

empathy to parents when they speak of their own stresses. Be responsive to parents' needs, and schedule conferences so that they can attend. Validate parents' efforts to work with children in reducing stress. Do not seek to place blame or to criticize unfairly the genuine attempts of parents to be supportive. (See Chapter 15 for additional information about working with families.)

How to Help Children Cope with Death or Divorce

1. *Use appropriate vocabulary when discussing death and dying.* Use the words "dead," "dying," and "died" when talking about death. Avoid analogies such as "dying is like going to sleep" or euphemisms like "passed on," "lost," or "gone away." Children are literal in their interpretation of language. Thus, words that are meant to soften the blow may actually make the situation more difficult for them to understand.

2. *Describe death in terms of familiar bodily functions.* In describing what it means to be dead, point out that normal body functioning stops: the heart stops beating; there is no more breathing, no more feeling, no more emotions, no more loving, no more thinking, no more sleeping, no more eating (Furman, 1979). Death is not like anything else. It is not like sleeping, resting, or lying still, and parallels to these activities should not be made. Children who overhear statements such as "She looks so peaceful, as if she were sleeping" may dread going to sleep themselves for fear that they will not wake up. This is particularly true for children in the first or second stages of conceptualizing death, who still think that death may be temporary and reversible.

3. *Explain why the death has occurred, giving children accurate information.* Eventually, children ask, "Why did he (or she) die?" When talking to a child about a person

or an animal who died as a result of illness, explain that all living things get sick sometimes. Mostly, of course, they get better again. But there are times when they are so terribly sick that they die because their body cannot function anymore (Mellonie and Ingpen, 1983). When talking to children about a death that has occurred as a result of an injury, help them differentiate between mortal injury and everyday cuts and scrapes from which we all recover.

4. Explain death rituals as a means by which people provide comfort to the living. Children often are confused by the mixed messages that funeral customs communicate. For instance, children who have been told that a dead person feels nothing may find it disconcerting that soft, satin blankets and pillows have been provided. In their minds, these props are objects of comfort, and their presence reinforces the notion that death is like sleep. Adults can point out that articles such as these are for the aesthetic benefit of the mourners.

5. Answer children's questions about death matter-of-factly. Help children understand the details of death by responding calmly to queries about cemeteries, coffins, cremations, embalming, tombstones, skeletons, ghosts, and angels. Accept their questions nonjudgmentally. Answer simply and honestly. Sometimes, children's questions seem insensitive or bizarre, such as "When are *you* going to die?" or "Do worms eat the eyeballs, too?" If you recoil in shock or admonish the questioner, you add to children's perception that death is a secret topic, not to be discussed or explored. Things that cannot be talked about can be frightening to children, adding to the stress of the situation. Remember, too, that children learn through repetition, so they may ask the same questions over and over again. Each time they hear the answer, they are adding a new fragment of information to their store of

knowledge. Frequent questions do not necessarily indicate stress or fear, but rather, can reflect normal curiosity.

6. Respect the family's prerogative for giving children religious explanations about death. Avoid religious explanations. As a helping professional, you will work with children and families whose beliefs vary widely. It is your responsibility to respect those differences by allowing parents to tend to the spiritual needs of their own child. Be sensitive to the cultural mores of the families in your group. Insensitivity or ignorance can have disastrous results for children because your explanation may undermine what they have been told by a parent. The only exception to this rule is if you have been hired by a specific religious group to promote their philosophy. Then, because parents have chosen to send their child to you for religious teaching, it is appropriate for you to reiterate the philosophy of the institution. However, keep in mind children's age and level of comprehension when giving explanations.

Sometimes, children will say that someone told them: "Baby brother is an angel" or "When people die, they can return in another life as something else." When this occurs, the best response is: "You're wondering if that is true. Many people believe that. Many people believe other things, too, and as you get older, you will learn about them and will understand them better" (Furman, 1979:189).

7. Explain to children that divorce is the result of "grown-up problems." Tell children that adults get divorced because they can no longer find happiness in being together. Reassure youngsters that they are not responsible for the divorce, nor is it possible for them to bring their parents back together. Explain that although family members will be living in different households, they are still family, and the mother and father are still the child's parents.

8. Acknowledge the pain that divorce inevitably brings to children. Offer physical comfort; reflect children's emotions; remain available to children who wish to talk. Remember that the grieving process takes a long time, and children will vary in their reactions to it.

9. Talk to parents about the importance of explaining to children how divorce will affect their daily living. Parents who are caught up in a divorce may not realize that children benefit from knowing such concrete details as where they will eat and sleep, with whom they will live, and how much they will be able to see the noncustodial parent. Draw parents' attention to these facts and help them think of ways they might explain the issues to their children.

PITFALLS TO AVOID

All children and all families experience stress. As has been pointed out, reactions to stressors will depend heavily on individual and familial assessment of resources to meet demands. Following are a few of the pitfalls experienced by caregivers in working with children under stress.

Stereotyping of families. Caregivers, who as individuals carry with them their own perceptions and, possibly, very different resources, must be careful not to stereotype families based on composition, ethnicity, or financial resources. Much of a family's response in a stressful situation will depend on how they perceive a particular demand or crisis together with what they feel they can do to maintain their balance. It must be remembered that, although some individuals and families make what seem to be terribly poor decisions, they certainly are doing the very best they can given their current perceptions of their options and resources. In other words, people do not purposely or consciously "mess up" their lives; they always are striving toward equilibrium.

Skewed and inappropriate responses. Because withdrawn children cause us fewer problems in the classroom, there often is a tendency for helping professionals to see the aggressive or overly dependent child as the one who most needs our help. In these cases, we probably are responding as much to our own needs as to the needs we see in the children. Their behavior increases our own stress levels, prompting us to do something about it. What we model to children when they put us under pressure is far more important than what we say or "teach" about stress management. It helps to keep in mind that children who are at their worst often are those who have the poorest coping skills and are most in need of our understanding and help. The children who suffer quietly may be particularly vulnerable, and we need to be alert for the subtle cues they present. These children need help in dealing with overwhelming thoughts and feelings; they will need particular help in learning to communicate what is bothering them and in learning to cope with these stressors rather than run away from them.

Problems in the educational setting occur when we see only the irritating behavior in a child, not the child's distress. When we find ourselves getting angry about a child's negativism, we need to remember that this is the child's strategy for coping with a particular situation. Although we will want to guide the child toward finding a more positive strategy, we must remember that effective behavior changes do not occur overnight. They require patience, consistency, and firmness on the adult's part and the development of trust on the child's part. A sensitive approach to troubled children need not be seen as a "soft" approach.

Children do feel safer with a strong adult; what they don't need, however, is a punitive adult who strips them of their faulty defense mechanisms without providing anything more effective. This only makes an already vulnerable child feel more bankrupt and out of control.

Dictating "appropriate" responses. Although everyone experiences the same range of feelings, reactions to particular situations vary among individuals. Situations arise in which an adult may expect a certain reaction from a child, such as remorse, sadness, or tension. When the child does not respond in the expected manner, adults interpret the reaction as inappropriate. Remember, there are no right or wrong feelings. The adult's role is not to tell children how to feel, but rather to help them learn constructive ways of making their feelings known to others.

Pushing children to talk when they are not ready. The skills you have learned thus far emphasize verbal communication. Children, however, often show their distress through their behavior rather than through words. Although talking can help a troubled child, it must take place when the child is ready. Children vary in the time it takes them to reach this point. Thus, adults can let children know they are available, but should not pressure them into talking or make them feel obligated to talk in order to obtain the adult's approval. You can say things like "If you want to talk, I'll be around" or "Sometimes people feel better when they talk about their feelings." If a child seems hesitant or expresses a desire to be left alone, respect his or her need for privacy by following up with a statement like "I'll still be here if you want to talk later; and, if you don't, that's all right, too."

If a child rejects your offer for help, you may feel annoyed and unappreciated. In most cases, the child's response is based on his or her reaction at the moment and has nothing to do with you. Adults must be careful not to burden children further by stalking off in a huff or

otherwise demonstrating disappointment or exasperation.

Making a perfunctory diagnosis of a child's behavior. When helping professionals know that a child and his or her family are going through a stressful time, they may erroneously assume that all of the child's inappropriate behavior is a direct result of a particular stressor. For example, adults often are quick to say: "He's biting because his mother went back to work," "She has trouble making friends because her parents are divorced," or "She's complaining about an upset stomach—it must be because of jealousy over the new baby." Although the stressful situation at home may, indeed, be contributing to these behaviors, there also is a chance that other factors are involved. Adults must carefully consider the range of possibilities. For instance, the child who is biting may not know an alternative way of getting what he wants; the friendless child may not recognize other children's attempts to make contact, or may lack basic conversational skills; and the child with the stomachache may, in fact, be reacting to something she ate.

Looking for a "quick fix" or a superficial solution. When adults feel they don't have the time, the energy, or a ready solution to a particular problem, they sometimes fall into the trap of trying to get the situation over with as quickly as possible. This can be difficult for children because the adult's notion of a solution may not match the child's real need. For example, all of us, at one time or another, have seen adults trying to cajole or shame a crying child into being quiet. When this strategy fails, it is not unusual to hear the adult say coercively, "Either you stop crying, or I'll give you something to cry about!" At other times, adults may force children to prematurely confront a situation in the mistaken belief that this will make the child "get over" feelings of fear, revulsion, or unhappiness. Statements like "There's nothing to be afraid of," "Just get in there and do it," and "You'll get over it" are typical of this approach. In any case, the child's real feelings are neglected, and the adult is focusing on his or her own convenience. Helping professionals must recognize that helping is not always convenient and that emotional assistance takes time an energy. In addition, solutions do not necessarily come about within one encounter and may require repeated effort.

Failing to recognize your own limitations. As a helping professional, it is not always within your power to eliminate the source of a child's distress. Although you perform an important function when you provide emotional support, it may not be possible to alter the child's environment or to change the behaviors of others in the child's environment who are negatively affecting the child. It also is important for professionals to know where their sphere of influence ends and when it is time to link families with other helping professionals (see Chapter 16).

SUMMARY

There is growing concern by early childhood professionals and pediatricians about increasing levels of childhood stress. Two reasons for that concern are that we now believe that undischarged stress and prolonged periods of stress lead ultimately to disease and that stress-coping styles are learned in childhood.

Sources of childhood stress include the child's own personality as well as familial stressors such as death of a family member, marital transitions, intense work-force involvement of all adults in the family, and abuse. Also significant are extrafamilial stressors such as negative day-care experiences and stress experienced in the formal educational arena. Some professionals believe that children may be less valued in today's society, causing adults to hurry children prematurely into adultlike status.

Children react to stress physically, psychologically, and behaviorally. They learn positive or negative coping styles by watching significant adults in their environment. Strategies caregivers can use to help children cope more effectively with stress include using attending and responding skills, creating a supportive environment for children, developing children's active coping skills, and working with families to reduce children's stress.

Stress is inevitable. As our world grows more and more complex, our ability to adapt positively to both negative and positive stimuli also must grow more sophisticated. Childhood is the period during which much of that critical learning will take place—or not take place. Because today's children spend much of their time in day-care and educational settings, the influence of helping professionals working in those settings will be enormous. Although we cannot always improve a child's environment, we can provide every child with more effective tools for mastering that environment.

DISCUSSION QUESTIONS

1. With three or four of your classmates, compare one another's most common physical, emotional, and behavioral reactions when under pressure. How are your reactions similar? How are they dissimilar?
2. A parents' group requests that you bring a speaker to discuss childhood stress. What aspects of the topic do you believe ought to be covered if the speaker has only an hour?

3. If you were to assess your own personality type based on the brief discussion at the beginning of the chapter, would you say that you probably were an easy child to raise or a difficult one? If someone were to interview your family, what kinds of examples might they provide to support your conclusions?

4. In your own childhood years, were there any significant stressors that you can remember, such as the death of a pet, parental divorce, or loss of a friendship? Can you remember anything about your own reaction or the type of support you received from significant others around you?

5. Discuss: a. As many aspects of poverty as possible that you believe can contribute, either directly or indirectly, to increased stress in children's lives. b. Aspects of middle-class children's lives that differ from the experience of poverty that also may create stress.

6. A co-worker tells you: "All this stuff you read about children's stress is tiresome. We had stress growing up, too. Why make so much of it?" Share what you know about the importance of coping more effectively with stress.

7. Develop a brief activity or exercise that could be used in the classroom to help children relieve tension or fatigue. Demonstrate the activity to a group of at least three classmates.

8. Often, professionals focus on children of divorced families as children who may be distressed. Discuss the kinds of significant stressors that may exist in families that are intact but troubled—stressors that may be somewhat hidden.

9. Brainstorm with another person about the different kinds of helping agencies and professionals in your community that can provide support to distressed families and children. What are some factors that could limit a family's ability to get help from these resources?

10. Talk about aspects of a preprimary or primary program with which you are familiar that you believe are stress producing or stress relieving for the children in that program.

CHAPTER 11
Supporting Children's Development in Sensitive Arenas: Sexuality, Ethnicity and Handicapping Conditions

SOURCE: H. Armstrong Roberts

OBJECTIVES:

On completion of this chapter, you will be able to describe:

1. Types of sexual behavior and psychosexual development in children that sometimes are disturbing to adults.

2. Consequences related to the development of ethnic identity, preferences, and attitudes in children.

3. Issues surrounding the integration of handicapped children into formal group settings.

4. Skills for effective handling of developmental issues related to sexuality, ethnicity, and handicapping conditions.

5. Pitfalls in the handling of issues related to sexuality, ethnicity, and handicapping conditions.

A four-year-old boy in the housekeeping area of a large day-care center suddenly announces that the dolls are "going to make a baby." Putting one doll on top of the other, he tells two other children who are playing nearby, "Watch this!" and proceeds with a fairly demonstrative performance. The other two children watch with obvious fascination. As the teacher approaches, the child quickly picks up one of the dolls, purposefully ending the play episode.

Several children begin arguing over selection of a variety of small dolls representative of different ethnic groups. The hands-down favorites are the white and Asian dolls. An adult cheerfully suggests that no one has chosen any of the black dolls lying in the bottom of the box. "We can't. They're dirty and bad," responds one of the children. The adult is particularly surprised because the statement is made by a black child.

Kathy, a visually-impaired student who is being mainstreamed into a fifth-grade classroom, listens as two teams are chosen for kick ball during recess. She is not chosen by either team; when the teacher announces, "Kathy will want to play, too," there is an embarrassed silence, but no offer from either team to have Kathy join them.

Many helping professionals frequently feel genuine embarrassment, irritation, discomfort, and uncertainty in handling sensitive situations such as these. Because of personal emotions that automatically arise in response to their own moral sensibilities and past experiences, adults may find themselves reacting too intensely, avoiding or ignoring such behavior, or feeling momentarily confused about what might be the most effective response.

A serious by-product of excessive adult anxiety, discomfort, or rejection in such situations is the deleterious effect such reactions or avoidance may have on children's development—primarily the production of guilt, loss of self-esteem, or the reinforcement of negative attitudes, misinformation, and maladaptive behavior.

Conversely, adults who are able to maintain a sensitive, nonreactive, and matter-of-fact ap-

proach when handling sensitive events support positive psychosocial development and competence in the child. They are able to keep in mind the value and principles of establishing a positive corrective experience by viewing the child's behavior in terms of what the child is trying to express rather than in terms of the positive or negative qualities of the behavior itself (Yamomoto, 1972).

CHILDREN'S PSYCHOSEXUAL DEVELOPMENT

The Development of Sexual Attitudes

From infancy, all human beings have sexual feelings. A positive attitude toward sexuality means accepting these sensual feelings and urges as vital and proper rather than shameful (Briggs, 1975). Children's subsequent ability to handle such feelings effectively will depend on their earliest experiences. When infants are handled securely and tenderly during everyday events such as bathing and feeding, they learn that physical contact can be pleasurable. Later encounters involving psychological intimacy with significant others teach the child that interpersonal involvement is safe or dangerous, pleasurable or unpleasurable, depending on the extent to which important people are nurturing, nonjudgmental, empathic, supportive, and committed to promoting the child's well-being.

Similarly, children develop positive or negative attitudes toward their own bodies and bodily functions depending on adults' verbal and nonverbal reactions as they help children with everyday functions such as bathing, dressing, and elimination. If adults use words such as "nasty" or "dirty" to describe genital areas or elimination, children are apt to develop feelings that there is something unacceptable about them.

Masturbation. Although childhood masturbation is a fairly universal human experience, it can elicit major concern in some adults. Most children discover their genital areas quite by accident during infancy as they become acquainted with their own bodies through poking into openings and exploring their own extremities. Briggs (1975) outlines three stages of normal development related to masturbation, the first occurring as the child experiences an overall pleasant sensation on contact with the sensitive nerve endings in the genitalia and then actively strives to repeat the experience. It should be pointed out that, although it is pleasurable, the masturbatory experience in the young child is not qualitatively the same as that experienced by a sexually mature individual. In fact, young children can be seen deriving comfort from and enjoying similar sensations by stroking other, less provocative body parts such as their noses and ears, twisting locks of their hair, or rubbing pieces of soft material between thumb and finger. Adults who view masturbatory behavior as abnormal or precocious sexual behavior and therefore "wrong" may actively attempt to discourage such exploration through shaming, threatening, or punishing the child.

The second stage of masturbatory play occurs between three and five years of age, when children experience growing emotional attachment to the opposite-sexed parent and find gratification for these feelings through self-manipulation. Residues of these feelings, and subsequent behavior, can be found in children who frequently lean their bodies against a favored adult's or who spend increasing amounts of time sitting very close, touching the adult, combing or brushing his or her hair, or playing tickling games.

The third stage of normal masturbatory development occurs during preadolescence or adolescence in response to the emergence of hormonal surges and the appearance of secondary sexual characteristics, which invite renewed exploratory interest. Acts of self-stimulation may or may not continue in adulthood, depending on the individual's sexual

needs, outlets for satisfaction, and choice in selecting an outlet. Few persons today still believe old myths about the harmful consequences of masturbation; most regard them as misguided attempts to control natural impulses. Although many adults are uncomfortable seeing a child masturbate in public, more are becoming informed about the need to simply instruct the child that handling one's genitals should be a private act.

In any of these three stages, children may engage in masturbation consciously or unconsciously as a source of comfort when feeling tired, tense, anxious, stressed, bored, or isolated from others; when needing to go to the bathroom; to get attention; or because it simply evokes pleasurable feelings (Borland, 1984). Adults who grew up in environments in which such behavior was condemned may continue to carry with them a sense of shame that affects their adult sexuality. Such feelings usually tend to intensify their reactions to such behavior in others.

Sex play. This type of play also can be disturbing to many adults and often accompanies the second stage of masturbatory play for three- to five-year-olds. By this age, children have learned that there is an opposite sex. Most also have discovered that this opposite sex is equipped with different genitalia, which are interesting not only because of their markedly different appearance but also because they are used in a different way for elimination.

Because children are curious beings as well as sexual beings, it should come as no surprise that they may want to explore these differences and that they commonly do so during the course of playing "house," "doctor," and other childhood games. At this stage of development, children show interest in adult heterosexual behavior, in play focused on genital behavior, and in general activity that is active, vigorous, and exploratory (Samuels, 1977). Young children who have witnessed the actual birth of a younger sibling or who have watched a representation of a birth on television sometimes extend sex play to act out the birth process. Adults who work regularly with young children also occasionally see them using dolls and other toys to represent acts of intercourse or birth.

A potentially serious problem can occur as children sometimes choose to insert objects into each other's genital openings as part of their sex play. Although adults should acknowledge children's curiosity in such situations, they also should explain the harm that can be caused by putting objects into body openings, including other openings such as the eyes, mouth, nose, and ears (Borland, 1984). Adults should calmly set limits about sex play and redirect inappropriate behavior to another activity.

Children's curiosity about the human body should not be dismissed, and adults can help satisfy children's natural desires to learn more about their bodies and the bodies of others by answering questions in a simple and forthright manner. They also can share some of the excellent picture books that provide satisfactory answers to many of the questions children pose about sexual differences. Using correct terminology (for example, "penis" rather than "wee-wee") is an important part of teaching physiological facts and will take away the aura of unspeakable secrecy about sexual differences (Hendrick, 1984).

Peeping or voyeurism by children. Often considered in the category of "sexual disturbances," voyeurism usually occurs when children's natural curiosity about sexual differences has been seriously stifled. Some children who do not have opposite-sexed siblings, a natural laboratory for learning about sex differences, may use the day-care center or school bathroom to satisfy some of their curiosity. For this reason, directors of preprimary centers often purposely choose to leave the doors off toilet stalls. This can be upsetting for some parents who feel that such practices promote precocious interest in sexuality, although there is evidence to the con-

trary. Also, young children who have been taught that toileting should take place in absolute privacy may be somewhat stressed. For this reason, at least one stall should have a door.

Peeping and other deviant behaviors also can occur in children who have been sexually abused or chronically overstimulated sexually by witnessing adult homosexual or heterosexual activity. These children may go beyond covert behavior and become more openly aggressive sexually. When such behavior occurs in very young children, it can be shocking to adults, particularly when they view such children as entirely "innocent" and incapable of such thoughts and actions. A day-care aide described the experience of having a four-year-old boy begin unbuttoning her blouse as he sat on her lap listening to a story she was reading. When she asked him to stop what he was doing, he grinned and matter-of-factly told her, "I want to see your breasts." She notes: "I was amazed *and* shaken that this little four-year-old knew exactly what he was saying and doing. I'm still having a hard time dealing with it, and I find myself avoiding him."

Similarly, school officials in a midwestern middle school found it necessary to indefinitely suspend a sixth-grade boy who, despite intensive efforts by staff to get him to alter his behavior, repeatedly grabbed at female classmates' breasts and genital areas. Accompanying the inappropriate intimate gestures were explicit descriptions of what he planned to do with the girls sexually.

A male teacher in an elementary-school classroom found himself in a professionally threatening situation when one of the girls in his class repeatedly charged that he was making sexual advances toward her and other female students. Further investigation revealed that, in reality, the student was struggling with a sexually abusive situation at home and had been substituting feelings about her father's behavior in a desperate attempt to end what had become an intolerable situation for her.

Responding to unexpected behaviors. Although adults can be thrown temporarily off balance when children unexpectedly display behaviors such as exhibitionism, peeping, public masturbation, homosexual acts, and sexually explicit language, several "rules of response" should be kept in mind:

1. It is important not to overreact. It must be determined whether the act is an isolated one on the child's part in innocent response to some information or misinformation about socially acceptable sexual behavior or a fairly serious symptom of emotional and/or pathogenic disturbance. This may require continued observation and, if the behaviors are repeated, more detailed evaluation by other professionals.
2. Inappropriate behavior on the part of the child should be addressed by correcting any misunderstandings and by expressing clear expectations for children's behavior.
3. When the child's behavior appears to be the consequence of a sexual disturbance rather than just normal development, helping professionals should make a genuine attempt to investigate negative influences on the child that may be taking place in the other environments in which the child plays and lives. If such influences are found, caring adults should make every effort to provide the child with necessary protection and safety to see that such dangers are minimized and/or eliminated.

Troublesome Aspects of Children's Psychosexual Development

In addition to behaviors related to normal sexual development and those that appear to be outcomes of sexual disturbances in children, there may be aspects of psychosexual development or behavior in children that can be problematic for some adults. Perhaps most troublesome is the behavior of the effeminate boy or

excessively tomboyish girl. At the other end of the continuum, however, are those children who seem to play extremely stereotypical and rigid sex roles at the expense of developing a wider range of androgynous behaviors, that is, behaviors that are viewed as non-sex-specific. For example, an androgynous male would not see child care as solely a woman's responsibility; similarly, an androgynous female would view learning how to change a tire as beneficial and appropriate rather than as "masculine." Adults who themselves hold more androgynous views and see these as appropriate may be uncomfortable seeing children developing what they feel are narrow psychosexual viewpoints. Many of the myths about feminine and masculine psychological differences, such as that girls are more social or "suggestible" than boys, have lower self-esteem, are better at role learning, and are less analytical, have *not* been substantiated by research. Four psychosexual differences that do appear to hold up under scrutiny are the following (Maccoby and Jacklin, 1974; Hendrick, 1974):

1. Girls have greater verbal ability than boys, particularly beyond the age of eleven years.
2. Boys excel in visual-spatial ability, again a finding more consistently present in adolescence and adulthood than in early childhood.
3. Boys excel in mathematical ability, particularly from age twelve on.
4. Males are more aggressive, both physically and verbally.

This difference in aggressive behavior seems to be the most troublesome to deal with. Adults who do not support such a viewpoint or who are particularly threatened by a lot of vigorous activity may tend to suppress boys' natural vigor (Hendrick, 1984) rather than providing effective outlets for their energy. One third-grade teacher made wrestling and chasing games off-limit activities on the playground for the boys in her class. No other suggestions were made about what might replace such play, and when two of the boys in the class continued wrestling, she would order them to stand quietly against the building until they could think of something else to do other than "bully one another." Other children in the class who had been more compliant soon began to tease the two boys, who became labeled as the "bullies," with no intervention on the teacher's part. When one of the boys' parents expressed concern over the reputation her son was earning, the teacher countered with the explanation that "If other children could control themselves and find more acceptable outlets for their energy in using the playground equipment provided, so could the boys." In a study by Soderman and Phillips (1986), it was hypothesized that this unwillingness or inability of classroom teachers to deal with boisterous behavior has contributed to the overrepresentation of boys in special-education classes for the emotionally impaired and learning disabled. Males consistently outnumber girls in such programs by a ratio of 3:1 and, in some school districts, the ratio is as high as 20:0.

Links Between Sexual and Psychosocial Development

Physical changes experienced by children at puberty can significantly affect their psychosocial development, with body image and feelings of attractiveness closely related to pubertal status. As can be expected, patterns differ for boys and girls (Petersen, Tobin-Richards, and Boxer, 1983).

Early sexual development can be problematic for some girls. Although puberty typically begins for girls between the ages of eight and fourteen, it can occur earlier, resulting in breast development, the appearance of pubic hair, and the onset of menarche. There also is a significant growth spurt prior to and following menarche, with accompanying growth of axillary hair and widening of the hips. For a young girl, not understanding what is happening during men-

struation or having to deal with peer reactions to these changes can be troubling, particularly if classmates make inappropriate remarks or suggestions.

Males more often experience problems with self-esteem and unkind peer reactions when onset of puberty is delayed. Accelerated growth of the testes and scrotum usually occurs between ten and fourteen years of age, but may be delayed until as late as eighteen. Initial changes in male genitalia are followed by penis growth and an increase in height, with a growth spurt typically occurring between the ages of thirteen and seventeen and a half. When these developmental changes do not occur "on time," there can be a great deal of psychological distress in the young male who is eagerly awaiting them. First ejaculations usually occur during sleep. These *nocturnal emissions*, which are the body's natural way of discharging accumulated sperm being produced in the testes, may occur irregularly on several successive nights or months apart (Williams and Stith, 1980).

When these changes occur precociously or before the child understands that they are aspects of normal sexual development, they can be quite upsetting. Equally discomforting for other children is delayed maturation. Some children may be more open with helping professionals than with parents in asking questions related to their sexuality. Again, it is important for the professional to respond in a straightforward way, providing information that will help to alleviate the child's concerns.

Sex-Role Development

Children progress through a series of stages in acquiring sex-role concepts. This sequence depends on experience and intellectual maturity. Ages may vary from child to child, but the sequence always remains the same and may be described as follows (note the overlapping of the last three stages).

Stage one: general awareness of gender (birth to eighteen months of age). The first stage of sex-role development begins the moment a child is born, a name is selected, and exuberant adults ooh and aah over the "sweet, dainty baby girl" or the "big, strapping baby boy." Children listen to themselves frequently described as a boy or a girl and then hear sex-typed attributes associated with those labels. Although children of this age are not capable of producing elaborate speech, they take in much of the conversation directed at them. By eight months of age, the normal infant differentiates self from others, and there is evidence that he or she also may recognize other specific categories, such as size and sex (Lewis and Brooks-Gunn, 1972; Samuels, 1977).

Stage two: gender identity (eighteen months to three years of age). By this time, children have learned the gender labels boy, girl, he, and she and have begun to apply them to others with increasing accuracy. Children at this stage distinguish between the sexes entirely on appearance, depending on visual cues such as hairstyle, clothing, or activities. Children do not yet understand that under all those clothes, people have either male or female genitalia, and that it is by such characteristics that maleness and femaleness are truly distinguished. Thus, toddlers may insist that a female with a deep voice is a man and a male with long hair is a woman. The labels they are taught do not match the attributes they see. Initially, children are more certain of others' gender than their own because it is easier to observe others than oneself. But, by two or three years of age, they have learned to label themselves as a girl or a boy. Once this has been established, the child's sex identification appears to be fixed and irreversible (Brown, 1957; Hartley, 1964; Rutter, 1971; Money and Erhardt, 1973). As was pointed out earlier, it is at this stage that children realize that they and all other people are either male or female. Realization of this concept is called *gender identity*.

Stage three: gender stability (four to six years of age). The major milestone of this stage is for children to realize that boys always become men and girls always become women; boys cannot become women, and girls cannot become men. This is not something children inherently know; they must learn it. Studies in Canada, Sweden, and the United States indicate that few children attain this understanding prior to age six. Children demonstrate understanding when they can correctly answer questions such as "When you were a baby, were you a little boy or a little girl?" or "Two weeks from now, will you be a girl or a boy?" Those children who have well-established *gender stability* usually will react to such questions with a surprised look or retort that they find the questions silly.

Stage four: gender constancy (four to eight years of age). A more advanced concept is *gender constancy*. This involves children's recognition that gender is constant or permanent and does not vary despite changes in clothing, appearance, activity, or personal desire (Eaton and Von Vargen, 1981). Researchers have found that when they ask five- and six-year-olds questions such as "If Mary really wants to be a boy, can she?" or "If Mary cuts her hair short, would that make her a boy?" a majority of children fail to understand that because Mary is female, she will remain female regardless of how she feels about the prospect, what she wears, or how she looks. Although children may be aware of the difference between female and male genitalia, they often are confused about how outward appearances relate to basic masculinity and femininity (Kohlberg, 1966). Thus, this phase of development is a period of sex-role inflexibility. Children focus on the most obvious gender cues and therefore engage in what adults would interpret as stereotypical behavior. Numerous studies support the notion that rigid sex typing during this period is to be expected, and that attempts to minimize such behavior meet with only modest success.

Stage five: gender-role identification (six to eight years of age and older). Once children achieve gender constancy, it is to their advantage to be satisfied with their sex, whichever it is, and that usually is what happens. It is important to note that *gender-role identification* is different from gender identity, which occurs between eighteen months and three years of age. Gender identity refers to a *biological* (male-female) identification, and *gender role* refers to the behaviors and characteristics that become associated with a particular gender. In this stage, children begin to imitate in earnest same-sexed adults and peers and gravitate toward sex-typed clothing, games, and behavior. As the identification process continues, many children will describe their own sex in positive terms and use negative descriptors for the opposite sex (Slaby and Frey, 1978). Girls say: "Girls look nice," "Girls give kisses," "Boys are mean," and "Boys like to fight." Boys, on the other hand, are inclined to say things like "Boys work hard," "Boys are strong," "Girls are crybabies," and "Girls are weak." Some behaviors are not so stereotyped. Boys and girls alike feel that both sexes are able to run fast, not be scared, be the leader, or be smart. All these behaviors relate to children's attempts to accept and adopt the socially defined behaviors and attitudes associated with being male or female (Kostelnik, 1984).

As can be seen, development has a major effect on children's understanding of their place in society as a male or female and also in the roles they take on to express their maleness or femininity. However, identity and role taking also are shaped by children's environments and their experiences within those environments (Bandura and Walters, 1963; Freud, 1933). For example, there is evidence that abused children may develop significant difficulties in their sexual identification. Segal and Yahraes (1979:182) describe such a child:

Isolated from his peers and disinterested in the normal activities of typical boys . . . , he enjoyed making clothes for his Barbie dolls, with which he

played for hours on end. In the laboratory he often folded his arms high on his chest in an attempt, he said, to imitate breasts. Like many of the other abused children, he appeared anxious, forlorn, and frightened. . . . Under an early barrage of abuse from the outside world, he—and many of the other young victims—seemed to have lost his sense of identity and to have entered a prolonged and unresolved sexual crisis.

In the same vein, the young girl described earlier who projected her father's sexual advances onto her teacher was described by the school principal as remarkably masculine in both her appearance and her behavior. There seemed to be a conscious effort on her part to reject her own sexual identity and, in light of the stress she had been experiencing, that rejection became fully understandable.

Effects of Parental Absence on Psychosexual Development

Whether children's sexual identity is negatively affected by the absence of the same-sexed parent has received serious attention by researchers. Because the majority of children continue to be cared for by their mothers, almost all studies have examined the father's absence. Cross-cultural studies indicate that an early lack of opportunity for young boys to form an identification with their fathers was associated later with a higher frequency of aggression and violence and an almost total rejection of femininity in every form, almost as if these so-called masculine characteristics—physical strength, dominance, toughness, aggression—were being worn as badges in an "overboard" attempt to prove their masculine identity (Rorher and Edmonson, 1960). The result is that boys today, who more frequently grow up in the absence of their fathers, may be substituting the traditional masculine attributes with more socially costly attributes such as dominance, toughness, aggression, daring behavior, and even violence (Thompson, 1986).

In another study involving doll play, preschool boys whose fathers had been absent in the very early years played with dolls similarly to their female peers, and they expressed aggression primarily by verbal means rather than by the more typical physical means (Segal and Yahraes, 1979). A study of the college entrance examination scores of approximately 3,000 college males supported this emphasis on verbal skill enhancement (Carlsmith, 1964). A relationship was found between students' earlier experiences with paternal absence and a "feminine" tendency to score higher on verbal subscales of the test than on the mathematical sections. Conversely, males who had not experienced significant paternal absence were more likely to fit the male scoring norm. Hetherington's (1977) study of girls whose fathers had been absent revealed a tendency for these girls to have trouble with later heterosexual behavior, manifested by extreme shyness and anxiety about sex or by sexual promiscuousness and inappropriately assertive behavior with male peers and adults. Shyness and anxiety were more likely to be found in girls whose fathers had died, and sexually assertive behavior was found more often in girls whose fathers were absent because of divorce.

A child's ability to mesh his or her sex-role identity with biological gender, and the positive evaluation the child can or cannot bring to that merger, will have important implications in the development of that child's self-concept and his or her resulting social behavior. For this reason, "sex-role identification is probably the keystone of the self system and . . . should be well under way in childhood with an ever-increasingly appropriate view of and desire for the adult role for which the young person is biologically destined" (Yamomoto, 1972:129).

Helping professionals who work with children whose sexual behavior or identity seems to be on a divergent track have the responsibility of objectively sorting out those behaviors that seem to be consistent with normal development from those that are not. When behavior appears inappropriate, the child will need understanding combined with appropriate, supportive intervention. Helping professionals who are unsure about how to evaluate a child's sexual behavior and psychosocial development or how to implement a plan for altering behavior may need to consult professionals who have additional expertise.

Although we are living in an era of significant change regarding sexual values and roles, the restructuring of male-female concepts does not call for the abandonment of all current social definitions constituting masculinity and femininity. Helping professionals must, however, be aware of how their own personal convictions may affect their responses to children and their program planning for them. They also must have a clear grasp of the difference between a nonsexist curriculum and one that attempts to deny or destroy a child's basic valuing of his or her own sexuality (Hendrick, 1984).

THE DEVELOPMENT OF ETHNIC IDENTITY, PREFERENCES, AND ATTITUDES IN CHILDREN

Just as sex-role development appears to be age- and stage-specific, so is the development of *ethnicity,* or cultural awareness and sensitivity. Adults sometimes are caught off guard by disparaging remarks children may make about a person of differing racial or ethnic origin. Such remarks can be quite innocent in nature, simply reflecting the child's lack of experience and information, or they may be more intentionally hostile, such as when they demonstrate the development of a style of "humor" that debases different races, nationalities, or religions. This type of humor depends on a negative conceptualization of the disparaged group and cannot succeed unless the child has learned to think in terms of "good guys" and "bad guys" (McGhee and Duffey, 1983). There also are conscious slurs that result from a child's developing ethnocentrism (the exaggerated preference for one's own group and a concomitant dislike of other groups) (Aboud and Skerry, 1984).

It is entirely possible that some helping professionals, because of their own ethnocentrism, may occasionally find themselves fighting feelings of mild dislike or even strong hostility toward children, parents, and colleagues who belong to racial or ethnic groups dissimilar to their own. These feelings also can stem from socioeconomic differences between groups. Whatever the source, such feelings will consciously or unconsciously affect interactions, causing patronizing behavior, avoidance, or aggressiveness, which undermine the professional's effectiveness. Such reactions "affect both the minority-group children's attitudes toward themselves and other children's reactions to them" (Samuels, 1977:236).

How individuals develop such preferences and dislikes has been a topic of much research, most of it emerging since the Supreme Court's desegregation efforts in the early 1950s (Porter, 1971). Because children's development of self-concept is so heavily influenced by the interactions they have with others, including peers and nonfamilial adults, the attitudes those others hold about the child's racial group, social class, or religious sect will be critical. When a child perceives that his or her race, class, or religion has a negative social status, basic feelings of self-worth will suffer.

Early conclusions about racial awareness held that such perceptions, like gender awareness, first appear at about three years of age for both black and white children, although there is evidence that black children are sensitive to racial cues even earlier than are white children (Proshansky, 1966). These early positive or negative attitudes tend to increase with age, clearly showing more consensus and reliability at four years of age than at three and becoming fairly well ingrained in all children by the age of six. Moreover, although evidence is contradictory, it does lean toward white children

showing more preference for their own group and rejection of other groups than is seen in blacks, Mexican-Americans, or other minority groups (Miller, 1971; Milner, 1973; Porter, 1971; Aboud and Skerry, 1984). The dislike, mistrust, rejection, and stereotyping of racial and ethnic groups that later constitute adult racist attitudes clearly have their origin in early childhood.

Mechanisms that underlie the development of racist attitudes are multifaceted and include elements of direct learning, personality, cognition, perception, communication from the media and from important people in children's lives, and reinforcement of behavior. It is Katz's (1976) position that the perceptual, cognitive, and reinforcement parameters most strongly underlie the early development of ethnic attitudes, with perceived differences among groups being the primary prerequisite in the development of hostile intergroup attitudes. Challenging earlier theories (that attitudes are preceded first by ethnic awareness at ages three to four and then ethnic orientation at ages four to seven) as too simplistic, Katz presents the following eight overlapping but separable steps in the acquisition of racial attitudes:

1. Early observation of racial cues.
2. Formation of rudimentary concepts.
3. Conceptual differentiation.
4. Recognition of the irrevocability of cues.
5. Consolidation of group concepts.
6. Perceptual elaboration.
7. Cognitive elaboration.
8. Attitude crystallization.

Early Observation of Racial Cues

Obviously, the rudiments of ethnic awareness demonstrated by three-year-olds are not acquired overnight, but are supported by a combination and quantity of early observation and events taken in by way of the child's senses. This time of life (that is, prior to age three) is referred to as "pregeneralized learning," a period in which children have only vague or inconsistent preferences at best (Samuels, 1977).

Although a one-year-old is not developmentally capable of translating sensory cues into negative or positive assessments, there is evidence that the child's expressed and receptive understanding is modified by others in the environment who are continually correcting and differentiating for the child. Often, exaggerated positive and negative descriptors are used to help children polarize a variety of concepts, such as good and bad, male and female, dog and cat, night and day, black and white, big and small. If a child's environment is devoid of opportunities for exposure to different races, nationalities, and religions, the process of building a receptive store of cues for these concepts will be delayed. Generally, most infants observe skin-color differences during the period of stranger anxiety, usually prior to the first birthday (McDonald, 1970).

Formation of Rudimentary Concepts

Prior to the age of three or four, children begin to attach labels they hear adults use to certain ethnic groups. They also pick up on both direct and indirect evaluations of these groups by significant adults. ''He's dark because he's a black person. You need to stay away from him, or he'll cut off your ears.'' Less direct, but affectively important, are children's early experiences with lightness or darkness and the learned connotations, symbolic language, analogies, and similies associated with light and dark colors, which transmit rather dynamic messages: that white is associated with goodness and purity, black with evil and death; that there are ''black sheep'' in families; that black clouds are ominous clouds that spell trouble; that someone is as ''black as sin'' or as ''pure as the driven (white) snow.''

Some scientists believe that every child has experiences early in life that lead to the development of a preference for light rather than dark. Major needs are satisfied during daylight hours. Conversely, disorientation often is experienced in the dark due to loss of visual orientation and control so that darkness becomes associated with fear and lightness with the reduction of fear. ''In sum, what appears to be racial bias in the young preschooler is not racial in its origins —although it later becomes racial in its implications'' (Morland and Williams, 1976:266). Common assumptions that negative attitudes result solely from adult teaching must be rejected because of powerful influences on the child from many indirect sources (Morris, 1981).

Conceptual Differentiation

Once children have developed to the point at which they can place objects, people, and things into categories and have had labels provided to them for this classification, they experience both positive and negative perceptions of racial and ethnic concepts. As children respond to their observations, they receive verbal feedback from others that is both informational and evaluative. Most likely, particularly when children have fewer significant others around them, the feedback they receive will tend to be somewhat redundant, thereby facilitating the building of negative or positive attitudes. For example, Martin became very friendly with George, a light-skinned black classmate. When he asked his mother if George could come home to play after school, she responded negatively, saying she preferred that Martin not invite black children home. Martin, later appealing again to his mother, challenged her statement that George was black, noting that he didn't have black skin. ''Yes,'' replied his mother. ''But that isn't the only way you can tell someone is black. He has very broad lips and a black person's hair. He's black, all right. You just play with your own kind.'' Thereafter, Martin began looking at George and children like George in a different way. It is difficult to gauge the ratio of prejudicial and nonprejudicial experiences a child may have in developing racial and ethnic concepts. Unless more opportunities are purposefully provided for the structuring of positive examples, children can later become victims of a pile-up of these earlier indirect experiences, which, in combination with their developing and immature cognition, may later translate into a tendency toward a negative perception.

Recognition of the Irrevocability of Cues

The age at which children understand that an attribute such as race is immutable is not clear. This can be a particularly difficult thing for a child to learn, in that he or she learns that other cues do change over time. For example, children learn that short (young) people grow taller, that people can get permanents to make their hair curly or that curly hair can be straightened, that fat people sometimes become thin and thin people sometimes become fat (especially when they have babies—and then they become thin all over again!). Married people sometimes get divorced, and people change jobs. As was pointed out in the preceding section, children are able to grasp the concept of gender stability between four and six years of age. There is some evidence that the concept of racial stability may take place at about the same time. It is not uncommon for very young white children who have not yet developed the concept of irrevocability to believe that a black person's skin color can be washed or scraped off, or that like a suntan, it is not permanent.

Consolidation of Group Concepts

When both the perceptual components (such as the ability to identify both positive and negative instances) *and* the cognitive components of attitudes (such as the recognition of immutability) are functionally interrelated, the child finally has an accurate concept of a group. This process usually begins at about five years of age and may take a considerable period of time to fully develop, again depending on the child's environment and experiences. It also is at approximately five years of age that a "rejection"

stage begins, when children begin to rationalize their feelings aloud.

Perceptual Elaboration

In this stage, usually before the age of five, the child has developed an established concept of "us" and "them" related to racial cues. Children then expand, throughout elementary school, their perception of the differences that characterize particular groups. At the same time, intragroup differences become less important. For example, children may focus on the general differences between blacks, whites, and Asians in terms of skin color, eye color and shape, hair texture, shape of lips, and other facial characteristics and become less discerning about the wide variations among individuals within these out-groups, helping to build later faulty perceptions that "they all look alike."

Cognitive Elaboration

Cognitive elaboration is the process by which concepts or preferences become racial attitudes. It depends on the particular experiences, or lack of experiences, children have with out-group children and adults as well as the attitudes expressed by parents, teachers, and peers about people of other races. Prior to three years of age, children's minds are still receptive to positive teaching that corrects erroneous conclusions, explanations, stereotypes, and negative impressions (Morris, 1981). There is evidence that cognitive elaboration and differentiation with respect to ethnicity continues through the middle childhood years.

Spencer (1982) suggests that "Eurocentrism," that is, the white-biased choice behavior demonstrated by both black and white preschoolers, should not be interpreted as an indication of negative self-concept or low self-esteem in the black child prior to the onset of concrete operational thinking. More correctly, it reflects that minority-group children are affected by the majority group's values. Prior to the appearance of concrete operational thought, which generally appears after the preschool age, children lack the cognitive structures needed to make complex associations. Thus, a black child's preference for a white doll may simply be a reflection of "jumping on the bandwagon" rather than of poor self-esteem. The tendency for black children to identify with white groups decreases as children grow older or, perhaps, as they learn to "hide their negative feelings better" (Samuels, 1977:153).

In a recent study of the cognitive aspects of ethnic development, it was concluded that black children in America do not "hate" themselves, but many do achieve what can be considered a bicultural identity by eleven years of age, a condition that is viewed as positive and adaptive by those favoring integration and assimilation, but that is seen as destructive by black nationalists and separatists (Semaj, 1980).

Some black children whose skin color is indistinguishable from that of white people have difficulty identifying themselves as black at an age when other black children do (Clark, 1955). By five or six years of age, as they move into the realm of concrete operations, they begin to accept their social identification. A more recent study of 1,988 children in the third through twelfth grades revealed that, when socioeconomic differences and age were taken into account, black children showed higher self-esteem than did white children, apparently because of racial insulation created by the predominantly black social context in which they were reared (Rosenberg and Simmons, 1971). In other words, children "mirrored" themselves against significant others in their social world instead of reflecting society's relatively low regard for their social group (Williams and Stith, 1980). A black educator noted that "many black children spend all day long in environments where they feel they are not valued. But when they get home and back in their own neighborhoods, they know they're accepted, that they're all right."

Native American children may experience more difficulty. In a study of 233 Chippewa Indian children aged three to ten, by the age of ten, 36 percent of the children still asserted that they were white (Rosenthal, 1974). These children also evaluated themselves more negatively than did any other minority culture Rosenthal had studied. It was concluded that the subordinate role of the children's parents in white society, as well as negativity and repressed hostility in the parents, were "caught" by the children, who responded with self-deprecation and passive, apathetic, and ambivalent attitudes toward white people (Samuels, 1977). Similarly, a study of 1,374 black, Chinese-American, and white children five to seven years of age indicated that only the Chinese-American children failed to identify readily with their own race, although lightskinned black children were less inclined to show preference for their own race than were their darker peers. It is difficult to know why black children tend to be less likely than other minority-group children to develop poor self-esteem. Obviously, additional research is needed to better identify the aspects of socialization that dominate the process.

There also appears to be a paucity of research into the effects of "transplanting" single children from one culture to another, as has been the case with many Korean children. Questions must be asked about the timing and effect of interrupting the sequence of development of ethnic identity and racial attitudes in such children, many of whom find themselves members of what ordinarily would constitute an out-group. Increases in the numbers of adoption cases involving black children and white adopting parents raise similar questions.

Many studies that have examined children's attitudes toward their own ethnicity and others' have failed to account for socioeconomic status, making it difficult to determine to what extent poverty (or the lack of it) becomes the dominant factor in children's feelings about group membership. It also must be noted that many measures of self-concept, particularly those involving self-evaluating techniques, are problematic with respect to reliability.

Attitude Crystallization

Noting that the child's mind does not remain beautifully diverse and open indefinitely, Katz (1976) notes that attitude fixing probably takes place at approximately nine or ten years of age, with in-group preferences increasing thereafter. The child's ethnic values, in response to prior cultural conditioning, have now become largely intransigent and are not likely to change unless he or she is forced to rethink them because of a significant change in social environment.

There is evidence that what goes on in the classroom in the relationships between teachers and certain students may reinforce negative attitudes about minority-group membership. According to a 1973 report by the United States Commission on Civil Rights, substantial disparities existed in the way teachers behaved toward minority-group children. These children's ideas were accepted and used less often; they were given fewer positive responses and asked fewer questions; and they were less inclined to be engaged in noncriticizing talks with teachers.

Helping professionals may find themselves prejudiced against any number of things, including skin color; ethnic, racial, or religious background; physical appearance of students; or the life-styles of students' families. The challenge is to genuinely accept these legitimate differences in people and not to try always to move others' values and attitudes over to the professional's side of a particular scale.

Clearly, the helping professional's ability to respond positively to children of all racial and ethnic origins is important both for the self-esteem of individual children and for the overall environment, which affects attitude development in all the children. Williams and Stith (1980) have astutely noted that, although children from lower-class homes or from racial

or ethnic minority groups are commonly thought of as culturally deprived, they really are not until they leave their own home and neighborhood environments. It is only then that children may find themselves inadequately prepared. Although they have vast stores of knowledge, it may not be the knowledge that is valued; although they have a broad array of skills, they may not be the skills that are considered useful or, perhaps, appropriate by mainstream society. Today, certain ethnic minority groups constitute the greatest share of the 29 percent high-school drop-out rate in the United States, with 45 percent of all Hispanic children and 33 percent of all black children never finishing school.

In summary, the child's development of ethnic and racial identity and out-group attitudes begins in infancy, as soon as the child becomes perceptually aware of physical differences in people, and is primarily completed by the end of the primary-school years. The process is a complex one that is affected by parents' behavior and attitude, helping professionals' behavior and attitude, school curricula, religious practices, and the media (Semaj, 1980). Because children are more likely to encounter prejudice toward their ethnicity outside their homes, the impact of professionals' attitudes and their ability to structure supportive, accepting, and caring environments for all children is extremely important as a prerequisite to the prevention and reduction of prejudice.

ISSUES SURROUNDING THE INTEGRATION OF HANDICAPPED CHILDREN INTO FORMAL GROUP SETTINGS

Another group of children owning "minority status" in many educational and child-care settings are those who are handicapped in one way or another, but not severely enough to make them ineligible for membership in mainstream society. Although it has been estimated that approximately 10 percent of all people in the United States are handicapped, it is difficult to determine an exact number. Some handicapping conditions, such as Down's syndrome, cerebral palsy, missing body parts, blindness, or severe speech impairments, are easy to spot. Others, such as mild or moderate emotional impairment or learning disabilities, are more difficult to determine.

Categorization of Handicapped Children

Handicapping conditions are categorized in various ways, depending on whether the categorizing group is medically, educationally, or legislatively oriented. The term *handicapped* can be broadly defined as one or more instances of the following: "any condition which delays a child's normal growth and development";

FIGURE 11-1 Many children who are categorized as handicapped function well in the regular classroom when professionals are supportive.
SOURCE: David and Linda Phillips

"any condition which distorts (makes abnormal or atypical) a child's normal growth and development"; "any condition which has a severe negative effect on a child's normal growth and development or adjustment to life" (Allen, 1980:2). Major categories that are most useful to teachers, parents, and day-care personnel are identified as follows (Morris, 1980):

Mental retardation. Mental retardation is defined by significantly below-average intellectual functioning (an IQ score of 70 or below) existing concurrently with deficits in adaptive behaviors (developmentally appropriate skills displayed by a child in taking care of his or her own needs and carrying out social responsibilities).

Visual impairment. Some children's vision is so limited that it cannot serve as a channel for learning. Although it is rare for a child to be totally blind, an individual is considered to be legally blind when keenness of vision does not exceed 20/200 in the better eye with correcting lenses.

Hearing impairment. Hearing losses may be present that range from partial to severe. Individuals considered *deaf* are those whose hearing loss was so severe at birth or during the period of language development that normal language comprehension and expression have not been acquired. Individuals considered *hearing impaired* are those who retained enough residual hearing to develop language skills. It is estimated that more than 3 million, or 5 percent, of all school-age children in the United States have some degree of hearing loss.

Neurological impairment. Neurologically impaired children have specific, identifiable central nervous system (CNS) disorders or damage. Inclusive here are such conditions as cerebral palsy (CP) and epilepsy. CP, a nonprogressive disorder, usually is characterized by motor or movement dysfunction and some impairment of intellectual and perceptual development.

Epilepsy is characterized primarily by convulsions, either the more common and severe grand mal type, which last only a few moments, or the milder petit mal type, which is characterized by brief staring episodes, eyelid fluttering, or lapses in speech fluency. Although children who are hyperactive or hyperkinetic often are classified as neurologically impaired, it should be noted that rarely do overly active children have CNS disorders or damage.

Emotional disturbances. Emotionally disturbed children may display frequent or intense temper tantrums, inability to tolerate frustration, moodiness and withdrawal, difficulty in making friends, or "school phobia." Severe emotional disturbance also includes the conditions of infantile autism (extreme withdrawal from normal social interaction and exhibition of unusual or bizarre behaviors) and childhood schizophrenia (a cluster of psychotic or severely inappropriate or deranged behaviors).

Learning disabilities (LD) and developmental disabilities (DD). LD conditions, although difficult to define, are said *not* to be due to visual, hearing, or physical handicaps, mental retardation, or emotional disturbance. They include conditions related to brain injury, perceptual-motor impairment, minimal brain dysfunction or damage (MBD), dyslexia (difficulty in reading), or developmental aphasia (impaired ability to use or understand words).

DD conditions, as defined by federal legislation in 1969, are defined by the existence of the following conditions (Morris, 1980):

1. Mental retardation, cerebral palsy, epilepsy, or other adverse neurological condition.
2. Treatment needed similar to that required for the mentally retarded.
3. Evidence of the disability before the age of eighteen.
4. Expectation that the disability is long term and will continue indefinitely.

The severity of any of these handicapping conditions and the availability of community, school, and family resources will determine whether a child will be institutionalized or *mainstreamed*—that is, integrated into the social, recreational, and educational activities that nonhandicapped children experience. The mainstreaming of many of these children has been prompted by legislative action. For example, Public Law 92-924 (1972 Economic Opportunity Act) and Public Law 94-142 (Education for All Handicapped Children Act, enacted in 1975) mandate that 10 percent of all openings in Head Start programs go to handicapped children. The purpose of integration of the handicapped and nonhandicapped is twofold: to promote the acceptance of the handicapped through reduction and removal of social stigma and the enhancement of social competence of the handicapped so they can later live more comfortably and successfully in the mainstream of society.

In the ten years since Public Law 94-142 was passed to ensure that, to the maximum extent possible, handicapped children would be educated with the nonhandicapped, personnel in public schools, day-care centers, and other programs for children have made great strides in making these mandated "least restrictive environments" as available as possible to the handicapped. Architectural barriers and problems with transportation and toilet facilities have dramatically improved despite the expense involved. Formal preparation and in-service education for professionals who work primarily with nonhandicapped children now regularly include information and skill training regarding handicapping conditions, strategies for supporting the social integration of handicapped and nonhandicapped children, and techniques for modifying curricula for children with special needs. In-service programs to upgrade professional skills are increasingly directed toward enhancing professional competencies in classroom management of the handicapped, screening and evaluation, interpretation of clinical reports, agency referral, and the structuring of Individualized Educational Program Committees (IEPCs) and programs.

Handicapped Children in the Classroom

The challenges encountered by helping professionals involved in the integration of the handicapped often are similar to those attempting racial integration: melding those who are different from the majority successfully into the mainstream. Some children accomplish this with few problems; others experience increased conflict and isolation and accompanying loss of self-esteem. Placing students with special needs into the regular classroom can be:

the beginning of an opportunity. But it carries the risk of making things worse as well as the possibility of making things better for the integrating child. If the [process] goes badly, handicapped students will be more severely and directly stigmatized, stereotyped, and rejected. Even worse, they may be ignored or treated with the paternalistic care one reserves for pets. If [mainstreaming] goes well, however, true friendships and constructive relationships may develop between nonhandicapped and handicapped children, adolescents, and young adults. (Johnson and Johnson, 1980:90)

Additional concern evolves from evidence that handicapped children often are less assertive in the regular classroom (Goldstein, Moss, and Jardon, 1965); may exhibit negative, rather than positive, changes in behavior (Vacc, 1971); and suffer from peer rejection (Johnson, 1975; Bryan, 1974; Iano, et al., 1974).

Other observations of integration have been more positive, indicating that integrated programs give disabled children a chance to:

plan and learn with children who will someday be their co-workers, friends, and neighbors. Both groups [handicapped and non-handicapped] benefit most from being together on a regular basis during the years when their attitudes and perceptions

of themselves and others are most pliable. (Klein, 1975:318)

Children's perceptions of handicapping conditions. Social acceptance depends not so much on a child's handicapping limitations as on individual characteristics such as independence, friendliness, and other social skills. Successful integration also will depend on the helping professional's ability to structure the environment, paying as much attention to the social dynamics of the integration as to physical facilitation and curricular aspects (Guinagh, 1980). Young children are keenly aware of differences in other children and react in a variety of ways when they encounter a child who acts, moves, looks, speaks, or thinks differently. Because they are still learning the "rules" of life, and generalize about the rest of the world from their own experience, they often are strict conformists about what is acceptable and what is not. They tend to explain disabilities in terms of what they already know, and their attempts to resolve their own curiosity often involve the following (Ginsberg, 1976):

Identification with the handicapped child. Children have been observed taking two long blocks and using them for crutches; asking a parent for a helmet "just like the one" worn by a brain-injured classmate; and responding to a classmate born with only one finger on each hand with, "When I was a baby, I had only one finger, too."

Creating explanations for a handicap. In reference to a classmate who could not walk, a child was overheard saying, "Tommy is still a baby." Another child, while talking about a classmate with cerebral palsy, explained, "He didn't eat enough carrots." Another child told a teacher, "When Sally grows up, she's gonna hear *real* well."

Fears about their own intactness. Children may express this concern by avoiding a handicapped child. Children also have been noted in dramatic play making such statements as, "My arm's gonna get chopped off."

Recognition and observation of special characteristics. Children talk about and name the differences they notice in another child or person. Younger, preverbal children simply may point to a hearing aid, brace, or person in a wheelchair.

Acceptance. Children sometimes choose the handicapped child to play with, share with, or sit next to. They may show particular delight in a handicapped peer's achievements: "Look! Kenny got his own coat on."

Children's attitudes toward handicapped peers. Young children who have not learned negative social attitudes toward handicaps, which typically appear after the age of five, will not automatically reject a child simply on the basis of a disability. They are open to social models portrayed by adults and thus are able to learn positive attitudes toward disability when a positive model is provided through the adults' actions, words, nonverbal behaviors, and explanations.

Supporting the fact that individual differences and experiences cannot simply be ignored in the blending of human beings in social situations, Laing (1967:63) noted that "human beings relate to each other not simply externally, like billiard balls, but by the relations of the two worlds of experience that come into play when two people meet."

Negative attitudes toward handicapped peers exhibited by children aged five and older often exist before these children have experiences with mainstreaming (Johnson and Johnson, 1980). These are natural responses to first impressions and to the labeling process that fosters stigmatization. The process that occurs in the actual interaction between the handicapped and the nonhandicapped children will determine whether this initial rejection will be reinforced or replaced by greater acceptance.

Such acceptance will result from interaction within:

> a context of positive goal interdependence, which leads to (a) promotive interaction and feelings of psychological safety; (b) differentiated, dynamic, realistic views of collaborators and oneself; (c) positive cathexis [concentration of psychic energy] toward others and oneself; and (d) expectations for rewarding future interaction with classmates. (Johnson and Johnson, 1980:92)

Rejection, on the other hand, results from interaction within a context of negative or no goal interdependence; this promotes:

> oppositional interaction and feelings of psychological rejection and threat, and no interdependence results in an interaction with peers. Both lead to (a) monopolistic, static, and stereotyped views of classmates; (b) negative cathexis toward others and oneself; and (c) expectations for distasteful and unpleasant future interactions with other students. (Johnson and Johnson, 1980:93)

Further interaction then tends to reinforce what has already occurred unless purposeful intervention or chance swings the interactions in the opposite direction.

An actual observation of this process over a period of days was made by a researcher when Chris, a preschooler with a moderate-to-severe hearing loss, was being mainstreamed into a university preschool setting. To date, he had not been well accepted by the other children. Because he chanced to begin a spontaneous play episode that caught the interest of some of the children, he eventually "earned" his way into the group (Soderman, 1979:150–151):

> March 2. The subject spots a purple cape hanging in the dramatic-play area. He puts it on and begins pretending he is a vampire, moving about the room flapping his wings and "scaring" other children. He draws the attention of several other nonhandicapped children who decide they, too, want capes so they can be vampires (positive goal interdependence).

"Vampire play" grew in popularity for several days afterward. The head teacher allowed the children to wear the capes about the room instead of confining their play to the dramatic-play corner, which usually was encouraged.

March 7. Cameron takes Chris up to a student teacher, telling her, "I have a whole team of vampires. He's (pointing to Chris) on my team." Cameron then "attacks" a helping adult standing nearby. Chris copies him. Cameron spreads his "wings" over Chris, catching him and saying, "Gotcha, little vampire." He takes him to a locker and puts him inside roughly. Chris tries to "break out." Cameron indicates the other children to Chris and says, "Let's suck their blood." They are joined by David. Cameron catches Chris again, saying to David, "I caught the little bat; I caught the little vampire!" He then lets Chris go, saying to Chris and David, "C'mon, team. We're a whole team" (promotive interaction and feeling of psychological safety; positive cathexis or concentration of psychic energy toward others and oneself).

The subject is definitely a member of the team and, thus, on his way to becoming an integrated, mainstreamed member of the class. Should the head teacher have insisted that the play be maintained in the dramatic-play area or asked the boys to play something else "nicer" than vampire play, the moment may have been lost. The fragile nature of the process, chance happenings, and sensitivity on the part of the supervising adults can be seen in a subsequent observation and example of "expectations for reworking future interaction with classmates":

March 8. Chris has his "bat cape" on again. It is precious to him, and he searches for it as soon as he enters the room. It has been his key to getting into the group. When he attempts to climb on some larger equipment with it, a student teacher asks him to remove the cape because of safety. He declines to play on the equipment, rather than give up the cape. The student teacher is aware of the cape's importance and does not push the issue. If Chris takes the cape back to the dramatic-play corner while he climbs, someone else may take it, and he will have lost his key.

Guidelines for Integrating Handicapped Children into Formal Group Settings

The quality of the integrative process will differ significantly depending on the extent to which helping professionals recognize the interdependence between special-education, agency, and regular teaching staff; appreciate the long-range value of positive mainstreaming efforts; are able to collaborate with other professionals and adults who support the child's development; and are willing to make the additional effort needed to go beyond the mere maintenance of handicapped students in the nonspecialized setting.

The skills every teacher must master in dealing with typical variations among nonhandicapped children are needed even more when dealing with handicapped children (Ginsberg, 1976). The ability to provide specific enrichment and developmentally appropriate stimulation for these children requires classroom practices that include the following (Dunlop, 1977:29–31):

1. Open, sensitive, and honest classroom discussion of differences between children.
2. A teacher who focuses intensively on the development of positive learning sets, which involves expectations for the attainment of realistic goals.
3. Some time set aside each day to evaluate and plan for the progress of each child in the classroom.
4. Children allowed and encouraged to undertake activities independently.
5. Cooperative activities planned and built into the curriculum that will encourage social growth of all the children.
6. Parents involved in classroom activities whenever possible.

Four additional factors identified as critical to the success of integrating handicapped children into ongoing programs (Haring, Hayden, and Allen, 1971) are the extent to which:

1. The classroom provides for all needs of the child.
2. The child can become a contributing member of the group.
3. The physical facilities of the school are amenable to the child's needs.
4. The teacher with whom the child is placed understands and accepts him or her.

The readiness of a child to be mainstreamed is of particular concern to many professionals. A study by Abelson (1975) indicated that, although the majority of the teachers surveyed revealed a positive attitude toward integration, they were less comfortable about some handicapping conditions than others. Least desirable conditions were those that involved confinement to a wheelchair, upper-extremity problems, and blindness. Because regular and special-education settings from which the child may have come often differ greatly with respect to instructional format, behavioral expectations, teaching styles, physical design, and student socialization patterns, careful evaluation must be made prior to the integration effort of the student's competencies and what will be expected of him or her. Attention should be given to the student's ability to interact positively with others, obey classroom rules, and carry out tasks that are expected of the other children (Salend, 1984).

Clearly, the responsibility for successful integration cannot fall solely on the handicapped child. Some professionals have expressed concern that children somehow have to "qualify" with a certain readiness before they can be admitted to the mainstream.

The very concept of mainstreaming tends to imply that the mainstream is inaccessible and unamenable to change. This orientation puts the burden of change on those being introduced into the environment. The educator's task is seen as that of making children ready to enter the mainstream.

Mainstreaming must be conceived of not as changing the special child so that he will fit into the unchanged regular classroom, but rather as changing the nature of the regular classroom so that it is more accommodating to all children. (Sapon-Shevin, 1978:119–120)

There is no set formula for the successful integration of handicapped and nonhandicapped children. What is clear is that successful mainstreaming must be made a priority by the administrators, parents, and professionals who are involved, entailing a major commitment and effort on the part of the staff if efforts are to yield more than simply maintenance of the handicapped in nonspecialized settings (McLaughlin and Kershman, 1979). This commitment and effort must be actively geared toward providing the kinds of interactive and nurturing experiences that produce optimal growth in all areas of children's development.

SKILLS FOR SUPPORTING CHILDREN'S DEVELOPMENT RELATED TO SEXUALITY, ETHNICITY, AND HANDICAPPING CONDITIONS

Positive results in the development of children's attitudes and behaviors related to sexuality, ethnicity, and handicapping conditions can be accrued when adults adapt the following skills into their repertoire of interaction techniques.

1. Educate yourself about persons of varying cultural, religious, racial, and developmental backgrounds. Participate in community, social, or cultural events that represent different groups and find ways to become personally acquainted with at least one family of each racial and cultural group in your community. Take advantage of opportunities to broaden your familiarity with other groups through ethnic festivals, community-awareness programs involving the handicapped, or open events sponsored by religious groups other than your own. In addition, seek out establishments in your area, such as stores and restaurants, that offer artifacts and food representative of particular cultures. There are organizations and institutions in many cities and in universities that focus on international programs. These organizations also schedule films and lectures and distribute newspapers and magazines from other countries. You can visit a medical-supply store that caters to the handicapped and examine the different equipment that some individuals use to function more effectively. Finally, volunteer in programs in which you are likely to interact with people who are different from yourself. Look on these experiences not only as a way to help others who are different from you, but as an opportunity to broaden your own understanding.

2. Evaluate your own responses to the sensitive arenas described in this chapter. Pay careful attention to your nonverbal behaviors

as well. If you find yourself drawing away, making a face, or avoiding eye contact with a child who falls into any of the categories discussed or to one who brings up sensitive subjects, stop. Remember that in your professional role, you are obligated to treat all children with respect and sensitivity. Watch out for any tendency on your part to blame whole groups of people for what individuals do, and demand proof when you hear children repeat rumors that reflect on any group; do not tell stories, however funny, that reflect on any group, and do not laugh when others tell them. Show disapproval when others use hateful terms that slur any group (Clark, 1963). Review Chapter 3 for ideas on how to manifest these attitudes more effectively. In addition, monitor your verbal responses, making sure you do not dismiss or deny children's feelings and verbal expressions of these feelings. A re-reading of Chapters 4 and 5 may help you achieve this. It may also be useful to discuss situations that are difficult for you with a colleague or classmate as a way to clarify your own attitudes as well as to elicit further suggestions.

3. Build a positive social climate in which both similarities and differences are valued. Emphasize that each person has something valuable and unique to contribute to the group. Take advantage of the many children's books about individual differences as well as puppet play, films, videotapes, and filmstrips to promote growth in the understanding of others. Utilize resource people from the community, including those with varying racial and ethnic origins and handicapping conditions. Foster positive attitudes and attitude changes in school-age children by role playing and disability simulations. For example, wheelchairs can be borrowed from equipment companies to allow students to understand the difficulty involved in maneuvering a wheelchair. Glasses can be made with layers of yellow cellophane to simulate visual impairment. In addition to focusing on the religious, racial and ethnic, and developmental differences that can be found in others, however, it is necessary also to discuss similarities between people: that we all need friends, that we all have similar emotions, and that all people have both positive and negative qualities.

4. *Build a cooperative, rather than competitive, spirit within the group.* Encourage children to rely on one another and to seek each other's help in solving problems rather than depending on the adults in the setting. Use small, heterogeneous groups whenever possible, rather than competitive or individualistic learning activities, to foster the development of acceptance, rapport, and mutual understanding among children of different racial, ethnic, and developmental backgrounds. Structure activities in which children have opportunities to establish eye contact, talk with one another, and develop common goal structures. Provide needed support to guide these groups toward success and reasonable goal achievement, remembering that repeated failure by the group may result in discouragement and a tendency to blame lack of success on the weakest members of the group. Purposely plan activities that will highlight, at one time or another, the skills of all children in the program. For example, one paraprofessional had a blind student demonstrate her ability to get around the room and explain the kinds of cues in the room on which she relied for help. Students then were blindfolded and, with the help of another student to keep them safe, tried their luck at negotiating the same path, relying not on their sight but on the cues the handicapped student had identified. More ways to create such an atmosphere are presented in Chapter 14, Promoting Prosocial Behavior.

5. *Identify youngsters who have health-related problems or developmental delays.* Observe whether or not children are physically healthy. Become acquainted with and utilize screening strategies that can identify children having problems with adaptive behavior, motor development, language delays, and verbal comprehension and expression. When indicated, follow up with more in-depth study with the help of the child's parents and other helping professionals.

6. *Learn about what goes on in the children's lives away from the program and take this into account when planning for them.* Find ways to build links between your program and other elements of the child's mesosystem. For example, a teacher working with Dominic, a child who was being mainstreamed into her afternoon kindergarten class, decided to follow up on a comment by the bus driver that the child was falling asleep while being transported to the school. She discovered that Dominic, in addition to his handicapping condition, was dealing with incredible role strain for a five-year-old. He was spending his mornings in a very structured, intensive special-education setting where, because of his relatively greater amount of residual hearing, he was considered by his peers to be a leader. Following lunch and the bus ride to kindergarten, he was thrust into a situation in which he was having difficulty being accepted by his nonhandicapped peers, who thought he "talked funny." In short, he was "at the top of the heap" in the morning and very much at the bottom in the afternoon. In addition to the psychological strain he was experiencing in dealing with his contrasting status in the two very different educational settings, it was observed that he frequently was expected to make up missed work in the special-education setting, which interrupted his valued free time with the other children. The problem was compounded when he

moved each day from the kindergarten class to a baby-sitter's home where he waited with his sister until 11:00 p.m. to be picked up by his mother, who was working evenings. The situation obviously called for a conference between parents and professionals and a restructuring of Dominic's schedule. In addition, the adults in each setting had to adjust their expectations to respond more appropriately to the child's needs.

7. *Respond thoughtfully to children's questions about sexuality, ethnicity, and handicapping conditions.* Listen carefully to determine what it is they really want to know. Clarify the question by reflecting before answering. For example, if a child asks the question "Is Timmy still a baby?" about a seven-year-old who can't walk, you would want to clarify with, "You mean, 'How come Timmy can't walk yet?'" After determining the child's purpose, answer the question at a level he or she can understand. Often, in an effort to be comprehensive, adults over-explain, giving children more information than they need. Give short, precise, clear answers in language that the child understands. Use simple phrases and familiar analogies. Then, check to see what the child thinks you have said by asking him or her to paraphrase your answer. "Tell me in your own words why Sandy talks the way she does." Work from there to expand the child's understanding, if necessary. Don't give more information than children ask for; allow them time to assimilate what already has been said.

In responding to preschooler's questions, remember this age group's "magical" and egocentric thinking processes. They are trying to make sense of a new and unfamiliar piece of information about other human beings. In doing so, they will rely on their own experiences, fears, and fantasies and directives from parents to assimilate the information. Be alert to what is behind children's questions. They may simply misunderstand an issue or want additional information, or they may genuinely fear some aspect of the situation. Reassure children when they seem to be overly concerned, and watch for evidence that the child is more comfortable once the explanations have been given.

You may have to answer the same question several times for very young or overly fearful children. When questions about another child's physical, ethnic, or developmental differences are repeatedly asked in that child's presence, redirect the curious child to discuss the issue with you privately.

8. *Use correct vocabulary when referring to body parts, cultural groups, or handicapping conditions.* Words like vagina, penis, and breast describe specific parts of the body, which should be as accurately labeled as other body parts. To do otherwise demeans the body and teaches children that sexual organs are not natural but are things to be ashamed of. Likewise, certain cultural groups prefer to be called by a particular name. For instance, some people prefer to be known as black Americans, others as Afro-Americans; some as Indians, some as Native Americans. If you are not sure about the preferences of the families in your group, find out. Similarly, describe a child as hearing impaired rather than saying that her ears are broken. Point out that another youngster has cerebral palsy rather than the "shakes." In each of these situations, it is better to be truthful and precise when speaking with children than to try to sidestep the sensitive arenas through euphemisms or inaccurate terminology.

9. *React calmly to children's sex play.* Reflect children's interest in their own bodies and the bodies of others. Give them information that will satisfy their curiosity, such as the names of their body parts and how they function. Set limits on behavior that is inappropriate or dangerous, such as fondling another child's genitalia, masturbating in public, or putting something in a child's vagina or anus. For instance, a child who is

masturbating might be told: ''Touching yourself like that feels good. That's something that people wait to do when they are alone. I'm worried you're missing the other activities that we have. You can choose between playing at the art table or in the space station.'' Likewise, if in the course of playing doctor, a child tries to take the rectal temperature of a classmate by poking him with a pipe cleaner under his pants, step in immediately. Reflect, ''You're pretending to be a doctor,'' and continue with a personal message: ''I'm worried that you will hurt him with the pipe cleaner. It is important not to put objects inside of someone's body. You can pretend to take his temperature like this.'' (Demonstrate an appropriate alternative.)

10. Provide natural opportunities for children to learn more about their sexual development. For very young children, the bathroom at the preschool or day-care center is an ideal place to ask questions, observe similarities and differences, and learn that body parts and body functions do not have to be hidden behind closed doors. Allow preschoolers to use the bathroom in one another's presence if they wish. Also, provide dolls with anatomically correct genitalia for them to play with. Use books to communicate information to older children. Act as a resource for answering their questions and clearing up misunderstandings. Avoid using plants and animals as a substitute for discussing human reproduction. The latter is quite different from the former, and children have difficulty inferring meaning from metaphorical information (Borland, 1984).

11. Remain alert for valuable learning experiences that may be created spontaneously by the children. Be flexible enough to let them progress without interruption. At times, children's interactions with materials and with one another capture their interest to

FIGURE 11-2 Adults should provide children with accurate information about their bodies; using the correct vocabulary to refer to body parts is a must.
SOURCE: Photo by David Kostelnik

such an extent that our own best laid curricular plans are usurped. When this happens, assess whether allowing children to deviate from intended activities will allow other learning or needed social adaptations to occur. Sometimes, as illustrated by the following example, a spontaneous event can be far more valuable than the planned one:

A student teacher commented to her head teacher that, although the children were not very socially accepting of a young classmate with a hearing impairment, they certainly were curious about the hearing aid she wore. In response, the head teacher suggested that the student prepare a "lesson" for the children to teach them how a hearing aid worked.

Subsequently, the student teacher set up on one of the tables a display of vibrating objects, including a tuning fork and xylophone, which she invited the children to examine. While she was working with some of the children and the tuning fork, the child with the hearing impairment began looking at the xylophone, which also was a wheeled toy that could be pulled with a string. Instead of using the striking mallet on the toy, the child put the xylophone on the floor and began pulling it across the room, marching as she went. Several nonhandicapped children fell in line after her, marching and singing, "Down by the station, early in the morning . . ." The children who had been observing the tuning fork activity also fell in line, leaving the student teacher and her carefully constructed display of vibrating objects in favor of the march.

Later, at a follow-up session in which the teachers were discussing the success of the lesson, the student teacher explained that the display had been somewhat dismantled with the loss of the xylophone and departure of her "audience" but that she felt the children had more to gain by joining the march. When asked to elaborate on the reasons why, the student noted that the social interaction of the handicapped child with her nonhandicapped peers, although a primary objective in the mainstreaming of the child, had not been going well. "I just thought it was a great opportunity to let the children take care of something that's had me stumped." Much to the student's relief, her head teacher congratulated her on her rationale and her ability to capture the "teachable moment."

12. Help children develop appreciation for our diverse heritage as a society. As a part of the daily routine, sing songs, tell stories, play games, and engage in other activities that relate to the cultures represented by the children and staff in your group. If your group is homogeneous, introduce other customs anyway. It may be best to begin with groups that can be found in the wider community rather than cultures with whom children are unlikely to interact. Paper folding is a common Asian pastime. Making a piñata provides opportunities for Hispanic children to explore and discuss this custom. Making and eating potato latkes for a snack acquaints children with a Jewish custom. Using currency from other countries can become an interesting counting activity in a math class. An activity in which children try to carry a bundle on their heads or backs allows them to become familiar with how people in different cultures solve the problem of carrying a load from one place to another. Similarly, the day-care center that has accumulated footwear common to many societies, such as a variety of slippers and sandals, exposes children to the fact that, although many people protect their feet, the manner in which they do so may vary. It is better to integrate such activities into the **ongoing curriculum rather than to occasionally have a "Mexico day" or "black American week." The latter approach sensationalizes and makes artificial what, to the culture itself, is just a natural part of living.**

13. Help children develop pride in their own cultural heritage. Pronounce a child's name as his or her family pronounces it rather than anglicizing it. Honor differences in language and traditions. Serve foods that are familiar to the children's particular backgrounds, asking parents for suggestions and recipes. Allow children to bring in articles that are used in family celebrations and to explain to the group how they are used. Include dress-up clothes from a variety of cultures. Encourage parents to share such items as dolls, pictures, books, and music. The purpose of including such activities and items in the children's everyday classroom experiences is to help each child feel included and valued and to encourage the development of friendly and respectful attitudes toward all ethnic, racial, and cultural groups (Hendrick, 1984).

14. Utilize rules and consequences to let children know that purposeful slurs and unkind references to particular children or groups will not be tolerated. If youngsters seem to be using terms such as "homo" or "honky" without knowing what they mean, provide pertinent rationales for why such behavior is unacceptable to you. When children deliberately use such tactics to wound the self-esteem of another, they are engaging in hostile aggression. This should be stopped with a personal message, warning, and follow-through as necessary. Carry these out in a calm, firm tone.

15. Monitor all teaching materials and activities for racial, cultural, sex-role, sexual, religious, and developmental stereotypes. Continuously watch for ways in which the curriculum may inadvertently limit children's potential by socializing them to develop narrow perceptions of their own roles and abilities or those of others. Encourage boys and girls to participate in a wide range of enriching activities on the basis of their interests and developing skills rather than on outmoded ideas.

16. Respond immediately to children's verbal hostile aggression using parts two and three of the personal message. Taunting, teasing, using slurs, or making unkind references to other people are forms of hostile aggression. Stop them instantly. Use a calm, matter-of-fact tone, then go on to the warning and follow-through, if necessary. Thus, if Madeline calls Victorio a "wop," approach her immediately and in a quiet, firm voice, say: "I get upset when you refer to people using derogatory words like wop. It's unkind and disrespectful. Stop." Note that this variation on the personal message is to be used *only* with older children whose unkind words are purposeful. Complete personal messages are more appropriate with younger children, who may not understand the significance of their remarks or their impact on others.

PITFALLS TO AVOID

When utilizing the skills described, there are common pitfalls you must strive to avoid.

Overprotecting the minority or handicapped child. Whenever helping adults give special privileges to one child and not to others, they run the risk of alienating other children and hampering the potential development of the favored child. Rules should be changed to accommodate individual children only when there are safety issues involved, when the child's learning modes are inadequate for the task at hand, or when children are not emotionally able to meet the challenge set before them. When rule changes are necessary, simple, matter-of-fact explanations can be given to other children. In addition, they can be drawn into a discussion about how to make the rule change palatable, given the circumstances. Children's sense of fairness, particularly when they are asked their opinion about a problem, almost always incline them toward helpfulness. When rules are changed arbitrarily, however, and without apparent fairness, children can become resentful, rejecting, and hostile toward the other child and/or the supervising adult.

Failing to see negative interactions because they are not part of the success picture you have in

mind. It is tempting to ignore negativity or inappropriate behavior in the classroom because one feels it reflects on one's ability to adequately control the situation. The tendency is to overlook negative incidents or to make light of them when others who are concerned bring them to one's attention. Professionals may instead focus on superficial evidence that children are accepting one another when focused observation reveals a less positive picture. Incidents in which a child is being exploited, manipulated, isolated, or harmed (physically *or* psychologically) by children or adults in the setting must be addressed immediately by (a) interrupting the incident; (b) acknowledging the emotions of all individuals involved; (c) stating that exploitive and harmful behavior is not allowed under any circumstances; and (d) structuring alternatives that will lead not only toward promotive interaction and feelings of psychological safety but also toward positive acceptance of one another.

Overreacting to children's mouthing of stereotypes. When children parrot popular stereotypes, such as "She can't lift that; she's only a girl" or "Asians have no feelings," one's natural reaction is to become upset and to lecture children on the insensitivity or inaccuracy of what they have said. Although the intent of such admonishments is positive, the outcome often is negative. Children may become defensive, belligerent, or covert. A better approach is not to condemn but to quietly convey accurate information to children, such as "It would take a strong person to lift that box—a strong girl, or a strong boy" or "All people have emotions. Some people show their emotions more than others."

Inadvertently using stereotypical language. All people have phrases in their vocabulary that they use unthinkingly. Some of these may be unintentionally offensive. Referring to someone as an "Indian giver," describing the haggling process as "Jewing someone down," or saying you'll go out "Dutch" with someone are examples. In addition, consistently referring to "firemen," "postmen," and "salesgirls" reinforces sex-role stereotypes. More egalitarian terminology would include "firefighters," "postal workers," and "salesclerks." Similarly, beware of segregating males and females unnecessarily. It is not constructive to pit boys against girls in games or have children retrieve their art projects by having one gender go before the other. Use other attributes to designate subgroups, such as "Everyone with green socks may get their coats" or "All the people at this table may be dismissed."

Failing to effectively plan for and evaluate student progress. Although children's programs almost always have an evaluation component attached to them, occasionally these are summative in nature and based simply on how much the student was able to accomplish against a given standard in a given period of time. Too often, that standard is not based on the individual child's status or ability to achieve prior to the evaluation period but on predetermined, normative criteria. Thus, children who have ability deficits for one reason or another are certain to measure up poorly unless they are given reasonable mastery objectives based on their own ability. Because of the structuring of handicapped students' individualized education programs (IEPs), they are less likely than minority-group children to experience such problems, although significant periods of time elapse between planning and re-evaluation of the plans. Although there is much discussion about the pros and cons of individualizing learning and evaluation, insufficient attention to this element can set into motion a no-win situation for children who have special needs.

Failing to seek the support of administrators, parents, other professionals, and community members. Just as children work within a team situation in the classroom, professionals are part of a larger team of adults who support, to greater or lesser degrees, what goes on in the program. Helping professionals working with children who require additional resources, such as more time, understanding, patience, staff, and materials, must be able to justify those needs to other adults who are in positions to help, depending on how they perceive the special needs of these children relative to the needs of all the other children in the program.

It is probably a given that adults who work with children with special needs will need additional resources. When these are not forthcoming, there is a tendency toward burnout in the professional who views the problem as a lack of support. What is needed is more effective communication between helping professionals and the other adults who are in positions to support the program.

SUMMARY

Sensitive issues surrounding children's handling of sexuality, ethnicity, and handicapping conditions sometimes can cause the helping professional discomfort, irritation, embarrassment, or confusion in choosing the most effective response. When these feelings lead to avoidance, rejection, aggressiveness, or overprotectiveness on the part of helping adults, their ability to support children's development and competency building is significantly diminished.

Sexual behavior in children such as public masturbation, sex play, peeping, sex-oriented language, and sexually assertive moves toward an adult should be handled as matter-of-factly as possible, with the adult calmly guiding the child toward more appropriate behavior. Apparent deviations in psychosexual development, although sometimes troublesome to adults, may not be subject to alteration and call instead for understanding and a more thorough knowledge of the child's perspective. Severe sexual deviations should be handled by seeking the expertise of other professionals.

Children's attitudes toward other racial and ethnic groups, like sex-role development, appear to be age- and stage-specific, beginning first with emerging ethnic awareness at about the age of three and concluding with attitude crystallization when children are about nine or ten years old. Adults who work with children and parents of other racial and ethnic origins or

socioeconomic status occasionally may find themselves dealing with negative feelings based on their own ethnocentrism and experiences. Unless they can rise above these feelings, their professional effectiveness will be undermined, causing patronizing behavior, avoidance, or inappropriate aggressiveness. Such behaviors on the part of adults negatively affect children's self-esteem and developing ethnic attitudes. Conversely, positive behaviors on the part of the adult serve as an important prerequisite to prejudice prevention and reduction.

Integration of handicapped children into formal group settings also is an area requiring additional sensitivity on the part of the adult. The objectives of integrating children with handicapping conditions is twofold: to promote acceptance of handicapped children through stigma reduction and removal, and to enhance the social competence of handicapped children so they can later live more comfortably and successfully in the mainstream of society. The challenge for professionals involved in mainstreaming efforts is similar to that encountered by those attempting racial integration, that is, melding those who are different from the majority successfully into the mainstream. This potential for qualitatively improving the handicapped child's lot carries a greater risk of increased stigmatization, stereotyping, and rejection if the professional is not able to facilitate supportive interaction between handicapped and nonhandicapped children. Success will depend on the adult's own commitment to successful integration, his or her ability to structure the environment, and the attention she or he pays to social dynamics such as the development of goal interdependence between handicapped and nonhandicapped children and the production of positive psychic energy between children in the cooperative achievement of those goals.

Respecting the uniqueness of all persons is a positive statement confirming our ability to be truly human toward one another. Adults who interact on a day-to-day basis with children have the responsibility to surround those children with an accepting, nurturant, growth-enhancing environment, one that allows children to see themselves and others as fully functioning, competently developing human beings.

DISCUSSION QUESTIONS

1. The parent board of an all-white cooperative nursery school is considering offering a scholarship to a black preschooler for the coming year. What advantages and disadvantages do you see in such an arrangement? What kinds of preparation do you feel should be made prior to implementing such a procedure?

2. You have a Korean-American child in your third-grade classroom and find that he is being harassed on the way home by three of the more popular boys in the classroom. You arrange to meet with the three boys. How do you begin your discussion with them? Role-play this situation with three classmates who can take the part of the students.

3. You are teaching in a large, urban middle school. An eleven-year-old girl approaches you during lunch hour, saying that a young male security guard in the school tried fondling her and has been asking her if he can take her home after school. How do you respond to her? What action, if any, do you take?

4. You are holding an open house for parents. The father of a five-year-old boy approaches you and asks you what you think about letting boys play with dolls. He also asks, "How early can you tell whether or not a male is going to be gay?" State your initial response to him exactly as you would make it. Review the normative sequence in the development of gender identity as you might relate it to the father.

5. You have observed that one of the parents who has volunteered to tutor children with reading problems appears to be highly impatient with Kevin, a second-grader. This morning, you overhear her saying to him: "Your problem is laziness. That's why a lot of you black children aren't able to ever finish school. Is that what you want to happen to you?" How do you handle this situation?

6. As you round the corner into the "quiet" area reserved for reading, you discover two five-year-old boys examining each other's genitals. What are your initial thoughts? What do you say to the boys? Do you take any further action? If so, what?

7. One of the boys in your Cub Scout group appears to be extremely nervous. On picking him up after a meeting, his mother notices him touching his genitals. In front of the other boys, she crudely quips: "For crying out loud, Terry, quit playing with yourself. You're going to make it fall off!" You ask her if you can talk privately with her for a moment. What do you say to her?

8. You see one of the white preschoolers vigorously rubbing the arm of a black aide. When you ask about it, the aide laughs and says, "He's trying to rub off the dark color of my skin." How do you respond?

9. In the middle of the morning's activity, one of the children unexpectedly has a grand mal seizure. Following the episode, the rest of the children are visibly shaken, and some are crying. What do you say to them?

10. Children in the day-care center are having a snack of raisin toast and peanut butter. The student teacher has been instructed to serve only one piece to each child until all children have been served. You notice that Kendra, a child with Down's syndrome, has been sitting at the table for quite a long time and is on her second piece of toast. When you ask the student about the situation, she says, ''I know the rule, but I feel sorry for her.'' Verbalize your response exactly as you would make it to the student teacher.

CHAPTER 12
Influencing Children's Social Development via the Physical Environment

SOURCE: H. Armstrong Roberts

OBJECTIVES:

On completion of this chapter, you will be able to describe:

1. The management process and its role in structuring the physical environment.

2. Decision-making processes in caregivers and children.

3. The adult's role in structuring the physical environment.

4. The influence of the daily schedule on children's behavior.

5. The influence of room arrangement on children's behavior.

6. How to select and organize materials to promote social development.

7. How to change the daily schedule or room arrangement with minimal disruption.

8. How to help children become decision makers and managers of their own environment.

Classroom A: The bulletin board has a colorful, commercial display focusing on bicycle safety. A few mounted pictures of children's drawings are on the other bulletin board, along with a chart with names on one side and stars in boxes for achievement of tasks. Tables, shelves, and bookcases are clean and orderly. The children's desks are arranged in rows facing the front blackboard, where work for the day is listed. The teacher's desk faces the children from the front of the room.

Classroom B: The bulletin board displays a painting on butcher paper of a parade. The animals, vehicles, and people in the parade vary somewhat in size and character, indicating that a number of artists worked on the project. On the other bulletin board, a chart is posted that lists classroom jobs and the team of children responsible for the tasks that month. The rest of the space holds twenty-two crayon drawings beneath the title "What Safety Means to Me." The evidence of children's "dusting in the front" of books and objects on the shelf can be seen. Similarly, evidence can be seen of paint incompletely removed from a table, and the storage area is a little cluttered. The children's desks are arranged in groups of four or six, with half the children in each group facing the other half. The seats swivel to face the chalkboard at the front of the room, where the day's work has been written. The teacher's desk is in the corner near the supply cabinet.

These two classrooms are used effectively by both children and adults. Yet, the differing physical environments suggest different social climates. Such assumptions can be made without ever seeing the children or the teachers by focusing on observable characteristics of the setting. For example, in classroom A, one can surmise that orderliness and individual achievement are high priorities. This is evidenced by the immaculate furnishings, neat rows, and star chart. Clearly, the children's attention is directed primarily toward the teacher rather than toward one another. A different impression is conveyed by classroom B. Here, the emphasis is on group collaboration, peer interaction, and self-expression. These characteristics

are obvious from the projects that are displayed, the arrangement of the children's desks, and the childlike efforts at room maintenance. Based on this analysis of the two classrooms, one can see that important, albeit dissimilar, social skills are learned by the youngsters who occupy them. This is because the teachers involved have made different decisions about how to manage the physical environment. Competent teachers create dissimilar environments because they value some goals more than others. These judgments are neither good nor bad, merely different.

Structuring is the term given to this form of management and is the focus of this chapter. It includes ways of managing time, space, and materials to promote children's social development. To understand structuring, you first must understand the management process itself.

THE MANAGEMENT PROCESS

Management consists of purposeful behavior involving the creation and use of resources to achieve goals. Management itself is a skill that can be learned and requires thoughtful consideration of all its component parts: making decisions, setting goals, planning, implementing the chosen plan, and assessing the outcome.

Motivations for Management

Why is it necessary to manage the physical environment in which adults and children interact? Adults manage in order to meet the *needs* of children (Maslow, 1954). *Physiological needs*, such as an adequate diet, enough sleep, and appropriate room temperature, must be satisfied in order for children to survive and to function. *Safety needs*, such as freedom from physical danger and fear, can be met by the judicious use of resources. *Social needs* include the child's need for acceptance and a sense of belonging, and *esteem needs* include self-respect, recognition, and status. Something as simple as a pair of mittens may meet the physiological need for temperature control of the hands, the safety need to prevent frostbite, social needs in that the child can play outside with other children, and esteem needs in that by joining in the outdoor play, the child is perceived as a contributing group member.

Adults also manage in order to meet *demands* from external sources. All facilities that provide care or education for children must be either licensed or inspected by the state. Demands for fire safety, tornado or fire drills, and sanitary handling of food and waste require management responses. The number and kinds of demands vary according to the nature of the program. For example, literacy is a demand made by school boards that would not be required in a recreational setting.

Adults also manage in order to satisfy *values*. Values permeate all aspects of human thought and action and define what is worthwhile and desirable. Values are all-inclusive, deeply internalized personal qualities and beliefs that direct action (Nickell, Rice, and Tucker, 1976). Because values are so pervasive and important in professional decision making, much of Chapter 16 is devoted to this topic. Values such as human dignity, equity, justice, and sociability are repeatedly emphasized in this book.

A *concern* is the affective side of a value. Concerns may be voiced in personal messages. When an adult says, ''I'm concerned that you will fall if you run downhill on the gravel path,'' he or she is expressing a concern related to the value of health and the need for safety. Other concerns are expressed nonverbally by organizing space, materials, and other resources to promote children's social development by controlling the physical setting. A summary of the motivations for management is presented in Table 12-1.

Establishing Goals

In the classrooms described at the beginning of this chapter, the teachers' clear value differences regarding sociability and orderliness influenced their decisions about the arrangement and maintenance of the room. Values clearly influence which goals people set and attend to. A *goal* is an end that can be accomplished. Some goals can be readily achieved in a short time; others are long-term endeavors that require years to accomplish.

Most beginning helping professionals work in programs in which the goals already have been set. Goals that reflect the demands of the

TABLE 12-1 Examples of Related Motivations for Management

MOTIVE	DEFINITION	EXAMPLE
Need	Essential for function or survival	Safety
Demand	Required by law or by individual programs	Regulations to protect children
Value	Desired quality	Beautiful environment or objects
Concern	Affective component of a value	Worry about the exposed cement at the base of a climber
Standard	Degree of goal attainment	Absence of accidents

community, the needs of the children, and the values of the organization will have been established. The problem for the entering professional is to manage the available resources to meet the long-term goals of the program.

Some goals that adults have for their own professional development are to enjoy their interactions with children; to minimize the frequency of limit setting and follow-through; to be effective in meeting the expectations of the organization that employs them; and to have enough energy at the end of the day to be able to have a satisfying personal life. Information on structuring the physical environment can contribute to meeting these ends.

A *standard* is a measure of quality, quantity, or method of goal attainment. Standards for academic achievement are set by schools and are measured by grading practices. Standards for health and safety of food and drugs are established by the federal government. Adults continuously set standards for children's behavior; some standards are determined by the program itself. For example, kindergarten children are expected to learn to sit quietly while a story is being read. Other standards are set by helping professionals as they implement the program. For example, in some classrooms, kindergarten children are expected to move from place to place without talking to one another. In other classrooms, conversation while moving is both expected and encouraged. In either case, the standards for noise generated by the children can be influenced by the structuring of the physical environment.

Decision Making

Decision making permeates the entire management process and is influenced by the needs, values, goals, and standards of the decision makers (Nickell, Rice, and Tucker, 1976). The steps in making a decision include:

1. Identifying the problem; recognizing the need for a decision.

2. Obtaining information and formulating alternatives.
3. Considering consequences; projecting possible outcomes.
4. Choosing a course of action.

Recognizing the problem requires observation and awareness of the long-term goals. For example, Mr. Yuhle noticed that there were five chairs at a table where only two children could work successfully with the scales. To *formulate alternatives,* he quickly gathered information. There were no more scales in the storage area. He rapidly *considered potential outcomes.* To do nothing to prevent congestion at the table might promote interpersonal conflict and little learning with the scales. After considering the last alternative, he *chose* to remove the extra chairs from the area. Such decisions are made frequently in the course of a day and are consistent with the long-range goal of helping children work together cooperatively and happily. The process of structuring the physical environment is the same regardless of the magnitude of the problem.

Most problems that arise in working with children require high-speed responses. Many of these decisions have been presented in earlier chapters and taught as skills. Other high-speed decisions can be made by using decision rules.

Decision rules. General practices that can be applied in many instances and that often shorten the time involved in determining a course of action are called *decision rules* (Deacon and Firebaugh, 1981). Some sample decision rules that have been used by early-childhood teachers are as follows:

1. Safety first!
2. The job at hand is less important than the child doing it.
3. Minimize the need for limit setting by organizing the environment.
4. Never do for children what children can do for themselves.

Giving Children Choices

Children also practice decision making and management from toddlerhood on. When adults offer them choices, children feel good about themselves and have an opportunity to practice decision-making skills: generating alternatives, seeking information, considering consequences, and, eventually, accepting responsibility for the outcome (Hendrick, 1984; Maccoby, 1980; Veach, 1977).

Collaborating with children requires enlisting them in the management process from the beginning. Setting goals, planning, determining standards, and deciding how and by whom the activity should be supervised all are part of the total process. Young children may participate in only a small part of the process, such as choosing between two acceptable alternatives; older children can engage in all aspects of management. The role of the adult is to demonstrate, explain, and guide the process. Children learn to manage by doing and are more likely to "own" the decisions they themselves make. Involved children are less likely to resent the consequences of decisions that turn out to be less desirable than anticipated when they have made them themselves.

Group decision making takes more time than individual decision making, and supporting the process with a group of children takes even longer. When adults decide to let the children choose as a group, they also have committed a substantial time resource to the process. Extensive communication is required in order to arrive at a decision. However, the time is well spent because children are more committed to a course of action if they have participated in determining it. Some decisions that groups of children might make are which song to sing, which game to play, whether to participate in a fund-raising activity, or how a holiday should be celebrated. Some groups of children are allowed to participate in choosing displays to make, rearranging furniture, and organizing storage.

Most decisions that involve management of the physical environment, time, and energy can be made in the absence of children and comprise the second part of this chapter. The goals of providing a safe, healthy environment in which children can learn to live and work together cooperatively are assumed, as these are common to most programs for children.

Developing a Plan

Once a goal is determined, a plan of action is needed to implement it. The planning may be done by an individual or by a small group and must take into account the resources that will be needed, the people that will implement the plan, the time frame in which it will be implemented, and some criteria or standard for evaluating it.

Some plans are comprehensive and complex. The daily schedule is of this type. The sequence of events, the adult responsible for the events, and the activities necessary to carry out the program or curriculum are complex. Other plans are quite simple and may become routines or habits for the children and adults. An example of a simple plan is a diapering schedule that merely indicates which adult checks the diapers of which infant and at what time.

How a plan of either variety can be initiated, carried out, and evaluated is illustrated in the following scenario. Mrs. Rouge's goal was for the three-year-olds in her day-care center to independently wash their hands clean. She noted that the children did not have very clean hands when they sat down to lunch even though the rule had been made clear. Implementing the consequence of sending them back to wash again did not help, so she observed the children washing to determine where the difficulty lay. She noticed that the shorter children had difficulty reaching the water, as their armpits just reached the edge of the sink; the taller children could reach the water, but had difficulty handling the soap, which frequently shot from their hands onto the floor. Based on this observation, she realized that the children were unable, rather than unwilling, to comply with the rule.

Mrs. Rouge decided that the best way to address the problem was not to set more limits, but to change the environment. Her method of altering the environment was to put something under the sink for the children to stand on so they all could reach it better. She also chose to modify the soap by drilling a hole through each bar and attaching it to the faucet with a string. She reasoned that even if the soap were to slip from their hands, the children would be able to retrieve it easily.

Next, she listed the steps for changing the current procedure and implementing the new one:

1. Discuss the new procedures with the staff.
2. Ask for volunteers to set up the platform and prepare the soap.
3. Assemble the materials needed to do the tasks.
4. Begin implementing the procedure by telling the children about it.
5. Assign staff to the bathroom to encourage children to follow the procedure. Ask staff to demonstrate the procedure as necessary.

In this instance, planning included an analysis of the problem and depended on Mrs. Rouge being able to break down the task into its component parts. The plan addresses the substance of the problem and includes a means for carrying out the solution. Effective communication with both the staff and children will be necessary to put the plan into effect. Materials, equipment, skill, time, and knowledge are the resources being used in this management task.

A plan may be used over an extended period of time or it may be designed for a single instance, such as a plan for creating a new facility or school. The planning process involves many decisions, as each step has numerous feasible alternatives.

Implementing and Evaluating the Plan

Direct action is necessary to implement the plan. The most complex or interesting plans are a waste of time if they are not carried out to completion. Clearly, some type of control is required at this stage. Some generally accepted ideas about the nature of control are as follows (Smith, 1971):

1. Develop a plan with clearly defined limits.
2. Consider acceptable variations of the plan.
3. Develop a procedure to check the current status in relation to the planned status.
4. Adjust supervisory behavior if the plan is not being implemented as anticipated.

The whole point of control is to keep children's and adults' behavior in line with the goals of the plan. This requires *organization*—structuring the materials and the people's roles in such a way that the plan can be implemented. Second, implementing requires *facilitating* the process—initiating and sustaining the action—and, finally, it requires *coordinating* the activities of all involved. Sometimes, activities may be clustered; sometimes, they may overlap. The helping professional must assume leadership if a group is implementing the plan or individual responsibility if other adults and children are not involved.

Supervision. If tasks are delegated, their completion must be supervised. Usually, tasks are delegated so that the work can be done rapidly and easily. However, actions may be assigned to people based on their need or desire to learn how to do a task. For example, the job of drilling holes in the soap was given to an assistant teacher who expressed an interest in learning to use a drill.

Supervising children or adults in implementing a plan requires that clear directions be given before the task is begun; also, someone must carefully observe the task being carried out so that errors can quickly be detected and corrected and those being supervised can proceed with confidence.

Supervising includes giving *feedback.* This may be as simple as remaining in the area to answer questions once the task is under way or as demanding as observing the step-by-step process in detail. In either case, it is important to provide information to individuals about their performance ("Alex, step up on the block so you can reach the sink"; "Rachel, you were able to get all the paint off your hands by yourself"). In some cases, the fact that supervision is taking place is obvious, as when adults give children step-by-step directions to follow and then watch as those directions are carried out. On other occasions, adults may perform related tasks in order not to appear to be hanging over the children's heads when the plan is put into operation. Thus, Mrs. Rouge may wash out paintbrushes while observing the children wash their hands.

Two approaches to supervision have been identified: *guiding,* which utilizes the facilitation dimension, and *directing,* which utilizes the action dimension. Usually, with children, guiding is the preferred approach. In guidance, the focus is on the child rather than the task, and the overall intent is to let the child learn the process gradually while building both skill and confidence. Directing is required when the primary focus is on completion of the task rather than the feelings of the child. It is used when some technical aspect of the task is important or when the standard for the end product is very high. For example, a 4-H sewing leader asked an eight-year-old to rip out a seam two or three times and do it over because the gathers of the skirt for her project were not quite even. In this case, the child's feelings of failure and frustration were less important to the adult than the final product. Another leader, who was more concerned that the child enjoy the process of sewing than that she produce a garment of the highest standard, chose to guide the distribution of gathers before the first stitching and, when the resulting garment was wearable, but

not perfect, she did not ask the child to rip out and redo the seam.

Directing as an approach to supervision of children is most appropriate when issues of health and safety are involved. Guiding usually involves more flexibility of standards and the slow acquisition of technical competence. It is preferred when children are participating in the management process and when the consequences of not accomplishing a task to a predetermined standard are not too severe. The adult who controls by directing tells children what to do and how to do it; the adult who controls by guiding makes suggestions, generates alternatives, and helps children to determine standards.

Supervision using guiding strategies, then, becomes an ongoing discussion about the goals and the means for achieving them. Although it takes longer, this method is effective in helping children to learn the management process.

Checking involves examining the activity to see how it is progressing. It is a necessary component of either approach to supervision. Does the outcome compare favorably with the desired standard? Often, the process of checking entails the setting of new goals and the use of different management processes, or it may generate new information. In the management of Mrs. Rouge's plan to improve the cleanliness of children's hands, she checked for both the cleanliness of the hands and the children's independence in washing. She also checked for the frequency of demonstrations by staff and the feedback adults gave to children. The use of limit setting and the frequency of adult-child conflict also were noted.

Adjusting means changing the plan when necessary to increase the probability of reaching the goal. Adjusting a management plan may require substituting one material for another. For example, staff members complained that the blocks chosen to go under the sink slipped, presenting a safety hazard. Mrs. Rouge adjusted by replacing the blocks with a low bench that had skid-resistant feet. Four categories of adjustment are possible: making little or no change; rearranging procedures according to a predetermined goal, plan, or standard; changing the standard; or shifting the underlying goal (Gross, Crandall, and Knoll, 1980).

Many decisions are made in the process of implementation. For example, one staff member questioned the standard for clean hands. She applied an aesthetic value to the situation ("They don't look too bad"); however, Mrs. Rouge was working to satisfy a health value. It was necessary to bring new information to the staff member's attention—that clean hands are the single most effective measure for the prevention of disease.

Evaluation.   Evaluating the overall project cannot be left to chance. Did the bench help children to reach the sink easily? Was there an overall decrease in limit setting in the washing-up period? Did children develop and maintain a procedure for washing their hands that became habitual after a month or so? Did the staff feel satisfied that the children's hands were clean?

Questions relating to overall satisfaction with a plan's outcome must be considered. Evaluating the implementation and outcome of a plan may help in establishing new goals to work toward, but, equally important, it will provide adults and children an opportunity to recognize success.

To this point, the discussion of management has been limited to the management of routine events and simple changes in the physical environment. Now, management concepts will be applied to the management of time, space, and materials.

MANAGEMENT OF TIME

Time is a concept that has individual, physical, and cultural interpretations. It cannot be saved or stored, but is only perceived in relation to change. Time is the one resource that is equally distributed to all people. Infants function first in biological time; the markers are changes in behavioral state, hunger, or comfort. Adults value time as a resource and are concerned with helping children to function within the cultural definitions of time that adults use. One way adults help children to use time efficiently is by teaching them a sequence of behaviors, or a habit, for activities that are repetitious and are used regularly. Sometimes, adults become angry with children when they are slow to develop a desired habit. At such times, the child either may not know an appropriate sequence of behaviors, or the sequence is so new that he or she must concentrate closely on each action in the sequence.

A typical example of not knowing an appropriate sequence is when a kindergarten child puts on her or his boots before the snow pants, or when the first garment put on by the child is the mittens. The helping professional may not realize that the parents may have dressed the child every day and that the mittens are the only garment the child has ever put on independently. Adults can become irritated when such incidents make the group wait, mostly because they do not realize that the situation requires teaching rather than demanding and limit setting.

Another way adults help children learn the cultural meaning of time is by organizing events into predictable sequences or routines.

The Daily Schedule

Schedules are organized time segments related to the program. In a summer camp, for instance, blocks of time will be set aside for maintenance of the environment, meals, rest, group sports, swimming, and crafts. These blocks of time are arranged in a certain order, with children moving from one activity to another in a predictable pattern.

Even the youngest infant establishes a rhythmic pattern of sleeping, eating, playing, and quietly observing the surroundings. This regular pattern of behavior varies among children within a family and varies more among different families. Some schedules are more flexible than others. When a child first enters a formal group setting, the familiar patterns developed within the family often must be altered to fit the new situation. This change results in distress and confusion and often is referred to as the initial adjustment to the program. The problems of adjustment are ameliorated as children and families incorporate the new pattern into their behavior.

The daily schedule or routine supports the child's ability to act autonomously. Events can be predicted; expectations for behavior are clear. The need for constant guidance in what to do and how to do it is minimized, so the child's dependence on adults is decreased.

Routines, however, must be learned. Adults first must adapt to the toddler's schedule, then gradually teach the child to function within a group schedule. Young children take longer to learn routines than older ones. They simply have more difficulty remembering. Children under six years of age may take as long as a month to adapt to a new daily schedule. Children in the elementary grades often adjust in two weeks or less; at this age, a pictorial chart or written schedule may help them to adjust more quickly.

Routines may be flexible, allowing a little more time to finish an activity if the change is compatible with the requirements of other program segments. Sometimes, however, as when large groups of children must use the same resources, schedules must be quite rigid. The use of the swimming area in a summer camp requires that all children must arrive, enter, and leave the water in an orderly fashion if standards of safety are to be maintained; every group must operate on clock time if all groups are to be able to swim each day. In contrast, in an after-school family day-care center where the pool is part of the family home, children may swim whenever adult supervision is available; a rigid clock-time schedule is unnecessary.

The predictability of a routine offers emotional security to young children. After a distressing encounter with another child, Cara, age four, chanted the daily schedule several times: "First we play, then we wash, then we have a snack, then we hear a story, then we go outside, and *then* my mama comes to take me home." After each repetition, she appeared more cheerful and ultimately was able to participate comfortably for the rest of the day. Young children also will comprehend the sequence of the daily routine before understanding the concept of time. Ross, three and a half years old, was distressed when his mother left him at the day-care center. He played for about 45 minutes, then asked if the children could go outside. This was a drastic change of schedule—usually, outside play was the last activity of the day—but the teacher allowed Ross and two other boys to go outside with an assistant. Ross played happily for a few minutes, then informed the adult that his mother would be there soon to pick him up! He had erroneously inferred that playing outside caused his mother to arrive because of the contiguity of the events.

A good schedule is continuous, fluid, and goal directed. It has blocks of time that allow children to finish tasks and provides for individual differences in speed. Waiting is minimal, and the transitions in which the whole group must participate are as few as possible. A *transition* occurs when one time block is finished and another begins. Transitions usually occur when children move from one room to another or when there is a complete change of materials. In Cara's verbalization of her routine, she located all the transitions by saying "then." In public schools, transitions occur before and after recess and lunch and also may occur between activities, such as between math and social studies.

Generally, there is a marked increase in the number of interaction problems between children and between adults and children during transitions. Children may be confused about

FIGURE 12-1 Teachers can accommodate differences in children's working speeds by not requiring them to complete all tasks in unison.
SOURCE: © Susan Lapides 1984

how to behave after one activity is over and before another begins. Older school-age children use this time for conversation and play, with a resulting increase in noise. Therefore, decreasing the number of transitions results in less probability of interaction difficulties.

Short attention spans and differences in working speed can be managed by grouping a variety of activities together in a larger time period and allowing children to change activities individually. For example, in a second-grade room, a teacher combined reading groups, workbook activities, and selected games involving one or two children into one block of time. In programs for very young children, a large variety of materials usually is available at any

one time. In any case, the goal is to meet the individual needs of children; strategies and standards for doing so differ according to program demands.

When multiple adults are involved, the schedule should be supplemented with a flow-chart that assigns adults to tasks, areas, or other responsibilities that will facilitate the supervision of children. A sample flowchart and schedule for a 2½ hour preschool program is illustrated in Table 12-2. Such a plan should be posted so that all adults know when they are supposed to be in a given area as well as what activity should come next. As can be seen, the divisions of time for adults are more frequent than the transitions for the group of children.

TABLE 12-2 Schedule and Flowchart for a 2½-Hour Program

SCHEDULE		CARL	JOHN	EVELYN
Arrival	9:00	Greet children	Help children with coats	Set up art activity
Free play	9:15	General supervision; blocks	Supervise dramatic play	Supervise art and bathroom areas
	9:30			Clean up art; general supervision
	9:45	Introduce new Lotto game		
	10:00	Supervise picking up of table toys	Supervise cleanup of dramatic-play area	Support cleanup where needed
Snack	10:15	Assist in bathroom	Prepare snack; set out juice	Encourage children to wash up
	10:25	All adults sit with children for snack		
Large group	10:40	Call children to story time	Clear snack	Supervise settling for story
	11:00	Announce outdoor time	Assist in locker area	Dress for outside; go outdoors to receive children
	11:10	Help last child prepare art to go home	Go outside; supervise tricycles	Supervise swings and slides
	11:15	General supervision outdoors		
Depart	11:30	Greet parents		Go indoors to clean up room
	11:40		Go indoors; help Evelyn	
	11:45	All children have left; discuss day together		
	12:00	Lunch for adults		

In addition, adults are stationed in areas before children enter, and they leave with the last child. The children in this group will experience an even flow of events without a lot of confusion. The nature of the schedule varies with the type of program, the ages of the children, and the number of adults involved. Sometimes, more complex schedules are developed to incorporate weekly events.

The schedule in Table 12-2 was carefully planned so that children will have the maximum opportunity to interact with one another and make small decisions and so that adults will be able to help and support children in their activities as they supervise the classroom. The head teacher will check to see that the plan is implemented and will communicate any adjustments to other staff members should the need arise.

Rate and Intensity of Programs

The speed, rate, or *pace* of a program is one of the most noticeable features in programs for children. Practically speaking, it is the number of activities per unit of time and is related to the overall purpose of the program and the length of time the children are in the program. For example, in a slow-paced child-care center where children are present between nine and ten hours each day, children probably will be able to predict specific activities and routines, and only one or two novel experiences may occur each week. However, in a fast-paced program, a child might anticipate one or two novel experiences each day. In addition, faster paced programs usually are more *intense,* with greater numbers of adults and more adult involvement in children's activities. Low-intensity programs are relaxed, and a common adult role is observation, with occasional guidance. Most programs for children have segments of the schedule that are faster in pace and more intense than other segments, with lower intensity periods occurring during segments in which fatigue is expected.

The intensity and pace of programs vary according to the population served, the length of time children spend in the program each day, and the goals and philosophy of the program. A classroom for gifted children operates at a faster pace than does a regular classroom; a classroom for mentally impaired children operates at a much slower pace. The intensity of the latter may be much greater than that of the former, however, because the knowledge and skill levels of the children require greater adult involvement.

The pace and intensity of programs affect children's interactions because these dimensions affect *fatigue.* The phrase "tired and cranky" reflects the common knowledge that fatigue influences children's ability to cope with social interactions. A child who is able to solve interpersonal problems when rested may simply cry or become distraught if required to face the same situation when tired.

The following are possible explanations for fatigue (Gross, Crandall, and Knoll, 1980):

1. Bodily changes resulting in *impairment* that might be the result of "running hard" for a long time.
2. *Frustration* with one's inability to cope with a situation.
3. *Boredom* with the activity.
4. The normal wear and tear of life due to *stress.*

Individual children will respond differently to the same program. It is quite possible to have some children in a program frustrated, others bored, and still others exhausted from the stress of working under pressure to keep up. Factors that influence the rate at which children can function are motivation, health, knowledge, skill, practice, age, stamina, habit, and the number of people involved in an activity (Nickell, Rice, and Tucker, 1976). The skillful swimmer is more efficient than the less skillful one and is not as tired at the end of 30 laps as the less skillful swimmer is at the end of 5. Crowded conditions are more tiring than those in which the density is lower. Interacting continuously with someone is more tiring than sporadic contact during the day. Interruptions lead to frustration and to fatigue.

Synchronization. Adults who plan programs for children must take into account individual differences so that children have the greatest probability of success. Planning schedules, activities, and equipment so that children can operate efficiently and at a pace and intensity suitable for their temperaments requires the thoughtful management of time and material resources. General schedules should be sufficiently flexible to meet these individual differences, and the availability and usability of the resources should be adapted to children's specific needs. However, all programs are influenced by general factors that limit the helping professional's ability to achieve this goal.

The following are general factors influencing time allocation (Swick, Brown, and Robinson, 1983):

1. The particular theories and philosophies that are valued.
2. The needs, strengths, and weaknesses of the adults in the setting.
3. Physical characteristics of the facility that houses the program.
4. The availability and skills of staff.
5. The expectations of the parents who have selected the program.
6. The particular children who are being served.

The facility and the management of space and materials are within the limited control of the helping professional and therefore will be examined next.

MANAGEMENT OF SPACE AND MATERIALS

Buildings, furnishings, materials, and elements of the natural environment are concrete, visible resources that can be managed to facilitate the social development of children. The physical environment in which children play and learn has much to do with the presence or absence of disruptive behavior (Mehrabian, 1976). Many ''discipline problems'' in classrooms can be traced directly to the arrangement and selection of furnishings and materials (Olds, 1977). On the other hand, self-control develops in a well-designed and well-arranged physical space (Day, 1975). The general consensus of researchers and theorists is that a well-designed environment creates a positive, supportive setting for the group using it (Marcu, 1977).

Facilities

Usually, such things as location, buildings, parking lots, and plumbing are taken for granted by the new professional. Rarely are beginning professionals required to develop plans for construction or renovation; yet, attributes of the facilities themselves influence the daily program and the frequency of limit setting. Factors such as construction materials, lighting, ventilation, temperature control, safety from environmental hazards, environmental noise, and actual layout and dimensions of the space influence children's behavior.

Safety. To protect children, states define standards for environmental safety for private-sector programs. Day-care centers, camps, and other settings in which children spend prolonged time away from their parents must be licensed. Minimum standards typically are set for fire safety, sanitation, water, and food preparation. Most states also have standards that prohibit overcrowding and ensure adequate supervision by establishing maximum acceptable adult-to-child ratios (Evans, Shub, and Weinstein, 1971).

The temperature of the environment should be comfortable for the level of activity. Ideal room temperatures are determined by the age of the children and the type of activity in which they are engaged. Infants are most comfortable between 78°F and 80°F (warm skin temperatures), but older children engaged in vigorous activity might be too warm at 68°F. Temperatures that are either too warm or too cold have health consequences for everyone.

Professionals who work with groups of children should be familiar with the standards and procedures for ensuring their safety and should support the maintenance of the standards. For example, an exit should not be blocked by trash waiting to be carried out while children are in the building; rooms should be clean, and children should be taught sanitary practices when the group is doing cooking projects;

fences and climbing equipment should be regularly checked for necessary repairs. Adults who work directly with children are likely to be the first to see areas that need improvement and can initiate the management process. Failure to use ordinary caution and to maintain established standards is considered negligence.

Interior design. The general principles of quality design apply to environments for young children. Unfortunately, many schools and hospitals have been constructed using "hard" architecture (Sommer, 1974). The spatial arrangements are similar to those of a factory, with ease of maintenance enjoying the highest priority. Frequently, the spaces are unattractive, make people feel closed in, limit movement, and reverberate with sound. Fortunately, modifications can be made.

Walls. Light colors with bright accents are a big improvement over dark or dirty walls. As most people know, color hue and intensity influence distance perception and the general atmosphere of a room. Wall surfaces that are covered with easily washed paint or with wallboard that has a hard, cleanable, fire-retardant surface work well. Children invariably leave fingerprints on surfaces and often can clean up after themselves if the wall texture is appropriate.

Sound control. Noise is absorbed by soft materials like carpet, draperies, ceiling and wall tile, and pillows. A certain level of noise is to be expected as children talk and move about. However, reverberating noise and yelling and screaming adults and children are not normal. If adults need to raise their voices to be heard when children are behaving appropriately, some modification of the environment must be made. Street noise also may filter in, adding to the general noise level. On the other hand, soft music played during quiet activities increases auditory interest, and recordings of the natural environment, such as waves washing ashore or birds singing, enhance the nap-room environment in a child-care setting.

Variation in texture usually influences the sound level and tends to humanize the environment. Hard surfaces on floors are useful in art areas, kitchens, bathrooms, and entrances and where children play in sand or water. Carpets are easier to sit on and are softer to land on if a child falls from an indoor climber. In the block corner, a firm-surfaced carpet reduces noise without reducing the stability of blocks. One enterprising teacher hung three tumbling mats on a cement wall. This solved the problem of storing the mats when they were not in use, decreased the reverberation of noise in the basement room, and added color and texture to the wall. Public schools and other formal settings for children often have carpeted and hard-surfaced floors, and most administrators will allow staff to bring additional rugs into such settings.

Lighting. Adequate lighting is necessary for children to perform detailed tasks, but it also can be boring and monotonous to be in a brightly lit space all the time. Lower lighting, and lighting dispersed around the room, are most conducive to social interaction (Meers, 1985). Although artificial lighting has not been found to affect performance, nearly everyone prefers sunlight to artificial light (Meers, 1985). Windows provide light and interest because outdoor scenes change throughout the year. The use of dimmer switches rather than off-on switches gives the adult greater control, especially if switches are available for various areas of the room (Marion, 1981). The use of dimmer switches in schools is rare, but they are inexpensive and easy to install.

Vertical and horizontal space. Varying a room's height by building a platform in a corner can increase the total available floor space and add interest to less usable space. Wells can be constructed in the floors of buildings, as can low platforms, both of which clearly separate visual space as well as adding visual interest. These dimensions are more difficult for the helping professional to change, but they should be explored if any major renovation to facilities is being considered because vertical relationships between people do influence interactions. Higher position in space represents greater power, and children get much satisfaction from looking down from greater heights to the people below. This concept was explored more fully in Chapter 3.

Arranging Furnishings and Equipment

A supportively built environment allows children to control their surroundings when appropriate and permits and encourages movement so that children can interact freely with objects and people (Marion, 1981). Because safety always is of highest priority, adults should plan environments to minimize risk for children.

A supportive environment is arranged into *learning centers,* or areas that provide for individual, small-group, or large-group activities (Day, 1975). When these are organized, physical limits are clear and regulate the use of materials and the behavior of children (Olds, 1977). The number and kinds of areas needed is determined by the age of the children and the size of the group (Alward, 1973). If an *activity space* is defined as that occupied by a child using a material, then the number of activity spaces for a block area may be four or six because that number of children could reasonably use the blocks at one time. To prevent waiting, it is recommended that there be roughly one-third more activity spaces than there are children (Marion, 1981). For a group of 20 children, areas that could accommodate a total of 27 children would be needed.

Private space. A private area is a space designed for one child, or maybe two, to which the child can retreat from social interaction. In one second-grade classroom, the teacher had painted an old bathtub red and filled it with pillows. A child in that area, usually reading or simply watching others, always was left undisturbed. A private area of this type is not to be used for punishment or time-out but to provide a sense of relaxation, comfort, and privacy in the midst of a public environment. Another kind of private area is a study carrel. Commercial carrels are desks with shelves and walls built around three sides. The same effect can be achieved by using three sides of a refrigerator box and opening it to put in a mobile desk.

Small-group space. A small-group area is designed for fewer than eight children. In most programs for young children, four to six children may be playing together (housekeeping, blocks, water play) or engaged in studying (insect collections, number lotto, weighing cubes). A small-group work area should have spaces for sitting and a surface for working (Alward, 1973). Primary-school teachers generally conduct reading groups in a small-group area with the children sitting in a circle or around a table. Some areas of this type, such as an art area, are specialized so that materials may be stored on adjacent shelves. Areas are more flexible when their use is not predetermined and materials may be brought into or removed from the area.

Large-group space. Most settings have an area that can accommodate all of the children at one time. This type of indoor space usually is used for a variety of activities: language arts, creative dance, group discussion, games, and music.

Boundaries. Activity spaces have clear boundaries. Usually, furnishings and low room dividers are used to mark separations in areas. Boundaries also may be established by using tape on the floor or by visual limitations such as placing a sheet over a shelf of toys. The most difficult boundaries for children to recognize are those that are totally symbolic. Verbal or symbolic boundaries are made when teachers tell children not to look at or speak to the person sharing a table with them. Each area may be further differentiated by distinctive materials, such as books, comfortable, child-sized chairs, and

FIGURE 12-2 This large-group area has clear boundaries and makes use of the element of softness to enable children to attend to the teacher.
SOURCE: H. Armstrong Roberts

cushions in one area and tables, chairs, and board games in another.

Areas also should be arranged within the room so that activities do not conflict with one another or offer distractions. Quiet activities should be separated from more vigorous ones. For example, it is better to locate a study carrel near a work area or the independent reading area than near the block or game area. The number, type, and arrangement of activity areas are within the control of the helping professional. Activity areas can be added, removed, or relocated to facilitate the achievement of program goals.

Activity areas are as useful outdoors as indoors. Usually, boundaries are established outdoors by varying the surface. Asphalt may be used on a ball court or a tricycle path, grass on the playing or running field, and sand or wood chips under climbing equipment. Boundaries

also are defined by large open spaces between activity areas. When outdoor space is shared by different groups and when the boundaries are formed by constructions such as sidewalks and fences, helping professionals have less control of the way space is used. Constructed boundaries, however, are clear to children and provide greater safety. Within well-defined activity areas, adults can influence social interaction by the use of mobile equipment and materials, such as the addition of water or shovels and pails to a digging area.

Pathways. Activity areas also must be arranged so that movement between areas is easily accomplished without interfering with the activities in progress. Such pathways need to be sufficiently wide to allow children to pass one another without physical contact. Usually, 30 to 36 inches is adequate indoors; outdoors, wider pathways are necessary to avoid collisions when children run. In some rooms, the area designated as the large-group area also serves as a means of access to other activity areas. Sometimes, the pathway is like a hallway without walls, with the large-group area at one end and small-group and private spaces arranged on either side of a central pathway.

Storage. Storage is essential to all programs. Stored items should be sorted, placed at the point of first use, and arranged so that they are easy to see, reach, and grasp and easy to replace by those who use them most often (Nickell, Rice, and Tucker, 1976). Storage units should be planned to fit the items to be stored. Mobile storage units equipped with casters can be used to set boundaries. Materials that are used regularly should be readily accessible from pathways or activity areas. Storage of equipment and materials used outdoors should be suitable in size and accessible from the playground areas. Some storage space that is inaccessible to children also is desirable. Cleaning compounds, medicines, power tools, and other potentially harmful substances and equipment should be stored where children cannot get to them. Less frequently used materials and equipment also may be stored well away from the program area.

Controllable Dimensions

The physical setting is composed of a number of dimensions involving the facility, the furnishings, and the materials used by children: soft-hard, open-closed, simple-complex, intrusion-seclusion, high mobility–low mobility (Jones, 1981). The particular combination of these dimensions varies according to the type of program (hospital, playroom, YMCA recreation area) as well as the goals of the program and the philosophy of the adults. These dimensions determine the overall comfort and atmosphere communicated by the physical environment.

Softness. The *soft-hard* dimension describes the responsiveness of the texture to the touch. A wooden desk chair is hard, and an upholstered chair is soft; asphalt is softer than cement, but turf is more responsive than either. Malleable materials such as sand, water, and play dough are softer than rigid materials such as blocks, books, or tricycles. Hardness usually is associated with efficiency and formality, and softness is associated with relaxation and comfort.

Openness. The *open-closed* dimension describes the degree to which the material itself restricts its use. When something is closed, both the goal and the mode of relationship are constrained. For example, puzzles, form boards, and tracing patterns are closed. These materials also have been described as ''reconstruction materials,'' indicating a predetermined end product (Whiren, 1977). Relatively open materials, or basic construction materials such as large blocks or Tinker Toys, allow greater alternatives in outcome. When a material is open, such as clay or mud, neither the alternatives nor the outcomes are limited. In furnishings, a storage cabinet would be closed if it were too high or if visibility of its contents were impeded. A relatively open cabinet would be low but with unlocked doors or glass doors. An open cabinet is low, visible, and available for use. More open settings encourage curiosity and exploration, and completely closed settings prohibit such behavior altogether.

Complexity. The *simple-complex* dimension describes the material in terms of the number of alternatives that can be generated. A simple unit has only one obvious alternative (a ladder), but when it is combined with other materials or parts to increase its complexity, children are able to use it imaginatively (two ladders hinged at the top, or a ladder and a large box). A ''super unit'' has three or more parts (ladder and two climbing triangles, or a water table with a water wheel and containers). Children tend to play cooperatively with complex and super units more frequently than with simple units, which often elicit solitary or parallel play activity. For older children, an Erector Set with wheels and motors is a semi-open, complex unit that will keep a small group solving problems for hours. Complexity encourages deep exploration, and variety encourages broad exploration. Formal group settings need some of each so that children will focus on an activity for an extended period of time, which is more likely with complex activities, but also can move to other alternatives for a change of pace.

Seclusion. The *intrusion-seclusion* dimension describes the permeability of two types of boundaries: the boundaries between the program and the things and people outside it and the boundaries between people and things inside the program. A university-based laboratory school, for example, ordinarily has a lot of people coming into its classroom, as would a teaching hospital with a pediatric play program. People do not just look; they usually come inside and do something. These programs have much more intrusion than most others. A city classroom in a warm climate may have the windows open for ventilation, permitting traffic noise and factory fumes to enter. This is another kind of intrusion. Many classrooms have no seclusion within them. Children who are overcome by the stress of continuous interaction in a large group act up, cry, or daydream to escape for short periods. Private areas, as described earlier, are spaces in which children would have a degree of seclusion; small-group spaces are partially secluded.

Mobility. The dimension of *high or low mobility* is simply the dimension of potential movement. A child on a large climber is using large muscles; another, coloring with a crayon, is mostly sedentary but does have the opportunity for limited movement of the hands and arms. American children are getting heavier and are not in as good physical condition as children were a generation ago. Concern for physical fitness may influence professionals in all learning environments to plan programs with greater emphasis on motor development. Children who have the opportunity to choose some sedentary activities and some active pursuits usually choose both in the course of the day. Prolonged sedentary activity causes children to wriggle to ease their muscles and to become bored and restless regardless of the interest or importance of the activity. Daily schedules should provide for a balance between vigorous movement, moderate activity, and more quiet pursuits. When children's need for mobility is taken to account, the selection of equipment and the use of space usually is changed.

Each of the dimensions varies by degrees and may vary over the course of a year or within a single day. Each dimension affects the social relationships of children in the setting. An open, moderately secluded, soft environment with low-to-moderate mobility is a conversation area, much like a living room, in which children can relax and interact informally. If children have a moderately complex task, such as preparing a skit for a 4-H demonstration, they are likely to cooperate in doing it; however, if they have a set of simple, discrete tasks, such as those involved in preparing a poster, they are much more likely to divide up the labor and work independently. The combination of setting quality and activity have an important impact on the nature of social relationships among children. In either activity, intrusion might occur if an adult were to enter the activity and give directions. Usually, setting the task and providing occasional guidance is all that is necessary for such situations.

Structuring for Goals

The environment should suit the goals of the program and the objectives set by the helping professional. If the leader of a toddler-parent learning group wanted to have the children move to music in a group, a moderately soft (adult lap on carpet) and closed (nothing on open shelves; toys in closed cupboards) large-group area is most appropriate. Such an activity, although simple for preschool children, is complex for toddlers who may be interacting with other adults and children for the first time in addition to getting guidance from someone other than parents. Mobility is high, so sufficient space is needed to avoid collision. Seclusion is provided by the availability of the parent's lap if the activity becomes overwhelming. Changing one dimension would affect the patterns of social interaction. For example, if the toys were out on open shelves, adults would spend most of the interaction in setting limits and redirecting the children. Children would have little opportunity to observe other toddlers and would have less pleasant experiences with other adults.

Adult behavior also is influenced by the physical environment. Whenever equipment distribution restricts children's activity or access to the materials, supervisory behavior in adults increases in frequency (Polloway, 1974). In a third-grade classroom, children who had desks arranged in small clusters screened by dividers, a conversation area, and a private space where children could be alone had longer attention spans, were less distractable, and answered more problems correctly than did the comparison group. The seclusion in this classroom was substantially higher than in a less successful room. The teacher, however, was much more mobile, spending one-fifth as much time at her desk as her counterpart and using considerably fewer behavior restrictions (Zifferblatt, 1972). The amount of space also influences the amount of verbal and nonverbal controlling behavior used by adults. When the density of children increases, so does the frequency of limit setting (Phyfe-Perkins, 1982). Adults who can decrease controlling behavior have more opportunities to engage in satisfying social interactions with children and are better able to meet program goals as well.

The furnishings, room arrangement, and general quality of the physical environment are important components of the setting. In addition, the materials used by children and the way they are managed influences interpersonal relations between children and between adults and children. The word *materials* includes everything that children use in the program: textbooks, pencils, art supplies, tennis rackets, tableware, or toys.

Choosing Appropriate Materials

Adults can promote competent and independent behavior in children by providing a moderately rich assortment of exploratory materials (White and Watts, 1973; Stallings, 1975). It also is desirable to structure the environment and organize the materials to enhance all aspects of the child's development as well as to meet basic needs (Day, 1975). Thus, appropriate use of materials can support the development of independence and self-control. However, materials also may be a prime cause of many disruptive behaviors (Olds, 1977).

Developmentally appropriate materials. Materials should reflect the goals of the program and the various levels of competence of children. Adults would think it strange if someone gave a chemistry set to a five-year-old. Not only would the child be at risk of swallowing some of the chemicals, but in all probability, the set would quickly be destroyed. However, the same set given to a twelve-year-old could provide hours of pleasure and instruction. Frequently, materials intended for older children create potential risks for younger ones. In addition, when older children use equipment and materials designed for young children, they lose interest because there is no challenge, and they find new, often destructive ways to use them.

Structurally safe materials. Materials should be examined for potential safety hazards. Sturdiness, durability, craftsmanship, and appropriate construction materials all contribute to safe products. For example, a metal climbing frame may be a sensible, safe purchase for three- to five-year-olds, but a wooden one would be much safer for toddlers and young preschoolers in cold climates. Young children tend to put their tongues on the metal in winter and can become stuck to it and badly injured. Tricycles available in local stores are not as sturdily constructed as those designed specifically for use by groups of children. Nontoxic art materials are available and should replace toxic substances for children of any age.

Maintenance of equipment is necessary to ensure continued safety. Eventually, even the most sturdy toys break down. Maintenance in terms of cleanliness is especially important for young children, who are likely to put things in their mouths. Care also should be taken to see that materials aren't likely to cause choking. If an object is small enough to get into a toddler's mouth and has a diameter between that of a dime and a quarter, it might get stuck in the throat.

Materials that work. Children become frustrated when equipment and materials do not operate. The wheels of trucks should turn; scissors should cut; finger paint should be thick, and the paper heavy enough or glossy so that it doesn't fall apart. Materials that do not work cause frustration in young children, which sometimes leads to disruptive behavior. Materials should suit the task for older children as well. It is nearly impossible to trace accurately through standard typing paper; tracing paper and paper clips make the job much easier. Children cannot use basketballs, kick balls, or volleyballs that are underinflated. Seeing that all materials are usable is the responsibility of the adult.

Complete materials that are ready to use. Puzzles should have all their pieces. If one gets lost, it can be replaced by molding in some plastic wood to fit the hole. One ten-year-old was extremely upset when, after working on a hooked pillow cover for weeks, she discovered that there was insufficient yarn in the kit to complete it. Incomplete materials lead to unnecessary feelings of failure and frustration.

In addition, when materials need to be brought out by an adult for a demonstration or for children's use, they should be assembled in advance so that children don't have to wait while the adult rummages around in a cupboard or drawer for a pair of scissors or a bit of wire. Waiting children usually lose interest or become disruptive. Complete preparation by the adult includes some plan for cleaning up, so having a damp sponge in a pan would be appropriate preparation for a messy activity. In this way, the adult never needs to leave the group of children and can offer continuous guidance.

Organizing materials. Storage should be where the material is most frequently used or where it is first used and located in logical areas. If children know where something is located, they can go and get it themselves to complete a project. This is especially important for common items like paper, crayons, scissors, and the like.

Materials also should be stored so that children can take care of them. For example, taping shapes of unit blocks on the back of a cupboard so that children know where to put each size and shape encourages independence. Materials that have many pieces, like beads, small math cubes, or Cuisenaire rods, should be placed in sturdy containers such as plastic shoe boxes or tiny laundry baskets because the cardboard boxes soon wear out. In this way, children can keep all materials that go together in one place.

Attractively displayed materials. Neatness and orderliness are aspects of attractiveness. Older children often enjoy cleaning classroom cupboards that have become jumbled. Materials are easier to find and more inviting if they are not crammed into a crowded area. Young children simply have difficulty in perceiving the figure-ground dimension of some shelves of materials.

Materials that are displayed in a moderately empty space on the shelf are most likely to be used. Some materials should be available to children and displayed on low, open shelves. Puzzles in a puzzle rack or laid out on a table ready for use are more appealing than a large, heavy stack of them (Whiren, 1977).

Appropriate size of equipment and materials. Tables, chairs, desks, or other equipment add to the comfort and decrease the fatigue of children if they are sized correctly. Adults also should have at least one chair that fits them to sit on occasionally.

Fewer problems would be encountered at mealtime if preschool children were offered six-inch plates, salad forks, and four- or five-ounce glasses to use. Serving dishes (soup bowls) with teaspoon servers would enable children to serve themselves amounts of food that they can reasonably consume. Using small, unbreakable pitchers for milk and juice encourages independence as well. Cleaning one's plate is much more feasible, as is tasting a tiny portion of everything, when children determine portion size for themselves. Children who are entering the growth spurt around the ages of eleven or twelve might reasonably use large, divided trays that can hold substantial servings.

Young children spend much time in adult-sized environments. Therefore, in programs designed for them, the environment and all the materials should be appropriate for their sizes. Long mirrors in a toddler room should be mounted horizontally, just above the molding on the wall near the floor; for preschoolers, mirrors can be set vertically, but again, low. The height of sinks, toilets, and drinking fountains can be adjusted by building platforms around adult-sized facilities, or child-sized fixtures can

be installed. If materials, equipment, and furnishings are appropriate in size, children can act more independently and develop good habits.

Quantities appropriate to the number of children. If there are enough materials for a particular activity, children can work without conflict. If there is an insufficient supply, either the number of materials should be increased or the number of children using them decreased. For example, if a third-grade teacher has 12 books and 14 children, she can either hold two consecutive sessions of 7 children and use the books on hand or get 2 more books. Either solution is better than having children rush to the reading area in order to get a book for themselves. Toddlers do not comprehend sharing. In addition, a toy being played with by another child is more appealing than one on a shelf. Duplicate toys allow the desires of the toddler to be met without conflict.

The number of materials that should be made available during free play in an early-childhood program also is related to the number of children. Usually, the total number of play units should be 2½ times the number of children (Whiren, 1970). A *play unit* is an object or set of objects needed by a child to use the material effectively. A book is one play unit; a small set of Tinker Toys or a small set of Lego blocks is one unit; a doll with its clothes and blanket is one unit. Having an adequate number of play units allows the child to use a variety of materials in one play space. In a complex, open area such as a housekeeping area, there may be four spaces for children and ten or more play units, enabling children to engage in cooperative sociodramatic play for an extended period of time without conflict. With fewer play units, the children either would compete for the materials or would discontinue the activity sooner.

Adequate supplies of materials are necessary for any program regardless of the children's age if children are to be reasonably successful. If hospitalized children paint ceramics, each child needs a figurine or plaque to paint on and paint within reach. Sharing paints between beds is not practical because of the distance involved and lack of mobility of children in traction or receiving intravenous feeding.

SKILLS FOR INFLUENCING CHILDREN'S SOCIAL DEVELOPMENT VIA THE PHYSICAL ENVIRONMENT

Management is a process in which some change occurs. Good management means changing in order to meet short- and long-range goals. You will be able to apply the management process to many problems in professional practice. In this section, we will discuss how to formulate and change a daily schedule, how to teach a habit, how to arrange and alter activity areas, and how to influence behavior by adding objects to or removing them from the environment.

How to Establish a Daily Schedule

1. Plan the schedule in detail and write it down. Write a time sequence in 15-minute intervals starting 30 minutes before children arrive and ending 30 minutes after they leave. Include all events that are predetermined, such as meals, naps, recess, or special activities. Estimate the time needed for these activities and mark it off on the paper. Estimate the time needed to get the children to and from each of these events and mark it off. Now, you have large sections of time that can be used for other program goals.

List activities that are appropriate to your program. Cluster together those activities that children can do during the same time period. Consider factors such as noise, mobility of children, and individual differences in pace. Allow sufficient time for the slowest child to complete an activity and enough variety so that children who finish sooner can do something other than wait. Estimate the time needed for each cluster or each activity period. These activity periods may involve total group participation or may include small-group and individual activities. Enter these estimates into the plan. (A complete schedule was presented in Table 12-2.)

If there are multiple adults, discuss the plan and determine which adult will supervise which activities. Determine the timing of movements of adults. In general, adults should precede children or move with them from one place to another. Write this into the plan. Determine who will make the decisions as to implementing the schedule with the children.

Identify the advance preparation that needs to be done before the children arrive and the cleanup after they leave. Assign tasks to adults, or fit some cleanup tasks into the activities themselves. Write these into the schedule as well.

2. Describe the daily schedule to children. Tell children the sequence of events before they occur. Communicate with parents of toddlers about the schedule prior to the children's entry into the program. Older preschool children may simply be told the broad schedule; grade-school children should be told the schedule, or the schedule should be posted in writing when they arrive. In all cases, the basic sequence of events should be clear.

3. Tell children in advance that a transition will occur. Simple statements such as "It will be time to put your things away in five minutes" allow children an opportunity to finish their projects or organize their materials.

Give clear signals that a transition has begun. A nonverbal signal such as an open palm raised high may indicate to children to assemble at that place. Playing a song or a chord on an instrument also may indicate a transition. Straightforward directions also can be used, such as "Push your chair under the table, and walk outdoors."

4. Walk children through the schedule on their first day or assign another child to escort them when moving between unfamiliar places. A new child in camp or in a hospital setting will not automatically know where specific facilities are, regardless of the child's age. Assign an adult to the activity area, ready to begin the activity when the first child arrives.

5. *Send children to an activity rather than away from one.* Use phrases such as "You may go to the playroom and paint" instead of "You don't need to stay in this room all the time."

Communicate with other adults if slight changes in the schedule are necessary so that children do not get confusing messages. Say: "Mrs. Carter, I will be delayed in getting to the playroom for about five minutes. Will you keep the children here or send someone with them?" rather than just arriving late.

6. *Evaluate the effectiveness of the schedule at regular intervals.* Make the first assessment at the end of the first three or four weeks of implementation. Continue to assess the schedule every three to four months after that. Frequently, a change of season results in a change of schedule. Switching outdoor and indoor activities according to seasonal variations is typical.

Observe children for signs of boredom and stress throughout the adjustment period. If these signs persist after three weeks, consider altering the program content, the space, or the pace and sequence of the daily program. Make notes of when signs of fatigue, stress, or boredom appear. Sometimes, these relate to particular situations or events that can be readily altered.

How to Change the Daily Schedule

1. *Establish clear goals before altering the schedule.* Know why the alteration is taking place.

2. *Communicate the revised plan to the staff.* Make necessary alterations in staff assignments. If whole clusters of activities are being reorganized, a written plan will be necessary, but if you are switching one cluster with another, this may not be needed.

3. *Tell the children about the new schedule in advance.* Encourage children to ask questions. Discuss any new signals that you will use to indicate transitions.

4. *Carry out the new schedule and allow a substantial period of time before evaluating it according to the new goals.* Expect children to be confused, disorganized, and possibly stressed when major schedule changes are made. Young children may take as long as three weeks to fully adjust to a major change in schedule; older children are likely to take several days. This transition period is a time for review of program materials, not a time to introduce novelty, especially for younger children.

5. *Monitor the results over time and make minor adjustments as necessary.*

6. *Evaluate the new schedule in terms of long- and short-term goals for the children as well as in terms of the new objectives.* Was the outcome worth the time, effort, and confusion involved?

How to Teach a Routine

Planned routines usually are taught to young children and usually relate to some aspect of daily life that is repeated regularly, such as self-help skills like eating, dressing, and storing daily supplies.

1. *Determine the need for the habit.* A routine is appropriate for an activity that is repetitive and time consuming but basically motoric in nature.

2. *Seek information about how to do the task efficiently.* Experienced professionals are a good source of information. Maria Montessori wrote out various skills of daily living, such as hand washing and table cleaning

and setting, in detail over her career. Observe an efficient adult do the task and write down each step in sequence. Note the placement of objects before and after use.

3. *Write out the steps in sequence.* Include all steps that a child would have to do to carry out the task.

4. *Try out the sequence on an adult or older child.* Give directions according to the sequence and ask the person not to do anything until told. Identify omissions and unclear directions, then revise the sequence.

5. *Discuss the sequence with other staff members to identify potential problems.* Post the sequence in the area in which children are most likely to need to use the habit.

6. *Give direct instructions to children using clear, simple ''do it'' statements.* These statements generally consist of a verb and a phrase. A sequence for putting on a coat for a preschool child follows:

Find your coat.
Take it out of the cubby.
Put it on the floor (with opening up).
Find the collar of your coat. (Point to it if necessary.)
Stand with your toes near the collar.
Put both arms in the arm holes. (Point.)
Lift your arms over your head (with arms in the coat).
Bring your arms down behind your back, and push your hands out of the sleeves.

Ordinarily, this sequence would continue until the child's coat was buttoned or zipped and the child was ready to go outside.

7. *Check on the children's daily progress.* Remind children of the next step in the sequence when they get partway through it and need help. Praise their successes.

8. *Adjust the time spent on the task.* Newly introduced tasks will take more time for children to complete than ones that have become habitual. Allow more time for unfamiliar tasks; shorten the time allocated as children become more proficient.

9. *Evaluate the procedure.* Determine whether the process is efficient and is helping you to reach your goals for children's social development. If it is, continue the practice; if it is not, adjust the plan. Once a habit is established, alter it only if absolutely necessary.

How to Arrange a Room

Classrooms, playrooms, gymnasiums, and other spaces are used for children's activities. Following are some general guidelines for initially setting up a room. However, the nature of the program and the nature of the space will greatly influence the specifics.

1. *Place activities that use water near a source of water if possible.* These activities might be water play, art, or food-preparation activities. Place related equipment and storage nearby. If water is not available in the room, place this center in a low-traffic area and bring water in pails.

2. *Place the cloaking area near the entrance to the room or in a hallway outside the room.* Provide for the storage of boots, mittens, clothing, and personal belongings with open shelving, cubbies, or lockers. A bench or seat for putting on boots also is needed here.

3. *Select an appropriate spot for large-group activities to take place.* Pick a section of the room where an electrical outlet is available so that audiovisual equipment can be used conveniently. Put a carpet in this area to define the space and to deaden noise.

4. Use storage units, seating, variation in flooring, and small dividers to form boundaries.

5. Place high-mobility activities in one section of the room and low-mobility activities in another section to minimize interference.

6. Allow space for moving from one activity to another without going through the middle of an activity area.

7. Place materials and equipment in areas where they are most frequently used.

8. Put seating in areas according to the number of children who are to use the area. The size of the private area should be very small, with room for just one. The number of chairs at a table in a work area will be determined by the number that can work at a particular activity. Remove extra chairs. Sketch out a plan to use the space first, then move the furniture. When in doubt as to sizes or fit of major furnishings, measure them and the space before moving them.

How to Change the Qualities of the Room

Given the inflexible nature of objects and rooms, there are basically two kinds of things you can do. You may *add* something, or you may *take* something *away*. These options apply to the controllable dimensions discussed earlier, to furnishings, and to materials.

1. Determine whether or not the physical environment supports your goals for the children. Consider such factors as softness, openness, complexity, mobility, and seclusion.

2. Add or subtract objects in the physical environment to achieve specific goals related to children's social development.

a. To increase the softness of the room, add draperies, rugs, pillows, upholstered furniture, stuffed animals, and activities using pliable materials such as papier-mâché, water, sand, and play dough. To add hardness, remove these things.

b. To increase the openness of the environment, add open shelves, remove the doors of cupboards, or place materials within the reach of children. Add construction materials such as blocks, art supplies, and the soft materials mentioned earlier.

c. To decrease the openness, shut cupboard doors or cover open shelving with a sheet. Provide materials that require one correct response, such as puzzles or workbooks.

d. To increase complexity, add related elements to a unit. For example, a teacher of ten-year-olds had 12 activity cards to do in sequence related to fairy tales that children could complete in an individual activity area. Books, paper, pens, paints, and a variety of other materials were available to use. For little children, hats or dress-up clothing may be added to the housekeeping area or dinosaurs to the sand-play area.

e. To promote simplicity, remove all materials except those absolutely necessary for the task. The simplest room is an empty one, which would be ideal for playing games; complexity is provided by the number of children involved.

f. To increase seclusion, make the boundaries clearer, and stronger. Add dividers to the table so that children can't see one another; add small room dividers between activity areas. Add draperies or shades to the windows. These decrease the noise and visual intrusion from the outside. Add a sign outside the door directing visitors to the office.

g. To increase intrusion, remove the items just mentioned. Improve the access to outdoors, if possible, by allowing children to move in and out. Minimize the barriers between rooms of the building. Invite community members to the program; borrow materials from businesses for displays; use audiovisual materials that bring into the classroom experiences from distant places or times.

h. To increase mobility, remove objects such as tables and chairs to unclutter the space. Add activity areas to the room. Increase the number of materials that can be used at the same time and the number of simple activities.

i. To decrease mobility, add complexity and softness to the environment. Another alternative is to add seclusion to the environment. When programs have too much space and children are running around, boundaries that decrease the space being used, such as a row of chairs across a gym floor, work well.

j. To decrease noise, add softness and seclusion.

How to Maximize Safety

The safety of children is every adult's responsibility. Usually, the adults in charge of a program will have checked some of the following items and determined that they are safe. Taking simple precautions is much better than telling children to be careful or scolding them for playing near something hazardous. You always have the option of inquiring about a situation you think is unsafe.

1. Check the temperature of the hot water by turning the water on rapidly and letting it flow. If tap water is uncomfortably hot, draw this to the attention of the adult leader, advise children that the hot water is very hot, or adjust the flow and temperature of the water yourself for the children's use. Head teachers may check the thermostat of the hot water supply and adjust it to comfort and safety levels.

2. Check visible electrical outlets in rooms for very young children. Plastic caps should be in the outlets. When you use an outlet, remove the cap and place it nearby so that it may be returned to the receptacle as soon as you are finished.

3. Check the emergency procedures. Read the procedures for natural disasters such as tornados, earthquakes, or fire. These usually are posted in a conspicuous place. Locate all the exits that might be used in an emergency. Participate in fire drills according to established procedures; this is not the time to run an errand. Each disaster drill must be taken seriously: it may *not* be a drill. Remain with the children until normality is restored.

4. Place appliances near electrical outlets; avoid pathways where children walk. Children may trip over an extension cord, pulling the appliance and its contents onto themselves. Also, don't allow an appliance cord to hang over a counter in a room for infants. They will grasp and pull it.

5. Use extension cords that are large enough for the voltage of the appliance you are using. Usually, the extension cords used for household lamps are insufficient for an appliance that generates heat or uses considerable power, such as a space heater.

6. Remain with anything that is hot if children are present. Supervise the popcorn popper, a boiling teakettle, or an audiovisual appliance that is very hot. If you must leave the area and if another adult is not available to assist you, either take the children with you or place whatever is hot in a safe place out of the way.

7. Remove any material or equipment that appears to you to be unsafe. Eliminate a wiggly tricycle wheel, a ladder with a missing rung, or a record player with a frayed electrical cord. Peeling paint and wood splinters are common nuisances. When in doubt, be cautious.

8. Keep safety in mind when supervising activities. Some materials are potentially hazardous if used improperly but otherwise are safe. A stapler used properly is safe, but little fingers can get under the staple. Large blocks usually are safe, but a tall construction may require an adjustment of a lower block to ensure balance of the whole structure.

9. Place all cleaning compounds and medicines out of the reach of children. All programs will have a designated storage area for such substances. Be sure that they are returned to that location immediately after use.

10. Scan the environment inside and out for potential safety hazards when supervising children. Look at the spaces you habitually use so that hazards can be removed. People may throw beer bottles or cans into children's play spaces. Sometimes, when space is used by other people during other time periods, materials and equipment are left out that may pose a danger to the children. Remove these promptly.

11. Know the local and state legal guidelines and periodically check that they are being maintained.

How to Manage Materials

Problems with cleanup done by children can be minimized by organizing according to the following guidelines.

1. Store materials to be used by children in durable containers near the point of first use and so that they are easy to reach, grasp, and use.

2. Establish a specific location for materials so that children will know where to put them. Maintain the storage area in an orderly fashion so that children will know what it is

supposed to look like. Mark storage areas with words, symbols, or pictures as needed to identify materials that should be located there.

3. Check equipment and materials to be sure that they are complete, safe, and usable. Prevent the frustrating experience of trying to do something that simply is not possible. Repair materials and equipment promptly or remove them from use.

4. Demonstrate the proper care of materials. If necessary, tell the children exactly what to do while doing the task yourself, then take the materials out again so that the children can imitate the behavior. A camp leader may need to demonstrate the cleaning and folding of a tent several times before children learn to do it correctly.

5. Give reasons for the standards that you set. For example, say: ''Put the pieces in the puzzle box before putting it in the rack. That way, the pieces won't get lost.'' You might ask older children to read the numbers on the spine of a book and replace it exactly so that another reader can find it.

6. Supervise the process of putting materials away, giving reminders as necessary; praise children who are achieving the standard and those who are helping others to do so. Allow children to choose between two or three tasks. If they are unwilling to choose which task to do, assign a task and support the child through the process using the skills learned in Chapters 7 and 8.

How to Minimize Conflict Between Children and Adults

1. Provide only enough chairs for the maximum number of children that can participate in an activity. Children become confused if there are five chairs at a table, but only three children may participate in the activity. To avoid this problem, remove extra chairs.

2. Encourage children to personalize their space by letting them make room decorations, use the bulletin boards, or have a display area. Allowing children to help decorate the room minimizes graffiti and writing on the walls.

3. Provide for appropriate activities for a private space. Plan activities that children may do alone. This allows the child who needs some seclusion an opportunity to behave appropriately while withdrawing from the main flow of action.

4. Provide materials that are developmentally appropriate. Know the typical kinds of materials that children of the age you work with enjoy. Make these available. Avoid offering activities that are too simple or too difficult. Use information available from other professionals and from the literature if you are uncertain about the appropriateness of an activity.

5. Provide furnishings of appropriate size. Chairs that are either too high or too low are uncomfortable and induce unnecessary fatigue. Children have excessive difficulty in safely using equipment that is not sized correctly, such as scissors that are too long or a climbing structure designed for much younger children.

6. Have all the materials ready and all the equipment and furnishings in place when the program begins. This allows you to supervise the children continuously rather than leaving to get supplies.

7. Organize materials so that physical work is minimized both for children and for yourself. Observe children and other adults for ways to eliminate or simplify unnecessary work. For instance, use a tray to carry several items instead of making many trips.

8. Send children to an activity or an area rather than away from one. Give children a clear notion of what alternatives they may pursue. This can be done by giving a direction, such as "Put away your books and come to the large-group area," or by asking the child what he or she plans to do next. Avoid ending a statement by saying things like "You should finish up" or "You're all done." Neither statement helps the child decide what activities are open for him or her next.

How to Minimize Conflict Between Children

1. Provide materials in an appropriate number for the task and situation. In an open classroom, use the ratio of 2½ activity or play units per child. Check the number of spaces and the amount of materials available when mobility is excessive or when child-to-child conflict is frequent. Either too many or too few activities can produce this effect. Either add or remove activity areas and play units, based on your assessment.

2. For young children, especially toddlers, provide duplicate or near-duplicate play materials. When conflict over an item arises, substitute a duplicate or similar object for the one under contention.

3. Arrange the space so that children can get materials and take care of them without interfering with other children. Place furnishings so that children can move to and from storage without bumping into other people or asking them to move their activity.

How to Help Children Make Decisions and Manage Independently

1. Offer many different choices to children each day. Anticipate situations in which choices could be offered, and plan what those choices will be. For instance, if you know you will be reading a story to the group, consider giving children a choice about where to sit, whether they would like to follow up the story by writing a poem or drawing a picture, or what character they would like to portray in a re-enactment of the tale.

2. Take advantage of naturally occurring situations in which to offer choices. As you pass out plates, even if they all look the same, give children a choice of which one to use, or ask children which side of the table they would like to sit on or whether they would like to pass out the napkins or the spoons.

3. Offer choices using positive statements. Give children acceptable alternatives rather than telling them what they cannot choose. It would be better to say "You can use the blocks to make something like a road, a house, or a rocket" than to say "You can make anything except a gun." The former statement helps children to recognize what alternatives are available; the latter directs children's attention to the very thing you do not want them to consider.

4. Offer choices for which you are willing to accept either alternative the child selects. Pick alternatives with which you are equally comfortable. If you say "You can either water the plants or feed the fish," you should be satisfied with either choice the child makes. If what you want is for the child to water the plants, do not make plant watering optional. Instead, offer a choice within the task, such as watering the plants in the morning or just after lunch. These choices are presented as either-or statements or "you choose" statements. For example, "You can water either the big plants or the little plants first" or "You choose: big plants or little plants first?"

5. Allow children ample time to make their decisions. When making choices, children often vacillate between options. Allow them time to do this rather than rushing them. Give youngsters a time frame within which to think: "I'll check back with you in a few minutes to see what you've decided,"

"While you're finishing your painting, you can decide which area to clean up," or "I'll ask Suzy what she wants to do, and then I'll get back to you."

6. Allow children to change their minds if the follow-through on the decision has not yet begun. If Camille is trying to decide between the blue cup and the red cup and initially chooses the blue one, she should be allowed to switch to the red cup as long as her milk has not already been poured into the blue one or the red cup has not been given to someone else.

7. Assist children in accepting responsibility for the choices they make. Once children have made a decision and it is in process, help them stay with and follow through on their choice. For example, Kent decided he wanted to water the plants after lunch; a gentle reminder on his return that afternoon may help him to act on his decision if it seems that he has forgotten. Use a neutral tone and non-inflammatory language; say: "Kent, earlier you decided to water the plants after lunch. It's about time to do that now" rather than "Kent, how are you ever going to learn to be responsible if you don't follow through on your decisions?" Similarly, if you had already poured the milk into the cup Camille had chosen but she wanted to switch at that point, your role would be to help her live with the consequences of the decision. Reflect: "You changed your mind" or "You're disappointed that the red cup is gone." Talk about how the child may choose differently another time: "Today, you chose the blue cup. Tomorrow, you'll have another chance to choose. If you still want the red cup, you can choose it then." Comfort children who are unhappy about the results of their decision.

8. Allow older children to collaborate with you on major management problems such as storage of materials, proposed rearrangement of space, or planning of a holiday party. Involve children in the entire process: ''It's nearly Halloween; would you like to celebrate it? . . . What do we need to plan for?'' List all the options and discuss the time and work necessary to carry out the activity. If children obviously have forgotten an important part, point it out: ''Have you considered how long the games will take? Will we be finished in time to clean up the room before dismissal?'' Older children can serve in supervisory capacities such as team leader for the cleanup squad or chairperson of the refreshment committee. You still will need to check on all of the plans and implementation and provide gentle reminders when needed.

PITFALLS TO AVOID

In structuring the physical environment to enhance children's social development, there are certain pitfalls you should avoid.

Making too many changes at once. Children need security and predictability. Even though you can think of several major alterations to make, such as altering the daily schedule and rearranging the room, do them gradually. Younger children are more upset than older children by major changes.

Evaluating too soon. Sometimes, when new materials are added, rooms changed, or schedules altered, you will anticipate an immediate positive result. Young children usually are very active as they refamiliarize themselves with the area. Increased noise and confusion can be expected immediately, with improvements more discernible after three weeks.

Failing to supervise. Never leave children unattended by an adult. Children may misuse materials usually considered safe. Even if you are just gone for a minute, a situation that could endanger a child may occur at that time. In addition, children may lose interest and behave inappropriately.

Planning inadequately. Don't initiate major adjustments in the daily schedule or room arrangement on the spur of the moment. Of course, you can add materials, such as a plant, books, or toys. But impulsive major changes upset children, especially younger ones. Follow the guidelines.

Sketch major furnishings on a floor plan before moving heavy items. If they don't fit, you will have to move them again, thereby increasing your fatigue and frustration.

Adhering rigidly to the plan. When you have evaluated the situation and it is clear that the plan won't work, either adjust the plan, modify it, or give it up. Sometimes, the very best plans don't work out as anticipated and must be adjusted.

Assuming that a child knows how to do a routine. Learn to distinguish whether a child does not know how to do something or is refusing to do it. Children do not automatically know how to dress, undress, wash, put away materials, or clean cupboards. If you are supervising a child, teach the child how to do a task correctly rather than criticizing the child's best effort. Comments such as ''Didn't your mother teach you anything?'', ''If you can't do it right, don't do it at all'' or ''Can't you even wipe a table? I'll do it myself'' are all inappropriate. Instead, use comments like ''You are having a hard time with that. I'll show you how and you can finish it.''

Assuming that nothing can be done. Sometimes, you may go into a room and assume that the present arrangements can't be improved. You may not be able to do much, but most spaces can at least be made attractive and can be personalized. When you don't know whether the materials, furnishings, or decorations can be changed, ask someone in authority. Usually, an extra pillow or small table is no major problem. Such things may be available.

Failing to communicate your plans to other adults and to children. When engaging in any aspect of the management process, change is involved. This requires communication to all parties. Everything will run more smoothly if adequate preparation of children and adults has been accomplished.

Allowing children complete freedom to choose. No one can do whatever they want. There are limits to all things. Children need to collaborate and be involved in decisions, but giving them complete freedom places a burden on them that they are not yet prepared to carry. Children who are given the opportunity to "do anything" may not even be able to generate choices. This complete freedom of choice is stressful for children, and they will become confused and distressed. This distress usually is accompanied by noise and disorder as all the children try to determine if you really mean that they can do *anything*.

SUMMARY

The process of managing resources to achieve the goals of the program was discussed. Motivations for establishing goals and standards are the needs of the children and adults in the programs as well as the external demands of the community. Decision making permeates the management process and can be taught to even the youngest children. Planning and implementing change that is goal-directed may be time consuming but leads to satisfaction and to new management strategies.

General management processes were applied specifically to time management in programs for children. Special consideration was given to the importance of predictability and routine for children's sense of security and emotional adjustment to the environment.

The process of management also was applied to the selection, storage, and use of materials and to the arrangement of space. The quality of the environment influences social interaction among children and adults and can be manipulated to meet program goals.

Skills were described for establishing and changing schedules and room arrangements and for promoting efficient use of materials. Techniques were presented for adding to or subtracting from the environment as a means to facilitate social interaction. Finally, skills were described for helping children to become responsible decision makers and participants in the management process.

DISCUSSION QUESTIONS

1. Describe the management process as simply as you can so that someone who does not know the vocabulary would understand.
2. Why do the principles of management seem to be so familiar and easy to grasp while adults obviously have difficulty in making everyday decisions?

3. Why might the standards of order and efficiency differ among similar kinds of programs in different settings?

4. Describe how the decision-making process is applied to each step of the management process in a program for young children.

5. Why do adults involve children in the decision-making process? How does it influence their social development?

6. Explain the role of communication between adults who work with children, various strategies by which it can be facilitated, and situations in which it might be problematic.

7. Why would a decision rule such as "The job at hand is less important than the child doing it" become widely accepted among professionals and be frequently repeated to professionals in training?

8. Explain how the management of time and of the daily schedule is related to children's social and emotional development. Is it important throughout childhood? Why?

9. Explain the importance of having a private space in programs for groups of children.

10. Select any activity for children and identify all the opportunities for children to make choices in carrying out the activity. Identify alternatives that are unacceptable to you, and state your reasons.

11. Think back over your own childhood and recall instances in which you were denied opportunities to make choices. How did you feel? How did you behave? Did the adults make explanations to you? How did they behave?

CHAPTER 13
Supporting Children's Friendships

SOURCE: H. Armstrong Roberts

348

Randy, eight years old, is the pariah of the school playground. He regularly pushes, hits, and trips his classmates. During group games, he runs to the center of the circle, grabs a ball, and dares the other youngsters to catch him. His loud, aggressive behavior has earned him a reputation as a bully, and most children avoid him whenever they can.

Four-year-old Alisha is reserved and very quiet around her peers. She often can be seen standing on the fringe of an activity, simply watching. Even when invited to join the play, she usually shakes her head "no." After several such refusals, children have stopped asking and now generally ignore her.

To the casual observer, Randy and Alisha seem worlds apart. Yet, both are typical examples of children who have difficulty making friends. Until recently, helping professionals observing children having these problems may have felt sorry for them, but assumed there was little they, as adults, could do to improve the situation. We now know that adults can support children as they try to establish friendly relations with peers and help them increase their chances for success (Asher, Oden, and Gottmann, 1977; Combs and Slaby, 1978).

Why Friends Are Important

Children become increasingly interested in having friends as they grow older. By first grade, many report that it is almost intolerable to be without a friend (Hendrick, 1984). Why is this so?

One reason is that people need satisfying relationships with others to receive affection, comfort, stimulation, attention, praise, opportunities for shared activities, and social comparison (Buss, 1980). Children derive these benefits from both adults and peers, but in different ways.

Society has defined certain expectations for each party in the adult-child relationship. Interactions between adults and children are characterized by a difference in status. Adults'

refined skills, accumulated knowledge, and greater experience make them authority figures to children. Whether the relationship involves parent and child, teacher and pupil, or coach and player, adults are supposed to function as leaders and experts and children are expected to respond as followers and novices. Although these relationships can be marked by love and respect, they are basically unequal. That is, children must respond to adult initiatives (Youniss, 1980). These roles are clearly defined, and children have few chances to change them.

Peer relationships, on the other hand, give children special opportunities to learn among equals. With friends, a child can be expert in one circumstance and learner in another. Each child has chances to lead, to follow, to contribute ideas, to respond to suggestions, to negotiate, and to compromise.

Because society has few formal guidelines for children's interactions with peers, they can take risks with one another they would not attempt with elders. They can more easily speak up, disagree, exert their will, ignore a request, or bargain for power. They can afford to experiment with different behaviors, to seek new friends if they are rejected, or to develop new interests (Rubin, 1980). Thus, it is with peers that children learn the give and take that will influence their future relationships as adults (Hartup, 1982).

Peer relations also help children understand and value their own traits, attitudes, and skills by providing natural comparisons with age-mates: Am I tall? Am I a good singer? Will people listen to my ideas? Are there things I can do that others cannot? Am I the only one who has trouble with spelling? Does anyone else feel scared in the dark? Through their observation and interactions with peers, children check the validity of what they believe and feel about themselves (Asher, 1978).

Peer relationship provide an opportunity for children to learn new skills and refine current ones. Children know what is relevant to other children and so offer support and guidance in arenas overlooked or disdained by adults. The ability to spit between the teeth, jump double Dutch, balance on a skateboard, and clear the screen in Space Invaders are examples of accomplishments children may value. Age-mates can teach these things to one another unself-consciously and without the total disparity in status that marks the adult-child relationship. Additionally, only youngsters can truly appreciate the satisfaction and status that accomplishing such milestones represents.

Finally, it is in the peer group that children achieve a sense of belonging. They feel valued and important to people beyond their own family. Because friends offer support and affection by choice, they assure the child that he or she is a lovable, desirable companion.

For all of these reasons, children want and need friends. It is no surprise that much of their time and energy is devoted to answering the question "Who will be my friend?"

What Happens When Children Cannot Find a Friend

Because all relationships have their ups and downs, children eventually experience the woe of rejection by someone they wish would be their friend. Even children peers describe as popular are rebuffed about 30% of the time (Gottman and Parkhurst, 1979). This is a natural and normal part of growing up. When rejection occurs, children's reactions vary greatly from matter-of-fact acceptance to real anguish: one child will become depressed; another will do anything he or she can to regain the lost friendship; a third will immediately begin looking for a replacement (Rubin, 1980). Regardless of the response, the impact of this loss on the child should not be underestimated. Upset feelings should not be dismissed lightly, nor should children be chastised or ridiculed when friendships do not work out. It is usual for most children to recover in a reasonable time and engage in other productive relationships.

There are some children, however, who are consistently rejected by their peers or who themselves reject all possible friendship choices. This can be a problem for both the child and society because there is evidence that the quality of peer relationships in childhood has a major effect on adjustment in later life. Friendless children are unhappy children and have more than their share of difficulties as they grow older (Roff, Sells, and Golden, 1972; Cowen, et al., 1973; Furman and Buhrmester, 1982). For instance, they are more likely than their more popular counterparts to:

Become juvenile delinquents.
Drop out of school.
Receive a dishonorable discharge from the military.
Experience psychiatric problems.
Commit suicide.

No one knows for sure whether friendlessness causes these serious problems or whether the behavior traits that lead to delinquency and emotional instability also lead to peer rejection. In either case, there is a strong relationship between children's ability to form close friendships, later feelings of self-satisfaction, and the capacity to get along with others.

Although completely friendless children are rare, many youngsters grow up wishing they had more friends. For instance, one national study showed that 18 percent of the third-, fourth-, fifth-, and sixth-graders interviewed reported having no friends or only one friend (Gronlund, 1959). More recently, when grade-school children were asked to name three children they would choose for a friend, 10 percent of the youngsters were chosen by no one. An even larger percentage reported feeling lonely.

For many children, the critical factor is not how many friends they have, but the quality of the peer relationships they establish (Stocking, Arezzo, and Leavitt, 1980). Some children want many friends, and others are happy with only a few. Clearly, all children think having friends is important, and many wish they had more satisfying relationships with others.

CHILDREN'S CHANGING IDEAS ABOUT FRIENDSHIP

What exactly is a friend in the eyes of a child? Do children see their friends in the same way adults view theirs? What many adults may not know is that children's concept of friendship—their notion of how it works, their expectations, and the rules that govern their actions toward friends—changes over time.

Harvard researchers Robert and Anne Selman (1979) theorize that all children pass through a sequence of five overlapping stages. Each stage is characterized by its own distinct logic, which becomes increasingly complex as children mature.

In the beginning stages, children are preoccupied with their *own* emotions, with the physical characteristics of their companions, and with what is happening here and now. In the later stages, children are more sensitive to the desires and concerns of others, they appreciate psychological traits such as humor and trustworthiness, and they think about the future of their relationships as well as the present. Children progress from the first stage to the last as a result of age; increasing intellectual, physical, and language abilities; and accumulated experience.

Many children have temporary difficulties when their ideas about friendship lag behind or move far beyond those of their peers. These problems are reduced once children and their age-mates catch up to one another. In the meantime, children may choose to associate with younger or older peers who are in the same stage of thinking. Adults cannot necessarily accelerate children's progress through the sequence, but they can attempt to understand children's behavior by knowing more about their philosophy of friendship at each stage.

Stage Zero: Momentary Playmates (Three to Seven Years of Age)

Young children call ''friend'' those peers with whom they play most often or who engage in similar activities at a given time. In this way, children define their friends by proximity (''He's my friend; he lives next door''). In addition, friends are valued for their possessions (She's my friend. She has a Cabbage Patch doll'') or because they demonstrate visible physical skills (''He's my friend because he runs fast'').

Because children of this age are egocentric, they think only about their own side of the relationship. Consequently, they focus on what they want the other child to do for them. They have no thought of their own duties to the relationship and so do not consider how to match their behaviors to the other child's needs. Moreover, it is common for youngsters to assume that friends think just the way they do. If this proves false, they become very upset.

Stage zero youngsters are better at initiating an interaction than they are at responding to others' overtures. Hence, they may inadvertently ignore or actively reject other children's attempts to join their play. This can happen even when the nay-sayer has expressed interest in finding a friend. We have observed that this phenomenon happens most often once the play has been established. By that time, a solitary player or group of children has centered on carrying out the play episode in a particular way, which includes only those currently involved. It then becomes difficult for them to expand their thinking to envision how the newcomer could be included. Their refusal to allow another child access to their play is a cognitive dilemma, not a deliberate act of cruelty.

Stage One: One-Way Assistance (Four to Nine Years of Age)

In stage one, children identify those age-mates as friends whose behavior pleases them. For some children, good feelings are engendered by a playmate who will give them a turn, share gum, offer them rides on the new two-wheeler, pick them for the team, or save them a seat on the bus. For others, pleasure comes from having another child accept the turn, the gum, the ride, inclusion on the team, or the seat. Because each friend is concerned about whether his or her wants are being satisfied, neither necessarily considers what to do to bring pleasure to the other. If, by chance, their individual wants and behaviors are compatible, the friendship lasts. If not, the partners change in short order.

Hence, at this stage, children's friendship choices are based on their current need and therefore can change if those needs change or are not satisfied. For example, Lily initially may choose to play with Carmen because Carmen has lots of ideas and takes responsibility for directing the play. Lily is happy because she can play without having to think up what to do next. Carmen also is satisfied because there is no question as to who is in charge. Over time, as Lily has a chance to observe how Carmen asserts her will, she too may venture to test her own assertiveness. In the meantime, Carmen, who also has been observing and practicing, may grow tired of such a passive playmate. If the girls do not respond to each other's changing needs, chances are they each will select a new companion. It may take a short or a long time for a relationship to reach this point, and it is children, not adults, who are the best judge of when to change a relationship or move on.

Another characteristic of stage one is that children try out different social roles: leader, follower, negotiator, instigator, comic, collaborater, appeaser, comforter. As part of this process, they experiment with a variety of behaviors that may or may not match their usual manner. Thus, it is normal for children who are practicing their roles to manifest extreme examples of them. That is, a child who wants to be more assertive may become bossy and overbearing; a child who discovers the benefits of comedy may become silly or outrageous.

By the time youngsters reach this stage, their desire to have a friend is so strong that many prefer to play with an uncongenial companion rather than play alone. They will try almost anything to initiate a relationship and may attempt to bribe or coerce another child to like them by saying: "If you'll be my friend, I'll invite you to my party," or "If you don't let me have a turn, I won't be your friend." Children who resort to such tactics are not malicious, but are merely experimenting with what works and what does not.

Stage one also is notable for the fact that boys play with boys and girls play with girls. This occurs because children continue to focus on outward similarities, and gender is an obvious way of determining likeness.

Although youngsters concentrate much of their energy on the friendship process, they have difficulty maintaining more than one close relationship at a time. An outgrowth of their struggle to identify friends is that they become preoccupied with discussing who is their friend and who is not. This is when children can be overheard to say, "You can't be my friend; Mary's my friend." Pairs change from day to day and frequently are determined by who gets together first, by what people are wearing, or by a newfound common interest.

Stage Two: Two-Way, Fair-Weather Cooperation (Six to Twelve Years of Age)

The thinking of children at stage two has matured to the point at which they are able to consider both points of view in the friendship. This leads to a notion of justice that dictates how the relationship should proceed.

Children expect friends to be "nice" to each other and often trade favors as a way of helping each other satisfy their separate interests: "You helped me yesterday; I'll help you today"; "We're playing my game first and then your game." They recognize that each person should benefit from the relationship and that the friendship will break up if this does not occur: "If you call me names again, I won't be your friend"; "That's not fair! I waited for you yesterday." Friends are concerned about what each thinks of the other and evaluate their own actions as they feel the other might evaluate them: "Steve will like me if I learn to catch better"; "Nobody will like me with this fuzzy permanent."

It is in this stage that conformity in dress, language, and behavior reaches a peak as children try to find ways to fit in with the group. As a result, it becomes very important for children to carry a super-hero lunch box, wear corn rows, or take swimming lessons. Why? Because "All the other kids have one (or do it)." As can be seen from these examples, the emphasis throughout this period is similarity. Forming clubs is a natural outgrowth of this. Clubs, although short lived, have elaborate rules, and the major activity involves planning who will be included and who will be excluded. To further confirm their unity, friends share secrets, plans, and agreements.

Friendships tend to develop in pairs. In particular, groups of girlfriends are loose networks of best-friend partnerships; male friendship groups are characterized by broader interaction patterns and fewer best-friend relationships (Hartup, 1980). Within both male and female groups, friends are very possessive of each other, and jealousy over who is "friends" with whom is quite pronounced.

Stage Three: Intimate, Mutually Shared Relationships (Nine to Twelve Years of Age)

Stage three marks the first time that children view friendship as an ongoing relationship with shared goals. Now, children are collaborative rather than simply cooperative. This means they are not concerned with the tit-for-tat reciprocity that marked the previous stage; rather, they become involved in each other's personal lives

and have a stake in each other's happiness. They gain satisfaction from the emotional support they enjoy within the relationship. On this basis, friends share feelings and help each other solve personal conflicts and problems. They reveal thoughts and emotions to each other that they keep from everyone else. Friendship has now become intimate and the best-friend relationship a crucial one. Because this is such an intense learning experience, children often only focus on one best friend at a time. It is natural for them to become totally absorbed in each other. Such friendships are both exclusive and possessive. In other words, friends are not supposed to have another close friend, and they are expected to include each other in everything. Friends do share approved acquaintances but are not allowed to pursue a relationship with someone one of them does not like. The greatest betrayal comes when someone breaks these rules. Only after children have developed friendship to this point are they able to branch out and have close ties with more than one peer at a time.

Stage Four: Mature Friendships (Twelve Years of Age and Older)

For persons at the mature-friendship stage, emotional and psychological benefits are the most valued qualities of friendship. Friends are not as possessive of each other as they were in previous stages; they can have some dissimilar interests and can pursue activities separately. Children in this stage are able to allow their friends to develop other close relationships as well. Thus, they can have more than one friend at a time and can have friends who are not friends with each other. In this way, friendship becomes a bond that involves trust and support. These elements sometimes are attained by coming together and sometimes by letting go. As a result, friends now are able to remain close over long distances, over long periods of time, and in spite of long separations.

Choosing Friends

Eric and Sandy are like peas in a pod; they dress alike; they talk alike; they act alike. They are the best of friends.

Sasha and Tabitha are as different as night and day. One is short, one is tall; one is boisterous, one is quiet; one likes cats, one likes dogs. Still, they are inseparable.

Adults often wonder why children choose the friends they do. Name, physical appearance, race, gender, age, ability, and attitudes all are cues children consider in selecting a potential friend. For instance, names go through cycles of popularity. Children who have names other youngsters like often are viewed as the most desirable playmates, and those who possess unpopular names are not as sought after (McDavid and Harari, 1966). The attraction of a particular name varies according to culture and geographic region. In recent years, Linda, Stephen, David, Jennifer, and Lisa have been among the names that many American children found most appealing (Beadle, 1973). On the other hand, names such as Frances, Hugo, and Bertha seem to carry with them certain social risks. It should not be too surprising that the names children prefer are those that occur most frequently in the population (Lansky, 1984). One possible explanation is that such names are familiar ones, and children may feel more comfortable approaching a child whose name is not entirely new to them (Asher, Oden, and Gottman, 1977). Although it is not preordained that children with unusual names will be friendless, they may have to work harder at making advances to their peers rather than waiting to be approached first.

Physical appearance and likeness. Another factor that contributes to children's friendship selection is personal appearance. Children who are overweight, mentally retarded, handicapped, slovenly, or physically unattractive are less likely to be chosen as friends than are youngsters who fit children's concept of beauty (Hartup, 1982; Langlois, 1985). Interestingly, the same standard of beauty is held by children of all ages and cultures and fits many of the stereotypes promoted through the popular media (Cross and Cross, 1971). Long hair, fine features, and wide eyes set far apart are some of the attributes many children find appealing. Children attribute the positive qualities of friendliness, intelligence, and social competence to those they consider attractive. Likewise, they associate negative attributes with peers they think of as unattractive (Dion and Berscheid, 1974; Lerner and Lerner, 1977).

Children also pick their friends based on race and are most likely to choose friends from their own racial group (Shaw, 1973). However, parental attitudes do influence how children feel about making friends with someone of another race or culture. If children perceive their parents as accepting of racial differences, they are more likely to include children of different racial or ethnic backgrounds among their friends.

FIGURE 13-1 Children who have common interests and opportunities to interact informally become friends. SOURCE: Joel Gordon 1980

Gender and age also are dominant considerations in who is "friends" with whom. Children prefer same-sex, same-age peers throughout childhood and even at a very early age tend to exclude opposite sex and non-agemates from their play (Hartup, 1982; Singleton, 1974). Although friendships between males and females do occur, same-sex friendships tend to be more lasting and stable over time. This is due in no small measure to the reinforcement children receive from adults and peers for choosing friends of their own gender (Fagot, 1977; Serbin, Tonick, and Sternglanz, 1977). When friendships develop between children of different ages, it usually is because the participants are developmentally similar in some ways. For instance, shy children who have less confidence in their interaction skills may seek out younger friends with whom they feel more comfortable socially (Zimbardo and Radl, 1982).

Friends also may resemble one another in terms of achievement, physical or cognitive skill, and degree of sociability (Cavallaro and Porter, 1980). Consequently, it is not unusual to see children choose as friends peers who share their love of sports, reading, chess, or stamp collecting. Nor is it uncommon for bright, agile, impulsive, or outgoing children to seek friends much like themselves. In addition to searching for likenesses, youngsters often choose as friends those peers whose characteristics complement their own personality and capacities (Rubin, 1980). This often involves attributes that they themselves lack and for which the other child can serve as a model. Thus, loud children and quiet children, active children and passive children, serious children and cut-ups may choose one another as friends. Yet, even when this occurs, one must remember that these youngsters have found enough common ground that they see more similarities than differences in each other.

Concurrently, when children who are dissimilar in some fashion discover that they share like attitudes, they feel more positive about one another. This awareness facilitates friendly relations between children who initially perceive themselves as totally different. Such knowledge has been found to promote increased friendships among children of differing races and between nonhandicapped and handicapped youngsters (Byrne and Griffit, 1966; Insko and Robinson, 1967).

Children look for obvious external clues to determine who they will choose for a friend. This means that adults will see children select friends who are most like them: boys will pick boys; girls will pick girls; black children will stay together and so will whites. This explains the cliquishness that develops in groups. Adults who want children to experience the rewards of friendships with children of the opposite sex, of another race, or whose abilities do not match their own must provide opportunities for the children to recognize more subtle similarities. Specific strategies for achieving this aim are presented in the skills section of this chapter.

MAKING FRIENDS

External attributes, such as name, physical appearance, race, gender, and age attract certain children to each other initially. It is at this point of attraction that the enterprise of making friends begins. Making friends involves three distinct processes: making contact, maintaining positive relationships, and negotiating conflict.

Making Contact

Before a friendship can "get off the ground," one person must make an approach and another must respond. How this contact is carried out influences each child's perception of the other. Children make good impressions when they engage in the following actions (Gottman, Gonso, and Rasmussen, 1975; Stocking, Arezzo, and Leavitt, 1980):

Smile and speak pleasantly or offer greetings.	"Hi" or "Hey! What's up?"
Ask for information.	"What's your name?" or "Where's the cafeteria?"
Respond to others' greetings and inquiries.	"I'm new, too" or "Come with me. I'll show you."
Offer information.	"My name's Rosalie. This is my first day at Central."
Invite participation.	"Wanna play catch?" or "You can be on our team."

By these signals, children are able to let others know that they want to be friends. Another behavior widely interpreted as a friendly overture is imitation. Children enjoy being imitated and are apt to be friendly toward peers who copy their actions (Guralnick, 1976; Hartup, 1978; Widerstrom, 1982). Thus, children can slowly move into a game or activity by matching their behavior to that of the other players.

From this discussion, it can be seen that youngsters who are cordial elicit positive reactions and are better accepted by their age-mates (Charlesworth and Hartup, 1967; Kohn, 1966). This is true whether the child is the initiator or the respondent. Yet, although the logic of acting pleasantly in order to gain friends may seem obvious and the related strategies self-evident, many youngsters fail to make the connection. These are children whose timing is off or who have the right idea but an inappropriate way of showing it. They may be truly unaware of the importance of such strategies or may fail to recognize how or why their behavior affects others as it does. Whatever the explanation, such children often attempt to make contact by grabbing, pushing, barging in, whining, threatening, ignoring, begging, criticizing, or being bossy (Leiter, 1977; Stocking, Arezzo, and Leavitt, 1980). Children who rely on these approaches are rejected frequently. As their lack of success becomes more habitual, they tend to withdraw or become hostile. Both reactions exacerbate their difficulties (Asher and Renshaw, 1981). Over time, they develop a reputation of being unfriendly or undesirable as a playmate. As a result, not only are their own attempts at contact rebuffed, but the other children stop initiating contacts with them as well. This causes the offensive youngsters to be further isolated and have fewer opportunities for positive interactions. Hence, it becomes increasingly difficult for such children to break out of this maladaptive pattern of behavior on their own. In cases such as these, adults can help children learn to make more positive contacts and hence improve their chances of finding a friend.

Maintaining Positive Relationships

The positive behaviors that characterize successful beginnings continue to be important as the relationship grows. Popular children of all ages are described by peers as sensitive, kind, flexible, and fun to be with (Hartup, 1970; Roff, Sells, and Golden, 1972). The following techniques characterize their interactions with others:

Expressing interest.	Smiles, nods, establishes eye contact, asks related questions.
Cooperating.	Takes turns, agrees to share something, agrees to work together.
Expressing acceptance.	Listens to another child's ideas, adopts another child's approach to a play situation.
Expressing affection.	Hugs, holds hands, or says: "I like you" or "Let's be friends."
Expressing empathy.	"That's a neat picture you made," "You look

	sad; want me to sit with you while you wait?''
Offering help and suggestions.	''Maybe we could try it this way.'' ''I'll hold the box while you tie it.''
Praising playmates.	''That was a great hit.'' ''Neat idea! I think it'll work.'' ''You're pretty.''

Children who use these tactics actively demonstrate respect and affection for others. This has the happy outcome of making them desirable companions because people seek out friends who are enjoyable (Stocking, Arezzo, and Leavitt, 1980). Thus, it is true that positive behaviors elicit positive responses, which in turn reinforce children's efforts and prompt them to continue their successful actions.

In the same way that positive cycles are established, so, too, are negative ones. Children who are aggressive or uncooperative or who act silly, show off, or display immature behavior irritate, frustrate, and offend their peers. They tend to further isolate themselves by daydreaming or escalating their negative behavior (Asher and Renshaw, 1981; Gottman, Gonso, and Rasmussen, 1975).

Similar problems arise when children try to act appropriately but misjudge how to do it. They may rely on insincere flattery, express their affection too roughly (giving bear hugs), or communicate their appreciation too effusively. Others miss the mark by constantly correcting rather than suggesting or taking over instead of merely helping. In any case, these behavior patterns sabotage children's efforts to maintain friendships over time.

Negotiating Conflict

Perhaps the most severe test of a relationship occurs when the friends disagree. How the conflict is managed on both sides determines to a large extent whether the friendship will continue or be abandoned. Children who use constructive ways of resolving differences, while still meeting their own needs, are most successful in pursuing lasting relationships (Gottmann, Gonso, and Rasmussen, 1975). This is because they are able to save face and at the same time take into account another person's perspectives. Children who are so passive that they never stand up for themselves lose self-respect and, eventually, the respect of peers. Those who respond aggressively also are rejected. Neither extreme is conducive to eliciting positive reactions.

There is a strong correlation between children's effective use of negotiation skills and their ability to communicate accurately (Rubin, 1972). Successful conflict negotiation depends on all parties having a common idea of the source of the problem and being able to express to others their ideas for a solution (Asher, Oden, and Gottman, 1977) Children who use threats, shame, or coercion to force a solution violate these fundamental requirements. Consequently, other children begin to avoid them or retaliate in kind. Successful negotiators are children who implement the following strategies (Stocking, Arezzo and Leavitt, 1980):

Express personal rights, needs, or feelings.	''I want a chance to pick the movie this time.''
Listen to and acknowledge others' rights and feelings.	''Yeah, you *have* been waiting a long time to see that movie.''
Suggest nonviolent solutions to conflicts.	''Let's flip for it.''
Explain the reasoning behind a proposed solution.	''This way, we each get a chance.''
Stand up against unreasonable demands.	''No, you got to pick the last time. Now, it's my turn.''
Accept reasonable disagreement.	''Okay, I hadn't thought of that.''

| Compromise on solutions. | "Let's see both, or go swimming instead." |

Improving Children's Friendship-Making Skills

Because the distinction is so clear between successful friendship-making strategies and those that are not, you may wonder why any child would choose techniques doomed to fail. Children are not born automatically knowing the best ways to make friends. They must learn by observing others, by practicing, by experimenting with a variety of social behaviors, and by experiencing the consequences of their actions (Dodge, 1983). Children who are better observers and more accurate evaluators of what is effective and what is not acquire friends more easily than those who make poor observations and assessments or those who have poor role models at home or among peers. This does not mean the children who experience difficulty have no chance for improvement. On the contrary, there is encouraging evidence that children can learn how to make productive contacts, maintain positive relationships, and manage conflicts constructively (Asher and Renshaw, 1981; Kostelnik and Stein, 1986; Ladd and Oden, 1979).

The behaviors designated as successful for each phase of the friendship-making process are, in fact, skills that children can learn and then adopt for their own use. Three methods adults can use to teach children these skills are to model them for children via friendship skits, to assist youngsters in role-playing friendship skills themselves, and to train children to use friendship skills by way of friendship coaching.

Friendship skits. Research has shown that children improve in their ability to assimilate friendship skills when they have a chance to watch enactments of them while a narrator points out instances of their use (Evers and Schwarz, 1973; O'Connor, 1972). Such skits frequently are presented to children using puppets, dolls, or small figures. A majority of the studies conducted thus far have involved filmed demonstrations; however, these are not easily available to most practitioners. Fortunately, research has shown that live demonstrations with props are a good substitute (Kostelnik and Stein, 1986).

Role-playing friendship skills. A variation on skits with props is to have children role-play each character's part and then report their feelings and reactions to each role (Spivack and Shure, 1974). Onlookers and participants then discuss what transpired and suggest alternate courses of action. Through role-playing, children try out various roles and experience the consequences associated with them in a risk-free, "pretend" situation. They also obtain concrete examples of social behavior that are easier to recognize than those offered through discussion alone.

Friendship coaching. For some children, the methods just described are not enough to help them assimilate the social skills that lead to peer acceptance. These are youngsters who, over time, demonstrate an inability to pick up and act on cues they receive from age-mates. In some cases, they are totally unaware of how to endear themselves to peers. In other circumstances, they can describe relevant social behaviors but do not demonstrate them in their own interactions. Such children have shown to benefit from direct, individual instruction or *coaching* (Feshback, 1978; Kostelnik and Stein, 1986; Oden and Asher, 1977). A variety of coaching methods have been developed. All include the same basic steps: discussion, demonstration, practice, and evaluation.

SKILLS FOR SUPPORTING CHILDREN'S FRIENDSHIPS

Children vary in the degree to which they will find adult support necessary and beneficial. However, all children profit when adults create an environment in which their friendships are respected and encouraged. The following guidelines will help you create such an environment for the children with whom you work.

1. Provide opportunities for children to be with their friends informally,—to talk, to play, and to enjoy one another's com- *pany.* In group settings, develop a daily routine that includes planned times when children can respond to one another freely. Don't fill every minute with adult-oriented tasks and enforced silence. Also, these planned times should not consist solely of transitions between activities or structured talking times like "circle time" or "show and tell." Unstructured time spent with peers is neither wasted nor uneducational. Rather, it provides rich opportunities for children to practice social skills and to learn more about themselves.

FIGURE 13-2 Shy children gain confidence when playing with younger children whose social skills more nearly match their own.
SOURCE: H. Armstrong Roberts

2. *Plan ways to pair children in order to facilitate interactions.* Pairing children gives them a chance to practice their friendship-making skills in a relatively risk-free situation. Assign children to do jobs together or have them carry out a joint project as a way to create common interests. Children feel closer when they see themselves working toward a collaborative goal. Finally, encourage parents to carpool or to invite agemates home for a visit as another way to provide contact and opportunities for discovery of common interests. When you first team two children, point out some similarities you have observed or give them an opportunity to discover some for themselves. This is particularly true when pairing children who outwardly seem much different. Remember that it is the perceived similarities that cement a friendship.

3. *Pair a shy child with a younger playmate who is less sophisticated socially.* Begin by pairing him or her with a younger child of the same gender. Gradually, include agemates of the same and opposite sex. This arrangement enables the shy child to practice social skills with a nonthreatening, often openly approving younger admirer (Zimbardo and Radl, 1982).

4. *Take children's friendships seriously.* Listen when children talk about their friends. Reflect their involvement and concerns. Ask questions to show your interest. Never minimize the importance of children's friendships by ignoring, dismissing, teasing, shaming, or denying children's emotions.

5. *Carry out group discussions that focus on children's self-discovered similarities.* First, set the scene by having children discuss their reaction to an adult-posed condition, for instance, ''Things I like best.'' Then, invite each child to answer a question such as ''Paul and I both like . . . or ''I like the Mets and so does . . .'' This tactic helps children recog-

nize peers with whom they share similar attitudes, interests, and concerns.

6. *Help children learn each other's names.* Because names are a basic form of recognition, children feel most comfortable making contact with peers whose names they know. Less common names can become familiar if you refer to each child by name. Make sure you know how to pronounce every child's name correctly and that you do not avoid using names that are unfamiliar or unattractive to you. Use children's names when you praise them as a way to create a positive image of each child to the group.

7. *Give children on-the-spot information to help them recognize the friendly overtures of others.* Children often overlook or misinterpret the friendly advances of other youngsters because they are so involved in what they are doing that they are unable to recognize the positive nature of the approach. Instead, they may interpret the newcomer as a potential competitor for space or materials and thus feel threatened rather than pleased. Be alert for such occurrences. Step in if you see a child rebuff another without giving a reason. Paraphrase the newcomer's positive aim. Then, let the child decide for himself or herself whether the contact is welcome. Do not force a youngster to accept the attentions of another if the idea continues to be repugnant.

Frequently, however, children will be more receptive to another's overtures once the friendly intentions are made clear. For example, Matt was an active four-year-old who longed for a friend. He frequently talked with teachers about who his friends might be. Yet, his actions often contradicted his words. One day, he had the entire block area to himself. He worked for a long time building a bus. As he was busily ''driving to Chicago,'' Courtney arrived on the scene and asked if she could go, too (the perfect opportunity for a friendly contact!). Matt scowled and said, "No." Courtney repeated her request and was again rebuffed. This time she said: "Well, I'll just stand here on the corner until someone gets off. Then, I'll get on." Matt looked confused. At this point, an adult approached and said: "Matt, you're having fun driving to Chicago. Courtney is telling you she would like to play. She wants to be a passenger on your bus. That way, she can be your friend." Matt looked pleased and relieved. He had not recognized the cues Courtney was using to signify her interest in his game. Information provided by the adult put a whole new light on the situation, and the two children played "bus" for most of the morning.

8. Help children recognize how their behavior affects their ability to make friends. Frequently, children are unaware of the link between what they do and how other people react. Offer information to make this association more clear. For instance, Steven pushed Daisy to get her attention. She stalked off. He became angry when she rejected him. The adult noted his surprise, took him aside, and said: "It seems as if you want to be friends with Daisy. Pushing hurts. When you push her, it makes her so angry that she doesn't want to play with you. Friends don't hurt each other. Next time, you could say her name and tell her what you want." The adult gave Steven important information that he had not picked up very well on his own. This information would have to be repeated several times and in several different circumstances before Steven could really follow the advice. If the negative pattern persisted, Steven would be a likely candidate for the coaching strategies discussed later in this chapter.

Information need not be confined to corrections. Tell children about the positive skills they exhibit so they can repeat them another time. For instance, if you notice children sharing, taking turns, smiling at each other, or coming to a compromise, point out the positive effects these actions have on their relations with one another: "You two figured out a way that you could both wash the blackboards. That was a friendly way to settle your disagreement."

9. Get children involved at the beginning of a play episode so they will not be viewed as interlopers. Children who hang back before attempting to join a group often are penalized because once the group has been established, it is difficult for its members to imagine any other configuration. If you notice that certain children are hesitant to become involved and subsequently are shut out, try one of the following approaches.

First, plan ahead with the child and help her or him identify an activity to choose as soon as play groups begin to form. In this way, the child will not have to cross any social barriers but instead will be an initial participant. If this is too difficult for the child, an alternative is to help her or him move into the group with you. To do this, you might choose a potential role and approach the activity within the role. For instance, if several children are pretending to fly to the moon, you could walk toward them, saying: "Carol and I will be Mission Control. We'll talk to you up in the spacecraft." As Carol becomes more comfortable and the group more accepting, gradually back out of the play. Do not be surprised if at first Carol walks out when you do. With your continued support, she eventually will feel more relaxed and be able to maintain her membership in the group on her own.

A second tactic is to advise a hesitant child to play near the desired group and at the same type of activity. Gradually, the group may allow that child to join them and become their friend. An alternative to this approach is to help the child build a new group by inviting other children to draw, build, compute, or cook with her or him.

10. Help children endure the sorrows of friendship. When a potential friend rejects them, an old friend snubs them, or a good friends moves away, children have a real sense of loss. Their feelings range from misery to frustration to fury—all of which are normal reactions. As an adult, you cannot assuage the child's feelings, no matter how much you would like him or her to be spared. You can accept the child's emotions, reflect them, and talk about them, if the child so desires. You also can offer your condolences: "I'm sorry you and Tricia weren't able to patch up your differences. It's really sad to lose a friend." Another important way to provide support is to not push children into new relationships before they are ready.

The strategies just described are simple ones that build on skills you have learned in previous chapters: reflection, giving information, and supporting children's play. The conflict-negotiation skills you have recently learned also facilitate friendly relations among children. These approaches are relatively informal and are easily integrated into day-to-day interactions. Later, we will explore two additional techniques that are more formal and require advanced planning: presenting friendship activities to children and friendship coaching.

11. Carry out group discussions that high-light friendship-related facts and principles. Refer to Table 13-1 for examples of friendship facts and principles appropriate for children aged two through twelve and to Appendix A for a more comprehensive listing. Introduce one or two concepts at a time for children to explore. You may stimulate their thinking by reading a book, telling a story, or showing them pictures that relate to the ideas you have chosen. Prompt discussion through the use of open-ended questions such as "How does it feel when a good friend

moves away?", "What can you do when a friend hurts your feelings?", or "How can you let someone know you want to be friends?" Listen carefully. Reflect children's answers. Offer relevant information as openings in the conversation occur. Do not be concerned with obtaining a "correct" answer or reaching consensus. Instead, focus on allowing children to explore each idea in their own way. Provide every youngster with an opportunity to contribute, but avoid pressuring children into talking if they prefer not to. Summarize key points of the discussion, either aloud or on paper, for the children to refer to later.

How to Design Skits that Demonstrate Friendship Skills

Children as young as two and a half years of age have shown interest in watching short dramatizations. Children of that age benefit most when professionals simply act out a scene and then explain it. Older preschoolers and grade-school children benefit from additional group discussion as well

1. Choose a friendship skill to teach. It usually is best to focus on only one skill at a time. This way, children can more easily identify the exact behavior being demonstrated.

2. Choose the medium through which the skill will be demonstrated. Dolls, pictures, and puppets all are good choices. Children learn best from concrete examples that include props they can point to, handle, and discuss.

3. Outline a script that consists of five parts. The script should include a demonstration of the skill, a demonstration of lack of the skill, an explanation by the adult, discussion by the children, and an opportunity for children to use the props to make up their own version of the skit. The best skits are only a few lines long.

TABLE 13-1 A Partial Listing of Friendship Facts and Principles

Friends Defined

1. Friends are people who:
   a. Like you.
   b. Like to be near you.
   c. Seek you out.
   d. Say, "I like you."
   e. Invite you to play with them or use their things.
   f. Like to talk with you.
2. Some friends are members of your family; some are outside your family.
3. Friends may be like you in many ways and different from you in others.
4. Friends may be of any age.
5. Friends may live near each other or far away.
6. People experience different feelings about their friends.
7. Sometimes, friends hurt each other's feelings.
8. Sometimes, friends can forgive each other and sometimes, they cannot.
9. Having a friend:
   a. Makes people feel good.
   b. Gives people someone with whom to share ideas, play, and work.
   c. Gives people someone with whom to share secrets.
   d. Gives people someone with whom to share feelings.
10. Sometimes, friendships end.
11. It can be sad or confusing when someone no longer wants to be your friend.
12. People can make new friends.

Making and Keeping Friends

13. People's behavior affects their ability to make or keep friends.
14. There are obvious ways in which people use their bodies that let others know they want to be friends. These include: smiling, playing near someone else, and looking directly at the person with whom they are speaking.
15. People feel friendly toward people who:
    a. Express an interest in what they are doing.
    b. Share.
    c. Listen to their ideas.
    d. Let them do some things their way.
    e. Have interesting ideas.
16. People feel less friendly toward people who:
    a. Hurt them.
    b. Make fun of them.
    c. Grab their things.
    d. Tattle on them.

4. Write out the statements and questions you will use to stimulate discussion in the group. Discussion will revolve around which character was demonstrating the skill and which was not, how viewers arrived at their conclusions, and what skill they would suggest the characters use the next time.

5. Rehearse the skit in advance. Gather your props. Practice the skit, privately or with friends. Revise the skit until you can do it from memory and feel comfortable about carrying it out.

6. Present your skit to children either in a group situation or in a one-to-one interaction. Speak clearly and with expression. Elicit group discussion. Listen carefully and accept children's answers nonjudgmentally. If children are way off track, give them information that will clarify the situation and make a mental note to revise your skit to make the point more clear next time. Praise children as they watch and again as they discuss what they have seen.

7. Later in the day, evaluate how well your skit got your point across. If it seemed that children were interested and were able to generate relevant conversation about the selected topic, plan to repeat the same skit using different props and dialogues the next time. Over time, gradually introduce new information for youngsters to consider. If children were disinterested, determine whether they were distracted by things in the environment or whether your activity was unappealing. Observe children carefully or ask their opinions as a way to find out. Children will not be attentive if the skit is too advanced or too babyish, if you fumble or seem tense, or if you press too hard for one "right" answer.

A sample of a type of skit that can be effective with young children is outlined in Table 13-2. It illustrates a scenario designed to teach friendship-initiation skills. Such vignettes could be adapted to illustrate any of the friendship skills discussed in this chapter.

8. Encourage older children to make up skits of their own that dramatize a problem with friends. Sometimes, children between ten and twelve years of age will be willing to enact their skits for peers or for younger children. The same procedures just discussed apply, regardless of the age of the skit planner.

How to Teach Children to Role-Play

Most children aged four through twelve enjoy role-playing. However, it cannot be assumed that they automatically know how to do it. Rather, helping professionals must teach youngsters how to take on a role prior to expecting them to glean factual information or insights from enacting a vignette or from watching one carried out by others. This can be accomplished using the following strategies.

1. Explain what role-playing is. Define it as a particular way of pretending in order to present a lesson. Describe roles as parts children play in a scene. Tell youngsters they may now act out how they would feel in a given situation or how they think another person might feel under those circumstances. Point out to the children that for each role-play episode, some youngsters will be taking on roles while others watch, and everyone will have a chance to discuss the results. Show them the boundaries of the physical area in which the enactment will take places as well as any props available to the actors.

2. Set the scene. Present a theme, script, or problem for the role-players to act out. You may also suggest certain emotions for them to portray. Give each child a specific role to play and a few hints about related actions or words that might characterize their role.

TABLE 13-2 Sample Skit for Teaching a Friendship Skill

General Instructions

Seat children in a semicircle facing you. Make sure everyone can see your face and hands and the space directly in front of you. If you are sitting on the floor, it is useful to kneel so you are more easily visible to the children. If you are sitting in a chair, a low bench or table can be used to display the props. As the script unfolds, manipulate the dolls in corresponding actions. Be expressive with your face and your voice. Use dialogue for the characters that seems appropriate for the situation; use different voices for each character.

Materials

Two dolls (or puppets); several small, colored blocks.

Focus

This skit incorporates friendship facts and principles 1, 26, 27, 28, and 29.

Procedure

Adult: Today, we are going to talk about friends. Here are two dolls. We are going to pretend that these dolls are real children just like you. Their names are Max and Gus. They are four years old and go to a school just like ours. Watch carefully and see what happens when Gus and Max try to be friends.

Set up one doll (Gus) as if "playing" with several blocks. Place second doll (Max) facing Gus but at least a foot away.

Adult: Here is Gus. He is playing alone with the blocks and is having a good time. Max sees Gus and would really like to play with him, so he watches Gus very carefully. Gus keeps playing; he doesn't look up. Max feels sad. He thinks Gus doesn't want to be friends.

Questions for discussion:
1. Who was playing?
2. Who wanted to play?
3. Did Gus know Max wanted to play?

As children answer these questions, provide information to help in their deliberations; "Gus was so busy playing, he didn't look up. That means he never even saw Max standing there. He didn't know Max wanted to play. Watch again and see what Max does differently this time.

Adult: Here is Gus. He is playing alone with the blocks and is having a good time. Max sees Gus and really would like to play with him. So, he watches Gus very carefully. Gus keeps playing. He doesn't look up. Max walks over to Gus and says: "Hi. I like your building. I'll help you get some more blocks."

Questions for discussion:
1. Who was playing?
2. Who wanted to play?
3. Did Gus know Max wanted to play?
4. How could he tell?
5. What will Gus do next?
6. Let's think of some other ways Max could let Gus know he wants to play.

(table continued)

TABLE 13-2 *(continued)*

As children suggest ideas, paraphrase them and write them down where all the children can see them. Accept all ideas regardless of originality, correctness, or feasibility. If children have difficulty thinking of ideas, prompt them by providing information: "Sometimes, when people want to play, they can say: Hi. I want to play, or they can ask a question like, What are you building? This lets the other person know they want to be friends. What do you think Max could do?" Once children have suggested their ideas, replay the scene using each suggestion, one at a time. Ask the children to predict how Gus will react in each case. Play out the scene as they suggest. Provide further information as appropriate: "John, you said Max could help Gus build. Let's try that." (Maneuver the dolls and provide appropriate dialogue.) "Tell me what you think Gus will do now."

3. Help the role-players get into character. Allow youngsters to select a prop or costume item as a way to further establish their roles. This step is critical for children younger than seven years of age who otherwise might have difficulty enacting and sustaining a role. Young children may need to hang a picture or symbol around their neck if the role is abstract or a good prop is not available.

4. Watch the role-players attentively. Applaud their efforts.

5. Discuss what occurred during the role-play episode. Elicit comments both from the participants and the observers. Refer to the friendship facts presented in Table 13-1 as a way to support and extend the discussion.

6. Ask children to develop alternate scenarios. Have youngsters act these out, then discuss the varying outcomes.

7. Summarize the key points of the children's discussion. Identify similarities in their thinking as well as differences. Highlight the one or two major points that seemed most important to the group.

How to Carry Out Friendship Coaching

Coaching begins when you have determined that a child has fallen into a destructive pattern of interactions or is unhappy with his or her inability to make friends and seems at a loss for what to do next. Coaching consists of short, regularly scheduled sessions with the child in which you work on particular friendship skills together. Your approach is very similar to that suggested for use with children in groups. The difference is that you are working with one child at a time and giving that child specific, on-the-spot feedback about his or her performance. Some children may need considerable help with several skills, and others may progress rapidly with more limited intervention.

1. Select a skill to work on. Identify a friendship skill that will address the child's particular difficulty. It can be challenging to narrow your choice to one skill if you see a child who seems to be doing "everything" wrong: ignoring peers, rejecting them, grabbing, pushing, interrupting, taking over, teasing. It is tempting to plan a complete make-over. However, trying to do too much all at once usually ends in frustration and failure. A better approach is to work on one problem area at a time. In this way, both the child and you experience success each step of the way. This encourages continued efforts and may ease the way for learning in related areas.

2. Initiate coaching. Experts emphasize the importance of selecting a neutral time to begin coaching rather than immediately following a disagreeable encounter. Otherwise, the targeted child may feel singled out and react defensively (Stocking, Arezzo, and Leavitt, 1980). Your goal is to have children perceive these sessions as enjoyable activities, not as the negative consequence of their behavior. Initiate the coaching session by taking the child aside at some dispassionate time and saying: "Robert, today you and I are going to have a special time together. Come with me and I'll tell you all about it."

3. *Describe the skill to the child.* Introduce the skill you are going to focus on, such as expressing acceptance, by describing it in observable terms rather than generalizations.

Appropriate: "When you want someone to be your friend, it is important to listen to his (her) ideas. That means looking at him (her) and not talking while he (she) is trying to tell you something."

Inappropriate: "When you want someone to be your friend, you should act more interested."

4. *Demonstrate the skill.* Model the behavior or point it out in other children who are playing so the child can actually see what you are talking about: "Here, I'll show you. Tell me one way we could play with these puppets and I will listen to your idea" or "Look at Jeremy—he's listening very carefully to what Sondra is saying."

5. *Provide a rationale for the skill.* Give the child a reason for why the new behavior is important: "When you listen to people's ideas, it makes them feel good. That helps them to like you better."

6. *Tell the child to practice the skill.* Have the child rehearse the skill with you. It usually is helpful if the child can first differentiate between examples of good and poor skill

usage. Again, you can demonstrate or use puppets and dolls: "Here are two puppets, Rollo and Gertrude. Rollo is telling Gertrude an idea. Watch and listen. Tell me how well Gertrude shows Rollo she wants to be friends." After several demonstrations, Robert can then rehearse the new behavior by role-playing with you or another child or by manipulating the dolls and puppets himself. This opportunity to practice helps children feel more comfortable with their new skills. They can more directly experience what it is like to be both the recipient and the initiator of varying social behaviors. As a result of this phase, children may suggest their own ideas about other ways to demonstrate the skill. They also have a chance to ask questions and discuss their emotions and reactions.

7. *Evaluate the child's use of the skill.* Praise children's efforts and improved performance throughout the practice session. Point out instances of the child's appropriate use of the skill. Commend the child for trying. Provide physical support through smiles and hugs.

In addition, offer corrective feedback aimed at improving the child's use of the skill. Focus on behaviors: "You listened to some of my ideas. You didn't hear them all. Let's try again."

8. *Repeat the coaching procedure several times.* Change the props and the hypothetical circumstances more than once. Remember that children vary in the rate at which they learn new behaviors. Some will progress quickly; others will move at a much slower pace. As you see each child increase his or her use of the targeted skill in day-to-day interactions, you should praise their efforts and offer some on-the-spot information that will help them polish their performance. As improvement becomes evident, plan to introduce a new skill for the child to work on or, if that is not necessary, gradually fade out the

coaching sessions. Coaching should not be ended abruptly at the first signs of progress. Children need the continued feedback and reinforcement such sessions offer in order to maintain their use of each skill. As they experience more and more success with peers, the natural environment will become rewarding enough that the coaching sessions are no longer the child's primary source of reinforcement.

Children who need coaching are those who have not acted on the subtle cues present in the everyday environment; therefore, the adult must make those cues more blatant and focus the child's attention on them. The professional's role goes beyond discussing and pointing out appropriate skills to include the elements of practice and evaluation. These latter steps are critical, both in the session and outside of it.

PITFALLS TO AVOID

Regardless of whether you are supporting children's friendships individually or in groups, informally or in structured activities, there are certain pitfalls you should avoid.

Barging in too quickly. When adults see children struggling over friendship issues, such as who will play with whom, or when adults see children using hurtful or inappropriate means of making their friendship preferences known, it is tempting to step in as a mediating figure immediately.

No one likes to see children hurting each other's feelings. On the other hand, children benefit when they have an opportunity to try out strategies and solutions on their own. Unless there is some physical danger that should be dealt with quickly, it is important to take a moment to observe the situation and to thoughtfully determine what form of intervention is best. At times, simply moving physically closer to the situation defuses it. In other instances, direct use of the strategies described in this chapter is more appropriate. Regardless of which course you follow, remember that the more children practice friendship skills with the least help from you, the more quickly they will learn how to be successful in their interactions with peers.

Missing opportunities to promote friendly interactions among children. Adults sometimes become so centered on interacting with the children themselves that they fail to recognize opportunities to help children increase their friendship skills with peers. For example, an adult who is carrying on a conversation with one child may view the arrival of a second child as an interruption or may carry on two separate conversations simultaneously. A better approach would be to use reflections or provide information that would help the children talk to each other as well as to the adult:

Juan: We went to the store last night.

Anita: We had pizza for dinner.

Adult: You both did interesting things last night. Juan, tell Anita what you saw at the store.

Insisting that everyone be "friends." Although it is natural for adults to want children to like each other, it does not always turn out that way. Instead, children in groups tend to form close relationships with only a few children at a time. Liking someone is not something that can be dictated; insisting that everyone like each other not only is unrealistic but denies children's real emotions. In every group, there are people who rub each other the wrong way. Part of what children can learn is how to interact constructively with the people they like best *and* the people they like least. Adults must show children alternative acceptable ways of making their preferences known.

Requiring everyone to be together all the time. It is a mistake to think that friendship is built on constant companionship. Although familiarity does breed common interests, forcing children to play together when they do not really want to detracts from, rather than enhances, their relationships. With this in mind, adults are cautioned to allow children opportunities to engage in solitary activity and to help each child to constructively explain his or her desire for privacy to curious or well-meaning peers. In addition, adults should aid the child who is rebuffed by a peer who would rather be alone. This can be accomplished by explaining the nay-sayer's desire for privacy and by helping the youngster who is turned away to find an alternate activity or companion.

Breaking up children's friendships. At any time in the late preprimary and early elementary years, a child will develop a best-friend relationship. During this time, the two children involved become inseparable. Adults often worry that this closeness is interfering with the children's ability to develop other friendships. As a result, adults frequently decide to intervene by limiting the children's time together. This is a mistake. As children begin to develop "special relationships," it is natural for them to center on the object of their admiration.

It must be remembered that when children first become interested in making friends, their main goal is simply to be included in group activities. However, once this has been accomplished, children begin to want to have an influence on their relationships. In other words, they want others to listen to their ideas, accept their suggestions, and involve them in decision making. From the children's viewpoint, this is a relatively risky process. So, they seek the security of a one-to-one relationship within which to test their skills. In friendship pairs, risks are reduced because the two children involved come to know each other well and therefore are more accurate in predicting another's reaction. In addition, they build up a history of good times, which helps them weather the bad times that are sure to occur. It takes a long time for children to work through these needs. When adults interrupt the process, they deprive children of important opportunities to learn the true meaning of friendship. Adults should allow children to experience this important phase of relationship building.

Failing to recognize children's friendship cues. Children may use inappropriate behaviors in their efforts to make friends. For instance, children may taunt to initiate an interaction, physically force other children out of an area to have exclusive access to a favored peer, or try to coerce a friend into rejecting another as a way of confirming their own friendship bond. On the surface, these may appear to be straightforward limit-setting situations. However, an observant adult will recognize that the issue relates to friendship and will seize the opportunity to help the erring child learn more constructive friendship skills such as better ways of making contact or expressing affection.

SUMMARY _____

Friendships with peers are important events in the lives of children and offer them unique opportunities to develop socially, emotionally, and intellectually. Some children make friends easily; others do not. The repercussions of not having a friend or of being dissatisfied with the relationships one does have represent severe difficulties in childhood, which can last through maturity. Completely friendless children are rare, however, evidence does indicate that many children wish they had more or better friends.

Adults may wonder whether children really understand what friendship means. Although children's ideas about what constitutes friendship are different from adults' and change as children mature, it is clear that even very young children are interested in having friends who are like them in age and experience and who share their intellectual and physical abilities. Increased facility in communicating also has an impact on children's relationships. Children progress from an egocentric view of relationships to one of mutual support and caring.

When first choosing a friend, children focus on obvious attributes such as name, physical appearance, race, gender, age, ability, and attitudes. In general, it can be said that children seek out friends whom they perceive as being similar to themselves. At times, these likenesses are apparent only to the children involved.

The social skills children display also have a major impact on their ability to make and keep friends. Making friends is not an automatic or magical process. Children who "win friends and influence people" know how to make contact, maintain positive relationships, and negotiate the inevitable conflicts that arise. These are skills that some children learn on their own but with which many children need help.

Adults can play a vital role in increasing children's friendly behavior. This can be accomplished through informal, day-to-day techniques, planned activities, or structured coaching sessions.

DISCUSSION QUESTIONS

1. A Chinese proverb states, "One can do without people, but one has need for a friend." React to this statement, discussing the reasons why people need friends.
2. Think about a childhood friend. Describe what attributes made that person important to you.
3. Think about an adult in your childhood whom you considered a friend. Compare the characteristics of that relationship with peer relationships you have experienced over the years.
4. Describe how children's ideas of friendship change over time. Describe children you know who fit into each stage and explain your conclusions.
5. Describe two children you know—one who seems to have many friends and one who seems to have no friends. Discuss what variables might be influencing each child's situation.
6. As a group, develop a friendship skit aimed at teaching children how to make contact with a potential friend. In addition, generate at least five discussion questions.
7. Pretend you have been invited to a parent meeting to describe friendship coaching. Outline what you might say to parents regarding the rationale for this technique as well as its component parts.
8. Refer to the friendship facts and principles in Appendix A. Identify those that seem most appropriate for children in stage two of friendship conceptualization. Identify those that would be more relevant for children in stage three.

9. Identify a child you know who might benefit from friendship coaching. Describe the area in which coaching would be most useful and explain how you would implement the coaching procedure.
10. Identify the pitfall in this chapter to which you think adults are most susceptible and describe ways to avoid it.

CHAPTER 14
Promoting Prosocial Behavior

SOURCE: © Ulrike Welsch

OBJECTIVES:

On completion of this chapter, you will be able to describe:

1. Major categories of prosocial behavior.

2. How children benefit when they act prosocially.

3. Prerequisite abilities and skills related to prosocial behavior.

4. Gender, age, cultural, and environmental factors that influence prosocial behavior.

5. Strategies to increase children's prosocial behavior.

6. Pitfalls to avoid in promoting children's prosocial behavior.

helping	sympathizing	rescuing
sharing	encouraging	defending
giving	sacrificing	reassuring
cooperating	aiding	comforting

All of these terms describe aspects of prosocial behavior. They are the opposite of antisocial conduct, such as selfishness and aggression, and represent the positive aspirations of society. These acts of kindness assist, support, or benefit others and often are executed without the doer's anticipation of external rewards (Moore, 1982). At times, they also involve some risk to the individual performing them, such as when a person defends a friend in a situation that is either physically or socially dangerous. One's inclination to engage in or refrain from such actions is learned and practiced as a child and is carried into adulthood. Thus, childhood is an optimal period for the development of prosocial attitudes and conduct.

Prosocial behavior falls into two major categories: cooperation and helpfulness. *Cooperation* involves people working together to achieve a common purpose (Bryan, 1975; Staub, 1978). It is exemplified by a group of fifth-graders coordinating their efforts to paint the scenery for the class play or by several preschoolers working together to put away the blocks. In this way, individuals adopt group goals as their own and share in the work as well as the outcome.

Helpfulness is the act of assuaging other people's distress or facilitating their work or play (Marcus and Leiserson, 1978). People alleviate distress when they remove its cause, when they rescue a victim, or when they defend someone under attack. They facilitate by sharing information or materials and by giving physical assistance. Thus, children are helpful when they dispose of a spider that is frightening to someone else, catch a friend's hand who has tripped, stand up for a child against jeering teammates, give half their sandwich to someone who has none, or lend a hand to carry a heavy load. Such help can be either instrumental (assisting with

a task) or psychological (providing emotional support) (Whiting and Pope, 1973; Severy and Davis, 1971).

Most children display both cooperative and helpful behaviors in their interactions with others. Typically, younger children exhibit far fewer prosocial acts than do olders ones. Yet, regardless of age, children's interactions tend to be more positive than negative. For instance, data suggest that the ratio of children's prosocial behaviors to antisocial acts is no less than 3:1 and may be as high as 8:1 (Moore, 1982). This means that for every negative behavior, youngsters average three to eight positive actions. Benefits to recipients seem fairly obvious; one also must ask what, if any, advantages accrue to those children who behave kindly toward others.

Values to Children of Acting Prosocially

Children who engage in prosocial behavior develop feelings of satisfaction and competence from assisting others. When youngsters help with the family dishes, share information with a friend, comfort an unhappy playmate, or work with others to achieve a final product, they come away thinking: "I am useful. I can do something. I am important." By helping, sharing, comforting, and cooperating, they have an impact on their world. The resulting perception of being capable and valuable contributes to a healthy self-image (White, 1960; Coopersmith, 1967). Kindness also serves as a sign of affection or alliance (Marcus and Leiserson, 1978). It induces positive feelings in recipients and so provides entree into social situations or strengthens ongoing relationships. Children whose behavior is characterized by helping and cooperating therefore maximize the number of successful social encounters they experience. Moreover, young people who help others or cooperate with them also better their chances for eliciting help or cooperation when they need it (Marcus, 1977). Children who seldom offer assistance or who work only for personal gain frequently are left to their own devices when confronted with difficult situations.

In addition, when children are the beneficiaries of any type of prosocial action, they get a closer look at how such behaviors are carried out. Each episode serves as a model from which they derive useful information to apply to future encounters. If children are only infrequently on the receiving end of prosocial acts, they have fewer opportunities to learn about them. Recipients also have chances to learn how to respond positively to the kindness that others extend to them (Marcus and Leiserson, 1978). Individuals who never learn this skill eventually receive fewer offers of comfort and support. As a result, there are times when they suffer needlessly because they are unwilling or unable to seek help or cooperation from those who are in a position to give it.

Besides benefiting the individual, prosocial behavior has advantages for groups as well. Group settings in which children are encouraged to be cooperative and helpful result in more friendly interactions and productive group efforts than settings in which little attention is paid to these values (Gazda, et al., 1973). Moreover, routine or tedious chores, such as cleanup, are more easily managed (Marcus and Leiserson, 1978). When everyone pitches in, tasks are quickly accomplished and no one person feels overly burdened. An added benefit is that youngsters begin to develop a positive group image in which they view both themselves and other group participants as genial and competent.

Steps to Acting Prosocially

At one time, it was thought that if children could only be taught to think prosocially, the appropriate actions would automatically follow. Unfortunately, kind thoughts have not been significantly linked to prosocial acts (Bryan and Walbek, 1970). Although even kindergarteners can explain that sharing, taking turns, and working together are good things to do, they do not necessarily act in these ways when to do so would be appropriate. Children must move beyond simply thinking about what is right; they have to go through a series of steps: becoming aware that help or cooperation is needed, deciding to act, and carrying out the prosocial act.

Step one: recognition. Youngsters first must become aware of a situation in which someone would benefit from help or cooperation (Baron, Byrne, Griffitt, 1974). They also must accurately interpret what they see and hear. This means recognizing typical distress signals such as crying, sighing, grimacing, or struggling as well as correctly identifying verbal cues: ''This is too much for me to do all by myself,'' or ''If we work together, we'll finish faster.'' Recognition in circumstances like these often causes children to respond empathically. That is, they feel the distress or frustration of the person in need and then respond. Initially, their reaction is to mimic the distress signals by crying or sighing themselves. Later, toddlers, preschoolers, and school-age children become more adept at coupling their emotional response with some gesture of assistance (Zahn-Waxler, Radke-Yarrow, and Brady-Smith, 1977; Zahn-Waxler, Friedman, and Cummings, 1983).

Step two: decision. Once children identify a person in need, they are faced with the decision of whether or not to act. They are most likely to respond to people they like or admire (Staub, 1978). In addition, children's mood influences which choice they make. Children in a positive frame of mind are most likely to act, and those in negative or neutral moods are less so (Hoffman, 1982; Strayer, 1980). A possible explanation for these differences is that youngsters who themselves are extremely upset may be too preoccupied with their own feelings to reach out to another. Children who are detached, as may be the case in neutral situations, have not been sufficiently aroused.

Children's interpretation of their responsibility to the potential recipient is a third factor that influences their actions. Initially, reciprocity is the principle that guides children's judgments. They feel responsible for helping or cooperating with someone who has extended these kindnesses to them in the past (Rosenhan, 1972). Moreover, they also will act if they anticipate that there will be some future reward to them, such as the helper becoming their friend. This type of thinking is most characteristic of children younger than seven years of age and is referred to as *normative altruism*. Eventually, children act in response to the needs of another without thought of personal gain. They reason: "It isn't right for someone to have to do so much all by themselves," "I wanted her to be happy," or "She looked like she was frightened." This is called *autonomous altruism*. It has been noted in the conduct of some preschoolers and kindergarteners, but it is more common in older children and adults (Rosenhan, 1972; Leahy, 1979). Based on these trends, scientists have speculated that as children mature, they become more aware that self-interest often is incompatible with acting for the good of another person (Baldwin and Baldwin, 1970). According to this idea, children decide to intervene even if no tangible benefit to themselves is evident.

Step three: action. If children assume responsibility for helping or cooperating, they must then select and perform a behavior they think is appropriate to the situation. Their conduct in such circumstances is influenced by two abilities: perspective taking and instrumental know-how (Moore, 1982). In *perspective taking*, children recognize what would be useful to someone else whose needs may not mirror their own at the moment. Toddlers who offer Mommy their well-chewed cracker as a way to assuage her distress over the mess made by the puppy mean well, but do not understand what is truly needed to rectify the situation. Their ineffectiveness is not surprising because they have limited role-taking skills. As these abilities emerge, preschoolers and youngsters in the lower elementary grades become better equipped to help and to cooperate in situations in which the setting is familiar or the circumstances of distress resemble something they themselves have experienced (Yarrow, Scott, and Waxler, 1973). Eventually, children ten years of age and older also become able to project appropriate responses in unfamiliar situations (Forbes, 1978).

However, goodwill alone will not fix a damaged library book. One also must know something about the most appropriate tape with which to repair the binding or the best way to erase crayon marks from the pages. This is called *instrumental know-how* and involves having the knowledge and skills necessary to act competently. Children who have many skills at their disposal are the most effective in carrying out their ideas. Those who have few skills may have good intentions, but their efforts often are counterproductive or inept. Moreover, children who initially are the most prosocial also are the most likely to engage in some antisocial behaviors. Due to their inexperience, they do not readily discriminate appropriate actions from inappropriate ones. As a result, the youngster who pats another in an effort to comfort may, a few minutes later, be the one who grabs or shoves (Moore, 1982). Gradually, children become more aware of what differentiates these two types of behavior and so become better able to initiate actions that are useful and appropriate.

Children may experience difficulty in proceeding through any one of the three steps just described. For instance, youngsters may overlook or misinterpret cues that convey another person's need for help or cooperation. They also may miscalculate when determining what behaviors are suited to the situation. A child who is trying to comfort may shove a favorite storybook in another child's face, hug so hard that it hurts, or say something lacking tact, like "Well, you don't smell *that* bad." Young helpers may miss the mark by adding water to the acrylic paint to make it go further or by using toothpaste to scrub the windows because they have heard that it cleans so well. In a similar vein, youngsters attempting to defend someone may become aggressive or "catty" as a way to show their favor. At times, children may assume that cooperation means giving up all of one's own ideas or settling for mediocrity in an effort to please everyone or that dissent is totally inappropriate. These are all natural mistakes children make in learning how to be kind to one another. As children mature and gain experience, these become less frequent.

Gender, Age, and Cultural Influences on Prosocial Behavior

As with many other developmental domains, scientists have tried to determine whether a person's potential to be prosocial can be predicted by gender or age. The vast majority of studies have failed to find any significant sex differences in children's likelihood either to be prosocial or to respond positively to the prosocial overtures of others (Mussen and Eisenberg-Berg, 1977; Honig, 1982). Age, on the other hand, does have an obvious impact. Yet, different behaviors follow different trends as children mature. For example, in our society, most children's abilities to nurture and share become steadily greater as they reach middle childhood (Bryan, 1975; Green and Schneider, 1974). In contrast, rescuing and cooperating show an initial increase but take a downward turn in the later elementary school years (Madsen, 1971; Staub, 1970). Such mixed results deserve further attention from the reader.

Nurturing and sharing. Although prosocial behavior is not a dominant characteristic of the preschool years, even very young children have been observed attempting to comfort someone who is crying or in obvious distress (Moore, 1982). One-year-olds' fledgling efforts are aimed at giving affection through pats and hugs or of-fering something, such as a teddy bear, that they themselves find comforting. As they approach the age of two, children's advances become more differentiated and sophisticated. They give suggestions, say sympathetic things, umpire fights, and stand up for victims (Zahn-Waxler, Iannotti, and Chapman, 1982). For the next two years, there seems to be little change in the degree to which preschoolers express sympathy for others or make attempts to help (Zahn-Waxler, Radke-Yarrow, and Brady-Smith, 1977). Then, between the ages of four and thirteen, significant increases in such actions become evident (Mussen and Eisenberg-Berg, 1977). This gain is a result of children's improved awareness of the needs of others and their growing ability to determine what deeds might be interpreted by another as comforting and supportive.

Sharing follows a similar trend. Although toddlers and preschoolers sometimes share, their frequency of sharing is relatively low compared with older children. They are more likely to share with adults than with peers. Gradually, youngsters' sharing abilities become greater, with the most dramatic changes occurring between six and twelve years of age (Staub, 1979; Honig, 1982). There are several reasons why older children share more easily. First, their more advanced intellectual abilities enable them to recognize that it is possible for two people to legitimately want the same thing at the same time, that possessions shared can be retrieved, and that sharing often is reciprocated. They also understand that there is a difference between sharing (which means temporary loss of ownership) and donating (which is permanent), and can understand, as well as make clear to others, which of the two is intended (Smith, 1982). In addition, they have more skills at their disposal that allow them to share in a variety of ways. If one approach, such as taking turns, is not satisfactory, they have options to fall back on like bargaining, trading, or using an object together. These youngsters also have had the opportunity to learn that sharing is viewed favorably by those around them, so they may use this strategy to elicit positive responses. Finally, older children find it easier to part with some items because they differentiate among the values of their possessions. Something that is no longer their "pride and joy" or something that seems to have little value can be given away. The same cannot be said for toddlers and preschoolers. They are attached to everything they own and treat most objects as having high value, making it more difficult to relinquish them. Hence, four-year-old Michael, who rides the tricycle and then runs off to dig in the sand, may protest loudly when another child gets on the trike. To Michael, the tricycle is his and he is loathe to give it up even though he has lost interest in it. An older child would not find it as painful to surrender the tetherball if she saw the swing as more appealing. Likewise, a three-year-old might have trouble parting with ten pennies because they seem like a lot of money, whereas a nine-year-old would more readily give them up because 10¢ no longer represents a great sum (Hall, Perlmutter, and Lamb, 1982).

Rescuing and cooperating. Toddlers and preschoolers sometimes become involved in rescuing and cooperating. However, these behaviors are more common in children older than four or five years of age. Rescue actions, such as eliciting help from an adult for a child in distress or offering direct personal assistance, increase steadily until about the age of nine. After that, these efforts become fewer (Staub, 1970). One explanation for this trend is that in the early elementary-school years, children who are aroused to help someone in trouble center on assisting the victim to the exclusion of all else. Older children, on the other hand, are more capable of considering multiple issues. They can think about aiding someone and also about the repercussions of that action. Therefore, they become hesitant to intervene if rescuing involves breaking a known rule or risking disapproval from adults or peers (Staub, 1978). For example, children may fail to help an injured

bird if it is outside a gate that marks a boundary they are not allowed to cross.

Similarly, cooperation is most evident in the early school years. Later, children tend to become competitive and less cooperative (Madsen, 1971; Madsen and Connor, 1973). In fact, youngsters seven to nine years of age typically are less cooperative than children between the ages of four and five and, at times, choose to compete even when cooperation would better help them achieve their aims. At first glance, this seems puzzling because as children become less egocentric and better skilled, they should be more capable of cooperative interactions. However, it is less mysterious when one considers that, by the time they are eight or nine years old, most American children are well aware of the values placed on individual achievement and competition. These values often are in direct opposition to working together toward a common goal. Thus, by this age, children may choose the individualistic behaviors, which are more likely to be rewarded.

In contrast, neither kibbutz-reared Israeli children, Hopi children, Chinese children, nor Mexican children become less cooperative as they get older (Madsen, 1971). These cultures are more group oriented and hence produce children who are more likely to be cooperative. Besides differences among cultures, there are differences between rural and urban environments. For instance, in the United States, Israel, Colombia, New Zealand, and Mexico, urban children tend to be less cooperative than their rural counterparts.

Scientists have studied this phenomenon and have postulated that the following societal characteristics are most conducive to the development of sustained prosocial behavior in the young (Mussen and Eisenberg-Berg, 1977):

1. Emphasis on considering others, sharing, and working together.
2. Simple, kinship-oriented social structure.
3. Women playing an important role in the economic structure of the society.

4. Extended families living together.
5. Early assignment of tasks and responsibilities to children in the family.

Looking at these characteristics, it is not surprising that in the United States, with its complex social organization, individualistic orientation, small families, and minimum responsibilities given to children, a child may become less cooperative in preadolescence. At the same time, it is obvious that prosocial behavior does not altogether disappear at this age and that some children do develop a strong inclination to help and to cooperate. The influence of adults constitutes the one factor that most strongly influences whether a child becomes more or less prosocial.

Adult Influences on Prosocial Behavior

Adults have a major impact on the degree to which children learn to be helpful and cooperative. One way they do this is by creating an immediate environment that either facilitates or inhibits the development of children's prosocial behavior (Schmuch and Schmuch, 1975; Honig, 1982). In group settings, the atmosphere most likely to promote nurturing, sharing, cooperating, and rescuing has the following characteristics (Staub, 1978):

1. Participants anticipate that everyone will do his or her best to support one another.
2. Both adults and children contribute to decisions made, practices, and procedures.
3. Communication is direct, clear, and mutual.
4. Individual differences are respected.
5. Expectations are reasonable.
6. People like one another and feel a sense of belonging to the group.
7. There is an emphasis on group as well as individual accomplishments.

Adults shape such an environment by using an authoritative discipline style, by modeling prosocial behavior, by rewarding children's attempts at prosocial actions, and by instructing children in prosocial values or skills.

Discipline strategies. Nurturant adults who utilize an authoritative approach to discipline promote prosocial behavior in the children with whom they interact (Honig, 1982). For example, children of authoritative parents tend to collaborate with others to achieve goals, are more likely to share, and are sympathetic when other children need help (Baumrind, 1977). Such adults teach prosocial values by applying other-oriented reasoning and explaining why they consider this type of behavior desirable. These techniques promote development of the empathy, competence, and rationales children need in order to behave prosocially.

On the other hand, youngsters whose parents use withdrawal of love or assertion of power to discipline children are far less likely to act helpfully, generously, or sympathetically (Baumrind, 1977; Hoffman, 1977). Children of permissive parents tend to be self-indulgent; children of authoritarian parents are obedient, but seldom take the initiative to do something unless it is dictated. Neither of these attitudes fosters empathy, which is the prerequisite for prosocial behavior. Nor do they encourage youngsters to implement positive actions that may not result in a tangible reward.

Modeling. Hearing about prosocial behavior is effective, but seeing it in action makes the lesson more vivid. Youngsters who frequently observe people cooperating, helping, sharing, and giving are most likely to act in those ways themselves (Grusec and Arnason, 1982; Marcus and Leiserson, 1978). Thus, adults who model such actions, either with other adults or with children, help to increase children's prosocial conduct.

Although everyone has the potential to be a prosocial model, certain people are more likely to be imitated than others. Children emulate the people in their lives who are friendly, responsive, supportive, and who are in a position to administer both rewards and consequences (Mussen and Eisenberg-Berg, 1977). Models who are aloof, critical, directive, punitive, or powerless commonly are ignored. In addition, prosocial modeling has its greatest impact when what adults say is congruent with what they do (Bryan and Walbek, 1970; Yarrow, Scott, and Waxler, 1973). Researchers have found that when there is inconsistency between words and deeds, the model is less credible and may even prompt children to engage in fewer prosocial acts (Presbie and Coiteux, 1971; Midlarsky, Bryan, and Brickman, 1973). This follows the old adage "Actions speak louder than words."

Hence, adults who urge children to lend one another a hand but seldom offer assistance themselves show children that helping is not really a high priority. Likewise, if they lecture about the virtues of cooperating and sometimes do so, but grudgingly, youngsters are quick to learn that collaboration is distasteful. Furthermore, adults who insist that children always be truthful, yet tell "little fibs" when it is convenient for them, show children that lying is acceptable even when they say it is not. The result in all cases is that children become less inclined to help or cooperate. On the other hand, when children observe adults acting prosocially and deriving obvious pleasure from their actions, imitation becomes more likely (Midlarsky and Bryan, 1967, 1972; Yarrow, Scott, and Waxler, 1973).

Rewarding prosocial behavior. A prosocial environment is one in which such conduct is likely to be rewarded. Technically, all adults have to do is watch for instances of children being kind and then enact positive consequences. Yet, adults commonly fail to make the most of this strategy for one of two reasons. First, they may take children's prosocial behaviors for granted and not reward them adequately or often enough. Second, adults may inadvertently reward actions that actually counteract helpful or cooperative behavior.

In order to avoid these problems, adults must remember that prosocial behaviors are learned and are subject to the same conditions that characterize other learning episodes. That is, children must be motivated to learn and to feel successful. Neither of these criteria is met when adults ignore children who are trying to figure out what the positive expectations are or spend the majority of their time correcting them. Instead, adults must take as much care to enact positive consequences as they do to follow through with corrective ones. Furthermore, cooperation among children will be undermined if adults rely on competition as their primary means for motivating children. Youngsters are encouraged to compete rather than cooperate when they are told: "Let's see who can put the most blocks away," "Whoever gets the most words right gets a star," or "The nicest picture will go in the showcase." In each instance, youngsters are quick to determine that there will be only one winner and that helping or cooperating with someone else will sabotage their own chances for coming out on top. On the other hand, such situations could be modified to make it easier for the youngsters to cooperate by focusing on group accomplishments rather than on individual achievement: "Let's see how well we can all work together to put these blocks away," "I'll check the board to find out if the class got more words right today than it did yesterday," or "When you're finished painting your pictures, we'll go out and hang them in the hall." These conditions clear the way for youngsters to come to one another's assistance or to work together as appropriate (Marion, 1981). In addition, group-administered rewards encourage children to work as a team to achieve a common aim (Bryan, 1975). Putting a star up for each book read by the group or for each act of kindness helps keep track of the children's progress as a whole and directs their attention to what an entire group can achieve. Thus, it is effective to monitor the group's progress and then enact positive consequences when certain "benchmarks" are obtained rather than always rewarding youngsters individually (Staub, 1978). This approach has been found to lead to friendlier, more cooperative behavior among the participants (Altman, 1971; Bryan, 1975).

Direct instruction. Children's prosocial behavior also increases when they have been trained to think and act prosocially (Honig, 1982; Shure and Spivack, 1978; Staub, 1971). Such training focuses on the individual skills that lead to helping and cooperating. Recognizing prosocial behavior when it is displayed, identifying the needs of another, anticipating the consequences of acts, and generating multiple solutions to interpersonal problems are all prosocial skills.

A variety of strategies have been used to teach these to children of varying ages. Some include:

1. Discussing the value of prosocial behavior and giving examples of how children themselves can act prosocially (Dinkmeyer, 1970; Bessel and Palomares, 1970).
2. Telling stories that illustrate prosocial principles (Yarrow, et al., 1973).
3. Demonstrating prosocial behavior using small figures, dolls, puppets, televised vignetes, or live models (Yarrow, Scott, and Waxler, 1973; Friedrich and Stein, 1975; Kostelnik and Stein, 1986).
4. Getting children to re-enact previously observed prosocial actions (Friedrich and Stein, 1975).
5. Having children role-play situations in which they take on the behaviors of helper and helpee (Staub, 1971).
6. Teaching children games that promote cooperation and awareness of others (Altman, 1971).
7. Creating opportunities for children to help or cooperate in real-life situations (Shure and Spivack, 1978; Marcus and Leiserson, 1978).

Although each of these techniques seems to have a positive effect on children's thinking, it has been clearly demonstrated that discussion alone does not lead to increased prosocial activity (Honig, 1982). Talk leads to talk. That is, youngsters who listen to adults extol the virtues of responding prosocially soon recognize the societal norm of social responsibility. They discuss it knowledgeably and, more often than not, also express agreement with such expectations (Bryan and Walbek, 1970). Yet, there is little increase in the number of prosocial acts they perform.

In contrast, youngsters who actively participate in tasks or situations that enable them to rehearse prosocial skills demonstrate greater instances of such behaviors in similar circumstances (Honig, 1982; Marcus and Lieserson, 1978). These findings hold true from preschool through preadolescence, particularly for youngsters younger than six years of age. The opportunity to physically re-enact appropriate behaviors in relevant situations helps children better remember both the behavior and the cues that signal what conditions apply in a given circumstance. For example, when Heidi watches a skit in which she must use a variety of cues to decide which puppet needs help, she is better equipped to recognize when help is needed in a real-life situation. Thus, the most productive approach for direct instruction is to combine verbal descriptions and explanations with practice of corresponding actions.

As can be ascertained from the preceding discussion, there are numerous ways for adults to promote prosocial behavior among children. Some of these, such as using an authoritative style of discipline and modeling and rewarding prosocial actions, are aimed at creating an environment in which helpfulness and cooperation are nurtured and expected. Formal instruction also can be used to teach children prosocial attitudes and behaviors. Specific techniques related to each of these are presented next.

SKILLS FOR PROMOTING PROSOCIAL BEHAVIOR IN CHILDREN

Creating a Prosocial Environment

Using the skills you have learned in previous chapters will help you create an atmosphere that is conducive to the development of prosocial behavior. Some additional strategies include the following.

1. Take advantage of naturally occurring opportunities to label children's prosocial acts. When children clean the guinea pig's cage, tell them they are showing concern for the animal's well-being. When Theresa announces that she received a get-well card during her recent absence, point out that sending the card was the way someone chose to comfort her. Explain that youngsters who remain quiet while a peer gives a report are helping him or her to concentrate. When children take turns, mention that this is a way of cooperating with one another. All of these instances enable you to highlight prosocial behavior rather than lecturing or moralizing about it.

2. Point out instances in which an unintentional lack of kindness was shown and describe an alternate, prosocial approach. Through inexperience or thoughtlessness, people sometimes are inconsiderate, selfish, uncooperative, or uncharitable. When this happens, point out to children the effects that behavior had on the person to whom it was directed and describe a more appropriate action. Thus, if youngsters laugh when one of them trips and drops his or her lunch tray, they should be told that their response was unkind because it caused embarrassment and that it would have been more considerate to have helped the child get up and clean up. Likewise, should children see an adult continually interrupt another person, the antisocial nature of this act could be discussed and alternatives suggested.

3. Create opportunities for children to cooperate. Each day, include projects and routines that require the efforts of more than one person. Assign children to work together to feed the animals rather than doing it yourself or having one child perform the task alone. Allow children to set up the science experiment together rather than having it ready beforehand. Ask several youngsters to collaborate on a mural rather than giving each his or her own section to paint.

4. Create opportunities for children to help. Give children some responsibility for the care and maintenance of their environment. Although it may be easier for adults to do some tasks themselves, children gain valuable helping experience if they have real work to do.

Periodically, assign youngsters to help one another. Make sure each child has a chance to be both helper and helpee. This can be done individually or in groups. For instance, in gymnastics, children could take turns "spotting" one another on the mat, or one group of youngsters could be taught a math game to teach to another group, who in turn could help them work a crossword puzzle. Encourage children to help one another as occasions arise.

When children ask you to help, try instead to find another child who could fulfill that role. Lifting a child to reach the glue for a playmate instead of getting it yourself, enlisting the aid of age-mates in comforting an unhappy child, or requesting information from a peer in response to a child's question are all examples of this strategy.

5. Explain potential or current deviations from rules that are made in order to promote helping responses. Because many older children fail to help someone in distress because they are worried about breaking known rules, anticipate potential exceptions to certain rules and inform children of these. Youngsters could be told: ''The rule is that when I leave the room, all of you are to stay in your seats. However, if anything ever happens that frightens you, you could go next door and get Ms. Jones.'' In addition, tell children why a traditional rule was ignored in a particular circumstance: ''Normally, the rule is that everyone stays on our side of the yard, but the bunny looked like he really needed help. So, I took Jennifer and John with me to help untangle him.''

6. Reward prosocial behavior. Remain alert to children's attempts to be helpful, cooperative, or kind. Avoid taking these actions for granted or waiting for dramatic episodes before administering a reward. Instead, acknowledge small kindnesses, such as when children move out of the way, help to carry something, play together without bickering, share an idea, or offer encouragement to someone else. Show approval and appreciation by smiling and using positive personal messages.

7. Administer group rewards. Think of situations that have the potential for children to work together. These may be newly introduced conditions (such as a special project) or circumstances that traditionally have focused more on individual achievement. For instance, if you have emphasized each child taking care of his or her own area or materials, plan to change this routine to encourage youngsters to work together to clean up a larger area. Implement your plan. Afterward, praise children for their cooperation and helpfulness.

8. Demonstrate a variety of prosocial behaviors. Adults who share, help, cooperate, comfort, and rescue illustrate the importance of these behaviors as well as how to carry them out. In order to make the most of this method, carefully examine your own

FIGURE 14-1 Prosocial behavior is fostered when children have opportunities to help one another.
SOURCE: Photo by Patty Charles

behavior with children and with other adults and then set an example for children to follow. Although it may seem easiest to comfort, rescue, or help children, do not forget to share and cooperate as well. Making a banner for the ward, picking a name for the volleyball team, or building with unit blocks are all situations that lend themselves to modeling cooperation. Allowing a child to borrow your book or distributing portions of a birthday cake made for you by a friend are ways for you to share.

9. Demonstrate constructive ways of responding to other people's prosocial behavior. Regardless of whether you are interacting with children or adults, and in spite of whether or not you want help, a positive response contributes to the prosocial environment. If you desire the help that is offered, say, "Thank you" with a pleased expression on your face. If you would rather do something on your own, or if the proposed assistance would not be helpful, do not simply brush the person aside. Instead, acknowledge the kindness and explain that this is something you would like to do yourself or describe an action that would be more useful. In both cases, you are modeling appropriate ways of either accepting or declining help. These are important actions for children to observe.

10. Be positive when engaging in prosocial behavior. Because children tend to imitate adults who seem to enjoy giving help and cooperation, exhibit obvious pleasure in prosocial situations. Smile and say things like, "It makes me feel good to help you."

11. Point out the prosocial behaviors modeled by yourself and others. Children are better able to understand the prosocial models they see when their behavior is explained. Provide children with such information by saying things like: "Arthur was having a hard time coming up with words for his song, so Lamont is helping him by making a list of some that rhyme," "Sally is worried about getting her x ray, so I'm going to go in with her," or "Randi and Mike have decided to use the workbench together. Randi will use the hammer while Mike uses the saw. Then, they'll trade."

Direct Instruction Related to Prosocial Behavior

Receiving direct training in helping and cooperating leads to an increase in children's prosocial behavior. Such instruction can be provided through on-the-spot teaching in naturally occurring situations or through preplanned activities. In both cases, the role of the adult is to teach children basic facts about helping and cooperating, to demonstrate applications to real-life situations, and to give children a chance to rehearse related skills. Each approach has certain elements in common but also unique characteristics that must be understood in order to implement them successfully.

On-the-Spot Instruction

As you will recall, there are three steps involved in behaving prosocially; awareness, decision making, and action. The main focus of on-the-spot instruction is to assist children at any point beyond which they seem unable to proceed.

1. Observe children for signs of prosocial behavior. Watch children carefully. Take note when they show consideration for another person, when they attempt to assist someone, or when they join forces, even briefly. All too often, adults focus on children's negative behaviors; the one big fight Christopher had stands out in their mind and, as a result, they overlook that at one point in the day, he offered help to someone and later appeared distressed at the despair of a friend. Both of these behaviors are signs that Christopher is learning to think of people other than himself.

2. Make children aware when someone needs help or cooperation. There are times when children fail to recognize distress signals or other signs that indicate that help or cooperation is desired. Rectify this by giving children relevant information to assist them in becoming more attuned to the circumstances at hand. If Marianne seems oblivious to Barney's struggle to carry a heavy board, say: "Look at Barney. He's working awfully hard. He looks like he could use some help." Likewise, if children are outside trying to pick teams and several youngsters are laughing at a private joke, it may be difficult for others to hear whose name is being called. As a result, those who are straining to listen may try to elicit cooperation by telling the jokesters to ''pipe down,'' or ''shut up.'' Such language could easily be misinterpreted by those to whom it is directed or even seen as a challenge to continue. Information from you at this point would be useful: ''You are having a good laugh. It's hard for other people to hear. They're just asking you to cooperate by being a little quieter.''

3. Teach children signals they might give to elicit help or cooperation from others. In the preceding example, youngsters who were trying to get their loud age-mates to cooperate used an antagonistic strategy, which could have backfired. They, too, could benefit from some basic information, such as: ''When you yelled at them, it just made them get louder. It might have been better to walk over and explain why you wanted them to be quiet.'' Toddlers and preschoolers, as well as youngsters in highly charged situations, respond best to direct suggestions. Offer these in the form of script or sample words that they might use: ''Tell Marianne, 'This board's too big for me to carry alone.' '' With your support and encouragement, most school-age children who are not passionately involved in a situation will be able to generate their own ideas for what to say.

4. Point out situations in which people could decide to help or cooperate. At times, children are aware that someone needs their help or cooperation, but don't know what to do next. This is when you can highlight that a prosocial decision can be made by saying something such as: ''Janice looks like she needs your help. We can decide to help her,'' or ''Mr. Crouch wants us all to work together on this project. We'll have to decide whether or not to do that.''

5. Discuss situations in which it would be best to decide not to cooperate. Help children sort out the reasons for such decisions. These would involve circumstances in which people or property are endangered or moral codes are violated. For example, joining together for the purpose of stealing, cheating on an exam, or spray-painting the lavatory walls would be inappropriate cooperative efforts.

6. Assist children in determining what type of help or cooperation is most suitable for a particular situation. Once children show some signs of wanting to help or cooperate, aid them in deciding what action to take. Provide information for them to consider, such as: ''Sometimes, when people are unhappy, it helps when someone hugs them or says nice things to them,'' or ''Sometimes, people feel satisfaction from attempting to do something that is difficult, and their pleasure is spoiled if another person takes over.'' Demonstrations also are useful. Showing a child how to crank the foot of a hospital bed up and down, illustrating to children how one person can steady a mannequin while another puts the clothes on, or demonstrating how it takes two people to make the computer game work are all ways to make these types of discussions more concrete. In addition, discuss ways children can support another person's efforts without offering direct, physical assistance. Point out the importance of a reassuring smile, the ''thumbs-up'' sign, or cheering from the sidelines. These are all ways children can provide comfort and encouragement. Finally, teach children to ask questions such as: ''Do you want help?'', ''How can I help you?'', ''What do you need?'', and ''What would you like me to do?'' This enables children to acquire information about what kind of behavior another person might perceive as helpful or cooperative in a given situation.

7. Work with children to evaluate the results of their actions. Children learn a lot from taking a retrospective look at what they have done as close to the event as possible:

"Did jumping on the box solve the problem?"

"Did Leslie feel better after you talked to her?"

"What happened when you let David finish on his own?"

"How could you tell that Celeste appreciated what you did?

"Were there enough of you, or did you need more people to work on that project?"

"Were you able to give Raymond all the information he needed?"

"How do you think it worked out for everybody to have a five-minute turn with the microscope?"

If children are unable to assess their own performances, offer some information yourself or help them glean information from others. This evaluation could be conducted during a private conversation with a child or as a group assessment of group effort. Regardless of how well their prosocial venture worked out, praise children for attempting it.

8. Encourage children to accept kindness from others. Sometimes, children are unaware of or misinterpret other children's attempts at prosocial behavior. Thus, Tricia may not realize that when Audrey takes over, she is actually trying to help, nor may she understand that Sam's apparent lack of decisiveness is his way of trying to cooperate. In situations like these, point out what is really taking place.

In addition, there are children who, wanting to be independent or self-sufficient, actively reject assistance, reassurance, or sympathy. Frequently, they neither cooperate nor expect cooperation from others. Their rationale is that they expect nothing and give

nothing. In reality, such youngsters often fear rejection or "taking a chance on" someone. These children need to experience kindness before they can extend it to those around them. Because their actions put other children off, it is you who must reach out. Do not fail to provide unreceptive youngsters with the same courtesies or offers of help and encouragement that you might grant to a more appreciative child. This is the first step in helping them become more accepting of prosocial behavior from someone else.

9. Support children when their attempts at kindness are rebuffed. At times, children's enthusiasm is dashed if their offer of help is refused or an action they thought was helpful turns out not to have been. If this happens, acknowledge the child's disappointment or frustration and discuss the situation. If you can, offer information that might assist the child in understanding the outcome. If you do not know why their attempt failed, be supportive and sympathetic.

All of the preceding strategies can be used individually, on separate occasions, or in combination. Which specific technique is called for depends on the particular circumstance in which you are involved. This is illustrated in the following real-life scenario:

SITUATION: Kenton and Josh, two six-year-olds, are playing with a construction toy that has many interconnecting pieces. Josh builds an elaborate vehicle, which Kenton admires.

Kenton: Make me one like yours.

Josh: Well, if I make it, it'll be mine.

Kenton: But I want one. Make me one.

Josh: Then it'll be mine!

Kenton: I can't get the pieces to fit.

At this point, it is obvious that Kenton is unsuccessfully trying to elicit Josh's help. Now is when the adult intervention is appropriate.

Adult: Josh, Kenton is asking you for help. Sometimes, when people help, they do the job for someone. However, it sounds like you think if you make the car for Kenton, it will have to be yours. Another way people help is by showing someone how to do it. That way, Kenton can make his own car with your help. How does that sound to you?

Josh: Okay.

Kenton: Yeah.

Josh demonstrated how his car went together. Once this was well under way, the adult commented briefly on the boys' cooperative behavior as well as on Josh's willingness to help a friend.

In this situation, the adult enabled one child to become aware of another child's signals and provided information about a possible course of action. She also rewarded the children for demonstrating prosocial behavior. Later in the day, she could take a moment to informally talk with Kenton and Josh about their reactions to the helping episode. Another type of direct instruction involves teaching prosocial behavior through planned activities.

Planned Activities

Planned activities are lessons adults develop in advance and carry out with children individually or in groups. The best activities are not necessarily the most elaborate; rather, they are those that have been well prepared and then implemented in ways that are sensitive to children's interests and needs. The following illustrates how best to accomplish this.

1. *Decide what prosocial facts or behavior you want to teach.* Choose three or four important facts or principles for children to consider. Refer to Appendix B for samples related to helping and to Appendix C for those related to cooperation.

2. *Think of many different ways the prosocial facts or behavior you have chosen might be presented to children.* Lessons that include both discussion and active participation are the most effective. Active participation means getting children physically involved in the activity by handling props, moving about, and talking rather than simply listening. Some examples of successful activities include:

a. Reading and telling stories that have a prosocial theme.
b. Dramatizing prosocial situations through skits, using puppets, dolls, or stand-up figures.
c. Discussing with the children prosocial events that have occurred in the formal group setting.
d. Role-playing prosocial episodes. Sample topics might include how to ask for help or cooperation, how to decide whether help or cooperation is needed, determining what type of action would be most helpful or cooperative, and how to decline unwanted help.
e. Discussing scenes from magazines, books, or posters. The discussion might involve identifying who was helped, who provided help, and how the help was carried out or pointing out cooperative and uncooperative behaviors.
f. Playing cooperative games such as ring-around-a-rosy with toddlers or carrying out a scavenger hunt with older children in which groups of children search for things as a team rather than competing as individuals.

g. Turning traditionally competitive games such as Bingo into cooperative group efforts.

h. Creating group projects, such as a class book or mural, to which everyone contributes.

3. Select one of your activity ideas to develop further. Make a realistic assessment of what props are available, how much time you will have, the physical setting, and the number of children you will be working with at one time. For instance, do not choose a story that takes 20 minutes to read if you only have 10 minutes in which to work. Likewise, if the only setting available is a bustling waiting room, or the only time available is when children may be hungry or preoccupied with other responsibilities, it is not appropriate to plan activities that require intense concentration.

4. Develop a plan of action that outlines the prosocial activity from start to finish. Write this plan down as a way to remember it and further think it through. Include what you will say to introduce the activity, any instructions you may have to give, how you will handle materials, how you will have children use them, the sequence of steps you will follow, and how you will close. Anticipate what you will say or do if children seem disinterested or unable to carry out your directions.

5. Gather the materials you will need. Make any additional props that are necessary.

6. Implement your plan. Utilize skills you have learned in previous chapters related to nonverbal and verbal communication, reflecting, asking questions, playing, and developing skits to enhance your presentation.

7. Evaluate your activity in terms of immediate and long-term prosocial outcomes. Typical evaluation questions include: Who

FIGURE 14-2 Clearly, these children are proud of their cooperative project.
SOURCE: H. Armstrong Roberts

were the children who participated? What did children actually say or do in this activity? How did children demonstrate interest or disinterest? Later in the day, did children refer either to the activity or the prosocial facts and principles covered in the activity in their conversation or play? Over time, do children spontaneously demonstrate prosocial behaviors highlighted by the activity?

8. Repeat the same prosocial activity, or a variation of it, at another time. Children learn prosocial concepts through repeated exposure over time. Therefore, do not expect to see immediate behavior change or the adoption of prosocial skills in their everyday interactions after just one or two presentations of particular facts and principles.

Sample Activities

We now present four prosocial activities to give you examples of how to formulate your own. Helping activities are presented in Table 14-1, and activities aimed at teaching cooperation are depicted in Table 14-2.

TABLE 14-1 Sample Helping Activities

ACTIVITY 1

Activity Name:	Sharing a Lump of Clay
Goal:	To help children reach consensus on how the clay is to be used
Focus:	Helping facts and principles 1, 2, 4, 14, and 26 (refer to Appendix B)
Materials:	A two-pound lump of clay, a table with five chairs (one for an adult, four for children), one plastic knife, one pair of scissors, one twelve-inch length of wire

Procedure:

1. Place a lump of clay in the center of the table.
2. Neutralize the clay by keeping one hand on it. Say: ''I have one big ball of clay, and there are four children who want to use it. Tell me how everyone can have a chance.''
3. Listen to children's ideas; elicit suggestions from everyone.
4. Clarify each child's perspective by paraphrasing his or her ideas to the group. Follow up with, ''And what do you think of that?''
5. Remain impartial throughout this process. Do not show disapproval of any child's idea, regardless of its content.
6. Remind children as necessary that the first step in playing with the clay is deciding how that will take place.
7. If children become bogged down, repeat pertinent helping facts and principles.
8. Summarize the solution when it has been achieved.
9. Praise children.
10. Carry out the agreed-upon solution.

ACTIVITY 2

Activity Name:	Helping Decisions
Goal:	To teach children to recognize situations in which people need help, and to determine appropriate ways of helping
Focus:	Helping facts and principles 7, 8, 9, 10, 11, 12, 13, 16, 17, 18, 24, and 25 (refer to Appendix B)
Materials:	Eight to ten pictures selected from magazines that show people or animals who need help in some way or people who are being helped in some way. These should be large enough for four or five children to be able to see them two or three feet away and should

TABLE 14-1 *(continued)*

be mounted on cardboard. Pictures should depict a variety of ages, cultures, and helping situations.

Procedure:

1. Select one picture at a time for discussion. Keep other pictures face down.
2. Introduce the activity by saying: ''I have several pictures here about helping. Look at this one: somebody needs help.''
3. Prompt discussion with questions and statements such as: ''Tell me who needs help? How did you know? Is there anyone in the picture who could help? What could they do? Who has another idea? What do you think this man will do if someone tries to help? Why might the man not want her to help him? What might you do if you had the same problem as the people in the picture?''
4. Paraphrase children's suggestions and ideas and elicit reactions from other youngsters in the group.
5. Accept all the children's suggestions and praise them for working so hard at figuring out who needs help, who could help, and what should be done.
6. Should the discussion falter, provide useful information by repeating pertinent helping facts and principles.
7. Repeat the procedure with additional pictures.

TABLE 14-2 Sample Cooperation Activities

ACTIVITY 3	
Activity Name:	Group Box Sculpture
Goal:	To give children the opportunity to cooperate spontaneously
Focus:	Cooperating facts and principles 1, 2, 3, 4, 5, 11, and 13 (refer to Appendix C)
Materials:	Boxes, cartons, and containers of various sizes and shapes (these could be provided by the adult, or children could be asked to bring one or more to contribute to the project); glue; masking tape; staple gun; stapler; poster paint; brushes; newspapers; towels; sponges buckets; scissors; markers; crayons; glitter; fabric swatches; wallpaper. There should be a wide variety of materials but a limited supply of each.
Procedure:	1. Set up the activity prior to the children's arrival by placing all of the materials in the center of the project area—crayons in one bin, markers in another, scissors in another, and so on. This will encourage youngsters to share materials more than if each child had his or her own personal supply.
	2. Introduce the activity by explaining that many people will work together to make a group sculpture. No one person will be in charge. Instead, everyone must work as a team. There are many materials available, and children may use any of them.

TABLE 14-2 *(continued)*

3. Stand back and allow children to figure out how to proceed.

4. Provide momentary help by giving relevant information related to the concepts or by mediating any conflicts that arise. Children should be allowed to work out their own disagreements if this can be accomplished without physical danger.

5. Point out instances of cooperation, compromises that are made, and other prosocial behaviors that are exhibited.

6. Keep the project and give children a chance to talk about their role and the role of others producing it.

(Note: This project may take more than one day to complete.)

ACTIVITY 2

Activity Name: Tree Planting

Goal: To enable children to experience three phases of cooperation: planning, implementing a plan, and sharing in the outcome.

Focus: This activity has the potential to incorporate all of the cooperation facts and principles presented in Appendix C.

Materials: A tree at least five feet tall, shovels, wheelbarrow, hose, and water source.

Procedure:

1. Introduce the project by explaining that the children will have an opportunity to plant a tree. This will be a cooperative effort in which everyone will share in the planning, the planting, and the enjoyment.

2. Select an appropriate spot to plant the tree. Discuss with preschoolers what the tree requires in terms of light and space and where they might most enjoy having a tree. Help school-age children do some fact finding related to the kind of tree, the type of soil it needs, how extensive its root system will be, and how that might affect power lines, water mains, sidewalks, and other plants.

3. Allocate jobs for young children. Draw up a predetermined list of jobs and elicit their ideas for how the tasks could be divided. Some of these would include digging the hole, watering the ground prior to planting, transporting the tree to its new location, feeding the tree, lowering it into the hole, balancing it, refilling the hole, and tamping the soil. Allow older children to participate in formulating their own roster of chores as well as in determining who will be responsible for each.

4. Plant the tree, following the plan.

5. Elicit ideas and help from as many children as possible and provide pertinent information by reiterating the cooperation facts and principles. Point out examples of cooperation in the group. Carry out discussions regarding children's emotions and reactions.

(Note: The degree of complexity of this project is open ended. The activity could be simplified by having a smaller tree, limiting the size of the group, and minimizing the decisions to be made; it could be expanded by having

TABLE 14-2 *(continued)*

the children determine what kind of tree to plant, having them earn the money to buy the tree, or having them plant a large area in saplings.)

In addition to the types of activities just described, the helping and cooperating facts and principles presented in Appendices B and C lend themselves to demonstrations and skits similar to those discussed in Chapter 13. Sample topics might include how to ask for help or cooperation, how to decide whether help is needed, what type of help would be best, and how to decline unwanted help.

PITFALLS TO AVOID

Whether you are teaching children prosocial behavior by creating an atmosphere that is conducive to acts of kindness, providing on-the-spot instruction, or using planned activities, there are certain mistakes to avoid.

Failing to recognize children's efforts to behave prosocially. Children who are just learning to help and cooperate may be awkward in their attempts or may initially pursue a course of action that, at first, bears little resemblance to kindness. When this happens, adults may misinterpret these behaviors as purposefully uncooperative or unhelpful. Although limits on potentially harmful behavior are appropriate, children should receive support for their good intentions as well as information on how to improve their performance. This means it will be necessary to ascertain what a child was trying to achieve before taking corrective action. Thus, if children are adding water to the acrylic paint or scrubbing the window with toothpaste, don't automatically assume that their motives are to ruin the materials or to strike out at you. Instead, ask questions such as: "What were you trying to do?", "What did you think would happen?", or "Why are you. . . ?" If they give an indication that their intent was to be helpful, acknowledge their efforts and explain why what they are doing is not as useful as it could be and what they could do instead. These same strategies can be employed in any situation in which a child is attempting to help, cooperate, comfort, or rescue via some inappropriate means.

There will be occasions when you do set a limit or enforce a consequence only to discover later that the child truly was trying to help. If this happens, go back to the child, explain that you now understand what he or she was trying to do, and discuss why corrective action was necessary. Give the child specific ideas about what to do instead.

Bringing a prosocial model's behavior to a child's attention through negative comparisons. As has been stated previously, children are more likely to imitate models whose behavior is pointed out to them. However, adults should not use these situations to make unfavorable comparisons between the model's behavior and that of the child. Statements like "Look at Roger. He's so polite. Why can't you be more like that?" make the child feel defensive rather than receptive and do not make imitation likely. A better approach would be to say: "Roger accidentally bumped into Maureen, so he said, 'Excuse me.' That was a very polite thing to do.'' The first statement was an evaluative remark aimed at shaming the child; the second provides factual information in a nonjudgmental way.

Coercing children to engage in insincere prosocial behavior. It is not uncommon for adults who are trying to teach children consideration to manipulate them into expressions of kindness that the youngsters do not really feel. This is illustrated by the parent who insists that twelve-year-old Raymond ''be nice'' and give Aunt Martha a kiss, even though the child has protested that he doesn't like to do it. He complies, not to be kind to Aunt Martha, but to avoid trouble. Similar difficulties arise when children are prodded into saying they are sorry when, in fact, they are not. Again, youngsters learn that apologizing is the quickest way out of a dilemma rather than a sincere expression of remorse. Likewise, children who are urged to bestow false compliments on others as a way to charm them are learning that hypocrisy is acceptable. In order to avoid these undesirable outcomes, adults must refrain from being preoccupied with the outer trappings of kindness at the expense of helping children develop the empathy that is necessary for true kindness to occur. Hence, it would be better to give the child information about the other person that might prompt empathic feelings: ''Aunt Martha is glad to see you. She loves you very much. It would make her feel good to know that you care about her, too,'' ''When you were trying to practice with your crutches, you banged Jerry in the leg. That hurt a lot,'' or ''You told me you thought Carrie's spider was neat. She'd probably like to hear that from you.''

Making children share everything, all the time. There is no doubt that sharing is an important interpersonal skill that children should learn about. Unfortunately, there are times when adults promote this virtue too enthusiastically. They make children give up items that they have really not finished using as soon as other children want them. For instance, Elizabeth was using three grocery bags to sort the food in her ''store.'' One bag was for boxes, one was for cans, and one was for plastic fruit. She needed all three bags. Helen approached and asked if she could have one of the bags to make a ''dress.'' Elizabeth protested, but the adult insisted that Helen be given a bag. The adult dumped out the fruit and gave a sack to Helen. In this case, Elizabeth had a legitimate right to finish using the bag. It would have been easier for her to share it willingly once her game was over. A better approach would have been to say: ''Elizabeth, when you are finished playing your game, Helen would like a chance to use a bag. Tell her when you are ready.''

A variation of this problem occurs when adults arbitrarily regulate turntaking as a way to get children to share. For example, as soon as a child gets on a tricycle, the adult admonishes, ''Once around the yard, and then you'll have to get off so someone else can have a turn.'' This approach is utilized in a well-meaning effort to avoid conflict or to be fair. However, it often ends up with no child feeling truly satisfied. Furthermore, it requires constant adult monitoring. Instead, allow children to fully use the materials to which they have access. It would be better, if at all possible, to expand the amount of equipment available so that youngsters are not pressured into having to give up something with which they are deeply involved. If this is not possible, prompt empathic feelings by pointing out that others are waiting and would like a turn, too. Finally, remember to praise children when they finally relinquish what they have been using to someone else. Point out how their actions pleased the child who wanted to be next.

SUMMARY

Cooperation and helpfulness are the two major categories of prosocial behavior. Cooperation involves people working together toward common goals, and helpfulness involves alleviating distress or facilitating others' work or play. This help can either be instrumental or psychological. Youngsters who behave prosocially develop feelings of satisfaction and competence, have many successful encounters, and get help and cooperation from others in return. They learn to respond positively to offers of help and cooperation from others as well. Groups in which prosocial behavior is fostered are friendlier and more productive than those in which it is ignored.

To behave prosocially, children first must become aware of situations in which help or cooperation would be beneficial. Then, they have to decide if and how they will help or cooperate, and finally, take the action (or lack of action) they have decided on. Desiring to act prosocially and knowing how best to do it are not necessarily learned at the same time. As children mature and gain experience, they become more proficient at matching their prosocial actions to the needs of others.

Age and culture influence children's prosocial behavior; gender does not. In our society, nurturing and sharing increase with age; rescuing and cooperating behaviors first increase and then show a downward trend. Children in cultures that value group living steadily increase in cooperativeness as they mature. Similarly, in many studies, rural children are more cooperative than urban children. Particular societal characteristics either prompt or inhibit prosocial conduct.

The most profound influences on children's helpful and cooperative behavior are the discipline strategies adults use, the behaviors they model, the behaviors in children they reward, and the prosocial values and skills they teach. Teaching children kindness can be accomplished through creating an atmosphere conducive to prosocial actions, through on-the-spot instruction, and through planned activities.

DISCUSSION QUESTIONS

1. Identify the two major categories of prosocial behavior. Discuss their similarities and differences, using examples from real life.
2. In small groups, talk about the benefits and risks of behaving prosocially. When appropriate, tell about some personal instances in which you did or did not behave prosocially and the consequences of those behaviors.
3. Geraldo is working hard at constructing a bridge out of tongue depressors. He seems to be having difficulty getting it to stay up. Patrick is watching.
   a. Delineate the steps Patrick will go through in acting prosocially toward Geraldo.
   b. Discuss all the possible choices Patrick will have to make and the potential outcomes of each decision.
4. Describe the influence of age on children's prosocial behavior. Discuss the emergence and the increase or decline of particular types of prosocial behaviors as children get older. Give reasons based on your understanding of children's development.
5. Discuss cultural influences on children's prosocial behavior. Describe experiences in your own upbringing to illustrate. Describe particular family or social values that had an impact.

6. Describe the attributes of the atmosphere of a formal group setting that facilitate the development of children's prosocial behavior. Discuss specifically how the discipline strategies you have learned thus far contribute to this atmosphere.

7. Describe six ways in which adults can model cooperation. Discuss how children can translate these techniques into their own behavior.

8. Using examples from the formal group setting in which you work, describe instances in which adults:
   a. Rewarded children's prosocial behavior.
   b. Overlooked children's prosocial behavior.
   c. Punished children's prosocial behavior.
   Discuss any aftermath you observed, either immediately or within a short time.

9. Discuss the role of direct instruction on children's prosocial behavior. Relate specific skills that foster helping and cooperating to particular strategies for teaching these skills.

10. In a small group, describe the most common pitfalls you have encountered when attempting to promote children's prosocial behavior. Discuss ways to avoid these in the future.

CHAPTER 15
Working with Parents

SOURCE: H. Armstrong Roberts

OBJECTIVES:

On completion of this chapter, you will be able to describe:

1. A rationale for forging effective relationships between parents and helping professionals.

2. A variety of methods for communicating with parents.

3. Skills for working more effectively with parents.

4. Pitfalls to avoid in working with parents.

This year, Mrs. Seitner has 26 children in her third-grade class. If she gets to know their parents very well, she will find out that:

Of six parents who are single, three are welfare recipients who are struggling just to meet their children's basic needs. One of these parents is just twenty-four years old and has two other children.

One parent is a reading specialist.

Fourteen mothers are employed full-time. Four more are working part-time. Two fathers are unemployed.

One set of parents operates a large apple orchard and cider mill.

Two parents are stepparents, and another has adopted an emotionally impaired adolescent.

Two others are considering divorce.

One parent faces recurring bouts of depression.

Another parent is eager to share some art experiences with the children if asked but is too shy to offer.

Two parents are abusive.

What these parents have in common is an emotional investment in their children and a link with Ross Elementary School through Mrs. Seitner. Other than that, without getting to know them better, we cannot be sure what they expect from their children, from the program, or from Mrs. Seitner.

Mrs. Seitner has come to understand that parents, as a group, vary greatly—in family structure, in their attitudes toward school, and in their expectations, needs, and values. She knows that although the overwhelming majority of American children still live in nuclear families, there are growing numbers of teenage and never-married parents, bi-nuclear or blended families, older parents, and, most dramatically, single-parent families. Over half of all mothers are in the work force, with employment pressures usurping the time they have available to spend with their children and

participate in the school setting (Berger, 1981). In the last ten years that Mrs. Seitner has been at Ross Elementary, she has watched these social changes strongly reflected in the families whose children attend the school.

This year, some parents will choose to become only minimally involved in Mrs. Seitner's program. These may be parents who are disenchanted with or hostile to helping professionals, social-service programs, or educational institutions; those who are overwhelmed with personal responsibilities; and a few who have become apathetic and generally unresponsive because of past insensitivity on the part of an educator. Mrs. Seitner is aware that parent involvement in the school setting, each parent's ability to reinforce what is taught in the classroom, and parents' expectations for their children, the program, and the staff have a direct correlation to their children's scholastic performance and self-concept. For that reason, she takes seriously the challenge of encouraging *all* parents to become involved in her program.

A RATIONALE FOR FORGING AN EFFECTIVE PARENT–HELPING PROFESSIONAL PARTNERSHIP

Linking Parents and Professionals: Why Do It?

Parent involvement is "a process by which parents and helping professionals learn together and function as facilitators of each other in their efforts to make life more meaningful for children and themselves"(Swick and Duff, 1978:6). Although this involvement usually takes place in the center or school setting, it also can take place in the child's home. Forging this important link between consumer and producer is critical if helping professionals are to (a) understand the needs and expectations of children and parents; and (b) establish shared goals and objectives that can lead to appropriate and stable programs to meet those needs and expectations (Cattermole and Robinson, 1985).

In some schools and centers, teachers and administrators are hesitant, skeptical, and occasionally even hostile about encouraging parent participation, not wanting to deal with additional pressures, scrutiny, scheduling problems, and permutations of ideas that accompany such involvement (Johnston and Slotnik, 1985). However, research indicates that this attitude may not be in the best interests of the child, the parents, or the program.

Parent Involvement as a "Consumer Right"

Many parents today expect to play an active role in the shaping of their children's education and extrafamilial care because they feel that becoming involved is a responsibility as well as a right and because their taxes or direct payments help finance schools, hospitals, and day-care centers. Active involvement also provides parents with more accurate and timely information about what goes on in the formal group setting. More often than not, it sparks feelings of grassroots ownership and a sense of control that keeps parents from feeling apathetic, alienated, or cynical about such programs.

Benefits of Parent Involvement

When parents believe that their own involvement is important, they are more likely to communicate to the child the importance of these programs (Nedler and McAfree, 1979). As can be expected, parents' perceptions of their influence in program decision making and of the quality of parent-professional relationships are positively related to their satisfaction with and their children's success in the program (Bronfenbrenner, 1977; Schaefer, 1972; Revicki, 1982).

Hence, "empowered" parents are more inclined to support the financial operation and policy of these programs when called on to do so. Strong parent-professional links that truly become resources to the helping professional also may serve to relieve some of the job stress and dissatisfaction currently being felt by many helping professionals, who increasingly are considering early retirement and professional alternatives (Stewig, 1985).

Current studies of parent involvement support the view that it creates a stronger and more comprehensive experience for children and is one of the most important elements in arranging an optimal learning environment (Allen, 1983; Herman and Yeh, 1982). Direct benefits to children include more individualized attention; the opportunity to relate to other adults, some of whom may be ethnically or culturally different from their own parents; and wider acquaintance with specialized knowledge and talents (music, carpentry, career and job information, hobbies, and crafts). Parents themselves also benefit from such involvement, often manifesting more positive parenting behavior both during and following involvement, which also enhances the development of other children in the family (Berger, 1981).

Government Support for Parent Involvement

Evidence of the government's support for parent involvement can be found in the mandate to include parents in all phases of Project Head Start, in the education of handicapped children (Public Law 94-142), and in agency-provided day care. Federal interagency day-care guidelines require that whenever an agency provides day care for 40 or more children, there must be a policy advisory committee whose membership must be composed of no less than 50 percent parents or parent representatives selected by the parents (Honig, 1979).

FORMING THE PARTNERSHIP

Differences that May Separate Parents and Professionals

Making parents feel an integral part of their child's education and care may not come naturally to the helping professional, and there are no guarantees that the home and formal group setting will not be pulling in opposite directions. There are many differences between helping professionals and parents that, without skillful handling on the part of the professional and cooperation by the parents, might make it difficult for them to work side by side. Teachers and professional caregivers are trained to work with children; most parents must rely on their own experiences of growing up, some of which may no longer be relevant in today's world. The professional has the interests of all the children in the group to consider; the parent naturally is more interested in the welfare of his or her own child. Professionals are paid to do what they do; parents are not. Because of these factors, professionals automatically are granted authority, status, and defined roles, which parents often must do without. Whenever parents come into a formal group setting for children, no matter how powerful they may be in another setting, they often feel they are "on someone else's turf."

Identifying Goals of Home-School Linkages

Hymes (1974) identified two aims of an active home-school relationship, which can reasonably be generalized to other parent-helping professional relationships. These are:

1. To bring about between teachers and parents a common understanding of what children are like—how they grow; how they behave; the problems they face, and how to help them meet these challenges.

2. To bring about between teachers and parents a common understanding of good education—what it looks like; how it operates; what it requires; what it avoids; and what it strives for.

Hymes notes that, although "working with parents" sounds very positive, making the necessary flow of ideas, energy, creativity, and leadership a reality involves a two-way process, with adjustments in attitudes that many helping professionals are unwilling to make. This means that each social-service system *and* each individual program should have a planned, systematic structure for communicating with and involving parents, with each connection, event, and arrangement carefully thought through before implementation (Williams, 1985). This does *not* mean having the professional arbitrarily predetermine all of the goals. What is called for is the hard work of setting common goals and objectives, generating a set of reasonable alternatives, and putting the plan to the test with the cooperative involvement of both parent and professional. Finally, there must be planned evaluation, conducted in a manner that is nonthreatening to each party: How well were goals realized? How can the available energies of parents and professionals be more effectively joined and utilized to strengthen their mutual support for the children and for one another?

Forging Relationships

The manner in which helping professionals forge relationships with parents is vitally important because these initial encounters lay important groundwork that may shape or reinforce parents' attitudes about other social programs. Parents of preschool- and kindergarten-age children traditionally have been more closely involved with their children's teachers than have parents of older children. However, parent involvement as children mature should not be viewed as less important, and professionals serving older children should make more intensive efforts to gain parent participation.

Although parent-professional linkages obviously are desirable and beneficial, it cannot be assumed that more commitment to the concept will result in successful implementation. Both parents and professionals must be willing to look at their roles from the other's perspective and in ways that will allow for the development of sensitivity toward one another's responsibilities and needs. Professionals can prepare the climate for this to happen only by establishing open communication with parents from the very beginning of their relationship.

METHODS OF COMMUNICATING WITH PARENTS

Communication, often defined as the art of passing along or exchanging information, is, unfortunately, not always done very artfully. Although communication usually is thought of in positive terms, as in "Communication is the key" or "The solution is communication," it is clear from the real-life experiences we have that communication can be both positive and negative. Much depends on the manner in which it happens, the prior relationship of those who are communicating, and how satisfied the parties are afterward with both the process and the result. Positive communication between professionals and parents is crucial if any system is to function for the benefit of the child and satisfaction of the parent.

Unless professionals make an active effort to supply accurate information, parents will rely on two methods for evaluating what is going on in the formal group setting, both of which may be faulty: (a) what their children tell them (Cattermole and Robinson, 1985); and (b) whatever else they can glean from the media. In addition, parents who have learned very little about the educational process since they themselves were

in school will compare that information with their own recollections of what school was like or what they think it should be like (Rutherford and Edgar, 1979). Hence, they may come to faulty conclusions when their children say: "We didn't have to do anything today. We had a substitute" or "Miss Jenison is mean. She yells at everybody!" Similarly, when parents read in the newspaper that third-graders in their district are scoring below children in a neighboring district in reading and math, they may conclude that instruction is poorer in their own district. Although the truth may be that the testing results were influenced by advance preparation of the students in the other district or skewed by a large influx of non-English-speaking children in their own system, they can only make their conclusions from the information they have. One teacher who provided parents with opportunities to share their concerns with him noted that parents asked him "why their children were painting the classroom (a very special free-time project), trading lunches (an experience in bartering), getting points for being good (a token system), and engaging in sensitivity training (he was teaching them to button their clothes and never did understand what the parent was talking about). In all of these cases, the parents were basing their perceptions of classroom activities on what they had learned from their children" (Rutherford and Edgar, 1979:14). For this reason, relevant information must be communicated accurately and clearly. Jargon commonly used among professionals (time on task, behavioral objectives) should be avoided as much as possible because it serves as a barrier in both written and oral communication.

Sharing Information About General School Policy and Operation

Although some parents never will get into the school, center, or community program, almost all of them want to know as much as possible about general policy and program operation. This information includes items about the program calendar (including conference dates, scheduled holidays, professional in-service days, and so on); transportation schedules and routes; names and telephone numbers of program staff (it helps to include photographs so that parents can readily identify staff members at group meetings); general program procedures with respect to tardiness, absences, and illness; lunch and snack menus; screening and assessment dates; fees assessed for meals and special activities; rosters of other participants and their birthdates; car-pool information; field trips; and rules related to discipline. Much of this information may be shared in a parent handbook that is distributed at the beginning of the program year, in written notices that go home with children, or in newsletters that are periodically sent home to parents. Written communication that goes out to parents should be of high quality. These should generally be typed and should be attractively formatted and edited *carefully* for any errors.

Increasingly, with the advent of cable television, school districts and other community-service groups are purchasing media time and distributing information of this type on special channels that parents are made aware of through advertisements in the local newspaper. Information also can be transferred over the radio and by telephone networks, although these tend to be less reliable than communications mailed directly to the home. Group meetings, such as parent orientation meetings at the beginning of the year, serve as a more interactive mode of transferring information and can be helpful in getting information to non-reading parents. Again, there will be parents who are unable or unwilling to attend a public meeting. A comprehensive effort to communicate information to all parents probably will call for a combination of written and oral methods. If there are sizable groups of non-English-speaking parents, efforts should be made to have the information translated for them.

Sharing Information About Children's Progress

It is very important to parents to have an accurate and sensitive exchange of information about how well their children are progressing. This type of information differs from information about school policy in that two-way, rather than one-way, communication should predominate. Also, this information must be delivered in such a way as to keep it confidential. The most common methods for sharing information about children's progress are informal notes and telephone calls, report cards, samples of the child's work, parent-teacher conferences, and home visits.

Informal contacts. Informal notes and calls should be used for reporting both satisfactory and unsatisfactory progress so that the parent isn't instantly put on alert when receiving a note or call from the professional. In fact, the positive note or telephone call can go a long way in reinforcing the efforts of both parent and child in the educational process.

Report cards. Report cards or periodic notices serve as a "safety net" for parents who cannot attend conferences but who are interested in their child's progress and development. If these are used, they should contain a section where parents can record their own comments, note that they have looked at the report, and register any questions or concerns they may have about the contents. These should be returned to the professional and kept during the school year but eventually sent home for the family to keep. Copies of the reports should be kept in children's cumulative folders so that if there are concerns at a later date about a child's progress, professionals and parents may refer to the records. Comments by professionals should always be honest but made in such a way as to eliminate any value judgment that later could skew opinions of other educators. "Kevin has become very lazy about turning in his homework'' is inappropriate. A more effective comment might be, ''Kevin has turned in 5 out of 22 homework assignments this marking period.''

Work samples. Samples of a child's work can be shared with parents during conferences at the center, taken home periodically by the child, or presented by the professional during a home visit. Professionals should make sure, for both the child's and the parents' sake, that there are positive as well as critical comments (suggestions for improvement) on the papers and that an adequate sample of work is saved so that impressions by the parent will be accurate. If only the child's best work is saved, parents may be a bit confused when a child's grade does not reflect the sample. Similarly, it would be unfair to save only the worst output of the child in order to make a point about poor performance.

Work samples that are to be presented during a home visit or conference can be gathered into a booklet or folder by the child and teacher. This allows children to see their own progress over a period of time, particularly when a teacher takes time to look at the booklet with the child and points out where progress has been made. The booklet can serve as a useful tool for professionals and parents to decide together what kinds of reinforcement or additional experience the parent could provide if the child isn't achieving what he or she potentially could.

Parent conferences. Parent conferences often are the backbone of parent-professional communication and usually are scheduled two or three times a year. They provide excellent opportunities for two-way communication in which the parent and helping professional can clarify any misunderstandings and work together as a team to structure a home-center learning experience for the child.

Every possible effort should be made to accommodate parents who have tight schedules or, because of number and spacing of children in the family, more than one center and professional to visit. Cordial notices reminding parents of the scheduled dates and offering several time slots (morning, afternoon, and evening, if possible) should be sent home in advance of the conference. Parents should be given an opportunity to indicate whether they have children in other classes in the center or school so that a mutually agreeable meeting time might be arranged. Following return of the form from the parent, schedules should be made up and sent to parents, indicating the exact time and place of the conference and asking parents to call if the time assigned will be difficult for them. Suggestions might be made about issues for parents to consider before meeting with the professional. For example, Mr. Kendall is considering adding an after-school program if there is enough interest by parents. Giving them some time to think about the idea prior to the conference would be beneficial.

Before parents arrive, the room in which the conference is to be held should be structured to ensure privacy and to eliminate any physical barriers between the professional and parent. If the conference is to be held in a day-care center, preschool, or elementary school, adult-sized chairs should be made available. These should be placed beside a table, which can be used for cups and materials. It is preferable that the professional not sit behind a desk because this arrangement gives a clear message of unequal status and may interfere with two-way communication.

Chairs can be placed in a hallway to accommodate parents who are waiting. Coffee or punch could be served by a volunteer (this could be a retired person in the community). The volunteer also could have parents fill out name tags and provide any relevant materials, such as a child's work folder, for parents to look through while waiting to see the teacher. Displays, reading material, and exhibits also can be set up for parents. Time schedules should be strictly adhered to so that parents' time commitments are respected. If a parent feels the need to talk longer about a particular problem, another appointment should be made. Responsibility for staying within the time limit is the professional's; when only a few minutes are left, the professional should make some move toward wrapping the session up, alerting the parent that the conference is coming to a conclusion and encouraging him or her to make some final comments or schedule an additional appointment. The professional can stand when the time is up, walk the parent to the door (thanking them for coming), and greet the parent who is scheduled next.

Obviously, what goes on between the professional and the parent during the conference is important. Professionals will want to think very carefully about their objectives for the conference, such as documenting the child's progress, explaining the program, learning more about the parent and child, allowing the parent to share her or his thoughts and feelings, and structuring some common goals for the child's benefit. The professional should know the parents' names and should not assume that their last name is the same as the child's. The conference should begin and end on a positive note, and professionals should allow parents adequate time to talk. Comparisons between the child and other children in the family or class should not be made. Concrete examples of the child's work and behavior should be available to support specific comments by the teacher. Although the tone of the conference should be relaxed, professionals should be able to bring the conversation back on track if it wanders. Professionals will want to call on their nonverbal communication skills (see Chapter 3), using appropriate eye contact and body language that says to the parent: ''I'm glad you're here. I'm listening; I'm interested. Tell me more.''

Although professionals will want to share exactly how the child is functioning in the program, they should not use words such as shy, below average, lazy, uncooperative, mean, or selfish in describing a child's behavior to a parent. Appropriate, more descriptive substitutes might be such phrases as ''watches for a while before participating,'' ''is easily distracted,'' or ''concentrates on one part of the task and does not look at the entire picture.'' Professionals should avoid telling parents that their child ''has a problem.'' Even if this is so, it is not just the child's problem. The statement probably should be phrased, ''I need your help in figuring out a better way to help Sally with . . .'' (Berger, 1981).

Home visits. Many of the communication skills described here also will be helpful when professionals make home visits. Home visits were popular in rural America, lost some ground as the country became more industrialized, and now are enjoying a renaissance (Swick and Duff, 1978). In fact, in some federally funded programs, home visits are mandated.

Professionals arrange to visit parents and children in their homes for several reasons. First, such contacts are a visible way of demonstrating interest in the child and the family as well as a willingness to step out of the formal group setting into an environment in which parents are in charge. In addition, home visits give helping professionals an opportunity to meet siblings and other people who live in the home and to observe family interactions. Finally, a visit to the child's residence may open channels of communication between the child's two important microsystems, home and school.

Many parents also appreciate this form of communication because it gives them a chance to meet the professional personally and privately. Additionally, when made prior to the child's entry into the program, home visits give children an opportunity to meet the helping professional in a familiar and comfortable setting. An added benefit is that when youngsters arrive at the formal group setting, there is already someone there whom they know.

In spite of all these advantages, home visits are not without drawbacks. They are time consuming for the professional and often require them to travel long distances or make visits in the evenings or on weekends. Reasons parents cite for disliking home visits are that they are ashamed of the place they live in or of their housekeeping, they are worried that their children may misbehave during the visit, they find such contacts as intrusion, or they interpret them as judgmental.

Thus, professionals need to think very seriously about whether a home visit will enhance their relationship with a child and his or her parents or detract from it (Croft, 1979). If the former seems to be the case and a home visit is planned, certain proprieties must be observed.

When planning a home visit, professionals first should establish the purpose for the visit. Because considerable time, energy, and expense is involved, the visit should accomplish a goal that can be achieved in no other way. It also should promote a more positive relationship between the parent, professional, and child.

Parents should work with the professional in setting the time, and the professional should arrive at that specified time. Many of the suggestions given for structuring a conference in the formal setting also apply to the home visit. In addition, professionals need to remain composed when family behaviors are at odds with their own ideas about family life. No visit should last more than an hour unless the family has previously invited the teacher to stay for a meal or a family event. The professional should follow the visit with a note of thanks to the family for allowing him or her to come, including a positive but sincere comment of some sort. Finally, the professional should think back over the visit to analyze how well objectives were met and to determine how the visit could have been improved (Swick and Duff, 1978). When a parent consistently makes excuses about why a visit cannot be arranged or cancels scheduled visits, the professional may wait to become better acquainted with the parent in other ways before attempting to set up a visit again.

Sharing Information About the Educational Process

Parents discuss what goes in early childhood centers and their local school system over the bridge table, on the telephone, at the grocery store, and at the office. They are concerned about the changes that are made, certain curricula that are instituted, staff behavior, and requests for greater funding. To ensure that parents have accurate information on which to base their discussions, professionals need to share new developments in education. This calls for translating research findings and educational or developmental theory into terms that can be understood by nonprofessionals. Although this may sound like a big job, professionals usually can draw on a large bank of resources to help them in this effort. Experts in areas such as health, counseling, legal problems, physical fitness, consumer problems, child psychology, safety, and nutrition often can be found in the community or in neighboring communities. Librarians, physicians, university and college faculty, family-service agency personnel, cooperative extension service staff, police officers, nurses, dentists, and a number of other community business people who understand current issues affecting the growth and development of children often are pleased to share such information with parents. Films and filmstrips on a variety of subjects can be ordered. A library for parents can be set up in an empty room if one is available. Included could be books; magazine articles; relevant journals; children's educational toys that could be loaned out; and filmstrips and videotapes, if equipment is available. This room also could serve as a lounge for teachers and professionals, where some excellent informal communication could go on.

Parent visits to the program. Besides structuring public and informal opportunities for parents to learn more about the program, and perhaps more important, programs should have an open-door policy with respect to parents.

FIGURE 15-1 Many parents appreciate an occasional opportunity to observe or participate in classroom activity.

Observation of what goes on in the program provides parents an excellent opportunity to see typical routines and procedures, something that can't truly be observed in a "back-to-school night," for instance, when teachers are not really teaching and the students are not there interacting with one another. In order to provide the best kind of experience, parents should be asked to telephone ahead to let the professional know they are coming in case a field trip or some other, more unusual event is being planned. At that time, the professional could ask parents a little more about what they might like to observe and inform them of any limitations that would be put on the observation (for example, no direct interaction with children). The observation should include a follow-up session in which parents have an opportunity to ask questions and clarify anything they didn't understand about what they saw or heard.

Clearly, communicating effectively with parents requires a variety of professional skills, such as considerable savvy in structuring adult-education programs, interpersonal skills for working with individuals and groups, and knowledge of strategies for motivating parents to move beyond simple information exchange and into the realm of more intense involvement in the extrafamilial processes that affect their children's lives.

SKILLS FOR WORKING WITH PARENTS

Building an effective parent-professional bond is a developmental process that the helping professional can facilitate by using the following strategies:

1. Build rapport with parents. Be as friendly as you are businesslike. Say "Hello" and smile when you see parents. Parents need attention every bit as much as their children do. Get to know them as individuals as much as possible. Find out what their special interests, skills, hobbies, and burdens are. Share some of your own thoughts and feelings with parents that will help them to view you as a human being as well as a professional. What you communicate non-verbally is as important as what you say aloud to parents. If you always appear rushed, parents will be hesitant about approaching you. If your eyes flit elsewhere when talking with them (your watch, the door, the children), they will feel you aren't listening to them. This also will be true if your speech is hurried or if you interrupt them to share *your* point of view before they have had an adequate opportunity to say what they want. Let them know that you are genuinely interested in a partnership that will benefit their child. All of the interaction skills that have been discussed in detail in previous chapters work as well with parents as with their children and should be actively employed.

2. Encourage involvement by every parent. Encourage each parent to participate in some aspect of the program, no matter how small. Involvement opportunities should include alternatives to working directly with children at school because not every parent is able or desires to work in the classroom. Other tasks might include preparing materials at home, planning field trips or visits by resource people, making telephone calls, coordinating fund-raising activities, or addressing newsletters. Asking parents to do specific tasks often is successful because long-term commitments are not required. Telephone calls from you or an enthusiastic volunteer will have better results than requests by form letter.

Show that you are pleased with *all* efforts that are made. Remember to positively reinforce those efforts by a verbal thank you, a written note, and/or public confirmation. Whenever possible, facilitate attendance at program events by providing alternative meeting times, child-care volunteers, and transportation networking for parents who need a ride. Be especially alert for the parent who is making an obvious effort to become more involved but is confused about how to do so. Sensitivity will be needed as you and the parent decide what kind of contribution will be satisfying to him or her and helpful to the children's program. Try to match skill levels to responsibilities as closely as possible so that parents don't become bored or frustrated. Stress to all parents the importance of following through on commitments that are made. Develop meaningful tasks (not just busywork!) that can be done at home for parents who are unable to promise scheduled time but who do want to become involved. Stay in touch with parents who "drop out," letting them know that you miss seeing them.

3. Acquaint parents with program philosophy and direction. This can best be achieved by a home visit, a parent orientation session just prior to the beginning of the program, and/or a printed handbook that can be referred to later. Share what you have planned for the children in simple and clear terms. Explain what kinds of assessment tools will be used during the year, and discuss any experimental programs or materials planned that might depart from the ordinary. Not every parent will agree with your goals and teaching style. Some may be quite hostile if your ideas about interacting with and disciplining children differ greatly from theirs. Whenever there is an issue about which parents could take sides or question your rationale, share the information or research on which you based your decision. For example, if you know that there has been controversy in the past about whether religious holidays should be observed, research the issue and decide ahead of time how you want to handle this in your program. Be prepared to support your position by using facts rather than relying on your intuitive feelings. In discussing controversial issues, be prepared to re-evaluate your position when parents present evidence that is more persuasive than your own; hold your ground, however, if the evidence is not more persuasive or if making a change would be damaging to the children. Use an authoritative (based on reason and cooperation) rather than an authoritarian (bossy, directive, coercive) approach, which may alienate parents.

4. *Communicate basic information.* Give parents a map and a tour of the center or school if they are unfamiliar with the layout, showing volunteers additional rooms (such as bathrooms, copy centers, lunchrooms, and auditoriums) in which they may be working. Explain attendance and discipline policies, additional services that are available (after-school care, health care, speech therapy, remedial and tutorial programs), and policies related to unscheduled center closings or natural disasters. Provide a program calendar that includes scheduled holidays, parent-professional conferences, and parent-teacher council meetings. Explain procedures related to entering and leaving the building, signing in for volunteer work, parking regulations, use of materials, arrangements for children's and volunteers' meals, use of the telephone, and who to contact (supply a telephone number) when they or their

children cannot attend. If extra fees are to be assessed, explain how the money is used and when payment is due. Share possible alternatives, such as free lunch allowances or breakfast, when there is financial difficulty. Give parents a list of various community agencies that can be helpful in times of stress. For each agency, include a contact person and telephone number.

5. *Become proficient at eliciting needed information from parents.* Have parents fill out intake forms prior to the beginning of the program that indicate with whom the child resides, who should be contacted in an emergency, whether there are custody issues, if there are siblings in other parts of the program, and whether there are any health issues (allergies, hearing or vision difficulties) or family issues about which you should be informed. If the child is to be picked up from school by another adult, ask to have that person identified. Encourage parents to let you know when unplanned events occur in the family that are unsettling to the child and that may affect the child's behavior at the center or at school. Also, explain that you would appreciate hearing from parents if the child seems particularly upset about something that has happened in the program that you may be unaware of, such as something that occurred on the playground, in a bathroom, or in a hallway that the child was reluctant to tell an adult about.

6. *Deal with sensitive issues tactfully.* Whether you are dealing with problems related to abuse, uncleanliness, tardiness and absenteeism, disease, discipline, or some other area that may arouse strong feelings, the best approach is to remain calm and focus on the issue and what can be done to remedy it. Such topics should never be discussed when others are present. Rather, you should schedule an appointment with the parent as quickly as possible to discuss the problem.

When another professional, such as an administrator or mental-health professional, is asked to attend the meeting, the parent should be told in advance that another person will be present. Confidentiality must be respected. The problem, the way the parent responded to it, or any difficulties in conflict resolution should never become a topic of conversation in the lounge or with other members of the community.

7. When conflict resolution is necessary, make it as positive as possible. Confronting someone about something on which you disagree never is pleasant. However, unless conflicts are faced and resolved, relationships usually deteriorate. Conflict can be negative or positive. Positive conflict resolution is based on ideas, issues, values, and principles. Negative efforts to resolve conflict usually involve attacks on personality, vindictiveness, and personal power struggles. In working through conflict areas with parents, try to compromise wherever possible. Treat the parent with respect no matter how negative she or he may become. Use all the skills you have learned in this book to help you understand and take into account the parent's point of view when expressing your own. Find common ground; focus first on those things about which you agree. For instance, your assessments of what a particular problem entails may be alike, even though the solutions proposed may be widely divergent. Being sensitive and empathic does not weaken your own position or convictions. It only allows the other person to feel that he or she has been listened to fairly. Listen to the parent until you "experience" his or her side of the issue. Listen to the *content* of that person's ideas, the *meaning* the issue has for him or her, and the *feelings* he or she has about it. When asking questions in order to gain more information about a parent's feelings or attitudes, do so in a nonthreatening manner. When you have heard what the

parent has to say, and if you still believe there is an issue that needs discussion, state your views, needs, and feelings, but do it this way:

a. Be brief.
b. Avoid loaded words and phrases like "always" or "never."
c. Avoid words that accuse and evaluate, such as "stubborn," "uncooperative," or "vicious."
d. Don't withhold important information or exaggerate.
e. Focus on the issue, not on personalities, hearsay, or what happened in the past.
f. Use personal messages rather than accusations. As you will remember, a personal message includes:
   (1) A reflection.
   (2) A clear statement of how you feel.
   (3) The behavior that has caused you to feel that way.
   (4) A reason why the behavior or event is upsetting to you ("I have been trying to get hold of you for several days. I would like to talk to you about Evan's reluctance to approach other children. Let's work out a time to get together").
   (5) What you want the person to do instead.

Sometimes, it is not possible to use a reflection because you do not know the person's point of view. If this is the case, still make sure to include the other steps.

If it is clear that parents are unable to deal reasonably with the problem at the time, indicate that you believe it would be best to set up another meeting in the near future after everyone has had a chance to think about what has been said. It also may be necessary to call in an objective third party, or arbitrator, who is acceptable to both the professional and parent. If parents are abusive, either on the telephone or in person, the professional should let the parent know that this behavior is not helpful in reaching a resolution and therefore is not acceptable. The meeting or telephone call should then be terminated. A subsequent contact should involve the presence of another professional who might provide added experience, objectivity, or protection.

8. Establish clear guidelines about areas of responsibility. Parents who are asked to take care of tasks they consider to be part of the professional's responsibility (*"You're getting paid to do this, not me!"*) may become alienated or reluctant to remain involved. Teachers who use volunteers should carefully outline a rationale for delegated responsibilities and communicate those reasons to parents. In order to ensure task completion and a smoothly running operation, clear, well thought out guidelines ought to be drawn up as to whether the professional or parent is to take primary or secondary responsibility in any given situation. Also, parents may wonder who is to take charge when trouble erupts. Again, professionals need to set clear guidelines for parents who volunteer in the group setting or who serve as paid aides. In handling disruptive situations, particularly when their own child is involved, parents may hesitate to act without the teacher's permission or may overreact because of embarrassment. Many parents and professionals have found the following guidelines both fair and useful:

a. Parents are in charge of the "home front." In other words, when a professional is making a home visit, or in a setting unrelated to the school program, parents are in charge of their own children and should take action when necessary. Exceptions would include events such as a field trip or center pic-

nic. In these cases, school or center rules would apply.

b. Parents who are acting as volunteers or as paid aides in the program should take responsibility primarily for children other than their own and leave the handling of their own children to another volunteer or the professional. If this is the accepted procedure, adults in the classroom should be quick to attend to problems involving another volunteer's child. For example, if Mrs. Sanchez is attempting to read a story to a group of children and her own child continually interrupts, the professional or another volunteer should move swiftly to deal with the situation.

9. Give credit and recognition for contributions, both great and small. Continually let parents know how much you appreciate the time and effort they contribute, not just because their help allows you to do a better job, but also because the children benefit so greatly (Berclay, 1977). A personal thank you is important; in addition, schools and centers often hold dinners or teas to honor contributing parents and introduce them at assemblies and other school programs. Their contributions are described in newsletters that go out to all parents or in community newspapers, and they are presented with tangible items such as pins, certificates, plaques, and thank-you notes from students. Parent volunteers often become advocates for the program because of their personal investment—as long as they feel appreciated. If they begin to feel their contributions are not valued, however, they also can become a school's greatest critic.

10. Ask for evaluative feedback from parents during the year. One of the best ways to let parents know that their input counts is to provide several opportunities for them to evaluate your performance and what they believe is happening in the program. One informal and ongoing method is to provide a suggestion box somewhere outside the classroom where parents can drop anonymous or signed suggestions for change. Although you would like to think that you have been honest and open enough that they feel free to share their thoughts and feelings with you, opportunities for anonymous feedback still should be made possible. In addition to this, brief surveys and questionnaires can be sent home for parents' response. This probably should be done just prior to conference times, noting on the form that there will be a drop box for responses outside the classroom door or that surveys can be put into the suggestion box at any time or returned via children. This prompts parents to examine their feelings and ideas about how the program is serving their child before they come into the conference and also gives the professional additional feedback that parents may be reluctant to share during the conference.

At some point, share with parents (in a group meeting or through a newsletter) some of the changes that have come about because of the input you have received from them. Again, don't just assume that if you begin changing a bulletin board more frequently, or begin getting children ready to leave earlier so parents don't have to wait, the parents will notice. Let them know that you intend to act on some of their suggestions, and provide evidence when you have done so.

11. Work together with parents to reduce children's stress.

Once children move into a situation in which they receive a significant portion of their care from adults other than their parents, all of the adults then become linked in the delicate responsibility of guiding their socialization. In order for this to be a cooperative linkage, the adults must be willing to share with one another what they believe the others need to know about a child in order to most effectively support the child's needs. This calls for frank, open communication that is conducted in a non-threatening, nonjudgmental manner. Whenever one adult seeks to place blame or to unfairly criticize the genuine attempts of another adult to be supportive, the thread that links them together is weakened significantly. Professionals can be most helpful to parents when they:

Let parents know when a child is manifesting signs of distress.

Remain alert for signs of parental stress.

Share information with parents about the effects of childhood and adult stress through seminars or newsletters.

Listen empathically to parents when they speak of their own stress.

Let parents know they want to work cooperatively with them to support them and their child.

Acknowledge parents' efforts to work cooperatively to reduce a child's level of distress.

These skills are discussed in more detail in Chapter 10, Helping Children Cope with Stress.

12. Eliminate nonconstructive criticism of parents or children.

One point that must be underscored is that sometimes, professionals can be sensitive to the feelings of the children they serve but quite insensitive to the same range of feelings in adults. Parents also are subject to anger, jealousy, fear, and resentment. When a professional approaches a parent in a domineering, threatening, blaming, or angry manner, he or she puts that person on the defensive, thereby severely reducing the chance to work together cooperatively for the benefit of the child. When offering constructive suggestions, ask yourself the following questions (Simon, 1978):

1. Can this person be responsive to what I have to say?
2. Has he or she heard it before?
3. Will it make any difference if they hear it again?
4. Can I word it in such a way that it will be less threatening?
5. Am I willing to work with the person in a supportive way to effect some change, recognizing that change does not always come quickly or easily?
6. Do I have any helpful alternatives to suggest?
7. How would I feel if I were in this person's situation?

When all of these questions have been asked, any criticism that still seems justified is likely to be delivered in a more constructive way.

Acknowledge parents' efforts to work with you. Again, parents enjoy recognition from important others in their lives (that's you!) that the energy they have spent has been worthwhile. Confirmation on your part that you've really been successful in tackling a problem together will prompt future cooperation.

13. When integrating children with special needs, utilize the child's parents as a primary resource. Children's special needs may range from the need for a more stable family or economic situation to the need for help in adjusting to a physical or mental handicap. Find out all you can about the family structure and the child's specific abilities and disabilities from the parents' perspective. The two most common concerns of parents of children with learning disabilities are the social acceptance and future of the child (Montgomery, 1982). Parents who have not yet fully accepted what the child's condition

will mean in the long run may need your help in working with other professionals who can provide additional information. Some parents may not accept a diagnosis that has been made on a marginal condition and may think that if the child were only pushed a little harder to produce, there would be no problem.

You also will have to be supportive and responsive to parents of nonhandicapped children. They may have questions and concerns about the presence in the group of a handicapped child or a child with other special needs. Such concerns are to be expected. Parents may worry that their own child may not get enough attention or may pick up "weird behavior." If you become defensive or intimidating or make parents feel guilty for having "negative" feelings, you probably will construct unwanted barriers. Respond as honestly as possible to both open and hidden concerns. For example, a parent might ask, "Things going pretty smoothly this year with all the changes?" If your were to respond, "Not bad," leaving it there, the interaction probably would end, cutting off the parent's opportunity to share his or her concerns. If, however, you respond: "Not bad. How are parents looking at them?", you leave an opening for the parent to bring out his or her own concerns in the context of a general response. Make yourself available to answer questions, and invite parents into the classroom to observe for themselves. Let parents know that you are interested in their questions and feedback and that you value openness.

Professionals are cautioned not to fall into the trap of condescending to or feeling sorry for either a "disadvantaged" or a handicapped child or parents (Croft, 1979). The child and family may have adjusted to the situation very well and feel proud about it. Many, in fact, become more resourceful for having done so. Sometimes, it is not the disabling event itself that continues to stress some children and families, but rather their perspective of how much the situation affects their well-being and how others feel about them as a result. The focus of the professional must be on the child's current strengths and needs and on implementing well-conceived goals for enhancing development and meeting the needs.

14. Contribute to parents' growth and development by scheduling parent education seminars and workshops. Address some of the critical issues identified by parents as well as some you believe need to be brought to their attention. As Thomas Gordon said, "Parents are blamed, not trained" (1974:1). The aim of parent education is to help parents become more knowledgeable about child rearing and about family life as it affects children (Nedler and McAfree, 1979).

15. Know the limitations of your own expertise and ability to help. Parents often view educators as bastions of wisdom and may ask for advice about personal and family problems as well as information about child rearing. Subjects can range from how to stop a child from wetting the bed to procedures for turning in a neighbor they suspect of child abuse. Sometimes, you will want to offer an idea that has worked in the past for another parent or suggest a helpful reading. However, when you do not have an appropriate answer, admit it. You should then be prepared to suggest referrals to trained specialists, particularly when the problem seems to suggest there may be a serious situation in the offing.

How to Help Parents of Preprimary Children in Dropping Off and Picking Up Their Children

Young children sometimes have conflicting emotions about having their parents leave, particularly when they are first being introduced to a formal group setting, during periods when the family is going through a significant change (mother entering the work force, father leaving because of divorce), and often following holiday recesses. Children balk because they're feeling insecure about what may happen while they're in the program. Also, parents are the most significant persons in their lives and, quite frankly, they enjoy being around their parents more than anyone else. Also, children new to an educational setting do not know how much "fun" school can be, so it does little good for the parents or professional to plead that case. Children only know that they are in a place they would rather not be and that their "security person" is leaving them with unfamiliar people who cannot, at least at that moment, quite fill the void.

Parents who are introducing children to a new setting and new people should plan, if possible, on spending some time in the setting with the child to help her or him become more secure. Although not all parents can rearrange their work schedules, the possibility ought to be suggested at the parent orientation meeting held prior to the opening of the center or school.

Personality differences in children make it difficult to design foolproof guidelines for separating, but the following procedure provides useful information to share with parents.

1. Give parents ideas about how to help their children prepare for their participation in the program. Suggest that they visit the building together, play on the playground, or drive or walk past the program site prior to the first day. Advise parents to tell the child that he or she will be attending the center or class and to describe in detail some of the things that will be going on each day. Encourage parents to bring the children to any orientation that might be offered.

FIGURE 15-2 This parent may need support from the helping professional in making the separation from her son.
SOURCE: © Susan Lapides 1983

2. Give parents specific guidelines for how to initiate the separation process once they arrive at the center or classroom. The first step is for parents to find a material that looks interesting to them and to begin playing with it. This shows children that the setting is a fun, safe place to be. Note that it has not been suggested that children be asked: ''Do you want to paint a picture?'' or ''Do you want to build with blocks?'' Youngsters often perceive such questions as pressure to separate and therefore resist the invitation. After five or ten minutes, if children have not become involved, parents can include them by saying something like: ''I can't decide just where to put this block. What do you think?''

3. Encourage parents to gradually remove themselves from direct interaction with their child. This step involves having the parent say something like: ''You're having a *really* good time here. I have to write a letter (read this book, work on a paper). I will sit on that bench (near the door but inside the room). I'll be there if you need me.'' If the child follows the parent to the chosen spot, a compromise is possible. The parent might say: ''I'll work here for 5 minutes. Then, I will join you.'' When the child becomes able to play comfortably for 20 minutes without checking on the parent, the parent can tell the child that he or she is going to the ''secretary's office'' for 5 minutes. It is important for the parent to then leave, even if the child protests, emphasizing that he or she will return. The parent must then reappear at the appointed time. This lets even the unhappy child know that the parent will do what he or she has promised to do. Parents can then spend an increasingly lengthy time away from the room. Once children can participate for at least 30 minutes without crying the whole time, parents can plan to leave their children at the appointed hour and pick them up when the program is over. Tell parents to anticipate the need for additional time to work through any separation problems with their child. Adapt the preceding routine to the parents' time constraints as necessary. Do not try to coerce parents into spending more time than they are able or make them feel guilty if they cannot stay as long as you might like.

4. *Encourage parents to leave promptly once they have said goodbye.* Lingering departures or unexpected reappearances heighten children's anxiety by making the environment unpredictable. Escort parents to the door, if need be, and assure them that you will call them later in the day to explain how the child is getting along.

5. *Physically intervene if necessary to help parents and children separate.* Frequently, parents wait for children to give them permission to leave. They try to obtain this permission with statements like: ''Don't you want to stay here with all your friends?'', ''You don't want me to lose my job, do you?'', or ''You want me to be proud of you, don't you?'' Children seldom cooperate in this effort. At this point, you should step in and say: ''Carla, your mom is leaving now. I'll help you find something to do.'' Then,

take the child to an activity. Assure the parent that this is part of your job and that you expect that eventually the child will become happily involved.

6. *Caution parents to resist the temptation to sneak away as soon as the child becomes involved with an activity.* This damages the child's confidence in the parent and reinforces the idea that the school or center is not a place to be trusted. It can create a real sense of abandonment and terror in a child and may later trigger a fresh and more intense outburst.

7. *Alert parents to potentially harmful ways of dealing with separation.* Some of these include pressuring children, shaming them, or denying their feelings. Sometimes, parents admonish their children to ''behave themselves,'' ''be good,'' or ''act nice.'' These cautions, although well intended, put pressure on children at a time when they least need additional worries. It is better for parents to say: ''Have fun!'', ''Have a nice day,'' or ''I love you. See you after outdoor time!''

In addition, children's anxiety increases when adults say: ''Mommy will feel bad if you don't stop crying,'' ''I feel sad when you don't like the school,'' or ''Nobody likes to play with a crybaby.'' These tactics do nothing to relieve the child's despair. Children who are sad or angry about separation should not be burdened with the additional responsibility of making other people feel better.

Finally, phrases like ''Don't worry'' or ''Don't cry'' intensify rather than soothe children's feelings of distress. Such statements indicate that the child's feelings are wrong or unimportant, rather than helping him or her find a constructive way to cope. It is better to acknowledge a child's true feelings, no matter what they are.

8. Agree to telephone distraught parents to reassure them when their child has adjusted to the separation, if necessary. Occasionally, the parent has more difficulty leaving the child than the child has in leaving the parent.

The procedure outlined here may be accomplished in half an hour or one day, or it may take several weeks. Some children will enter a room confidently, wave goodbye to their parents, and immediately settle into an activity. When they don't, these guidelines can be activated.

9. Support the parent and the child as needed in other transitions. Separating from children is not the only point at which parents experience problems with children in the program. Sometimes, the same kinds of behaviors are seen in children when parents participate in the setting (for example, in a cooperative nursery) or return to take them home. When this happens, the behavior probably springs from other causes. A child may show off or become aggressive or clinging when his or her parent is working for the day, simply not wanting to share the parent with other children. At pick-up times, the child may be involved in an activity and not want to be interrupted. The child may be cranky, tired, out of sorts, and even angry with the parent for leaving. At times like this, it is not helpful for professionals to make comments like: "I can't understand why Sammy is acting this way. He's an angel when you're not here" or "He's been so good all morning." These are "killer" statements that can make parents feel extremely upset. Parents may worry that they have less control over their children than do other parents or professionals or that the bond they have with their child is being weakened by their absence. Professionals should reassure parents that this behavior is normal in children. End-of-the-day transition procedures, such as caregivers alerting children that their parents are present and that they can get ready immediately or play for five more minutes, are helpful to parents. Some schools or centers even offer a lounge where parents can have a cup of coffee and relax a moment while the child and his or her belongings are readied for departure.

PITFALLS TO AVOID

Despite your best efforts, working with parents will not always be easy. It becomes more difficult when a few parents are insensitive, overbearing, threatening, rude, or unfair when trying to get the center or school to respond to their wishes. When professionals respond in kind, situations can deteriorate quickly. Helping professionals must always keep in mind that working constructively with parents is a critical and necessary part of the total process of working with children. There are certain pitfalls to be avoided.

Failing to recognize parents as consumers. Often, helping professionals consider the "center" or "school system" as their only employers. They fail to recognize the major investment most parents have made in their children in terms of love, money, time, and energy. They also forget that parents and other adults in the community fund professionals' salaries and that local control in education and child care is still highly valued by the American people. Simply acknowledging this fact is not enough. Helping professionals must hold themselves accountable, not just to the children they serve and the settings in which they work, but to the taxpayers in their locale who make such programs possible.

Failing to recognize parents as resources.   Don't assume that family behavior can be predicted by the neighborhood in which the family resides or any other general characteristic. Professionals can gain a great deal of insight into how a child functions by learning more about the parents' feelings, thoughts, behaviors, and values: How do they feel about this child? Are they proud or disappointed? What are their hopes for him or her? What kinds of models are they? What are their attitudes about education and educators? What kind of physical and emotional environment constitutes home for the child? What type of guidance procedure is used, and are interaction patterns primarily positive or negative?

With respect to at least one child in the program, each parent is an unqualified expert. You can simply give lip service to that concept, or you can make it work for you and the child by making up your mind to form real partnerships with parents. You can ask their advice when you have hit a dead end in helping the child, communicating honest feelings and admitting when you don't know the answer: "How do you get Jenny to hang up her coat? I'm having a tough time doing that." With especially shy children, most of the year could go by before you get a handle on the child's likes, dislikes, and interests. A parent often can provide a valuable shortcut to obtaining this information.

Responding only to the needs of parents with whom you feel comfortable and avoiding parents of different ethnic, racial, or cultural backgrounds.   Parents who are different from the majority of the other parents or who don't speak fluent English may shy away from becoming involved in the group setting because they feel they have little to offer. Others may sense, fairly or unfairly, a condescending or standoffish atti-

tude on the part of the professional. You must, first of all, examine your own attitudes with respect to minorities and people who depart from the mainstream. You will want to check whether predominant views you hold are more myth and stereotype or are true of that particular segment of the population. For example, there are wide variations in attitudes and values in all ethnic groups. Thus, it would be dangerous to generalize from one person to another just because they share similar ethnic backgrounds. Socioeconomic status probably accounts for wider differences between families than do ethnicity or culture (Croft, 1979). You will want to make an effort to study ethnic groups and cultures that differ from your own by traveling, taking classes, and taking advantage of social opportunities to interact with people who have other attitudes and value systems.

If you have had few personal experiences with certain ethnic groups and cultures, getting the "inside story" may be difficult. If parents feel that you have some sort of ulterior motive for getting to know them better, it will be impossible for you to get beyond a superficial relationship with them. If parents feel that you see them as "deficient," they naturally will close themselves off, and an important resource will be lost to you.

For instance, one young woman who applied for a Head Start position was excited about working with "those" children. What she hadn't counted on was that her job also required her to work with parents. However, armed with some of her best ideas from a parent-teacher interaction class she had taken in college, she marched in the first evening to share some of her expertise. The parents hadn't come prepared to receive it and had other things on their minds. She said the next day to one of her colleagues, "All they wanted to do was sit and talk and drink coffee!" She and the parents never were able to get beyond that, and the young woman lasted only the rest of the year in that position. Instead of working to meet parents where they needed her to meet them, she indignantly waited for them to "show some interest in their kids." However, their need to talk to one another about *their* concerns had to come first.

Professionals must be careful not to come across as the "expert" when working with parents, pushing what they know and where they learned it. They also need to remember that the attitudes they hold about parents often are transferred unconsciously to the children of those parents, perhaps negatively affecting the children's opportunities in the program and their self-esteem. Children come to school valuing their home and parents. They soon learn to view parents as others may view them, at least in the school setting. If their own particular ethnic group or culture is never represented in the textbooks they read or in the materials they use, they may formulate erroneous ideas about the worth of their own culture and ethnicity. Adults can use ethnic and cultural differences to build strength into the program, or they can choose to ignore them. The status quo can become the mark everyone shoots for, or differences can be positively highlighted in order to introduce children early to a richer world.

Allowing special-interest groups or powerful parents to determine all policy and program direction. Just as shy children in a classroom sometimes can be overshadowed by their more outgoing classmates, parents who are strong in numbers but not very articulate or vocal may need your help in protecting their concerns. If you are interested in representation from all families, you will have to make special efforts, through telephone and paper surveys and questionnaires, to assess the views of all parents when program issues are under consideration.

Any request or concern of parents should be studied to see:

a. How representative it is of all parents.
b. Whether it is a legitimate concern.
c. How feasible it is, given present resources of the school and needs of the children.
d. What adaptations would have to be made and what kinds of additional resources would have to be gathered in order to implement the idea.
e. How it would fit over the long term into overall program goals.
f. Consequences to students, parents, and the school or center system.
g. Benefits that might follow implementation.
h. How the administration would respond to such a proposal.

Until any proposal has been analyzed in this way, helping professionals need to move slowly in responding to pressure from special-interest groups.

Forgetting that parents have other roles that require their time and energy. The reaction of young children who run into their teachers at the supermarket or elsewhere in the community is often amusing to adults. The children seem absolutely amazed that the teacher can be anywhere but in the classroom and in the role of teacher. Ironically, professionals and parents hold like perspectives, unless they happen to travel in similar social circles that allow them to meet one another frequently outside the educational setting. Parents and professionals tend to think of one another narrowly and only in terms of the role each plays in their interactions. Thus, when parents think of helping professionals, they may forget that these people also are parents, spouses, adult children, voters, and home owners. Similarly, helping professionals can forget that although parents may play the parenting role 24 hours a day, other roles can and do become more dominant in their lives during that 24-hour period. They, too, experience the pressure of meeting job demands, maintaining a home, nurturing intimate relationships with persons other than their children, furthering their education or training, responding to their own parents' needs, and performing a wide variety of community obligations. An effective home-school relationship can only be built on a mutual understanding that parents are not simply parents and professionals are not simply professionals (Swick and Duff, 1978). The expanded roles that each play bring problems as well as added dimensions to the common goal they share, that is, facilitating children's development.

Failing to establish clear goals and objectives for involved parents. It is hard to imagine any parent today having unlimited time to spend involved in a center or school setting. Thus, it is frustrating to them when the purpose of their involvement is unclear. Professionals need to respect the effort that involvement requires on the part of parents, who could easily spend the time taking care of other obligations. Exercise skill in group process and management so that goal-setting sessions and the implementation of ideas move along at a reasonable pace. Time schedules and flow charts outlining action sequences and persons taking responsibility should be posted publicly and sent home to involved parents. Expectations agreed on should be well spelled out, and any materials needed should be discussed and ordered well in advance. Volunteers should be given adequate space in which to work, with as few interruptions as possible. When a volunteer is working with a specific child and the child is absent, the professional should contact the volunteer as soon as possible.

Working with parents only in a group format and neglecting to deal with individual needs. Some professionals feel that they have met their "obligation" in working with parents if they have an orientation meeting at the beginning of the year, bring in a couple of speakers for group presentations, and have a year-end meeting recognizing parent contributions during the year. No effort is made to deal with parents individually unless a parent calls for an appointment or the performance of the child necessitates the teacher contacting a parent. As was pointed out in the section on communicating with parents, connections can be made with parents in a variety of ways, both formally and informally, to ensure a better match between program and child and adequate opportunities for information exchange and evaluation.

Being inflexible and/or insensitive to the needs of financially troubled parents, working parents, single parents, teenage parents, divorced parents, stepparents, parents of handicapped children, and bilingual or migrant families. Professionals sometimes are seen as distant and unfeeling about the pressures many parents face in their everyday lives. Notices arrive home regularly reminding parents to put their children to bed early, to provide a quiet place to study, and to be sure that children eat a balanced diet. Parents whose homes are small and crowded, those who are unemployed, and those who are going through painful marital transitions or other unexpected crises must experience additional distress when receiving these reminders.

Most teachers do not get specific training to deal with troubled families (Croft, 1979). Although some professionals will have themselves experienced some of these difficulties, the sensitivity, understanding, flexibility, and insightfulness needed are characteristics that would be difficult, if not impossible, to teach in the college classroom. However, everyone can learn to be empathic. One way to do this is to gain as much information as possible from the parents' perspective and then picture yourself in the same situation (Croft, 1979).

When helping professionals have done their homework with respect to the families they serve, they will be aware of some of the many individual situations creating strain and hardship for parents. When they fail to be sensitive, parents' feelings of inadequacy, guilt, and alienation inevitably will increase as they find themselves unable to meet given expectations. Often, parents will never question the reality of the expectation, only their inability to respond adequately. Many parents will attempt to deal with this added pressure by putting as much distance as possible between themselves and the program (Nedler and McAfee, 1979). Although teachers need not restrict the kinds of general information they send to parents, they do need to filter criticism very carefully and have direct, individual contacts with parents who are troubled. These parents need to know that someone is concerned about *them*; professionals must verbalize this, noting that they can certainly understand if the parent needs additional support during that particular time.

Overreacting to negative parents. The less confident we are of our own position regarding a controversial issue, the more we will tend to become defensive when our views are challenged. As experience and continuing education allow us to integrate what we know about children and families with what others know, we will become more relaxed and open when others present a different, even hostile viewpoint. When we overreact to a critical and negative parent, we exhibit our fear of being proven wrong, our uncertainty, and our confusion.

A parent can make an important point, one that is based on very good intentions and might truly be helpful; however, she or he may deliver it in such a negative manner (blaming, sarcastic, derisive) that we fail to really listen. A message delivered in such a way that it puts the receiver in a highly charged emotional state often fails to be heard. Professionals need to work hard to stay calm in such a situation, to actively listen and to perhaps reflect to the parent: ''You're really angry. I think we need to talk about that, but I *am* hearing what you're saying about the need for a better information-delivery system, and I believe you're

right.'' Occasionally, hostile remarks and behavior by a parent may have little to do with the professional or with what is really going on in the program. The parent may be feeling overwhelmed or out of control in other important areas and may see no other outlet for expressing his or her frustrations. Some careful probing, combined with understanding responses, sometimes can help such a person to understand what is happening and re-evaluate his or her behavior.

Allowing yourself to be drawn into squabbles between parent volunteers, or between parents and other professionals. Remember that in every conflict, there may be two sides to the story. Sometimes, parents will share in confidence a personal difficulty they are having with another family member, another professional, or some other person familiar to both of you. It is natural for the person presenting his or her view of the situation to see himself or herself as the persecuted, not the persecutor, and to want you to agree with that viewpoint. Without siding with the person, you can serve an important function by just listening. Refrain from giving advice in this kind of situation. Allow the person to talk through his or her thoughts, feelings, and ideas without trying to influence the person in a particular direction. When it is clear that the person is not handling the situation very well or objectively, it is helpful to have handy the name and telephone number of another professional who might be trained to offer more guidance.

Stereotyping parents who are neglectful or abusive as ''bad'' parents. Parents or parent surrogates who mistreat their children usually are victims themselves of economic, social, or personal mental health problems (Swick and Duff, 1978). These families need special help in coping with the pressures they face, and the parents are no less needy than their children. Helping these families does not mean ignoring what is happening. It can literally be deadly (and *is* illegal) to ignore abuse cases. You must follow center or school guidelines immediately if you suspect abuse; in the case of neglect, approach the parents sensitively and positively to see what kinds of emotional or educational assistance might help them turn the situation around. For example, one teacher suspected that a seven-year-old girl in her first-grade class was a neglect case. The little girl was clearly in the lower twenty-fifth percentile as far as height and weight and was much smaller than even her younger classmates. On investigating, the teacher found that the mother had been reared in the South in a family with strong traditions about how family members were to be fed. Older males in the family were to be served first, then younger males, followed by daughters. The mother was to eat what was left, if anything. The mother, who was almost skeletal, obviously had been following the rules. Moreover, she received little income from her husband and was unsure about how to get assistance. The teacher helped this mother link up with the agency whose help she needed, providing transportation for her to make the necessary applications.

Failing to yield the spotlight to parents. Some professionals tend to exploit parents who become involved in their programs. They do most of the talking, planning, and setting of goals, and the parents do all the listening and "dirty work." It is clear who the general is and who makes up the infantry. When it comes time for rewards, the general is right there, giving little credit to the troops who really got the job done.

In order to avoid this kind of scenario, professionals need to involve parents right from the beginning in any decision making that affects their involvement. Events can be planned that allow parents to act as experts. As has been suggested before, there also should be public confirmation of what the parents contribute as well as personal thanks from the professional, who ought to keep as low a profile as possible.

Being overly critical of a child's performance. In attempting to give information honestly and clearly, some professionals overload parents with detailed reports of their child's failures, problems, and inadequacies without mentioning what is being done to correct the situation. As a result, parents are left with the notion that they are at fault for their child's behavior in the program. This strategy tends to alienate parents. Only enough information about problems should be shared to enlist the parents' assistance in establishing and implementing common goals.

When a handicapped child is being mainstreamed into the program, parents should not have to hear how "different" their child is from the other children. Parents usually know about the child's special difficulties and need to hear more about how the child is progressing by advantageous use of his or her strengths. The parents of a handicapped child described their conference with a teacher in rather graphic terms: "She stabbed us over and over and then turned the knife so that we'd be sure to feel the pain." Given this treatment, some parents give up in despair, and others become adversaries. Neither is in the best interest of the child or the program.

SUMMARY

Parent involvement is a process by which parents and helping professionals learn together and function as facilitators in each others' efforts to make life more meaningful for children and themselves. When professionals and parents forge a strong link between home and school, children benefit in higher achievement and self-worth. Also, parents who are made to feel an integral part of their children's education are more likely to support educational efforts in the community.

There are two prerequisites to parent involvement: trust between professionals and parents and a belief by the professional that parents *should* be involved in childhood programs. Rutherford and Edgar (1970:x) feel that the latter rule cannot be compromised: "Parents believe they are a crucial component of education; the government believes it; and research supports it. Unless teachers share this belief, however, there can be no effective teacher-parent cooperation."

The role of the professional is not to prescribe parent involvement without input from parents; goals and activities should fit well with parents' needs and abilities. Nor should parents who choose to participate minimally be made to feel guilty.

Parents want information about general program policy and operation, their children's progress, and changes and developments in the educational process. Unless professionals make an active effort to supply accurate information, parents will rely on two methods for evaluating what's going on in the program, both of which may be faulty: (a) what their children tell them; and (b) what they get from the media.

Communicating effectively with parents requires a variety of professional skills. These include considerable savvy in adult-education programming, interpersonal skills for working with individuals and groups, and knowledge of strategies for motivating parents to move beyond simple information exchange and into the realm of more intense involvement in childhood programs.

DISCUSSION QUESTIONS

1. You are being interviewed for the position of director of a large, urban day-care center. A board member asks how you intend to involve parents in your program. How do you respond?
2. One of your co-workers complains that parent involvement is more trouble than it is worth. Convince him or her of the benefits that can be gained by children, parents, and helping professionals when parents participate.
3. What kinds of negative attitudes on the part of parents and professionals can get in the way of an effective partnership? In your estimation, what does it take to alter these attitudes?
4. Discuss the kind of information you feel is most important to share with parents and what you feel are effective ways of delivering such information to them.
5. You have been asked by your director (principal) to consider making home visits this year. Discuss your feelings about them, citing the pros and cons of such visits. Complete your discussion with a decision about whether or not you will make home visits, citing the primary reason for your decision.
6. A group of parents approach you, suggesting that you set up a series of educational programs for them. Describe the procedure you would use in structuring such a series and ways in which you would involve parents in this effort.
7. You receive a telephone call while at home from a very angry parent who accuses you of irresponsible behavior during a recent field trip. Role-play this situation with another classmate who takes the part of the parent. Utilize the skills that were described in Chapter 9.

8. You have a child who is not adjusting very well to his mother leaving him each morning. The child is at a table, putting together a puzzle but keeping a wary eye on his mother. She says to you, ''Is it all right if I leave now?'' What do you say?

9. You realize how important an orientation meeting is for parents at the beginning of the year. When you approach the administrator of your program about setting one up, she tells you that turnouts in the past have been very poor and, unless you have a creative plan for getting parents to turn out, she does not want to schedule an orientation. What kind of plan could you share with her?

10. Parents seemed to be very enthusiastic about becoming involved in your program at the beginning of the year. Lately, however, you notice that parents are not showing up regularly, and those who do seem disgruntled. Discuss how you might assess what has gone wrong.

CHAPTER 16
Making Judgments

OBJECTIVES:

On completion of this chapter, you will be able to describe:

1. What a judgment is.

2. Judgment questions related to goals, strategies, and standards.

3. Variables that influence the judgments helping professionals make.

4. The priority principles involved in making a judgment.

5. What constitutes extreme behavior and why it occurs.

6. What constitutes child abuse and why it occurs.

7. Judgment skills related to day-to-day decision making, children's extreme behavior, and child abuse.

8. Pitfalls to avoid in making judgments.

SOURCE: © Susan Lapides 1983

The children in the hospital playroom are told that at the end of the session, everything must be put back where they found it. When cleanup time is announced, all the children pitch in to help. A few minutes later, they proclaim the job finished. As Mr. Walters, the childlife specialist, surveys the room, he notices that although tables are clean and everything has been put away, the cupboards are disheveled and not all of the markers have been capped. Looking at the children's beaming faces, he ponders, "Should I make them do more, or should I accept the job they've done?"

While observing children on the playground, Ms. Curtis notices that Alexandra, who frequently is the butt of classroom jokes, once again is being teased. She wonders, "Should I intervene, or will that make matters worse?"

The day-care provider, working at the sink, hears four-year-old Jonathan's cup fall. She turns to see milk all over the floor. Jonathan blames the spill on his imaginary friend, Boo. The adult thinks, "Should I treat this as a deliberate lie, or should I go along with him?"

The teacher observes that over the past several days, Yuri has been pulling her hair out. The child's mother has witnessed the same behavior at home. Together they wonder, "Is this something serious or a passing phase?"

For the second time this month, Stuart comes to the center badly bruised. Again, he claims he fell down the stairs. The director muses, "Is this really the result of an accident, or could it be a sign of abuse?"

Every day, helping professionals are faced with making judgments such as these. That is, they must evaluate a particular state of affairs and then decide what to do. Some of the situations they encounter demand on-the-spot decision making; others allow time for longer deliberation. Some involve relatively minor incidents; others are much more serious. Some call for maximum intervention, others for only minimal interference or none at all. Yet, hurried or meticulously planned, small or large, involving more or less direct action, all judgments affect the lives of children and adults.

The best judgments are those that helping professionals make consciously. For example, it is better for Mr. Walters, the childlife specialist, to praise the children for a job well done because he has *decided* this is the best course of action than to do so unthinkingly. In this way, his judgment becomes a calculated response to a specific circumstance.

Essentially, all judgments involve the same progression of steps found in any decision-making model:

1. Assessing the situation.
2. Analyzing possible strategies in response to it.
3. Selecting and implementing a strategy or combination of strategies.
4. Evaluating the resulting outcomes.

For Mr. Walters to reach his decision, he first would have to formulate a picture of what was happening. This would mean taking into account the children's lack of familiarity with the playroom, the anxiety many of them felt at being in a hospital setting, his supervisor's penchant for neatness, how major or minor were the things left undone, the children's display of pride, his knowledge that no one would be using the playroom again until tomorrow, and his own feelings of pleasure that the children had worked together.

Next, he would have to contemplate what possible responses were available to him. Some of these included accepting the children's work without comment, having them redo the work, singling out particular children as being either more or less successful, reprimanding them all for being too slipshod, and praising the children for working together willingly.

The subsequent step of deliberately selecting one or more of these responses would be based on Mr. Walters' analysis of the potential outcomes of each. In this case, the analysis would probably occur on the spot and would involve trying to envision which response would best support his overall aim that children feel comfortable in the hospital environment.

Making these kinds of predictions would be challenging because many of the prospective outcomes would be ambiguous. That is, some would be unknowable and some would include both positive and negative aspects that would be hard to weigh. For instance, Mr. Walters could not be sure whether making the children redo the work would seem reasonable to them or would make them feel defeated. Nor could he be certain how youngsters with whom he was unfamiliar would react to a scolding. Similarly, even if he praised the children for their efforts, it is possible that some youngsters would view his words as false because they would recognize the discrepancy between their own performance and a really clean room.

From this discussion, it can be seen that formulating a judgment carries with it certain risks and no guarantees. Yet, as uncertain as the process is, going through these steps makes it more likely that the adult's actions will match his or her aims. Furthermore, evaluating the outcomes that actually occur once an option is carried out provides additional information that can be used as input for future judgments.

Because judgments are influenced both by the situation and by the person who is deciding how to proceed, any two persons faced with formulating a judgment about the same circumstance might make entirely different, yet equally good, decisions. Hence, judgments are so personal and so situation-specific that we will not attempt to present prescribed answers to a variety of scenarios. Rather, our aim is to point out what variables to consider when making a judgment as well as how to think through the judgment process.

The What and Why of Judgments

The majority of judgments helping professionals make relate to goals, strategies, or standards. Consideration of each of these prompts certain questions that adults must answer and that affect the actions they take.

Goals. Adults in formal group settings have in mind certain goals aimed at enhancing children's social development. Typical goals include fostering children's independence, promoting their consideration of others, improving their ability to make friends, and increasing their capacity for controlling impulsive behavior. Each of these represents a desired outcome, the achievement of which contributes to increased social competence. None are wholly attained within the setting or time period during which a helping professional works with a particular child. However, forward movement toward the goal represents progress.

When adults establish goals, their interactions with children gain purpose. That is, they have an end result to work toward, rather than operating haphazardly with no purpose in mind. Helping professionals differentiate their goals as general or specific, long range or short range, more or less important, and independent of or interdependent with other aims (Deacon and Firebaugh, 1981). Furthermore, they develop goals for individual children as well as goals for the entire group. Sometimes these multiple aims are compatible; sometimes they are in direct opposition to one another. Therefore, adults must make many judgments regarding their goals. Some of the questions to be asked include:

What are the appropriate goals for each child?

Is a goal that is appropriate for one child also suited for another?

What should be done when pursuit of a goal for an individual runs counter to one established for the group?

Is a particular goal still valid?

What should be done when one goal for a child seems incongruent with another?

What factors necessitate changing a goal?

What makes one goal more important than another?

It is questions such as these that Mrs. Torez must consider when, during a class discussion, Jesse blurts out an answer without raising his hand. Her goal for the group has been for children to exercise greater impulse control and demonstrate it by waiting to be called on. Yet, Jesse is a shy child who Mrs. Torez has been encouraging to become more assertive. Should her response be geared toward supporting the group goal or the one established for Jesse? Is there a way to address both goals without compromising either? What Mrs. Torez does will be based on her judgment of the situation.

Strategies.   In order to pursue their goals for children, adults implement particular strategies. These strategies encompass practices that are carried out either explicitly or implicitly, in a premeditated or spontaneous fashion, and in a targeted or pervasive mode. At times, different techniques may be chosen to achieve the same goal; at other times, similar strategies may be utilized to pursue different goals. The judgments helping professionals make regarding strategies are many. Some of these involve determining:

Which strategy is best suited to achieving a particular goal.

Whether the potentially most effective strategy actually is feasible.

How compatible the strategies implemented for one goal are with those for another.

How long to continue implementing a strategy before judging its effectiveness.

Whether or not a planned strategy is being carried out as originally intended.

Whether a strategy can stand alone or whether it must be carried out in conjunction with other strategies.

A situation in which judgments about strategies must be made arises when Mr. Chvasta considers T. J.'s persistent misbehavior in the group. For the past several months, the adult has been trying to get T. J. to exhibit fewer instances of antisocial behavior. He has tried several options, none of which has had the desired effect. Recently, he has begun to wonder whether he has used too many different approaches, too rapidly. He also wonders whether his efforts to contend with T. J. have led him to neglect other children, prompting them to act out. The conclusions Mr. Chvasta reaches and what he will do about them depend on the judgments he makes.

Standards.   As mentioned in Chapter 12, success in accomplishing goals is assessed via standards. People establish standards when they decide that a certain amount of a behavior or a certain quality of behavior represents goal attainment. Behaviors that do not meet these criteria are indications that the goal has not yet been achieved. The measurement of standards may be formal or informal, known by children or unknown by them, purposeful or intuitive on the part of the adult. Questions that focus on judgments about standards are as follows:

What standards should be established?

Should the same standard apply to all children?

When or why should a standard be changed?

When competing standards exist, which standards should prevail?

How well does a child's behavior meet a given standard?

Thus, Ms. Cree is making a judgment regarding standards when she decides whether or not Billy has met the conditions of time-out. He has been sitting still, but he has been singing under his breath the entire time. Standards also are the issue when Mr. Walters, the childlife specialist, has to determine whether the children's definition of a clean room is good enough to accept. Likewise, Mr. Heller is thinking about standards when he tries to determine how many questions a child must answer correctly in order to receive a star. His dilemma over whether rewards should be based on the percentage correct for the whole class or on the percentage of improvement of each child also is a question of standards. In each case, final determinations regarding an acceptable level of performance will come about as the result of adult judgments.

VARIABLES THAT AFFECT JUDGMENTS

Goals, strategies, and standards are fluid. Goals that are accomplished are replaced by other goals, and those that obviously are unattainable are revised; strategies that are outmoded or ineffective are changed; standards that no longer fit are altered (Nickell, Rice and Tucker, 1976). Because none of these remains constant forever, helping professionals continually make judgments about them. Their judgments are influenced by three variables: their personal values, their knowledge of how children learn and grow, and their assessment of the situation at hand. Let us examine each of these influences more closely.

Values

Underlying each judgment a helping professional makes are his or her values. Values are the qualities and beliefs a person considers desirable or worthwhile (Berns, 1985). As such, values are deeply internalized feelings that direct people's actions (Nickell, Rice, and Tucker, 1976). For instance, adults for whom honesty is a value set goals for children with that value in mind. Some of these might include telling the truth, not cheating on tests, and completing one's work without copying. To achieve these goals, these adults implement related strategies such as rewarding children who tell the truth, separating children who are taking tests, and teaching children appropriate sources

for getting help as a substitute for copying. In addition, they apply related standards to determine how well their goals have been met. For instance, an adult might allow a preschooler to tell a "tall tale" but refuse to accept a fabrication from a fifth-grader. He or she might expect 100 percent of the students to keep their eyes on their own papers during an exam and monitor students' homework to determine that none of their answers were exactly the same. Not only do adults' values influence their goals for children, but they also affect how adults interpret and appraise children's behavior. As a result, an adult may view children who tell tall tales with less favor than children who refrain from such practices.

Because values cannot be seen, their presence can only be inferred from what people do (Deacon and Firebaugh, 1981). For instance, Mary Gonzales frequently reminds children about the value of telling the truth and doing their own work. She often carries out activities in which children must discriminate between fact and fancy. She reveals her emotions rather than hiding them, and she encourages children to describe their true reactions even when they are in opposition to her own. If a child copies another's work, he or she is told to do it over. Based on her actions, one might surmise that the value of honesty is important to her. On the other hand, were she to ignore minor incidents of cheating, tell fibs herself, or attempt to deny children's emotions, her behavior would indicate that honesty was not critical to her. Even if she were to say that it was, her actions would belie her words.

How values develop.   Values are a product of socialization. Families, society, culture, teachers, religion, friends, and the mass media all contribute to one's belief system. In this way, every facet of a person's environment has a direct or indirect impact on his or her thinking. Because value acquisition starts in the cradle, it is the family that has the first, most immediate, and most profound influence on this process. Family members, through their day-to-day interactions, transmit to the young fundamental notions of living. As children mature, these beliefs are supplemented by inputs from their mesosystems, exosystems, and macrosystems. All of these combine to form a particular orientation that individuals internalize and that guides them throughout their lives (Deacon and Firebaugh, 1981).

Because each person's ecological milieu is unique, no two people have exactly the same value system. Values differ across cultures, between families in the same culture, and among individual family members. This means there is no one correct set of values to which all persons subscribe.

Prioritizing values. People develop a system of values that often is hierarchical, ranging from most critical to least important. The order of importance is determined by whether a person treats a particular value as *basic* (one that is absolute regardless of context) or *relative* (one that depends on context for interpretation). It is thought that basic values usually take priority over relative values, and relative values take on more or less importance depending on the situation (Deacon and Firebaugh, 1981). In Mary's case, the basic value of honesty pervades everything she does. Therefore, choices between being forthright, circumspect, or deceitful usually result in the former being selected.

However, a value's hierarchy is not always so linear, with each value being placed above or below another. Rather, several values may occupy the same level of importance at the same time. These values may be compatible or contradictory. The similar weight shared by a cluster of competing values explains why people sometimes experience value conflicts. For instance, a person may equally value honesty and kindness. At times, he or she may be caught in the dilemma of whether to tell the truth, perhaps hurting someone's feelings, or to be less than truthful in order to be kind. Which

path is pursued will be based on the person's judgment in that particular circumstance.

Recognizing one's own values. Becoming cognizant of one's own personal values enhances one's professional performance. Helping professionals who are consciously aware of their values are in a good position to examine them. They can better determine when conflicting values exist within themselves and take systematic steps to resolve dilemmas. Additionally, it is possible for them to determine whether their actions are congruent with the values they espouse. This makes it more likely that they will be consistent in their interactions with children and their families. For all of these reasons, clarifying one's own values is an important step in becoming a helping professional.

Conversely, ignorance of one's values impedes one's capacity to function in formal group settings. Values may have been formulated unconsciously as the result of misinformation or unsound principles (Gross, Crandall, and Knoll, 1980). Because these values are not at a conscious level, they cannot be checked for validity. Moreover, the adult cannot make a deliberate link between unconscious values and the goals, strategies, and standards he or she employs in varying situations. Consequently, the approaches he or she chooses may support some values but undermine others or may be incompatible with the actual values under which the individual would like to operate. Also, inasmuch as the adult lacks a clear guide for his or her behavior, reactions may be haphazard and unpredictable.

Respecting clients' values. Helping professionals also must be sensitive to the differing values held by the children and families with whom they work. They cannot expect their clients' values to exactly mirror or always be compatible with their own. When educators, counselors, recreational leaders, social workers, or childlife specialists are confronted with dissimilarities between their values and those of their clients, their task becomes one of finding ways to work with them that demonstrate respect for their belief systems. Regardless of what action is eventually taken, children, families, and professionals all must perceive that social rewards have been gained.

Separating values from goals, strategies, and standards. Although variations in values are common between helping professionals and their clients, there are times when professionals mistake differences in goals, strategies, and standards for value conflicts. In reality, it is possible for dissimilar goals, strategies, and standards to be applied in response to the same value. For example, Mrs. Williams values competence and has a goal for her son, Webster, to be able to handle social situations with greater proficiency. She teaches him to establish his rights through physical force and considers his winning a fight as a positive indication of his abilities. Mrs. Pritchard, his teacher, shares the same value and goal, but her tactics and standards differ. She teaches Webster to use words to establish his rights and views his avoidance of physical confrontation as a measure of achievement. In this case, the dissimilar approach between parent and teacher is based not on conflicting values, but on differing means. Although values are almost impossible to debate, strategies can be negotiated. The two adults do have common ground. If Mrs. Pritchard recognizes this, she will have a positive base from which to approach the parent. If she does not see this shared perspective, her efforts to influence the parent could result in failure.

In addition to an understanding of values, there are two other variables that affect the judgments helping professionals make. The first involves how well they take into account children's current level of functioning; the second is whether they look at each situation in context.

Knowledge of Child Development and Learning

When adults make judgments about goals, strategies, and standards related to children's behavior, they must weigh such variables as the child's age, what the child's current level of comprehension might be, and what experiences the child has had. Although age is not an absolute measure of a youngster's capabilities and understanding, it does serve as a guide for establishing appropriate expectations. For instance, adults who know that preschoolers do not yet have a mature grasp of games with rules would not view a four-year-old who spins twice or peeks at the cards in a memory game as a cheater. Subsequently, they would not require very young children to adhere to the rules of a game in the same way they might expect grade-schoolers to. Likewise, awareness that seven- and eight-year-olds normally spend much time verbally designating who is "friends" with whom would keep adults from castigating youngsters who engage in this practice. Rather, their strategy for improving peer relations might consist of group discussions aimed at encouraging children to discover similarities with others in the group.

The kinds of previous knowledge and skills a child brings to a situation should also be taken into account. Obviously, children with little or no exposure to a particular situation or skill should not be expected to pursue exactly the same goals or perform at the same level of competence as youngsters whose backlog of experience is greater. For instance, goals for a field trip to a farm for children from the inner city would be different from those established for youngsters from a rural area. Standards related to dressing independently would be different for a two-year-old from those for a six-year-old, not only because of differences in age, but because the older child has had more practice. Furthermore, a child who has lived all her life in Florida would not initially be expected to demonstrate the same degree of skill in putting on a snowsuit as would a child from a northern climate, where such clothing is commonplace. In instances such as these, helping professionals use children's development and experience to guide their judgments.

The Situational Context

Adult judgments do not take place in a vacuum. Rather, they are made within an ecological milieu, which is influenced by several factors. Some of these include time, human resources, material resources, the physical environment, and the specific details of the behavioral episode itself. The goals, strategies, and standards finally decided on are all affected by these constraints. For instance, under normal circumstances, Ms. Omura's goal is to foster independence among the children in her class. Ordinarily, children are given the time to make their own decisions, to repeat a task in order to gain competence, and to do as much as possible for themselves. However, these goals and strategies have to be modified during a tornado drill, when the goal of safety supercedes that of independence. Under such circumstances, children have no choice about taking shelter, nor can they take their time dressing themselves. As a result, slow dressers get more direct assistance than is customarily provided.

Similarly, Mr. Ogden might think that the best strategy for helping an impulsive child is constant, one-to-one monitoring by an adult. Yet, he concludes that he would be unable to implement this approach because of demands on his own time and the lack of other adults who might serve in this role.

The impact of contextual factors also is evident when a social worker who ordinarily advocates sharing, but who also knows that Michelle has recently become a big sister, allows her to keep all of the watercolors to herself one day. He realizes that this child already is sharing many things for the first time—attention at home, her room, and even some of her things.

In his judgment, asking her to share on this occasion is unnecessarily stressful, so he does not oblige her to follow the rule for now.

Physical resources and available time also affect judgments. This explains why the presence of a huge mud puddle on the playground could be viewed as either a place to avoid or an area of exploration. Which judgment is made depends in part on what kind of clothing the children are wearing, whether soap and water is available for cleanup, whether it is warm enough to go barefoot, and whether there is enough time for children to both play in the mud and get cleaned up before the next activity period.

Judgments often involve establishing priorities from among competing interests. Some of these include self-interest versus children's interests, individual interests versus group interests, and the interests of one person versus those of another. People also may experience conflicts within their own value system that cloud their ability to make a definitive judgment. Although there are no absolute rules for distinguishing among these, there are some general principles helping professionals can use when faced with difficult decisions.

Priority Principles

The following principles are arranged in a hierarchy from most to least important. Each one has higher priority than those that follow it. All of them serve as rules of thumb for which priorities will take precedence in a given circumstance. These principles came about as a result of our experiences with families and children and through discussions with helping professionals representing a variety of backgrounds.

Principle A. *Strategies that preserve children's safety take precedence over all others.* The overriding concern of every helping professional is children's physical and mental welfare. If one must choose between an option in which a child's health and well-being can be maintained and other, more efficient, easier, or less involved options in which safety is in question, there *is* no choice. The adult is ethically and morally obligated to pursue the safest alternative.

SITUATION: The fifth-grade science class is doing an experiment with heat that involves the use of Bunsen burners. The children, working in small groups, are running behind schedule in their task. Another class is due to arrive in a few minutes. While surveying the room, the teacher notices that a few children, still working, have taken off their protective goggles. The adult feels caught between wanting them to get the experiment over with in time and feeling that she should enforce the safety standards. Even though there are only a few minutes remaining, and making the children don the goggles will cause a delay, the appropriate course is clear, as mandated by principle A: safety first.

Principle B. *Priority is given to the approach that promises the most positive and the least negative outcome.* Although all goals, strategies, and standards have some benefits and some drawbacks, it is best to eliminate the most negative options and choose from among those that are most favorable. Sometimes, the best option has the largest number of benefits. Sometimes, an option is best because its negative aspects are less deleterious than the other alternatives under consideration.

SITUATION: During a conference with the director of the day-care center, Mrs. Leeper (one of the parents) reveals that her father is terminally ill and is not expected to live much beyond the new year. She has not yet shared the news with her children and has approached the center director for advice. Together, they identify the benefits of telling the children about the situation right away, such as giving the

children lead time to deal with the tragedy, a chance to say goodbye to their grandfather, and an opportunity to share in a family experience; a chance for Mrs. Leeper to gain family support; and the relief of not having to keep it a secret. Drawbacks to telling the children include causing everyone to feel sad during the holiday as well as the difficulty of introducing a topic about which she feels uncomfortable and with which the children have had little experience. The two adults also explore the pros and cons of not telling. Favorable aspects of postponing the disclosure are that the children probably will have an uninterrupted holiday and that the mother will not have to deal with the issue right away. The negative impacts of this approach include the mother's heightening anxiety, her inability to share a very traumatic period of her life with loved ones, the potential shock to the children, and their probable distress over sensing that something is wrong but not knowing what it is.

Taking all of these factors into account, Mrs. Leeper makes the judgment that it is better to tell them than to remain silent. In her opinion, the benefits of telling right away outweigh both the benefits of not telling and the negative aspects of making the announcement.

Principle C. *When faced with a situation in which the child's needs and the adult's needs differ, priority is given to meeting the child's needs, unless doing so compromises the adult's basic values.* In other words, when adults' and children's interests compete, children's interests have the higher priority, except when the adult would find pursuit of those needs unlivable.

SITUATION: Children at the Jefferson School are rehearsing for a spring concert. The music teacher is especially anxious for the youngsters to put on a good show because music teachers from several other districts will be in the audience. While listening to the opening number, she realizes that Sandra sings loudly and enthusiastically, but off key. She debates whether or not to allow the child to sing. She knows that other teachers have told such youngsters to mouth the words without making a sound. At the same time, she is aware of how much Sandra is anticipating singing at the concert. Based on her understanding of principle C, she rejects restricting Sandra's participation in favor of allowing her to sing. In this case, the adult permitted the child's needs to come before her own.

SITUATION: Kathy's brother was killed in a traffic accident by a car driven by a black woman. Although the accident happened over a year ago, Kathy still harbors great anger toward all black people. Today when she passes out the spelling papers, she calls each black child "nigger." The teacher recognizes Kathy's need to express her emotions, but interprets the child's actions as a violation of her own basic value of respect for people of all races. Thus, guided by principle C, she chooses to forbid Kathy to use derogatory language in her presence.

Principle D. *When making a judgment that involves choosing one goal from among several contradicting goals of equal weight, priority is given to the goal that the adult has fewest opportunities to address in day-to-day encounters.* Often, situations arise in which it is possible to concentrate on reinforcing only one of several competing goals. Pursuit of one goal would negate another goal. When this happens, it is best to pursue the goal that is less often addressed.

SITUATION: Jorge received $10 from his grandmother for his birthday. He took the entire amount and bought his mother a blue velvet pillow painted with a naked woman in a suggestive pose. He is proud of his purchase and pleased to be giving his mother a gift. His mother is touched that he so selflessly used his money for someone other than himself, but also is concerned with his poor choice and lack of fiscal awareness. She realizes that she must focus on one aspect of the situation or the other.

If she tries to deal with both by thanking him and then having him return the inappropriate purchase, she would, in fact, diminish the genuineness of her praise. She must choose between the value she places on prosocial behavior and her value related to money management. After much thought, following the premise of principle D, she thanks Jorge for the pillow and says nothing about the inappropriate image. She decided that she would have many future opportunities to teach fiscal responsibility but would have fewer chances to reward Jorge's gift giving.

Principle E. *When choosing between two strategies, one that supports short-term goals but impedes long-term goals and another that has the opposite effect, priority is given to pursuing long-term goals.* At times, strategies that lead to either short- or long-term goals conflict. When this happens, one should choose those that best contribute to the long-range outcome.

SITUATION: The children from the center have been on a walking field trip. They are tired, and the adults are anxious to get back—it has been a long afternoon. The group has reached the middle of the block. The school building is right across the street, and there is no traffic in sight. The leader considers jaywalking, but realizes that such an action would detract from her long-range goal of teaching children the appropriate way to cross the street. Her decision to have the children walk several extra yards to the corner, thereby using the crosswalk, is based on her understanding of principle E.

Principle F. *When faced with competing group and individual needs, priority is given to the approach that best satisfies each. If no mutually satisfying option is available, individual needs take precedence over group needs, unless meeting the needs of a single person jeopardizes group functioning.* On occasion, an option that would benefit a child at that point in time will be at odds with what would be optimal for the group as a whole. Sometimes, it is possible to blend these needs through a combination of strategies. At other times, this is not so feasible and a choice must be made between primary benefit for one or the other. Under these circumstances, helping professionals should select the strategy that favors the individual. The only exception is when by doing so, the damage to the group is too great.

SITUATION: The children are seated in a group, listening to a story. Suddenly, the adult becomes aware that Leslie is sobbing quietly. The adult interrupts the story, saying: ''Leslie, you look unhappy. What's wrong?'' The child continues to cry without answering. The adult is torn between the group's desire to hear the story and the child's need to be comforted. In accordance with principle F, she comforts the child.

SITUATION: Vito has little self-confidence. The one area in which he excels is building with blocks. Day after day, he builds elaborate structures and then begs that they remain standing, undisturbed. At first, the adult honors Vito's wishes, even though it limits other children's access to the blocks. She reasons that it is more important for Vito to feel good about an accomplishment than for the group to use the materials. However, over time, the adult notices that the youngsters are becoming increasingly upset about their limited opportunities to build. Although no one seems to resent Vito, children are really starting to feel shortchanged. Using principle F, the adult decides to limit how long a structure can remain standing as well as Vito's monopolization of the blocks. She offers him a choice of using the blocks exclusively for a few minutes or using them for a longer time in conjunction with other children.

Principle G. *When choosing between options that have equally positive and negative outcomes, priority is given to the one that is most personally satisfying.* At times, all of the alternatives one generates seem to have about the same number of benefits and drawbacks. There may be no particular option that is clearly the most or least desirable. In cases such as these, helping professionals should select the option with which they are most comfortable. This principle has been included so that adults have some guide for what to do when no alternative stands out. A decision based on this principle is preferable to remaining indecisive and avoiding a conscious judgment.

SITUATION: The adult is reading books to the group. There is time for one more story before they go home. Half of the children want a dinosaur story; half prefer one about space. Both are worthwhile tales, and selecting only one means that some children may be dissatisfied. The adult decides to read the dinosaur book because he finds it amusing. He has made his choice based on principle G.

Using the priority principles just described is an effective way of thinking through the judgment process. These principles can be applied to a wide range of scenarios involving both on-the-spot decision making and more long-term deliberations. Moreover, these principles are valid in dealing with issues of varying magnitude. For this reason, we feel they can be generalized to most of the day-to-day judgments helping professionals have to make.

However, some situations call for judgments that are so specialized that they must be addressed separately. Two such situations involve making judgments about children's extreme behavior and making judgments related to child abuse. In both cases, the essential judgment to be made is whether or not the condition exists. If the answer is no, the preceding principles apply. If the answer is affirmative, there are precise guidelines for what to do next. We will now focus on each of these special cases in turn.

JUDGMENTS ABOUT EXTREME BEHAVIOR

Sometimes, helping professionals find themselves in a quandary, trying to decide whether a child's behavior warrants the attention of additional behavioral or medical experts. On one hand, a child's actions may be so baffling or so dysfunctional that the adult fears that ignoring them could have serious consequences. On the other hand, he or she worries about alarming the family, offending them, or asking them to commit to what may be a significant outlay of time or money. Torn between both sides of the issue, the helping professional may find it impossible to make a conscious decision. Fortunately, there are guidelines available to enable professionals to make such judgments with more assurance.

What Constitutes Extreme Behavior

Dr. Louise Guerney, a clinical psychologist in the College of Human Development, The Pennsylvania State University, has developed criteria for determining what behaviors should be considered extreme (1984). It is from her work that we have drawn the material for this portion of the chapter. Dr. Guerney notes that some behaviors are extreme by virtue of their mere presence. Others are designated as extreme because they exceed the normal boundaries one would expect in relation to a child's age. How intense a behavior is and how generalized it becomes are additional factors one must take into account when determining whether behavior is extreme. Other variables that influence one's judgment include the effect the behavior has on the child's present or future functioning and how resistant the behavior is to modification.

Presence of self-destructive behaviors or sudden, drastic changes in behavior patterns. Self-destructive acts and behaviors that represent a sudden shift in a child's functioning are danger signs. Their very appearance should prompt immediate intervention. Self-destructive acts are those that children inflict on themselves and that result in physical injury or mental damage. This is exemplified by the youngster who disfigures herself by scratching; by the child who bangs his head, causing contusions; and by the child who deliberately courts danger as a thrill-seeking device. In each case, the behavior is too serious to be allowed to continue.

Another cause for concern is a child's normal behavior pattern changing suddenly or radically. A generally happy, responsive child who becomes withdrawn and fearful, a habitually mild-mannered child who overnight becomes volatile, and a child who begins complaining of unrelenting stomachaches are all showing evidence of extreme behaviors. Because these actions are so out of character, they signal a need for closer scrutiny.

Age. Frequently, a behavior is considered extreme if it reappears or continues to exist long after one would expect a child to have outgrown it. Although it is typical for two-year-olds to have temper tantrums, even frequent ones, nine-year-olds do not usually behave this way. Thus, if a nine-year-old repeatedly resorted to explosive outbursts, it would be obvious that the behavior should be categorized as extreme. Likewise, if an eight-year-old suddenly begins bed-wetting, a behavior more typical of infancy and toddlerhood, this turn of events would deserve serious attention.

Intensity of the behavior. The intensity of a behavior involves its frequency and duration. Problem behaviors are generally considered normal if they appear only occasionally or briefly. However, they are labeled extreme if they occur frequently or if they last for protracted periods of time. For instance, it is not unusual for preschoolers to periodically seek the comfort of blanket and thumb when frightened or tired. On the other hand, were three-year-old Michael to spend the majority of his waking hours pacifying himself in this manner, the behavior would be considered extreme. Whether parents or the professional with whom the child comes in regular contact should seek outside help would depend on how long the problem lasts. There are times when extreme behaviors are short lived. That is, they appear for a few days, and then children gradually return to their original behavior patterns. Such instances are viewed as temporary crises that require adult support but not necessarily outside intervention. However, should the behavior endure, some serious exploration of the child's situation, with the help of an expert in such matters, would be in order.

Breadth of the behavior. Indiscriminate manifestations of behavior often are considered extreme. That is, certain actions that might be considered normal if their appearance were limited become abnormal when they pervade all aspects of a child's life. For instance, it is common for youngsters aged four through nine to tell untruths to protect themselves in incriminating situations or to make themselves seem more interesting. Although hardly exemplary, their resorting to lies under duress or in moments of self-expansiveness should not be categorized as extreme. On the other hand, there are a few children who rely on falsehoods in virtually all situations, regardless of whether they are in obvious trouble or in a circumstance in which absolute adherence to the facts is unimportant. These youngsters tend to lie about many things even when the truth would serve them better. Lying in this form is indiscriminate and should be examined in conjunction with a behavioral expert to determine how it could be modified.

Effect on the child's present and future functioning. Behaviors that have the potential to

hamper children's growth or development should be treated as extreme. This is exemplified by children who repeatedly force themselves to throw up after eating, those who are so hostile they cannot let anyone get close to them, and youngsters who become so centered on getting good grades that they resort to cheating, lying, and sabotage of others' work to better their own standing. Likewise, diabetic children who deliberately avoid their medication or habitually eat forbidden foods fall into this category. Young people who are so shy that they literally have no friends or acquaintances also are enmeshed in an extreme, counterproductive pattern of behavior. In each case, consultation with parents and behavioral experts is recommended.

Resistance of the behavior to change. Resistance for more than a short time (usually several weeks) to *reasonable* efforts to correct a common, everyday problem is a sign that the behavior has become extreme. "Reasonable efforts" refers to adult use of relevant, constructive strategies aimed at eliminating negative actions while simultaneously promoting desirable alternate behaviors. It also implies consistency. That is, the problem behavior must receive attention on a predictable basis, and the strategies employed must be used often enough and long enough that a behavior change is likely. Within this definition, a child who periodically experiences negative consequences for being out of his seat, but who at other times is inadvertently rewarded for wandering, is not demonstrating resistant behavior but rather the effects of the adult's lack of predictability. On the other hand, were the child to experience appropriate consequences over a two-month span but still habitually wander the room, this could be taken as evidence that the behavior had become extreme.

Similarly, a developmental task for all young children is to become toilet trained. Although the optimal period for this to occur varies among individuals, it is accepted that by about three years of age, most children will have begun this training. Yet, some children resist learning to use the toilet. Initial resistance is common and should not be a signal for alarm. However, there are youngsters whose resistance continues to mount such that bladder or bowel control is still not achieved into the grade-school years. Under these conditions, the behavior can appropriately be described as extreme.

Frequently Reported Sources of Extreme Behavior

When adults are confronted with children's extreme behavior, they often wonder where it comes from and why it occurs. Although the variables influencing any single child may differ widely, three of the most commonly reported sources include physiological factors, childhood fears, and childhood depression (Fitch, 1985; Guerney, 1984).

Physiology. It has been suggested that some children who exhibit extreme behavior do so as a result of protein, vitamin, or mineral deficiencies in their diet (Wunderlich, 1973). For instance, children who are deprived of essential B vitamins have impaired concentration, resulting in a shorter attention span and a lack of task commitment. Other researchers claim that biochemical irregularities, such as glandular disorders (Eames, 1962) and hypoglycemia (Roberts, 1969), are related to the maladaptive behavior patterns some children display. Over the past several years, scientists also have discovered that some genuinely extreme, non-compliant behavior is related to neurological disfunction. Hyperactivity, which involves impulsive, uncontrolled behaviors as well as exceedingly active behavior not typical of the majority of children, is the most common of these (Cook and Armbruster, 1983). For instance, brain damage, which may result from birth complications or a later head injury, can make it difficult for a child to sit still. Brain

dysfunction may contribute to a child's need for constant motion and an inability to relax (Berger, 1980). Although not all hyperactivity is physiologically based, the preceding findings indicate that this sometimes is the case. Another extreme behavioral problem that results from neurological difficulties is La Tourette's syndrome. Children with this condition display many tics (repeated involuntary movements, such as eye blinking), which may be accompanied by the shouting of obscenities and the production of loud and/or strange noises. All of these behaviors are actually beyond the child's ability to control. Although it is not common, this condition has been included here to underscore the point that some extreme behaviors can be related to physical dysfunctions. In cases such as these, assistance from specially trained professionals is necessary.

Childhood fears. Another source of extreme behavior in children is fear. All children at one time or another become afraid of certain places, people, things, or events. Even if extreme in intensity for days or sometimes weeks, these fearful episodes usually are of a relatively short duration. (Refer to Chapter 5 for a review of typical childhood fears and what to do about them.) Time, along with adult empathy and support, will dissipate most of these.

Yet, there are times when fears persist for such long periods and permeate so many areas of a child's life that they interfere with the child's ability to function. Such extreme fears are called *phobic disorders*. They are persistent, unfounded, out of proportion to the actual danger or threat, and lead to maladaptive behavior (Fitch, 1985). Most often, this maladaption takes the form of extreme withdrawal. For example, seven-year-old Veronica reached a point where she was terrified at the mere prospect of coming in contact with anything fuzzy. Initially, Veronica had expressed a fear of mice. Gradually, her fear extended to encompass most fuzzy objects, such as stuffed animals, blankets, and the fur collar on her coat. As time went on, she became hysterical at the touch of a cotton swab and when asked to use yarn in a weaving project. Ultimately, her anxiety prompted her to resist leaving the sanctuary of her home, from which most of the offending items had been eliminated.

A common phobic disorder during the grade-school years is known as school refusal, or *school phobia* (Alexander, Roodin, and Gorman, 1980; Kessler, 1972). Although many youngsters experience some anxiety about school, about 16 out of every 1,000 develop such severe anxieties that they become physically ill at the prospect of going to school each day (Gelfand, Jenson, and Drew, 1982; Kennedy, 1965). Their resistance to school becomes extreme: screaming, crying, and tantrums are common, as are severe stomachaches, headaches, and sore throats. The child's distress may be directly related to incidents at school (a scolding from a teacher, a bullying classmate, embarrassment over poor work) (Ambron and Salkind, 1984). It also may be caused by other factors not so easily discernible, such as fears that develop from a misunderstood conversation or the chance remark of a friend (Kostelnik, Stein, and Whiren, 1984). In either case, the child's reaction is to attempt to withdraw from all school contacts.

Occasionally, rather than trying to resolve fear through withdrawal, some youngsters try to master it directly. In the process, they often overreact, engaging in potentially harmful activities. For example, following a period of extreme fear of fire, some children set fires. They reason that their ability to produce a flame at will and to extinguish it themselves demonstrates their power over it.

A third worrisome way that some children cope with fear is to develop an obsession or a compulsion. Undesired, recurring thoughts are called *obsessions*. These are persistent preoccupations: ideas children cannot get out of their heads (Ambron and Salkind, 1984). Impulses to repeatedly perform certain acts are called *com-

pulsions* (Fitch, 1985). Everyone exhibits some obsessive or compulsive behavior at some time, and in their mildest forms, neither of these is a problem. For instance, the childhood chant ''Step on a crack, break your mother's back; step on a line, break your mother's spine'' prompts some children around the age of seven or eight to keep their eyes glued to the sidewalk, compulsively avoiding the fateful cracks and lines. This is a game involving great ritual into which children enter happily with no feeling of inner coercion (Kessler, 1972). They believe in the power of the chant enough to honor it, and yet, they do not really think a misstep will cause injury.

However, if a compulsion or obsession begins to interfere with a person's functioning and is one from which he or she derives no pleasure or social benefits, it is judged extreme. For instance, ten-year-old Jessica was obsessed with the thought of having to urinate even though there was no physical basis for her concern. Her obsession caused her to make as many as 50 trips to the bathroom each day. Often, once she got there, she was unable to produce even a drop. When Jessica was denied access to the bathroom as often as she wanted, her anxiety over a possible accident drove her to tears. She became so preoccupied with this one biological function that she was able to think of little else.

How a child's compulsion might disrupt his or her life is illustrated by Craig, whose elaborate rituals at mealtime prevented him from enjoying his lunch. It also made him seem ''weird'' to age-mates, causing them to avoid him. Before allowing himself to take a bite, Craig felt compelled to unfold his napkin a certain way and then refold it several times. Next, he spread it out with the corners in a particular position. Each corner was then carefully torn off and placed in a neat pile to the left. He had equally time-consuming routines for the preparation of his sandwich and milk. If the procedure was interrupted, Craig became quite upset and began over again.

All of the fear-related circumstances just described exceed the bounds of normalcy. When these kinds of episodes take place, the attention of behavioral experts is called for.

Childhood depression. A source of extreme behavior that has become increasingly prevalent in the two-to-twelve age group is childhood depression (Kashani and Simonds, 1979). Behaviors associated with this phenomenon range from affective ones, such as sadness, continual crying, withdrawal, inability to concentrate, lack of interest in life, and feelings of defeat, to physical manifestations such as severe and fre-quent stomachaches or headaches for which there seems to be no physiological basis. Additional symptoms to be aware of, as well as how to help children deal with childhood depression, were described in Chapter 10, Helping Children Cope with Stress. The topic is reintroduced here because sometimes, extreme misbehavior can be a symptom of depression. It shows itself in such acting-out behaviors as stealing, fighting, or defiance. These and other destructive acts are characterized by excessive disobedience and unrelenting resistance to change. It must be remembered that all children occasionally disobey for a variety of reasons and

FIGURE 16-1 Prolonged sadness that has no link to immediate events may be a sign of childhood depression.

SOURCE: David Strickler/Monkmeyer Press Photo Service

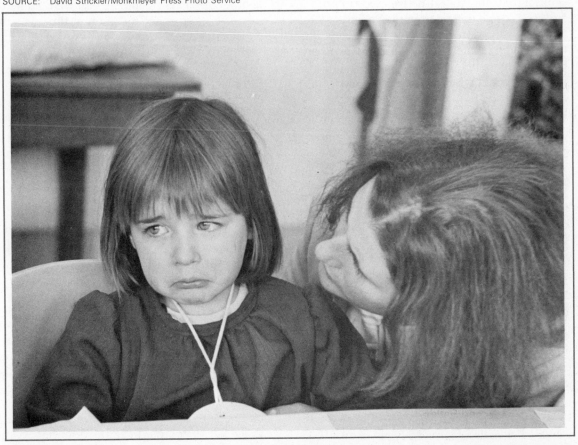

that noncompliance does not, in and of itself, mean that a child is suffering from depression. Rather, outside help is warranted when unremitting, intense, hostile disobedience occurs over a long period of time.

JUDGMENTS REGARDING CHILD ABUSE

When helping professionals believe that a child in their care has suffered the trauma of child abuse, their emotions run high. Initially, they may experience disbelief, horror, anger, or panic. If they allow these feelings to dictate their reaction, their response will not be constructive. Incredulity may cause them to ignore a serious problem; shock may immobilize them; rage may prompt them into a destructive mode of action; and panic could detract from their ability to deal with the situation coherently. At times like these, helping professionals must be able to control their emotions and make a calm, rational judgment about whether there is, indeed, child abuse. In order to make such a judgment, they first must understand the nature of child abuse and the signs to look for.

Defining the Phenomenon

Most generally, abuse can be described as any behavior by a person in a child's microsystem or mesosystem that cripples his or her efforts to achieve potential as a human being (Zigler and Rubin, 1985). Under this umbrella statement fall such diverse forms of maltreatment as child neglect, physical or verbal violence, sexual assault, molestation, and exploitation. Legally, every state has its own definition of these acts. For our purposes, we will focus on two major categories of child abuse: physical and sexual. Within our framework, a child is considered to be any person under eighteen years of age.

Physical abuse is defined as any nonaccidental injury sustained by a child resulting from acts of omission or commission by a parent, guardian, or caregiver (Burgess, 1979). Acts of omission refer to the failure of adults to provide adequate food, clothing, shelter, and medical and emotional care to children. Acts of commission involve direct actions that result in injury to youngsters. Whipping children, tying them up, locking them in closets, throwing them against walls, scalding them, and shaking them violently are some of the more commonly occurring examples.

Children who are abused sexually are "coerced to engage in sexual activity through subtle deceit, bribes, or outright threats and force" (Koblinsky and Behana, 1984:4). Most incidents of child sexual abuse involve genital fondling, oral-genital contact, or sexual abuse of the breasts or anus. Sexual intercourse is another, albeit less common, occurrence (Finkelhor, 1979; Peters, 1976). At other times, sexual abuse does not consist of direct contact. Rather, youngsters are made to exhibit themselves or to watch the exhibition of an adult (Michigan Council for the Prevention of Child Abuse and Neglect, 1985). They also may be subjected to obscene phone calls or sexually explicit language (Shay and Murphy, 1984). In each of these cases, children's current levels of functioning are damaged and there is a potential threat to their future well-being. At one time, it was thought that such detrimental acts occurred seldom and were perpetrated by a few "sick" people in our society. We now know better.

Scope of the Problem

It has been reported that approximately 200,000 children are abused in the United States each year. Table 16-1 contains a breakdown of child abuse by type. Of the cases documented, approximately 2,000 children are so badly injured that they die (Leavitt, 1983; American Association for Protecting Children, 1985). These figures are based on reported cases; the real numbers undoubtedly are higher because much abuse is never brought to the attention of the authorities. Thus, professionals in the field estimate that approximately 1.5 million children actually are affected (Kaplan, 1986). These figures suggest that at least one out of every ten young people will experience violation of their person during the childhood years. According to the law of averages, this means that a helping professional may come in contact with about two such children during a 12-month period. This is not to say that an abused child will be found in every formal group setting. It does underscore the fact that sometime during their career, helping professionals will have to make a judgment that a child is a victim of abuse. In fact, the problem has become so widespread that all 50 states now have laws requiring that suspected cases of child abuse be reported. Furthermore, in most states helping professionals are legally responsible for any injury to a child that comes about because the professional failed to make such a report (Mnookin, 1978).

The Abusers

Who would beat, bash, burn, choke, neglect, rape, sodomize, or otherwise assault a child? Are the perpetrators of such hideous deeds psychopathic monsters? Overwhelmingly, the evidence says, no. Rather, they are ordinary people who, for any number of reasons, subject children to humiliating or physically injurious acts. Child abuse cuts across all ages, both genders, all races, all social classes, all family structures, and all socioeconomic groups. There are no characteristics that infallibly separate abusers from nonabusers, victims from nonvictims. Although certain conditions may be more or less highly related to abuse, their existence alone is not an absolute indicator of whether or not abuse will occur. Rather, it is a combination of variables that determines actual outcomes.

Physical abusers. Parents who physically abuse their children are not crazy people. Only 10 percent actually suffer from a serious psychotic disorder (Steele, 1980). The remainder are adults who claim to care for their children, although the care they offer frequently is marred by violence or neglect.

Initially, scientists assumed that abusive parents would display specific personality traits that might distinguish them from their nonabusing counterparts. Over time, it was found that they were somewhat more impulsive, immature, self-centered, hypersensitive, and troubled (Leavitt, 1983; Zigler and Rubin, 1985). Yet, the investigations in which such findings

TABLE 16-1 Types of Abuse Suffered by Children in the United States in 1984 (Based on Reported Cases)

TYPE OF ABUSE	PERCENT OF CHILDREN
Major physical injury (broken bones; injuries requiring hospitalization, surgery, or stitches)	3.4
Other physical injury (welts, contusions, abrasions, burns, concussions)	20
Sexual maltreatment	13.1
Neglect	53.9
Emotional maltreatment	9.9
Other	0.4

Source: American Association for Protecting Children, News Release, November 8, 1985.

were reported were not always conclusive or unanimous (Wolfe, 1985). More definitive data have been generated by studies that focused more on the parents' behavior and attitudes toward their children. From these, it has been found that abusive parents often inaccurately assume intentionality in children's behavior and consider normal child behavior as "difficult" (Kempe and Helfer, 1972; Kempe and Kempe, 1978). Thus, a mother may be convinced that a school-age child who fell down and scraped his knee did so deliberately just to upset her. These parents frequently have unreasonable expectations for children's behavior and distorted perceptions of what children should be able to do at a given age (Martin, 1978). For instance, a parent might become incensed when an infant does not stop crying on demand or when a three-year-old proves incapable of getting her own lunch. Abusive parents also tend to believe in physical punishment and are afraid that without it, their children will be spoiled (Steele, 1983). They exhibit a low tolerance for stress, possess a poor repertoire of life skills, and express general dissatisfaction with the parental role (Kelly, 1983). In an overwhelming number of cases, they have experienced poor relationships with their own parents, often having been abused as children themselves (Spanier, Lerner, and Shea, 1982).

Finally, situational factors within and outside the family play a significant role in the likelihood of abuse occurring (Belsky, 1980). For example, abuse is most common in families in which finances are severly strained (regardless of socioeconomic status). More than 50 percent of all cases have been linked to this factor (Spanier, Lerner, and Shea, 1982). Other stressful life events such as divorce, unemployment, family conflict, overcrowding, lack of a support system, or drastic changes in status and role create the conditions in which abuse may eventually take place. It also has been discovered that abusive families frequently are isolated families. Their family boundaries tend to be rigid and closed (Garbarino, 1977). That is, they

have little access to parenting information that might be of use to them or to potential resource people and have no real means of social comparison, either for their children or for themselves. This isolation exacerbates, and sometimes causes, many of the problems they experience.

Most recently, it has been hypothesized that abuse actually occurs as a result of an interactive effect among all of the variables just described: the adult's personality, his or her lack of parenting skills, unrealistic expectations, and situational characteristics (Wolfe, 1985). The volatile nature of the encounter may be heightened by the child's own attributes, such as temperament or physical appearance. How and why this occurs will be discussed shortly.

Sexual abusers. For many years, parents and helping professionals have warned children to stay away from strangers. Most often, the child molester has been portrayed as a classic "scary person": an unfamiliar, middle-aged male in a raincoat who hangs around parks or schools waiting to tempt a lone child with candy (Shay and Murphy, 1984). Unfortunately, this scenario does not cover the most common situations in which children are at risk. In reality, in 80 percent of child sexual abuse cases, the child knows the offender, and in 50 percent, the offender is a member of the child's own household (MacFarlane, 1978). When sexual abuse by strangers does occur, it is most likely to happen in a single episode, during warm-weather months, outside, in an automobile or a public building. On the other hand, abuse perpetrated by family members or acquaintances is apt to occur repeatedly, at any time, and at home (Peters, 1976). In these cases, force or bribery seldom is used. Instead, the child may submit to the adult's requests in deference to the adult's perceived status in the family or from a desire to please.

Families in which the father or father figure abuses a daughter represent the most common incidents of abuse. These families often are plagued by dysfunctional relationships, especially between spouses. The adult male frequently has low self-esteem and is weak and resentful rather than virile or oversexed as in the common stereotype. Although some mothers do not recognize the situation, others are aware but unable to face their predicament and so must deny what is happening. In fact, once the abuse becomes known, it is not uncommon for family members to turn against the victim, blaming her for the disruption. Circumstances such as these can go on for years if no intervention is forthcoming.

The Victims

The majority of physical-abuse cases are initiated during the preschool years (Kempe and Helfer, 1972). This is a time when children have little power to retaliate and have fewer people to tell. Generally, parents do not physically abuse all of their children. Instead, one victim is singled out. It often is the child's own personal characteristics that contribute to his or her being selected. For instance, physically unattractive infants, premature or low-birth-weight infants, and children who began life unwanted are more likely to be abused than youngsters who were not born under these negative circumstances (Spanier, Lerner, and Shea, 1982). Likewise, physically or mentally handicapped youngsters, as well as those who are considered temperamentally difficult, are more likely to become victims of abuse (Friedrich and Boriskin, 1976; Parke and Collmer, 1975; and Spinetta and Rigler, 1972). Finally, there is evidence that youngsters who are frequently disruptive and noncompliant are treated more abusively than those who are more passive.

Although 10 percent of all victims of sexual abuse are younger than five years of age, the majority are school-age and adolescent children, with the average age being eleven years (Sgroi, 1975). Females are victimized at a much higher rate than males (the estimated ratio is 10:1). Hence, overwhelmingly, victims are young girls, and perpetrators most often are adult males (Canavan, 1981). Although females are primary targets, it should not be forgotten that boys also are victims of abuse and that adult females can be abusers. Unlike physical abuse, child sexual abuse often extends to more than one victim within the same family (MacFarlane, 1978). These sexual encounters often begin with innocent touching and progress to fondling and then to overt sexual stimulation. Forcible rape rarely occurs. Instead, there often are pleasurable overtones to the interactions, which contribute to children's confusion over what is happening to them. The most susceptible youngsters are those who lack information about sexual abuse and what to do if it occurs (Koblinsky and Behana, 1984). Likewise, children who have low self-esteem, those who have been taught to blindly obey adults, and those who are poorly supervised are more likely candidates for victimization (DeFrancis, 1969; Sanford, 1982).

Effects on victims. An obvious outcome of either physical or sexual abuse is injury. For example, it has been reported that abusive acts are the fourth most common cause of death in children five years of age and younger (Wolfe, 1985). Other problems include fractures, lacerations, internal injuries, pregnancy, and venereal disease. Physical and sexual abuse have been correlated with truancy, running away, drug and alcohol abuse, sexual promiscuity, psychological distress, physical complaints, dramatic behavior changes, depression, suicidal tendencies, violent crime, inability to trust others, guilt, and anger (Adams-Tucker, 1982; Conte, 1982). In addition, one can only begin to calculate the cost to society of caring for victims, incarcerating perpetrators, and the loss of productive family functioning. Perhaps most significantly, this phenomenon has been tied to abuse in future generations. Thus, left unchecked, child abuse perpetuates itself for years to come. All of these factors make early detection crucial. Because of the close contact helping professionals enjoy with the children in their care, they play an important role in identifying victims of abuse.

Signs of Abuse

Several signs may indicate possible child abuse. Some relate to the child's appearance, others to the child's behavior, and still others to what the child says. Certain family indicators also should be considered. The presence of one sign alone does not automatically signal abuse. However, if one or more are present, they should be interpreted as a warning that additional attention is warranted (Kaplan, 1986). These signs are summarized in Table 16-2.

Reporting Child Abuse

Some helping professionals are reluctant to report child abuse because they assume that making a report automatically will result in an arrest or in the child being removed from the home (Beezer, 1985). The U.S. National Center on Child Abuse and Neglect (1977) has tried to dispel these misgivings by emphasizing that reporting child abuse does not represent a punitive action but rather the beginning of a rehabilitative process whose aim is to protect the child and support the family microsystem.

Professionals must remember that reports signal only the suspicion that abuse has occurred. Helping professionals who, in good faith, document signs of abuse and relay them to the proper authorities are acting as an advocate for the child.

The reporting process is straightforward. Although particular institutions and government jurisdictions have their own individual procedures, most include:

1. A disclosure of the suspicion to a designated person within the program.
2. A verbal report to the social agency responsible for children's protective services in a particular community. This report is conveyed either directly by the individual who has the suspicion or indirectly through a designated spokesperson. In either case, the identity of the person who originally suspected abuse is kept confidential and is revealed only with his or her consent.
3. A written report to the social agency with which verbal contact was initiated. This usually occurs within two to three days. The written statement contains essential information, usually is brief, and is written in the person's own words rather than in legalistic terms.
4. An interview with the child. This is most common when sexual abuse is suspected. Youngsters usually are interviewed in the presence of someone they trust; in many cases, this is the helping professional in whom they confided.
5. Continued investigation. From this point on, the case falls within the jurisdiction of a protective service worker. Although contact with the helping professional is desirable, the burden of responsibility has now shifted to the protective service worker.

This chapter has focused on factors that influence judgments helping professionals make. We have concentrated on three distinct categories: judgments in day-to-day encounters, judgments about children's extreme behavior, and judgments regarding child abuse. Specific skills associated with each of these now follow, as do the pitfalls that should be avoided.

TABLE 16-2 Signs of Child Abuse: Physical, Behavioral, Verbal, and Family Indicators

PHYSICAL ABUSE

Physical Indicators

Bruises

    Bruises on the face, lips, or mouth; on large areas of the back, torso, buttocks, or thighs; on more than one side of the body

    Bruises of different coloration, indicating that they occurred at different times

    Bruises that are clustered

    Bruises that show the imprint of a belt buckle, coat hanger, strap, or wooden spoon

Welts

Wounds, cuts or punctures

Burns

    Rope burns on arms, legs, neck, face, or torso

    Burns that show a pattern (cigarette, iron, radiator)

    Burns on the buttocks or genitalia

    Caustic burns

    Scalding-liquid burns

Fractures

    Multiple fractures in various stages of healing

    Any fracture in a child younger than two years of age

Bone dislocations

Human-bite marks

Neglect

    Child is consistently dirty, hungry, or inappropriately dressed for the weather

    Child has been abandoned

    Child has persistent medical problems that go unattended

Behavioral Indicators

The child:

    Is wary of physical contact with adults

    Flinches when adults approach or move

    Exhibits a dramatic change in behavior

    Shows extreme withdrawal or aggression

    Indicates fear of parents or caregivers

    Consistently arrives early and stays late

    Is consistently tired or falls asleep during the day

    Is frequently late for school or absent

    Is under the influence of alcohol or drugs

    Begs or steals food

    Shows a limited capacity for experiencing pleasure or enjoying life

TABLE 16-2 *(continued)*

PHYSICAL ABUSE

Verbal Indicators

The child:

Reports injury by parents or caregiver

Offers inconsistent explanations for injuries or condition

Offers incredible explanations for injuries or condition

Makes comments such as: ''Can I come and live with you?'', ''Do I have to go home?'', ''My mom/dad doesn't like me''

Reports not having a place to sleep and/or enough to eat

Family Indicators

The family:

Maintains a filthy home environment

Is socially isolated from the rest of the community

Is extremely closed to contacts with school or child's friends

Refuses to allow child to participate in normal school activities (physical education, social events)

Offers inconsistent, illogical, or no explanation for child's injury or condition

Shows lack of concern about child's injury or condition

Attempts to conceal child's injury or condition

Describes the child as evil, monstrous, or incorrigible

Reports or uses in your presence inappropriate punishments (denial of food, prolonged isolation, beating)

Consistently speaks demeaningly to the child

Abuses alcohol or drugs

Reacts defensively to inquiries regarding the child's health

SEXUAL ABUSE

Physical Indicators

The child:

Is pregnant

Shows signs of venereal disease

Has blood in urine

Has genitals that are swollen or bruised

Shows presence of pus or blood on genitals

Has physical complaints with no apparent physical cause

Has torn or stained underclothing

Shows rectal bleeding

TABLE 16-2 *(continued)*

SEXUAL ABUSE

Behavioral Indicators

The child:

Persistently scratches genital area

Has difficulty sitting on chairs or play equipment (squirming, frequently readjusting position, frequently leaving seat)

''Straddle walks'' as if pants were wet or chafing

Suddenly loses appetite

Suddenly reports nightmares

Shows extreme withdrawal or aggression

Shows wariness of contact with adults

Shows inappropriate seductiveness with adults or other children

Shows a sudden lack of interest in life

Withdraws into fantasy behavior

Regresses to infantile behavior such as bed-wetting, thumb sucking, or excessive crying

Shows limited capacity for enjoying life or experiencing pleasure

Is promiscuous

Runs away

Is frequently truant

Exhibits knowledge of sexual functions far beyond other children in his or her peer group

Suddenly withdraws from friends

Verbal Indicators

The child:

Complains of pain in the genital area

Reports incidents of sexual contact with an adult or older child

Reports having to keep secret a game with an adult or an older child

Expresses fear of being left alone with a particular adult or older child

Reports: ''She/he fooled around with me,'' ''She/he touched me,'' or ''My mother's boyfriend/my father/my brother/my aunt does things to me when no one else is there''

Family Indicators

The family:

Exhibits an obvious role reversal between mother and daughter

Is socially isolated from the rest of the community

Is extremely closed to contacts with school or child's friends

Demonstrates extreme discord

Refuses to allow child to engage in normal social interactions

SKILLS FOR MAKING JUDGMENTS

How to Make Day-to-Day Judgments

1. Become aware of values that are important to you. Think about decisions you have made in your own life in terms of the values they represent. Try to determine what basic beliefs govern your interactions with children and their families. Figure out if there are discernible patterns to the kinds of choices you make. Discuss your ideas with friends and colleagues. Compare your reactions with theirs, and try to articulate why you have chosen a particular path. Take advantage of formalized opportunities to engage in values clarification.

2. Comprehensively assess situations in which a judgment must be made. Make an initial survey that includes the following factors: recognition of the child's perspective, awareness of your own affective state, consideration of the child's age and past experiences, and an analysis of the situational context.

SITUATION: Brian approaches the lunch table with dirty hands. When you remind him to wash, he says, "But I already washed my hands three times."

Child's emotions: Frustration, annoyance, discouragement, surprise

Your reactions: Disbelief, uncertainty about what to do next, concern about the child's health, apprehension about the example being set for others, sympathy for the child's efforts

Other factors to consider:

a. Brian has had several unhappy interactions today.

b. Brian usually forgets to wash his hands altogether.

c. Children in the group have been questioning some of the rules.

d. Your last interaction with Brian involved a confrontation.

e. The cook is signaling that lunch is on the table.

Because this type of analysis covers so much territory, you may think it can only be incorporated in judgments that allow time for long-term deliberation. Actually, this process also can be applied to on-the-spot decision making as well. At first, you may feel so pressured in a situation that you think of some, but not all, of the critical variables. However, as you gain experience, you will become more adept at quickly considering multiple factors when making a judgment.

If you are in a situation in which you are an observer and in which safety is not in question, take a few moments to sort out the issues prior to acting. Should you be in a circumstance in which an immediate response is expected, use an affective reflection and the middle portion of the personal message (that is, your emotions and the reasons for them) to identify aloud the child's perspective and your own. If, at that point, you need a few more moments to think, tell the children so: "You're anxious to go in swimming. I'm in a real quandary; I know it's hot, but I'm not sure how to keep an eye on all of you. Let me think about it for a minute, and then I'll decide what to do."

3. Consider alternative strategies in terms of their potential outcomes. Imagine various responses to a particular situation. Predict the possible impact of each on the child, on yourself, and on others. Think about how each outcome would either support or impede your current goals for all parties. The following illustrates this process in relation to the preceding example about Brian.

Possible actions to take:

1. Acknowledge Brian's efforts and let him proceed to lunch.

2. Acknowledge Brian's efforts, explain your own concerns, and tell him to rewash his hands.

3. Acknowledge Brian's efforts, acknowledge the difficulty of the task, and offer to help.

Possible outcomes:

1.a Brian will feel successful and therefore will be more likely to remember the rule in the future.

1.b Other children may notice that Brian didn't have to wash as thoroughly as they did and will not have faith in your rules.

1.c Brian will feel successful, but you may still feel uncomfortable about the dirt on his hands.

1.d You and Brian will get to lunch on time.

1.e You will avoid another confrontation with Brian.

2.a Brian may feel discouraged that his efforts were not good enough.

2.b Brian's pride in having washed his hands may be replaced with resentment.

2.c You will be involved in another confrontation with Brian.

2.d Children will perceive that your standards are the same for everyone.

2.e You and Brian will be late for lunch.

2.f Brian's hands may become cleaner.

2.g Brian may interpret that you think he's lying.

3.a All of the outcomes identified for option (2),

3.b Brian's feelings of incompetence may be assuaged by your support.

3.c Brian will have the opportunity to learn more about how to wash his hands properly.

FIGURE 16-2 Children need time and practice to perfect their skills; mistakes are a natural part of the process.
SOURCE: © Susan Lapides 1981

4. Select and implement a strategy or combination of strategies that supports your overall goals for children and that is based on your priorities for the situation. Keep in mind the goals you are working toward for each child and for the group as a whole. In addition, use the priority principles outlined in this chapter to help you sort out what is most important in a given instance. Use the goals and priorities you identify as the basis for action.

In regard to Brian's case, were the adult to determine that safety was not a major issue, other considerations would have to be made. For instance, the professional's long-range goal for Brian might be to help him to feel more confident. A goal for the entire group might be individualism. Thus, the adult may interpret that this is a situation in which priority principles C and E are relevant. Based on all these factors, he or she would be led to judge that acknowledging Brian's efforts and letting him proceed to lunch is the most appropriate action.

On the other hand, were the adult to interpret the situation as one involving safety, then priority principle A would prevail, signaling the necessity of implementing options

(b) or (c) (having the child rewash, either alone or with help). Selection of the former or the latter would depend on whether the adult judged the situation to be one of noncompliance or lack of knowledge.

5. Include nonintervention as a strategy option. Taking no action in a situation can be the result of a considered judgment on your part. For example, on the playground, Myron drops a hard line drive. "Oh damn," he says. Miss Delmar, who overhears this, considers many options: lecturing Myron, having him apologize for using a curse word, sending him off the field, or ignoring the incident. She surveys the situation. Myron looks surprised and chagrined that he dropped the ball. He is seemingly unaware of the epithet. The adult does not really feel offended because his words were more an exclamation of surprise than true profanity. Also, it is unlikely that anyone else heard him. Considering the excitement of the situation, Myron's embarrassment over his fielding error, and the context of the game, she judges that the best goal for Myron is to have another chance catching. Every option other than ignoring the episode probably would impede achievement of this goal, so she makes a second judgment not to intervene.

6. Adopt standards that take into account children's age and experience. Apply your understanding of child development and learning to your expectations for children's performance. Do not expect children to perform perfectly the first few times. Allow them to make mistakes. Observe youngsters carefully to determine what they can and cannot do, then set your standards accordingly. As they become more adept, increase your expectations gradually. It is with this in mind that the adult may have judged Brian's "almost-clean" hands as "clean enough" for the time being. However, several days hence, the standard could be raised because Brian would have had additional opportunities to increase his skill.

7. Reassess situations in light of new information. Remember that you can make different judgments regarding your goals, strategies, and standards as you acquire new knowledge. This may mean selecting an option you had previously discarded or developing an entirely new one. For instance, the judgment to allow Brian to proceed to lunch might be changed if you overheard him bragging to a friend that on his way out of the bathroom, he saw a dime at the bottom of the toilet, which he reached in to get.

8. Evaluate the judgments you make. Take time to assess the effectiveness of your thinking and of corresponding actions. Consider whether the potential outcome became reality. If so, ask yourself whether it contributed to progress toward a desired goal. If the anticipated effect did not occur, reflect on what contributed to the incongruous result and what might be done instead. Discuss your deliberations with a colleague or supervisor.

9. Learn from judgment errors. Sooner or later, you will make a judgment that you will come to regret. When this happens, mentally review the circumstances under which you made it. Consider what prompted your response and what other options were available to you at the time. Try to determine what went awry, and figure out what you might do if you had the decision to make again. Sometimes, you will conclude that you made a bad judgment and that another option would have been better. On other occasions, you will deduce that the judgment was right at the time, even though the outcome was negative or stressful. Mentally catalogue relevant information for future use. Then, move on. It is counterproductive to unceasingly agonize over a past judgment.

10. Support colleagues who have made poor judgments. When fellow staff members have made a judgment and it has turned out poorly, offer comfort and encouragement. Be available as a sounding board and listen to their evaluation of what went into their decision. Help them sort out what went wrong and brainstorm remedial strategies or alternate approaches for the future.

11. Identify values you and another person hold in common when differences in goals, strategies, and/or standards exist. Talk over conflicts in approach that arise. Explore thoroughly the other person's perceptions by asking him or her to describe his or her understanding of the situation and overall purpose within it. Listen carefully and quietly, avoiding jumping to conclusions, interrupting, or giving your opinion prematurely. Use the reflective listening skills you have learned to convey interest and acceptance. Look beyond the details of what people are saying to the essence of their message. Find common aims at this level. Then, proceed to negotiate the goals, strategies, and standards that might be acceptable to both of you.

In most cases, this type of clarification should contribute to mutual understanding and a more unified approach. If you recognize that you have a true conflict in values, acknowledge this state of affairs. Then, determine what you will have to do to make the situation livable.

How to Deal with Children's Extreme Behavior

1. Get to know the children in your group prior to making a judgment that any one of them is exhibiting extreme behavior. Although the mere presence of some behaviors is enough to signal a problem, most can be identified as extreme only because they represent a major deviation from the child's customary pattern. For this reason, it

is important that you give yourself enough time to determine what is typical for each child. Thus, the loud outbursts from a child that initially were startling may seem less unusual over time or may represent a brief episode rather than a prevailing mode of interaction for that child. Similarly, the extremely quiet behavior of one youngster might be normal and functional for him or her; the same demeanor in a usually exuberant child could be seen as a legitimate cause for concern.

2. Make a concerted effort to change a behavior by using appropriate guidance techniques before judging it extreme. Use the skills you have learned in previous chapters as your initial means of addressing problematic behavior. Be consistent in your approach, and allow enough time (usually several weeks) for your strategies to have a fair chance of success. Ask a colleague to review your plan and/or to observe its implementation in order to judge whether it is appropriate and whether you are carrying it out effectively. If you discover that a child's continued exhibition of a problem behavior is the result of a faulty plan or ineffective implementation, make the corresponding revisions.

3. Confirm your judgment that a child's behavior is extreme. Make an objective record of the child's behavior over time. Then, refer to books that describe age norms. If the behavior is not categorized as appropriate for the child's age, check to see if it is typical of other ages, particularly younger ones. If the latter turns out to be the case, remember that children under stress often regress. Although you should continue to monitor such behavior, do not consider it extreme unless it persists over a long period of time. However, should the child's activity not be described for any age group, it is possible that if falls outside appropriate limits, irrespective of age. To determine if this is the case, carefully observe other children of comparable age while they are both active and quiet. If no other children manifest the behavior in question, talk to an experienced and trusted colleague who has worked with many children effectively. Also, consult your supervisor or other co-workers whose job responsibilities encompass this type of consultation. Check to see if they agree that the behavior is outside of that considered acceptable for the child's age and circumstances. If others agree that the behavior seems extreme, seek out a reputable professional for consultation.

4. Communicate to the family your concern that their child's behavior is extreme. When making the initial contact, whether in person, by telephone, or by written message, express your concern matter-of-factly and request a meeting with the parent(s). On one hand, avoid going into elaborate detail; on the other hand, avoid sounding secretive and mysterious. Both tactics can only serve to alarm the parents or make them feel defensive. You might say something like: "I've been observing Charles for the last several days and have become concerned about his sudden disinterest in interacting with the other children. Normally, he's quite outgoing, and his withdrawal has persisted for some time. I'd like to set up a time to discuss this with you in more detail."

When the meeting takes place, be prepared to provide concrete examples of the behavior in question. Find out if the same behavior occurs at home and whether or not the parent considers it atypical. If, as the conference proceeds, you reach the conclusion that indeed, the behavior is extreme, share this observation with the parents(s) and provide a rationale for your judgment. Be prepared to suggest specific courses of action the parent(s) could take.

5. Seek out or recommend the type of professional who could deal most appropriately with a particular problem. Determine with the family who will contact the consulting professional. If the behavior may be physically based, as in problems with eating, elimination, sleeping, too much or too little energy, or obvious depression, first contact a physician. If no physical difficulties are found, consult next with a behavioral specialist.

If an extreme behavior is obviously unconnected to physical sources, begin with a behavioral expert, such as someone trained in speech therapy or learning disabilities. These people are more likely to be familiar with behavioral problems than would many physicians. Further, reputable, competent behavioral specialists would be aware of conditions to which physical difficulties could contribute and would suggest medical consultation in such instances.

Check on potential community resources such as child-guidance clinics, college psychological clinics, school guidance counselors, community mental health agencies, social-service agencies in your area, intermediate school districts (umbrella agencies that offer special services across school districts), and programs specializing in youngsters whose problems are similar to the one you have tentatively identified for a particular child. Even when an individual program may not exactly suit your needs, personnel there may be able to direct you to a more appropriate source.

6. Provide emotional support to families who are seeking outside help for their child's extreme behavior. The referral process often takes a long time, resulting in anxiety or frustration for families. Offer words of encouragement or sympathy, and be willing to listen to familial complaints and lamentations. Use reflective listening skills to communicate your understanding. Take additional action, if possible, to speed up the process.

7. Follow up on your recommendation that a child or family receive outside services. If you have agreed to contact a medical or behavioral expert, do so promptly. Make the contact directly or through the channels dictated by your agency or program. Periodically, check on the progress of your referral and make sure that contact actually is made. Should the family assume primary responsibility for seeking help, communicate with them regularly to ascertain what has transpired.

8. Provide accurate, relevant information to the consulting professional. Share your observations of the child's behavior, either verbally or in writing. Make available records you have kept regarding his or her behavior pattern, or summarize them in a report. Invite the outside expert to observe the child within the formal group setting. Offer to meet with him or her and the family.

9. Coordinate the way you deal with the child's extreme behavior in the formal group setting with the way it is being handled by the family and by the consultant to whom the child has been referred. Find out what action has been recommended. Discuss with the consultant and the family the feasibility of adapting your program to the consultant's recommendations as well as ways in which your actions can complement theirs. For instance, if it has been decided that certain behaviors will be rewarded and others ignored at home and in the therapy session, follow the same guidelines, if possible. Provide feedback to all adults involved in the plan regarding the child's progress in your setting. Make relevant suggestions for changes and revisions in the plan. Also, ask for feedback regarding your own performance. Maintain periodic contact with both the consultant and the family throughout this time.

How to Deal with Child Abuse

1. Find out the appropriate procedures for reporting child abuse. Read the laws of your state regarding child abuse, including what constitutes abuse, the persons or agencies to whom such cases should be referred, who is legally obligated to report abuse, and what safeguards exist for those reporting. Although all 50 states mandate reporting suspected cases and protect helping professionals from legal prosecution when making reports in good faith, the specifics of who is bound to report, who is notified, and how it is done vary. For example, the Michigan Child Protection Law requires all school administrators, teachers, counselors, social workers, nurses, physicians, dentists, audiologists, law-enforcement officers, and duly regulated child-care providers to make an oral report of *suspected* child abuse or neglect to the local department of social services.

In addition to obtaining this legal knowledge, find out the reporting protocol of the formal group setting in which you are employed. If you are required to make a report through a designated person, determine how you will be appraised that your report has been filed. Also, ask what role you are expected to play in subsequent action. Should the policy require that you report your suspicions directly to the authorities, find out who they are. (Often, these are described as "children's protective services.") If you are unable to locate the authorities in your community, contact one of the nationwide emergency numbers provided in Appendix D.

2. Watch for signs of child abuse. Use the physical, behavioral, verbal, and family indicators outlined in Table 16-2. Pay attention to children. Look at them. Listen to what they say. Be alert for changes in a child's physical condition or demeanor. Believe children when they persistently complain that they are hungry, that they "hurt down there," or that cousin Billy beat them with a strap (Hendrick, 1984). Most children do not make up stories about abuse or molestation (Shay and Murphy, 1984).

3. *Document your suspicions.* Keep written notes about the sign that caused you to suspect child abuse and the date on which it occurred. If more than one sign is present, record each of them.

4. *Promptly report suspected cases of child abuse.* Should a child or family display a combination of signs that you have been trained to recognize as indicative of child abuse, report it. Do not delay in the hope that conditions will change or that you were wrong. Do not vacillate about what to do. Once the suspicion is there, the subsequent action is clear.

5. *Reassure children who have revealed that they are victims of abuse.* Say something like: "It was hard for you to tell me about this" or "You're upset your momma knocked your tooth out. I'm really glad you told me." Let them know that you believe what they have said and that no harm will come to them from you for reporting the incident. Reflect their feelings of confusion, worry, anger, or guilt. Allow them to talk out their feelings and to describe individual incidents with as much or as little detail as they want. Remain receptive and supportive of abused children no matter how uncomfortable or distressed you may feel. On the other hand, avoid pumping children for details that are beyond their capacity or willingness to reveal at a given time. Express your sympathy about what has happened, but at the same time, do not berate the child's family. Even youngsters who have been ill treated often feel a loyalty to family members. They may withdraw if they perceive that they must defend their family to you.

Many children feel guilty regarding their role in the abusive situation. They may conclude that because they are "no good" or "ugly" or "so bad," the adult had no choice but to abuse them. Attempt to rectify these misperceptions by stating that what happened was not the child's fault. Instead, it was the adult's behavior that was inappropriate. Explain that sometimes, adults become angry, confused, or lonely, but that beating children, tricking them, or subjecting them to unwanted fondling is wrong.

6. *Talk to children about physical touching.* Begin with infants, and continue throughout the childhood years, to use feeling words to describe physical interactions. Use affective reflections to provide children with information about how touching affects them and others. Say things like: "A hug feels good," "Pinching hurts," "You were happy when Jeremy scratched your back," or "You didn't like it when Marion hit you." Such reflections form the foundation for a "touch vocabulary" that can be expanded as children develop (Shay and Murphy, 1984). Familiarizing children with these specialized words is the first step in teaching personal safety.

7. *Teach children personal safety.* It is widely believed that some sexual abuse can be prevented by directly teaching children ways to avoid exploitive touching. Refer to the personal safety facts and principles in Appendix E for ideas on relevant and accurate facts to present to children. Use these facts and principles as the basis for discussions with children and to give you ideas about appropriate material for activities and skits. Review Chapters 13 and 14 for guidelines on how to construct these. Adapt your presentation to match children's understanding and experience. For example:

a. Initiate a discussion in which children talk about touches that make them feel good and touches that make them feel bad. Introduce the idea of confusing touches: those that start out feeling good but that eventually become uncomfortable (tickling, bear hugs, petting). Point out that no one has the right to use bad touch or confusing touch with another person. Tell children that if someone tries to touch them in ways they do not like, they can say "*No*," get away, and then tell someone they trust.

b. Set up a skit in which one character tries to trick another character into doing something. With very young children or older youngsters who have had little prior training, begin with obvious tricks unrelated to sexual abuse. As the children begin to understand the notion of a trick, introduce skits that address inappropriate touching (for example, bribery, keeping a "secret," or flattery). Emphasize the point that it is not okay for people to force children to touch them or to trick children into touching them. Teach children that if a person tries to trick them into touching him or her or into doing things the child does not understand, the child can say, "*No*," get away, and tell someone he or she trusts.

c. Play the "What if . . . ?" game as a way to check children's understanding of how to respond in dangerous situations. Make up pretend episodes, such as: "What if the man down the street asks you to come in and see the new puppies?", "What if your baby-sitter asks you to keep a secret, especially from your mom and dad?", or "What if you have a fight with your friends in the park and a nice lady you don't know offers you a ride home?" Reflect children's answers and provide accurate information as appropriate. Ask open-ended questions to further extend the discussions.

8. *Treat families with sensitivity even when child abuse is suspected or has occurred.* If you have been the source of a child-abuse report, contact the family after it has been made. Inform them that you suspect that their child has been subjected to physical or sexual abuse. Explain that you are legally bound to report such suspicions and that you wanted them to know you had done so. Indicate that you would like to be supportive of the family in any way they might find acceptable. Expect a hostile or incredulous reaction, particularly if the parents themselves have been involved in the abuse. Avoid berating the family or spending a great deal of time trying to justify your actions to them. The purpose of this contact is not to humiliate them or to try to get them to repent, but to indicate that you respect them enough that you would not do something behind their backs.

Should parents choose to respond to you, either in defense of their actions, to explain extenuating circumstances, or to accuse you of misrepresenting them, listen nonjudgmentally. Use the reflective listening skills you have learned to accomplish this.

Keep confidential all matters related to the case. Do not gossip or disclose tantalizing tidbits to other parents or to staff members who are not directly involved. Refuse to answer questions from curious people who have no legitimate right to the information.

If you are in a situation that requires continued contact with the family, treat them casually and civilly. Acknowledge their presence, speak to them, and be genuine in your interactions. This means not being effusive or more friendly than you have been in the past. Talk about day-to-day affairs rather than "the case."

9. *Be aware of help available in your community for parents who indicate they are on the brink of abuse.* Promising studies show that 80 percent of all abusing parents can be helped so that they no longer resort to physical violence (Kempe and Kempe, 1978). This is an indication of how important it is to refer parents to people and programs designed to assist them. Find out as much as you can about such support programs in your area. Identify short-term alternatives such as hot lines, sources of respite care, parent groups, educational opportunities, and workshops. In addition, keep a file of long-term options including local individual and family therapists, mental-health agencies, and religious and social-service programs, as well as such nationally recognized groups as Parents Anonymous and Parents United (see Appendix D).

PITFALLS TO AVOID

There are many guidelines to remember in deciding how to make a judgment. The skills just covered describe the behaviors you should exhibit. The pitfalls that follow describe behaviors you should avoid.

Failing to make a conscious judgment because of time pressures. Sometimes, helping professionals are so rushed that they think they cannot take the time to figure out what to do. Instead, they react instinctively. Occasionally, their intuitive responses are correct and fit well into a comprehensive approach to the child and the group. More often, they satisfy short-term ends but do not comprehensively address long-term goals. Although it is not always feasible to ponder over what to do, it is possible to incorporate the judgment process somewhere in the situation. Even if this can be done only in retrospect, assessing one's judgment is a valuable professional skill. Moreover, unless safety is the issue, it is better to postpone one's reaction in order to think it out than to respond haphazardly. Frequently, time spent in an initial assessment that leads to a successful approach is less than that accumulated over time in failed efforts.

Staying with a poor judgment too long. At times, people become ''wedded'' to a selected option because they have invested so much time and energy in making that judgment. They fail to recognize signs that a goal or standard does not fit, that a strategy useful under other circumstances is not effective in this instance, or

that a plan simply is not working. If they continue to ignore these cues, the situation will deteriorate. The best way to avoid this pitfall is to keep alert to changes in the situational context and to remain receptive to new information. Continual re-evaluation of judgments made also is essential, as is a willingness to let go of unproductive approaches.

Failing to recognize one's limitations. Helping professionals err when they imagine themselves as the only person capable of helping a child even when the child's problems call for skills beyond their own. This mind set can be the result of any of the following:

1. They may think they are the only ones who care enough to handle the child appropriately or who understand the child well enough to know what to do.
2. They may jealously guard their role in the child's life and perceive other helping professionals as interlopers.
3. They may not recognize the seriousness of the child's situation.
4. They may interpret consultation with an outside expert as an indication of their own inadequacy.
5. They may think they possess skills that, in fact, they do not.

In any case, this type of thinking is not conducive to creating the most favorable climate for the child's development. Helping professionals who find themselves resisting making a referral, even when all signs indicate that doing so is in the best interest of the child, must examine their attitudes. If they find that their lack of enthusiasm relates to any of the reasons just described, reconsideration is in order.

Neglecting to clarify one's own role in relation to the consulting professional. Working with an outside consultant requires a coordination of efforts. Children benefit most when they are handled consistently throughout their mesosystem. This mean that professionals in the formal group setting must have a clear understanding of what expectations, if any, the consultant has for their performance. It is not enough to have a vague picture of what is required. Instead, one must develop a precise list of expectations. It is therefore important to clarify mutual goals and the strategies and standards that will support them.

Not following the recommendation of a consultant long enough to allow it to work. One of the most common pitfalls in working with an outside consultant is to prematurely abandon a mutually agreed-on plan. Having finally taken the step of calling in an outsider, the helping professional may expect instant results. When these are not forthcoming, he or she gives up in disappointment. To avoid succumbing to this form of disillusionment, it is best to formulate, in conjunction with the consultant, a time line along which progress will be measured. Knowing that a particular approach might have to be employed for several weeks or even months before a change can be expected increases one's patience and makes setbacks easier to bear.

Ignoring signs of abuse. Sometimes, in an effort to avoid dealing with a difficult situation or because they wish it were not so, helping professionals overlook obvious cues that abuse has occurred. If a child exhibits bruises and reports that his mother beat him, the professional may think, "Oh, all children get paddled sometimes." When a youngster's vagina is raw and bleeding, the adult attributes it to masturbation. Should a child continually be dirty and smell bad, the adult passes it off as typical of that cultural group or social class. Children are not served well when adults reach these conclusions, which are based not on the facts but on their own psychological and emotional defenses. Every sign that could indicate abuse must be taken seriously. Children should not be made to suffer because adults are afraid to face reality.

Threatening families one suspects of child abuse. Occasionally, rather than reporting a case of probable child abuse, helping professionals try to intervene directly with the family. They confront family members, saying things like: "If you do this again, I'll have to report you" or "Promise me you'll stop, and I won't report you." Their motives may be self-serving (wishing to avoid legal entanglements) or well-meaning (hoping to save the family embarrassment). In either case, these tactics are ill advised and should not be used. Rather, helping professionals should follow the procedures outlined in the skills section of this chapter.

Purposely frightening children as a way to teach personal safety. Adults who are trying to teach children to be careful about strangers and exploitive touching may deliberately overgeneralize their warnings so that youngsters become fearful of everyone and all forms of physical contact. Describing in lurid detail horrible incidents of abuse, treating all situations as unsafe, and failing to distinguish "good touch" from "bad touch" contributes to this negative perception. It is not healthy for young people to feel always in jeopardy. Instead, they must be exposed to a balanced view in which caution is promoted, but complete terror and distrust is avoided.

SUMMARY

Helping professionals continually make judgments for and about the children with whom they work. These encompass long- or short-range judgments, judgments adults have time to evaluate carefully and those that must be made immediately, and judgments that have profound or relatively minor effects. All judgments must be made consciously.

In making any judgment, helping professionals go through several steps. First, they assess the circumstance; next, they think about possible actions in response; eventually, they must select one or a combination of strategies, which they then put into action. Finally, helping professionals evaluate the results of their decisions and use this information to guide future judgments. Although no outcome can be guaranteed, following this process makes a measured judgment more likely. Furthermore, the probability is greater that the adult's goals, strategies, and standards for children will be congruent.

Goals represent milestones on the path toward achieving social competence. Strategies are the specific practices adults employ to pursue their goals for children. Standards are used to determine the degree to which goals have been achieved. Developing, implementing, and evaluating goals, strategies, and standards calls for a multitude of judgments.

Several variables affect the judgments people make. Among these are their values. Values are not directly observable but are inferred from an individual's behavior. People acquire values through the socialization process. They develop a value hierarchy in which values are prioritized. This can be a complex process, and it explains why individuals experience value conflicts. Understanding one's own values leads to more conscious behavior and helps individuals to respect the values of others as well as to separate values from goals, strategies, and standards.

A second variable that affects judgments helping professionals make is their knowledge of child development and learning. A third is the context of the situation in question. Because judgments often involve establishing priorities from among a range of possibilities, it is important to adopt and follow principles for how to set these priorities.

The preceding discussion has dealt with everyday kinds of judgments. Two arenas require specialized judgments: children's extreme behavior and child abuse. The judgment to be made in each case is whether or not the condition exists. Once this is determined, there are specific actions helping professionals should follow. The factors that go into a judgment of whether children's behavior is extreme are: the presence of self-destructive acts or a sudden shift in a child's functioning; inappropriate behavior for the child's age; persistently intense behavior; indiscriminate evidence of particular behaviors; impairment of a child's present or future functioning; and resistance of the behavior to change. Extreme behavior often can be attributed to physiological causes, children's fears, and childhood depression.

Judgments about suspected child abuse are critical for children's health and well-being. Physical abuse is a nonaccidental injury that results from acts of omission or commission by a parent, guardian, or caregiver. Sexual abuse exists when youngsters are forced or persuaded to engage in sexual activity by an older child or adult. There are differences between the victims of physical and sexual abuse as well as between the perpetrators of these two forms. Some of the effects of abuse on its victims are injury, truancy, dramatic behavior changes, psychological distress, guilt, and anger. The need for early intervention is critical, so, helping professionals must become familiar with the signs of abuse. For each type, there are physical, behavioral, verbal, and family indicators. All states have specific reporting guidelines that helping professionals must learn.

There are specific skills helping professionals can learn to enable them to make day-to-day judgments, judgments involving children's extreme behavior, and judgments about child abuse. In addition, there are behaviors that helping professionals should avoid when making these types of judgments.

DISCUSSION QUESTIONS

1. Discuss the relationship between helping professionals' values and their goals, strategies, and standards for children. Give some examples from your own life.
2. In a small group, discuss a value that you hold. As best you can, trace its origin and how it has affected a judgment you have made.
3. Discuss the priority principles outlined in this chapter. Make comments either in support of or in opposition to:
   a. The order in which they are presented.
   b. A specific principle or principles.
   c. How they should or should not be applied.
4. Define what is meant by extreme behavior. Describe four factors that must be taken into account when making a judgment about whether or not a behavior is extreme. Discuss three pitfalls to avoid in making this kind of judgment.
5. Discuss how a child's fear may result in extreme behavior. Describe the judgments a helping professional must make in such a case.
6. Define what is meant by physical abuse. Discuss who are the most likely victims and the most likely perpetrators. Discuss what you would do if you suspected physical abuse.
7. Define what is meant by sexual abuse. Discuss who are the most likely victims and the most likely perpetrators. Discuss what to do if you suspect sexual abuse.
8. Talk in a small group about the similarities and differences in the judgments you would make in cases of suspected physical or sexual abuse.
9. Discuss what signs would alert you to a case of possible physical abuse. Discuss the signs that would alert you to a case of possible sexual abuse.
10. Discuss the similarities and differences in judgments you would make on a day-to-day basis and those you would make when dealing with extreme behavior or child abuse.

APPENDIX A
Friendship Facts and Principles

Friends Defined

1. Friends are people who:
   a. Like you.
   b. Like to be near you.
   c. Let you play with them.
   d. Seek you out.
   e. Hold your hand; hug you; pat you on the back.
   f. Say, "I like you."
   g. Invite you to play with them or use their things.
   h. Like to talk with you.
   i. Care about what happens to you.
   j. Wait for you.
   k. Notice when you are absent.
   l. Miss you when you aren't around.
   m. Help you do things.
   n. Let you help them.
   o. Try to keep you from being hurt.
   p. Share secrets with you.
   q. Listen to your ideas.
   r. Pay attention to your feelings.
   s. Decide with you where to play.
   t. Decide with you what to do.
   u. Help you solve a problem.
   v. Like you even after you do things they don't like.
   w. Forgive you.
   x. Sometimes let you have your way even when it's not their way.
   y. Comfort you when you are feeling unhappy.
   z. Come over to visit.
   aa. Ask you to visit them.
2. Some people are friends, some are acquaintances, and some are strangers.
3. Some friends are members of your family; some are outside your family.
4. Friends may be like you in many ways and different from you in others.
5. Friends may be of any age.
6. Friends may live near each other or far apart.
7. Friends may see each other frequently or only once in a while.
8. Friends can remain friends even when they are not together.
9. Some friends are people, some are animals, some are toys, and some are pretend.
10. Friends may have different ideas about things: sometimes, friends agree; sometimes, they disagree.
11. Friends may enjoy doing some things together, some things with other people, and some things by themselves.

12. People vary in the number of friends they have.
13. People can have more than one friend at a time.
14. The same person can be a friend to more than one person.
15. People do not always like all the people their friends like.
16. People experience different feelings about their friends.
17. Sometimes, friends hurt each other's feelings.
18. Sometimes, friends can forgive each other; sometimes, they cannot.
19. Having a friend:
    a. Makes people feel good.
    b. Gives people someone with whom to share ideas, play, and work.
    c. Gives people someone with whom to share secrets.
    d. Gives people someone with whom to share feelings.
    e. Gives people someone to listen to and someone to listen to them.
    f. Gives people someone to comfort and someone to comfort them.
    g. Gives people someone to care for.
    h. Gives people the opportunity to help each other.
20. Sometimes, friendships end.
21. There are many different reasons why a friendship may end.
22. People have different feelings when friendships end.
23. It can be sad or confusing when someone no longer wants to be your friend.
24. People can make new friends.
25. Friends can be found in many different places.

Making and Keeping Friends

26. People's behavior affects their ability to make or keep friends.

27. There are obvious ways people use their bodies to let others know they want to be friends. These include smiling, playing near someone else, and looking directly at the person with whom they are speaking.
28. There are obvious ways people use words to let others know they want to be friends. These include offering greetings, offering information, and responding in a positive way to the greetings and questions of others.
29. When people use less obvious ways to show they want to be friends, it is sometimes hard for others to figure out their message.
30. People feel friendly toward people who:
    a. Express an interest in what they are doing.
    b. Take turns.
    c. Share.
    d. Listen to their ideas.
    e. Let them do some things their way.
    f. Have interesting ideas.
    g. Think their ideas are interesting.
    h. Like to do some of the same things.
    i. Keep their secrets.
    j. Trust them.
    k. Stick up for them.
    l. Notice the nice things they do.
    m. Are thoughtful.
    n. Think of ways to solve problems without hurting others.
31. People feel less friendly toward people who:
    a. Hurt them.
    b. Make fun of them.
    c. Grab their things.
    d. Tattle on them.
    e. Cheat.
    f. Lie to them or about them.
    g. Always insist on their way.
    h. Gossip about them.

APPENDIX B
Helping Facts and Principles

1. Helping is a way of acting toward others that changes things for the better.
2. There are two major kinds of helping: aiding someone in distress and assisting people in their work or play.
3. Ways to aid people in distress include removing the cause of their distress, rescuing them, defending them, and comforting them.
4. Ways to assist people in their work or play include sharing materials and information and providing physical assistance or encouragement.
5. All people can give help; all people can receive help.
6. People who help are more likely to receive help themselves when they need it.
7. Some situations in which people need help are:
   a. When a job is too big to do by themselves.
   b. When they are frightened.
   c. When they don't know how to do something they want to do.
   d. When they need food, clothing, or shelter.
   e. When they don't have all the information they need.
   f. When they are in danger.
   g. When they are lonely.
   h. When others are interfering with their work or play.
   i. When there are limited resources available.
8. People may be showing they need help when they:
   a. Cry.
   b. Frown.
   c. Groan.
   d. Sigh.
   e. Look confused (wrinkle their brow, stare, shake their head).
   f. Pound their fist or stomp their foot.
   g. Shout.
   h. Crumple something.
   i. Run away from something.
9. People may tell you they need help by:
   a. Saying, "Help me."
   b. Asking who, where, when, what, which, how, or why questions.
   c. Saying such things as: "I'm worried," "I'm hungry," "I'm tired," "I need

you,'' ''This is too much for me,'' ''I'm afraid,'' ''I can't do this by myself,'' ''I'm confused,'' ''I don't know,'' ''I'm uncomfortable,'' ''I wish I had a friend,'' ''They're bothering me,'' or ''I need . . .''

10. Some ways of removing the cause of distress are:
    a. Taking it away.
    b. Taking the person to a different place.
    c. Helping the person figure out how to solve the problem.
11. Some ways of rescuing are:
    a. Offering personal assistance.
    b. Telling someone else about the problem.
    c. Getting someone else to help, too.
12. Some ways of defending are:
    a. Telling the truth.
    b. Explaining things.
    c. Giving new information.
    d. Telling someone to stop hurting someone.
    e. Standing up for a companion.
13. Some ways of comforting are:
    a. Hugging.
    b. Patting.
    c. Staying nearby.
    d. Talking and listening.
14. Some ways of sharing materials are:
    a. Taking turns.
    b. Dividing them.
    c. Trading one item for another.
    d. Using the item together.
15. Some ways of sharing information are:
    a. Telling something you know.
    b. Finding out about something another person wants to know.
    c. Lending someone a book, a magazine, or a picture.
    d. Directing someone who doesn't know to someone who does know.
    e. Telling someone where to find the information.
16. Some ways to provide physical assistance are:

    a. Doing something for someone (telephone, translate).
    b. Lifting, carrying, holding, or pulling something for, to, or with someone.
    c. Giving someone something they need (a bandage, a book, a pencil).
17. Some ways of encouraging people are:
    a. Telling them they did something well.
    b. Telling them you believe they can do something.
    c. Recognizing their efforts at trying.
    d. Working with them to try again.
    e. Figuring out with them what went wrong and how to correct it.
18. Helping is a way of showing kindness, consideration, caring, respect, and concern.
19. When people see someone who needs help, they decide whether to help or not.
20. Sometimes, helping means doing something that other people won't like.
21. People who help are more likable.
22. Some people find it easy to seek and accept help.
23. Some people find it difficult to seek help or accept it.
24. Deciding what would be most helpful depends on several factors:
    a. How willing a person is to receive help from the helper.
    b. What relevant skills or information the helper has.
    c. Whether someone else is available who could be more helpful.
25. Sometimes, behaviors that are helpful in one situation are not helpful in others.
26. Helping involves thinking of another person as well as oneself.
27. Sometimes, people are aware of being helped; others may be unaware.
28. Sometimes, helpers want the person to know that they are helping, and at other times, they would rather the person didn't know.
29. Sometimes, help is planned; sometimes, it is spontaneous.

30. Sometimes, help involves a lot of time and effort; sometimes, it is less demanding.
31. Sometimes, it is helpful to do something; sometimes, it is helpful to stop doing something or to refrain from doing something.
32. Sometimes, people want to be helped; sometimes, they would rather do things without help.
33. Sometimes, one person helps; sometimes, a few people or many people help.
34. Sometimes, people help people they know; sometimes, they help people they've never met; sometimes, they help people they hear about.
35. Sometimes, help is given directly; sometimes, it is given through another person or organization.
36. Sometimes, the helper finds out how successful the help was; sometimes, he or she does not.
37. Sometimes, people help using ideas they are familiar with; sometimes, people create new ideas in order to help.
38. Helping can be fun, boring, satisfying, frightening, risky, interesting, convenient, or inconvenient.
39. When help is rejected, people sometimes feel sad, embarrassed, annoyed, relieved, surprised, or hurt.
40. People who never help may have trouble getting help when they need it.
41. When help isn't acknowledged, the helper doesn't always know the outcome of the help.
42. People being helped can give information to the helper that makes the help more effective.
43. People don't always know whether or not they need help.
44. People don't always know what the helper could do to help them.
45. People who help are called helpful.
46. People who do not help are called unhelpful.
47. Unhelpful people often:
    a. Ignore people in distress.
    b. Contribute to people's distress.
    c. Interfere with someone's plans or activities.
    d. Keep information or materials to themselves.
    e. Discourage people.

APPENDIX C
Cooperating Facts and Principles

1. Cooperation involves people working together toward a common goal.
2. There are times when a person's own goals and the group's goals are not the same.
3. When individual and group goals don't match, people can choose to:
   a. Place personal goals second to those of the group.
   b. Proceed independently toward their own goals.
   c. Change their own goals to match those of the group.
   d. Attempt to change group goals to match their own.
4. People cooperate when they are willing to:
   a. Listen to each other's ideas.
   b. Take each other's ideas into account when forming an opinion or making a plan.
   c. Try out someone else's ideas.
   d. Compromise.
   e. Take turns using things.
   f. Take turns expressing themselves.
   g. Take turns getting their way.
5. People who cooperate are called cooperative.

6. People who seldom cooperate are called uncooperative.
7. Uncooperative people often:
   a. Insist on having their own way regardless of what other people want.
   b. Reject the ideas of others without considering whether those ideas are good or bad.
   c. Interfere with the group's ability to plan or carry out a project by making fun of other people's ideas, refusing to listen, refusing to do things they are asked to do, or finding fault with all suggestions other than their own.
8. People who cooperate with others are more likely to receive cooperation in return.
9. People can be cooperative in one situation and uncooperative in another.
10. There are some tasks that can be accomplished better when people work together than when one person works alone.
11. People enjoy working with others to accomplish a task.
12. People tend to like cooperative people more than uncooperative people.

13. Cooperating is a way people show their concern or affection for other people.
14. Cooperating involves thinking of people other than yourself.
15. Sometimes, cooperation is planned; sometimes, it's spontaneous.
16. There are many factors that contribute to whether or not people feel like cooperating:
    a. Their mood—people are more cooperative when they feel happy than when they feel unhappy or angry.
    b. How much they care about the person who needs their cooperation.
    c. How strongly they feel about their own goals, which may or may not be compatible with those of others.
    d. Whether or not they anticipate personal benefit from cooperating.
17. It is easier to cooperate in some situations than in others.
18. Sometimes, people cooperate even when they don't feel like it.
19. People can cooperate with people they know and with people they don't know.
20. People can cooperate with one other person at a time, with a few other people at a time, or with several other people at a time.
21. It is more convenient to cooperate at some times than at other times.
22. Sometimes, working with others makes projects go faster; sometimes, it makes them go slower.
23. People are more willing to support a project they have been part of.

APPENDIX D
Organizations Which Address Child Abuse

American Association for Protecting Children (a division of the American Humane Society)
9725 East Hampden Avenue
Denver, CO 80231
(303) 695-0811
Emphasizes the political expression of citizen's views, researches child abuse, rates programs, and issues data on abused children.

National Committee for Prevention of Child Abuse
P.O. Box 2866
Chicago, IL 60609
(312) 663-3520
Provides information for people who want to find solutions to child abuse, including sexual abuse. Stresses preventive efforts, gives referrals, and offers volunteer opportunities.

Parents Anonymous (an affiliate of the National Committee for Prevention of Child Abuse)
P.O. Box 2866
Chicago, IL 60609
(800) 421-0353 [in Illinois, (312) 663-3520]

A crisis-intervention program for parents who abuse their children. Operates a hot line and provides referrals to local chapters.

Parents United
840 Guadelupe Parkway
San Jose, CA 95110
(800) 422-4453
A resource for sexual-abuse victims, perpetrators, and their families to call for referrals to local affiliates in 50 states and Canada.

Parents Without Partners
7910 Woodmont Avenue
Bethesda, MD 20814
(800) 638-8078
A national support group for single parents and their children with over 1,000 local chapters. Provides various social and educational programs.

APPENDIX E
Personal Safety Facts and Principles

Beginning Facts and Principles

1. Your body is your own.
2. You have a right to the privacy of your body in dressing, bathing, and sleeping.
3. When anyone touches you in a way you don't like, you can say, "*No!*"
4. There are many kinds of touch: some touches make you feel good; some touches make you feel bad.
5. No one has the right to touch you in a way that hurts or feels frightening or confusing.
6. No one has the right to force or trick you into touching them. Some kinds or hurtful tricks include:
   a. Telling children something that isn't true.
   b. Pretending to know you or your parents.
   c. Promising you treats.
   d. Offering to give you a ride.
7. When anyone touches you in a way that you don't like, tell someone you trust about it right away, even if you've been told to keep it a secret.
8. It's not fair for an adult or older child to touch you in a way that you don't like. If an adult or older child touches you in a way that's not fair, it is not your fault.
9. Sometimes, people try to trick children into doing things that aren't good for them. Sometimes, people who try to trick children seem nice at first.
10. If someone tries to trick you, tell someone else about it right away, even if you've been told to keep it a secret.
11. Good secrets are about happy surprises and can be fun to keep for a little while.
12. Bad secrets are about things that make you uncomfortable, confused, scared, or unhappy. If someone wants you to keep a bad secret, tell someone you trust right away.
13. People you trust are the people with whom you always feel safe.
14. A stranger is a person whose name you don't know; you don't know where they live, and your parents don't know them either.
15. If someone you don't know does anything

that seems strange or frightening, you can:
a. Run.
b. Yell or scream, "Leave me alone—you're not my father (mother)!"
16. If someone you *do* know does something that seems frightening or confusing, you can:
a. Yell or scream, "Leave me alone!"
b. Run and find someone you trust and tell them what happened.
c. If the person you tell doesn't believe you, find someone else to tell right away.

Intermediate Facts and Principles

1. Sometimes, pleasant touches become unpleasant or confusing:
a. Holding someone's hand feels good, but it hurts if your hand is squeezed too hard.
b. Tickling can be fun, but tickling too hard or for too long can be upsetting.
2. Sometimes, you feel like being hugged or kissed; sometimes, you don't. You can tell someone how you feel.
3. When you feel like giving a hug or a kiss, first ask if it's okay. If someone says, "Yes," give them a hug or kiss. If someone says, "No," don't give them a hug or kiss.
4. Parents worry when they don't know where their children are. It's important to always be where your parents think you are.
5. Being lost is a scary feeling. When your parents can't find you, they worry too.
6. When you're lost, there are some strangers you can ask for help:
a. Ask a mother with children.
b. Ask another child to take you to his or her mom or dad. Tell them you're lost.
c. Tell a salesclerk or cashier that you can't find your mom or dad.
d. Tell a person wearing a uniform, such as a police officer or a mail carrier.
e. Tell one of these people your phone number so they can call home for you.
7. Parents often have private code words that they tell only the people who are allowed to take you away with them.
8. If you have a code word, your mom or dad will never send a stranger to get you who doesn't know your family's special code word.
9. If someone says your parents sent them and doesn't say the code word, don't go with them. Tell someone you trust what happened.

These facts and principles were developed by Donna Howe, Instructor, Department of Family and Child Ecology, Michigan State University, 1985.

REFERENCES

Abelson, A. G. "Measuring Preschool Readiness to Mainstream the Handicapped." Ann Arbor, Mich: Early Intervention Project for Handicapped Infants and Children, 1975.

Aboud, F. E., and S. A. Skerry. "The Development of Ethnic Attitudes." *Journal of Cross Cultural Psychology* 15, no. 1, 3 (1984): 3–34.

Adams-Tucker, C. "Proximate Effects of Sexual Abuse in Childhood: A Report on 28 Children." *American Journal of Psychiatry* 139 (1982): 1252–56.

Adler, A. *Practice and Theory of Individual Psychology.* New York: Harcourt, Brace and Company, 1923.

Ainsworth, M. D. S. "The Development of Infant-Mother Attachment." In *Review of Child Development Research*, Vol. 3, edited by B. M. Caldwell and H. N. Riccuti, Chicago: University of Chicago Press, 1973.

Aldis, O. *Play Fighting.* New York: Academic Press, Inc., 1975.

Alexander, T., P. Roodin, and B. Gorman. *Developmental Psychology.* New York: Van Nostrand Reinhold Co., Inc., 1980.

Allen, K. E. *Mainstreaming in Early Childhood Education.* New York: Delmar Publishers, Inc., 1980.

Allen, K. E. "The Parent-Teacher Partnership in Programs for Young Children." *Resources in Education* 7 (1983).

Allman, I., and D. A. Taylor. *Social Penetration: The Development of Interpersonal Relationships.* New York: Holt, Rinehart & Winston, 1973.

Altman, K. "Effects of Cooperative Response Acquisition on Social Behavior During Free Play." *Journal of Experimental Psychology* 12 (1971): 385–95.

Alward, K. R. *Arranging the Classroom for Children.* San Francisco: Far West Laboratory for Educational Research and Development, 1973.

Ambron, S. R., and N. J. Salkind. *Child Development.* New York: Holt, Rinehart & Winston, 1984.

American Association for Protecting Children. News Release. Denver, Colo., 8 November 1985.

Anderson, H. H., and J. E. Brewer. "Studies of Teachers' Classroom Personalities." *Applied Psychology Monographs* 6 (1945).

Asher, S. R. "Children's Peer Relations." In *Social and Personality Development*, edited by M. E. Lamb. New York: Holt, Rinehart & Winston, 1978.

Asher, S. R., S. L. Oden, and J. M. Gottman. "Children's Friendships in School Settings." In *Current Topics in Early Childhood Education*, Vol. 1, edited by L. G. Katz. Norwood, N.J.: Ablex Publishing Corp., 1977.

Asher, S. R., and P. Renshaw. "Children without Friends: Social Knowledge and Social Skill." In *The Development of Children's Friendships*, edited by S. R. Asher and J. M. Gottman. New York: Cambridge University Press, 1981.

Ashton, R. "The State Variable in Neonatal Research: A Review." *Merrill-Palmer Quarterly* 19 (1973): 3–20.

Azrin, N. H., and W. C. Holz. "Punishment." In *Operant Behaviors: Areas of Research and Application*, edited by W. K. Honig. New York: Appleton-Century-Crofts, 1966, 380–447.

Bach, G. R., and H. Goldberg. *Creative Aggression.* New York: Avon Books, 1974.

Bakeman, R., and J. Brownlee. "The Strategic Use of Parallel Play: A Sequential Analysis." *Child Development* 51 (1980): 873–78.

Baker v. Owen, 39 F. Suppl. 294 (M.D.N.C. 1975), Off'd U.S.—96 S. Cet. 210.

Balaban, N. *Starting School.* New York: Teachers College Press, 1985.

Baldwin, C. P., and A. L. Baldwin. "Children's Judgements of Kindness." *Child Development* 41 (1970): 29–47.

Bandura, A. "The Role of the Modeling Process in Personality Development." In *The Young Child: Reviews of Research*, Vol. 1, edited by W. W. Hartup and N. L. Smothergill. Washington, D.C.: National Association for the Education of Young Children, 1967.

Bandura, A. *Aggression: A Social Learning Analysis.* Englewood Cliffs, N. J.: Prentice-Hall, Inc., 1973.

Bandura, A., and W. Mischel. "Modification of Self-Imposed Delay of Reward Through Exposure to Live and Symbolic Models." *Journal of Personality and Social Psychology* 2 (1965): 698–705.

Bandura, A., D. Ross, and S. A. Ross. "Imitation of Film-Mediated Aggression." *Journal of Abnormal and Social Psychology* 66, no. 1 (1963): 3–11.

Bandura, A., and R. H. Walters. *Social Learning and Personality Development.* New York: Holt, Rinehart & Winston, 1963.

Bandura, A., and R. H. Walters. *Social Learning Theory.* Englewood Cliffs, N. J.: Prentice-Hall, Inc., 1977.

Baron, R. A., D. Byrne, and W. Griffith, *Social Psychology.* Boston: Allyn and Bacon, Inc., 1974, 231–32.

Bateson, G. "The Message 'This Is Play'." In *Child's Play*, edited by R. E. Herron and B. Sutton-Smith. New York: John Wiley & Sons, Inc., 1971.

Bauer, D. H. "An Exploratory Study of Developmental Changes in Children's Fears." *Journal of Child Psychology and Psychiatry* 17 (1976): 69–74.

Baumrind, D. "Effects of Authoritative Parental Control on Child Behavior." *Child Development* 37 (1966): 887–907.

Baumrind, D. "Child Care Practices Anteceding Three Patterns of Preschool Behavior." *Genetic Psychology Monographs* 75 (1967); 43–88.

Baumrind, D. "Socialization and Instrumental Competence in Young Children." *Young Children* 26, no. 2 (December 1970): 104–119.

Baumrind, D. "Note: Harmonious Parents and Their Preschool Children." *Developmental Psychology* 4 (1971): 99–102.

Baumrind, D. "Socialization and Instrumental Competence in Young Children." In *The Young Child: Review of Research*, Vol. 2, edited by W.W. Hartup. Washington, D.C.: National Association for the Education of Young Children, 1972.

Baumrind, D. "Current Patterns of Parental Authority." *Developmental Psychology Monographs* 4 (1973): 1.

Baumrind, D. "The Development of Instrumental Competence Through Socialization." In *Minnesota Symposium on Child Psychology*, Vol. 7, edited by A. D. Pick. Minneapolis: University of Minnesota Press, 1973.

Baumrind, D. "Socialization Determinants of Personal Agency." Paper presented at the biennial meeting of the Society for Research in Child Development, New Orleans, April 1977.

Baumrind, D. "Some Thoughts About Childrearing." In *Child Development: Contemporary Perspectives*, edited by S. Cohen and T. J. Comiskey. Itasca, Ill.: F. E. Peacock, Publishers, Inc., 1977.

Beadle, M. "The Name of the Game." *New York Times* (21 October 1973): 18–132.

Becker, W. C. "Consequences of Different Kinds of Parental Discipline." In *Review of Child Development Research*, Vol. 1, edited by M. L. Hoffman and L. W. Hoffman.

New York: Russell Sage Foundation, 1964, 164–208.

Becker, W. C., S. Engelmann, and D. R. Thomas. *Teaching: A Course in Applied Psychology.* Chicago: Science Research Associates, 1971.

Beckwith, L. "Relationships Between Infants' Vocalizations and Their Mothers' Behaviors." *Merill-Palmer Quarterly* 17 (1971): 211–26.

Beebe, B., and D. Stern. "Engagement-Disengagement and Early Object Experiences." In *Communicative Structures and Psychic Structures*, edited by N. Friedman and S. Grand. New York: Plenum Publishing Corporation, 1977.

Beezer, B. "Reporting Child Abuse and Neglect: Your Responsibility and Your Protections." *Phi Delta Kappan* 66, no.6, 2 (1985): 434–36.

Bell, S. M., and M. D. Ainsworth. "Infant Crying and Maternal Responsiveness." *Child Development* 43 (1972): 1171–90.

Beller, E. K. "Teaching Styles and Their Effects on Problem-Solving Behavior in Head-Start Programs." In *Critical Issues in Research Related to Disadvantaged Children*, edited by E. H. Grotberg. Washington D.C.: ERIC Research in Education, 1969.

Beller, E. K. "Adult-Child Interaction and Personalized Day Care." In *Day Care: Resources for Decisions*, edited by E. H. Grotberg. Washington, D.C.: Office of Economic Opportunity, 1971, 229–64.

Belsky, J. "Child Maltreatment: An Ecological Integration." *American Psychologist* 35 (1980): 320–55.

Belsky, J., and L. Steinberg. "The Effects of Day Care: A Critical Review." *Child Development* 49 (1978): 929–49.

Benson, H. *The Relaxation Response.* New York: William Morrow & Co., Inc., 1970.

Berclay, C. J. *Parent Involvement in the Schools.* Washington, D.C.: National Education Association, 1977.

Berg, W. K., C. D. Adkinson, and B. D. Strock. "Duration and Frequency of Periods of Alertness in Neonates." *Development Psychology* 9 (1973): 434.

Bergan, J. B., and R. W. Henderson. *Child Development.* Columbus, Ohio: Charles E. Merrill Publishing Company, 1979.

Berger, E. H. *Parents As Partners in Education.* St. Louis, Mo.: The C. V. Mosby Company, 1981.

Berger, K. S. *The Developing Person.* New York: Worth Publishers, Inc., 1980.

Berkowitz, L. "Control of Aggression." In *Review of Child Development Research*, edited by B. Caldwell and H. Riccuti. Chicago: University of Chicago Press, 1973, 95–141.

Bernard, S., and L. W. Sontag. "Fetal Reactivity to Tonal Stimulation: A Preliminary Report." *Journal of Genetic Psychology* 70 (1947): 205–210.

Berndt, T. J. "The Effect of Reciprocity Norms on Moral Judgments and Causal Attribution." *Child Development* 45 (1974): 1322–30.

Berns, R. M. *Child, Family, Community.* New York: Holt,

Rinehart & Winston, 1985.

Bernstein, B. "Social Class and Linguistic Development: A Theory of Social Learning." In *Education, Economy and Society,* edited by A. Halsey, J. Floud, and C. Anderson. New York: Prentice-Hall, Inc., 1961.

Bertenthal, B., and K. W. Fischer. "Development of Self-Recognition in the Infant." *Developmental Psychology* 14 (1978): 44–50.

Bessell, H. *Methods in Human Development: Theory Manual.* San Diego, Calif.: Human Development Training Institute, 1970.

Bessell, H., and J. Palomares. *Methods in Human Development.* La Mesa, Calif.: Human Development Training Institute, 1970.

Bishop, N. "A Systems Approach Toward the Functional Connections of Attachment and Fear." *Child Development* 46, 801–17.

Blanck, P., and R. Rosenthal. "Developing Strategies for Decoding 'Leaky' Messages: On Learning How and When to Decode Discrepant and Consistent Social Communications." In *Development of Nonverbal Behavior in Children,* edited by B. S. Feldman. New York: Springer-Verlag New York, Inc., 1982.

Block, J. "Personality Development in Males and Females: The Influence of Differential Socialization." *Socialization Influencing Personality Development.* Berkeley, Calif.: University of California Press, 1979.

Bloom, B. S., J. T. Hastings, and G. F. Madaus. *Handbook on Formative and Summative Evaluation of Student Learning.* New York: McGraw-Hill, Inc., 1971, 118–32.

Bloom, L., K. Lifter, and J. Brazelton. "What Children Say and What They Know: Exploring the Relations Between Product and Process in the Development of Early Words and Early Concepts." In *Language Behavior in Infancy and Early Childhood,* edited by R. Stark. New York: Elsevier/North Holland, 1981.

Blurton-Jones, N. "Categories of Child-Child Interaction." In *Ethological Studies of Child Behavior,* edited by N. Blurton-Jones, Cambridge, England: Cambridge University Press, 1972, 97–128.

Blurton-Jones, N. "Rough-Tumble Play Among Nursery School Children." In *Play: Its Role in Development and Evolution,* edited by J. Bruner, A. Jolly, and K. Sylva. New York: Basic Books, Inc., Publishers, 1976, 352–63.

Boggs, S. T. "The Meaning of Questions and Narratives to Hawaiian Children." In *Functions of Language in the Classroom,* edited by C. B. Cazden, V. P. John, and D. Hymes. New York: Teachers College Press, 1972.

Boneau, C. A. "Paradigm Regained: Cognitive Behaviors Restated." *American Psychologist,* 29 (1974): 297–309.

Bongiovanni, A. "A Review of Research on the Effects of Punishment: Implications for Corporal Punishment in the Schools." Paper presented at the Conference on Child Abuse, Children's Hospital National Medical Center, Washington, D.C., February 1977.

Borke, H. "Interpersonal Perception of Young Children: Egocentrism or Empathy?" *Developmental Psychology* 5 (1971): 263–69.

Borke, H. "Chandler and Greenspan's Ersatz Egocentricism: A Rejoinder." *Developmental Psychology* 7 (1973): 107–9.

Borland, D.C. "Human Sexuality in the Home." *Two to Twelve* 2, no. 1 (1984): 1–4.

Borton, T. *Reach, Touch, and Teach.* New York: McGraw-Hill, Inc., 1970.

Boss, P. "Normative Family Stress: Family Boundary Changes Across the Life Span." *Family Relations* (29 October 1980): 445–50.

Bower, G. "Mood and Memory." *American Psychologist* 36 (1981): 128–48.

Bowlby, J. *Attachment and Loss. Vol. 1: Attachment.* New York: Basic Books, Inc., Publishers, 1969.

Brackbill, Y. "Obstetrical Medication and Infant Behavior." In *Handbook of Infant Development,* edited by J. D. Osofsdy. New York: John Wiley & Sons, Inc., 1979, 76–125.

Brenner, A. *Helping Children Cope with Stress,* Lexington, Mass.: D.C. Heath & Company, 1984.

Bretherton, I. "Representing the Social World in Symbolic Play: Reality and Fantasy." In *Symbolic Play,* edited by I. Bretherton. New York: Academic Press, Inc., 1984, 1–41.

Bridges, K-H. B. "Emotional Development in Early Infancy." *Child Development* 3 (1932): 324–41.

Briggs, D. C. *Your Child's Self-Esteem.* New York: Doubleday & Company, Inc., 1975.

Bronfenbrenner, U. "Who Needs Parent Education?" Paper presented at the Working Conference on Parent Education, Mott Foundation, Flint, Mich., 30 September 1977.

Bronfenbrenner, U. *The Ecology of Human Development* Cambridge, Mass.: Harvard University Press, 1981.

Bronson, G. W. "Infants' Reactions to Unfamiliar Persons and Novel Objects." *Monographs of the Society for Research in Child Development* 37, 1972 (3, Serial No. 148).

Brooks, J. B. *The Process of Parenting.* Palo Alto, Calif.: Mayfield Publishing Co., 1981.

Brophy, J., and J. Putnam. "Classroom Management in the Elementary Grades." In *Classroom Management. Yearbook for the National Society for the Study of Education,* edited by D. Duke. Chicago: NSSE, 1979, 182–216.

Broughton, J. "Development of Concepts of Self, Mind, Reality and Knowledge." *New Directions for Child Development* 1 (1978): 75–100.

Brown, B. "Slim Talk: A Strange Mirror of the Mind." *Psychology Today* 8 (1974): 8.

Brown, B. "Parents' Discipline of Children in Public Places." *The Family Coordinator* 28, no. 1 (1979): 67–73.

Brown, D. G. "Masculinity-Femininity Development in Children." *Journal of Consulting Psychology* 21 (1957): 197–202.

Brown, P., and R. Elliot. "Control of Aggression in a Nursery School Class." *Journal of Experimental Child*

Psychology 2 (1965): 103–7.

Brown, R., and U. Bellugi. "Three Processes in the Child's Acquisition of Syntax." *Harvard Educational Review* 34 (1964): 133–51.

Bruner, J. S., R. R. Oliver, and P. Greenfield. *Studies in Cognitive Growth*. New York: John Wiley & Sons, Inc., 1966.

Bryan, J. H. "Children's Cooperation and Helping Behaviors." In *Review of Child Development Research*, Vol. 5, edited by E. M. Hetherington. Chicago: University of Chicago Press, 1975, 127–80.

Bryan, J. H., and N. Walbek. "Preaching and Practicing Generosity: Children's Actions and Reactions." *Child Development* 41 (1970): 329–53.

Bryan, T. "An Observational Analysis of Classroom Behavior of Children with Learning Disabilities." *Journal of Learning Disabilities* 7, no. 1 (1974): 26–34.

Bubolz, M. M., J. B. Eicher, and S. Sontag. "The Human Ecosystem: A Model." *Journal of Home Economics* 71, no. 1 (Spring 1979): 28–31.

Buck, R. "Spontaneous and Symbolic Nonverbal Behavior and the Ontogeny of Communication." In *Development of Nonverbal Behavior in Children*, edited by R. S. Feldman. New York: Springer-Verlag New York, Inc., 1982, 28–62.

Bugental, D. "Interpretations of Naturally Occurring Discrepancies Between Words and Intention; Modes of Inconsistency Resolution." *Journal of Personality and Social Psychology* 30 (1974): 125–33.

Bugental, D., L. Caporael, and W. A. Shennum. "Experimentally Produced Child Uncontrollability: Effects on the Potency of Adult Communication Patterns." *Child Development* 51 (1980): 520–28.

Bugental, D., J. W. Kaswan, and L. R. Love. "Child Versus Adult Perception of Evaluative Messages in Verbal, Vocal and Visual Channels." *Developmental Psychology* 2 (1970): 367–75.

Bugental, D., J. W. Kaswan, and L. R. Love. "Perception of Contradictory Meanings Conveyed by Verbal and Nonverbal Channels." *Journal of Personality and Social Psychology* 16 (1970): 647–55.

Bugental, D., L. Love, and R. Gianetto. "Perfidious Feminine Faces." *Journal of Personality and Social Psychology* 17 (1971): 314–18.

Bugental, D., et al. "Child Versus Adult Perception of Evaluative Messages in Verbal, Vocal and Visual Channels." *Developmental Psychology* 2 (1970): 367–75.

Burgess, R. L. "Family Violence: Some Implications from Evolutionary Biology." Paper presented at the annual meeting of the American Society of Criminology, Philadelphia, Pa., November 1979.

Buss, A. "Sociability, Shyness, and Loneliness." Paper presented at the American Psychological Association Convention, Montreal, Canada, August 1980.

Buss, A. H., and R. Plomen. *A Temperament Theory of Personality*. New York: John Wiley & Sons, Inc., 1975.

Butterfield, and G. N. Siperstein. "The Mouth of the Infant." In *Third Symposium on Oral Sensation and Perception*, edited by J. F. Bosma. Springfield, Ill.: Charles C. Thomas, Publisher, 1972.

Byrne, D., and W. A. Griffit. "A Developmental Investigation of the Law of Attraction." *Journal of Personality and Social Psychology* 4 (1966): 699–702.

Cairns, R. B. *Social Development: The Origins and Plasticity of Interchanges*. San Francisco: W. H. Freeman & Company, Publishers, 1979.

Caldwell, B. M. "Aggression and Hostility in Young Children." *Young Children* 32 (January 1977): 4–13.

Campos, J. J., et al. "Socioemotional Development." In *Handbook of Child Psychology*, Vol. 2, edited by P. H. Hussen. New York: John Wiley & Sons, Inc., 1983.

Camras, L. A. "Facial Expressions Used by Children in a Conflict Situation." *Child Development* 48 (1977): 1431–35.

Canavan, J. W. "Sexual Child Abuse." In *Child Abuse and Neglect: A Medical Reference*, edited by N. S. Ellerstein. New York: John Wiley & Sons, Inc., 1981, 233–53.

Canter, L. and M. Canter. *Assertive Discipline*. Santa Monica, Calif: Canter and Associates, Inc., 1983.

Carkhuff, R. R. *Helping and Human Relations: A Primer for Lay and Professional Helpers. Vol. 1: Selection and Training*. New York: Holt, Rinehart & Winston, 1969.

Carlsmith, L. "Effect of Early Father Absence on Scholastic Aptitude." *Harvard Educational Review* 34 (1964): 3–21.

Carroll, J. J. and M. S. Steward. "The Role of Cognitive Development in Children's Understanding of Their Own Feelings." *Child Development* 55 (1984): 1486–92.

Carter, E. A., and M. McGoldrick. *The Family Life Cycle: A Framework for Family Therapy*. New York: Gardner Press, Inc., 1980.

Cattermole, J., and N. Robinson "Effective Home/School Communication—From the Parents' Perspective." *Phi Delta Kappan* 67, no. 1, 9 (1985): 48–50.

Cavallaro, S. and R. Porter. "Peer Preferences of At-Risk and Normally Developing Children in A Preschool Mainstream Classroom." *American Journal of Mental Deficiency* 84 (1980): 357–66.

Cazden, C. B. *Language in Early Childhood Education*. Washington, D.C.: National Association for the Education of Young Children, 1972.

Chaikin, A. L., and U. J. Derlega. *Self-Disclosure*. Morristown, N. J.: General Learning Press, 1974.

Chance, P. *Learning Through Play*. New York: Gardner Press, Inc., 1979.

Charles, C.M. *Elementary Classroom Management*. New York: Longman, Inc., 1983.

Charlesworth, R., and W. W. Hartup. "Positive Social Reinforcement in the Nursery School Peer Group." *Child Development* 38 (1967): 993–1003.

Chernow, F. B., and C. Chernow. *Classroom Discipline and*

Control: 101 Practical Techniques. West Nyack, N. Y.: Parker Publishing Co., Inc., 1981.

Chomsky, N. *Syntactic Structures.* The Hague: Mouton Publishers, 1957.

Chukovsky, K. "The Sense of Nonsense Verse." In *Play: Its Role in Development and Evolution,* edited by J. S. Bruner, A. Jolly, and K. Sylva. New York: Basic Books, Inc., Publishers, 1976, 596–602.

Clarizio, H. *Toward Positive Classroom Discipline.* New York: John Wiley & Sons, Inc., 1980.

Clarizio, H. *Contemporary Issues in Educational Psychology.* Boston: Allyn and Bacon, Inc., 1981.

Clark, K. B. *Prejudice and Your Child.* Boston: Beacon Press, 1955, 1963.

Clarke-Stewart, A., S. Friedman, and J. Koch.*Child Development: A Topical Approach.* New York: John Wiley & Sons, Inc., 1985.

Clarke-Stewart, A., and J. B. Koch, *Children: Development through Adolescence.* New York: John Wiley & Sons, Inc., 1983.

Cohen, B., J. S. De Loache, and M. S. Strauss. "Infant Visual Perception." In *Handbook of Infant Development,* edited by J. D. Osofsky. New York: John Wiley & Sons, Inc., 1979, 393–438.

Coleman, J. "Learning Through Games." In *Play: Its Role in Development and Evolution,* edited by J. Bruner, A. Jolly, and K. Sylva. New York: Basic Books, Inc., Publishers, 1976, 460–63.

Coleman, J. C., and C. L. Hammen. *Contemporary Psychology and Effective Behavior.* Glenview, Ill.: Scott, Foresman & Company, 1974, 462–63.

Coletta, A. J. *Working Together: A Guide to Parent Involvement.* Atlanta: Humanics, Ltd., 1977.

Combs, M. L., and D. A. Slaby. "Social Skills Training with Children." In *Advances in Clinical Child Psychology,* edited by B. Lakey and A. Kazdin. New York: Plenum Publishing Corporation, 1978.

Comstock, G. "Types of Portrayal and Aggressive Behavior." *Journal of Communication* 27 (1977): 189–98.

Comstock, G. "New Emphases in Research on the Effects of Television and Film Violence." In *Children and the Faces of Television: Teaching, Violence Selling,* edited by E. L. Palmer and A. Dorr. New York: Academic Press Inc., 1980, 129–44.

Conn, L.K., et al. "Perception of Emotion and Response to Teacher's Expectancy by Elementary School Children." *Psychological Reports* 22 (1968): 27–34.

Conte, J. "Sexual Abuse of Children: Enduring Issues for Social Workers." *Journal of Social Work and Human Sexuality* 1 (1982): 17–25.

Cook, R. E., and V. B. Armbruster. *Adapting Early Childhood Curricula.* St. Louis, Mo.: The C. V. Mosby Company, 1983.

Coopersmith, S. *The Antecedents of Self-Esteem.* Princeton, N. J.: Princeton University Press, 1967.

Cotler, S. B., and J. J. Guerra. *Assertion Training.* Champaign, Ill.: Research Press, 1975.

Cowen, E. L., et al. "Long-Term Follow-Up of Early Detected Vulnerable Children." *Journal of Consulting and Clinical Psychology* 4 (1973): 438–46.

Craig, G. J. *Child Development.* Englewood Cliffs, N. J.: Prentice-Hall, Inc., 1979.

Crary, E. *Without Spanking or Spoiling: A Practical Approach to Toddler and Preschool Guidance.* Seattle, Wash.: Parenting Press, 1980.

Croake, J. W. "The Changing Nature of Children's Fears." *Child Study Journal* 3 (1973): 91–105.

Croft, D. J. *Parents and Teachers: A Resource Book for Home, School, and Community Relations.* Belmont, Calif.: Wadsworth, Inc., 1979.

Cross, J. F., and J. Cross "Age, Sex, Race, and the Perception of Facial Beauty." *Developmental Psychology* 5 (1971): 433–39.

Crow, G. A. *Children at Risk.* New York: Schocken Books, Inc., 1978.

Damon, W., ed., *New Directions for Child Development: Moral Development.* Vol. 2. San Francisco: Jossey-Bass, Inc., Publishers, 1978.

Damon, W. *Social and Personality Development.* New York: W. W. Norton & Company, 1983.

Danish, S. J., and A. L. Hauer. *Helping Skills: A Basic Training Program.* New York: Behavioral Publications, 1973.

D'Augelli, A. R., et al. *Helping Skills: A Basic Training Program.* New York: Human Sciences Press, Inc., 1980.

Day, B. *Open Learning in Early Childhood.* New York: Macmillan, Inc., 1975.

Dayton, G. O., et al. "Developmental Study of Coordinated Eye Movements in the Human Infant. I. Visual Acuity in the Newborn Human: A Study Based on Induced Optokinetic Nystagmus Recorded by Electro-oculography." *Archives of Ophthalmology* 71 (1964): 865–70.

Deacon, R., and F. Firebaugh. *Family Resource Management: Principles and Applications.* Boston: Allyn and Bacon, Inc., 1981.

DeCarie, T. G. *The Infant's Reaction to Strangers.* New York: International Universities Press, Inc., 1974.

DeCasper, A. J., and W. P. Fifer. "Of Human Bonding: Newborns Prefer Their Mothers' Voices." *Science* 208 (1980): 1174–76.

DeFrancis, V. *Protecting the Child Victim of Sex Crimes Committed by Adults.* Denver, Colo.: American Humane Association, 1969.

Desor, J. A., O. Maller, and L. S. Green. "Preference for Sweet in Humans: Infants, Children, and Adults." In *Taste and Development: The Genesis of Sweet Preference,* edited by J. M. Wuffenback. Bethesda, Md.: U.S. Department of Health, Education, and Welfare, 1977, 161–72.

Devoney, C., M. J. Guralnick, and H. Rubin. "Integrating

Handicapped and Nonhandicapped Preschool Children: Effects on Social Play." *Childhood Education* 50 (1972): 360–64.

DiCaprio, N. S. *Personality Theories: Guides to Living.* Philadelphia: W. B. Saunders Company, 1974.

Dillon, J. T. "Using Questions to Depress Student Thought." *School Review* 87 (November 1978): 50–63

Dillon, J. T. "To Question and Not to Question During Discussion: Non-Questioning Techniques." *Journal of Teacher Education* B, no. 6 (1981): 15–20.

Dinkmeyer, D. *Developing Understanding of Self and Others (DUSO).* Circle Pines, Minn.: American Guidance Service, Inc., 1970.

Dinkmeyer, D., and G. D. McKay. *Systematic Training for Effective Parenting.* Circle Pines, Minn.: American Guidance Service, Inc., 1976.

Dion, K. K., and E. Berscheid. "Physical Attractiveness and Peer Acceptance Among Children." *Sociometry* 37 (1974): 1–2.

Dittrichova, J., and K. Paul. "Behavioral States in Infants." *Ceskoslovensko Psychologie* 15 (1971): 529–38.

DiVesta, F. J. *Language, Learning and Cognitive Processes.* Monterey, Calif.: Brooks/Cole Publishing Company, 1974.

DiVesta, F. J., and J. P. Rickards. "Effects of Labeling and Articulation on the Attainment of Concrete, Abstract, and Number Concepts." *Journal of Experimental Psychology* 88 (1971): 41–49.

Dobson, J. *Dare to Discipline.* Wheaton, Ill.: Tyndale House Publishers, 1970.

Dodge, K. A. "Behavioral Antecedents of Peer Social Status." *Child Development* 54 (1983): 1386–99.

Dolgin, K. "The Importance of Playing Alone: Differences in Manipulative Play Under Social and Solitary Conditions." In *Play As Context*, edited by A. Cheska. West Point, N. Y.: Leisure Press, 1981, 238–47.

Dollard, J., et al. *Frustration and Aggression.* New Haven, Conn.: Yale University Press, 1939.

Doyle, P. "The Differential Effects of Multiple- and Single-Niche Play Activities on Interpersonal Relations Among Pre-schoolers." In *Play As Context*, edited by A. Cheska. West Point, N. Y.: Leisure Press, 1981.

Drabman, R. S., and M. H. Thomas. "Does T.V. Violence Breed Indifference?" *Journal of Communication* 25 (1975): 86–89.

Drake, J. D. *Interviewing for Managers: Sizing Up People.* New York: American Management Association, 1972.

Dreikurs, R. *The Challenge of Child Training: A Parent's Guide.* New York: Hawthorn Books, Inc., 1972.

Dreikurs, R., and P. Cassel. *Discipline Without Tears.* New York: Hawthorn Books, Inc., 1972.

Dreikurs, R., and V. Soltz. *Children: The Challenge.* New York: Hawthorn Books, Inc., 1964.

Dunlop, K. "Mainstreaming: Valuing Diversity in Children." *Young Children* 33, no. 5 (1977): 26–32.

Eames, T. H. "Physical Factors in Reading." *The Reading Teacher* 15 (1962): 427–32.

Eaton, W. O., and D. Von Vargen. "Asynchronous Development of Gender Understanding in Preschool Children." *Child Development* 52 (1981): 1020–27.

Eckerman, C. "The attainment of interactive skills: A major task of infancy." Colloquium address given at the University of Virginia, Charlottesville, October 1978.

Eddy, J. M., and W. F. Alles. *Death Education.* St. Louis, Mo.: The C. V. Mosby Company, 1983.

Egan, G. *The Skilled Helper.* Monterey, Calif.: Brooks/Cole Publishing Company, 1975.

Eiferman, R. "Social Play in Childhood." In *Child's Play*, edited by R. Herron and B. Sutton-Smith. New York: John Wiley & Sons, Inc., 1971, 270–97.

Eisenberg, N. "Sex-Typed Toy Choices: What Do They Signify?" In *Social and Cognitive Skills: Sex Roles and Children's Play*, edited by M. Liss. New York: Academic Press, Inc., 1983, 45–74.

Ekman, P. "Cross-Cultural Studies of Facial Expression." In *Darwin and Facial Expression*, edited by P. Ekman. New York: Academic Press, Inc., 1973.

Ekman, P., and W. Friesen. "The Repertoire of Nonverbal Behavior: Categories, Origins, Usage, and Coding." *Semiotica* 1 (1969): 49–98.

Ekman, P., W. Friesen, and P. Ellsworth. *Emotion in the Human Face: Guideline for Research and Integration of Findings.* New York: Pergamon Press, Inc., 1972.

Elkind, D. *The Hurried Child—Growing Up Too Fast Too Soon.* Reading, Mass.: Addison-Wesley Publishing Company, Inc., 1981.

El 'Konin, D. "Symbolics and Its Functions in the Play of Children." In *Child's Play*, edited by R. Herron and B. Sutton-Smith. New York: John Wiley & Sons, Inc., 1971, 221–30.

Ellis, M. J. *Why People Play.* Englewood Cliffs, N. J.: Prentice Hall, Inc., 1973.

Emde, R. N., T. J. Gaensbauer, and R. J. Harmon. "Emotional Expression in Infancy: A Biobehavioral Study." *Psychological Issues* 10, no. 1 (1976): 3–198.

Engen, T., and L. P. Lipsitt. "Decrement and Recovery of Responses to Olfactory Stimuli in the Human Neonate." *Journal of Comparative and Physiological Psychology* 59 (1965): 312–16.

Emmich, D. E. "Nice Guys Don't Finish Last Here." *The Clearing House* 57, no. 5, 1 (1984): 205–8.

Epstein, H. "Growth Spurts During Brain Development: Implications for Educational Policy and Practice." In *Education and the Brain*, edited by J. Child and A. Mersey. Chicago: University of Chicago Press, 1978.

Erikson, E. H. *Childhood and Society.* Rev. ed. New York: W. W. Norton & Co., Inc., 1950, 1963.

Etaugh, C. "Introduction: The Influences of Environmental Factors in Sex Differences in Children's Play." In *Social and Cognitive Skills: Sex Roles and Children's Play*, edited by M. Liss. New York: Academic Press, Inc., 1983, 1–21.

Evans, E. B., B. Shub, and M. Weinstein. *Day Care*. Boston: Beacon Press, 1971.

Evers, W. L., and J. C. Schwarz. "Modifying Social Withdrawal in Preschoolers: The Effects of Filmed Modeling and Teacher Praise." *Journal of Abnormal Child Psychology* 1 (1973): 248–56.

Fabes, R. A. "How Children Learn Self-Control." *Two to Twelve* 2, no. 5 (May 1984): 1–3.

Fagen, R. *Animal Play Behavior*. New York: Oxford University Press, 1981.

Fagot, B. "Consequences of Moderate Cross Gender Behavior in Preschool Children." *Child Development* 48 (1977): 902–7.

Fagot, B. "Reinforcing Contingencies for Sex Role Behaviors: Effect of Experience with Children." *Child Development* 49 (1978): 30–36.

Fein, G. "Play with Actions and Objects." In *Play and Learning*, edited by B. Sutton-Smith. New York: Gardner Press, Inc., 1979, 69–82.

Feldman, R. S., L. Jenkins, and O. Popoola. "Detection of Deception in Adults and Children via Facial Expressions." *Child Development* 50 (1979): 350–55.

Feldman, R. S., J. B. White, and D. Lobato. "Social Skills and Nonverbal Behavior." In *Development of Nonverbal Behavior in Children*, edited by R. Feldman. New York: Springer-Verlag New York, Inc., 1982, 257–78.

Feshbach, N. D. "Empathy Training: A Field Study of Affective Education." Paper presented at the annual meeting of the American Educational Research Association, March 1978.

Feshbach, N. D. and S. Feshbach. "Children's Aggression." In *The Young Child: Review of Research*, Vol. 2, edited by W. H. Hartup. Washington, D.C.: National Association for the Education of Young Children, 1976.

Feshbach, S. "Aggression." In *Carmichael's Manual of Child Psychology*, edited by P. Mussen. New York: John Wiley & Sons, Inc., 1970, 159–259.

Feshbach, S., and R. D. Singer. "The Effects of Fear Arousal and Suppression of Fear upon Social Perception." *Journal of Abnormal and Social Psychology* 55 (1957): 283–89.

Field, T. M., and E. Ignatoff. "Interaction of Twins and Their Mothers." Unpublished manuscript, University of Miami, 1980. As referred to by Campos, et al., "Socioemotional Development." In *Handbook of Child Psychology*, Vol. 2, edited by P. Mussen. New York: John Wiley & Sons, Inc., 783–916.

Finkelhor, D. *Sexually Victimized Children*. New York: Free Press, 1979.

Fitch, S. K. *The Science of Child Development*. Homewood, Ill.: The Dorsey Press, 1985.

Flavell, J. H. *The Developmental Psychology of Jean Piaget*. New York: Van Nostrand Reinhold Co., Inc., 1963.

Flavell, J. H. *Cognitive Development*. Englewood Cliffs, N. J.: Prentice-Hall, Inc., 1977.

Flavell, J. H., and J. F. Wohlwill. "Formal and Functional Aspects of Cognitive Development." In *Studies in Cognitive Development: Essays in Honor of Jean Piaget*, edited by D. Elkind and J. H. Flavell. New York: Oxford University Press, 1969, 67–120.

Flygare, T. J. "The Supreme Court Approves Corporal Punishment." *Phi Delta Kappan* 59 (1978): 347–48.

Forbes, D. "Recent Research on Children's Social Cognition: A Brief Review." In *New Directions for Child Development*, edited by W. Damon. San Francisco: Jossey-Bass, Inc., Publishers, 1978.

Fraiberg, S. *The Magic Years*. New York: Charles Scribner's Sons, 1968.

Fraiberg, S. *Insights from the Blind*. New York: Basic Books, Inc., Publishers, 1977.

Freud, S. "The Psychology of Women." In *New Introductory Lectures on Psychoanalysis*. Translated by James Strachey. New York: W. W. Norton & Co., Inc., 1965.

Freud, S. *A General Introduction to Psychoanalysis*. Garden City, N. Y.: Doubleday & Company Inc., 1938.

Freud, S. *Jokes and Their Relation to the Unconscious*. New York: W. W. Norton & Co., Inc., 1960.

Friedman, M., and R. H. Rosenman. *Type A Behavior and Your Heart*. New York: Ballantine Books, Inc., 1974.

Friedrich, L. K., and A. H. Stein. "Prosocial Television and Young Children: The Effects of Verbal Labeling and Role-Playing on Learning and Behavior." *Child Development*, 46 (1975): 27–38.

Friedrich, W. N., and J. A. Boriskin. "The Role of the Child in Abuse: A Review of the Literature." *American Journal of Orthopsychiatry* 46 (1976): 580–90.

Frodi, H. L., J. Macaulay, and P. R. Thome. "Are Women Always Less Aggressive Than Men? A Review of the Experimental Literature." *Psychological Bulletin* 84 (1977): 634–60.

Fromm, E. *The Art of Loving*. New York: Harper & Row, Publishers, Inc., 1956.

Frye, D. "Developmental Changes in Strategies of Social Interaction." In *Infant Social Cognition: Empirical and Theoretical Considerations*, edited by M. Lamb and L. Sherrod. Hillsdale, N. J.: Lawrence Erlbaum Associates, Inc., 1981.

Furman, E. "Helping Children Cope with Death." *Young Children* 33, no. 4, (May 1978): 25–32.

Furman, W., and D. Buhrmester. "The Contribution of Siblings and Peers to the Parenting Process." In *Child Nurturance, Vol. 2: Patterns of Supplementary Parenting*, edited by M. J. Kostelnik, et al. New York: Plenum Publishing Corporation, 1982, 69–100.

Gage, N. L. "Judging Interests from Expressive Behavior." *Psychology Monographs* 66, no. 18 (1952).

Gagné, R. W. *The Conditions of Learning*. New York: Holt,

Rinehart & Winston, 1977.

Galambos-Stone, J. *A Guide To Discipline.* Washington D.C.: National Association for the Education of Young Children, 1976.

Gall, M. *Minicourse Nine: Higher Cognitive Questioning, Teachers' Handbook.* Beverly Hills: Macmillan Educational Services, Inc., 1971.

Garbarino, J. "A Preliminary Study of Some Ecological Correlates of Child Abuse: The Impact of Socioeconomic Stress on Mothers." *Child Development* 47 (1977): 178–85.

Garbarino, J., and G. Gilliam. *Understanding Abusive Families.* Lexington, Mass.: D. C. Heath & Company, 1980.

Gardner, J. K. *Developmental Psychology.* Boston: Little, Brown & Company, 1981.

Gardner, R. A. *The Parent's Book About Divorce.* Toronto: Bantam Books, Inc., 1977.

Garvey, C. *Play.* Cambridge, Mass.: Harvard University Press, 1977.

Garvey, C., and R. Berndt. "Organization of Pretend Play." *JSAS Catalog of Selected Documents in Psychology* 1, ms. no. 1589 (1977).

Gazda, G. M. *Human Relations Development—A Manual for Educators.* 2d ed. Boston: Allyn and Bacon, Inc., 1977.

Gazda, G. M., W. Childers, and R. Walters. *Interpersonal Communication: A Handbook for Health Professionals.* Rockville, Md. Aspen Systems Corp., 1982.

Gazda, G. M., et al. "A General Review of Related Research Literature." *Human Relations Development: A Manual for Educators.* Boston: Allyn and Bacon, Inc., 1973.

Gecas, V. "Parental Behavior and Dimensions of Adolescent Self-Evaluation." *Sociometry* 34, no. 4 (1971).

Gecas, V., J. M. Colonico, and D. L. Thomas. "The Development of Self-Concept in the Child: Mirror Theory Versus Model Theory." *Journal of Social Psychology* (1974): 466–82.

Geldhard, F. "Some Neglected Possibilities of Communication." *Science* 131 (1960): 1583–84.

Gelfand, D. M., W. R. Jenson, and C. J. Drew. *Understanding Child Behavior Disorders.* New York: Holt, Rinehart & Winston, 1982.

Ginott, H. G. *Between Parent and Child.* New York: Avon Books, 1969.

Ginsberg, H. "And We Can Learn Together: Some Thoughts on Mainstreaming Children with Special Needs." Integration project. East Lansing, Mich.: Michigan State University, 1976.

Glasser, W. *Schools Without Failure.* New York: Harper & Row, Publishers, Inc., 1969.

Glick, P. "Marriage, Divorce and Living Arrangements: Prospective Changes." *Journal of Family Issues* 5 (1984): 7–26.

Glorziady, N. P., and L. G. Romano. "Parent Teacher Conferences: Indispensible for the Middle School." *Middle School Journal* 14, no. 1, 11 (1982): 7,30–31.

Gnagey, W. "Controlling Classroom Misbehavior." What Research Says to the Teacher Series. Washington, D.C.: National Education Association, 1975.

Goffman, E. *Interaction Ritual.* Chicago: Aldine Publishing Co., 1967.

Goldstein, H., J. W. Moss, and L. J. Jardon. *The Efficacy of Special Class Training on the Development of Mentally Retarded Children.* Urbana, Ill.: Institute for Research on Exceptional Children, 1965.

Goodson, B., and R. Hess. *Parents As Teachers of Young Children: An Evaluative Review of Some Contemporary Concepts and Programs.* Stanford, Calif.: Stanford University Press, 1975.

Gordon, T. *Parent Effectiveness Training.* New York: Peter Wyden, Inc., Publisher, 1974.

Gordon, T. *Parent Effectiveness Training.* New York: The Times Mirror Co., 1975.

Gottman, J., J. Gonso, and B. Rasmussen. "Social Interaction, Social Competence and Friendship in Children." *Child Development* 46 (1975): 709–18.

Gottman, J., and J. Parkhurst. "A Developmental Theory of Friendship and Acquaintanceship Processes." In *Minnesota Symposia on Child Psychology,* Vol. 13, edited by W. A. Collins. Hillsdale, N. J.: Lawrence Erlbaum Associates, Inc., 1979.

Green, F. P., and F. W. Schneider. "Age Differences in the Behaviors of Boys on Three Measures of Altruism." *Child Development* 45 (1974): 248–51.

Green, K., R. Forehand, and R. MacMahon. "Parental Manipulation of Compliance and Noncompliance in Normal and Deviant Children." *Behavior Modification* 3, no. 2 (1979): 245–66.

Gregory, D. *Nigger: An Autobiography.* New York: E. P. Dutton, Inc., 1964.

Griffin, H. "The Coordination of Meaning in the Creation of a Shared Make Believe." In *Symbolic Play,* edited by I. Bretherton. Orlando: Harcourt Brace Jovanovich, Inc., 1984.

Gronlund, N. E. *Sociometry in the Classroom.* New York: Harper & Row, Publishers, Inc., 1959.

Gross, I., E. Crandall, and M. Knoll. *Management for Modern Families.* Englewood Cliffs, N. J.: Prentice-Hall, Inc., 1980.

Gruendel, J. M. "Referential Extension in Early Language Development." *Child Development* 48 (1977): 1567–76.

Grusec, J. E., and L. Arnason. "Consideration for Others: Approaches to Enhancing Altruism." In *The Young Child: Reviews of Research,* Vol. 3, edited by S. G. Moore and C. R. Cooper. Washington, D.C.: National Association for the Education of Young Children, 1982.

Grusec, J. E., et al. "Learning Resistance to Temptation through Observation." *Developmental Psychology* 15 (1979): 233–40.

Guerney, L. *Foster Parent Training: A Manual for Parents.* University Park, Pa.: The Pennsylvania State University, 1975.

Guerney, L. *Parenting: A Skills Training Manual.* 2d ed. State College, Pa.: Ideals, 1980.

Guerney, L. "Understanding Children's Extreme Behaviors." *Two to Twelve: Current Issues in Children's Development* 2, no. 5 (May 1984): 7–9.

Guinagh, B. "The Social Integration of Handicapped Children." *Phi Delta Kappan* 52, no. 1, 9 (1980): 27–29.

Guralnick, M. J. "The Value of Integrating Handicapped and Nonhandicapped Preschool Children." *American Journal of Orthopsychiatry* 46 (1976): 236–45.

Haith, M., and J. Campos, eds. *Handbook of Child Psychology.* Vol. 2. New York: John Wiley & Sons, Inc., 1983, 783–916.

Hall, E., M. Perlmutter, and M. Lamb. *Child Psychology Today.* New York: Random House, Inc., 1982.

Hall, E. T. *The Silent Language.* Garden City, N. Y.: Anchor Press/Doubleday, 1959, 1981.

Hall, E. T. *The Hidden Dimension.* Garden City, N. Y.: Doubleday & Company, Inc., 1966.

Haring, N. C., A. H. Hayden, and K. E. Allen. "Programs and Projects: Intervention in Early Childhood." *Educational Technology* 11 (February 1971): 52–61.

Harris, M. "Children with Short Fuses." *Instructor* (November 1980): 170–71.

Harris, P. L., T. Olthof, and M. M. Terwogt. "Children's Knowledge of Emotion." *Journal of Child Psychology and Psychiatry* 22, no. 3 (1981): 247–61.

Harrison, A., and L. Nadelman. "Conceptual Tempo and Inhibition of Movement in Black Preschool Children." *Child Development* 43 (1972): 657–68.

Harter, S. "A Cognitive-Developmental Approach to Children's Expression of Conflicting Feelings and a Technique to Facilitate Such Expression in Play Therapy." *Journal of Consulting and Clinical Psychology* 45, no. 3 (1977): 417–32.

Harter, S. "Children's Understanding of Multiple Emotions: A Cognitive-Developmental Approach." Address given at the ninth annual meeting of the Piaget Society, Philadelphia, Pa., 1979.

Harter, S. "The Perceived Competence Scale for Children." *Child Development* 53 (1982): 87–97.

Harter, S. "Developmental Perspectives on the Self-System." In *Handbook of Child Psychology,* Vol. 4, edited by P. H. Mussen. New York: John Wiley & Sons, Inc., 1983.

Hartley, R. E. "A Developmental View of Female Sex-Role Definition and Identification." *Merrill-Palmer Quarterly* 10 (1964): 3–16.

Hartup, W. W. "Peer Interaction and Social Organization." In *Carmichael's Manual of Child Psychology,* Vol. 2, edited by P. H. Mussen. New York: John Wiley & Sons, Inc., 1970.

Hartup, W. W. "Aggression in Childhood: Developmental Perspectives." *American Psychologist* 29 (1974): 336–41.

Hartup, W. W. "Children and Their Friends." In *Issues in Childhood Social Development,* edited by H. McGurk. London: Methuen, Inc., 1978.

Hartup, W. W. "Peer Interaction and the Process of Socialization." In *Early Intervention and the Integration of Handicapped and Nonhandicapped Children,* edited by M. J. Guralnick. Baltimore Md.: University Park Press, 1978.

Hartup, W. W. "Peer Relations and Family Relations: Two Social Worlds." *Scientific Foundations of Developmental Psychiatry.* London: Heinemann Medical Books, 1980.

Hartup, W. W. "Peer Relations." In *The Child: Development in a Social Context,* edited by C. B. Kopp and J. B. Krakow. Reading, Mass: Addison-Wesley Publishing Co., Inc., 1982.

Hartup, W. W. "Peer Relations." In *Handbook of Child Psychology,* Vol. 4, edited by P. H. Mussen. New York: John Wiley & Sons, Inc., 1983.

Haswell, K. L., E. Hock, and C. Wenar. "Techniques for Dealing with Oppositional Behavior in Preschool Children." In *Curriculum Planning for Young Children,* edited by J. F. Brown. Washington, D.C.: National Association for the Education of Young Children, 1982.

Havighurst, R. J. *Developmental Tasks and Education.* New York: Longman, Inc., 1954.

Hawley, R. C., and I. L. Hawley. *Achieving Better Classroom Discipline.* Amherst, Mass.: Education Research Associates, 1981.

Hay, D., H. Ross, and B. D. Goldman. "Social Games in Infancy." In *Play and Learning,* edited by B. Sutton-Smith. New York: Gardner Press, Inc., 1979, 83–108.

Heatherington, E. M. "Divorce: A Child's Perspective." *American Psychologist* 10, no. 34 (1979): 851–58.

Hendrick, J. *The Whole Child: Early Education for the Eighties.* St. Louis, Mo.: The C. V. Mosby Co., 1984.

Henley, N. *Body Politics: Power, Sex and Nonverbal Communication.* Englewood Cliffs, N. J.: Prentice-Hall, Inc., 1977.

Herman, J., and J. P. Yeh. "Some Effects of Parent Involvement in Schools." *Resources in Education* 2 (1982).

Hetherington, E. M., M. Cox, and R. Cox. "Beyond Father's Absence: Conceptualization of Effects of Divorce." In *Contemporary Readings in Child Psychology,* edited by E. M. Hetherington and R. D. Parke. New York: McGraw-Hill, Inc., 1977.

Hewitt, L. S. "The Effects of Provocation, Intentions and Consequences on Children's Moral Judgments." *Child Development* 46 (1975): 540–44.

Hicks, D. "Imitation and Retention of Film-Mediated Aggressive Peer and Adult Models." *Journal of Personality and Social Psychology* 2 (1965): 97–100.

Hildebrand, V. *Guiding Young Children.* New York: Macmillan, Inc., 1985.

Hill, R. "Schema of Interdependent Ecological Systems Shaping both Directly and Indirectly the Development of Families and Children." Paper presented at Michigan

State University, May 1985.

Hoachlander, E. G., and S. P. Choy. "Work Based Attendance: A New Approach to Expanding Parental Choice in Education." *Phi Delta Kappan* 66, no. 1, 9 (1984): 57–61.

Hoffman, M. "Affective and Cognitive Processes in Moral Internalization." In *Social Cognition and Social Behavior: Developmental Perspectives,* edited by E. T. Higgins, D. N. Ruble, and W. W. Hartup. New York: Cambridge University Press, 1983.

Hoffman, M. L. "Parent Discipline and the Child's Consideration of Others." *Child Development* 34 (1963): 573–85.

Hoffman, M. L. "Moral Internalization, Parental Power, and the Nature of the Parent-Child Interaction." *Developmental Psychology* 5 (1967): 45–57.

Hoffman, M. L. "Parent Discipline and the Child's Moral Development." *Journal of Personality and Social Psychology* 5 (1967): 45–47.

Hoffman, M. L. "Moral Development." In *Carmichael's Manual of Child Psychology,* Vol. 2, edited by P. Mussen. New York: John Wiley & Sons, Inc., 1970, 262–360.

Hoffman, M. L. "Developmental Synthesis of Affect and Cognition and Its Implications for Altruistic Motivation." *Developmental Psychology* 11 (1975): 607–22.

Hoffman, M. L. "Empathy, Role-Taking, Guilt, and Development of Altruistic Motives." In *Moral Development and Behavior: Theory, Research and Social Issues,* edited by T. Lickona. New York: Holt, Rinehart & Winston, 1976.

Hoffman, M. L. "Personality and Social Development." *Annual Review of Psychology* 28 (1977): 295–321.

Hoffman, M. L. "Development of Prosocial Motivation: Empathy and Guilt." In *The Development of Prosocial Behavior,* edited by N. Eisenberg-Berg. New York: Academic Press, Inc., 1982.

Holmes, T., and R. Rahe. "The Social Readjustment Rating Scale." *Journal of Psychosomatic Research* 11 (1967): 213–18.

Holzman, M. "The Use of Interrogative Forms in the Verbal Interaction of Three Mothers and Their Children." *Journal of Psycholinguistic Research* 1, no. 4 (1972): 311–36.

Hom, H. L., Jr., and S. L. Hom, "Research and the Child: The Use of Modeling, Reinforcement/Incentives, and Punishment." In *Aspects of Early Childhood Education: Theory to Research to Practice,* edited by D. G. Range, J. R. Layton, and D. L. Roubinek. New York: Academic Press, Inc., 1980.

Honig, A. S. *Parent Involvement in Early Childhood Education.* Washington, D.C.: National Association for the Education of Young Children, 1979.

Honig, A. S. "Prosocial Development in Children." *Children* 37, no. 5 (July 1982): 51–62.

Honig, A. S. "Compliance, Control and Discipline." *Young Children* 40, no. 3 (March 1985): 47–51.

Hoversten, G. H., and J. P. Moncur. "Stimuli and Intensity Factors in Testing Infants." *Journal of Speech and Hearing Research* 12 (1969); 687–702.

Hutt, C. "Exploration and Play in Children." In *Child's Play,* edited by R. Herron and B. Sutton-Smith. New York: John Wiley & Sons, Inc., 1971.

Hyde, J. S. "How Large Are Gender Differences in Aggression? A Developmental Meta-Analysis." *Developmental Psychology* 20 (1984): 722–36.

Hyman, I. A., and J. D'Alessandro. "Good, Old-Fashioned Discipline: The Politics of Punitiveness." *Phi Delta Kappan* 66 (September 1984): 39–45.

Hyman, R. T. *Questioning in the Classroom.* Urbana, Ill.: Document Reproduction Service, 1977, 1–14 (catalog. no. ED 138-551).

Hymes, J. I. *Effective Home School Relations.* Sierra Madre, Calif.: Southern California Association for the Education of Young Children, 1974.

Iano, R. P., et al. "Sociometric Status of Retarded Children in an Integrative Program." *Exceptional Children* 40, no. 1 (1974): 267–71.

Ingraham v. Wright, 95 S. Ct. 1401, at 1406, citing 525 F.2d. 909 (1976), at 917.

Insko, C. A., and J. E. Robinson. "Belief Similarity Versus Race As Determinants of Reactions to Negroes by Southern White Adolescents: A Further Test of Rokeach's Theory." *Journal of Personality and Social Psychology* 7 (1967): 216–21.

Irwin, D. M., and S. G. Moore. "The Young Child's Understanding of Social Justice." *Developmental Psychology* 5, no. 3 (1971): 406–10.

Irwin, N., ed. *Children at the Center.* Cambridge, Mass.: Abt Associates, Inc., 1979.

Ivancevich, J. M., J. H. Donnelly, and J. L. Gibson. *Managing for Performance.* Plano, Tex.: Business Publications, Inc., 1983.

Izard, C. E. *Human Emotions.* New York: Plenum Publishing Corporation, 1977.

Izard, C. E. "The Primary of Emotion in Human Development." Paper presented at the biennial meeting of the Society for Research in Child Development, Boston, April 1981.

Jabs, C. "Is that Baby Scowling? Smiling? Crying?" *McCalls* 112, no. 10 (July 1985): 78–113.

Jackson, N., H. Robinson, and P. Dale. *Cognitive Development in Young Children.* Monterey, Calif.: Brooks/Cole Publishing Company, 1977.

Jensen, L. C., and K. M. Highston. *Responsibility and Morality.* Provo, Utah: Brigham Young University Press, 1979.

Johnson, D. W., and R. T. Johnson. "Integrating Handicapped Students into the Mainstream." *Exceptional Children* 47, no. 2, 10 (1980): 90–98.

Johnson, G. O. "A Study of Social Position of Mentally Retarded Children in the Regular Grades." *American Journal of Mental Deficiency* 55 (1975): 60–89.

Johnson, K. R. "Black Kinesics: Some Nonverbal Communication Patterns in Black Culture." *Florida FL Reporter*

57 (1971): 17–20.

Johnson, R. *Aggression in Man and Animals*. Philadelphia: W. B. Saunders Company, 1972.

Johnston, M., and J. Slotnik. "Parent Participation in the Schools: Are the Benefits Worth the Burden?" *Phi Delta Kappan* 66, no. 6, 2 (1985): 430–33.

Jones, E. *Dimensions of Teaching-Learning Environments*. Pasadena, Calif.: Pacific Oaks, 1981.

Jones, S. J., and H. A. Moss. "Age, State, and Maternal Behavior Associated with Infant Vocalizations." *Child Development* 42 (1971): 1039–51.

Jourard, S. M. "An Exploratory Study of Body-Accessibility." *British Journal of Social and Clinical Psychology*, no. 5 (1966): 221–31.

Jourard, S. M. *The Transparent Self*. Rev. ed. Princeton, N. J.: Van Nostrand Reinhold Co., Inc., 1971.

Kagan, J. "Reflection-Impulsivity." *Journal of Abnormal Psychology* 71 (1966): 17–24.

Kagan, J. *Change and Continuity in the First Two Years: An Inquiry into Early Cognitive Development*. New York: John Wiley & Sons, Inc., 1971.

Kagan, J. "The Effect of Day Care on the Infant." In *Policy Issues in Day Care. Summary of 21 Papers*. Washington, D.C.: U.S. Department of Health, Education, and Welfare, 1977.

Kagan, J. "The Psychological Requirements for Human Development." In *Family in Transition*, edited by A. S. Skolnick and J. H. Skolnick. Boston: Little, Brown & Company, 1977.

Kagan, J., and H. A. Moss. *Birth to Maturity*. New York: John Wiley & Sons, Inc., 1962.

Kaplan, H. B., and A. D. Pokorny, "Self-Derogation and Psychosocial Adjustment." *Journal of Nervous and Mental Disease* 149 (1969): 421–34.

Kaplan, L. J. *Oneness and Separateness: From Infant to Individual*. New York: Simon & Schuster, Inc., 1978.

Kaplan, P. S. *A Child's Odyssey: Child and Adolescent Development*. St. Paul, Minn.: West Publishing Co., 1986.

Kashani, J., and F. Simonds. "The Incidence of Depression in Children." *American Journal of Psychiatry* 136 (1979): 1203–5.

Kastenbaum, R. J. *Death, Society, and Human Experience*. St. Louis, Mo.: The C. V. Mosby Company, 1981.

Kato, S. *A History of Japanese Literature*. Tokyo: Kodansha International, 1979.

Katz, L. G. *Teacher-Child Relationships in Day Care Centers*. Urbana, Ill.: ERIC Document Reproduction Service, 1972 (catalog no. ED 046-494).

Katz, L. G. "What is Basic for Young Children?" *Childhood Education* 54, no. 1 (1977): 16–19.

Katz, L. G. "The Professional Early Childhood Teacher." *Young Children* 39, no. 5 (July 1984): 3–10.

Katz, P. A. "The Acquisition of Racial Attitudes in Children." In *Towards the Elimination of Racism*, edited by R. A. Katz. New York: Pergamon Press, Inc., 1976.

Keller, A., L. H. Ford, Jr., and J. A. Meachum. "Dimensions of Self-Concept in Preschool Children." *Developmental Psychology* 14 (1978): 483–89.

Kelly, J. A. *Treating Child Abusive Families: Intervention Based on Skills Training Principles*. New York: Plenum Publishing Corporation, 1983.

Kelman, H. C. "Compliance, Identification and Internalization: Three Processes of Attitude Change." In *Groups and Organizations: Integrated Readings in the Analysis of Social Behavior*, edited by B. L. Hinto and H. J. Reitz. Belmont, Calif.: Wadsworth, Inc., 1958.

Kempe, C. H., and R. E. Helfer. *Helping the Battered Child and His Family*. Philadelphia: J. B. Lippincott Company, 1972.

Kempe, R. S., and C. H. Kempe. *Child Abuse*. Cambridge, Mass: Harvard University Press, 1978.

Kenden, A. "Some Functions of Gaze Direction in Social Interaction." *Acta Psychologia*, 26 (1967): 22–63.

Keniston, K. "Do Americans Really Like Children?" *Childhood Education* 52, no. 1, 10 (1975): 4–12.

Kennedy, W. A. "School Phobia: Rapid Treatment of Fifty Cases." *Journal of Abnormal Psychology* 70 (1965): 285–89.

Kessen, W., J. Levine, and K. A. Wendrich. "The Imitation of Pitch in Infants." *Infant Behavior and Development* 2 (1979): 93–100.

Kessler, J. W. "Neurosis in Childhood." In *Manual of Child Psychopathology*, edited by B. Wolman. New York: McGraw-Hill, Inc., 1972.

Key, M. R. *Paralanguage and Kinesics*. Metuchen, N. J.: Scarecrow Press, Inc., 1975.

Klein, H. A. "Early Childhood Group Care: Predicting Adjustment from Individual Temperament." *Journal of Genetic Psychology* 13, no. 7 (1980): 125–31.

Klein, J. W. "Mainstreaming the Preschooler." *Young Children* 7 (1975): 317–27.

Klineberg, O. *Race Differences*. New York: Harper & Brothers, 1935.

Klinnert, M. D. "Infants' Use of Mothers' Facial Expressions for Regulating Their Own Behavior." Paper presented at the biennial meeting of the Society for Research in Child Development, Boston, April 1981.

Koblinsky, S., and N. Behana. "Child Sexual Abuse, The Educator's Role in Prevention, Detection, and Intervention." *Young Children* 39, no. 6 (September 1984): 3–15.

Kohlberg, L. "Development of Moral Character and Moral Ideology." In *Review of Child Development Research*, Vol. 1, edited by M. L. Hoffman and L. W. Hoffman. New York: Russell Sage Foundation, 1964.

Kohlberg, L. "Moral Stages and Moralization: The Cognitive-Developmental Approach." In *Moral Development and Behavior*, edited by T. Lickona. New York: Holt, Rinehart & Winston, 1976.

Kohlberg, L. A. "A Cognitive Developmental Analysis of Children's Sex Role Concepts and Attitudes." In *The Development of Sex Differences*, edited by E. E. Maccoby.

Stanford, Calif.: Stanford University Press, 1966.

Kohn, M. "The Child As a Determinant of His Peers' Approach to Him." *Journal of Genetic Psychology* 109 (1966): 91–100.

Koocher, G. "Childhood, Death, and Cognitive Development." *Developmental Psychology* 9 (1973): 369–75.

Korner, A. F. "The Effect of the Infant's State, Level of Arousal, Sex and Centogenetic Stage on the Caregiver." In *The Effects of the Infant on Its Caregiver,* New York: John Wiley & Sons, Inc. 1974, 105–21.

Korner, A. F., and E. B. Thoman. "Visual Alertness in Neonates As Evoked by Maternal Care." *Journal of Experimental Child Psychology* 10 (1970): 67–68.

Korner, A. F., and E. B. Thoman. "The Relative Efficacy of Contact and Vestibular Proprioceptive Stimulation in Soothing Neonates." *Child Development* 43 (1972): 443–53.

Korner, A. F., et al. "Characteristics of Crying and Non-Crying Activity of Full Term Neonates." *Child Development* 45 (1974): 953–58.

Kostelnik, M. J. "An Evaluation of a Program to Teach Young Children a Feeling Word Vocabulary." Master's thesis, The Pennsylvania State University, 1977.

Kostelnik, M. J. "Evaluation of a Communication and Group Management Skills Training Program for Child Development Personnel." Ph.D. diss., The Pennsylvania State University, 1978.

Kostelnik, M. J. "Evaluation of an In-Service Multi-Media Training Program in Discipline Skills for Teachers of Young Children." Paper presented at the annual meeting of the National Association for the Education of Young Children, Atlanta, Georgia, November 1983.

Kostelnik, M. J. "Children and Sex Stereotypes." *Two to Twelve* 2, no. 1 (January 1984): 4–7.

Kostelnik, M. J., and P. D. Kurtz. *Communication and Positive Guidance Skills for Teachers of Young Children.* 3d ed. East Lansing, Mich.: Michigan State University Press, 1986.

Kostelnik, M. J., and L. C. Stein, "Effects of Three Conflict Mediation Strategies on Children's Aggressive and Prosocial Behavior in the Classroom." Paper presented at the annual meeting of the National Association for the Education of Younger Children, Washington, D.C., 14 November 1986.

Kostelnik, M. J., L. C. Stein, and A. P. Whiren. "Mid-Year Crisis: What to Do When Children Don't Want to Come to the Center Anymore." *Day Care and Early Education* 1, no. 2 (1982): 42–45.

Kostelnik, M. J., A. Whiren, and L. Stein. "Living with He-Man: Managing Superhero Fantasy Play." *Young Children* 41, no. 4 (1986): 3–9.

Krasner, L., and M. Krasner. "Token Economics and Other Planned Environments." In *Behavior Modification in Education: The Seventy-Second Yearbook of the National Society for the Study of Education, Part 1,* edited by C. C. Thoresen. Chicago: University of Chicago Press, 1972.

Kuczen, B. *Childhood Stress: Don't Let Your Child Be a Victim.* New York: Delacorte Press, 1982.

Labov, W. *The Study of Nonstandard English.* Urbana, Ill.: National Council of Teachers of English, 1970.

Ladd, G. W. "Effectiveness of a Social Learning Method for Enhancing Children's Social Interaction and Peer Acceptance." *Child Development* 52 (1979): 171–78.

Ladd, G. W., and S. L. Oden. "The Relationship Between Peer Acceptance and Children's Ideas About Helpfulness." *Child Development* 50 (1979): 402–8.

LaFrance, M., and C. Mayo. "Racial Differences in Gaze Behavior During Conversations: Two Systematic Observational Studies." *Journal of Personality and Social Psychology* 33 (1976): 547–52.

Laing, R. *The Politics of Experience* New York: Ballantine Books, Inc., 1967.

Lamb, M. E. "Developing Trust and Perceived Effectance in Infancy." In *Advances in Infancy Research,* Vol. 1, edited by L. P. Lipsitt. Norwood, N. J.: Ablex Publishing Corp., 1981.

Lamb, M. E. "The Development of Social Expectations in the First Year of Life." In *Infant Social Cognition: Theoretical and Empirical Considerations,* edited by M. E. Lamb and L. R. Sherrod. Hillsdale, N. J.: Lawrence Erlbaum Associates, Inc., 1981.

Lamb, M. E., and D. Baumrind. "Socialization and Personality Development in the Preschool Years." In *Social and Personality Development,* edited by M. E. Lamb. New York: Holt, Rinehart & Winston, 1978.

Lamb. M. E., and J. Campos. *Development in Infancy.* New York: Random House, Inc., 1982.

Lamb, M. E., and M. A. Easterbrooks. "Individual Differences in Parental Sensitivity: Origin, Components and Consequences." In *Infant Social Cognition: Theoretical and Empirical Considerations,* edited by M. E. Lamb and L. R. Sherrod. Hillsdale, N. J.: Lawrence Erlbaum Associates, Inc., 127–54.

Lane, D. M., and D. A. Pearson. "The Development of Selective Attention." *Merrill-Palmer Quarterly* 28 (1982): 317–37.

Langlois, J. H. "From the Eye of the Beholder to Behavioral Reality: The Development of Social Behaviors and Social Relations As a Function of Physical Attractiveness." In *Physical Appearance, Stigma and Social Behavior,* edited by C. P. Heiman. Hillsdale, N. J.: Lawrence Erlbaum Associates, Inc., 1985.

Lansky, B. *The Best Baby Name Book.* Deephaven, Minn.: Meadowbrook Press, Inc., 1984.

Leahy, R. "Development of Conceptions of Prosocial Behavior: Information Affecting Rewards Given for Altruism and Kindness." *Developmental Psychology* 15 (1979): 34–37.

Leathers, D. G. *Nonverbal Communication Systems.* Boston: Allyn and Bacon, Inc., 1976.

Leavitt, J. E. "Helping Abused and Neglected Children." In *Early Childhood Education*, edited by J. S. McKee. Guilford, Conn.: Dushkin Publishing Group, Inc., 1983, 49–51.

Lee, L., and J. Charlton. *The Hand Book*. Englewood Cliffs, N. J.: Prentice-Hall, Inc., 1980.

Lefkowitz, M. M., et al. *Growing Up to Be Violent: A Longitudinal Study of the Development of Aggression*. New York: Pergamon Press, Inc., 1977.

Leiter, M. P. "A Study of Reciprocity in Preschool Play Groups." *Child Development* 48 (1977): 1288–95.

Lenneberg, E. H. "Speech As a Motor Skill with Special References to Monophasic Disorders." In "The Acquisition of Language." *Monographs of the Society for Research in Child Development* 29, no. 1 (1964): 115–27.

Lepper, M. R. "Social Control Processes, Attributions of Motivation and the Internalization of Social Values." In *Social Cognition and Social Behavior: Developmental Perspectives*, edited by E. T. Higgins, D. N. Ruble, and W. W. Hartup. New York: Cambridge University Press, 1983.

Lerner, R. M., and J. V. Lerner. "Effects of Age, Sex, and Physical Attractiveness on Child-Peer Relations, Academic Performance, and Elementary School Adjustment." *Developmental Psychology* 13 (1977): 585–90.

Levenstein, P. "Cognitive Development Through Verbalized Play: A Mother-Child Home Program." In *Play: Its Role in Development and Evolution*, edited by J. Bruner, A. Jolly, and K. Sylva. New York: Basic Books, Inc., Publishers, 1976, 286–99.

Leventhal, H. A. "A Perceptual-Motor Processing Model of Emotion." In *Advances in the Study of Communication and Affect. Vol. 5: Perception of Emotion in Self and Others*, edited by P. Pliner, K. Blankstein, and I. M. Spigel. New York: Plenum Publishing Corporation, 1979.

Levinger, G., and J. D. Snoek. *Attraction in Relationships: A New Look at Interpersonal Attraction*. New York: General Learning Press, 1973.

Levitan, T., and J. D. Chananie. "Responses of Female Primary School Teachers to Sex-Typed Behaviors in Male and Female Children." *Child Development* 43 (1972): 1309–16.

Lewis, M. "State As an Infant-Environment Interaction: An Analysis of Mother-Infant Interaction As a Function of Sex." *Merrill Palmer Quarterly* 18 (1972): 95–121.

Lewis, M., and J. Brooks-Gunn. *Self, Other and Fear: The Reaction of Infants to People*. Princeton, N. J.: Educational Testing Service, 1972.

Lewis, M., and J. Brooks-Gunn. *Social Cognition and the Acquisition of Self*. New York: Plenum Publishing Corporation, 1979.

Lewis, M., and C. Michalson. "The Child's Social World." In *Emotion and Early Interaction*, edited by T. Field and A. Fogel. Hillsdale, N. J.: Lawrence Erlbaum Associates, Inc., 1982.

Lewis, M., and L. A. Rosenblum, eds. *The Development of Affect*. New York: Plenum Publishing Corporation, 1978.

Lewis, W. C., R. N. Wohlman, and M. King. "The Development of the Language of Emotions: II. Intentionality in the Experience of Affect." *Journal of Genetic Psychology* 120 (1972): 303–16.

Lively, W. J., and D. B. Bromley. *Person Perception in Childhood and Adolescence*. London: John Wiley & Sons, Ltd., 1973.

Long, J. D. *Making It 'Til Friday*. Princeton, N.J.: Princeton Book Co., Publishers, 1981.

Lorenz, K. *On Aggression*. Translated by M. K. Wilson. New York: Harcourt Brace Jovanovich, Inc., 1966.

Lowe, M. "Trends in the Development of Representational Play in Infants from One to Three Years: An Observational Study." *Journal of Child Psychology* 16 (1975): 33–48.

Lundell, K. T. *Levels of Discipline: A Complete System for Behavior Management in the Schools*. Springfield, Ill.: Charles C Thomas, Publisher, 1982.

Luria, A. R. *The Role of Speech in the Regulation of Normal and Abnormal Behavior*. London: Pergamon Press, Inc., 1961.

Luria, A. R., and F. Yudovich. *Speech and the Development of Mental Processes in the Child*. London: Staples, 1959.

Lytton, H. "Correlates of Compliance and the Rudiments of Conscience in Two-Year-Old Boys." *Canadian Journal of Behavioral Science* 9 (1977): 242–51.

Lytton, H. "Disciplinary Encounters Between Young Boys and Their Mothers and Fathers: Is There a Contingency System?" *Developmental Psychology* 15 (1979): 256–68.

Maccoby, E. E. *Social Development-Psychological Growth and the Parent-Child Relationship*. New York: Harcourt Brace Jovanovich, Inc., 1980.

Maccoby, E. E. "Socialization and Developmental Change." *Child Development* 55 (1984): 317–28.

Maccoby, E. E., and C. N. Jacklin. *The Psychology of Sex Differences*. Stanford, Calif.: Stanford University Press, 1974.

Maccoby, E. E., and C. N. Jacklin. "Sex Differences in Aggression: A Rejoinder and Reprise." *Child Development* 51 (1980): 964–80.

MacFarlane, A. *The Psychology of Childbirth*. Cambridge, Mass.: Harvard University Press, 1977.

MacFarlane, K. "Sexual Abuse of Children." In *The Victimization of Women: Sage Yearbooks in Women's Policy Studies*, Vol. 3, edited by J. R. Chapman and M. Gates. Beverly Hills, Calif.: Sage Publications, Inc., 1978, 81–109.

Machotka, P., and J. Spiegel. *The Articulate Body*. New York: Irvington Publishers, Inc., 1982.

Madsen, C. H., Jr., and C. K. Madsen. *Teaching Discipline: Behavioral Principles Toward a Positive Approach*. Boston, Mass.: Allyn and Bacon, Inc., 1981.

Madsen, M. C. "Developmental and Cross-Cultural Differences in the Cooperative and Competitive Behavior of Young Children." *Journal of Cross-Cultural Psychology*

2 (1971): 365–71.

Madsen, M. C., and C. Connor. "Cooperative and Competitive Behavior of Retarded and Non-Retarded Children at Two Ages." *Child Development* 44 (1973): 175–78.

Mahler, M., S. Pine, and A. Bergman. *The Psychological Birth of the Human Infant.* New York: Basic Books, Inc., Publishers, 1975.

Mallick, S. K., and B. R. McCandless. "A Study of Catharsis of Aggression." *Journal of Personality and Social Psychology* 4 (1966): 591–96.

Marcu, M. "Environmental Design and Architecture: The Friendly Environment Versus the Hostile Environment." *Children in Contemporary Society* 1, Special Issue 11 (1977): 3–5.

Marcus, R. F. "A Naturalisitic Study of Reciprocity in the Helping Behavior of Young Children." Paper presented at the biennial meeting of the Society for Research in Child Development, New Orleans, March 1977.

Marcus, R. F., and M. Leiserson. "Encouraging Helping Behavior." *Young Children* 33, no. 6 (September 1978): 24–34.

Marcus, R. F., S. Tellenen, and E. J. Roke. "Relation Between Cooperation and Empathy in Young Children." *Developmental Psychology* 15 (1979): 346–47.

Marion, M. *Guidance of Young Children.* St. Louis, Mo.: The C. V. Mosby Company, 1981.

Marion, M. "Child Compliance: A Review of the Literature with Implications for Family Life Education." *Family Relations: Journal of Applied Family and Child Studies* 32, no. 4 (October 1983): 545–55.

Martin, H. "A Child-Oriented Approach to Prevention of Abuse." In *Child Abuse: Prediction, Prevention, and Follow-Up,* edited by A. W. Franklin. London: Churchill Livingstone, Inc., 1978, 9–20.

Martin, R. *Legal Challenges to Behavior Modification.* Champaign, Ill.: Research Press, 1975.

Maslow, A. H. *Motivation and Personality.* New York: Harper & Row, Publishers, Inc., 1954.

Mattick, I. "The Teacher's Role in Helping Young Children Develop Language Competence." *Young Children* 27 (1972): 133–39.

Maurer, A. "Maturation of Concepts of Death." *British Journal of Medicine and Psychology* 39 (1966): 35–41.

Maurer, A. "All in the Name of the 'Last Resort': The Abuse of Children in American Schools." *Inequality in Education: Center for Law and Education,* No. 23. Cambridge, Mass.: Gutman Library, 1978.

Maurer, D., and L. Heroux. "The Perception of Faces by Three-Month-Old Infants." Paper presented at the International Conference on Infant Studies, New Haven, Conn., 1980.

May, R. *Power and Innocence: A Search for the Sources of Violence.* New York: W. W. Norton & Co., Inc., 1972.

McBride, S. "The Culture of Toy Research." In *Play As Context,* edited by A. Cheska. West Point, N. Y.: Leisure Press, 1981, 210–18.

McCarthy, P. R., and N. E. Betz. "Differential Effects of Self-Disclosing Versus Self-Involving Counselor Statements." *Journal of Counseling Psychology* 25, no. 4 (1978): 251–56.

McClelland, D. "Testing for Competence Rather Than Intelligence." *American Psychologist* 28 (1973): 1–14.

McClintock, C. G., J. M. Moskowitz, and E. McClintock. "Variations in Preferences for Individualistic, Competitive and Cooperative Outcomes As a Function of Age, Game Class and Task in Nursery School Children." *Child Development* 48 (1977): 1080–85.

McCord, W., J. McCord, and A. Howard. "Familial Correlates of Aggression in Non-Delinquent Male Children." *Journal of Abnormal and Social Psychology* 62 (1961); 79–93.

McDavid, J. W., and H. Harari. "Stereotyping of Names and Popularity in Gradeschool Children." *Child Development* 37 (1966): 453–59.

McDonald, M. *Not by the Color of Their Skin: The Impact of Racial Differences on the Child's Development.* New York: International Universities Press, Inc., 1970.

McGhee, P. *Humor: Its Origin and Development.* San Francisco: W. H. Freeman & Company, Publishers, 1979.

McGhee, P. E., and N. S. Duffey. "Children's Appreciation of Humor Victimizing Different Racial-Ethnic Groups." *Journal of Cross-Cultural Psychology* 14, no. 1 (1983): 29–40.

McKay, D. "Introducing Preschool Children to Reading Through Parent Involvement." *Resources in Education* 1 (1982).

McLaughlin, J. A., and S. M. Kershman. "Mainstreaming in Early Childhood." *Young Children* 34, no. 4, 5 (1979): 54–66.

McNiel, D. *The Acquisition of Language.* New York: Harper & Row, Publishers, Inc., 1970.

Mead, D. E. *Six Approaches to Child Rearing.* Provo, Utah: Brigham Young University Press, 1976.

Meers, J. "The Light Touch." *Psychology Today* 19, no. 9 (1985): 60–67.

Mehrabian, A. *Nonverbal Communication.* Chicago: Aldin-Atherton, 1972.

Mehrabian, M. *Silent Messages.* Belmont, Calif.: Wadsworth, Inc., 1971.

Mehrabian, M. *Public Places and Private Spaces: The Psychology of Work, Play and Living Environments.* New York: Basic Books, Inc., Publishers, 1976.

Meichenbaum, D. *Cognitive Behavior Modification: An Integrative Approach.* New York: Plenum Publishing Corporation, 1977.

Meichenbaum, D. H., and J. Goodman. "Training Impulsive Children to Talk to Themselves: A Means of Developing Self-Control." *Journal of Abnormal Psychology* 77 (1971): 115–26.

Mellonie, B., and R. Ingpen. *Lifetimes.* New York: Bantam

Books, Inc., 1983.

Mendler, A. N., and R. L. Curwin. *Taking Charge in the Classroom*. Reston, Va.: Reston Publishing Co., Inc., 1983.

Michigan Council for the Prevention of Child Abuse and Neglect. *Reporting Child Abuse and Neglect in Michigan*. Lansing, Mich: MCPCAN, 1985.

Midlarsky, E., and J. H. Bryan. "Training Charity in Children." *Journal of Personality and Social Psychology* 5 (1967): 408–15.

Midlarksy, E., and J. H. Bryan. "Affect Expression and Children's Imitative Altruism." *Journal of Experimental Research in Personality* 6 (1972): 195–203.

Midlarsky, E., J. H. Bryan, and P. Brickman. "Aversive Approval: Interactive Effects of Modeling and Reinforcement on Altruistic Behavior." *Child Development* 44 (1973): 321–28.

Miller, J. "A Comparison of Racial Preferences in Young Black and Mexican-American Children. A Preliminary View." *Sociological Symposium* 7 (1971): 37–48.

Miller, L. C. "Fears and Anxiety in Children." In *Handbook of Clinical Child Psychology*, edited by C. E. Walker and M. C. Roberts. New York: John Wiley & Sons, Inc., 1983.

Miller, P., and C. Garvey. "Mother-Baby Role Play: Its Origins in Social Support." In *Symbolic Play: The Development of Social Understanding*, edited by I. Bretherton. New York: Academic Press, Inc., 1984, 101–30.

Milner, D. "Racial Identification and Preference in Black British Children." *European Journal of Social Psychology* 3 (1973): 281–95.

Mischel, W. *Introduction to Personality*. 2d ed. New York: Holt, Rinehart & Winston, 1976.

Mischel, W. "How Children Postpone Pleasure." *Human Nature* 1 (1978): 51–55.

Mischel, W., E. G. Ebbesen, and A. R. Zeiss. "Cognitive and Attentional Mechanisms in Delay of Gratification." *Journal of Personality and Social Psychology* 21 (1972): 204–18.

Mischel, W., and C. J. Patterson. "Substantive and Structural Elements of Effective Plans for Self-Control." *Journal of Personality and Social Psychology* 34 (1976): 942–50.

Mnookin, R. H. *Child, Family and State: Problems and Materials on Children and the Law*. Boston: Little, Brown & Company, 1978.

Mohr, D. M. "Development of Attributes of Personal Identity." *Developmental Psychology* 14 (1978): 427–28.

Money, J., and A. Ehrhardt. *Men and Women: Boys and Girls*. Baltimore, Md.: The Johns Hopkins University Press, 1973.

Montgomery, E. "To Parents of Children with Learning Disabilities—Some Insights from a Teacher's Perspective." *Journal of School Health* 52, no. 2, 2 (1982): 116–17.

Moore, N. V., C. M. Everton, and J. E. Brophy. "Solitary Play: Some Functional Reconsiderations." *Developmental Psychology* 10 (1974): 830–34.

Moore, S. G. "Prosocial Behavior in the Early Years: Parent and Peer Influences." In *Handbook of Research in Early Childhood Education*, edited by B. Spodek. New York: Free Press, 1982, 65–81.

Moore, S. G., and F. Olson, "The Effects of Explicitness of Instruction on the Generalization of a Prohibition in Young Children." *Child Development* 40 (1969): 945–49.

Moos, R. H. *Human Adaptation: Coping with Life Stresses*. Lexington, Mass.: D. C. Heath & Company, 1976.

Morland, J. K., and J. E. Williams. *Race, Color, and the Young Child*. Chapel Hill, N. C.: University of North Carolina Press, 1976.

Morris, J. B. "Indirect Influences on Children's Racial Attitudes." *Educational Leadership* 1 (1981): 286–87.

Mowrer, O. H. "Freudianism, Behavior Therapy, and Self-Disclosure." In *Personality: Readings in Theory and Research, 2d ed.*, edited by E. Southwell and M. Merbaum. Monterey, Calif.: Brooks/Cole Publishing Company, 1971.

Moyer, K. E. *The Physiology of Hostility*. Chicago: Markham, 1971.

Mueller, E., and T. Lucas, "A Developmental Analysis of Peer Interaction Among Toddlers." In *Friendship and Peer Relations*, edited by M. Lewis and L. Rosenblum. New York: John Wiley & Sons, Inc., 1975.

Muir, D., and J. Field. "Newborn Infants Orient to Sounds." *Child Development* 50 (1979): 431–36.

Murray, A. D., et al. "The Effects of Epidural Anesthesia on Newborns and Their Mothers." *Child Development* 52 (1981): 71–82.

Murray, E. J. *Motivation and Emotion*. Englewood Cliffs, N. J.: Prentice-Hall, Inc., 1964.

Murray, J. P. *Television and Youth: 25 Years of Research and Controversy*. Boys Town, Nebraska: Boys Town Center for the Study of Youth Development, 1980.

Mussen, P., and N. Eisenberg-Berg. *Roots of Caring, Sharing, and Helping: The Development of Prosocial Behavior in Children*. San Francisco: W. H. Freeman & Company, Publishers, 1977.

Nagy, M. H. "The Child's Theory Concerning Death." *Journal of Genetic Psychology* 73 (1948): 3–27.

National Institute for Mental Health. *Guideline for Talking to Children about Death*. Washington, D. C.: NIMH, 1979.

Nedler, S. E., and O. D. McAfee. *Working with Parents*. Belmont, Calif.: Wadsworth, Inc., 1979.

Nelson, R. E. "Facilitating Children's Syntax Acquisition." *Developmental Psychology* 13 (1977): 101–7.

Neugarten, B. "Adaptation and the Life-Cycle." *The Counseling Psychologist* 6, no. 1 (1976).

Newman, B. M., and P. R. Newman. *Infancy and Childhood*. New York: John Wiley & Sons, Inc., 1978.

Nickell, P., A. Rice, and S. Tucker. *Management in Family Living*. New York: John Wiley & Sons, Inc., 1976.

O'Connor, R. D. "Relative Efficacy of Modeling, Shaping

and the Combined Procedures for Modification of Social Withdrawal." *Journal of Abnormal Psychology* 79, no. 3 (1972): 327–34.

Oden, S., and S. R. Asher. "Coaching Children in Social Skills for Friendship Making." *Child Development* 48 (1977): 495–506.

Olds, A. R. "Why Is Environmental Design Important to Young Children?" *Children in Contemporary Society* 1, Special Issue 11 (1977): 5–8.

Openshaw, D. K. "The Development of Self-Esteem in the Child: Model Theory Versus Parent-Child Interaction." Ph.D. diss., Brigham Young University, Provo, Utah, 1978.

Opler, M. K. "Cultural Induction of Stress." In *Psychological Stress,* edited by M. H. Appley and R. Trumbull. New York: Appleton-Century-Crofts, 1967, 209–41.

Orlick, T. *Winning Through Cooperation.* Washington, D. C.: Acropolis Books, Ltd., 1978.

Osofsky, J. D., and K. Conners. "Mother-Infant Interaction: An Integrative View of a Complex System." In *Handbook of Infant Development,* edited by J. D. Osofsky. New York: Wiley-Interscience, 1981, 519–48.

Ostfeld, B. M. "Children's Fears: What They Are and What Causes Them." *Day Care/Staff Development Program.* New York: Curriculum Development, Inc., 1971.

Ostwald, P. F. *Soundmaking: The Acoustic Communication of Emotion.* Springfield, Ill.: Charles C Thomas, Publisher, 1963.

Olweus, D., et al. "Testosterone, Aggression, Physical and Personality Dimensions in Normal Adolescent Males." *Psychosomatic Medicine* 42 (1980): 253–69.

Packard, V. *Our Endangered Children.* Boston: Little, Brown & Company, 1983.

Papalia, D. E., and S. W. Olds. *Human Development.* New York: McGraw-Hill, Inc., 1981.

Papousek, H., and M. Papousek. "Mothering and the Cognitive Head Start: Psychobiological Considerations." In *Studies in Mother-Infant Interaction,* edited by H. R. Schaffer. London: Academic Press, Inc., 1977.

Parke, R. D. "Effectiveness of Punishment As an Interaction of Intensity, Timing, Agent Nurturance, and Cognitive Structuring." *Child Development* 40 (1969): 213–36.

Parke, R. D. "Some Effects of Punishment on Children's Behavior." In *The Young Child,* Vol. 2, edited by W. W. Hartup. Washington, D.C.: National Association for the Education of Young Children, 1972.

Parke, R. D. "Rules, Roles, and Resistance to Deviation: Explorations in Punishment, Discipline, and Self-Control." In *Minnesota Symposia on Child Psychology,* Vol. 8, edited by A. Pick. Minneapolis: University of Minnesota Press, 1974.

Parke, R. D. "Punishment in Children: Effects, Side Effects and Alternate Strategies." In *Psychological Processes in Early Education,* edited by R. Hom and R. Robinson. New York: Academic Press, Inc., 1977.

Parke, R. D. "Some Effects of Punishment on Children's Behavior—Revisited." In *Contemporary Readings in Child Psychology,* edited by R. D. Parke and E. M. Hetherington. New York: McGraw-Hill, Inc., 1977, 208–19.

Parke, R. D., and C. W. Collmer. "Child Abuse: An Interdisciplinary Analysis." In *Review of Child Development Research,* Vol. 5, edited by E. M. Hetherington. Chicago: University of Chicago Press, 1975, 509–90.

Parke, R. D., and J. L. Duer. "Schedule of Reinforcement and Inhibition of Aggression in Children." *Developmental Psychology* 7 (1972): 266–69.

Parke, R. D., and S. Murray. "Reinstatement: A Technique for Increasing Stability of Inhibition in Children." Unpublished manuscript, University of Wisconsin, 1971.

Parke, R. D., and R. H. Walters. "Some Factors Determining the Efficacy of Punishment for Inducing Response Inhibition." *Monograph of the Society for Research in Child Development* 32, no. 109 (1967).

Parmelee, A. H., W. H. Werner, and H. R. Schultz. "Infant Sleep Patterns from Birth to 16 Weeks of Age." *Journal of Pediatrics* 65 (1964): 576–82.

Parten, M. B. "Social Participation Among Preschool Children." *Journal of Abnormal and Social Psychology* 27 (1932): 243–69.

Parten, R. L. "How Effective Are Your Questions?" *The Clearing House* 52 (February 1979): 254–56.

Patterson, G. R. "The Aggressive Child: Victim and Architect of a Coercive System." In *Behavior Modification and Families, Vol. 1: Theory and Research,* edited by E. J. Mash, L. A. Hamerlynck, and L. C. Handy. New York: Brunner/Mazel, Inc., 1977.

Patterson, G. R., J. A. Cobb, and R. S. Ray, "A Social Engineering Technology for Retraining the Families of Aggressive Boys." In *Issues and Trends in Behavior Therapy,* edited by H. E. Adams and I.P. Unikel. Springfield, Ill.: Charles C Thomas, Publisher, 1973, 139–224.

Patterson, G. R., R. A. Littman, and W. Bucker. "Assertive Behavior in Children: A Step Toward a Theory of Aggression." *Monographs of the Society for Research in Child Development* 32 (1967): 1–42.

Peake, T. H., and D. Egli. "The Language of Feelings." *Journal of Contemporary Psychotherapy* 13, no. 2 (Fall/Winter 1982): 162–74.

Pearsall, P. "De-Stressing Children: Wellness for Children." *Offspring* 25, no. 2 (1983): 2–9.

Peck, C. A., et al. "Teaching Retarded Preschoolers to Imitate the Free-Play Behavior of Nonretarded Classmates: Trained and Generalized Effects." *Journal of Special Education* 12 (1978): 195–207.

Peck, P. J., and R. V. Havighurst. *The Psychology of Character Development.* New York: John Wiley & Sons, Inc., 1960.

Peller, L. "Models of Children's Play." In *Child's Play,* edited by R. Herron and B. Sutton-Smith. New York: John Wiley & Sons, Inc., 1971, 110–25.

Pelletier, K. R. *Mind As Healer, Mind As Slayer*. New York: Dell Publishing Co., Inc., 1981.

Peters, D. L., and J. Belsky. "The Day Care Movement: Past, Present, and Future." In *Child Nurturance*, Vol. 2, edited by M. Kostelnik, et al. New York: Plenum Publishing Corporation, 1982.

Peters, D. L., and M. J. Kostelnik. "Day Care Personnel Preparation." In *Advances in Early Education and Day Care*, Vol. 2, edited by S. Kilmer. Greenwich, Conn.: JAI Press, Inc., 1981.

Peters, J. "Children Who Are Victims of Sexual Assault and the Psychology of Offenders." *American Journal of Psychotherapy* 30, no. 3 (1976): 398–421.

Petersen, A. C., M. Tobin-Richards, and A. Boxer. "Puberty: Its Measurement and Its Meaning." *The Journal of Early Adolescence* 3, no. 1, 2 (1983): 47–62.

Phyfe-Perkins, E. *Effects of Teacher Behavior on Preschool Children: A Review of Research*. Urbana, Ill.: ERIC Document Reproduction Service, 1982 (catalog no. 194).

Piaget, J. *The Origins of Intelligence in Children*. New York: International Universities Press, Inc., 1952.

Piaget, J. *Play, Dreams and Imitations in Childhood*. New York: W. W. Norton & Co., Inc., 1962.

Piaget, J. *The Moral Judgment of the Child*. New York: Free Press, 1965. (Originally published in 1932.)

Piaget, J. "The Rules of the Game of Marbles." In *Play: Its Role in Development and Evolution*, edited by J. Bruner, A. Jolly, and K. Sylva. New York: Academic Press, Inc., 1976, 411–41.

Piaget, J., and B. Inhelder. *The Psychology of the Child*. Translated by H. Weaver. New York: Basic Books, Inc., Publishers, 1969.

Plutchik, R. "A Language for Emotions." *Psychology Today* 16 (February 1980): 68–78.

Plutchik, R. *Emotion: A Psychoevolutionary Synthesis*. New York: Harper & Row, Publishers, Inc., 1980, 152–72.

Polloway, A. M. "The Child in the Physical Environment: A Design Problem." In *Alternative Learning Environments*, edited by G. Coates. Stroudsburg, Pa.: Dowden, Hutchinson and Ross, 1974.

Porter, J. D. *Black Child, White Child: The Development of Racial Attitudes*. Cambridge, Mass.: Harvard University Press, 1971.

Postman, N. *The Disappearance of Childhood*. New York: Dell Publishing Co., Inc., 1982.

Presbie, R. J., and P. F. Coiteux. "Learning to Be Generous or Stingy: Imitation of Sharing Behavior As a Function of Model Generosity and Vicarious Reinforcement." *Child Development* 42 (1971): 1033–38.

Prescott, E. *A Pilot Study of Daycare Centers and Their Clientele*. Washington, D.C.: U.S. Government Printing Office, U.S. Department of Health, Education, and Welfare, Children's Bureau, publication no. 428, 1965.

Proshansky, H. "The Development of Intergroup Attitudes." In *Review of Child Development Research* Vol.2,

edited by L. W. Hoffman and M. L. Hoffman. New York: Russell Sage Foundation, 1966.

Raffini, J. P. *Discipline: Negotiating Conflicts with Today's Kids*. Englewood Cliffs, N. J.: Prentice-Hall, Inc., 1980.

Reichenbach, L., and J. C. Masters. "Children's Use of Expressive and Contextual Cues in Judgments of Emotions." *Child Development* 54 (1983): 993–1004.

Resnick, L. "Teacher Behavior in an Informal British Infant School." *School Review* 81, no. 1 (1972): 63–83.

Rest, J. "Morality." In *Carmichael's Manual of Child Psychology*, 4th ed, New York: John Wiley & Sons, Inc., 1983.

Revicki, D. "The Relationship Among Socioeconomic Status, Home Environment, Parent Involvement, Child Self-Concept and Child Achievement." *Resources in Education*. 1, (1982): 27–33.

Rheingold, H., and K. Cook. "The Contents of Boys' and Girls' Rooms As an Index of Parents' Behavior." *Child Development* 46 (1975): 459–63.

Rich, J. M. "Discipline, Rules and Punishment." *Contemporary Education* 55, no. 2 (1984): 110–12.

Richards, C. S., and L. J. Siegel. "Behavioral Treatment of Anxiety States." In *Child Behavior Therapy*, edited by D. Marholin. New York: Gardner Press, Inc., 1978.

Ridley, C. A., and S. R. Vaughn. "The Effects of a Preschool Problem Solving Program on Interpersonal Behavior." *Child Care Quarterly* 12, no. 3 (Fall 1983): 222–30.

Ritchie, F. K., and I. J. Toner. "Direct Labeling, Tester Expectancy, and Delay Maintenance Behavior in Scottish Preschool Children." *International Journal of Behavioral Development* 7, no. 3 (1985): 333–41.

Roberts, H. A. "A Clinical and Metabolic Reevaluation of Reading Disability." *Selected Papers on Learning Disabilities, Fifth Annual Convention, Association for Children with Learning Disabilities*. San Rafael, Calif.: Academic Therapy Publications, Inc., 1969.

Roedell, W. C., R. G. Slaby, and H. B. Robinson. *Social Development in Young Children: A Report for Teachers*. Washington, D.C.: National Institute for Education, U.S. Department of Health, Education, and Welfare, 1976.

Roff, M., S. B. Sells, and M. M. Golden. *Social Adjustment and Personality Development in Children*. Minneapolis: University of Minnesota Press, 1972.

Rogers, C. R. "The Necessary and Sufficient Conditions of Therapeutic Personality Change." *Journal of Consulting Psychology* 21 (1957): 95–103.

Rogers, C. R. *On Becoming a Person*. Boston: Houghton Mifflin Company, 1961.

Rohwer, W. D. "Cognitive Development and Education." In *Carmichael's Manual of Child Psychology*, 3d ed., edited by P. H. Mussen. New York: John Wiley & Sons, Inc., 1970.

Rorher, J. H., and M. S. Edmonson. *The Eighth Generation*. New York: Harper and Brothers, 1960.

Rosenberg, M. *Society and Adolescent Self-Esteem*. Princeton, N. J.: Princeton University Press, 1965.

Rosenberg, M., and R. G. Simmons. *Black and White Self-Esteem: The Urban School Child.* Boston: American Sociological Association, 1971.

Rosenhan, D. L. "Prosocial Behavior of Children." In *The Young Child: Reviews of Research,* Vol. 2, edited by W. W. Hartup. Washington, D.C.: National Association for the Education of Young Children, 1972, 340–60.

Rosenhan, D. L., and G. M. White. "Observation and Rehearsal as Determinants of Prosocial Behavior." *Journal of Personality and Social Psychology* 5 (1967): 424–31.

Rosenthal, B. G. "Development of Self-Identification in Relation to Attitudes Toward the Self in Chippewa Indians." *Genetic Psychology Monographs* 90 (1974): 43–141.

Rothbart, M. K. "Measurement of Temperament in Infancy." *Child Development* 52 (1981): 569–78.

Rowe, M. B. "Pausing Phenomena: Influence on the Quality of Instruction." *Journal of Psycholinguistic Research* 3 (1974): 203–33.

Rubin, K. H. "Relationship Between Egocentric Communication and Popularity Among Peers." *Developmental Psychology* 7 (1972): 364.

Rubin, K. H., T. Maconi, and M. Hornung. "Free Play Behaviors in Middle and Lower Class Preshoolers: Parten and Piaget Revisited." *Child Development* 47 (1976): 414–19.

Rubin, Z. *Children's Friendships.* Cambridge, Mass.: Harvard University Press, 1980.

Rushton, J. P. "Generosity in Children: Immediate and Long-Term Effects of Modeling, Preaching and Moral Judgments." *Journal of Personality and Social Psychology* 31 (1975): 459–66.

Rushton, J. P. "Socialization and the Altruistic Behavior of Children." *Psychological Bulletin* 83 (1976): 898–913.

Rutherford, R. B., and E. Edgar. *Teachers and Parents.* Boston: Allyn and Bacon, Inc., 1979.

Rutter, M. "Normal Psychosexual Development." *Journal of Child Psychology and Psychiatry and Allied Disciplines* 11 (1971): 259–83.

Rutter, M. "Parent-Child Separation: Psychological Effects on the Children." *Journal of Child Psychology and Psychiatry and Allied Disciplines* 12 (1971): 233–60.

Safier, G. A. "A Study of Relationships Between Life and Death Concepts in Children." *Journal of Genetic Psychology* 105 (1964): 283–94.

Salend, S. J. "Factors Contributing to the Development of Successful Mainstreaming Programs." *Exceptional Children* 50, no. 5, 2 (1984): 409–16.

Saltz, E., and J. Brodie. "Pretend-Play Training in Childhood: A Review and Critique." In *The Play of Children: Current Theory and Research,* edited by D. Pepler and K. Rubin. New York: S. Karger, 1982, 97–113.

Samuels, S. C. *Enhancing Self-Concept in Early Childhood.* New York: Human Sciences Press, Inc., 1977.

Sanford, L. *The Silent Children.* New York: McGraw-Hill, Inc., 1982.

Sapon-Shevin, M. "Another Look at Mainstreaming: Exceptionality, Normality, and the Nature of Difference." *Phi Delta Kappan* 60, no. 10 (1978): 119–20.

Sawin, D. B. "Assessing Empathy in Children: A Search for an Elusive Construct." Paper presented at the biennial meeting of the Society for Research in Child Development, San Francisco, March 1979.

Sayles, L., and G. Strauss. *Managing Human Resources.* Englewood Cliffs, N. J.: Prentice-Hall, Inc., 1981.

Scarr, S. *Mother Care—Other Care.* New York: Basic Books, Inc., Publishers, 1984.

Schacter, S., and J. E. Singer. "Cognitive, Social and Physiological Determinants of Emotional States." *Psychological Review* 69 (1962): 379–99.

Schaefer, E. S. "Parents and Educators: Evidence from Cross-Sectional, Longitudinal, and Intervention Research." *Young Children* 4 (1972): 227–39.

Scheflen, A. *Body Language and the Social Order.* Englewood Cliffs, N. J.: Prentice-Hall, Inc., 1972.

Scherer, M. W., and C. Y. Nakamura. "A Peer-Survey Schedule for Children: A Factor Analytic Comparison with Manifest Anxiety." *Behavior Research and Therapy* 6 (1968): 173–82.

Schickedanz, J. A., D. I. Schickedanz, and P. D. Forsyth. *Toward Understanding Children.* Boston: Little, Brown & Company, 1982.

Schlichter, C. L. "The Answer Is in the Question." *Science and Children* 20, no. 5 (February 1983): 8–10.

Schmuch, R. A., and P. A. Schmuch. *Group Processes in the Classroom.* 2d ed. Dubuque, Iowa: W. C. Brown Group, 1975.

Schultz, E. W., and C. M. Heuchert. *Child Stress and the School Experience.* New York: Human Sciences Press, Inc., 1983.

Schultz, W. *Profound Simplicity.* New York: Bantam Books, Inc., 1979.

Sears, R. R. "The Growth of Conscience." In *Personality Development in Children,* edited by I. Iscoe and H. Stevenson. Austin: University of Texas Press, 1960.

Secord, D., and B. Peevers. "The Development and Attribution of Person Concepts." In *Understanding Other Persons,* edited by T. Mischel. Oxford: Blackwell Scientific Publications, Inc., 1974.

Seefeldt, V., and J. Haubenstricker. "Patterns, Phases, or Stages: An Analytical Model for the Study of Developmental Movement." In *The Development of Movement Control and Coordination,* edited by J. A. Kelso and J. E. Clark. New York: John Wiley & Sons, Inc., 1982, 309–18.

Segal, J., and H. Yahraes. *A Child's Journey.* New York: McGraw-Hill, Inc., 1979.

Selman, R. L. "Social-Cognitive Understanding." In *Moral Development and Behavior: Theory, Research and Social Issues,* edited by T. Lickona. New York: Holt, Rinehart & Winston, 1976.

Selman, R. L. *The Growth of Interpersonal Understanding.* New

York: Academic Press, Inc., 1980.

Selman, R. L. "The Child As Friendship Philosopher." In *In the Development of Children's Friendships*, edited by J. M. Gottman. Cambridge, England: Cambridge University Press, 1981.

Selman, R. L., and D. F. Byrne. "A Structural Developmental Analysis of Levels of Role-Taking in Middle Childhood." *Child Development* 45 (1974): 803–6.

Selman, R. L., and A. P. Selman. "Children's Ideas about Friendship: A New Theory." *Psychology Today* 13 (October 1979): 71–114.

Selye, H. *Stress without Distress*. New York: The New American Library, Inc., 1974.

Semaj, L. "The Development of Racial Evaluation and Preference: A Cognitive Approach." *Journal of Black Psychology* 5, no. 2 (1980): 59–79.

Serbin, L. A., I. J. Tonick, and S. H. Sternglanz. "Shaping Cooperative Cross-Sex Play." *Child Development* 48 (1977): 924–29.

Severy, F. J., and K. E. Davis. "Helping Behavior Among Normal and Retarded Children." *Child Development* 42 (1971): 1017–31.

Sgroi, S. M. "Sexual Molestation of Children." *Children Today* 4, no. 3 (1975): 18–21.

Shaffer, D. R. *Developmental Psychology: Theory Research and Applications*. Monterery, Calif.: Brooks/Cole Publishing Company, 1985.

Shanab, M. E., and K. A. Yahya. "A Behavioral Study of Obedience." *Journal of Personality and Social Psychology* 35 (1977): 550–86.

Shantz, C. U. "The Development of Social Cognition." In *Review of Child Development Research*, Vol. 5, edited by E. M. Hetherington. Chicago: University of Chicago Press, 1975.

Shantz, D. W., and D. R. Voyandoff. "Situational Effects on Retaliatory Aggression at Three Age Levels." *Child Development* 44 (1973): 149–53.

Shapiro, E. K., and E. Weber. *Cognitive and Affective Growth: Developmental Interaction*. Hillsdale, N. J.: Lawrence Erlbaum Associates, Inc., 1981.

Shaw, M. E. "Changes in Sociometric Choices Following Forced Integration of an Elementary School." *Journal of Social Issues* 29 (1973): 143–57.

Shay, S. W., and S. L. Murphy. "Scary People: When Touching Is Not Okay." *Two to Twelve: Current Issues in Children's Development* 2, no. 1 (January 1984): 7–9.

Sheppard, W. C., and R. H. Willoughby. *Child Behavior*. Chicago: Rand McNally & Company, 1975.

Sherman, J. A., and D. Bushell, Jr. "Behavior Modification As an Educational Technique." In *Review of Child Development Research*, Vol. 4, edited by F. D. Horowitz. Chicago: University of Chicago Press, 1975, 409–62.

Sherrod, L. "Issues in Cognitive-Perceptual Development: The Special Case of Social Stimuli." In *Infant Social Cognition: Empirical and Theoretical Considerations*, edited by M. E. Lamb and L. Sherrod. Hillsdale, N. J.: Lawrence Erlbaum Associates, Inc., 1981, 11–36.

Shotwell, J., D. Wolf, and H. Gardner. "Exploring Early Symbolization: Styles of Achievement." In *Play and Learning*, edited by B. Sutton-Smith. New York: Gardner Press, Inc., 1979, 127–56.

Shure, M. B., and G. Spivack. *Problem-Solving Techniques in Childrearing*. San Francisco: Jossey-Bass, Inc., Publishers, 1978.

Siegel, A. F., and L. G. Kohn. "Permissiveness, Permission, and Aggression: The Effects of Adult Presence or Absence on Aggression in Children." In *Child Development and Behavior*, edited by F. Rebelsky and L. Dorman. New York: Alfred A. Knopf, Inc., 1970, 234–42.

Simon, S. B. *Negative Criticism*. Niles, Ill.: Argus Communications, 1978.

Singer, J. L. *The Child's World of Make Believe: Experimental Studies of Imaginative Play*. New York: Academic Press, Inc., 1973.

Singleton, L. "The Effects of Sex and Race on Children's Sociometric Choices for Play and Work." Urbana, Ill.: University of Illinois Press, 1974. (ERIC Document Reproduction Service catalog no. ED 100520.)

Slaby, R. G., and K. S. Frey. "Development of Gender Constancy and Selective Attention to Same-Sex Models." In *Social Issues in Developmental Psychology*, 2d ed., edited by H. Bee. New York: Harper & Row, Publishers, Inc., 1978.

Slaby, R. G., and R. D. Parke. "The Influence of a Punitive or Reasoning Model on Resistance to Deviation and Aggression in Children." Unpublished manuscript, University of Wisconsin, 1968.

Smart, M. S., and R. C. Smart. *Children: Development and Relationships*. New York: Macmillan, Inc., 1977.

Smilansky, S. *The Effects of Sociodramatic Play on Disadvantaged Preschool Children*. New York: John Wiley & Sons, Inc., 1968.

Smith, A. I. "Nonverbal Communication Through Touch." Ph.D. diss., Georgia State University, 1970.

Smith, C. A. *Promoting the Social Development of Young Children*. Palo Alto, Calif.: Mayfield Publishing Co., 1982.

Smith, C. T. "The Relationship Between the Type of Questions, Stimuli and the Oral Language Production of Children." *Research in the Teaching of English* 11, no. 2 (1979): 111–16.

Smith, P. K. "A Longitudinal Study of Social Participation in Preschool Children: Solitary and Parallel Play Reexamined." *Developmental Psychology* 14 (1978): 517–23.

Smith, P. K., and M. Green. "Aggressive Behavior in English Nurseries and Play Groups: Sex Differences and Response of Adults." *Child Development* 46, no. 1 (1975): 211–14.

Smith, R. E. *The Subtle Revolution*. Washington, D.C.: The Urban Institute Press, 1979.

Smith, S. T. "Personality Traits, Values, Expectations and

Managerial Behavior." Master's thesis, The Pennsylvania State University, 1971. As quoted in I. Gross, E. Crandall, and M. Knoll, *Management for Modern Families.* Englewood Cliffs, N. J.: Prentice-Hall, Inc., 1980, 32.

Soderman, A. "Interaction Within a Typical and Hearing-Impaired Preprimary Setting: An Intensive Study." Ph.D. diss., Michigan State University, 1979.

Soderman, A. "Dealing with Difficult Young Children: Strategies for Teachers and Parents." *Young Children* 40, no. 5, 7 (1985): 15–20.

Soderman, A. "Helping the School-Age Child Deal with Stress." *Focus* 10, no. 1 (1985): 17–23.

Soderman, A., and M. Phillips. "The Early Education of Males: Where Are We Failing Them?" *Educational Leadership* 44, no. 3 (November 1986): 70–72.

Soderman, R. "Getting Ready for Middle School." *Two to Twelve* 2, no. 8, 8 (1984): 8–9.

Sommer, R. *Tight Spaces: Hard Architecture and How to Humanize It.* Englewood Cliffs, N. J.: Prentice-Hall, Inc., 1974.

Soroka, S. M., C. M. Corter, and R. Abramovitch. "Infants' Tactile Discrimination of Novel and Familiar Stimuli." *Child Development* 50 (1979): 1251–53.

Spanier, G. B., R. M. Lerner, and J. A. Shea. "Parent and Child Development." In *Human Development 83/84,* edited by H. E. Fitzgerald and T. H. Carr. Guilford, Conn.: The Dushkin Publishing Group, Inc., 1982.

Spencer, M. B. "Preschool Children's Social Cognition and Cultural Cognition. A Cognitive Developmental Interpretation of Race Dissonance Findings." *Journal of Psychology* 112 (1982): 275–86.

Spinetta, J. J., and D. Rigler. "The Child-Abusing Parent: A Psychological Review." *Psychological Bulletin* 77 (1972): 296–304.

Spitz, R. A. "The Role of Ecological Factors in Emotional Development in Infancy." *Child Development* 20 (1949): 145–55.

Spivack, G., J. Platt, and M. Shure. *The Problem-Solving Approach to Adjustment.* San Francisco: Jossey-Bass, Inc., Publishers, 1976.

Spivack, G., and M. B. Shure. *Problem-Solving Techniques in Childrearing.* San Francisco: Jossey-Bass, Inc., Publishers, 1974.

Spivack, G., and M. B. Shure. *Social Adjustment of Young Children: A Cognitive Approach to Solving Real-Life Problems.* San Francisco: Jossey-Bass, Inc., Publishers, 1974.

Sroufe, L. A. "Wariness of Strangers and the Study of Infant Development." *Child Development* 48 (1977): 731–46.

Sroufe, L. A. "Social Emotional Development." In *Handbook of Infant Development,* edited by J. Osofsky. New York: John Wiley & Sons, Inc., 1979.

Sroufe, L. A., and M. J. Ward. "Seductive Behavior of Mothers of Toddlers: Occurrence, Correlates and Family Origins." *Child Development* 51 (1980): 1222–29.

Sroufe, L. A., and E. Waters. "Attachment As an Organiza-

tional Construct." *Child Development* 48 (1977): 1184–99.

Stallings, J. "Implementation and Child Effects of Teaching Practices in Follow Through Classrooms." *Monographs of the Society for Research in Child Development* 40, serial no. 163 (1975): 7–8.

Staub, E. "A Child in Distress: The Influence of Age and Number of Witnesses on Children's Attempts to Help." *Journal of Personality and Social Psychology* 14 (1970): 130–40.

Staub, E. "The Learning and Unlearning of Aggression." In *The Control of Aggression and Violence,* edited by J. L. Singer. New York: Academic Press, Inc., 1971, 93–124.

Staub, E. "The Use of Role-Playing and Induction on Children's Learning of Helping and Sharing Behavior." *Child Development* 42 (1971): 805–16.

Staub, E. *Positive Social Behavior and Morality: Social and Personal Influences.* Vol. 1. New York: Academic Press, Inc., 1978.

Staub, E. *Positive Social Behavior and Morality: Socialization and Development.* Vol. 2. New York: Academic Press, Inc., 1979.

Stayton, D. J., R. Hogan, and M. D. S. Ainsworth. "Infant Obedience and Maternal Behavior: The Origin of Socialization Reconsidered." *Child Development* 42 (1971): 1057–69.

Steele, B. "Psychodynamic Factors in Child Abuse." In *The Battered Child,* 3d ed., rev., edited by C. H. Kempe and R. E. Helfer. Chicago: University of Chicago Press, 1980.

Stein, A. H. "Imitation of Resistance to Temptation." *Child Development* 38 (1967): 159–69.

Stein, L. C., and M. J. Kostelnik. "A Practical Problem Solving Model for Conflict Resolution in the Classroom." *Child Care Quarterly* 13, no. 1 (Spring 1984): 5–20.

Steiner, J. E. "Facial Expressions in Response to Taste and Smell Stimulation." In *Advances in Child Development and Behavior,* Vol. 13, edited by H. W. Reese and L. P. Lepsitt. New York: Academic Press, Inc., 1979, 257–96.

Stengel, S. R. "Moral Education for Young Children." *Young Children* 37, no. 6 (1982): 23–31.

Stern, D. *The First Relationship: Infant and Mother.* Cambridge, Mass.: Harvard University Press, 1977.

Stewig, J. W. "Reaching for Links That Foster Strength and Stability." *Phi Delta Kappan* 66, no. 9, 5 (1985): 640–42.

Stocking, S. H., D. Arezzo, and S. Leavitt, *Helping Kids Make Friends.* Allen, Tex.: Argus Communications, 1980.

Stone, L. J., and J. Church. *Childhood and Adolescence.* New York: Random House, Inc., 1973.

Strayer, J. "A Naturalistic Study of Empathic Behaviors and Their Relation to Affective States and Perspective-Taking Skills in Preschool Children." *Child Development* 51 (1980): 815–22.

Sullivan, H. S. *Concepts of Modern Psychiatry.* Washington, D.C.: William Alanison White Psychiatric Foundation, 1957.

Suomi, S. "The Perception of Contingency and Social

Development." In *Infant Social Cognition: Theoretical and Empirical Considerations,* edited by M. E. Lamb and L. Sherrod. Hillsdale, N. J.: Lawrence Erlbaum Associates, Inc., 177–204.

Sutton-Smith, B., and S. Sutton-Smith. *How to Play with Your Child and When Not To.* New York: Hawthorn Books, Inc., 1974.

Swartzman, H. *Transformations: The Anthropology of Children's Play.* New York: Plenum Publishing Corporation, 1978.

Swartzman, H. "The Socio-Cultural Context of Play." In *Play and Learning,* edited by B. Sutton-Smith. New York: Gardner Press, Inc., 1979, 239–57.

Swaze, M. C. "Self-Concept Development in Young Children." In *The Self-Concept of the Young Child,* edited by T. D. Yawkey. Provo, Utah: Brigham Young University Press, 1980.

Swick, K. J., M. Brown, and S. Robinson. *Toward Quality Environments for Young Children.* Champaign, Ill.: Stripes Publishing Company, 1983.

Swick, K. J., and R. E. Duff. *The Parent Teacher Bond.* Dubuque, Iowa: Kendall/Hunt Publishing Co., 1978.

Sylva K., S. Bruner, and P. Genova. "The Role of Play in the Problem-Solving of Children 3–5 Years Old." In *Play: Its Role in Development and Evolution,* edited by J. Bruner, A. Jolly, and K. Sylva. New York: Basic Books, Inc., Publishers, 1976, 244–61.

Thibault, J. W., and H. H. Kelley. *The Social Psychology of Groups.* New York: John Wiley & Sons, Inc., 1959.

Thomas, A., and S. Chess. *Temperament and Development.* New York: Brunner/Mazel, Inc., 1977.

Thomas, A., S. Chess, and H. Birch. *Temperament and Behavior Disorders in Children.* New York: New York University Press, 1968.

Thomas, R. M. *Comparing Theories of Child Development.* 2d ed. Belmont, Calif.: Wadsworth, Inc., 1985.

Thompson, D. C. "A New Vision of Masculinity." *Educational Leadership* 43, no. 4 (1986): 53–56.

Thompson, D. F., and L. Meltzer. "Communication of Emotional Intent by Facial Expression." *Journal of Abnormal and Social Psychology* 68, no. 2 (1964): 129–35.

Toepfer, C. "Brain Growth Periodization: Curricular Implications for Nursery Through Grade 12 Learning." Paper presented at the annual meeting of the Association for Supervision and Curriculum Development, St. Louis, Mo., March 1981. (ERIC Document Reproduction Service catalog no. ED204 835 EA 013 727.)

Toner, I. J., R. B. Holstein, and E. M. Hetherington. "Reflection-Impulsivity and Self-Control in Preschool Children." *Child Development* 48 (1977): 239–45.

Toner, I. J., L. P. Moore, and B. A. Emmons. "The Effect of Being Labeled on Subsequent Self-Control in Children." *Child Development* 51 (1980): 618–21.

Toner, I. J., R. D. Parke, and S. R. Yussen. "The Effect of Observation of Model Behavior on the Establishment and

Stability of Resistance to Deviation in Children." *Journal of Genetic Psychology* 132 (1978): 283–90.

Tonkova-Yampolskaya, R. V. "On the Question of Studying Physiological Mechanisms of Speech." *Pavlov Journal of Higher Nervous Activity* 12 (1962): 82–87.

Trabasso, T., N. L. Stein, and L. R. Johnson. "Children's Knowledge of Events: A Causal Analysis of Story Structure." In *Learning and Motivation,* Vol. 15, edited by G. Bower. New York: Academic Press, Inc., 1981.

Tracy, R. L., and M. D. S. Ainsworth. "Maternal Affectionate Behavior and Infant-Mother Attachment Patterns." *Child Development* 52 (1981): 1341–43.

Trause, M. A. "Stranger Responses: Effects of Familiarity, Strangers' Approach and Sex of Infant." *Child Development* 48 (1977): 1657–61.

Tribe, C. *Profile of Three Theories.* Dubuque, Iowa: Kendall/Hunt Publishing Co., 1982.

Tronick, E., et al. "The Infant's Response to Entrapment between Contradictory Messages in Face-to-Face Interaction." *Journal of the American Academy of Child Psychiatry* 17 (1978): 1–13.

Turiel, E. "The Development of Concepts of Social Structure: Social Convention." In *The Development of Social Understanding,* edited by J. Glick and A. Clarke-Stewart. New York: Gardner Press, Inc., 1978.

Turiel, E. "Social Regulations and Domains of Social Concepts." In *Social Cognition,* edited by W. Damon. New Directions for Child Development Series, no. 1. San Francisco: Jossey-Bass, Inc., Publishers, 1978.

Turner, P. "Teacher Level of Questioning and Problem Solving in Young Children." *Home Economics Research Journal* 8, no. 6 (July, 1980): 399–404,

U.S. Bureau of the Census. *Current Population Reports.* Washington D.C.: U.S. Government Printing Office, p-20, no. 399, 1985.

U.S. National Center on Child Abuse and Neglect. *Child Abuse and Neglect Report 7.* Washington, D.C.: Department of Health, Education, and Welfare, February 1977.

Vacc, N. A. "A Study of Emotionally Disturbed Children in Regular and Special Classrooms." In *Conflict in the Classroom: The Education of Children with Problems,* edited by N. J. Long, W. C. Morse, and L. G. Newman. Belmont, Calif.: Wadsworth, Inc., 1971.

Veach, D. M. "Choice with Responsibility." *Young Children* 32, no. 4 (May 1977): 22–25.

Visher, E. B., and J. S. Visher. *Stepfamilies: A Guide to Working with Stepparents and Stepchildren.* New York: Brunner/Mazel, Inc., 1983.

Volkmar, F. R., and A. E. Siegel. "Responses to Consistent and Discrepant Social Communications." In *Development of Nonverbal Behavior in Children,* edited by R. Feldman. New York: Springer-Verlag. New York, Inc., 1982, 231–56.

Vuorenkoski, U., et al. "The Effect of the Cry Stimulus on

the Temperament of the Lactating Breast of Primipara: A Thermographic Study." *Experientia* 25 (1969): 1286–88.

Vuorenkoski, U., et al. "Cry Score: A Method for Evaluating the Degree of Abnormalities in the Pain Cry Response of the Newborn Young Infant." *Quarterly Progress and Status Report*. Stockholm: Speech Transmission Laboratory, Royale Institute of Technology, April 1971.

Walker, H. M. *The Acting-Out Child: Coping with Classroom Disruption*. Boston, Mass.: Allyn and Bacon, Inc., 1979.

Wallerstein, J. S., and J. K. Kelly. *Surviving the Breakup—How Children and Parents Cope with Divorce*. New York: Basic Books, Inc., Publishers, 1980.

Watson, M. W., and K. W. Fisher. "Development of Social Roles in Elicited and Spontaneous Behavior During the Preschool Years." *Child Development* 18 (1980): 483–94.

Weilbacher, R. "The Effects of Static and Dynamic Play Environments on Children's Social and Motor Behaviors," In *Play As Context*, edited by A. Cheska. West Point: N. Y.: Leisure Press, 1981, 248–58.

Weiss, R. S. *Going It Alone—The Family Life and Social Situation of the Single Parent*. New York: Basic Books, Inc., Publishers, 1979.

Weitz, S. "Attitude, Voice and Behavior: A Repressed Affect Model of Interracial Interaction." *Journal of Personality and Social Psychology* 24 (1972): 14–21.

Welch, R. A. "Severe Parental Punishment and Delinquency: A Developmental Theory." *Journal of Clinical Child Psychology* 5 (1976): 17–21.

Weston, D. R., and E. Turiel. "Act-Rule Relations: Children's Concepts of Social Rules." *Developmental Psychology* 16 (1980): 417–24.

Whaley, D. L., and R. W. Malott. *Elementary Principles of Behavior*. New York: Appleton-Century-Crofts, 1971.

Whiren, A. P. "The Preschool: Planning for a New Day." *Parent Cooperative Preschool, International* 12, no. 1 (Spring 1970).

Whiren, A. P. "Establishing Routines for Young Children As a Framework for Learning." *Early Childhood Newsletter*. Michigan State University, Cooperative Extension Service, January–February 1977.

Whiren, A. P. "Table Toys: The Underdeveloped Resource." In *Ideas That Work with Young Children*, Vol. 2, edited by L. Adams and B. Garlick. Washington, D.C.: National Association for the Education of Young Children, 1979.

White, B. *The First Three Years of Life*. Englewood Cliffs, N. J.: Prentice-Hall, Inc., 1975.

White, B. L., and J. C. Watts. *Experience and Environment: Major Influences on the Development of the Young Child*. Vol. 1, Englewood Cliffs, N. J.: Prentice-Hall, Inc., 1973.

White, R. W. "Competence and the Psychosexual Stages of Development." *Nebraska Symposium on Motivation*. Lincoln, Neb.: University of Nebraska Press, 1960.

Whiting, B., and C. Pope. "A Cross-Cultural Analysis of Sex Differences in the Behavior of Children Ages Three

to Eleven." *Journal of Social Psychology* 91 (1973): 171–88.

Wickelgren, L. W. "Convergence in the Human Newborn." *Journal of Experimental Child Psychology* 5 (1967): 74–85.

Widerstrom, A. "Mainstreaming Handicapped Preschoolers." *Childhood Education* 58, no. 3 (January–February 1982): 172–77.

Williams, H. B. "The Need for Public Relations Programs in the Middle Schools: Communicating about the Critical Years." *Middle School Journal* 16, no. 3, 5 (1985): 19–30.

Williams, J. W., and M. Stith. *Middle Childhood*. New York: Macmillan, Inc., 1980.

Withall, J., and W. W. Lewis. "Social Interaction in the Classroom." In *Handbook of Research on Teaching*, edited by N. L. Gage. Chicago: Rand McNally & Company, 1963.

Wolfe, D. A. "Child Abusive Parents: An Empirical Review and Analysis." *Psychological Bulletin* 97, no. 3 (1985): 462–82.

Wolff, P. H. "Observations on the Early Development of Smiling." In *Determinants of Infant Behavior*, Vol. 2., edited by B. Foss. London: Methuen, 1963.

Wolff, P. H. "The Causes, Controls, and Organization of Behavior in the Neonate." *Psychological Issues* 5, no. 1 (1966): 7–11.

Wolff, P. H. "The Role of Biological Rhythms in Early Psychological Development." *Bulletin of the Menninger Clinic* 31 (1967): 197–218.

Wolff, P. H. "The Natural History of Crying and Other Vocalizations in Early Infancy." In *Determinants of Infant Behavior*, Vol. 4, edited by B. M. Foss. London: Methuen, 1969.

Wolff, P. H., S. R. Levin, and E. T. Longobardi. "Motoric Mediation in Children's Paired Associate Learning: Effects of Visual and Tactual Contact." *Journal of Experimental Child Psychology* 64 (1972): 176–83.

Wolfgang, C. H. *Helping Aggressive and Passive Preschoolers Through Play*. Columbus, Ohio: Charles E. Merrill Publishing Company, 1977.

Wolman, R. N., W. C. Lewis, and M. King. "The Development of the Language of Emotions: Conditions of Emotional Arousal." *Child Development* 42 (1971): 1288–93.

Wunderlich, R. C. "Treatment of the Hyperactive Child." *Academic Therapy* 8 (1973): 375–90.

Yamomoto, K. *The Child and His Image*. Boston: Houghton Mifflin Company, 1972.

Yarrow, L. "Should Children Play with Guns?" *Parents* 58 (January 1983): 50–52.

Yarrow, M. R., P. Scott, and C. Z. Waxler. "Learning Concern for Others." *Developmental Psychology* 8 (1973): 240–60.

Yinger, J. *Problem Solving with Children*. San Francisco: Far West Laboratory for Educational Research and Development, 1975.

Youniss, J. *Parents and Peers in Social Development*. Chicago: University of Chicago Press. 1980.

Zahn-Waxler, C., S. L. Friedman, and E. M. Cummings. "Children's Emotions and Behaviors in Response to Infants' Cries." *Child Development* 54 (1983): 1522–28.

Zahn-Waxler, C., R. Iannotti, and M. Chapman. "Peers and Prosocial Development." In *Peer Relationships and Social Skills in Childhood,* edited by K. H. Rubin and H. S. Ross. New York: Springer-Verlag New York, Inc., 1982.

Zahn-Waxler, C., M. Radke-Yarrow, and J. Brady-Smith. "Perspective Taking and Prosocial Behavior." *Developmental Psychology* 13 (1977): 87–88.

Zahn-Waxler, C., M. Radke-Yarrow, and R. A. King. "Child Rearing and Children's Prosocial Initiations Toward Victims of Distress." *Child Development* 50 (1979): 319–30.

Zifferblatt, S. M. "Architecture and Human Behavior: Toward Increased Understanding of a Functional Relationship." *Educational Technology* 12 (1972): 54–57.

Zigler, E., and N. Rubin. "Why Child Abuse Occurs." *Parents* 60 (November 1985): 102–218.

Zimbardo, P. G., and S. L. Radl. *The Shy Child.* Garden City, N. J.: Doubleday & Company, Inc., 1982.

Zuckerman, M., et al. "Controlling Nonverbal Cues: Facial Expressions and Tone of Voice." *Journal of Experimental Social Psychology* 17 (1981): 506–24.

INDEX